D0340398

A GOTHIC TREASURE TROVE

A GOTHIC TREASURE TROVE

SELECTED
AND CONDENSED BY
THE EDITORS OF
READER'S DIGEST

THE READER'S DIGEST ASSOCIATION, INC.
Pleasantville, New York
Cape Town, Hong Kong, London, Montreal, Sydney

The acknowledgments that appear on page 640 are hereby made part of this copyright page.

First Edition

Library of Congress Cataloging in Publication Data
Main entry under title: A Gothic treasure trove.
Contents: Moonraker's bride/by Madeleine Brent — The golden unicorn/by Phyllis A. Whitney — Kirkland revels/by Victoria Holt — [etc].
1. Horror tales, American. 2. Love stories, American.
3. American fiction — 20th century. 4. American fiction — Women authors.
5. Horror tales, English. 6. Love stories, English.
7. English fiction — 20th century. 8. English fiction — Women authors.
9. Gothic revival (Literature) I. Reader's Digest Association.
PS648.H6G68 1987 813'.0872'08 85-25734
ISBN 0-89577-228-0

Printed in the United States of America

Contents

MOONRAKER'S BRIDE

A CONDENSATION OF THE NOVEL BY

Madeleine Brent

ILLUSTRATED BY ROBERT McGINNIS

Seventeen-year-old Lucy Waring felt more Chinese than English. After all, she had never seen England, but she had lived her entire life in China, the orphaned daughter of English missionaries. Then one day a fair-haired stranger rode up to the mission school that was Lucy's home with a parchment map and a riddle he was trying to solve. It was a day that would change Lucy's life forever—a day in a series of days begun many years before that was to entwine her destiny with that of a beautiful English mansion called Moonrakers. The first tendril of danger was even then reaching out from the other side of the world to draw her there . . . as the Moonraker's Bride.

Madeleine Brent's witty, resourceful heroines are the delight of readers everywhere.

CHAPTER ONE

ON THE MORNING OF that day in March 1899, the Year of the Boar—the day the ugly stranger came to Tsin Kai-feng—I opened my eyes at dawn and felt a pang of despair to find that nothing had changed. I suppose this was foolish of me, for I had learned long ago that troubles rarely disappear overnight. Mine were most unlikely to do so.

I had fifteen girl-children and Miss Prothero to feed, and the larder was empty but for some potatoes and a few pounds of millet. There was only one answer. I would once again have to make the journey into the town of Chengfu and steal some money.

I shivered, pulling the worn blanket up about my shoulders and huddling down on the straw mattress that lay between me and the scrubbed floor-boards. It would be useless for me to try begging in the streets of Chengfu. The people might consider begging an honorable profession because it gave them an opportunity to show charity, but the Beggars' Guild was very strict. Although I spoke Chinese as well as they did, having spoken it all my life, they still counted me among the *yang kuei-tzu*—the foreign devils. Indeed, the one time I had tried to beg, a year ago when I was still sixteen, three men of the guild caught me. Luckily I managed to say something to make them laugh, otherwise they might have cut off my ears. As it was, they only beat me with canes. After that, my shoulders were so stiff that I had to pretend to Miss Prothero that I had fallen and hurt my back.

Through the shutters I could hear the dawn chorus of birds in the courtyard, and knew that I was already late getting up. It was past six o'clock. The walk to Chengfu would take two hours each way, and there was much to be done before I could leave. In the long room I could hear the children already stirring, a whimper from Kimi, the baby, and the voice of Yu-lan soothing her. I got up, sponged myself with water from the bowl I had filled before going to bed, then put on my jacket and trousers and slipped my feet into my sandals. The thin quilting of my clothes was not very warm, but I knew that when I started working I would be warm enough.

The only mirror in the whole mission was in Miss Prothero's room. Over the past winter I had sold almost everything that was not a necessity. But on the wall of my cubicle was a long bronze shield, set in the plaster, and I kept this polished to use as a mirror. When Miss Prothero and her sister had begun their work in the village forty years earlier, they had established the mission in an abandoned Chinese temple. The ancient bronze shield was the only relic of that time, for all the effigies of Chinese gods had been removed long before I was born, even long before my father and mother had been sent out from England by the Christian China Mission to help the Misses Prothero. I had no memory of my parents. They had both died in a cholera outbreak a year after I was born, and so had Miss Adelaide Prothero, leaving only her sister, Victoria.

I liked my strange mirror. The curve of the surface distorted everything, taking away the ugliness of my big round eyes; the bronze disguised the freakish white color of my skin. When I looked in it I could pretend that I was quite pretty, with smooth yellow skin, nice narrow eyes and tiny bound feet. . . . I gave my hair a quick brush, then walked between the two rows of mattresses in the long room, calling to the children to wake up. The baby lay well wrapped in a desk drawer from the schoolroom. Beside her squatted Yu-lan, who at fourteen was the oldest girl we had. She looked up with a smile as I knelt beside her.

Yu-lan was a very pretty girl and had a kind nature. Not for the first time I thought what a pity it was that Miss Prothero would not let me sell Yu-lan as a laborer or a concubine. She would become one or the other anyway when she left the mission, though Miss Prothero always believed she had placed the girls in service with "a nice family." She still did not understand many of the ways the Chinese had followed for thousands of years. To me most of these ways seemed natural and inevitable. But when I looked at Kimi, I felt an ache in my heart at the thought that if her mother had not brought her to the mission, she would have been left outdoors at birth, to die of exposure. Strong sons would look after their parents when old age came, but girl-children were considered useless and often allowed to die soon after they were born. Most of the time I thought of myself as Chinese, but this was one custom I could not bear to dwell on.

"What is for breakfast, Lu-tsi?" asked Yu-lan. None of the children could pronounce Lucy properly.

"Today we have a change," I said, and smiled. "Instead of soybean milk and porridge we shall have porridge and soybean milk."

She gave a trill of laughter. The girls laughed at the simplest joke, repeated for the tenth time. "And for dinner?" she asked.

"Potatoes." There had been nothing but potatoes for dinner for a week now, and I had no heart to joke about it.

Yu-lan stood up, watching me with troubled eyes. "What will you do, Lu-tsi? The small ones are always hungry."

"None of you have gone hungry," I said angrily. "At least, not very hungry. And there's enough food for two days still."

"Where will you get food after that, Lu-tsi?"

I gave the only answer I could think of, the answer Miss Prothero had always given me whenever I asked such a question: "The Lord will provide." Then I went into the kitchen, thinking of what I would have to do that day in Chengfu, and hoping that at least the Lord would make sure I did not get caught while I was busy providing.

Ten minutes later I took Miss Prothero's breakfast to her. As she sat propped up in bed she looked so gray and shrunken that it was hard to recognize her as the plump, warmhearted woman who had been a mother to me almost since I was born. She and Adelaide had come to the village of Tsin Kai-feng forty years earlier for the Christian China Mission. By 1882, when my parents, Charles and Mary Waring, had been sent out to help, she and her sister were over fifty and were relieved that some of the work would be lifted from their shoulders. But within eighteen months the cholera took my parents and Adelaide. At the same time the Christian China Mission was beset by squabbles with other missionary bodies and withdrew from North China.

But Victoria Prothero remained, with no funds, twenty-two Chinese girls at the mission, and Lucy Waring, a year-old baby. Somehow Miss Prothero had risen above sorrow and weariness and braced herself to the task. She had a legacy from her father, meant for her old age back home in England. She transferred the money to a bank in Chengfu, and eked it out over many years to keep the mission going. Miss Prothero had many funny ways and strange ideas, but I loved her and admired her more than any other human being.

She had been unable to leave her bed now for six months, and I knew that she had little time to live. Dr. Langdon, the American doctor I had brought from Chengfu to see her, had told me so. I cried that night for the first time since I was very small. Then I dried my tears, realizing that the only thing to do was to protect Miss Prothero from all worry and difficulty during the time that remained to her.

Beyond that, I could not think at all. I remembered once asking Miss Prothero how she had managed to meet all the terrible troubles that had fallen upon her. She had answered, "Whenever you can't think what to do, Lucy dear, just do whatever comes next and go on from there."

As I laid the breakfast tray on her lap Miss Prothero gave me a vague little smile. There was a cup of tea, and a bowl of soybean milk and porridge to which I had added a sheep's liver, chopped up fine. I had got it from the farmer, Mr. Hsun, for clearing a ditch.

"Thank you, Lucy dear, that looks very nice." Her voice was feeble but steady. Then she frowned. "I do wish you would wear your nice dress, child." She was speaking of a dress she had made for me when I was six.

"It's being washed," I said. There was today's first lie for the Recording Angel to write down on Lucy Waring's page of his book. Miss Prothero had been much too busy keeping us all alive over the years to do much preaching, but once a day she had always read the Bible to us and given us a little talk, so I knew all about the Recording Angel. I never dared think how many pages he had used up on me. Apart from four trips to Chengfu for stealing, I had been telling lies to Miss Prothero for months now. Almost a year ago her memory had begun to fail. She did not realize that all her money had gone, though the bank manager had written to her saying there was no money left. That was when I had to start stealing.

Miss Prothero said, "Lucy, I don't like to see you in trousers all the time. You must remember that you are an *English* child. That does not make you *better* than a Chinese child, of course, but it is right to take pride in your own country."

"Yes, Miss Prothero." I sat down on the chair beside the bed. "Eat up your breakfast before it gets cold."

"Breakfast?" She looked down at the tray. "Oh yes. I'm afraid I'm not very hungry, Lucy."

"But Dr. Langdon says your medicine is only to be taken after meals."

She nodded vaguely, and began to eat. After a moment her expression became more alert. "Are you keeping everywhere clean and shining, Lucy? And the children too?"

"Yes, Miss Prothero. All the daily duties are being done."

"I haven't heard the morning hymn yet, dear."

"That comes later. After cleaning, and before breakfast."

"Of course. How silly of me." She suppressed a wince of pain. "Now for your reading, Lucy. Something from Miss Jane Austen would be nice."

Miss Prothero was determined that I should never forget the proper use of my mother tongue. Ever since I could read, I would read to her for half an hour each morning, and for an hour each evening we would indulge in what she called the art of conversation. I enjoyed the books, though often I was baffled by the stories, for they took place in the strange world of the foreign devils. The world I knew was made up of the mission and the nearby village of Tsin Kai-feng, which held only two or three hundred souls within its ancient mud-brick walls. The English world that Miss Prothero knew had no reality for me.

When I finished reading from *Pride and Prejudice*, I saw that Miss Prothero had eaten only half her breakfast and was lying back with her eyes closed. I thought she had fallen asleep, but as I put the book back on the shelf she said, "Have you planned the day's work, Lucy?"

"Yes, Miss Prothero. After breakfast I'll give the children lessons, and in the afternoon I'll see if Mr. Hsun can find half a day's work on the farm for the older ones." I hesitated. "I have to go to the bank in Chengfu this afternoon for some money."

Another lie, and there were more to come, I thought unhappily.

"Money? But you went for money only a month or two ago. Really, dear, you must be more thrifty. Money doesn't grow on trees, you know. Now run along. It must be nearly time for the morning hymn."

In the hall outside her bedroom I stood for a little while, shaking inside. I managed not to cry, and I was very glad of that. If the children saw me in tears they would think the world had come to an end.

I heard Yu-lan calling the children to assembly in the school hall, and I went to join them. Sitting down at the creaky old harmonium, I looked at the hymn Yu-lan had chosen. It was "Bread of Heaven." I could read no music, but I had learned to play four hymn tunes. I struck a chord and said, "Now children, sing very loudly, so Miss Prothero will hear. One, two, three . . . now!"

One way I knew I was a foreign devil was that I could follow a tune as Miss Prothero did. To the Chinese children the music meant nothing. They simply shrieked the words, all on the same note, and as fast as possible. There was no pause between verses, and I had to play and sing faster and faster to keep up. Yu-lan finished first, but I was close behind. Then we said the Lord's Prayer and went to breakfast.

For me the morning passed all too quickly. I dreaded the moment when I would have to set off for Chengfu. I sent Yu-lan to ask Mr. Hsun if he could offer any work. He kept her waiting for nearly an hour to mark her insignificance, then said he would pay for four of the big girls to come and trample the mud and straw together for bricks. That would at least buy some milk for Kimi.

At midday we ate hot mashed potatoes, and then I went to my cubicle. My hands already trembling, I pulled on my warm felt boots and the coat I had made from an old blanket, then settled a conical straw hat on my head. I liked the hat because it made me look more like everybody else. Then I went to the small wooden box at the head of my mattress. The box contained everything I treasured: a blurred photograph of my parents, a prayer book, some samplers my mother had made, and a piece of fading blue hair ribbon. There was also the picture.

The picture had held and haunted me ever since I had first discovered it three years before under a thick layer of dust in a recess of the cellar where we kept firewood. It was drawn boldly in black ink on very coarse canvas. It showed a fine house, standing on a ridge, with a line of trees to one side. Tall chimneys rose from a steeply pitched roof with straight gables, not with upturning eaves as in China. There were two rows of elegantly proportioned windows, and a handsome entrance. In front of the end gables were two parapets, with stone balls set on short pillars. Beneath the picture was the word Moonrakers.

Miss Prothero had no idea where the drawing might have come from. "It must have been here before my time," she said. "How strange."

"Is Moonrakers the name of the house, do you think?"

"I should think so, child. The word has a meaning, but I can't remember what. . . ."

Miss Prothero scarcely mentioned the picture again, but I was fascinated, not only by the picture itself but by the mystery behind it. Often I would try to make up a story to account for that strange drawing by an unknown hand. I was certain that the hand was English. The sketch had been made lovingly. Perhaps this was why seeing it restored me when I was troubled. The house held an uncanny attraction for me; my heart seemed to reach out toward it. I would sit and gaze at it, and when I put the picture away to set about whatever problem came next, there was a new quietness and hope in me.

But on this occasion, though I looked at the picture, I hardly saw it. My mind was too busy with Chengfu. As I put it away I heard Yu-lan calling, "Lu-tsi! Here is a foreign devil, with gold hair!"

I went to her. And then I saw him. His hair was the color of pale gold, his cold eyes blue as the summer sky. His face was weathered to a light bronze, and though his eyes were as round as my own he kept them narrowed as he looked about him. He wore breeches, a short topcoat and no hat. He looked like a man who had traveled for many days and slept by the roadside, but in spite of this he had the air of a man more accustomed to command than to obey.

The ugly stranger sat his pony at ease, just outside the north wall of the mission. As I drew near he consulted a slip of paper in his hand, then pronounced a few words that were meant to be Chinese. I said, "Good afternoon, sir. Can I help you?"

He leaned forward to peer at my face. "Take your hat off, girl," he said. As I obeyed he straightened in his saddle. "I'll be damned. You're English. What are you doing here?"

"I've always been here. I look after the children at the mission."

His brows rose. "Do you now? And how old are you?"

"Seventeen, sir."

"And your name, girl?"

"Lucy Waring, sir." Automatically I bobbed a little curtsy, as Miss

Prothero had taught us. Then something in my English blood sparked off anger and dislike toward this man for his brusqueness. I said, "Pray do not trouble to introduce yourself if it embarrasses you to do so."

He looked at me appraisingly for several seconds, then said, "Falcon. Robert Falcon." He swung down from his saddle. "I'm looking for a certain temple." Opening his coat, he took out a leather wallet and drew from it a folded parchment map. He spread this against his saddle. The map was hand-drawn in black ink. I saw one or two hills marked, a river, a few groves of trees, and a walled town or village. No names were lettered on the map.

"Some features are missing here," said Mr. Falcon. "There's a second map showing them, and the maps can't be read properly till the two are put together. But this is the area where the temple is supposed to be, and perhaps there's enough here for you to recognize the place."

I shook my head. "It could be one of a hundred places, sir. Small villages in China are very much alike. I only know it's not here, because the course of the river is wrong."

He shrugged, folded the parchment and put it away, then said, "Are you good at riddles?"

"I don't think so, Mr. Falcon. I haven't had much practice."

He gave a bleak smile. "Well, listen to one all the same:

"Above the twisted giant's knife
Where the windblown blossom flies
Stands the temple where fortune lies.

"Beyond the golden world reversed
Marked by the bear cub of the skies
Rest the sightless tiger's eyes."

He waited for me to speak. "I'm sorry," I said. "I don't understand."

He shrugged. "I wondered if the villagers here have a legend about a giant, preferably with a sword or a knife."

"Tsin Kai-feng has its legends, but nothing to fit your riddle, sir."

"Does nothing about it strike you?"

"No, sir. Only that it seems very bad poetry."

"I see. Well, this was written by my grandfather."

I felt the blood drain from my cheeks. I had insulted his ancestor. It was hard to imagine a worse offense.

He went on, "Don't look so stricken, girl. I doubt if he could have written a decent line of poetry to save his life—which was somewhat short in any event. The fool got himself killed in a duel when he was my age."

I heaved an inward sigh of relief. I had been thinking as a Chinese, knowing how they revered their ancestors. Evidently Mr. Falcon had no such feeling toward his forebears. He stood thoughtfully, a hand resting on the saddle, almost as if he had forgotten my presence. Then he strolled over to a piece of ground where the ashes from the kitchen range were put when we cleaned it out each week. He picked up a charred stick and made a bold black stroke with it on the wall of the mission.

I caught my breath with astonishment. Under the blackened stick a face began to appear on the wall, a clear picture made with only a few strokes: a man's face, lean-jawed and widemouthed. The thick, curly hair reached well down the cheeks, the nose was long, and a corner of the mouth curved up in a half smile. The eyes were just charcoal marks on rough stone, yet they lived, sparkling with a kind of wicked laughter.

Mr. Falcon tossed the stick aside and brushed his hands. With a jerk of his head toward the face he said, "Do you know him?"

I could only shake my head. Mr. Falcon walked back to the pony. "It's quite possible you'll see something of him one fine day," he said, his eyes grim. "If so, he'll ask the same questions I've asked, and recite the same riddle. I advise you not to mention that you've met me."

"But where's the harm in it, sir?" I asked.

"The harm? I'll tell you. He may think you've helped me, and that I've paid you not to help *him*. Then you wouldn't be safe, Lucy Waring, for that one's dangerous. He has a devious mind, and he's the most ruthless devil you're ever likely to meet."

He was tightening the pony's girth now, and as I watched I thought suddenly that he was bound to have some money. If I could beg a little from him, perhaps I would not have to steal for a week or more.

I had seen beggars at work. Hunching my shoulders, I let my head fall to one side. Then, dragging one foot, I limped toward him, whining, "Please, sir, please give me money. The mission lady is very ill, and I have fifteen children to feed. We have no food. Please . . ."

Next moment an open hand struck me across the face, so that I staggered. "How *dare* you!" His voice was low but hard. "You're not some starving peasant. You're a girl with advantages—it's in your face, your voice, the way you move. How dare you degrade yourself by begging!"

He put a foot in the stirrup and swung up into the saddle. I wanted to make him come and look in our larder and then ask him what advantages he thought I had. But I was too confused. As I stood with one hand to my aching cheek I was absorbing the fact that the ugly stranger and I lived in different worlds. In my world it was no dishonor to beg. But I partly belonged in his world also, for it was a heritage in my blood, and now I felt shame myself, so deep that I could use it to measure his contempt. "Mr. Falcon," I began, "I'm very sorry—"

Even as I spoke he turned the pony, dug in his heels and said, "Go, Moonraker." Then they were away, going down the hill at a good canter. I watched them skirt the village and turn south along the road that led away from Chengfu.

Moonraker. He had called his pony Moonraker. And in my box was that mysterious picture of a house called Moonrakers, drawn long ago by a hand quite as bold and skillful as Robert Falcon's.

CHAPTER TWO

YU-LAN WOULD BE IN charge while I was in Chengfu, so before I set out I told her, "I won't be home until well after dark. Just give the children whatever's left for supper." I hesitated, then went on, "And in case I'm delayed or—or something, you'd better have this."

Stitched into the hem of my jacket was a silver tael, my precious reserve for emergencies. I picked at the stitches with my fingernail, squeezed the coin out and gave it to Yu-lan. She stared at me in alarm. "But you *will* come back, Lu-tsi?"

"Yes, of course. But you're grown-up now. If something unexpected happens you'll be able to manage somehow. That tael will be enough to feed everybody for a few days, if you're careful. After that—" I quoted Miss Prothero: "You'll just have to do whatever comes next." Without waiting for an answer I opened the door and set off down the pathway.

The small village of Tsin Kai-feng stood in a wide loop of the river that ran below our hill. When I reached the village bridge I turned and looked back up at the mission, the only home I had ever known, with its long double-tiered roof curving up at the eaves, and a small marble pagoda, part of the original temple, rising from one corner. On one side was a big cedar; on the other, outside my window, were two ancient plum trees.

I turned and stepped out quickly along the road, trying to thrust away the sick feeling of fear in my stomach. I must not be caught stealing. I *must* not. Chengfu was governed by a very important person, a three-button mandarin whose name was Huang Kung. He was the terror of all wrongdoers and renowned as a hater of foreign devils. If I was caught, I would be beaten severely if I was lucky. More probably I would lose a hand, if the mandarin was in a bad temper when my case was tried.

Beyond the village the road wound between stony hills and then across a plain where the wind blew keenly. There were few people on the road so early in the year. I was glad of this, because the carts had not broken the frozen surface and churned it to mud.

At last I reached Chengfu. I always thought of it as a huge city, but Miss Prothero had told me that it would be lost in Peking or Tientsin. The streets were crowded with carts, rickshaws, people on donkeys, and occasionally a sedan chair of some important person. Just ahead of me was a woman driving geese. Another carried a huge load of logs on her back, held in a blanket that was brought forward in a band across her forehead. I always carried loads this way myself, and it was surprising how much weight I could bear.

I reached the square outside the House of Justice. People would gather here when a whipping or an execution took place. Once I myself had glimpsed the executioner, a grim figure in a black leather jerkin, carrying a big curved sword.

I had decided to do my stealing in the street of the goldsmiths, for they were rich and it seemed better to steal from them than from poorer people. The goldsmiths were also careful, so I knew my task would be dangerous. I suppose it was cowardice, but I decided that I would go first to see Dr. Langdon to ask for another bottle of Miss Prothero's medicine. Dr. Langdon was one of no more than half a dozen foreign devils in Chengfu, an American with gray hair and tired eyes who had come to China before I was born. He lived in part of a mansion now made into a number of small apartments. They all looked out upon a courtyard, and the latticed-paper windows were set in brightly lacquered frames.

Dr. Langdon had just finished seeing a patient when I arrived. He gave me a friendly smile and said, "Hello, young Lucy. Like some tea?"

I had to stop myself from protesting that an insignificant person like myself would not dream of putting an honorable elderborn to such trouble. I just said, "Thank you, Dr. Langdon. I'd like some tea very much."

He looked me up and down shrewdly. "You look as if you could do with something to eat. Take off your coat and sit down."

He made the tea and I asked him if I could have another bottle of the medicine. He nodded. "I'll make one up. I wish I could do more, but there's nothing anybody can do for her now, except keep the pain down."

It was strange to see a man making tea, even though I knew Dr. Langdon had no woman to do it for him. (Miss Prothero had told me that in England the men even allowed their wives to eat with them at the same table.) He gave me a plate with three sesame-seed pastries, told me to eat them all, then settled himself in a chair.

"How are you getting along at the mission?" he asked.

"It's difficult sometimes, Doctor, but we manage somehow."

He frowned almost angrily. "Why the devil haven't some of your English missionary people taken over?"

"We haven't been connected with any of the missionary societies for years, Doctor. Miss Prothero wrote to a society in Soochow months ago, asking for help, but nothing has happened."

He sipped his tea, then got up and began to pace the room. "I'm in China by my own wish, and Miss Prothero by hers. But what about you,

Lucy? You're an English girl. You should be home, being properly educated, not working like a slave to keep a few Chinese children alive."

I must have looked startled, for he went on, "Oh, they should be kept alive all right, but it's not *your* job. If the British Government only gave the missions as much as they spent on the Opium Wars here, or if the United States would only—"

He broke off with a shrug. "No, that's hardly fair. The Chinese themselves would never let hordes of us barbarians come in to clean up the country. But Lucy—there's trouble coming. One day soon the Chinese are going to decide they don't want foreign devils in their country any longer, and they'll start chopping off heads."

He stopped pacing and stood in front of me. "You *must* go home, Lucy. When trouble breaks, it's going to be bad. I'm going to write to your ambassador in Peking, and to an American missionary group. *Somebody* must take care of the children, so that you can go home."

I said, "Yes, Dr. Langdon," because it would have been bad manners to argue with an older male person, but the things he had been saying were quite impossible. Sometimes I had a very great longing to see the strange country called England, but I knew it could never happen.

"I wish I could help more," Dr. Langdon was saying as he mixed the medicine, "but I've just paid for new medical supplies and I'm right out of money—what Americans call broke." He stirred the mixture with a long glass rod. "Most of my patients are too poor to pay me."

He poured the medicine into a bottle. "There you are, young lady. As the pain gets worse, increase the dose. I'll come out to the mission next week if I don't hear from you before then."

I had eaten the pastries slowly, to make them last, and now I felt much less nervous about my stealing expedition. Perhaps hunger had made me more anxious. I put on my coat and thanked Dr. Langdon for the tea. "I have an errand to do," I said, "so may I call for the medicine on my way home, please?"

"Anytime. If I'm called out I'll leave it next door."

Remembering my English manners, I held out my hand, and dropped a little curtsy as he took it. He held my hand gently. Then he said, "I wonder if you know how pretty you are, Lucy?"

For a moment I went hot with shame, for I thought he was making fun of me, but then I saw he was quite serious. I realized that foreign devils must like girls who had round eyes and white skin.

Twenty minutes later I was walking along the line of shops where the goldsmiths worked, trying to decide which of them offered the most hope for me. Young apprentices pumped the bellows of the little brick furnaces while the smiths watched the molten gold or sat working at their benches.

Seeing no money or gold objects left carelessly in view, I turned and walked along the narrow alley behind the shops. If I could enter one from the back I might find a storeroom with something to steal. I tested the shop doors gently and found only one, at the end of the row, unlocked.

My heart was pounding. I had thought I might grow used to stealing, but instead I felt worse every time. I almost jumped out of my skin when something cold and wet touched my hand. I looked down and saw the nose of a stray dog, one of many in Chengfu. I shooed him silently away and for a few moments clasped my hands tightly together, trying to prevent them from trembling. Then I carefully eased the flimsy door open. Beyond lay a small room, with tools hanging on the walls, pots and pieces of old rope on the floor. There was nothing worth taking. Through a partly open door on the far side I could hear the tapping of the goldsmith's hammer.

I shut the back door and walked around to the street again. There was no apprentice in the shop. The goldsmith, a big man in a leather apron, was making a filigree brooch. I watched him fix it gently in the jaws of a wooden vise and pick up a slim steel tool. An idea suddenly came to me.

I hurried back around into the alley. The stray dog was still there. I coaxed him to the door, opened it cautiously, and reached inside for a piece of rope. I tied one end of the rope around his neck, then pushed him into the room and closed the door so that it jammed tightly on the free end of the rope. Then I ran quickly around to the front and lingered by the next shop, pretending to study the combs laid out there. Really I was watching the big goldsmith, and straining my ears for the sound I expected. The next moment it happened—a whining and barking from behind him. He jumped to his feet and ran into the back room. In three paces I was beside his bench. As I released the brooch from the vise I could hear the smith shouting and trying to open the back door to send the stray dog on its way. With the brooch clutched in my hand I turned to run.

Just then the smith's apprentice appeared, carrying his master's dinner. I barely had time to see the startled look on his face before we collided. The rice bowl flew from his hands, and I went sprawling on the floor of the shop.

The apprentice began to shout. I scrambled to my feet, but was wrenched around and saw the face of the goldsmith glaring down at me. The boy was crying, "She took the brooch, master! She has it in her hand!"

Still gripping my shoulder, the smith squeezed my hand open. "Foreign-devil thief!" he said fiercely. He buffeted the side of my head and I went reeling across the shop, hit the far wall and slithered down to the floor again. There seemed to be pain everywhere as I lay there, but it was small compared to the huge fear that possessed me.

A rough hand dragged me to my feet and shook me. One of the mandarin's policemen was standing over me. He asked me a question, but my mind was still fuzzy and I could only shake my head dumbly. I found myself being marched through the streets with the policeman's hand on my shoulder. As we walked he lectured me in an angry voice, saying that the mandarin Huang Kung knew how to deal with foreign barbarians who stole from the People of Heaven.

We came at last to the prison. A clerk wrote down the details of my crime. Then I was handed over to the jailer, a squat man who wore a broad leather belt with metal studs in it. On one hip hung a bunch of big keys that clanked as he walked, and on the other a curving sword in a leather sheath. He spent some minutes in a grumbling argument with the clerk, saying there was no more room in the women's section of the prison. In the end I was taken down some steps to a stone corridor with heavy grille doors. The cells were in pairs, each pair divided by iron bars running from floor to ceiling. There were men in these cells, some of them gambling through the bars. I wondered what they could be gambling with, then realized that a prisoner's money would of course be left with him so that he could offer bribes for better treatment. Bribery was an ancient Chinese custom.

At the end of the corridor was a rather small pair of cells. The jailer opened a door, pushed me inside, locked the door, then walked away muttering to himself. No doubt he would have preferred a male prisoner with coins in his pocket.

There was nothing in the cell but a stool, a dirty mattress and a bucket. I sat on the stool, in despair. How would Yu-lan manage at the mission? What would she do when Miss Prothero's medicine ran out? It might be several days before the mandarin decided to try my case. I would be found guilty, of course. And then . . .

A voice spoke to me in bad Chinese, just a few clumsy words. I looked up and saw that a man now stood by the bars separating his cell from mine. In the narrow beam of light from a small window high in the wall I saw his face, and felt a terrible shock. In spite of the two-day growth of bristle on his chin, I knew that this was the man whose face Robert Falcon had sketched in charcoal on the mission wall. This was the dangerous man he had warned me to beware of.

He was an inch or two taller than Mr. Falcon, but slighter in build. He wore slim riding trousers tucked into leather boots, and a warm sheepskin jacket. I rose and moved to the bars, taking off my hat. Shakily I said, "Good afternoon, sir."

"Good Lord. A girl—and English!" His voice was deep and lazy. "What the devil are you doing dressed up like that, and in jail?"

"I always dress this way, sir. And I'm here because I tried to steal a gold brooch and the man caught me." My cheeks grew hot with shame.

He chuckled mockingly. "Hard luck. Though I wouldn't have thought you were a girl who went in much for jewelry."

"I didn't steal it to wear. I have to take care of the children at the mission. We have no food or money left, and the Beggars' Guild beat me when I tried to beg. . . ."

He reached between the bars, and for a moment I was petrified. But he only cupped my chin gently in his hand and tilted my head so that the light caught my face. After the first moment I no longer felt afraid, and was able to look back at him.

At last he let me go. "Yours is the first English face I've seen for some time, and it's a tonic. Bring your stool up to the bars and talk to me for a while." He brought his own stool closer and I did the same. In the gathering gloom everything seemed completely unreal to me, and I wanted it to remain so, for it was less frightening than reality.

"We'd better introduce ourselves," he said. "I'm Nicholas Sabine, of many occupations and no fixed abode."

"I'm Lucy Waring and I live at the Tsin Kai-feng Mission."

"How do you do, Miss Waring."

"How do you do, Mr. Sabine."

We shook hands politely through the bars, and I said, "What subject would you like to talk about, sir?"

"Perhaps we could start with you, Lucy. May I call you Lucy?"

"Oh . . . Yes, of course. Please do." And I started to tell my story briefly, but he kept asking questions, so it was almost an hour before I had finished. Then he sat in silence for a long time, with his chin on his hand. Finally he looked at me, though the gloom had deepened so that we could only see each other dimly now.

"Your Miss Prothero is dying, the children will soon be starving, and you're here in jail. What happens now?"

"I hope I'll be tried tomorrow and just be whipped. But . . ." I tried to keep my voice steady. "I'm afraid they may cut off a hand."

Even in the semidarkness I saw the sudden flare in his eyes, and it was frightening. Now I knew it was true that this man was dangerous. But his voice was quiet. "Have you no friend here who can help you?"

"There's Dr. Langdon, but he has no money. Broke, he called it."

"Suppose he had money, what then?"

"Well, then he could go to the goldsmith and pay him, say, three sovereigns to withdraw his accusation. The prison clerk would have to be paid a sovereign to destroy the paper, and the jailer half a sovereign to forget he ever saw me. Oh, and a sovereign for the policeman. . . ." I felt drained of strength. It was hopeless.

But Mr. Sabine seemed to relax. "Let's call it six sovereigns," he said. He reached down inside one of his boots and drew out a leather cylinder as thick as a man's thumb. He twisted off the cap and tilted it; the next moment there was a glitter of gold in his palm. The strange purse seemed to be full of sovereigns, perhaps a hundred.

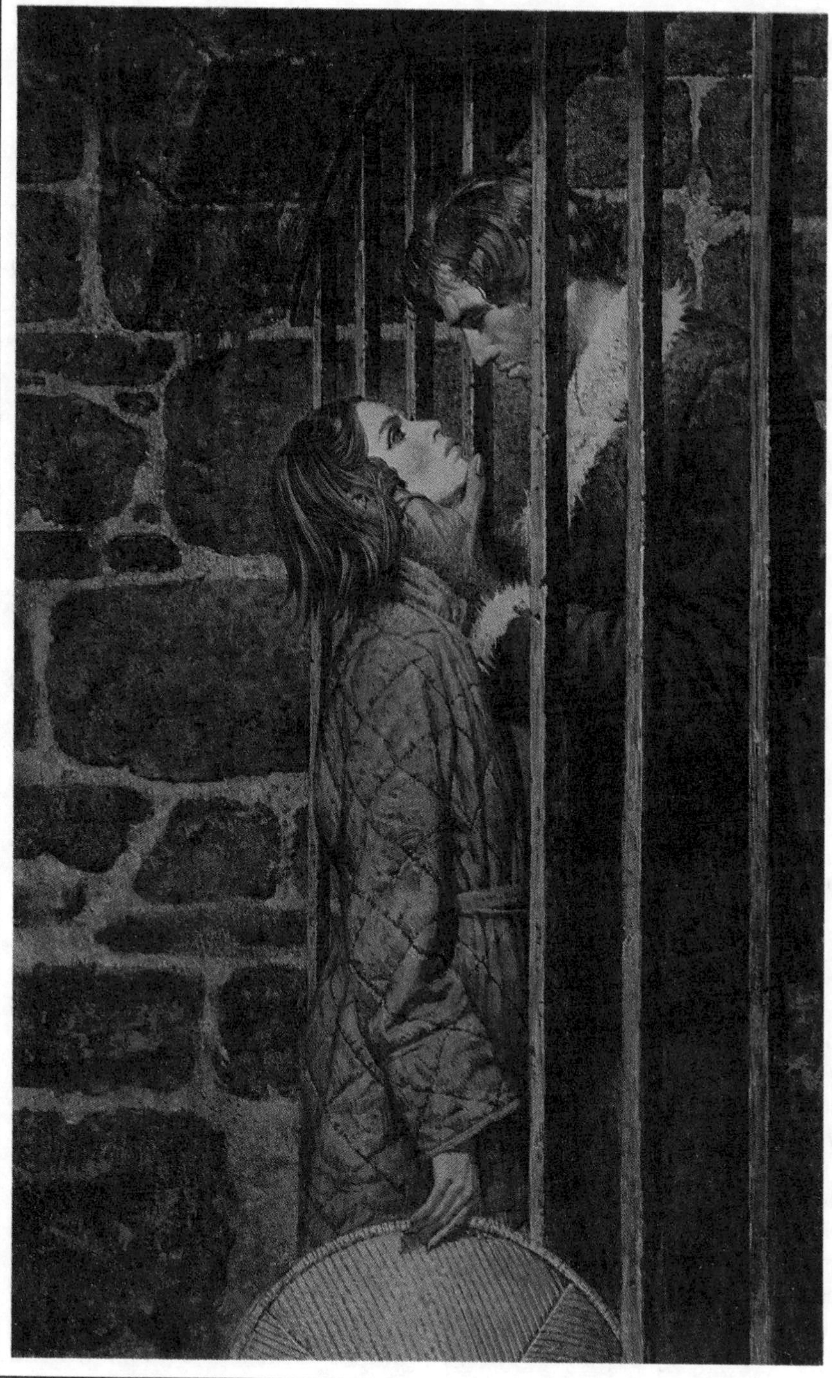

I stared at the gold coins in his hand. "But you *can't,*" I whispered. "I—I don't know why you're in prison, but if you've offended the mandarin you'll need all your money for yourself."

"If I had ten times as much it wouldn't be enough to change Huang Kung's mind." He grinned. "I came to China to find something, and in trying to find it I made a bad mistake. He has very special plans for me. He told me when I was taken to be examined by him. Come on, Lucy. Call the jailer and start bargaining."

Before I could reply there came the sound of feet in the stone-flagged corridor. The jailer appeared carrying an oil lamp, with Dr. Langdon following close behind. The jailer hung the lamp on a hook and said, "There she is. You can talk for a few minutes." Tossing a small coin in the palm of his hand, he spat contemptuously and trudged away.

Dr. Langdon was breathless, as if he had been running. "Oh my God, so it was true!" he said unsteadily. "I was told that a foreign-devil girl had been caught stealing. Oh Lucy! What have you done?"

I was too ashamed to speak. From the cell beside me Mr. Sabine said, "Introduce me to your friend, Lucy."

I think Dr. Langdon was too worried about me to show much surprise at finding an Englishman in the next cell, but his look when Mr. Sabine put six sovereigns in his hand would always remain in my memory. His tired, anxious face lit with relief, because he had been given the gold that would save me. He said, "I've no words to thank you."

"To hell with your thanks." Nicholas Sabine's voice was hard. "Why didn't *you* help her before she was driven to steal? This scrawny little monkey's alone in the world with a pack of kids and a dying woman dependent on her. She risks losing a hand just to keep them fed for a few more days, and nobody cares!"

"I care, Mr. Sabine." Dr. Langdon's tired voice held no resentment. "You're a young man and you don't know what China does to people. When a million or so die of starvation every year, it shouldn't dull your senses, but it does. I've been at fault regarding Lucy, but I'm going to send her home to England somehow, if it's the last thing I ever do."

Mr. Sabine glanced up at the tiny window. In the patch of sky beyond, the first stars were beginning to show. "It's getting on," he said. "Can you fix everything tonight?"

"Don't worry." Dr. Langdon patted the pocket where he had put the sovereigns. "When money's talking the Chinese are never sleepy." He turned to go, then paused and looked back. "I'm sure Lucy will thank you for herself, but I'm grateful on my own account, Mr. Sabine. I gave my last coin to the jailer to let me in, so if it wasn't for your generosity I'd have to turn to stealing myself. And I don't think I'd be very clever at it."

He went away down the corridor. I moved to the bars between the two cells. "I wish I could thank you properly, Mr. Sabine, but there aren't any words big enough."

He shook his head. "Lucy, you're a mystery to me. A riddle I'd like to solve." He looked at me with a half smile. "As a matter of fact, I came here to solve a riddle. Listen now, Lucy."

I was too dazed with all the shocks of the day to show surprise. I just stood looking at him as he recited the lines I expected:

"Above the twisted giant's knife
Where the windblown blossom flies
Stands the temple where fortune lies.

"Beyond the golden world reversed
Marked by the bear cub of the skies
Rest the sightless tiger's eyes."

I tried to think whether or not I should speak of my meeting with Robert Falcon. Finally I remained silent because I was too weary to launch into explanations.

"Does it sound like nonsense to you?" he said at last. When I nodded he gave a shrug and ran a hand through his hair. "And that's probably just what it is. Ah well, Nick Sabine's gambled once too often." He glanced at the window. "It'll take Dr. Langdon a while to arrange matters, so try to sleep, Lucy. I've some thinking to do."

He lay down on his mattress, and I went to my own. As I lay there, I wondered what Mr. Sabine meant by saying that he had gambled once too often. With a shock I realized my selfishness. I had scarcely thought of what might lie ahead for him, yet his very life might be in danger.

I must have fallen asleep, for I remember nothing more until I heard a voice calling, "Lucy. Lucy . . ." I saw Mr. Sabine crouching by the bars. I went across to him.

"Are you awake, Lucy?" he said. "Really awake?"

I rubbed my eyes. "Yes, Mr. Sabine."

"Then listen to me. Is there a Church of England clergyman in Chengfu?"

"There's old Mr. Tattersall. He stayed on after the Chengfu Mission closed. His little church was burned down, but he wouldn't leave. Dr. Langdon would be sure to know him."

"All right. Now, how old are you, Lucy?"

"Seventeen and a half."

"Is Miss Prothero your legal guardian?"

"No. I haven't really got anybody like that, Mr. Sabine."

He rubbed a thumb across his bristly chin and I saw wicked laughter sparkle in his eyes. "Lucy, will you do something for me?"

"Yes, Mr. Sabine. I don't suppose I can ever repay what you've done for me, but I'll do anything I can."

He reached through the bars and gently took my hands. "Well now, don't be shocked or afraid, because there's no need. What I'm going to ask you to do for me, if it can be arranged, is to marry me. I want us to be married tonight."

CHAPTER THREE

I FELT DAZED, AND although I was chilled by the cold of the cell my cheeks burned, for I thought he was mocking me. Then I saw there was no hint of mockery in his gaze. My mind seemed to splinter in confusion, and I stammered, "But—but why? Why would an English gentleman like you want to marry a young girl he doesn't know anything about?"

"I think I've learned quite a lot about you in a short time, Lucy Waring," he said thoughtfully. "But that isn't really the point. There's something that belongs to me, and if I have a wife she'll inherit it. Otherwise it might go to someone who's my enemy, and I'd do anything to prevent that."

"But your wife would only inherit when you die. And even if I agreed, I'm sure Mr. Tattersall would say to wait until you come out of prison."

Nicholas Sabine hesitated, then said almost apologetically, "The fact is, Lucy, I won't be coming out."

Horror flooded through me. "You're going to . . . to be *executed?*"

"Steady, Lucy." He tightened his hold on my hands to stop their trembling. "You see, I made a bad mistake. I was trying to find something that was hidden long ago and I searched in what I thought was a small temple. But it was Huang Kung's family tomb. How's that for bad luck?"

The blood drained away from my face. "But Mr. Sabine, the Chinese worship their ancestors. Their tombs are sacred!"

"So I gather. The soldiers who caught me made that very clear." Before I could say anything more we heard footsteps, and as we stood up Dr. Langdon appeared. He was smiling. The jailer clanked respectfully along beside him. A piece of gold had changed his manners very quickly.

"All's well," Dr. Langdon said with a sigh of relief. "You're free, Lucy. I don't know how to thank you, young man."

"I've suggested a way Lucy can repay me," Nicholas Sabine said briskly.

The jailer unlocked my door, and as I came out I said to him in Chinese, "Would you kindly permit us to talk with the foreign-devil prisoner for a few minutes, honored sir?"

He must have received a whole sovereign, for he grinned. "As long as you please," he said, and walked away down the corridor.

I was feeling so tired by now that everything seemed dreamlike. "Dr. Langdon," I said, "this gentleman wants me to marry him. Tonight."

Dr. Langdon blinked. "Are you crazy?" he asked Nicholas Sabine.

"No, Doctor. It's really quite simple. I have about twenty-four hours to live and I have pressing reasons for wishing to be legally married before I die. Lucy seems to be the only candidate." In a few sentences he repeated the story I had just heard.

Dr. Langdon winced. "My boy, you couldn't have made a worse enemy in all China than Huang Kung. He hates us foreigners."

"He dwelt on the details of my departure with great relish," Nicholas Sabine said calmly, "but there's nothing anyone can do about *that.* Can you help arrange my marriage to Lucy? She mentioned a Mr. Tattersall who could marry us."

Dr. Langdon took out a handkerchief and wiped his face. "Yes, but I don't like it. Dammit, Sabine, she's only seventeen."

"What the devil does that matter? She'll be widowed soon enough, and she'll be my heir. And there's something else. I've got about a hundred and twenty sovereigns left. You may need some to get the marriage arranged, but there should be a hundred left at least. It ought to help her keep those poor little brats at the mission alive for a while."

Dr. Langdon stood rubbing his chin. At last he said, "Well, Lucy?"

I was silent for a long time, trying to work things out. An unbearable sadness pressed down on me. I owed this man an enormous debt. He had shown me the one way in which I could repay him, and it would cost me nothing. On the contrary, it would free me for a long time to come from the dread of waking each morning and wondering how to feed the children. I had read the marriage service in Miss Prothero's prayer book, the vows I would have to make, promising to love and honor Nicholas Sabine until we were parted by death. I shivered. Finally I said, "If you want to marry me, Mr. Sabine, then I will."

"Thank you, Lucy," he said politely. "I'm very grateful."

He asked for pen and paper so he could make a will. Then we left him and took a rickshaw to Mr. Tattersall's house. Mr. Tattersall had gone to bed, but did not seem to mind being roused. He and Dr. Langdon talked for quite a while, and I had to confirm that I had no parent or guardian and that I agreed to the marriage. It took the old, white-haired minister some time to find all the papers he needed, but at last we made our way in rickshaws back through the dark and silent city to the jail.

Nicholas Sabine was at the door of his cell as we came down the corridor. For a small bribe the jailer brought Mr. Tattersall a chair and a little table. It was an eerie, unreal scene. For what seemed a long time, Mr. Tattersall asked Mr. Sabine questions and wrote on the papers he had brought with him. At last he was satisfied and ready to perform the ceremony.

The jailer had refused to unlock the door, even for another whole sovereign. It was more than his life was worth, he said, to give the foreign devil any chance of escape. So my marriage ceremony was performed through the bars of the cell door.

As I repeated my vows to Mr. Tattersall my voice sounded to me like that of one of the mission children, chanting English hymns without understanding them. Nicholas Sabine drew a signet ring from his finger, reached between the bars and took my hand, repeating the words after Mr. Tattersall as he slipped the ring on my finger. It was much too big, and I had to curl my finger to keep it on. In the flickering lamplight I saw that he was smiling gently at me as he spoke; but I was numb with the knowledge that this man I was marrying would soon be killed, and in a corner of my mind I heard Robert Falcon's words: "A devious mind . . . the most ruthless devil you're ever likely to meet."

I thrust the memory from me. I would not believe those words. Nicholas Sabine had shown me nothing but kindness. Even if the words were true, it no longer mattered now. The man I was marrying would never be a danger to anybody again.

Then Mr. Tattersall was speaking the final words: ". . . and live together in holy love unto your lives' end. Amen."

There was a silence. "Thank you, Lucy," Mr. Sabine whispered. "Now I'd like to kiss the bride." He drew my hand between the bars and touched it to his lips. Then, releasing my hand, he took a sheet of paper from his pocket. "Dr. Langdon," he said, "this is my will, leaving everything I possess to Lucy. It needs witnessing, if you'd be so kind."

Dr. Langdon took the will, and he and Mr. Tattersall signed it at the table. I was watching Nicholas Sabine—my husband, I realized with unbelief. He was looking toward the men at the table with devilish laughter now in his eyes, as if he had achieved some triumph of mischief. He said, "Will you keep Lucy's papers safe until you've arranged for her to go home to England, Doctor?" He drew the purse of sovereigns from his boot. "I think you'd better take charge of her wedding present too. She can ask you for whatever money she wants for as long as she's in China."

As he passed the purse through the bars I thought how mistaken he was to believe that I would soon be going to England. Nobody would come to take care of the children at Tsin Kai-feng, and I would never leave them.

Dr. Langdon said in a low, unhappy voice, "Is there anybody . . . who's to be informed?"

"About my death? There's no need for you to do anything. On the back of the will I've written the address of my solicitors in England. All Lucy has to do is to go to them, produce the papers and claim her rights. Now, will you take her away with you, Doctor? The poor child's as white as a sheet and nearly asleep on her feet." He reached through and put a hand on my shoulder. I wanted to thank him for saving me, and to say how sorry I was that he was to die, but my throat closed up. I think he understood. He said, "Lucy, I want you well clear of Chengfu tomorrow. Try not to think about any of this again until you're in England. It's just a dream, really. Good-by, Lucy."

FOR WHAT WAS left of that night I slept on a couch in Dr. Langdon's office. Early next morning, I was at the city gate with him, sitting on a small cart laden with provisions with a sturdy mule between the shafts. I had two sovereigns tucked away in the lining of my coat; the rest were safely hidden in Dr. Langdon's house. I said, "Will you do one more thing for me, Doctor? I'm trying not to think about . . . what will happen to Mr. Sabine today." My throat began to close up again. At last I said, in a rush, "But please, will you try to get his—his body, and take what money you need from the sovereigns to see that he's buried properly . . . ?"

My voice failed again. Dr. Langdon said, "Leave everything to me, Lucy. I'll do the best I can."

I nodded, still unable to speak, and set the mule to a steady plod. When I looked back, Dr. Langdon was standing to one side of the gate, his hand raised. I waved back, then settled to the journey. There was a great heaviness inside me. I tried to imagine seeing our larder full and the great fortune still in Dr. Langdon's safekeeping, but other pictures kept darting into my mind. My wedding ring hung around my neck on a piece of twine under my tunic; feeling it there brought to my mind pictures of the mandarin's soldiers coming to the jail to take Nicholas Sabine away for whatever cruel plans Huang Kung had made for him.

Yu-lan must have set someone to watch from a window, for I was only halfway up the hill when the children came pouring out, calling to me. I drove in through the gate, and as I got down from the cart all the little ones swarmed around me, tugging at my coat and twittering with joy.

"How is Miss Prothero?" I asked Yu-lan later, after everything had been stored away. "Did she eat all her breakfast?"

She looked at me sorrowfully from her beautiful almond eyes. "Lu-tsi," she whispered, "when I took breakfast to her this morning I found that she had died. I think it happened in her sleep. Lu-tsi, I have been so frightened, and praying for you to come home."

Everything seemed to rush away from me. With a great effort I brought the world into focus again. Tears were running down Yu-lan's cheeks. "You're a good girl," I said. "You've done very well."

She smiled through her tears. "I made the children sing the morning hymn. I thought she would want that."

"She'd be very proud of you. And the Recording Angel will write it down in big letters on the good side of his book."

Leaving Yu-lan, I went to Miss Prothero's room with a small, foolish hope that she had been mistaken. But, like me, Yu-lan had seen death too often to make any mistake. I tidied Miss Prothero's hair and put a clean nightdress on her. She was very light and it was easy to wrap her neatly in a blanket. Then I went down to speak to Yu-lan again.

"We'll get the children out of the way and carry her down to the chapel," I told her. The chapel was a tiny place at the back of the old temple building. "I'll have a coffin made in the village today, and tomorrow I'll take her into Chengfu on the cart. Mr. Tattersall will help arrange the burial. We'll say nothing to the children until it's all over. Today we'll set them to work spring-cleaning the whole mission."

It was a blessing to be so busy. It distracted me from my grief over Miss Prothero, and also from the horror of imagining what was happening to Nicholas Sabine. By evening I was so tired that I asked Yu-lan to see the children to bed, always an exhausting business.

I was in the kitchen when I heard the unmistakable sound of the big wooden gate of the mission creaking open. I ran to peer through the little peephole in the stout front door. In the clear moonlight I saw a big ox-drawn wagon moving through the gateway. A foreign devil rode beside the oxen, mounted on a pony, and on the wagon seat beside the Chinese driver was another foreign devil, a tall woman, heavily wrapped against the cold. In the back sat two young Chinese women.

As I opened the door the man rode up to meet me. "Don't be afraid," he said in English. "We're from the Anglican Mission in Tientsin. My name is Stanley Fenshaw." He turned and called, "This is the place, Margaret," then swung down from the saddle. He seemed about forty years old, with a square brown face creased with deep lines, a face stern but for the eyes, which were very bright and smiling. "You must be Lucy Waring."

"Yes, sir," I said. "I'm Lucy Waring."

He pulled off a glove and put a hand on my shoulder. "Well, Lucy—Miss Prothero has had to wait a long time for help. But her troubles are over now, and so are yours. We are here now."

I did not know whether to laugh or cry. After all the years of struggle, help had come less than a day after Miss Prothero's death. I opened the door wide. "Come in, sir. You must all be cold. I'll make some tea."

The tall woman had gotten down from the wagon, followed by the two young Chinese women. Fascinated, I saw she had red hair and green eyes. In the hall she threw back her cloak, rested her hands on her hips and stared fiercely about her. When she spoke, her accent was strange.

"A cluster of bairns in this auld ruin, and only a spinster in her seventies to see after them. There's good wurrk for us here, Stanley."

"Yes indeed." Mr. Fenshaw looked at me with a smile. "Perhaps you'll tell Miss Prothero we've arrived, Lucy."

I said, "I'm sorry, sir. Miss Prothero . . . she's been ill for months now, and last night she died."

There was a long silence. Mr. Fenshaw and his wife looked at one another and then back at me. "Ill for months?" Mr. Fenshaw said. "Do you mean you've been managing on your own?"

"Yes, sir. There isn't anybody else."

The red-haired lady moved toward me and put her arm around my shoulders. Her voice was softer now and seemed much less fierce as she said, "There's somebody else now, lassie."

DURING THE NEXT hour I showed Mr. Fenshaw and his wife over the whole mission, each of us carrying a bright new oil lamp from their wagon. The amount of stores they had brought with them made my precious supply from the morning seem very unimportant. The Reverend Stanley Fenshaw and his wife had been working for the past five years at the Anglican Mission in Tientsin, and spoke quite good Chinese. Mrs. Fenshaw talked to all the children and gave instructions to the two young Chinese nurses she had brought with her. Then I took the Fenshaws to the chapel, where Miss Prothero lay, and Mr. Fenshaw said some prayers for her.

Now we sat in Miss Prothero's room. "The whole place is as clean as a pin," Mrs. Fenshaw was saying, "and all the bairns with some flesh covering their ribs. You're a bonnie girl, Lucy Waring."

I did not know what "bonnie" meant, so I only smiled politely. Mr. Fenshaw jumped to his feet and began pacing, his hands clasped behind his back. "It chills me to think of such responsibility falling upon your young shoulders, my dear," he said. "Miss Prothero wrote several times to the mission in Tientsin for help, but unfortunately they could not respond. There's never enough money for all that needs to be done.

"Now, however," he went on, "an event has occurred which I regard as something of a miracle. An English gentleman living in the county of Kent, a Mr. Charles Gresham, has approached our London headquarters with a most unusual request. He is interested in receiving into his family a young English-speaking girl from North China. It appears that he has for many years made a scholarly study of the region. He promises that if we recommend a suitable young person he will make a substantial donation to our work. Our director in Tientsin remembered Miss Prothero's letters, in which she had spoken of you at some length. He therefore cabled London, asking if Mr. Gresham would accept an English girl who had lived all her life here. And Mr. Gresham was delighted."

I sat with growing fear as Mr. Fenshaw continued. "Our people made full inquiries about Mr. Gresham. He is married, with a family, and held in high respect. So you'll go to England, Lucy, live with a good family and be well cared for." He smiled, expecting me to show delight.

"That's . . . very kind." My voice was shaking. "But I—I'd rather stay here, please. I'm sure I could be useful to you."

Mr. Fenshaw looked a little sad at my response. "I'm afraid not, my dear. You see, Mr. Gresham is providing funds for our mission to take over the work here only if you go to England to live as one of his family. That is the arrangement. Now, would you have us go away and leave the children with only you to care for them through the years to come? Surely not, if you love them."

Hope died within me. It had been cowardly of me even to ask if I might stay. I had always believed that Miss Prothero was mistaken in refusing to sell our girls when they were too big to be kept at the mission. Now that I was the one to be sold I could scarcely complain. I wondered briefly what Mr. Gresham was like, and then hurriedly closed my mind against any further thought of him. I tried to smile. "Yes, I understand, sir. When must I go?"

"In a few days. I shall take you to the railway station at Yang-su myself. Our mission will send somebody to meet us there and take you to Tientsin." He smiled at me encouragingly. "You will be going home by ship, of course. It will be a year or two before this wonderful Trans-Siberian Railway is completed. Two of our people who are retiring to England, Dr. and Mrs. Colby, will accompany you. I'm sure you'll have a splendid time."

I said, "Thank you, sir," and stood up. My head felt very strange, as if my mind had curled up inside it and gone to sleep so that it could forget everything for a little while.

"Now off to bed with you, child," said Mrs. Fenshaw, not unkindly. "You must be tired out."

I slept deeply that night, but not well, for my dreams were troubled. In one I saw the house in the mysterious drawing, the house called Moonrakers. I entered it, and moved among English foreign devils who could not see or hear me, and who walked through me as if I were a ghost.

In the morning I took out the piece of canvas with the sketch of Moonrakers on it. Today it made me feel uneasy, almost afraid. I told myself that this was because it reminded me of the strange land where I would soon have to face a new life, and I put the sketch away.

For the next two days I felt almost as much like a ghost as I had felt in my dreams, for suddenly there was nothing for me to do. The mission began to run so easily that I felt miserable, realizing how poorly I had managed in the past. On the second day Miss Prothero was buried under the old plum trees near the wall of the mission where she had worked for so long. Mr. Fenshaw conducted the service.

On the third day I went to see Dr. Langdon in Chengfu. When he opened his door I saw that his face was drawn and there were dark hollows under his eyes. "Come in, Lucy. I didn't expect to see you so soon."

He began to make tea and it seemed that he avoided looking at me.

I said, "Please, Dr. Langdon . . . what happened about Mr. Sabine?"

"I was able to do as you asked," he replied, gazing at the kettle. "I'll take you up to the cemetery later, Lucy."

It was difficult to speak. "What happened? What did they do?"

He shook his head. "It's foolish of you to ask, Lucy. And it doesn't matter anymore. He told you not to think about it. Tell me your news of the mission. How's Miss Prothero?"

When I could get control of my voice I told him of all that had happened. He showed no surprise when I spoke of Miss Prothero's death, and as we drank our tea he listened to the rest with growing pleasure.

"So you'll be living with a good family in England," he said. "Well, that solves a lot of problems. But why aren't you excited, Lucy?"

"I suppose because I don't really want to go."

"It's best for you. China will be dangerous soon. If I were young I might clear out myself." He rose, and took a brown envelope and a single sheet of folded paper from a small cabinet. "In the envelope are the papers concerning your marriage, and the will. I went to visit Mr. Sabine after you left Chengfu that morning, to ask if there was anything more I could do. He wrote this note and asked me to give it to you."

I unfolded the paper. The message was written in a bold hand:

> Dear Lucy,
>
> I don't know when you will be going to England, but I would like you to delay saying anything about our marriage or approaching my solicitors until six months have passed. Also, would you leave some of your wedding-present money with Dr. Langdon? I want to repay him for his kindness, and I have nothing left of my own.
>
> Never change.
>
> With love from your devoted husband.
>
> Nick

There was a pricking behind my eyes, and I wished that I could cry. I did not think that the last line in the note was meant to mock me. More likely it was to mock himself, and I could almost see him grin as he wrote it.

"What does 'never change' mean?" I whispered.

"I guess it means that he liked you the way you are."

"I'll do as he asks, Dr. Langdon. And I want you to keep all the money. You need it for your work with the sick more than the mission does now."

He hesitated, then nodded reluctantly. "I'm deeply grateful, Lucy."

When we had finished our tea we walked up the hill to the English cemetery. Dr. Langdon led me to a new mound with a wooden cross on it.

The name Nicholas Sabine had been burned into the cross with a hot iron. We did not speak. I stood with my heart aching, almost glad to be leaving a China where men like Huang Kung had the power to do these terrible things. Some small white flowers were beginning to show with winter's end, and I made a little bouquet and laid it on the grave. I said, "Sleep in peace, Mr. Sabine." Then we walked silently down the hill.

When we said good-by in the street that led to his house, Dr. Langdon kissed me on the cheek. "Take care of yourself, Lucy. And if you think of me, try to think of me as a friend."

"How else would I think of you?"

He looked troubled and uncertain. "Well, you never can tell."

As I walked back to Tsin Kai-feng my thoughts returned to those last words of Dr. Langdon's. What could have been in his mind? I found no answer, but at least it kept me from thinking about my future, among strangers in a strange land. When I reached the mission, Mrs. Fenshaw came bustling into the hall and said, "Lucy, come have some dinner. Tomorrow will be a long day for you."

"Tomorrow?" My heart turned over.

She smiled and put an arm about me. "Aye. We've had a message from Tientsin. They're sending someone to take you there tomorrow. Your first step on the long road home."

CHAPTER FOUR

I SAW MY OWN country for the first time on a June evening, just before sunset. As we steamed up the English Channel, Dr. and Mrs. Colby and I and all the passengers were at the rail, gazing at the distant coastline. I felt curious and a little moved to be coming at last to the land of my own people, but also very nervous.

Although I now wore English clothes provided for me by the Tientsin Mission, I knew that I did not think like a proper English girl. At first I had found it impossible to move easily with the long skirts flapping around my ankles, and I still could not understand why I had to wear frilly cotton petticoats underneath. I had let my hair grow on the ten-week voyage, as I was told young English ladies did not wear their hair short. My cheeks had filled out and my nails, once chipped and broken, were now as neat and smooth as a mandarin's. In spite of all this, I knew that in many ways my mind was still patterned by my Chinese upbringing.

My happiest moments on the voyage were when the sun had gone down and I could find a quiet corner of the deck to be by myself under the stars. Then I would think about the children at the mission, and remember all the things we had done together. Sometimes I thought of Nicholas Sabine and that night in the prison. It seemed remote, as if it had all happened in another world. I remembered his last words to me: "It's just a dream, really." That was how it seemed to me now, just a dream. But I never thought of him without sadness. Perhaps he was a wicked man, as Robert Falcon had said, but he had the saving grace of laughter, and he had been so full of life.

The next day we sailed slowly up the Thames to the Royal Albert Dock. I grew more apprehensive with every moment. At last we were told we could disembark, and as we went down the gangway I was clutching Mrs. Colby's arm. All around us on the dockside excited reunions were taking place. I saw a man with a pale narrow face and thin dark hair move away from a little group of ladies and walk toward us. I judged him to be in his late fifties. As he reached us he smiled eagerly and said, "Good afternoon. May I ask if you are Dr. and Mrs. Colby?"

"We are indeed," said Dr. Colby. "And you must be Mr. Gresham."

Tucking his cane under one arm, Mr. Gresham shook hands with the Colbys. Then he turned his smile on me, a rather toothy smile that seemed too big for him. "Well, well, so this is Lucy Waring. Welcome to England, and to my family."

He put out his hand and I took it, dropping a curtsy as I did so, not realizing until it was too late that he had leaned forward and drawn me toward him a little, to kiss me on the cheek. The result was that as I came up I butted him slightly in the face with my head.

"Oh, I'm sorry!" I cried, and went crimson with embarrassment.

He gave a quick, flustered laugh, said, "My own fault entirely," then turned to the Colbys. "Will you all come and meet my family?"

Mrs. Gresham and her two daughters found themselves being introduced to a red-faced creature who stared at them wordlessly. Mr. Gresham kept laughing and talking, but I was so numb with shame that even when somebody asked me a question I made no reply. Mr. Gresham had a strange, mechanical smile that came on suddenly, then was switched off. After what seemed an eternity, Dr. and Mrs. Colby said good-by, and ten minutes later the four Greshams and I were on our way to Charing Cross Station for the trip to their home in Kent.

I had never before seen so many foreign devils all at once, and the train we boarded was huge and splendid compared to that in which I had traveled to Tientsin. I was wearing the best of my three dresses, but once in our compartment I realized how shabby I looked in comparison with the Gresham daughters in their beautiful silk dresses and their hats decorated with big colored plumes. I had never thought much about clothes before, but suddenly I was very conscious of my drabness, and this made me shrivel up inside even more.

The train moved off. There was silence in the compartment, except for the two girls whispering together. Mr. Gresham read his newspaper and Mrs. Gresham sat waving a small fan. She was small and plump, with lovely hair the color of sandalwood, blue eyes and a soft pink complexion. I tried to think of something to say to her, but my mind remained empty. I saw her close her eyes and sigh. When I thought of the impression I must have given so far, I could scarcely blame her for being anxious.

One of the two girls seemed to be about eighteen, the other a few years younger. Emily, the elder, was small and plump like her mother; Amanda, the younger, looked more like Mr. Gresham. The girls were now giggling, and darting little glances at me. At that moment I could almost have wished to be on a stealing expedition in Chengfu rather than there.

Suddenly Mrs. Gresham said sharply, "Stop that giggling at once, you two! Sit up straight and chat with Lucy, there's good girls."

They looked at each other helplessly for a moment, then Emily said to me, "Papa took us to see a comic opera about China, by Mr. William Gilbert and Sir Arthur Sullivan. It was called *The Mikado,* and he was the king there. Have you ever seen him? I mean, the real Mikado?"

I shook my head. I had never heard of him.

Amanda said to Emily, "It wasn't China, you silly, it was Japan."

"Don't be rude to your sister, dear." Mrs. Gresham fluttered her fan. "After all, I'm sure China and Japan are much of a muchness."

"I'm sorry, Mama," Amanda said without sounding sorry. She turned to me. "Who *did* you see in China, Lucy?"

I managed to find my voice. "Just people. Chinese people. I saw the mandarin Huang Kung once. He's a very important person."

"There! You see?" Mr. Gresham said hopefully. "Lucy's seen a mandarin. Isn't that nice?"

"There was a Lord High Executioner in *The Mikado,*" said Emily. "Did you ever see an executioner?" I nodded. "Did he have a big sword and cut people's heads off?" she asked with a giggle.

"Not always," I answered, my voice a little stronger now. "If you were a thief, he was only supposed to brand you with a hot iron. But Huang Kung's very strict—his executioner would cut your hand off."

Both girls stared, round-eyed. Emily made a mewing sound of horror.

"That's *quite* enough, Lucy!" Mrs. Gresham said in an agitated voice. "We don't want silly tales of that kind, thank you!"

I shrank back into myself, wondering what I had said wrong. Mr. Gresham gave me one of his sudden glassy smiles. "I expect you'll want to look out the window now, this being your first sight of England."

I gazed thankfully out the window, and gradually I began to take in the countryside, green as an emerald and so beautiful I could hardly believe my eyes. There were no flat plains of the kind I had always known.

Here the ground rose and fell, always gently. I saw giant horses with shaggy legs, working in the fields. Fine cows and sheep grazed on grassy slopes, and everywhere there were trees. Wildflowers grew along the hedgerows, and roses on the walls of little cottages.

What surprised me most was seeing no walls around the villages. In China even the smallest village was protected by a mud wall. Here all was open and unguarded. I sensed an atmosphere of peace lying like an invisible canopy over the land, and it had a strangely healing effect on me. It was as if the heritage in my blood carried with it an indefinable need that had been sleeping all those years. I suddenly knew myself to be a part of England, however strange she might appear to me.

Tears came unexpectedly to my eyes. Emily wrinkled her nose and said to Amanda in a loud whisper, "Look, she's a crybaby."

Mr. Gresham jerked his head up from his newspaper and glared. "How dare you, Emily!" he snapped. "That remark was most unkind."

Emily pouted as if about to cry herself. Mrs. Gresham said indignantly, "Charles, see how you've upset the poor pet."

"She is not a poor pet," Mr. Gresham replied irritably. "She is a young lady who should know her manners. You spoil her, my dear."

He gave me what I think was meant to be a reassuring smile, and resumed reading. Heavy silence fell. Without saying a word I had caused the family to be angry with one another again. I looked back out the window, scarcely daring to breathe. After several stops we came to a station called Chislehurst. Waiting for us there was a coachman with a big open carriage, and in this we set off along a lane that wound up a hill.

Amanda, the younger daughter, was sitting beside me. Suddenly she tucked a hand under my arm. "It must be so difficult to come to a strange country. If I were suddenly taken to China on my own, I think I'd be quite frightened."

I could almost have wept with gratitude. I turned and smiled at her, then I looked at Mr. Gresham, who sat facing me with his wife beside him, and the words came tumbling out. "I'm so sorry, Mr. Gresham. I know I've been stupid and impolite, but I didn't mean to be. I was nervous, and—and everything seemed to go wrong."

"Not at all," he said quickly. "Quite understandable, my dear. You'll soon settle down and feel at home." He sat back with an air of relief.

Mr. Gresham's house, High Coppice, stood on a ridge; beyond it the ground sloped down to a broad, wooded valley. The house was huge, and all straight lines. In China, rich people built their houses with upcurving roofs to harmonize with the spirits of earth and water and air, but at that time the only harmony I saw in High Coppice was the natural beauty of the ivy that mellowed the yellow brick walls.

The carriage halted outside the big front porch and a distinguished-looking white-haired servant, a butler, greeted his master. A less important servant, a young man in shirt sleeves, took my suitcase and carried it in. As we stood in the big hall, with the stairs rising to a gallery above, I looked about me in astonishment. I had never in my life seen so much furniture, so many pictures, mirrors, ornaments, statuettes. The only ornament in the mission, apart from one picture in the chapel, was my bronze shield, and this had survived only because I could not bring myself to chip it out of the wall and sell it.

Mrs. Gresham said, "Ah, Edmund dear, you're here." A man in his twenties, wearing a dark suit and a shirt with a high stiff collar, was coming down the stairs; obviously he was Mr. Gresham's son. He had the same pale narrow face, but where Mr. Gresham was almost jumpy in his movements, the son was sober and precise.

"Good evening, Mama," he said. "Was it a good trip? I see you've brought Papa's latest possession safely home." He gave me a carefully measured smile, but his reference to me as his father's possession had made me feel ill at ease again.

Mrs. Gresham said, "Yes, this is Lucy Waring. Lucy, I would like you to meet our son, Edmund."

"Welcome to High Coppice, Lucy," he said, and we shook hands.

"Edmund lives and works in London," said Mrs. Gresham, "but he has come down today especially to greet you."

"That's very kind of you, Mr. Gresham," I said.

"I think you would do better to call me Edmund." Another small smile. "Otherwise we shall invite a degree of confusion." He glanced at his father, who was now speaking with the butler.

"Edmund's a lawyer, he's very clever," Amanda said, swinging her handbag. "Mama, can I take Lucy up to her room?"

"Not 'can I,' 'may I.' " Mrs. Gresham sighed. "Very well, dear."

I was glad to escape from the hall. I felt happier with Amanda than with anybody else. She led me up the stairs and along a passage to a bedroom, twice as big as Miss Prothero's at the mission, with furniture in proportion. The huge wardrobe alone would have provided enough wood to keep our kitchen range going for a week.

"Take your hat off, and sit down while I unpack for you." Amanda busied herself with the clasps of my case. "Wasn't that journey *awful?* I'm sorry Emily was horrid to you. Now that she's eighteen, she's so stuck-up."

She began to lift the clothes from my case and lay them on the bed. "Oh dear, you haven't got many clothes, have you? And those you have got aren't very nice."

"They're what the mission in Tientsin found for me," I said.

Amanda held a dress in front of her and looked in the wardrobe mirror.

"I suppose they're missionary sort of clothes," she said. "I'll persuade Papa to buy you some new, pretty ones."

"Yours are beautiful," I said.

She looked at herself in the mirror again and fingered the pale blue silk of her skirt. "Yes, this is my best dress for traveling. But Emily has the nicest things, because she's Mama's favorite."

"You mean after the firstborn son? After Edmund?"

"Goodness, no! I don't think Mama really likes boys very much. I think she'd have been pleased if we'd *all* been girls."

I shook my head, bewildered. In China a girl-baby was often considered a disaster. It would take me a long time to understand this strange country.

At a tap on the door Amanda called, "Come in," and a maid entered carrying a copper jug of hot water with a cover to keep it warm. "Pour some in the washstand basin, Beattie," Amanda said. "Have you put out soap and towel? Everything Miss Lucy needs? Very well, that will be all."

The maid went out and Amanda said, "Mama and Papa have their own bathroom, but we're not allowed to use it. There's a hip bath in your cupboard. When you wake up in the morning, pull the bell ribbon, and when the maid comes tell her to bring hot water for your bath. There's lots of things I'll have to explain to you, but there's plenty of time. I'm going to change now—I won't be long."

When she had skipped away I sat down on the bed and stared about me in awe. Mr. Gresham was clearly an enormously rich man. It had struck me as strange that anybody should go to the expense of fetching a young girl from China, but now I realized he was rich enough to indulge whatever whim might take his fancy.

I removed my dress, washed my face and combed my hair afresh. Now that it was long enough I had begun to wear it in a thick plait. I put on another dress, patched at the elbow but not so dull as the other two. Then I went to the window. It looked out over beautiful gardens to the wooded valley below.

I gazed across the valley, and my mind whirled. Was I asleep and dreaming? On the far side of the valley stood a house I knew. The *only* English house I knew. There was a sketch of it on the old piece of canvas rolled up and still in my suitcase. Everything about it was the same as in my picture.

I became aware that Amanda had returned and was holding my arm. "Are you all right, Lucy? Are you all right?"

"I'm all right. I—I just felt dizzy for a moment."

"Perhaps your stays are too tight?"

"I don't wear them, they suffocate me. But please don't tell your mother. Mrs. Colby said it was wrong not to wear stays."

"I won't tell. You *look* as if you're wearing them, anyway."

I was unable to take my eyes off the house across the valley. "What do they call that house, Amanda?"

"Moonrakers." She giggled. "The Falcons live there, and Mama says it's just the right name for them. A moonraker is someone not right in the head. He sees the moon reflected in a pond and thinks it's a big round cheese lying there, so he gets a rake and tries to fish it out, and they call him a moonraker."

"Oh?" I said blankly. "And you said it suited the Falcons?"

"Yes, they are dreadful creatures who do all sorts of funny things. Edmund says they're very bohemian, whatever that means."

"Is Mr. Falcon a young man?" I asked.

"Oh no—he's about the same age as Papa. His wife's younger than Mama, though, and very beautiful. Then there's Robert, but he's abroad somewhere, and a younger son still at school."

I turned from the window. It was still hard to realize that only a mile away stood the house an unknown hand had sketched on canvas and left in the mission at Tsin Kai-feng. Robert Falcon had come to China from that house seeking something, with a useless map in his hands and a meaningless riddle on his lips. I wondered if I should tell Amanda now that I had met him in China, but I needed time to think about it first.

"Just now you called the Falcons dreadful creatures," I said.

She giggled again. "That's how we always speak of them. We hate them, and they hate us. It's been going on for years. A feud, Papa calls it."

"It must have begun for a reason," I said.

"It began when Mr. Falcon's father and Papa's father were young men in the army together, in India. They were great friends, but then they quarreled over something. They fought a duel with pistols, and killed each other. Papa and Mr. Falcon were just babies at the time, but the feud between their families has gone on ever since." She shrugged. "I suppose it isn't quite so bad now, but we still don't speak."

My head was beginning to ache with unanswered questions. What had Robert Falcon been seeking in China? What had Nicholas Sabine been seeking there? It must be the same thing, for they had both asked me the same riddle. And it must be something valuable, for China could be a dangerous place for foreign devils, as Nicholas Sabine had found.

"Come on," Amanda said. "I'll show you over the house."

I nodded, trying to empty my mind of speculation. Mr. Gresham had paid a lot of money for me, and I was living under his roof. There was enough for me to think about without racking my brains for an answer to a mystery I could not solve. My new life was about to begin, and I hoped fervently that I would be able to meet whatever new demands were made upon me without any further blunders. I could not know that before the evening was ended I would make the most dreadful mistake of all.

CHAPTER FIVE

AMANDA TOOK ME THROUGH the three floors of the Greshams' house, including the servants' quarters on the top floor. The servants outnumbered the people to be served, for Mr. Gresham employed two housemaids, a parlormaid and a lady's maid, besides the cook, the butler, the coachman, and the young footman. I noticed that the maids wore shoes with elastic sides, and Amanda told me that this was to avoid squeaking as they walked.

In the dining room we found the butler supervising the footman and the parlormaid as they laid the table for dinner. I now saw that the butler was much younger than his white hair had first made me think. His name, I had learned, was Marsh, and his manner was one of polite authority.

When we reached the drawing room I said, rather pink-faced, "Amanda, what are all those knives and forks on the dining table for?"

She stared at me. "For the different courses. Oh goodness, did you use chopsticks in China?"

"No, just spoons mostly."

"Well, just start with the cutlery on the outside and work your way inward. If you're not sure, watch what I do."

We spent half an hour looking at a photograph album, then Mr. Gresham and Edmund came in, followed by Mrs. Gresham and Emily. They were all beautifully dressed. Edmund seated himself in an armchair, leaned back, placed the tips of his fingers together and said, "You look very nice, Lucy. What a pretty dress."

Amanda sighed. "Men are so silly. Can't you see it doesn't fit her properly? It was made for someone else and it's been altered." She turned to her father. "Lucy must have some proper clothes, Papa. She hasn't anything that's suitable for paying calls."

"We shall have to see what can be done," Mr. Gresham said heartily. "Becky, my dear, I think that matter is to your address."

His wife agreed, but with little enthusiasm.

Emily was sitting on a couch, playing with a white kitten, and when there was a pause in the conversation Mrs. Gresham looked at me with a smile that seemed to be rather an effort, and said, "Do they have cats in Japan, Lucy?"

I was taken by surprise by the question. "I—I think so, Mrs. Gresham. We certainly have them in China."

"That is what I meant, dear. I think you should not be *too* ready to correct your elders, but we'll say no more for the moment. So you have cats in China. Do you like cats?"

"Well, they're better than no meat at all, Mrs. Gresham, but rabbit is much nicer."

Her eyes went glassy. I looked around and saw that everybody was staring at me with shocked expressions, while Emily clutched the kitten protectively to her. I said hastily, "I beg your pardon, I didn't realize you were talking about cats as pets. There are a lot of strays in China, and when there's a famine, we—"

"That will do, Lucy." Mrs. Gresham's voice was icy.

I sat looking down at my hands in my lap, the blood rushing to my cheeks. It was a relief when Mr. Marsh entered to announce that dinner was served. Although the sun had not yet set, the swan-necked gas lamps on the walls of the dining room had been lit. Mr. Gresham said grace, and a moment later the young footman and a maid began to serve dinner under Mr. Marsh's watchful eye.

Even if I had not felt too nervous to be hungry, I could never have eaten all the food that was offered for each course, but it was wonderful food, and as I became calmer I began to enjoy the dinner.

I was not drawn into the conversation, for which I was glad. Mr. Gresham talked very little. He had a faraway look in his eyes, as if reflecting on some weighty matter. When the maid and footman had withdrawn after serving a delicious dessert of peaches in syrup with cream, he seemed to emerge from his reverie. Leaning back in his chair, he dabbed his mouth with a table napkin and gave me one of his brief smiles. "No doubt it was a considerable surprise to you, Lucy, when you learned that you were to become part of an English family?"

"Yes, sir," I said meekly. I had been more distressed than surprised, but did not want to offend him by saying so.

"You'll never guess why Papa brought you here," said Amanda.

So far I had closed my mind to this aspect of my future because it made me nervous, but similar situations were long familiar to me as a bystander.

"Go on," Amanda said, "guess."

I hesitated. Everybody was looking at me expectantly, so I bowed my head politely to Mr. Gresham. "I know you paid a lot of money to the mission, sir. . . ." The phrases that came to my mind were the Chinese phrases I would have used had this been happening there, and I had to translate them as I went along. "I am greatly honored that you have chosen this insignificant person to be your concubine now that your wife is becoming old."

There was the most terrible silence, as if everybody had stopped breathing. Mrs. Gresham's eyes bulged with shock and indignation. My blood seemed to turn to ice, for I knew I had done something dreadfully wrong.

Mr. Gresham rose, his face dark with rage. *"How dare you?"* he said in a frightful whisper. "How *dare* you speak so, in front of my family? Have

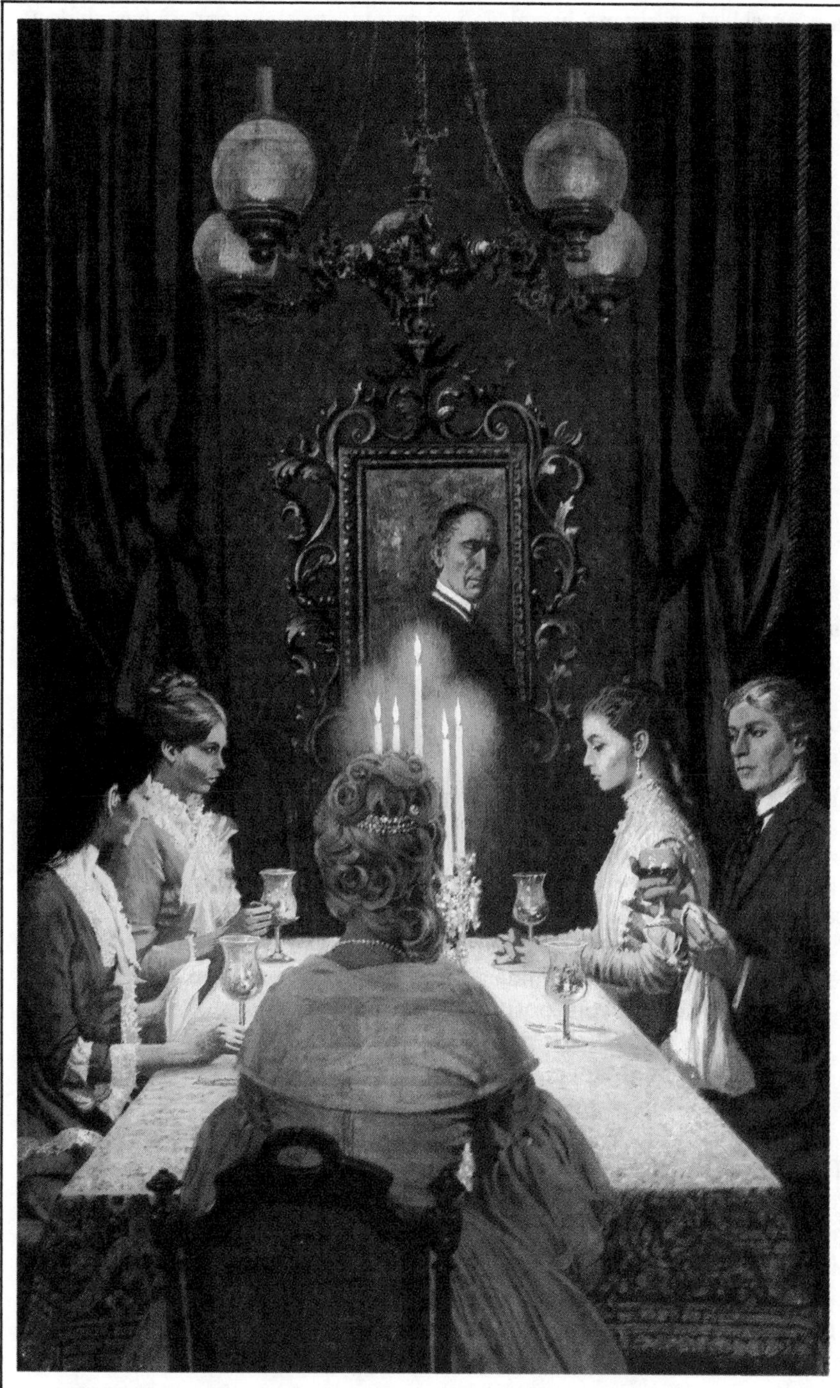

you no shred of shame in you?" He pointed to the door with a shaking hand. "Go to your room, miss! At once!"

Understanding broke upon me like a thunderclap. I had been a fool. I knew well that English gentlemen did not have concubines. But when I had been told that a rich man had bought me, I had at once assumed that it was for the same reason I would have been bought in China. I was so dazed by Mr. Gresham's anger that I could not find the strength to get to my feet.

"Father," Edmund murmured, "I think perhaps you should consider that in China—"

"Be silent, Edmund!" Mr. Gresham snapped. "You will make no defense of evil talk at my table. Miss! To your room at once!"

Behind me Mr. Marsh's voice said calmly, "If you please, Miss Lucy." He drew back my chair as I rose, and moved beside me to the door.

Mr. Gresham called harshly, "Leave us, Marsh. I'll ring if I want you."

"Very good, sir." The butler followed me out. Before the door closed I heard Mrs. Gresham say, in a rising wail of anguish, "Dear heaven, Charles, what kind of creature have you burdened us with?"

As I walked to the big staircase I felt a crushing despair. Then a voice behind me called to me. I turned and saw that Mr. Marsh was looking at me with an expression on his face in which I recognized, beyond the gravity, something of sympathy, and even of amusement.

"Don't distress yourself too greatly, Miss Lucy. I fancy Mr. Edmund already understands that your offense was not intentional but due to your background, and he will certainly argue the matter with the master when Mr. Gresham's anger has cooled a little."

I felt an upsurge of gratitude so powerful that tears stung my eyes. "You're very kind, Mr. Marsh."

He smiled. "Only the other servants address me in that way. You must call me Marsh."

"Oh, I couldn't, sir. You're an older male person, and . . ."

"You are no longer in China, Miss Lucy. For your own sake you must behave according to your position here."

"Yes. It's so difficult for me." My voice was shaking. "Whatever I say seems to make them angry. And Mrs. Gresham thinks I make up tales."

He flicked a tiny piece of fluff from his sleeve. "May I offer you some advice, Miss Lucy? You are now with an English family of the upper class. They have their virtues and their faults. One of their faults is a blindness to everything beyond the borders of their own little world. They believe in their hearts that God is an English gentleman, and it therefore follows that their customs have the stamp of divine approval."

I was astonished at the way Mr. Marsh spoke. He must have seen my surprise, for he went on, "You wonder at a servant who expresses himself in this way? Well, I was for many years in the army, and I served overseas a great deal. Like you, I have seen a hundred things that go beyond the imaginings of Mr. Gresham and his family. I also had the good fortune to serve as batman to an officer who was a scholar. We spent many long hours talking together over the years."

I was reminded of Miss Prothero making me practice the art of conversation. "I understand, Mr. Marsh—I mean, Marsh."

He smiled his approval, then went on, "The word concubine would never be spoken in front of English ladies. You have lived all your life in China, and I have no doubt you wore trousers, as they all do. Here, the sight of a woman in trousers would shock most people. Even the legs of a grand piano are draped because legs are deemed to be somewhat improper. If you refer to them, you must speak of 'lower limbs.' I hope this gives you some inkling of the shock which struck the family just now when you suggested that Mr. Gresham had bought you as a concubine?"

"Yes. Oh yes," I said feebly. "But you . . . you *were* joking about piano legs, surely?"

"I fear not, Miss Lucy." He glanced across the hall. "If I may advise you, try to carry on tomorrow as if nothing had happened. I'm sure you will find matters have improved. Avoid speaking of your life in China and devote yourself to learning the ways of this country." He gave me a little bow. "I'll wish you good night now, Miss Lucy, and see that some hot milk is sent to your room."

I was so touched by his kindness that I could hardly speak. "Thank you, Mr.—thank you, Marsh, with all my heart."

I went to my room, and the maid Beattie brought me hot milk. I sat up in bed, thinking that tomorrow I would make a new start and avoid further catastrophes. Sleep did not come easily, and I awoke soon after dawn. At half past seven there came a tap on the door, and before I could answer Amanda darted in, wearing a dressing gown. "Lucy, how *awful* you were last night! Emily told me a concubine is like another wife. No wonder Papa was furious!"

"Amanda, I truly didn't mean to insult your parents. I'm so used to the way people live in China that I—"

"That's what Edmund said. There was an awful commotion, but in the end Papa decided to do nothing more about it. . . . There's not much he *can* do. I mean, he can't send you back to China."

"I suppose not," I said, trying to hide my regret. "Amanda, why *did* your father bring me to England?"

"Oh, it's one of his schemes. He's always thinking of schemes to make us rich, but they never work. . . ." She giggled, then opened the door and darted out before I could question her further.

When I went downstairs Edmund was in the dining room and had already almost finished breakfast. I said a timid "Good morning."

"Good morning, Lucy." He studied me in a manner neither friendly nor unfriendly. "In England we serve ourselves breakfast from the dishes on the sideboard." He waved a hand in that direction. After I had taken some bacon and kidneys he rose from the table, saying, "You will excuse me. I must go to my office in London, and I have a train to catch. I suggest that last night's—ah—misunderstanding is best left alone. No doubt I shall see you again when I come down at the weekend. Good morning."

Only a few minutes after he had gone Mr. Gresham and Amanda arrived. The atmosphere during breakfast was uneasy, but still far better than I had dared to hope. Mrs. Gresham and Emily rarely rose before eleven, I learned. After breakfast Mr. Gresham said, "Time for your piano practice, Amanda. Run along now. I have matters to discuss with Lucy in my study."

He took me to a large room cluttered with a host of strange objects. Books were everywhere, even on the floor. There was a desk in one corner, piled with papers and bearing a large globe. A human skeleton hung from a bracket on one wall. A dusty telescope was mounted on a tripod near the window. There was a model steam engine on a shelf.

"Well now," Mr. Gresham said enthusiastically, waving an arm to encompass the room. "As you see, I am a keen student of the Orient."

I looked around the study for help in replying. On the globe I saw a ring had been drawn with red pencil around the province of Jehol in North China. On the wall beside the skeleton there were large-scale maps. On one I recognized the Gulf of Liaotung. The table near the fireplace held a large tray on which a landscape had been molded in some kind of clay.

"Come now," Mr. Gresham said with a touch of impatience, pointing to this. "Surely you see that this model represents the province of Shansi?"

"I'm afraid I've never been there," I said.

"Oh?" He gave me a blank look. "Well, never mind. I'm sure you are familiar with much else."

"I recognize that map of North China on the wall," I said, anxious to please, "and you've marked Jehol province on the globe, but a lot of your things aren't to do with China, Mr. Gresham. They would never display a skeleton, because it would be somebody's ancestor—"

"No, no, the skeleton has nothing to do with it," Mr. Gresham said testily. "That concerned an interest I have now discarded." He looked around the study as if vaguely surprised. "I seem to have some articles here that hark back to former interests, but ignore them, Lucy. We are concerned with *China*."

He took a small Oriental box out of his desk. "We are hunting for something, you see. You know China, so you are the right person to assist me in the search. Oh, I expect no miracles, Lucy. Perhaps it will take months of patient deduction."

I found all this very bewildering. "Do you mean you wish me to go with you to China to help find something?"

"Heavens no, child! Someone else will attend to the traveling. My task is to apply intellect to this affair." He gave a smug smile. "Deduction must come first, and you, with your knowledge of the East, will provide the framework in which the power of my intellect can operate." He opened the box and took out a slip of paper. "I will give you a strange clue to think upon," he said. "Now listen."

Before he had even begun to read from the paper I knew the words he would speak, but this foreknowledge did not diminish the shock.

"Beyond the twisted giant's knife . . ."

I knew the riddle by heart. Robert Falcon had recited it by the mission wall. And Nicholas Sabine in Chengfu prison. . . . Unwanted memories broke suddenly into my mind, seeming to sweep me back into the past. . . . I had laid a bouquet of flowers on Nicholas Sabine's grave, and I still had the ring and the papers. But I did not want him to linger in my memory, for it brought me an aching sorrow.

". . . Rest the sightless tiger's eyes," Mr. Gresham ended.

I drew a deep breath. "I know the riddle, Mr. Gresham. I've heard it before. In China. I met Mr. Robert Falcon there."

"What?"

"It's true, Mr. Gresham. Amanda's told me about the family that lives across the valley, and that the elder son Robert is abroad. Well, I met him in China, and he asked the same riddle."

"You met him? Did you help him? Did you tell him the answer?" There was as much anger as alarm in Mr. Gresham's voice.

"No sir," I said quickly. "I don't know what the riddle means."

He sighed with relief, then began to pace the study. "Extraordinary! But no—perhaps it's not so surprising that you met him, if the young whelp went out to search the area." He swung around to me. "Tell me all about it."

As briefly as I could, I told of my meeting and what had passed. Mr. Gresham rubbed his chin. "Did he show you a map?"

"Yes, but a lot of things were missing from it. He said they were on another map."

"I know. His was the Falcon map. We have the Gresham map. The two can only be read together." He picked up a rectangle of parchment. "Lucy—look. Can you remember the map young Falcon showed you?"

I gazed at the features drawn in black ink on the parchment and shook my head. He frowned, and waved a hand to indicate the globe, the books, and the carefully made miniature landscape. "I am gradually assembling facts, Lucy. If we persevere we shall be able to narrow down the search to a small area." He smiled one of his brief smiles. "My methods will prove superior to those of Robert Falcon, have no fear. I think it best first for you to know the whole story, so you will understand what I am trying to do. Have you heard of the Opium Wars in China?"

"Yes. Miss Prothero told me about them."

"Well, my father and John Falcon were young officers with the British Army in China in 1842. Both had been married the year before. During the campaign they were sent as couriers on a secret mission which took them through territory where two warlords were fighting each other for control. They skirted the battleground, and at dusk came on a dying man who had dragged himself away from the fighting. They could not understand a word he said, but from his fine uniform they concluded he was the defeated warlord himself. As they tried to tend his wounds he died."

Mr. Gresham moved to his cluttered desk and sat down. "There are many details we can never know . . . but on the dead man they found . . . something. A bag, a case, we don't know what, but it contained the dead warlord's personal treasure. Whatever it was, my father and John Falcon decided to take it rather than leave it on the body.

"They spent a week on the whole journey. We don't know their route, but I believe they stayed in a temple one night, because a temple is mentioned in the riddle. However, at some time they found that their presence had been discovered by enemy patrols, and they were in great danger of being caught. Therefore they hid the treasure."

Mr. Gresham looked at me, blinking rapidly. "After hiding the treasure they continued on their mission, and had the good fortune to complete it safely. Then, two months later, their regiment was withdrawn from China and sent to India. As they had had no chance to regain what they had hidden, John Falcon wrote a cryptic piece of doggerel to indicate the whereabouts of this hidden fortune, and both men made wills, which they gave to their commanding officer for safekeeping. Attached to each will was a brief account of their exploit, with a copy of the riddle, and one of the two complementary maps." Mr. Gresham grimaced. "All very romantic . . . They wanted to be sure that if anything happened to either of them, both families would share the fortune." He shook his head dolefully. "And then they quarreled over some foolishness. The upshot was a duel. Both men were mortally wounded."

He rose and began to pace the study again. "Now the two families are rivals for the treasure. It will go to whoever first lays hands on it. That hotheaded young fool Robert Falcon appears to be blundering about China in search of it. Well, let him waste his time! This battle will be won by intellect, Lucy." He tapped a finger to his temple.

Something was puzzling me. "Why haven't you or Mr. Falcon searched for the treasure before, Mr. Gresham?"

"Because we first learned of it less than two years ago! You see, the wills and the other documents were entrusted to an officer who was then killed in an uprising. They were sent home to his widow. She could never bring herself to go through his effects in detail, so they were stored away in her attic. More than fifty years later, her grandson found the two sealed envelopes, marked with the names of the two men. He took them to the War Office, who forwarded them to Harry Falcon and to me respectively. Until that moment, nobody had known of our fathers' exploit in China—and both families have been careful to keep the secret ever since."

But somebody outside the two families *did* know of the fortune, I thought. Nicholas Sabine had been seeking it too.

"If only we had some idea of what to look for," Mr. Gresham was saying. "For instance—is it large or small?"

"It can't be very big, Mr. Gresham. I mean, emeralds don't take up much room—even a small purse could hold a fortune."

I thought his eyes would start from his head. *"Emeralds?"* he cried. "How do you know? Did you tell Falcon? Were you lying to me just now? Answer me at once!"

"But—but it *says* emeralds in the riddle," I said. "Tiger's eyes, sir. That's what they call them round Chengfu. I thought you knew. I thought Mr. Falcon and *everybody* knew. Please forgive me for being so dense."

He threw up his arms in delight. "Thank heaven you were! It prevented you telling Falcon! I was right, you see—you don't realize how much you know, Lucy. But I shall draw it out of you. Your knowledge and my intellect will do the trick."

At luncheon Mr. Gresham proudly announced that with my help he had already discovered exactly what the treasure was. Though this did nothing to tell us *where* it was, he remained enthusiastically convinced that he was well on the way to success, and seemed to regard me more kindly.

I wanted to persuade Mrs. Gresham and Emily also to like me a little better, but I soon came to realize that the hope of my doing so was small. Edmund returned for the weekend, and I was pleased to see him because I felt that at least he did not positively dislike me. Sunday we attended matins at the village church. I had looked forward to this, sure that there I would be able to stop worrying about making blunders and be at ease.

It was in church that I first saw the Falcons. It seemed that the Falcons and the Greshams were the most important families in the village, for their pews were placed in front of the main congregation, facing one another. Mr. Falcon had the same fair hair as Robert, and wore a short beard. His wife was also fair, with a beautiful oval face crowned by honey-colored hair. Slender and graceful, she looked a happy person.

There were people with them, all dressed strikingly and seeming very full of self-confidence as they chatted in rather loud whispers before the service began. I heard Mrs. Gresham whisper to her husband, "They have some of their fast poet and painter friends staying the weekend with them, I see. How can they bring such scandalous people to church?"

There was only one anxious moment during the service. We were singing the *Te Deum*, and I was caught unprepared when a number of people stopped singing the line "Thou didst not abhor the Virgin's womb." Because the volume of singing suddenly dwindled, my own voice rang out loudly, and again I was aware of Mrs. Gresham's look of displeasure.

It was not until we were on our way home in the carriage that Mrs. Gresham let out a long hissing sound, as if she had been holding her breath all through the service. "Charles, that child chose to disgrace us in front of the whole village. Deliberately."

Edmund said, "You have no evidence that it was deliberate, Mama."

"Nonsense!" she snapped. "Lucy Waring, the words in that particular line of the *Te Deum* are not for the lips of ladies."

Bewilderment was added to my misery. Were wombs, like legs, for some reason considered improper? Mr. Gresham said nothing, but sat with his hand resting on his cane, glowering about him.

THAT FIRST WEEK at High Coppice set the pattern of my life there. Every morning I tried again and again to help Mr. Gresham make deductions from his clues. Every afternoon we paid or received "morning calls"—a strange name for visits made in the afternoon. I hated them. We made conversation while sipping tea and eating cucumber sandwiches. At first many questions were asked me about my life in China, but I had learned my lesson and never said more than a word or two in reply. So I was soon considered dull and uninteresting.

The evenings were spent in the drawing room, though often Mr. Gresham went to his study. This was a time for the ladies to gossip while they did needlework. Occasionally we would play pencil-and-paper games. The game I liked most was anagrams. Each of us in turn would give the others two or three short words, from which they had to make one long word.

Each weekend Edmund came down from London. I looked forward to this because he was always pleasant to me in his formal way. He seemed a man without real warmth, but he had a lawyer's sense of what was fair. However, my moments of pleasure were few. Day after day went by and I could not find one single thing to do that was in any way useful. It seemed wicked that I did not feel happy, for I was never hungry now, I had pretty clothes and every comfort, and no burdens of responsibility. Yet sometimes I lay in bed at night wondering how I could endure the years ahead, for I lived with people who had no need of me and who did not like me much, except perhaps for Amanda. I had always been needed before, and the children had loved me. This was what I missed.

Mr. Gresham slowly lost his enthusiasm for our daily task. I was not surprised, for we had made no progress at all, and Amanda had warned me that her father was a man of short-lived enthusiasms. But a frequent subject of conversation was still the need of both the Greshams and the Falcons to restore their fortunes. At first I could not believe it, but slowly I came to understand that Mr. Gresham lived on a private income, and his capital was dwindling as he used a little each year for living expenses. The same applied to Mr. Falcon, except that according to the Greshams he and his wife frittered their money away uselessly.

My failure to help solve the riddle of the warlord's treasure added to my uneasiness. I was another mouth to feed, and I gave nothing in return.

CHAPTER SIX

TOWARD THE END OF breakfast one morning, Marsh entered, and Mr. Gresham looked up and said, "Yes, what is it?"

"Good morning, sir. I have just heard from Beattie that she saw Mr. Robert Falcon passing through the village in a carriage yesterday afternoon. I felt you would wish to be informed."

"Ah! So the young fool's back from China, eh?" Mr. Gresham pulled at his chin and looked at Marsh with a touch of anxiety. "Did Beattie say how he looked? Did he have a look of *success?*"

"I questioned Beattie closely, sir. In her own words, he was 'all sort of broody,' and when another carriage got in his way he looked 'as black as Newgate's knocker.' "

Mr. Gresham gave a satisfied chuckle. "I expected nothing else. Nobody ever found a needle in a haystack by fumbling about blindfolded. You and I must resume our labors, Lucy. We've been somewhat remiss of late. Very well, Marsh. That will be all."

Mrs. Gresham and Emily had joined us at breakfast, which did not happen very often. When Marsh had gone Mrs. Gresham said, "Lucy, you realize that we do not acknowledge the Falcons, so if at any time you encounter Robert Falcon you must pass him by without recognition."

I felt a dull anger. I had no part in the feud and thought it both wrong and stupid to go on being enemies all these years. I felt sad too, for I would have liked to talk with Robert Falcon. He was a link with my past life.

I emerged from my thoughts to find that there was an air of excitement at the table. Mr. Gresham held a letter in his hand and wore a tantalizing smile, while Amanda and her mother were both speaking at once. "What does it *say*, Papa? Don't tease!" "Charles, has she been accepted?"

"All in good time. . . . First I had better explain to Lucy. In April, Amanda became too old to continue at the school here, so we have sought a place for her at a splendid college for young ladies at Cheltenham." He waved the letter. "She will start there in September."

Amanda exclaimed in delight, while Mrs. Gresham patted her hair and looked as smug as her husband. "Heaven knows how we shall afford it," he went on genially, "but if only Lucy will make a real effort and help me to deduce the whereabouts of the emeralds, then all problems will be solved."

I was glad for Amanda, but not for myself. She was my only friend in the family; without her I would be lonelier than ever.

For a week Mr. Gresham had me come to his study each morning to resume the weary task of poring over maps, books, and that maddening riddle. "This is the area," he said one day, spreading his hand on one of the wall maps. "Falcon was searching too far south. The boy's a fool."

"I don't quite see why he was wrong," I said, politely but incautiously. "There's no way to be sure, Mr. Gresham."

"Heavens, child, don't you ever listen to a word I say?" And suddenly it burst upon me. I had overlooked something so obvious that I could scarcely believe my own stupidity. I must have been gaping with shock, for Mr. Gresham said sharply, "What is it? Why do you look like that?"

"I've just thought of something," I cried. "Excuse me for a minute!"

I rushed from the study and ran up the stairs two at a time. Less than two minutes later I entered the study again. "It's this," I panted, and spread the limp and ancient piece of canvas on the desk. "I found this in the mission when I was quite small. You see? It's a sketch of Moonrakers."

He touched the canvas. "Good heavens. Why didn't you speak of it before?"

"I forgot. I think I was too worried about making mistakes here to remember anything else. But don't you see, Mr. Gresham? It means John Falcon was there, in our mission. He sketched Moonrakers there. So surely the mission must be the old temple where they hid the emeralds!"

He gazed down at the sketch, then shook his head slowly. "That's John Falcon's work, no doubt. He was something of an artist, and it runs in the family. But you're making a false deduction, Lucy."

"Surely not, Mr. Gresham, if we know John Falcon was there."

"Don't argue, child. The two soldiers were in China for months and moved about a great deal. There must have been scores of occasions for Falcon to make this sketch. Possibly he was quartered at the mission for a time. Above all, one simple fact puts your village out of court, Lucy. You have told me yourself that the river marked on young Falcon's map was different from the river there."

I felt almost sick with disappointment, but I could see that Mr. Gresham's reasoning was right. "I'm sorry," I muttered. "It came to me suddenly, and I was so excited I—"

"No harm done." Mr. Gresham shrugged. "And no good either." He picked up the canvas between finger and thumb, and handed it to me. "You'd better throw this away, Lucy. It's not a relic I wish to have in the house. Run along now, and we'll try again tomorrow. I think that another word-by-word examination of the riddle might be of use. We'll see."

I went to my room, guiltily determined that I would not dispose of the sketch. It was a treasured souvenir. Carefully I rolled it up and put it away.

After luncheon that day, when Amanda retired to her room to study, I went out to the terrace. This was a quiet time of day, Mrs. Gresham and Emily resting, Mr. Gresham dozing in the armchair in his study.

Marsh, returning from having a word with the gardener, stopped and said, "Good afternoon, Miss Lucy. May I ask if you're feeling more at home now?"

"I suppose so, thank you. I'm not quite so afraid of making blunders, but that's because I hardly say or do anything most of the time. I feel as if I were shut up in a cage."

He gave a sympathetic nod. "It's very difficult for you, Miss Lucy. Idleness is an art not easily learned. One must be born to it."

His dry manner made me laugh. I looked out over the gardens. It was a beautiful day. "Do you think I could go for a walk?" I said.

"A young lady does not go walking abroad on her own. But may I make a suggestion? If you take the path through the orchard you will find a footpath you can follow down into the valley. It's part of Mr. Gresham's land, so I think there can be no objection to your walking freely there."

I had not realized that the Gresham land extended beyond the gardens. "Will he be angry if I go without asking permission?"

"I shall be seeing the master very shortly myself. Leave the matter in my hands, Miss Lucy. I shall say the suggestion was mine."

I wanted to run forward and hug Marsh. He had helped me that first terrible evening of my arrival, and he had shown me nothing but kindness ever since. I restrained myself, but words came tumbling out before I could stop them. "Oh Marsh, you're so good to me and I do love you for it! I never knew my father, but if I could choose one, I'd want it to be you!" I stopped, afraid that I might have embarrassed him.

"That is the greatest compliment I have ever been paid, Miss Lucy," he said quietly, a glow of pleasure in his eyes. "And if I may presume to say so, I return your feelings of affection. You also have my respect, and that of all of us below stairs." He paused, then resumed his usual formal manner. "Now, when you reach the valley you will find that the path winds through tall bracken to a clump of trees with a wire fence and woods beyond. Don't go past the fence, Miss Lucy. That's Falcon land."

"I'll be careful. And thank you again."

"My pleasure, Miss Lucy." He smiled gravely, inclined his head and went into the house. As I walked through the gardens I thought how wonderful it would be to have a father like Marsh, someone who liked and cared about me.

Beyond the orchard the path led down between pines and silver birch. The smell was beautiful, and the sunlight slanting through the branches spread golden patterns on the grass. Below the trees the path followed a thick hedge for a while, then cut through a slope of high bracken. I walked slowly, enjoying every moment. Finally to my left I saw a wire fence, and realized that I'd almost reached the border of Mr. Gresham's land. As I turned reluctantly to go back, there came a scuffling from beyond a great bank of rhododendrons in front of me. Puzzled, I crouched low, peering through the thickly clustered leaves. In the dimness I glimpsed something white—a small face, topped by fair hair.

I moved closer to the wall of foliage and said, "Hello?"

From within a voice replied, "Wait a moment, please. I'm coming out." There was further rustling, then a big hanging branch was pushed aside and a small boy of nine or ten emerged from what appeared to be a tunnel running back through the bushes. He was dressed in knickers and a sweater, and he looked at me with sorrowful resignation. I knew that this must be Robert Falcon's brother, for his delicate features were so much like those of Mrs. Falcon.

"Are you going to tell them I'm here on their land?" he said anxiously, nodding back in the direction I'd come.

"No, I won't tell them."

"Thank you very much. They'd write to my papa, and then I wouldn't be able to come here again. I know who you are. You're Lucy Waring, the girl my brother Robert met in China. I'm Matthew Falcon." He put out his hand politely. "How do you do, Miss Waring?"

"How do you do, Matthew? Perhaps you'd better call me Lucy. It's more friendly."

"Yes, I'd like that. I haven't any friends here." He smiled at me and it caught at my heart; it seemed so long since I had known the simple warmth of a child's smile. "Would you like a cup of chocolate with me in my secret house?" He turned and nodded to the towering greenery behind him.

"Thank you, Matthew. I'd enjoy a cup of chocolate."

He pulled aside the leafy branch and we moved through a tunnel of foliage, emerging into a small clearing in the thick shrubbery, backed by a miniature cliff about twenty feet high. The clearing showed every sign of having been used for some time. There were half-coconuts hanging from low branches for the birds to peck at, a roughly made pen in which a tortoise and a hedgehog were sleeping, some bowls, and a lean-to shelter made of branches. There was a recess in the low cliff, not deep enough to be called a cave, but sufficient to give some shelter if it rained. Set in the recess was a square biscuit tin with a saucepan resting on top.

Matthew said, "It's all right for me to be here, because the fence stops against the bluff on that side of the rhododendrons and starts again on the other side." He pointed as he spoke. "So I can pretend this is Papa's land, and you can pretend it's Mr. Gresham's."

"I think it's all your own," I said. "After all, you found it, and it's really an in-between place."

"You're the only one who knows about it. Not even Robert knows." He knelt to lift the square tin from the spirit lamp it covered. "It won't be really a *cup* of chocolate. It's only a mug, and we have to share it."

"Then it's all the more kind of you to ask me."

He set a saucepan of water on the stove to heat. "I'd like to hear all about China. If I show you my zoo, will you tell me?"

"I'll tell you about China anyway, but I'd love to see your zoo."

"Come along then. I'm afraid it isn't very big." He took my hand. Suddenly I felt joyful; until a few months ago children had been taking my hand all my life.

"My tortoise and my hedgehog," he said. "I leave the pen open so they can get out, but there's always food and water and straw here while I'm at home during the school holidays." He led me across the clearing and parted some foliage. On a bed of grass wedged in the crotch of a thick branch was a thrush with one wing held in a splint made of thin cardboard.

"She's not really part of my zoo, because she'll fly away when her wing's better. I must find her some worms this afternoon." Still holding my hand, he showed me where at the edge of the clearing a trickle of water bubbled up among the rocks to make a tiny pool. He pointed to something by a big damp stone. "That's one of my frogs. There are two squirrels too, but I haven't seen them today. Oh, the water's boiling."

He ran back and turned off the spirit stove. Taking out a slab of chocolate, he broke off a piece, put it in a chipped mug, and added hot water and sugar lumps from his pocket. He stirred the liquid with a peeled stick, then stood the mug on a flat stone to cool while he made me a cushion of hay to sit on.

"The cocoa is nicer with milk," he said, "but I haven't any today." Handing me the mug, he sat down beside me comfortably.

I took a few sips, then said, "It's just right, Matthew. Here, your turn."

He was thoughtful as he drank a little chocolate. "I wish I could make a better splint for that thrush," he said at last. "The cardboard goes soft quickly, but wood's too heavy."

"What about whalebone?" There was plenty in my discarded stays. "I'll bring a piece next time I come."

He looked up. "Thank you so much. And I'm glad you're coming again. I'm here almost every day during the holidays, and I don't have to go back to school for nearly a month."

"But Matthew, if your parents don't know of this place, surely they must sometimes worry about where you've got to?"

"Oh, they know I like being in the woods. As long as I'm home in time for meals they don't mind. Papa says a boy has enough discipline at school—while on holiday he should do as he pleases as long as he doesn't cause any trouble."

"Your father sounds a very nice man."

"Yes. And Mama is nice too. I just wish they'd talk to me more, but they're busy painting and things like that, and they have lots of friends. Robert gets cross with Papa and Mama, though. He says they waste their time while the house goes to rack and ruin for want of money. He loves Moonrakers. That's why he went to China, to look for Grandfather's fortune. It would make everything all right if he found it, but he didn't."

As Matthew prattled on, a clearer picture of the Falcons began to form in my mind. I gathered that Mr. and Mrs. Falcon had little interest in the feud, but disliked the Greshams for themselves and so made no attempt to heal the breach. Robert regarded the Greshams as enemies since they were rivals for the fortune.

When we had drunk the last of the chocolate Matthew said, "I'm sorry to talk so much. I expect it's because there isn't usually anybody to listen. Will you tell me about China now?"

"Let me see. . . . I hardly know where to begin, Matthew." I looked up at the sky as I tried to order my thoughts, and was startled to see how far the sun had moved. "Oh my goodness, Matthew—do you know the time?"

"I heard the church clock strike just now. It must be half past three. Hasn't the time gone quickly?"

I took his hand. "I'm sorry, dear, but I dare not stay longer. Can I tell you about China another day?"

"Yes, of course, Lucy." He jumped to his feet and helped me up. "I don't want them to stop you coming again."

When I went to bed that night I felt happier than at any time since my arrival in England, but two days passed before I was able to see Matthew again. Then we spent most of our time talking about China while we put a whalebone splint on the thrush's wing. Soon everybody at High Coppice accepted the fact that I wandered away on my own sometimes, but since I remained within the grounds nobody seemed to mind. In truth, I think they were relieved to be without me.

TWO WEEKS LATER, on a Saturday, we all attended a church garden party on the fine lawns behind the vicarage. The small parish had only a few families of gentlefolk, and these circulated to chat with one another. So did the families of the shopkeepers and tradesmen, with the farm people forming yet another group. The Greshams and the Falcons had long experience of avoiding each other on such occasions, but all the same I wondered if I might catch a glimpse of Robert Falcon there. In fact, just as I was having trouble in manipulating the parasol Mrs. Gresham had insisted on my carrying, he appeared in front of me, raising his hat and smiling.

His face was still deeply tanned, and he looked very handsome in a gray jacket and fine-checked trousers with sharp creases. I was too surprised, and even alarmed, to wonder at the fact that whereas I had once thought of him as the ugly stranger, he now seemed handsome. It was only later I realized that living in England had changed my ideas.

"Miss Waring, how good to see you again," he said, with no hint of embarrassment. "And what a remarkable coincidence." He made a little bow, first to Mrs. Gresham and then to the rest of the family. "Your servant, ma'am. Young ladies. Good afternoon, sir."

I glanced urgently at Mrs. Gresham for help, but her face was blank with confusion, and Mr. Gresham was in no better shape. So, feebly, I said, "Good afternoon, Mr. Falcon."

Still smiling, he addressed Mr. Gresham. "No doubt Miss Waring has told you we met briefly in China. Will you be so kind as to permit me to steal her so that I may introduce her to my parents?" Mr. Gresham made a bewildered sound. Without waiting for more, Robert Falcon offered me his arm. I flashed a last look of appeal at Mr. Gresham, but he simply stood as if transfixed. So I had no alternative but to put my hand in the crook of Robert Falcon's arm, and next moment I was being introduced to his parents and Matthew. I glimpsed a twinkle in Matthew's eyes.

"Ever since Robert told us about you, I've wanted to meet you," said Mrs. Falcon. "I'm glad he has now taken the bull by the horns."

"More than one can say for old Gresham," Mr. Falcon said with amusement. "Robert, my boy, I think you may be the cause of him having a fit, by the look of him."

"Now Harry, behave yourself," his wife said gently. "Lucy lives with the Greshams. You mustn't embarrass her."

"Sorry," Mr. Falcon said cheerfully to me. "Well, have you been able to help Mr. Gresham find a solution to the mystery?"

"No, sir. I'm afraid I've been of little use."

"Oh, never say that. He should be content just to have you in the house. You're a pleasure to the eye, my dear."

Robert said, "If you've done with embarrassing her, Father, I suggest we stroll together for a while. I'm sure we'd all like to hear how Miss Waring is settling down in England."

For the next half hour we strolled and chatted, though I said very little myself. Every now and again I caught a glimpse of the Gresham family. Mrs. Gresham would beckon, and twice I tried to excuse myself. Each time Robert forestalled me by asking another question, and it seemed an eternity before he conducted me to where the Greshams sat taking tea.

"I really can't thank you enough for allowing me to renew old acquaintance with Miss Waring, sir," he said. "I speak for my parents also when I say it has been a pleasure." He bowed to us all.

As he moved away Mrs. Gresham let out a sound like that made by an enraged goose. Within five minutes we were in the carriage and the explosion came. I apologized, and even dared say I wished Mr. Gresham had not allowed Robert to lead me away, but my protests were brushed aside with a fine show of indignation.

On Sunday, the day after the garden party, Mrs. Gresham said I was not to accompany the family to church. She would explain to the vicar that I had a slight fever. Apparently everybody would understand that this was not true, but meant that Robert Falcon must not attempt again to breach the barrier between the two families.

At five o'clock on Monday I was taking tea in the drawing room with the family when Marsh entered carrying a silver tray with a card on it. Mrs. Gresham took the card and her eyes widened with shock.

"Robert Falcon?" she said angrily. "Good heavens, Marsh, you know very well that we are *never* at home to a Falcon!"

"Quite so, madam. However, the young gentleman brought what I understand is a very special gift for the master." He placed a long envelope on the tray and moved toward Mr. Gresham. "Under the circumstances I thought it my duty to ask the young gentleman to wait in the hall while I ascertained your wishes."

"Confound his impudence!" Mr. Gresham stood up, snatched the envelope from the tray and opened it, and a parchment slipped out. "Good heavens! This is the other map! This could answer all our problems. At least there can be no harm in seeing young Falcon for a moment, to hear what he has to say. Show him in."

Marsh went out. Mr. Gresham stood with his back to the fireplace, holding the lapel of his coat and striking a dignified position.

The door opened again. Marsh entered and stood to one side. "Mr. Robert Falcon," he announced.

CHAPTER SEVEN

HE WAS BEAUTIFULLY DRESSED, with a carnation in his buttonhole, his hat and cane in one hand. His manner was respectful.

"How very kind of you to receive me, ma'am." He greeted Mrs. Gresham first, then made a little bow to Mr. Gresham. "I hope I find you well, sir?" Another bow. "Your servant, young ladies."

Mr. Gresham cleared his throat. "I should be obliged if you would tell me the reason for this—ah—unexpected gift."

Robert smiled engagingly. "Sir, during my journey abroad I had time to reflect. I concluded it was a pity that our families should be bad friends as a result of events which occurred long ago. I come for a double reason. First, I extend the olive branch of peace, and in token of my sincerity I bring you the gift I believe you will be most pleased to receive."

Mr. Gresham weighed the map in his hand solemnly. "Does your father know of this?"

"Naturally, sir. I have his approval. I myself have tried to find the warlord's treasure, and failed. We hope that you may have greater success."

Mr. Gresham looked baffled. "Extraordinary," he muttered. "Most—um—unexpected. You mentioned a double reason, I believe?"

"I did, sir. I have a somewhat selfish reason for wishing to dispel the ill feeling between our families." He smiled at me. "I would like to be allowed to call upon Miss Lucy and hope you will give your permission."

I heard Emily squeak with surprise. Mrs. Gresham put a hand to her breast. Amanda gasped and wriggled. There was a long silence, during which Robert Falcon stood quite at ease, waiting, a polite smile on his lips.

"Ah . . . hum." Mr. Gresham sounded most uncertain. "Would you care to sit down, Falcon? Have some tea?"

"Thank you, sir, but I feel I've intruded long enough on this occasion. You will wish to give thought to my request." He smiled warmly again. "I shall await your decision with some anxiety, but rest assured my small gift is yours no matter what your answer may be." He turned to Mrs. Gresham. "With your permission, ma'am, I will take my leave."

Mr. Gresham, looking dazed, tugged at the bellpull, and by the time Robert had made correct good-bys to us all, Marsh was there to show him out. No sooner did we hear the sound of the carriage driving away than there was an outburst of excited chatter.

Emily was shrill with annoyance. "It's absurd! Why ever would he want to court Lucy? Mama, you'll never allow it, surely!"

"We must discuss this alone, Charles," Mrs. Gresham said. "I certainly don't want to be friends with the Falcons, but one must consider that Lucy's chances of marriage are not particularly glowing, and our responsibility for her may continue indefinitely."

Mr. Gresham, however, was exulting over the map. "Look, Becky! With this, Lucy and I can make a huge stride forward in our quest."

I was busy trying to untangle my thoughts. Did I want Robert Falcon to call upon me? This I knew was the first stage of courtship. Did I want to be courted? I was aware of an obscure yearning. In China I had heard girls of fourteen speak longingly of handsome young men in the village. Now I knew something of what they had felt. Yes . . . I would like to be held in the arms of someone who loved me. But Nicholas Sabine's face was suddenly clear in my mind's eye, and with it came an aching sense of loss.

With an effort I roused myself. "Excuse me, but I really would rather not have Robert Falcon call upon me, Mrs. Gresham."

Emily cried in triumph, "There Mama! Even *she* can see it's ridiculous for her to have a beau before I do!"

Mrs. Gresham looked at me coldly. "It would make a pleasant change, Lucy, if for once you were content to let your elders know best. Whether or not Robert Falcon shall call upon you is *our* responsibility, not a matter for a young girl to make up her own mind about."

Mr. Gresham looked up from the map. "We'll discuss it later, Becky. I want Lucy to come to the study so we can compare the maps."

Before and after dinner we traced out a new map with all the features from the old maps marked on it, but I could not identify it. It could have represented any of a dozen different places.

After the hope brought about by Robert's gift, Mr. Gresham's enthusiasm lasted for almost a week before dwindling again, though he was reluctant to admit this. "It's a matter of patience," he said. "Perhaps just one more clue will give us the pattern."

I thought wearily that one more clue would be of as little use as all the rest. I did not know then how wrong I was.

A note had been sent to Robert Falcon to say rather coolly that he might call upon me. I knew that Mrs. Gresham would never have allowed a Falcon to call upon her daughter Emily, but I was an extra young female who should be married off as quickly as possible to any young man of reasonable position who would have me.

Robert called twice a week, and we sat in the drawing room with Mrs. Gresham, making conversation. For me this was an ordeal. Robert was very good, talking freely and amiably. This smiling, attentive man was very different from the brusque, quick-tempered stranger I had met in China. I wondered which was the real Robert Falcon. Later, if Mrs. Gresham decided to let the courtship continue, I knew we should be left alone together for a little while during each visit. I hardly knew whether this would make things easier for me, or more difficult.

Then Matthew went back to his preparatory school, and amid great excitement Amanda was taken by her parents to the school for young ladies at Cheltenham. My life became more empty than ever. I desperately missed arriving at Matthew's secret house, to have him take my hand and show me some new feature of his zoo.

The best times now were when I was able to talk with Marsh for a little while. On one occasion I said, "There's something I thought of asking Mr. Gresham, but I'd like to know what you think of it first. You see, I've met

Dr. Cheyne once or twice when we've paid calls on his wife, and he seems a nice man. I wondered if I could help in his office and go on his rounds with him. He's always busy, and I could help with delivering babies."

For the first time I heard Marsh catch his breath in astonishment. "Delivering *babies?* Do you know what you're saying?"

"I've helped Miss Prothero deliver babies from when I was fourteen. After she was taken ill I had to do it on my own, so I'm quite good at it. And I can also stitch gashes, or splint broken fingers."

"You continue to surprise me, Miss Lucy. But I beg you not to mention your midwifery as a topic of conversation with the family."

"Oh, I won't. But I thought helping Dr. Cheyne would be all right. And, after all, ladies do have babies."

"Indeed. But the having of them is hardly acknowledged." Though his face remained straight, his eyes twinkled. "Many ladies feel that the good Lord might well have devised a less vulgar procedure. I'm afraid I must advise you against asking if you may help Dr. Cheyne. You will certainly be refused, and probably scolded for making such a suggestion."

This was a great disappointment to me. My spirits now fell even lower than before. It was Marsh in the end who came to the rescue, and in a very diplomatic way. Unknown to me, he approached Mr. Gresham and suggested that my behavior was less polished than a young lady's should be, owing to my growing up in the Far East. He therefore offered for the general good of the family reputation to devote an hour each day to coaching me in the finer points of custom and etiquette.

From then on, my hour with Marsh was the best time of the day. I listened carefully as he explained many bewildering matters of behavior, and practiced such things as the correct way to stir my tea, and how I should extend my hand to be shaken so that only the fingers were grasped. When he pretended to be a lady or a gentleman so that I could practice various formalities, we often had to stifle our laughter, but I learned quickly, for I knew that way we would have more time for chatting together. He told me of his years in the British Army, and listened with interest when I talked of my life in China.

I told him of Miss Prothero and Dr. Langdon. I would have liked to tell him about Nicholas Sabine, but though I trusted him completely, I had to carry out the wishes of the man I had married and keep silent until I had seen the solicitor in London.

There lay a huge problem. The six months I had been asked to wait had almost passed, and I was wondering how I could ever go to London without first explaining to Mr. Gresham. That, I knew, would be a very unpleasant occasion, and he might even refuse to let me go. But in the middle of October, Marsh again came to my rescue, this time by chance. He was allowed one day off each month, and in October he suggested to Mr. Gresham that it would improve my education if I were taken to London to see the sights.

Mrs. Gresham was dubious about allowing me to be escorted by a butler, but she was pleased with the results of Marsh's tuition and finally concluded that a visit to London would be a good thing for me. So Mr. Gresham gave Marsh money for the journey and for luncheon at a modest restaurant.

The day was a Wednesday. I packed the envelope containing my papers in my handbag, and we caught the ten-o'clock train. We had a compartment to ourselves. When the train pulled out of Chislehurst Station I said, "Marsh, will you do something very special for me? It's hard to explain, because it's a secret I can't tell you about until afterward. But I want to go to an address in Gray's Inn, a solicitor's office."

"A solicitor's office? I've no wish to pry into your business, Miss Lucy, but surely you should have spoken of this to the master?"

"I will, this evening. But you see, I promised a man in China faithfully that six months after leaving there I would . . . deliver some papers to a firm of solicitors, and not breathe a word to anybody until I'd done so."

Marsh's chin lifted. "A promise should always be kept. I imagine the man was English. Is he still in China?"

"In a way." My throat ached, and I swallowed hard. "I—I didn't want to tell you this part, but I must. He desecrated a tomb, and the mandarin had him killed. I saw his grave later."

"So this was the request of a dying man," Marsh said slowly. "Certainly you must not fail him, Miss Lucy. We shall go to Gray's Inn, and if Mr. Gresham is displeased, as I don't doubt he will be, then we shall meet his displeasure together."

I was startled. "Oh, Marsh! You'll get into trouble too!"

"Don't concern yourself on my account." He held my hand tightly for a moment. "If Mr. Gresham chose to dismiss me for helping fulfill a promise made to a man about to die, then I would prefer to serve another master."

I cried at that, slipping my arm through his and pressing my cheek against his shoulder, happy to know he was still my friend.

From Charing Cross we walked to Gray's Inn, past Covent Garden Market, where scores of laden carts jostled each other in seeming chaos, and then Holborn, where I saw my first steam omnibus. At any other time I would have been full of excitement at all the London sights, but the coming ordeal lay heavily upon me.

Gray's Inn was a big square, with tall houses around three sides of it and trees set in a large rectangle of grass in the middle.

"Do you wish me to come in with you?" Marsh said as we halted. "No doubt I can sit in a waiting room while you see the solicitor."

I hesitated, for I would have welcomed his support, but then I screwed up my courage. "I think I ought to do it alone."

"Very well." He nodded approvingly. "I shall wait on that bench under the tree." He pointed. "There is no need for you to tell me any more of this matter, Miss Lucy. I shall ask no questions when you rejoin me. I recommend that you act according to whatever advice the solicitor may give."

Two minutes later I stood outside a house that bore the brass plate of GIRLING, CHINNERY AND BRAND, the names on the envelope I carried. I could see Marsh settling himself on a bench under a plane tree. When I rang the bell, the door was opened by an elderly man in a black suit and white shirt with a very high collar. He invited me to enter, led me into a musty waiting room, asked me to be seated and inquired my business.

I drew a deep breath. "I am Mrs. Nicholas Sabine. My husband died abroad six months ago. He asked me to come here at this time, to see his solicitor. I have a number of papers with me."

The little man showed no surprise. "Quite so, Mrs. Sabine. Pray accept my sympathy. I am the firm's chief clerk, but your husband rarely called here, and I must confess I do not recollect him. May I ask which of the partners deals with his affairs?"

"Oh—you mean Mr. Girling, or one of the others?"

He smiled sadly. "There is no longer a Mr. Girling or a Mr. Brand with us. Several new partners have entered the firm since their day."

"I don't know which one Mr. Sabine dealt with. I'm sorry."

"Never mind, Mrs. Sabine. If you will be so good as to wait a few moments, I will inquire. There are some magazines to glance at. I fear *Punch* is not what it was. Far too radical. However . . ."

He left the room. I stared at *Punch,* but saw nothing. Five minutes later the clerk returned and conducted me to a door, where he tapped. Then he opened the door. "Mrs. Nicholas Sabine," he announced. I thanked him with a smile and went in.

Edmund Gresham rose from behind a desk. "Good morning, Mrs. Sab—" He stopped short, staring, as the door closed behind me.

Edmund? I froze with shock. Edmund was no less astonished.

"*You*, Lucy? What on earth does this mean?"

"I—I had no idea . . . Mr. Sabine didn't say it was you. I mean, the firm you work for. I—" I stopped in confusion.

Edmund moved around the desk and brought a chair forward. "Sit down, Lucy, and get your breath back. We must take this calmly." He returned to his chair and sat watching me. Slowly the worst of the shock faded. I had always known that Edmund was a partner in a firm of solicitors, but he had never mentioned its name. It was an astonishing coincidence that he should be Nicholas Sabine's solicitor . . . or was it? Nicholas had been seeking an answer to the riddle, so perhaps it was not so strange that he should have some connection with Edmund Gresham.

I was trying to decide where I should begin my story when Edmund said,

"I think it will be best if I ask a few questions. Now . . . first, did you come here on your own?"

I shook my head. "No. It's Marsh's day off, and he had permission to show me some of the sights of London. While we were on the train I asked him to bring me here. He's waiting on a bench outside."

"My parents know nothing of this?"

"No. I'll tell them when I get home. I couldn't tell them before, because I'd made a promise. You see—"

"Just a moment, Lucy. We'll come to the explanations later. First I want to establish the facts. You say you are Mrs. Nicholas Sabine, and that your husband is dead. Can you prove this?"

"Yes, Edmund."

I took the envelope from my handbag and gave it to him. There was a silence while he read each paper carefully.

"Hmm," he said at last. "These will certainly stand up in court if need be. Trust Nick to make a job of it." He took the letter Mr. Sabine had written to me before he died. "Do you know why he wanted you to delay for six months before coming to me?"

"No."

"I see. . . . Now, have you ever spoken of this to anybody? To Robert Falcon in particular?"

"No. I told Marsh I wanted to come here because of a promise I'd made in China to a man about to be executed, but I didn't say his name."

"Executed?" For the first time I heard a note of genuine feeling in Edmund's cool voice. "Was that how he died? My God . . . poor Nick. So he took one gamble too many at last."

My nerves had steadied again, and I felt it was my turn to ask a question. "You seem to have known Mr. Sabine quite well. Did you know about his going to China?"

Edmund gave me an unhappy smile. "It was I who engaged him to go. That was *my* way of trying to find the Gresham fortune. I was sure Nick Sabine would succeed if any man could, and I offered him one fifth of whatever he brought back." He looked down at my papers. "But it seems I was wrong. He won't be coming back."

I stilled the familiar ache that came with remembering the grave with my flowers on it. "Did you know him well, Edmund?"

He pursed his lips. "No man knew Nick well. A few women, perhaps. We were at school together, Nick and I and Robert Falcon."

"Robert Falcon!"

"Yes, to my regret. As you can imagine, Falcon hated me as a Gresham and did his best to make my life unpleasant. It amused Nick to protect me from him to a great extent." He shrugged. "But that's long ago now. I went on to study law. Nick preferred to enjoy himself. He was an adventurer—a gunrunner in South America, a riverboat gambler on the Mississippi. . . ." He tapped the papers in front of him. "And now I shall be obliged if you would tell me how all this came about, Lucy."

Even without the details, it took me a quarter of an hour to tell my story. Edmund listened carefully, making an occasional note on a pad of paper. It was not until my tale was told that he gave any sign of his personal feelings. Then he capped his pen, shook his head and exhaled a long breath. "I might have guessed Nick would never let Falcon come out on top," he said dryly.

"He said he wanted a wife to inherit something which an enemy of his might otherwise get. Was this enemy Robert Falcon?"

"Yes." Edmund stood up and paced slowly to the window. "They were always rivals, Nick and Falcon. Something about Falcon got under Nick's skin, and vice versa. They were always at each other's throats, on the playing fields or in class. Nick was a scholarship boy, and very poor. I think his father must have died when he was young, for Nick never spoke of him. His mother worked as a seamstress and I saw her only once. She died just before I went up to Cambridge. A scholarship boy is looked down upon, you know, by oafs with no brains but rich parents. Nick didn't give a damn, except with Robert Falcon."

Edmund turned back to his desk. "Now we'd better study this will. He leaves his whole estate to you." Edmund looked at me with the air of someone about to spring a surprise. "This means, among other things, that you will inherit Moonrakers in approximately one year's time."

My head reeled. "*Moonrakers?* But I don't understand. Moonrakers belongs to the Falcons, surely?"

"At present, yes. But Harry Falcon is a rather gay and reckless fellow. Against a short-term mortgage on Moonrakers he borrowed a substantial sum from a wealthy friend, named Ramsey. Should he fail to pay back the money in five years, Moonrakers would be taken over by Ramsey."

"But how does Mr. Sabine come into it?"

"The wealthy Ramsey fancied himself at the card table. Your husband, Lucy, belonged to the same London club and engineered a game which ran to high stakes. It's quite a dramatic tale, but the upshot was that Nick won the mortgage deed on Moonrakers. So when repayment falls due in a year's time, if Harry Falcon fails to meet it, the house will belong to you, as Nick's widow. But please note—as executor I am instructed to sell the property, if and when the debtor fails in his repayment."

If I felt anything at all, it was only a small sadness that Nicholas Sabine had made me his wife only to strike at his enemy.

"There is the rest of Nick's estate, of course," Edmund was saying. "He tended to spend money as fast as he made it, so I doubt that he'll have more than a thousand or two. But he always kept a reserve of stake money for his ventures. I'll consult his bank and let you know what to expect. Are you listening, Lucy?"

"I'm trying to, Edmund. Do you think your parents will be angry?"

"They will be amazed, of course. But when they hear the full story they will be well satisfied, for it means their responsibility for you will end when you have funds of your own. I advise that you continue your sightseeing with Marsh and return here at four o'clock, so that we can all go home together. Then I shall explain everything to Father myself."

"I'd be so grateful, Edmund. I've dreaded that part."

"You need worry no more. I urge you not to speak of this to anyone, not even to Marsh. If Robert Falcon came to know the secret, he might attempt some sort of delaying action to gain time. With Nick absent for so long, Falcon no doubt hopes he has met with some accident in China, as indeed he did. So not a word, Lucy." He smiled conspiratorially. "Let us take the Falcons by surprise when the time comes."

I did not share his pleasure. I did not want to take Moonrakers from the Falcons, but I could see no way of avoiding what Nicholas Sabine had set in motion.

Five minutes later I was with Marsh again. I told him that the solicitor had proved to be Mr. Edmund, and that we three would travel home together that afternoon, but explained unhappily that I was not allowed to say more.

"Put the matter out of your mind, Miss Lucy," he said gently. "I'm sure Mr. Edmund can be relied upon to do what is best for you."

That evening, when Emily and I had gone to bed, Edmund told his parents the strange story. At breakfast the next morning I could see that Mr. Gresham was full of suppressed excitement. When the meal was over he summoned me to his study. "Leave everything to Edmund," he said in a tense whisper as soon as the door was closed, "and next year you'll be able to send the Falcons packing. Since you are technically a widow of only six months, to encourage Robert Falcon is now out of the question. I shall write and tell him not to call again."

I felt an unexpected pang of disappointment. Robert's visits had been something of an ordeal, but he had been more friendly toward me than anyone except Marsh and Amanda and little Matthew Falcon.

DURING THE NEXT week or two I came to hate the occasional gloating look I detected on the faces of Mr. and Mrs. Gresham. They were reveling in the coming downfall of their enemies, and I knew I was to be the instrument of that downfall.

In the first week of November, Amanda came home for her half-term holiday. My pleasure at her return soon vanished, for she had become very condescending. I knew that with her good nature this would pass when she had gotten used to the novelty of becoming a young lady, but for the present it made us strangers. Through the servants I heard with dismay that Matthew Falcon had chicken pox and was being kept at school over the holiday, so I missed his longed-for company too.

On November 5 came the day when the English remember the Gunpowder Plot with bonfires and fireworks. Amanda pretended she thought Guy Fawkes Day childish, but when Mr. Gresham suggested that we should not trouble to celebrate it at High Coppice, she said that of course we must, because the servants enjoyed it so.

A bonfire had been prepared the day before on a piece of flat, open ground in the valley. Marsh was in charge and the servants were allowed to attend. The cook had given each of us packets of bread and butter, and some sausages were to be cooked later on a brazier near the bonfire. By six o'clock, when the fire was lit, it was quite dark. All the family were there, and well wrapped against the cold, we stood at some distance from the fire as flames leaped up to engulf Guy Fawkes's effigy with its ugly mask.

Soon there were rockets soaring into the sky, Amanda squealing with excitement, all her grown-up scorn of the occasion forgotten. Along the valley and on the far side I could see other fires, and from all around came the distant sounds of fireworks. The smoke thickened, and soon the valley was filled with a foggy haze. When fresh wood was put on our fire it produced such heavy coils of smoke that I found my eyes were smarting, and moved back some little way. As I stood alone, watching dreamily, I saw dark figures flitting here and there through the murk, and heard voices and laughter. It was as if time had stopped for me, while the rest of the world went on its way. I do not know how long I stood lost in this half-sleeping state, but suddenly I was no longer alone, for a man was walking toward me through the tendrils of smoke. It was Robert Falcon.

He stood in front of me, staring from those fierce blue eyes with an expression I could not fathom. Slowly he lifted his hands, reached out and, gripping my shoulders, drew me toward him. I did not resist. He held me close as he kissed my lips. There was a stirring within me. I found that my arms were about him, and knew that I was answering his kiss. Then he broke from me almost roughly, holding me at arm's length, staring at me as if wondering what he had done. I wanted to speak, but before I could find words he had let his hands fall, turned on his heel and walked quickly away.

In seconds he was lost to my sight in the smoke and darkness. I started after him, blundering over tussocks of grass. I had no clear idea of what I felt for Robert Falcon, but something must be said. He had come to me out of the darkness, held me in his arms and kissed me. Surely he could not go without a word?

In the thickening haze of smoke I crashed headlong into a bush. As I turned to move around it I glimpsed his figure moving past me, as if going up the valley side away from Moonrakers. I began to hurry after him and he must have heard me, for he stopped and turned his head, peering through the shifting wreaths of smoke. A feather of wind blew the gray coils aside, and in that moment my dreamlike state was shattered. This was not the face of Robert Falcon. This was the face of a man who lay buried on the other side of the world, the face of Nicholas Sabine.

I found myself half crouching, covering my face with my hands and wondering if I had gone mad. The image of his face still burned in my mind. I saw the thick black hair curling over the brow, the lean jaw and wide mouth. One thing only was different. The wicked laughter that had lived in his eyes was no longer there. Instead there was emptiness. Slowly I drew my hands down over my face and looked again.

Nothing. Darkness and curling smoke. Nothing more.

Had I seen a ghost, or lost my mind?

I broke into a stumbling run, trying to make a wide circle around the bonfire and go back to High Coppice, to be alone, away from this haunted place. Suddenly my foot came down on air, and I plunged forward, rolling down a steep slope, clawing thick clumps of grass helplessly for a handhold.

The slithering fall lasted only a few seconds. I was slowing down as the slope flattened, when my foot caught in some obstruction and I was swung around. Next instant a light seemed to explode in my head, and the world ceased to exist.

CHAPTER EIGHT

I WAS COLD TO the bone. There was a sharp pain above my left ear. I was lying on my side, on cold damp stone. I pushed myself into a sitting position and felt the lump on the side of my head where I had banged it. I had the sensation of rousing not from unconsciousness but from a dream. There was the lingering impression that I had been carried in strong arms, and that a voice had whispered to me. But the impression was fading.

Nausea swept me. Slowly I got to my knees and looked about. Then fear tore the breath from my lungs, fear that I was blind. For I could see no glimmer of light, whether from a star or from the fires along the valley. Only complete blackness. In panic I began to crawl, feeling for the tussocks that dotted the slope I had tumbled down, but there was no grass, only stone. This was not the place where I had fallen. Could I have stumbled some distance in a semiconscious state before collapsing again?

The air about me was strange. I realized that I could feel no breath of wind, hear no whisper of sound. I drew my coat more tightly about me, and

there came from it a faint rattling sound. A box of matches, less than half full . . . I had put it in my pocket before leaving the house, to light some of the fireworks with. I struck a match, and the sight of the flaring match head brought me relief so great that I almost wept. I was not blind.

I lifted the match. Beside me a curving rock wall stretched away for as far as the light of the match revealed. Opposite, perhaps twenty feet away, was another such wall, and above me a dripping roof of stone. The match burned my fingers and I dropped it. Now I knew where I was, and with the knowledge came fresh terror. I was in the Chislehurst Caves, a great maze of ancient tunnels, a labyrinth that had been explored for twenty miles without its limits being reached.

Whether I had been carried or had walked here unwittingly, I could not conceive how I came to be in the caves. The only entrance I knew of was close to Chislehurst Station, a mile or more away. There at certain times guides would take small parties on conducted tours, only a few hundred yards or so, for barriers were set up at a great many points to prevent people from going in too far and losing themselves in the maze of tunnels.

The cold was biting more deeply. I knew that if I did not find my way out I would die from exposure. Yet my hope of escaping from the labyrinth was so small that I hardly dared think about it. All I could do was to beat down the panic within me and try as doggedly as possible to make the best use of my one advantage—the matches. I dared not waste them.

I tried to think what else I might make use of. I had nothing in my pockets except a handkerchief and the packet of bread-and-butter sandwiches. I still wore my felt hat, with a long pin that had kept it on my head during my fall. Lifting my skirt I began to tear strips from my petticoat, fumbling in the darkness. When I had several strips I plaited them together in short lengths, then put all but one length in my pocket.

My teeth were chattering as I opened the packet of sandwiches and began to smear some of the butter on the plait of cloth, blessing the cook for her liberal hand with the butter. I drew out my hatpin and pierced the ungreased end of the plait, so that I could light it and hold it without burning myself. Then, striking one of the matches, I stood quite still. I could feel no breath of air, but as I watched, the flame was drawn a little toward my right. I put the match to the dangling, greasy plait of my torch. The material took the flame and began to burn slowly.

Without waiting for a second I set off along the tunnel, taking the direction in which the match flame had leaned. I might be wrong in thinking that whatever faint currents of air were in the tunnel would tend toward an aperture, but it was better to follow some pattern than to wander at random.

After only thirty paces I found myself passing the end of another tunnel, which ran at right angles. It was hard to detect which way the flame leaned, but I fancied that it was in the direction I had been going, so I ignored the side tunnel and walked on. After forty-seven paces I came to a point where the tunnel forked. The flame leaned very positively toward the left fork, and I followed that direction. Now I moved quickly for a hundred and twenty-three paces, for though the tunnel curved there were no branches. My torch died out, so I rubbed butter into another of the rag plaits.

After using up three torches I found myself in a section of the caves where many tunnels crossed. My eyes were becoming blurred with the strain of trying to detect the direction in which the flame was drawn when I passed each intersection. Sometimes it was hard to see any movement at all.

There was little butter left for the last torch. At first it refused to light, and then, when I teased open the plait to make it burn more easily, the material flared and was quickly consumed. I stood in the darkness, knowing that I had few matches left. . . . But the tiny spark that was dying on the charred torch grew suddenly brighter for a few seconds before vanishing completely. My heart jumped. Surely that meant there must be a definite current of air? I struck a match and watched the flame carefully. It flickered distinctly toward me, and that was absurd, for I was standing with my back to one wall. I turned, and there was nothing to be seen but a long, dark shadow on the wall. As I moved forward the match went out. I did not strike another, but groped onward.

My hands found it—an irregular aperture stretching from the ground to as high as I could reach, and no more than a yard wide. As I moved through the gap I felt air on my face, and hope leaped within me. I went forward, the passage winding through rock, rising at each step. I was in dread that the walls would narrow to a crack, but suddenly there was no stone hemming me in, and I felt the crunch of dead leaves underfoot.

I was in a thicket of bush and bramble. When I looked up there were stars beyond the pine branches spreading above me. I had never in my life been so glad to see the sky. I forced my way through the thicket, and in less than a minute I found myself in the open. I knew where I was now; I had often noticed these pine trees from a distance when making my way down to visit Matthew's secret house. They stood only a stone's throw from Mr. Gresham's land.

As I looked to my left along the valley I could see the glow of the Gresham family's bonfire. I climbed the slope, bypassing the fire by a good distance. I did not want to meet anybody, for I was weary to my soul.

When I entered the house there was nobody about. The hands of the clock stood at twenty-five minutes past seven, and I thought it must have stopped. But no, it was still ticking. I could not believe my tired, smarting eyes. I had fallen at about half past six, so in fact I had been in that dreadful labyrinth hardly longer than forty minutes.

I went to my bedroom, washed my face, changed my dress and lay down on the bed. The lump on my head throbbed, but the skin was not broken, and my hair hid the swelling. As I lay with a cold washcloth on my brow, thoughts churned in my head. So much had happened. There had been Robert Falcon, coming to me out of the darkness, kissing me, going away without a word. Then there had been Nicholas Sabine. But that was impossible, a trick of the imagination. Nicholas Sabine had died more than six months ago. Dr. Langdon himself had shown me the grave.

Who had carried me into the caves? Whoever had done so was an enemy, for it was only by good fortune that I had not wandered in darkness till I died. Was my enemy an unknown? a Falcon? or a Gresham?

All answers seemed to make little sense. Could Edmund, that precise man of the law, be working against me for some unfathomable reason? Or his father? What of Robert's father, or Robert himself? Not Robert. If he had wished to harm me he could have done so easily enough when he held me in his arms. Nicholas, then . . . But I had not seen Nicholas Sabine, only imagined him. There was just one other answer—that I had wandered without memory after my fall and stumbled upon the hidden entrance to the caves.

I heard sounds from below as the family returned to the house. I knew I couldn't tell anyone what had happened; the Greshams would never believe me, and even Marsh would find such a story hard to accept. A few minutes later Amanda knocked on my door and entered. I took the damp cloth from my brow. "So there you are!" she said. "What a thing to do, going off home without a word!"

"I'm sorry. It's just a headache. I'll be all right in the morning. Will you apologize to your parents? I don't think I'll come down to dinner."

"All right. My goodness, you do look pasty. . . ."

When Amanda had gone I lay with eyes closed, trying not to relive the terror I had known in the caves, and at last I fell into an uneasy sleep.

Throughout the next day I had a dull headache, but after another night's sleep I felt myself again. I closed my mind to my experience, partly because it seemed more and more unreal as time went by, but mainly from cowardice. I did not want to think about it.

At the end of the week Amanda went back to school. Christmas was little more than six weeks away, but to me that seemed a long, barren period. In the middle of November, Edmund told me he had received information from Nicholas Sabine's bankers; when the will was probated more than sixteen hundred pounds would come to me. After this I sometimes thought about running away from High Coppice. With so much money I could easily find somewhere to live and something useful to do, but such thoughts made me feel guilty. Although Mr. Gresham had brought me to England for his own purposes, I was still in his debt. I consoled myself with the thought that if I did leave the family I could at least repay my debt in money, and I knew that my going would be a relief to them all.

Meantime, my happiest moments were those devoted each day to Marsh's lessons. One day, in the second week of December, Marsh was late, and I busied myself finishing the last of the handkerchiefs I was embroidering as Christmas presents for the Greshams. When Marsh finally came in, I saw that his face was pale. He moved to one of the chairs. "May I sit down, Miss Lucy?"

"Oh Marsh, of course. Aren't you feeling well?"

He lowered himself into an easy chair. "I'm . . . not quite myself at this moment. Only a few minutes ago . . ." He fumbled in one of his pockets. "Beattie found this on the floor outside your room, and brought it to me. Is it yours, Miss Lucy?"

He held out his hand. On it lay the signet ring Nicholas Sabine had given me. I had always worn it on a thin piece of ribbon around my neck under my dress. "Yes, it's mine." I felt around my neck and drew out the piece of ribbon. "Look, the ribbon's broken."

"May I . . . make so bold as to ask how you came by this ring?"

I hesitated. "I can't tell you exactly. Mr. Edmund said I wasn't to tell anybody. But it was given me by the man who died in China. . . . Marsh, what's wrong? You look so shaken."

"I know this ring, Miss Lucy." His voice was very low. "It has an unusual design. I bought it in Hong Kong when I was a young soldier, and later gave it to my wife."

"Your *wife?* I didn't know you were married."

Marsh turned over the ring. He did not seem to have heard me. "That was long ago, and my initials were on it then. Now I see they have been replaced by the initials N.S." He looked up. "Would they stand for Nicholas Sabine?"

I stared at him, dumbfounded. "Yes . . . But how did you know?"

"Because Nicholas Sabine was my son."

I could hardly believe it. Yet I was sure Marsh would not lie to me. My heart went out to him as I saw the grief in his eyes. I sank down on my knees in front of him and took the hand that held the ring in both my own.

He drew in a long breath. "Was it Nick?" he asked steadily. "Not a different man who'd come by the ring in some way? Black, curly hair. A long jaw, like his mother. And eyes always laughing at some joke only he could see?"

I held his hand tightly. "It was Nick," I said. "I'm so very sorry, Mr. Marsh." The "Mr." came naturally to my lips. This kindly man had become more than a servant in the last few moments. Much more. "But how is it that his name was different from yours?"

"It's a sad and simple story," he said. "I married above myself, and my poor wife paid the price. I was a young soldier, signed on for twenty-one years. Most of that time I was abroad and my wife was alone, for when we married against her parents' will they rejected her. We had one child, Nicholas, and in the first ten years of his life I saw him only three times. After that, he did not wish to see me on the few occasions when I was on leave, and neither did his mother."

Mr. Marsh made a little grimace. "It was understandable that my wife should be embittered. On my soldier's pay she lived in poor London lodgings, and even then she had to work as a seamstress to make ends meet. But she brought the boy up well, and taught him the ways of a gentleman. He won a scholarship to a fine school."

I said, "Edmund told me that. Nick was his friend at school. Does Edmund know that you're Nick's father?"

He shook his head quickly. "No, nobody knows. At school Nick took his mother's maiden name, Sabine. You see, he grew up with a great contempt for me. He hated my being a soldier. I saw him for the last time when he was fourteen. . . . I used to send every penny I could spare, but my wife worked herself to an early grave for the boy, and I have always blamed myself. It is foolish to marry outside one's station in life. When I had served my time in the army and took this position, it was a shock to discover that Master Edmund was at the same school as Nick."

"Did your son never tell Edmund that you were in service here?"

"He didn't know. We didn't communicate. He wanted nothing to do with his father."

"That was very cruel of him," I said sadly.

"Perhaps. But it seemed to him that his mother was neglected, left uncared-for by her soldier husband who spent his life in foreign parts. He was right, of course. For the soldier's or sailor's wife, marriage is a lonely business."

There was a long silence. At last Mr. Marsh roused himself from his memories and looked at me. I was still holding his hand in my own. "Won't you be seated now, Miss Lucy?" he said, troubled. "It's not my place to sit here like this with you at my knee."

I did not move. "Yes, it is your place. It's strange to feel sad and happy at the same time, but I do. I'm sad for you about Nick, and sad for myself, but in another way I'm happy. I once said I wished you were my father. And Mr. Marsh, you *are* my father. I was married to your son. The ring was all we had for a wedding ring."

Mr. Marsh sat without moving for several seconds, then he rubbed his eyes with a finger and thumb, shaking his head slowly as if still trying to take in my words. "You . . . married Nick?" he said at last.

"Yes. That's when he gave me his ring, and I've worn it ever since."

I told him my own strange story now, and by the time I ended, Mr.

Marsh had recovered from the first shock of surprise, and a trace of happiness was beginning to show through his sorrow.

"Why, Lucy child, I am . . . a greatly honored man." He leaned forward to kiss my cheek. I put my arms around his neck and hugged him. He stood up, helping me to my feet. His eyes grew anxious. "We must keep this as our secret, Lucy. It would never do for the family to know that you are married to their butler's son."

I was startled. "I'm not ashamed of it!" I said hotly.

"It simply won't do." His voice was firm. "You have been accepted as one of the family. I am a servant. It would cause even greater difficulties than you face already. I beg you to be guided by me in this." He put the ring in my hand. "Here, child. I have a silver chain that belonged to Nick's mother. I'll bring it to you later, and you can wear the ring on it." He put a hand on my shoulder."We neither of us knew the boy well, but he was my son and he was your husband. It gives me pleasure to know you wear the ring he gave you." He drew himself up. "With your permission I will take my leave of you now, Miss Lucy." He inclined his head, moved with his usual unhurried pace to the door, and closed it quietly behind him.

I sat pretending to be busy with my embroidery in case anybody came in. I wanted to have no secrets from Mr. Marsh now, but I still could not tell him that I had seen, or imagined seeing, Nicholas Sabine here in England. I knew my mind must have played me false. Nick Sabine was dead. It would be cruel to speak to his father of what I had imagined.

It hurt me to keep secret from the family that Mr. Marsh was my father-in-law, but I realized he would be dismissed if Mr. Gresham learned the truth, and I could not let that happen while I had no money to help him till he found a new position. I would have to be patient, I decided, but as soon as I had some money I would beg Mr. Marsh to take me away.

Amanda came home a week before Christmas, and Matthew the next day. He was waiting in his secret house. It was a joy to see him. We made hot chocolate together, and with great pride he introduced me to a tame rabbit he had brought from school. The Falcons' gardener had made a hutch from an old crate and some wire netting.

I held the rabbit while he spread straw in the hutch and set out food and water. "We mustn't leave her for more than two days without bringing fresh food and water," I said. "And we ought to make a long leash of string, so that we can let her have a little run whenever we come."

"I shall come every day. Mama and Papa will have some friends staying over Christmas and they won't mind if I'm away for a little while, even on Christmas Day. I say, could you come then too, Lucy? We could have our own special party, just for a little while."

"I'd love to, Matthew, but I don't think it's likely I'll be able to, so you mustn't get cold waiting for me."

As I walked home I realized that it would seem the most terrible betrayal to Matthew when the Falcons lost Moonrakers—to me, his friend. Even to think of it made me despair. But there was nothing I could do, for Edmund was bound to carry out the terms of the will.

At dinner that night I suffered again the regular ordeal of watching Mr. Marsh serve the family, and of hearing Emily make a sarcastic remark when he asked if she would like another slice of roast beef. I went to bed feeling that more than anything in the world I wanted to get away from High Coppice and never come back.

On the evening before Christmas Eve the countryside lay under a great blanket of snow, which was still falling and gathering in high drifts. We sat in the drawing room after dinner, playing anagrams. Edmund, who had arrived later than expected from London because of the blizzard, had just given us an anagram to solve. The words were "string manor," and we had to make them into a single word.

I could not solve the anagram, and I began idly to wonder instead if it might be possible to make an English word from the name of a Chinese town. Hardly thinking what I was doing, I wrote down Tientsin on my little pad, then Tsin Kai-feng and Shanghai. . . .

"Oh, I give up," said Amanda. "Tell us your silly old word, Edmund."

"The word is morningstar." Edmund smiled a little smugly. "Not the morning star which shines in the sky, but the ancient weapon, like a club with spikes on it, called a morningstar."

"Oh, that's cheating! How do you expect us to know words like that? Papa—tell him not to be so mean!"

I did not hear Mr. Gresham's reply, for I was staring at the letters on my pad. A fragment of the riddle John Falcon had written almost sixty years before had suddenly leaped out at me, so clearly that I could not understand why I had never seen it before. And then, in the long strange moments of clarity that followed, other fragments of the riddle fell into place, like the last few pieces of a jigsaw puzzle.

I was about to cry out with excitement, when the drawing-room door opened and Mr. Marsh entered. Without waiting to be spoken to, he said urgently, "Excuse me, sir. A matter of some importance. Mr. Harry Falcon begs a moment of your time. An emergency."

For several seconds there was complete silence, then Mr. Gresham got slowly to his feet. "Harry Falcon? Here?"

"Yes, sir. Because of the snow upon his boots and his person, he is waiting on the porch. He seems greatly disturbed."

"Well . . . I'd better go and see what it's all about," Mr. Gresham said reluctantly. I was suddenly glad that the interruption had prevented me from blurting out my discovery, for now I was by no means sure that I wanted the Gresham family alone to know it. If the warlord's emeralds lay hidden where I now believed, I wanted the fortune to be shared by the two families, as their forebears had intended.

The game went on in a halfhearted fashion, and in ten minutes Mr. Gresham reentered the drawing room. He looked flustered. "It appears the little Falcon boy is missing," he said. "He was in the house an hour or so ago, but now he's gone. They're searching, but this blizzard makes all movement difficult. Falcon came to ask if the boy had taken shelter here, and then to ask for help in the search. I told Marsh to put a coat and boots on, and I've sent him off with Falcon." He looked at us almost guiltily. "I felt bound to cooperate under the circumstances."

"No question of that," Edmund said firmly, and stood up. "It's a bad business. The child won't survive long in such cold." He moved to the door. "I'll wrap up and search the lane."

All this I heard as if from a great distance, for I was stupefied by fear. Then something stirred in my benumbed mind. I cried out, jumped to my feet and ran to the door. "I know where he is!" I said frantically. "He's down in the secret house—he went there because of his rabbit! He was afraid it would die in the snow!"

Mr. Gresham gazed at me as if I had gone mad. Then with an angry set to his mouth he gripped me firmly by the arm and marched me back across the room. "How dare you! I hoped you had outgrown this wicked habit of making up fantasies!"

My voice was a croak. "It's not a fantasy, Mr. Gresham. Please come with me. There's a place in the valley. He has a zoo there, and I often go there to meet him when he's home from school."

"Rubbish!" Mr. Gresham's face was mottled with fury. "You would never dare to consort with the Falcon child."

"I'll—I'll go on my own if you won't help," I stammered.

"You will go nowhere except to your room. You are a wicked, lying young woman, and I regret the day I brought you to this house. Now go to your room *at once!* Not another word!"

With an enormous effort I took hold of myself. "Very well, Mr. Gresham. I apologize for making you angry." I went out, gathered up my skirts and raced up the stairs. Beattie was busy turning down the beds.

"Beattie! Come here." I ran on into my room. She followed, her eyes round with surprise. I was already struggling out of my dress. "I need some trousers, Beattie. Yes, *trousers.* Go and get me a pair from Mr. Edmund's room, the oldest you can find."

"Ooh, miss, I daresn't!"

"I'll say I took them myself. Please, it will save me time. The little Falcon boy is dying in the snow, and I know where, but they won't believe me."

She blinked, then said, "Right, miss. I'll be back in a jiffy."

Three minutes later she was in the hall below, keeping watch on the drawing-room door for me as I ran stealthily down the stairs. I had taken off my dress and petticoat, and put on three blouses and a woolen jacket under my topcoat. A pair of Edmund's trousers were belted about my waist with the strap from my suitcase, the bottoms tucked into the high felt boots I had brought with me from China. My hands were gloved, and under one arm I carried a folded blanket.

Before I had gone fifty yards across the gardens I began to wonder if I would ever reach Matthew's secret house. The snow was more than twelve inches deep and still falling heavily, slanting in the bitter wind. The stars were blotted out, but there was some reflected light from the great white blanket hiding the earth, and I was able to see a dozen or so paces ahead of me. I made steady progress moving downhill, but I did not dare think what the return journey would be like. I came at last to the shrubbery that hid Matthew's secret house. I shouted against the whine of the blizzard, *"Matthew! Matthew!"*

There was no answer. In the clearing beyond the ring of bushes the snow lay deep. I clambered forward to the low cliff wall, but there was no sign of him. I rubbed snow from my face and peered again through the darkness. Then I saw him, huddled in the recess, his arms curled about his head. A thin layer of snow already spread like a sheet over his hunched form.

"Matthew!" I knelt beside him, taking him by an arm. In the dim, eerie light I saw that his eyes were closed, and his face was like marble. I shouted and, holding him close, blew hot breath on his face and eyes. For a moment the lids half opened, then they closed again and he sagged in my arms.

I ached with cold, but now I felt an even deeper ache, for I knew that Matthew would never wake again unless I could bring him to warmth very soon. And I knew, too, that I could never carry him back up the hill to High Coppice. And there was no time to go for help. I knew with bleak certainty that whatever was to be done I would have to do alone.

I spoke to myself through frozen lips as I began to unfold the blanket. "Do what comes next, Lucy. First do whatever comes next, then go on from there!"

CHAPTER NINE

I SPREAD THE BLANKET on the snow and dragged Matthew to the middle so that he lay diagonally on it. Two corners I brought across his middle and knotted there. I took the other two corners, at his head and feet, brought them together and with numb fingers tied the ends in a big double knot.

Turning my back on Matthew, I went down on my hands and knees, then reached back, grasped the knot, and struggled to bring the loop of the blanket forward over my head. This was the way I had carried heavy burdens in China, the way the peasants did. Matthew was huddled in the blanket and resting against my back, with the loop acting as a sling around my forehead.

Somehow I crawled through the tunnel of bushes. Then I hunched my shoulders, tensed my neck, and used all the strength of my legs to stand up with my burden. Once I was on my feet and leaning forward against the pull of the blanket, Matthew's weight seemed much less formidable.

Well . . . I had done what came next. But what came next now? The answer slipped into my mind as I watched the snowflakes hurtling away from me, vanishing into the darkness. I had never traveled up the path through the woods to Moonrakers, but I knew it was a gentler slope and there should be no drifts on it.

Three times I strayed from the path, for it lay hidden under snow. I was bent double now under Matthew's weight. The muscles of my shoulders and neck burned, the breath rasped in my throat, and all the time I was desperately aware that Matthew, lying still and unmoving across my back, would be sinking deeper into the murderous coma by which cold claims its victims. Half a dozen times I knew that I could not take another step, then roused from a period of unawareness to find that I was still plodding on. It would never end. I would take a million steps, and still it would be only the beginning.

Despair grew within me as I found that the snow underfoot was becoming deeper. Slowly I reasoned that this must be because the trees were left behind and I was nearing the top of the ridge. . . . The top? I lifted my head and stared. Through the swirling flakes I could see the windows of a great house with every light burning and every curtain drawn back. Moonrakers. Two hundred paces away. I stumbled forward and fell. I moved on again, crawling on hands and knees, plowing a channel through the snow, my face sometimes buried. The weight on my back was a boulder, a mountain.

There was gravel beneath the snow; I felt it beneath my knees. I looked up. The great warm house was near now. Two figures with lanterns stood close together, as if speaking, then moved off in different directions. I lifted my head and shouted. My shout was a thin shrill noise.

One of the men stopped, turned, moved slowly toward me, lifting the lantern, then suddenly lunged forward with great strides and dropped to his knees beside me. I found myself looking up into the haggard face of Matthew's father.

"I've got him," I whispered. "In the blanket. Please, get him warm . . . quickly."

Then there was a great roaring in my ears, and my mind slid down a long dark slope into nothingness.

THE ACHING OF MY NECK AND BACK woke me. I was propped on pillows in a big four-poster bed, in a large room with a fire crackling in the grate. I put my arms outside the covers, and saw that I was wearing a pretty pink nightdress with lacy cuffs. Mrs. Falcon sat in a chair beside the bed, her beautiful face tired but calm.

I started up on one elbow. "Matthew? Is he all right?"

"Hush, dear. Matthew is safe." She stood up and took my hand. "It's more than three hours since Harry found you crawling through the snow with Matthew on your back. Dr. Cheyne has managed to get here, and he's seen you both. We sent word to the Greshams at once, so they know you're safe." Mrs. Falcon shook her head wonderingly. "We still can't understand how you could carry Matthew up out of the valley in that blizzard."

"I'm quite strong for my size, Mrs. Falcon."

"My dear, you're strong in your heart, where it counts most." Tears suddenly filled her eyes. She kissed my cheek. "God bless you, Lucy."

I was close to tears myself, with relief. "I am glad I could help, Mrs. Falcon. But I'm afraid Mr. Gresham is going to be terribly cross with me. . . . Please, need I go back tonight? I'm so tired, and . . ."

"Go back tonight? It's out of the question, Lucy. Dr. Cheyne said you must stay in bed until he's seen you again."

It was not until she had brought me a bowl of soup and watched me eat it that she allowed her husband and Robert to enter. I felt very foolish and awkward. Mr. Falcon still looked haggard from the hours of anxiety, but he smiled and kissed me on the forehead, and thanked me with warm simplicity. Robert seemed quite at a loss, grim-faced and troubled. He muttered a few stilted words, his manner so different from his usual confident air that I would scarcely have known him.

My sleep was deep and dreamless that night. When I woke the next morning, the curtains had been drawn back and I saw that the snow had stopped falling. My shoulders still ached, but I felt well, even hungry. A servant was sitting beside me, and as soon as I opened my eyes she hurried away to tell her mistress. Ten minutes later she returned with a breakfast tray, followed by Mrs. Falcon.

"Good morning, Lucy. I hope you slept well. Matthew is asking for you, but I said he must wait till the doctor has seen you."

As I ate my breakfast she stood by the window, looking out over the snow-covered valley and talking easily about the beauty and cruelty of nature. I responded readily, thinking how different this household seemed. Mrs. Gresham talked only of domestic matters and gossip.

Later that morning Dr. Cheyne came, a cheerful, red-faced man who took my pulse and temperature, and said, "Well, young lady, how'd ye do it? That little jaunt of yours would have put most people in bed for a week. You're out to ruin my business, is that it?" He turned to Mrs. Falcon.

"Keep young Matthew in bed another day if you please, ma'am. But if this one wants to get up, let her. She's a freak, that's what she is." He winked at me and departed.

An hour later, wearing one of my own blouses but in a borrowed skirt and shoes, I was in Matthew's room with Mrs. Falcon. He did not remember much of his ordeal the night before, in fact his main concern was for his rabbit. I promised to ask Robert to look after the rabbit, and this satisfied him. We left him to sleep.

In many ways Moonrakers was a shabby home, with old furniture and carpets a little threadbare, but it had an atmosphere I loved. Instead of rooms crammed with furniture there was spaciousness; instead of fussy knickknacks there were fascinating objects set on mantelpieces and tables: wood carvings; a slender vase holding stalks of strange dry grass, delicately arranged; a big stone, broken to show amethyst within it, and set on a beautiful wooden base. The Falcons had a studio in the house, and there were pictures everywhere, painted by them and their friends.

"Nothing of any value," Mr. Falcon said cheerfully as we settled down in the drawing room with cups of coffee. "Not unless one of our painter friends turns out to be an unsung genius. I was told the other day that I could make a pretty penny doing portraits of rich women, but I wouldn't like that." He turned in his chair as the door opened. "Ah, Robert. Any luck with the rabbit?"

"I found it alive. The hutch was almost buried, but I suppose the snow kept it warm, like an Eskimo igloo." Robert Falcon had recovered his old manner. Quite at ease, he crossed the room, took my hand and bent to kiss my cheek. "Already out of bed, Lucy? What an astonishing girl you are. And how nice it is to see you here."

"Hello, Robert. I'm very happy to be here." I had expected to feel embarrassed meeting him this morning, for we had seen almost nothing of each other since that moment in the darkness in the valley. But his parents created such a warm atmosphere that it was impossible to feel ill at ease. Before I could think what I was saying I added, "It's so different here, I don't like to think about going back to High Coppice."

Robert shot a glance at his father. "Can Gresham make her?"

Mr. Falcon scratched his beard. "If he's legally her guardian, I suppose he can."

"He isn't my guardian," I said, then added hastily, "but please don't think I was suggesting I could stay. I shouldn't have said—"

"Why not?" Mr. Falcon said. "You'll always be welcome here, Lucy." He smiled at his wife. "We could manage, couldn't we, sweetheart?"

"We always have, Harry." She turned her candid gaze on me. "I'd be very happy to have you, my dear."

I said reluctantly, "You're very kind. But Mr. Gresham brought me from China and has looked after me all this time. It wouldn't be right for me to come to you if he wants me to stay."

"We won't try to persuade you," Mrs. Falcon said quietly. "We think everyone should follow his own way of thinking." Her glance touched Robert. "As long as no hurt is caused to others."

Mr. Falcon chuckled. "I'll wager old Gresham considers us feckless. Well, perhaps Tina and I don't worry about material things as much as we should. Still, we live the way we want, cause no harm, and don't complain when life gives us a few buffets." He stood up, went to his wife, and bent to kiss her without any hint of embarrassment. "And we're happy, aren't we, sweetheart?"

I felt so glad for them that my eyes stung. I had never seen Mr. and Mrs. Gresham display such affection.

"Your happy-go-lucky philosophy is all very well, Father," Robert said amiably enough, "but one day you'll come to the crunch." His face grew somber. "It could well be next year."

Mrs. Falcon said, "That doesn't mean the end of the world, Robbie. Your father and I might take a cottage in Cornwall. I love Moonrakers, but a house isn't the most important thing."

"Moonrakers is important to me, Mother."

"I know. It's an obsession with you, and I wish it weren't. But perhaps Mr. Sabine will extend the mortgage when the time comes."

"Nick Sabine? Mother, the only chance we have of the mortgage being extended is if he never comes back from China. I've heard no word of his return, so perhaps we'll be lucky."

"Never wish him dead, Robbie," his mother said quickly. "That's an awful thing to hope for."

Robert shrugged. I felt guilty to be sitting in silence when there was so much I could have told them, but I simply could not find the courage to say that before the year's end I would inherit Moonrakers and they would have to go. I hoped that before that day something would happen to prevent what Nicholas Sabine had planned.

An hour later I was sitting in Matthew's room, playing snakes and ladders with him, when the front doorbell sounded. Then Mrs. Falcon came into the room. "I'm sorry, Lucy, but Edmund Gresham is waiting to see you in the drawing room."

I got to my feet reluctantly. "Then I'd better go down."

Edmund rose as I entered. We greeted one another awkwardly, then fell silent. For once Edmund seemed embarrassed. To fill in the silence I said, "I'm sorry I took your trousers, Edmund, but I could never have got through the valley wearing skirts."

"Quite so, quite so." He flushed. "Um—what I have to ask you, Lucy, is that . . . well, have the Falcons taken good care of you?"

"Oh yes, they've been wonderfully kind."

"I suppose it would hardly be possible for you to—er—stay? To be frank, it would be a relief to my parents if you did not return to us, Lucy. My father is not a logical man, and the fact that you were entirely right last night has not lessened his ill temper. Perhaps without realizing it, he is ashamed, and in the way of impulsive people he tends to convert this into anger. . . . The fact is, your presence creates an atmosphere of strain. My father is to blame for bringing you to High Coppice in the first place, and I have said so to him, plainly."

I could hardly speak for delight. "If he doesn't want me back, Edmund, Mr. and Mrs. Falcon have already said I could stay here."

It was hard to tell whether Edmund was more surprised or relieved. "Well, that is really most convenient, Lucy. Now there is something else I must say. Marsh returned some time after we found that you had left the house. He learned what had happened from Beattie, forgot his position as a servant, and—ah—criticized my father in terms more suited to a sergeant major than a butler. In the course of this—um—articulate expression of opinion, he revealed the astonishing fact that he is your father-in-law. No doubt this was the cause of his alarm and his justifiable anger."

"Yes, it's true, Edmund," I said. "I have Nick's signet ring, and Mr. Marsh recognized it. I didn't tell anybody, because I was afraid Mr. Marsh would have to leave High Coppice if I did."

Edmund tapped his fingertips together. "Quite so. In any event, he was dismissed on the spot, after his unfortunate behavior. He left the house this morning." Edmund drew an envelope from his pocket. "He asked me to bring you this note."

I was all thumbs, trying to open the envelope. "May I read it now, please?" Edmund nodded, and I unfolded the note.

> My dear Lucy,
>
> Thank God you and the little boy are safe. Please do not worry about me. I have my army pension and am sure that my old master, now an important person in the War Office, will help with a good recommendation. It would be a great joy to hear from you, and perhaps to meet occasionally if this can be arranged. My address will be 14 Ludford Road, Greenwich.
>
> With love from your affectionate father,
>
> Thomas Marsh

I looked up. "It's just to give me his address and tell me not to worry about him. Thank you for bringing it, Edmund."

"Not at all." He lowered his voice. "Will you be telling the Falcons that you were married to Nick, and will inherit Moonrakers?"

"I don't know. It's awfully difficult. Oh Edmund, must you do what Nick said? Couldn't the mortgage be extended?"

"Certainly not, Lucy." He looked shocked. "I am bound by law to follow Nick's instructions."

"Edmund . . . don't you think it would be good for both families to agree that if the fortune is ever found, it should be shared equally, the way your grandfathers intended?"

Edmund nodded. "It would be excellent, Lucy. But my parents would never agree, and neither would Robert Falcon. Besides, frankly, I don't think the emeralds will ever be found."

My feelings were divided. I was sure I knew now where the fortune lay, unless it had been removed from where it was first hidden. If I told the Falcons, it would be a betrayal of Mr. Gresham, and I had lived under his roof for the past seven months. Neither could I tell the Greshams, for the fortune seemed to be the one way to save Moonrakers for the Falcons, and this I wanted desperately.

Edmund stood up. "I'll have your clothes and belongings packed and sent across. I'll leave you now, Lucy."

"Edmund, please know how grateful I am for all your kindness. You've been very nice to me."

"Really?" He gazed out the window. "I've done my duty, but I can hardly take the credit for kindness. It's strange, but I don't seem to feel things most people do. You know, the law doesn't have any feelings, it simply tries to be just and fair. Perhaps I'm rather like the law."

A wave of pity for him touched me, but I could find nothing to say. After a moment I gave him my hand and wished him good-by.

AFTER THE SHOCK of Matthew's narrow escape from death, the Falcons sent telegrams to their friends canceling their previous arrangements for Christmas. Instead we spent it very quietly, and I soon discovered that living at Moonrakers was like living in another world. As Mrs. Falcon had said, each member of the family was free to do as he pleased, as long as no hurt was caused to others. I was allowed to help the servants, who were friendly people and seemed to count themselves fortunate to be in service with the Falcons. I learned to cook English dishes and helped with the dusting. I also spent time with Matthew until he returned to school.

Soon after Christmas I wrote to Mr. Marsh, and received an affectionate letter in return. At present he was working as a valet at the London house of his old master, who was now a lieutenant general at the War Office. He was delighted to learn that I was happily settled with the Falcons and hoped he might visit me soon, when he had a day off.

The first time I saw the Greshams again was at church. After the service, as the two families passed, I dropped a curtsy and said, "Good morning." Edmund raised his hat. Amanda, looking embarrassed, said, "Hello, Lucy." Emily ignored me. Mrs. Gresham inclined her head haughtily, and

Mr. Gresham half lifted his cane in vague acknowledgment. I was very glad to have this first meeting over, and it set a pattern for all future encounters.

After Matthew went back to school Robert began to court me again, or so it seemed. He sought my company, especially when we could be alone together, and was attentive and affectionate. Yet he never mentioned the strange occasion when he had kissed me by the bonfire, and I had the feeling that something held him back from saying what he really wished to say. I believed that sooner or later he might tell me that he loved me, and I wondered what I would do then. Whenever I saw Mr. and Mrs. Falcon together, I felt that I knew what love should be. There was a golden current flowing between them, as warm and natural as the sun's rays flowing to earth. I did not feel that for Robert, or any man.

Once Mrs. Falcon said to me, very gently, her eyes troubled, "If Robert asks you to marry him, I—I hope you won't accept."

I was startled, even hurt, but then I realized that while the Falcons were not wealthy, they were gentry, and Robert would be expected to make a good match. I said, "I hadn't thought about it before, Mrs. Falcon, but I understand your feeling that I wouldn't be suitable."

She looked at me quickly, and for a moment I thought she was about to protest, but she seemed to change her mind and said, "It's something like that, Lucy." The smile she gave me was a little tired.

Thus it was that when Robert finally asked me to marry him I was not unprepared. In a stumbling fashion I thanked him for the compliment he had paid me, and told him that perhaps I was not yet sufficiently grown-up to think of marriage.

He seemed in no way put out. "You're eighteen, Lucy, and far more grown-up for your age than most English girls. But I expect you need time to get used to the idea. I'll wait awhile, then ask again. Next week." He laughed, and left me to my confusion.

When I went to bed that night I could not sleep, so I lit the lamp, put on my dressing gown, and sat up in bed hugging my knees, trying to sort out my tangled feelings. The germ of an idea came stealing into my mind. . . .

I needed a way to save Moonrakers and at the same time ensure that the warlord's treasure would be shared between the Greshams and the Falcons. The answer, I thought, was simple. I would agree to marry Robert in return for his promise to share the fortune with the Greshams. And then I would tell him that I had solved the riddle. He could go to China and come back with the emeralds. When he returned and the fortune had been shared, he could pay off the debt on Moonrakers. Then I would marry him. And I would try with all my heart to be a good wife to him.

I took a writing pad and pencil from my chest of drawers, got back into bed, and began to write out the riddle, feeling that the secret should be set down on paper and not just kept in my mind.

"Above the twisted giant's knife
Where the windblown blossom flies
Stands the temple where fortune lies.

Beyond the golden world reversed
Marked by the bear cub of the skies
Rest the sightless tiger's eyes."

Then I began to write the solution: *The words "giant's knife" form an anagram. When the letters are twisted around they make "tsin kaifeng." My mission, which was once a temple, stands on a hill above Tsin Kai-feng.*

This was the discovery that had come to me that evening we played anagrams. Until that moment I had thought it impossible for our mission to be the temple of the riddle because the maps showed the river taking a different course. But then I remembered something I had once heard. Some thirty years before, the little river had been dammed and made to change course. The maps showed the terrain as it was then, not now. With this fact, and the sure knowledge that our mission was the right temple, the rest of the clues almost solved themselves. I wrote: *There are old plum trees a few yards from the north side of the mission. This would be "where the windblown blossom flies."*

I paused, remembering how I had often lain in bed of a summer's night, the window open, and watched the stars reflected in the bronze shield in the wall, the shield I used as a mirror. My pencil moved again: *"The bear cub of the skies" means the constellation known as the Little Bear. The brightest star of this group is the Pole Star, which shines through the window of a room onto a bronze shield set in the wall. When polished, this shield reflects like a mirror, and shows the world in reverse. "Beyond the golden world reversed" must mean behind this shield.*

I realized that I had not quite completed the solution, so I wrote: *"Tiger's eyes" is a phrase used for emeralds in this area of China.*

I folded the sheet of paper, sealed it in an envelope, and wrote Mr. Marsh's name and address on it. Then I wrote, "Private and confidential." I put the letter with my little collection of treasures in my old suitcase, and returned to bed feeling rather foolish and melodramatic. However, at least I had made sure that the secret would not be lost again. If it ever came into Mr. Marsh's hands, I knew he would do whatever he thought best.

The following week Robert again asked me to marry him. That morning I had decided that if the occasion presented itself I would carry through with my plan and accept his proposal in return for his promise to share the warlord's treasure with the Greshams. So it was that when Robert and I were in the drawing room that afternoon and he asked me again if I would marry him, I said, "Robert, before I can answer there's something I have to tell you—" At that moment the doorbell clanged loudly.

Robert said, "Go on then, little Lucy. Tell me."

"We'd better wait. I don't want to be interrupted in what I have to say, because—"

The door opened. Nellie, one of the maids, stood there with a startled look. "Mr. Robert," she burst out, "there's a gentleman to see Miss Lucy. He says . . ." Her voice faltered. "He says— Oh, I can't hardly tell you what he says, Miss Lucy!"

"Then I'll tell her myself," said a voice that brought me to my feet. A hand moved Nellie firmly aside, and Nick Sabine walked into the room. "I've come to collect my wife," he said.

Without the stubble of beard he had had in prison, his jaw looked longer and leaner than ever. Apart from this he was exactly as I remembered him, except that there were no laughing devils in his dark eyes. They were cold and without emotion.

It was impossible, but true. This was Nicholas Sabine, alive. Through the shock that engulfed my mind I felt a piercing shaft of relief and gladness. "Mr. Sabine . . . ?" My voice was barely a whisper. "Oh, you're *alive!* I'm—I'm so glad!"

"Are you, Lucy?" His eyes flickered over me. Something showed briefly in them. Sorrow? Bitterness? "Well, that's fine," he said. "Go and pack a case, will you?"

A sudden fear grew in me. If Nick Sabine was alive, then surely I *had* seen him that night of the fireworks, when somebody had carried me into the Chislehurst Caves. And that meant . . . My mind flinched from what it meant. With an effort I focused my eyes on the two men. Robert's face was as white as I knew my own must be.

"Your *wife?*" he said in a frightful whisper.

"My wife." Nick Sabine's voice was flat. "We married a few hours before I was due to be executed in Chengfu prison. It was all very legal. Ask Edmund Gresham. He's my lawyer and has all the papers. Better still, ask Lucy."

I nodded and whispered, "Yes, it's true."

Robert asked, "But why, Lucy?"

Long before I could find words to answer, Nick Sabine said, "The reason scarcely matters now. But if Lucy will be so good as to go and pack, I'll give you a brief narrative while I'm waiting."

The two men did not take their eyes from one another, and it was as if an unseen thunderbolt were forming in the air from the tension between them.

Robert's jaw jutted. "I'm not sure how the law stands, but I doubt if you could make her go with you against her will."

Nick turned to me. "Do you refuse to come with me, Lucy?"

I shook my head. No matter how it had come about, I had become Nick Sabine's wife. And besides, I feared what might happen here if I refused, for Robert stood leaning forward a little, with eyes burning, as if about to spring at his enemy.

Trying vainly to steady my voice I said, "I'll only be a few minutes, Mr. Sabine."

Idly he brushed his hat with his sleeve. "You'd better begin calling me Nick," he said.

CHAPTER TEN

As IF IN A dream I packed my suitcase and put on my coat and hat. Mrs. Falcon heard what had happened and came to help me, her eyes swimming with tears. As we worked I told her in stumbling phrases of that strange night in Chengfu prison. "I've wanted to tell you," I ended miserably. "I hate secrets, but I didn't know what to do."

She asked no questions, but held me tightly for a moment. "Robert has always told us Nick was a wicked man. I just pray that everything will go well for you, Lucy," she said.

Minutes later my husband was helping me step up into the carriage in which he had arrived. Robert had disappeared, but Mr. and Mrs. Falcon kissed me and said with forced smiles that they hoped we would visit them soon. Nick Sabine bowed, and climbed up beside me. As we reached the end of the drive I looked back and saw the Falcons waving. A moment later they had vanished from sight as we turned into the road.

My husband leaned back in his seat, his face expressionless. After we had gone half a mile, I said timidly, "Mr. Sabine, are—"

"Call me Nick," he broke in, absently watching the road. "It's usual between man and wife."

"I'm sorry. Nick . . . are you angry with me?"

He looked at me gravely. "Why should I be angry with you?"

"I don't know, but . . . please try to understand. All this time I thought you were dead, so it was an enormous shock to see you walk into the room just now. But I'm so very glad, Nick." I touched his arm. "It's wonderful that you escaped. However did you do it?"

"Dr. Langdon managed it," he said quietly. "He came back to the prison after he'd seen you off, and asked me if I'd care to risk being killed by him rather than by the mandarin's soldiers."

"I—I don't understand."

"Neither did I at first. There's a drug derived from opium. A large dose produces a state of coma so like death that even a doctor has difficulty in telling the difference. Often it *is* death. All the doctor can do is wait forty-eight hours and see if the patient comes out of the coma." He grinned, and for a moment I saw the devils in his eyes again and felt a throb of relief. "I agreed, of course, and I added some trimmings of my own. When the jailer came to my cell I was lying on the floor, one end of my belt looped round my neck. The other end, broken off, was dangling from the lantern hook in the ceiling. Before I took the drug I'd arranged it to look as if I had hanged myself and the belt had snapped under my weight.

"When the mandarin heard I'd hanged myself he sent doctors to make sure I was dead. They said I was. Then Dr. Langdon offered a twenty-sovereign bribe if he could take my body for burial in the English cemetery. Later that day a coffin full of stones was buried and old Tattersall conducted a funeral service. There can't be many clergymen who've married and buried the same man within twenty-four hours."

"He didn't know the truth?"

"No. He might have let it out. At the time I was lying in a coma in an old chicken coop at the back of Dr. Langdon's house."

I was perplexed. "But the doctor took me to your grave, and I put flowers there. Why didn't he tell me then?"

"Because I'd made him promise not to. I still had to get clear of the region without getting caught and it was a month before I could even stand up, let alone travel. If I did get caught I knew anybody in the plot would be executed." He smiled the lopsided smile I had first seen in charcoal on the mission wall. "After saving your hand, Lucy, I didn't want to cost you your head."

The coach halted at the station. Nick helped me down, relapsing again into a somber mood. The coachman carried my case onto the platform and I did not speak again until we were alone in a first-class compartment of a train bound for London. Then I said, "May I talk, Nick?"

He stared. "Do you feel you have to ask?"

"You seem so preoccupied."

"Talk if you wish." His eyes were hard. "And never ask my permission like that again."

I was bewildered. His words were at odds with his manner, and I could not begin to guess at his thoughts. But I had one very important question to ask. "When did you get back to England?"

He looked out the window. Then he said, "A week ago. I hid in Chengfu for months, getting my strength back. When I left I walked most of the way to Tientsin, wearing Chinese peasant clothes. That mandarin has a long arm, and I couldn't risk being recognized."

I was sure it was a lie. He had been in England on the night of the fifth of November. I said, "Did you write that letter, telling me to wait six months before going to the solicitors, just before you took the drug?"

He nodded. "I thought that if I survived I'd be home before the time came, but I hadn't reckoned on being ill for so long. I saw Edmund at his office yesterday, by the way." His grin came back. "He seemed to feel it was most thoughtless of me to be alive when he'd gone to such trouble in respect to my death. He tells me the treasure is in emeralds. Was that all the help you were able to give the Greshams?"

"Yes, it was." I hesitated. "Will you try again?"

He shook his head. "That enterprise is a dead duck. Especially with the people they call the Boxers starting to make trouble. They're a secret society and their aim is to destroy all foreigners."

"But the Empress would never let them attack the foreign devils!"

"You're out of touch, Lucy. Dr. Langdon told me that by winter's end she'll be encouraging her people to do so."

"Will Dr. Langdon and the mission be safe?"

"Sensible people will move into the legations in Peking before trouble really starts. Even more sensible ones will make for Tientsin, or any big port, where they'll have protection from the British Navy."

I sat lost in my thoughts. It was only when the train began to slow down that I came to myself, and as we stopped at Charing Cross I said, "Where are we going now?"

He took my case from the rack. "I've a small cottage in Chelsea. There are no servants. Will you be able to manage without?"

"Oh yes, of course, I always have." But his words brought a new thought to my mind, and when we were settled in a hansom cab I asked, "Did you know about . . . your father?"

"Being the Greshams' butler? Yes, I've known for years, but I've never spoken of it. And I know why he's no longer their butler. Edmund told me everything."

"Mr. Marsh thinks you're dead, Nick. I must write to him today."

"No need. Edmund has already written to say I'm alive and taking you home today." He frowned. "What I haven't yet fathomed is how you came to discover that he is my father."

I told him the story. "Look," I ended, "your father gave me a lovely chain for your ring." I reached inside my collar and drew out the ring. "The chain was your mother's once, like the ring."

He turned his head away. "Why do you wear the ring?"

"Because you were kind to me, I suppose. I've treasured it as a keepsake, and . . . well, because I was your wife. Have I made you angry? Don't you want me to wear it?"

He leaned back in his seat and closed his eyes. "No, you haven't made me angry." He said no more. After a few moments I took off my hat and leaned back myself, feeling too weary even to wonder what the coming hours and days would hold for me.

I woke from a doze when the cab halted outside a small, pretty house in a road leading north from the Chelsea Embankment. It had white walls and Virginia creeper growing almost to the low roof. Inside were two very pleasant rooms and a kitchen and scullery downstairs, with two bedrooms, a bathroom and a small storeroom above. The house was not heavily furnished, but the impression was one of comfortable elegance.

As Nick took me from room to room I exclaimed with pleasure. "It's beautiful," I said. "Just like a miniature palace, Nick."

"You're not hard to please, are you?" he said, setting down my suitcase in the larger bedroom. "I'll leave you to unpack. You'll find me in the drawing room."

There were two wardrobes. The first I opened was empty, presumably meant for me, together with an empty chest of drawers beside it. As I hung up my clothes I found it almost impossible to believe that less than three hours ago, at Moonrakers, Robert Falcon had been asking me to marry him, and now I was here with Nick Sabine, my husband, a man I scarcely knew. Why had Nick come to claim me? And why did he pretend that he had only recently returned to England? Since he might well have been the man who carried me deep into the Chislehurst Caves, I should have been in terror of him now, but I did not feel afraid. Nervous, yes, that was only natural, but not afraid.

I washed my face and tidied my hair, then made my way down to the drawing room. Here a gas fire burned brightly. There was a well-filled bookcase against one wall, newspapers and magazines piled on a side table. Nick sat in one of the armchairs, his legs stretched out toward the fire. He got to his feet as I entered.

"Have you had this house long, Nick?" I asked.

"I rented it over a year ago, but I have an option to buy. It's fairly well stocked, but if there's anything we need, just tell me." He took out his wallet and drew from it three five-pound notes. "Here, Lucy, for your personal needs . . . You'll find the larder reasonably full, but you can go round to the shops tomorrow. I settle up weekly with the tradesmen, but you'd better have a little for incidentals." He pushed another five-pound note into my hand. I held a kitchenmaid's wages for a year.

"You're—you're very generous," I stammered. "I won't be extravagant, I promise. What time will you have dinner?"

He shook his head. "I'm going out," he said, almost brusquely. "Just get whatever you want for yourself."

I stared in bewilderment. The clock above the mantelpiece stood at ten minutes past six. "Won't you be back for dinner?"

"No. I'll probably be in around midnight. I have my key, so go to bed when you feel like it." He moved to the door. There he paused, looking back at me with a brief smile. "Well, at least you're better off than you were in Chengfu prison."

He turned away. Seconds later I heard the front door close.

By ten o'clock that evening I had eaten my dinner, washed up, cleaned the kitchen and downstairs rooms, and was sitting by the fire in the drawing room reading. At half past ten I turned out the gas fire and went upstairs. Lying in the double bed, I waited for my husband to return, my mind turning over unanswerable questions. Why had Nick claimed me as his wife, brought me here, and then gone out for the evening on his own? Why did his mood change so?

An hour later I heard the front door open and close. Then came the sound of his feet on the stair. I held my breath, listening, but I did not feel afraid. I felt only a strange and heady excitement. I had left the door half open. I could hear Nick on the landing. He stopped at the door and there was complete silence for a moment or two. Then came the sound of the bedroom door on the far side of the hall being closed.

I got up, struck a match, and groped for the chain of the gaslight on the wall above me. The light came on with a faint pop. I went to the second wardrobe, the one I had thought was Nick's. It was empty. Slowly I climbed back into bed and turned out the light.

This was not *our* bedroom. It was mine alone.

DURING THE NEXT two weeks I was sometimes happy and at other times almost in despair. I loved keeping the little house spotless and cooking nice meals. I enjoyed going to the shops, walking beside the river. The atmosphere was gay and exciting.

But Nick remained a stranger, and I saw little of him. On most days he spent several hours at the London Metal Exchange, which was something to do with buying and selling copper and tin and such. When I asked him what he did he simply said, with one of his rare smiles, that it was a respectable way of gambling, and very profitable.

The evenings he spent at his club. Sometimes, for a few hours, he would be as intensely alive as I remembered him in Chengfu. Then he would perhaps spend an evening at home with me, or take me to a restaurant, and once we went to the theater. But, abruptly, a barrier would come down, transforming him into a man who seemed to find my very presence unbearable. At those times it was hard to hide the pain I felt.

One day, when he had gone off to the exchange, I suddenly had a great longing to see Mr. Marsh. Perhaps he could explain Nick's strange behavior and tell me what to do. I knew the address of his master, the officer he had attended in the army who was now Lieutenant General the Lord Shipley. It was in Duke of York Street, near Whitehall.

After an hour's walk I found the house. It was tall but narrow, and set in a terrace of similar houses. I guessed that this was a small establishment that Lord Shipley used for convenience when in London. He would have estates elsewhere. An alley led to the rear for tradesmen. The back door was opened by a plump lady wearing an apron and a mobcap. Even as I inquired for Mr. Marsh I heard his voice exclaim, "Lucy!" and the next moment he appeared behind the woman. "Lucy, what a wonderful surprise! Come in, my dear."

"Is it all right for me to be here?" I asked as I was ushered into the kitchen.

"Quite all right, child. My duties are light, and his lordship is at the War Office all day." He embraced me and took my hat and coat. "Mrs. Burke, this is my daughter-in-law, Lucy."

When Mrs. Burke left a little later to go to the shops, I told my story. Mr. Marsh listened with a puzzled frown. "I know there's no reason why he should like me," I ended, "but if not, then I just don't understand why he claimed me as his wife. He's never even kissed me."

Mr. Marsh sighed. "I know less of the boy than you do, Lucy. I can't even begin to understand why he acts so strangely."

We talked of other things for a while, until Mrs. Burke returned. I was disappointed to have found no help in understanding Nick, but realized that I had been foolishly optimistic even to hope for it. Mrs. Burke was a kindly woman and a great chatterbox. I was invited to stay for lunch, shown round the small but elegant house, then spent an hour copying some of her recipes. Time ran on, and it was almost four when I left.

By the time I reached home dusk had fallen. As I entered the house Nick came from the drawing room, newspaper in one hand, a cigar in the other. "You shouldn't be out so late, Lucy," he said.

"I walked over to see your father, Nick, near Whitehall and . . . I should have asked you, but I went on the spur of the moment. I'm so fond of him, and it made company for me today."

"I don't mind you going to see my father," he said. "But you *walked?* There and back?"

"I—I didn't want to spend your money on cabs, Nick," I stammered, "and it's only four miles each way."

"Will you never learn?" he cried furiously. "You have *rights*, Lucy. *Rights!* You're not in China now. You're not poor now. Never behave as if you had to account to me for what you spend."

I was greatly upset. "I'm sorry," I said, trying to keep my voice steady. "It wasn't that I thought you'd be angry if I spent money on a cab, Nick. I know you wouldn't. It's just that I—I have bad habits, I suppose. Please forgive me."

"Bad habits?" He drew a long breath, and the anger faded from his face. "There's nothing to forgive, Lucy. If ever I shout at you again, shout back at me. You're not a servant, not a possession. Mark that well, or you'll spend your life kowtowing to some pompous, condescending husband."

I said dazedly, "But Nick . . . you *are* my husband."

He blinked, disconcerted for a moment, then said in an odd voice as he turned back into the room, "Why, so I am, Lucy. So I am."

This was when I first wondered, with a sharp stab of alarm, if Nick's mind sometimes slipped across the border of normality. He had just spoken as if marriage for me lay in the future and with another man. If Nick suffered mental lapses from time to time, it would explain so much that bewildered me.

After a moment or two I said hopefully, "Will you be at home for dinner tonight, Nick? I have a new recipe to try."

He did not look at me, but studied the glowing tip of his cigar. "No, I'll be going out soon. Don't wait up for me, Lucy."

As TIME PASSED there was little change in the pattern of our lives. I wavered between hoping that my fear of Nick's being unbalanced was absurd and dreading that it was true. It was in the second week of June that I returned from shopping one morning to find a cab outside the house and Mr. and Mrs. Falcon standing there. I was overjoyed to see them, and we were soon settled comfortably in the drawing room with cups of coffee.

"We've had something of a shock," Mrs. Falcon said, looking at her husband. "That's mainly why we came to see you without writing first, Lucy. I hope Nicholas won't be angry at our calling."

"Oh no, Mrs. Falcon. What's happened?"

"We spent the past two weeks in Cornwall," Mr. Falcon said. "When we arrived home, we found Robert gone. He left no message but we believe he's taken a ship for the Far East, and we wondered if you could tell us anything about it, Lucy. With the troubles in China, we're rather worried."

"Robert's gone to China?" I said, astonished. I had begun to read *The Times* carefully, and it was clear that the Boxers were becoming more dangerous all the time. "That's a stupid thing to do now! What makes you think I might know about it, Mr. Falcon?"

"Well . . . there's a rather strange story you may be able to throw some light on. You remember Nellie, the maid? She tells us that one day she was cleaning and trimming the bedside lamp in your old room, Lucy. She scraped some sooty carbon onto the top sheet of a writing pad she found in the drawer beside the bed. When she had finished, she saw that the soot scattered on the paper had made some words stand out faintly—words that must have been written on the sheet above before it was torn off.

"Apparently the soot picked out the dents you'd made with your pencil on the sheet below. Nellie could only make out a few of the words, but they were something to do with a giant's knife. She was looking at the paper as she went downstairs, when she met Robert. She showed it to him and he became very excited. He took the paper, saying he would brush carbon from pencil lead over it, to make the whole message visible.

"And that was the last Nellie saw of the paper," Mr. Falcon concluded with a troubled frown. "Apparently Robert went away the very next day. We've inquired of the shipping agencies. Nothing has left direct for China in the last two weeks, but he could have taken passage to Bombay or Singapore and picked up another ship there. We're assuming that he found something to throw new light on that damn riddle, of course."

Mrs. Falcon put a hand on mine, her beautiful eyes anxious. "Do you know what was on the pad, Lucy?"

"It was the answer to the riddle." I explained what had happened. "I've never told anybody about it. I'm sorry. I wouldn't knowingly have done anything to put Robert in danger."

"You're not to blame at all," Mrs. Falcon said quickly. "Well, at least we know the truth, Harry. Better that than being in doubt."

"We can only do what parents do the world over. Worry and hope." He gave me a wry smile. "So you told nobody? I always knew you had good sense, child. That treasure has spawned nothing but hate and malice. We'd be glad to see it at the bottom of the ocean, Tina and I. But for Robert it means saving Moonrakers. He'd risk anything for that."

They left ten minutes later, promising to let me know if they had any news, and I spent the rest of the day in a troubled state of mind. When Nick came home that night I told him of their visit, then gave him the original sheet of paper.

"This is what the riddle means, Nick. I'm sorry if you feel I should have told you before. To be truthful, I've scarcely thought about it since you brought me here. And besides, I didn't want anybody to go off to China now, when there may be a war there soon. It would be madness."

He sat down and studied what I had written, then looked up. "Ironic to think that all those years when you were scratching for a few bowls of millet porridge you were sleeping with a fortune in your room." He grinned suddenly. "And now the bold Robert has gone off to seize the emeralds and save Moonrakers from my greedy clutches. Very interesting."

I was baffled by his good humor when he might so easily have been angry with me. "You don't mind that Robert might find the emeralds, Nick?"

"All part of the game." He shrugged, and handed me the sheet of paper. "Off to bed with you now. It's late. Good night, Lucy." He bent forward and kissed me on the cheek.

The next three days were the best I had known since coming to Nick's house. His good moods had never lasted so long before. I found myself daring to hope that whatever had afflicted him was past and done with, and that now we would come to a happy and normal life together, for over the past weeks I had found myself longing for our marriage to be complete. I knew that it was not proper for a young Englishwoman to feel as I did, but I was glad to be different.

On the fourth day, at breakfast, between my going to the kitchen and returning with more coffee, the change occurred. I came back to the dining room to find Nick staring down at his hands. His mouth was grim, and his newspaper lay crumpled on the floor as if he had thrown it down in anger.

Trying to keep anxiety out of my voice, I said, "Is anything wrong?"

"Eh?" He looked up, seeming hardly to see me. "Oh, never mind about more coffee. I'll be off now." He got up, went into the hall, and the next moment I heard the front door slam. Wearily I picked up the paper and folded it neatly. I spent the rest of that day wondering how he could change so quickly, and without apparent cause.

Nick did not come home that evening, and in the morning I found his bed had not been slept in. Then a messenger arrived from Nick's club with a note for me, dated the day before. It read:

> Dear Lucy,
>
> Sorry for such short notice, but I'm catching the night packet across the Channel and going on to China. There's an old score I have to repay. Go and see Edmund Gresham. He is authorized to provide whatever money you need, and will arrange a drawing account at the local bank for you.
>
> Never change.
>
> Love,
> Nick

The words blurred before my eyes. Nick had gone to China to repay an old score. He had followed his enemy, Robert Falcon. What score did Nick intend to repay? And how?

CHAPTER ELEVEN

For the next few days I kept house and performed my daily tasks like an automaton. By night I slept poorly and had bad dreams. By day I felt overwhelmed by my own helplessness. China was now a country torn by terrible strife, where anything could happen. I had a powerful presentiment that, if they survived, Nick and Robert would meet at Tsin Kai-feng. And when they met . . .

I remembered how enmity had pulsed between them when they faced one another in the drawing room at Moonrakers. If only I could go to Tsin Kai-feng myself, if only I could overtake them on the long journey, surely I could find some way to prevent their hatred ending in tragedy.

Eight days after Nick's departure I went to see Mr. Marsh. I chose a time when I knew Mrs. Burke would be out shopping, and told him all that had happened and all that I feared. "I'm going to China," I ended. "I know it sounds impossible, but it isn't really. Some ships are faster than others, and perhaps I'll be lucky in getting a quick passage. I'll draw money from the bank, then go to see a shipping agent. I *have* to get there in time."

"I don't think you realize how bad things have suddenly become in China," Mr. Marsh said gently. "My master told me last night. Peking is cut off, and the foreign embassies there are besieged. He has been put in charge of the matter at the War Office. It's a state of war, Lucy."

I was shocked by his news, but it did not lessen my particular anxiety. "Robert and Nick aren't the kind to turn back," I said.

He rubbed his brow. "Both of them are determined men. . . . But it would be different for a girl, Lucy."

With all the emphasis I could muster I said, "If you put the three of us down anywhere in China, I could travel faster than either of them. Please don't tell me the difficulties. I know them and I don't care."

He studied me, and nodded slowly. Then he sat up very straight, as if he had been struck by a sudden and startling thought. "I wonder if— Hmm . . . There's a chance, a good chance." He took my hand. "If I could stop you going, Lucy, I'd do it. But I know you, child. You won't be stopped. So the next best thing is to—" He broke off again and sat thinking. Then: "Go to see Mr. Edmund. Tell him you're closing up the house and he must arrange for somebody to keep an eye on it. Then go home and pack whatever you'd planned to take for the journey. Come back here at six o'clock this evening with your luggage. Will you do that?"

For the next few hours I was so busy with hurried preparations that I scarcely had time to puzzle over what Mr. Marsh could be planning. At six o'clock I presented myself as directed at the house in Duke of York Street. Mr. Marsh was very calm, and stood straight as a ramrod in front of me, looking me over almost as if inspecting a soldier on parade.

"Very good, Lucy," he said. "Now we are going up to see his lordship. Don't be frightened of him. His bark is much worse than his bite."

Lieutenant General the Lord Shipley was not in uniform. He was tall and very thin, with a bony face and deep-set eyes. His thin hair, brushed straight back, had been black but was graying now. In his hand he held a glass of brandy.

I curtsied and said, "Good evening, my lord."

A dark red flush crept slowly into the thin brown cheeks. He spoke in a shrill, angry bark. "Dammit, Marsh, she's a *female!*"

"Quite so, my lord. This young lady is Lucy Sabine, my daughter-in-law. May I explain myself, sir?"

"I think you'd better, Marsh."

"Thank you, my lord. Last night you spoke to me at some length about the situation in China, and if I may, I'll recapitulate for Lucy's benefit. The Empress has now swung her authority behind the Boxers. Hundreds of foreign refugees are besieged in the grounds of the British Legation in Peking, with only a handful of marines to protect them."

I listened with horror as Mr. Marsh went on. "As I understand the situation, my lord, a mixed force of British, French, and other nationalities is now marching on Tientsin, which is expected to fall quickly. They will then have to fight their way to Peking, a hundred miles distant, to seize the Empress and her council. Have I summarized the situation correctly so far, my lord?"

"You make a messy business sound simple, but carry on."

"Our forces in the Tientsin area have no communication with the people besieged in Peking. As you pointed out, sir, what the refugees in the British Legation there need is hope."

"Quite right." Lord Shipley turned to me. "Classic situation. Those people in Peking don't know what's happening. Every day they'll be getting shorter of food, water, ammunition. Now m'dear, a mainly civilian group in that situation can very quickly lose the will to resist. But if they *know* help is on the way, then they'll hold on somehow, even on a thimbleful of food a day. Understand?"

"Yes, sir. I can understand that very well."

"Good. Well, according to our troop commander out there, it's impossible to get any message through to Peking except by hand. And any foreigner trying to make the journey will get chopped up by the first group of Boxers he meets. We can't send a Chinese chap, because the ones who don't like the Boxers are frightened to death of them. Even if a Chinese agreed to go, we'd never be sure we could trust him."

He turned and fixed Mr. Marsh with a stern eye. "You told me you had someone who could be relied on to get through to Peking. What the devil d'you mean by telling me a yarn like that and then producing this—ah—very charming young girl?"

"My lord," Mr. Marsh said quietly, "until a year ago Lucy had lived all her life in China. She speaks the language as well as any native. You may remember some time ago I spoke of a young lady who came to High Coppice—"

"Hey?" Lord Shipley's eyebrows rose. "You mean this is the little girl at the mission, trying to feed those starving brats? The one who went out in the snow for young what's-his-name?"

"The same, sir. She is as used to hardship as any soldier. She thinks nothing of walking twenty miles in a day, and through a land infested with brigands. I would trust her with my life, sir." He smiled. "Indeed, I expect to do so, for it is my hope that you will allow me to accompany her."

Lord Shipley said to me, "Marsh is a canny soldier, so when he speaks like that I'm vastly impressed. But why should he be willing to expose his delightful daughter-in-law to such danger?"

"It's only because he knows I'm determined to go to China anyway, sir. I have very important reasons."

His eyes on my face, Lord Shipley said, "She really means it, Marsh?"

"Very much so, my lord. She is a most stubborn young person."

"Good. I like that." Lord Shipley chuckled. "A girl . . . now who would suspect a girl of acting as courier for the army? She'd have twice the chance of a man. Lucy, we'll give it a try! Now listen. *Crocodile* is a fast destroyer, waiting at Marseille. You can be there by dusk tomorrow, and she'll make Tientsin in twenty-two days. But you'll have to attend to my business before you attend to your own, young lady."

Twenty-two days! I had never dreamed of such speed. I could make the overland journey to Peking and still reach Tsin Kai-feng before Robert or Nick, even though Robert had left three weeks ago. I said, "I'm very grateful to you, my lord."

He stared down at me grimly. "I may well be sending you to your death, girl. But since you're set on going, I'll make the prize worthwhile. I fancy there must be well over a thousand souls under attack in Peking. A thousand lives, Lucy. So do your best. There's no one else we can send with your knowledge and experience."

He turned to Mr. Marsh. "You will accompany her to Tientsin, but she makes the journey to Peking alone. You couldn't hope to pass as a Chinese, and you'd jeopardize the whole mission."

Something flickered for a moment in Mr. Marsh's eyes, and then was gone. "Very good, my lord," he said. "May I suggest that you write out the authority for us to show the British commander in Tientsin, and the appropriate travel documents? We must be off within the hour if we are to catch the night Channel steamer."

I WAS THE only woman aboard *Crocodile,* and was given the first officer's cabin. The captain and his crew went out of their way to make our voyage as pleasant as possible, and treated us with marked respect. No questions were asked; even the captain did not know our mission.

When we stopped to refuel at Colombo, in Ceylon, Mr. Marsh went ashore and returned with a parcel. Next day there was a tap on my cabin door. When I opened it I stared in astonishment, for a Chinese coolie stood there, head bowed. He wore rough sandals, ragged trousers, a coarsely woven jacket, and a shapeless felt hat with a wide brim flopping down over his eyes. A moment later I saw that the "coolie" wore no braid, his jet-black hair was too short, and other things were amiss: the stiff-wristed way he held his hands, and the way the cheap peasant clothes hung on him.

"Who are you?" I said. The man lifted his head; it was Mr. Marsh. With his white hair dyed black he looked ten years younger, and the wicked twinkle in his eye reminded me of his son.

"I know I've a lot to learn before I can really pass for a Chinese," he said, "so the sooner you start teaching me, the better. These are makeshift clothes, of course. We can get real Chinese clothes in Hong Kong."

So he planned to go to Peking with me! "But Lord Shipley said—"

"I know. But I'm not a soldier now, so I can disobey orders. If I *can* pass as a Chinese, then you'll be safer on the journey. A young girl alone in a war-torn country—you'd be tempting prey for evil men, child."

"I know. But I'll be careful. And I can run very fast—"

"Just hear me out. Teach me how to be a Chinese peasant. We have time before we reach Tientsin. Then you can make the decision yourself. If I'm good enough, then take me with you. If not . . . then I'll abide by your judgment. For your own sake."

It was only to please him that I agreed. Up on deck I made him walk back and forth in his makeshift clothes. "*Anyone* would know you were a foreign devil," I sighed. "A coolie doesn't walk like a soldier. Hunch forward a little and let your hands dangle. . . . Now try moving at a little trot, leaning forward, then gradually slow down to a walk. Like this. It's a kind of shuffle. Oh dear, there's still something wrong. . . ."

Every day we practiced, and I became more hopeful, for Mr. Marsh seemed really to be entering into the skin of a Chinese peasant. As his walk improved I made him loll his head to one side and hang his mouth open, so that he looked simple-minded. During the evenings I taught him to sing an old Chinese children's song in a high, wavering voice. His performance became quite remarkable.

When we stopped at Hong Kong I bought old clothes, including coolie hats, for both of us, and saffron to rub into our faces. Later, when we were dressed for the part, I took Mr. Marsh ashore. He wore a braid made of my hair and dyed, and a rough leather patch over one eye. I made my own eyes look longer and narrower by using pencil black at the corners. He was Lu Yen now, and I his daughter.

Holding his hand, I led him along the narrow streets. He shuffled beside me, head wagging, and occasionally sang a few quavering lines of his little song. At several stalls I stopped to talk, and not a single person realized that we were anything other than a young Chinese girl from the North with a simpleton father. Now I knew that his presence with me on the journey would not add to the danger. In fact, a girl with her afflicted father might attract even less attention than a girl alone. It was wonderful to think that I would have his company on the journey.

We found Tientsin full of soldiers. The destroyer's captain sent two officers to accompany us to British headquarters, and Mr. Marsh presented his papers to the commanding officer, Colonel Strake, a small, stout, dour man. He read the letter from Lord Shipley with no enthusiasm. "The situation north of Tientsin is a damnable mess," he said. "These Boxer fellows are mad as hatters. They think their magic makes them immune to bullets, and they have the regular Chinese forces with them now. Badly organized, of course. So with any luck you'll sneak through their lines by night. Then you should follow the railway line to Peking." He tugged gloomily at his mustache. "Frankly I haven't much hope, but if by a miracle you do get through, tell the Minister that we'll be raising the siege by . . . say by the middle of August. Tell him to hang on till then and we'll be there."

Colonel Strake looked at me dubiously, then said to Mr. Marsh, "Do you seriously intend taking this young woman on such a journey?"

Mr. Marsh smiled. "Not exactly, Colonel. She's taking me."

LONG AFTERWARD, WHEN I was home in England and had married again, people who knew something of my adventures would sometimes ask about our journey to Peking, thinking that it must have been the most dangerous time of all. But the truth is that we never met with any serious danger.

We took with us a donkey, carrying food and water for four days, and two blankets. Mr. Marsh had a pistol hidden under his tunic. I had my felt boots, and I found a pair in Tientsin for Mr. Marsh—he said they were the best marching boots he had ever known. The Boxers wore red ribbons around their wrists and ankles, and a red sash. To show that we supported them, we tied cheap red scarves around our necks.

We left Tientsin that very night, and by dawn we had passed through the Chinese lines and were several miles north, moving parallel with the railway. Sometimes we met Chinese soldiers or groups of Boxers. Then I would pick up the end of a short rope tied to Mr. Marsh's arm, so that I seemed to be leading him as well as the donkey. He would loll his head and whine a snatch of his childish song, while I kept my head humbly bowed. We walked from dawn till dusk, covering about thirty miles, resting for a quarter of an hour every two hours. We slept in the open, for the nights were not cold.

Once we passed a small Buddhist temple with a group of Boxers outside, chanting spells and performing the strange ritual supposed to give them the power to turn aside bullets. When some of them glared suspiciously as we passed, I patted my red scarf, waved my arm and cried *"Sha! Sha!"* This war cry of the Boxers meant "Kill! Kill!" They shouted back and we passed without trouble.

At noon on the fourth day we came in sight of Peking, and settled down in a hollow beside the road to study a map of the city that Colonel Strake had provided. We marked where the Legation Quarter lay. When we entered the city's south gate an hour before sunset, there were soldiers and Boxers everywhere, mingling with the people, and the occasional sound of rifle fire. Nobody took any notice of us, and we made a slow circle of the

Legation Quarter, noting the positions from which the Chinese were firing on the defenders.

Often there would be no sound of shooting for half an hour or more; then would come a fusillade from the attackers, answered by no more than two or three shots from within the walls. It was a great relief to have Mr. Marsh with me, for he had a military grasp of exactly what was happening.

Two hours after sunset we began to move toward the wall of the Legation compound, keeping in the shadows. For the last fifty yards we crawled on hands and knees through a tangle of roughly made barricades, passing within thirty paces of a group of soldiers settling down for the night. At last we lay beside a low wall with only an empty road between us and the high wall of the compound. Mr. Marsh must have detected a British sentry position here earlier in the day, for now he cupped his hands about his mouth and spoke in a sharp, penetrating whisper. "Sentry!"

A low voice came from somewhere on the wall. "Who goes there?"

"Two friends. British. Hang a ladder down. We're coming in."

"Stand fast!" the voice snapped. "Identify yourself or I fire!"

This was our moment of greatest danger. Lying flat beside me, Mr. Marsh drew in a long breath. "Speak soft, you kettle-mender's scut, and say 'sir' when you address me, or I'll . . ." Then came a string of phrases so heavily larded with words I had never heard before that he might have been speaking a foreign language. But the soldier beyond the wall seemed to understand, for when Mr. Marsh paused there came a chuckle from the darkness and a voice said, "Hold on, friend. We'll drop the ladder."

There were faint scuffling sounds beyond the wall. Then the sentry's voice said, "Right—at the double!"

We rose and darted across the road. A rope ladder hung down the wall. I went over the top first, and tumbled onto a platform built against the side of the wall to form a firing position. Two figures stood waiting, one with a rifle pointed toward me. The other held a shielded lantern. The first said, "Blimey, it's a girl!"

The next moment Mr. Marsh came over the wall. The second man said, "Now then, who the devil are you?"

"Acting-Colonel Marsh," Mr. Marsh said haughtily. "Special emissary from the War Office. Who's in charge here?"

"Sir Claude MacDonald, sir," the man with the lamp said.

"Then take us to him at once, if you please."

"Yes, sir. May I ask, who is this Chinese girl?"

"She is English, my guide and aide-de-camp, and she has brought me safely from Tientsin in four days. Now take us to Sir Claude, and look sharp about it, young man."

Sir Claude MacDonald was a tall, thin-faced man with a wide mustache. When Mr. Marsh told him our story and showed him our papers of authority his relief was evident. "Thank God," he said quietly. "Everyone is in very low spirits here. We feared the outside world believed us already massacred, and that there would be no urgent attempt to reach Peking."

Mr. Marsh said, "Sir, Colonel Strake instructed me to tell you it will be another three weeks. I've observed the forces and the terrain between here and Tientsin, and I believe his estimate to be accurate."

Sir Claude smiled tiredly. "I've been wondering if we could last another seven days, but this news makes all the difference. We'll cut the food ration again, and make every bullet count. Be sure we'll hang on somehow, once everyone knows that rescue is certain."

It was not until the next day, after twelve wonderful hours of sleep, that I realized how much our coming meant to the defenders. Everywhere we went, men and women would stop us and ask anxiously if help was really on its way. A spirit of resolve seemed to sweep through the three thousand people within the walls of the Legation compound. More than a third of those under siege were Chinese converts who had been brought in from far and wide by missionaries when the troubles in China first began. I asked if the Fenshaws and the mission children had reached Peking, and learned to my dismay that nothing had been heard of them.

I had planned to leave Peking and strike northeast for Tsin Kai-feng as soon as I was rested, but Mr. Marsh said, "It's not only dangerous, Lucy, it's pointless. Robert Falcon may have reached Shanghai but he'll get no farther now. I doubt Nick has even reached China. And we're needed here. There'll be time enough when the siege is raised."

On the seventh day Mr. Marsh sought me out in the make-shift hospital where I was working. "A Chinese came in last night through a dry sewer, Lucy. He's from Tsin Kai-feng. You'd better come and talk to him. His English isn't up to much and I can't make out what he says."

The man was in one of the kitchens, greedily drinking a bowl of thin soup. I recognized him at once. He was Chang Li, the convert who had driven the oxcart when Mr. and Mrs. Fenshaw came to the mission. He began to express his amazement at finding me there, but I cut him short. "What has happened at the mission, Chang Li?"

"It is bad, Lu-tsi. I think they will die. Before the Boxers came, the Lady with Red Hair and her husband brought in much food, and there is the well for water. But the Boxers are camped in Tsin Kai-feng. For three weeks they have attacked. Forty, fifty of them. They shout they will kill us all, the children too, as they are contaminated by the foreign devils."

"Three weeks? How have you stopped them?"

"The outer wall is strong. Also they do not come from the north side, which is the most difficult to hold. They have some fear of it, we do not know why. And before the troubles the American doctor came from Chengfu with two rifles. He shoots with one rifle, and the husband of the

Lady with Red Hair shoots with the other. And then there is also another one, who came ten days since. He too has a rifle."

I said, "Who is this other one?"

"An Englishman. His name is Fal-con. He is very fierce and terrible. He came on a horse, dressed in the clothes of a Boxer he had killed, and with a red scarf about his head so none could see he was a foreign devil."

I turned to Mr. Marsh, barely able to speak for shock. "He says Robert is at the mission. They're holding it against a band of Boxers."

"How in the world could he have got there so quickly? And what's this fellow doing here now, Lucy? Ask him!"

Chang Li shrugged when I put the question. "We cannot hold. Fal-con sent me out by night three days ago to bring back help."

Ten minutes later Mr. Marsh and I stood before Sir Claude MacDonald. His face was lined, and even his mustache seemed to droop with weariness. "It's out of the question, Marsh," he said curtly. "I can't send a detachment to some mission ninety miles away. You must know that."

"I do, sir. I'm asking permission for Lucy and myself to go. We can get through."

"Please, sir!" I added urgently. "They're my children—I mean, I looked after them for years."

Tugging at his mustache, Sir Claude frowned, then nodded.

DISGUISED AGAIN, WE left the compound by way of the dry sewer that night, when clouds hid the moon. I carried the pistol myself, tied to my waist under my tunic, and we had a small sack with a little food and a bottle of water. Once clear of the siege area surrounding the Legation Quarter, we lay in a disused stable until dawn, then passed through the city gate without rousing any suspicion. Throughout the three-day journey to Tsin Kai-feng I felt dazed, as if I did not belong in my own body. It was hard to believe I was returning to the mission and that every life there was threatened; even harder to believe that Robert Falcon was there.

We made a half-circle around Chengfu shortly after midnight on the fourth night, and came to the mission from the north some two hours later. Lights flickered in the village below, but there were no signs of an attack in progress. We crawled toward the north wall. Briefly the moon emerged from a cloud bank, and we hugged the ground. I stared ahead, and almost gasped aloud. There, on the outer wall, faded but still clear even by moonlight, was the portrait of Nick Sabine. The soft charcoal must have been absorbed into the porous stone of the wall.

Clouds hid the moon again. Mr. Marsh lifted me and I clambered over the wall. Seconds later he dropped down beside me and we ran for the kitchen door. We were halfway there when Yu-lan's voice came from a window: "Doctor! They come from the north!"

I called in a fierce whisper, "Yu-lan! Let nobody shoot. This is Lu-tsi! Let us in quickly."

We hugged the wall beside the kitchen door, which was barred from inside. Yu-lan called tremulously, "Lu-tsi—is it truly you?"

"Yes, I am Lu-tsi. How else would I know your name? Or baby Kimi's? I have come with a friend. Let us in, Yu-lan."

"Wait, Lu-tsi, wait!"

A minute later the kitchen door was unbarred. As it opened I saw that a lamp hung from the ceiling, and on the far side stood Dr. Langdon, aiming a rifle at us. I took off my hat to show my face as I went in. He lowered the rifle, staring. His face was gaunt. "How on earth. . . ?" he croaked.

Mrs. Fenshaw appeared from behind the kitchen door. In her hand was a broom handle with a carving knife tied to one end. Her face was thinner, but the green eyes were as purposeful as ever. "Lucy Waring! What in heaven's name are *you* doing here? And who's this Chinese with you?"

Behind me Mr. Marsh closed and barred the door. I introduced him and told our story, how matters stood in Peking, and how we had carried the news that a relief army was coming to the rescue in another ten days or so.

Dr. Langdon exchanged glances with Mrs. Fenshaw. "Well, we'll just have to do our best. Once the troops take Peking this business will end, for the Empress will be bound to turn her troops against the Boxers."

From Yu-lan, who hugged me and cried and hugged me again, I learned that Mr. Fenshaw was manning a lookout post on the south side of the mission. Yu-lan and some of the older girls took turns watching at other windows to give warning of any attack. All windows were blocked by earth-filled sacks, with small holes left for keeping watch and shooting. The two Chinese nurses looked after the little children, cooked the dwindling supply of food and took their turn on watch.

"They've only twice attacked by night, thank God," Dr. Langdon said. "They don't seem to fancy it much. When they come by day they have to climb the slope from the village, so we have them in our sights for about three hundred yards. We've been able to drive them back before they reach the wall, but we have to hoard our ammunition."

At last I could ask the question I most wanted to ask. "Chang Li said an Englishman arrived two weeks ago. Is that right?"

Dr. Langdon nodded. "We'd have been finished without him. He reorganized our defense, and put fresh heart into us. We'd have no ammunition left if he hadn't made night sorties to steal from those devils in the valley." He looked at me strangely. "You know him, Lucy."

Mr. Marsh said, "We both know him, Doctor. May we see him?"

"He's lying with a bullet in his chest. It's not a fatal wound in itself, but the bullet's so placed that probing for it is going to be dangerous. Yet if I don't get it out, infection will kill him. Every hour counts."

I felt my stomach shrink from shock. "Please . . . may we see him?"

"Yes, Lucy. But even if he's conscious I doubt if he'll know you." Dr. Langdon took the lamp from its hook and Mr. Marsh and I followed him upstairs to the room that had been Miss Prothero's. A man lay on the bed, a dressing strapped over his left side. Dr. Langdon lifted the lantern, and I heard my own gasp of astonishment mingle with Mr. Marsh's.

The man who lay there with eyes closed was not Robert Falcon. It was my husband, Nick Sabine.

CHAPTER TWELVE

THE MOMENT OF DISBELIEF was engulfed by an aching of the heart so intense that it was like physical pain. I knelt by the bed and gently grasped his limp hand. "Nick," I whispered. "Dear Nick."

His eyes flickered open, but he gave no sign of recognition. His dry lips parted in a caricature of a smile. "Dreaming again," he croaked. "Of Lucy . . . the best of them all, Doc. They broke the mold when they made her. Too good for me . . . Don't ever tell how I loved her. Promise . . ." His eyes closed, and ragged breathing sounded loudly in the room.

Mr. Marsh turned to Dr. Langdon. "When did it happen?"

"Only a few hours ago." Dr. Langdon wiped sweat from his face with the back of his hand. "The Boxers brought up a small cannon today and fired into the mission. Smashed part of the chapel and breached a corner room. Three children were slightly wounded."

"But Nick has a bullet wound, you say?"

"Yes. When it grew dark he went out. He was gone for more than an hour. There was an explosion—he'd blown up the cannon with their own powder. We heard some rifle fire, and then he came over the wall. He even brought a small cask of gunpowder back with him. . . . God knows how, with that wound. He mumbled something about making bombs with it."

Mr. Marsh looked down at Nick. "That bullet has to come out," he said. "Do you have the equipment? And anesthetic?"

Dr. Langdon nodded. "I brought everything with me when I came here, but the bullet's awkwardly placed. I daren't probe for it in these conditions, my eyes aren't good enough, or my sense of touch."

Mr. Marsh said, "My eyes and hands are no longer young, either. But Lucy's are. Could she get forceps on that bullet under your guidance?"

"Lucy?" Dr. Langdon stared at me in the yellow light. "Can you do it, my dear?"

Stiff with fear, I was about to shake my head when Mr. Marsh said calmly, "Lucy can do whatever she has to do. She always has."

The next hour was to haunt my dreams for months to come. Under Dr. Langdon's instructions I scrubbed my hands in antiseptic while Mr. Marsh boiled surgical instruments in the kitchen. Dr. Langdon put Nick to sleep with ether. When I had removed the dressing and cleansed the whole area, I had to cut with a scalpel to make a path for the forceps. From that moment I stopped feeling terrified, and simply felt numb. I kept hearing Miss Prothero's voice in my head: "Just do what comes next, Lucy dear."

Mr. Marsh held the lamp, with a hand mirror belonging to Mrs. Fenshaw reflecting the light onto the wound. I made myself forget that this was Nick, forget even that this was a human being. Dr. Langdon talked quietly, telling me what to do, how to feel for the bullet with the forceps. Finally I held up the ugly piece of lead.

My knees felt suddenly like jelly. "No nonsense, Lucy!" said Mr. Marsh harshly. "There's more to be done."

I took a new grip on myself, and again followed Dr. Langdon's instructions, cleansing the wound and cleansing it yet again before putting in a tube for drainage and stitching the edges of the wound together. Then I put on a new dressing.

Dr. Langdon exhaled a long breath. "Good girl, Lucy. Whether he lives or dies, nobody could have done better."

As I stepped back from the bed the room seemed to be swaying beneath my feet. I turned to Mr. Marsh, and he caught me as I crumpled.

I WOKE TO find myself lying on a mattress in an upstairs room on the south side of the mission. I could hear rifle fire, and I sat up with a start. Mrs. Fenshaw was at the sandbagged window, peering through a hole from which a cone of bright sunlight streamed into the room. I scrambled to my feet and ran to join her. "Are they attacking?" I asked.

"Aye. There's a bunch of them coming up the hill." She moved her head so that I could look through the hole. Some twenty Boxers were running up the hill from the village, pausing sometimes to fire their rifles. I could see their red sashes.

"Why aren't we firing back?" I cried.

"Hush, child," she said briskly. "Your Mr. Marsh is in charge now. He's arranged a surprise for yon poor misguided devils."

The Boxers came on. When they were only some twenty paces away an object soared over the wall and landed among them with a loud explosion. Several men went down, and the rest turned tail.

Mrs. Fenshaw said, "That was a bomb your Mr. Marsh made. Gunpowder and nails rammed in a cocoa tin with a fuse stuck through the lid. They'll not come at us again today, I'm thinking. As a good Christian woman, I'm opposed to violence. But I'm a wee bit more opposed to letting bairns be butchered, so I'm hoping the good Lord will understand."

Mr. Marsh appeared in the doorway. "We hit them hard that time, ma'am. Your husband has a good aim. . . . Ah, Lucy, how are you?"

"Well, but I didn't mean to sleep so long. Is Nick . . . ?"

"Asleep and breathing comfortably. His fever's abating, Dr. Langdon says. Now child, don't cry." He put his arm about me. "You run along and sit with Nick. There won't be another attack for a long time, I fancy. Mrs. Fenshaw, will you take me round the defenses? I think there are some changes we could make."

Mrs. Fenshaw smiled. "I've never been overfond of the military, Mr. Marsh, but I confess it's a great comfort to have you here now. You're a formidable man."

They went off together, and I made my way to Nick's room. Yu-lan sat by him. She smiled a welcome. Nick's forehead was still hot, but he seemed to be in a deep, natural sleep. Yu-lan left, and I sat watching my husband.

If I could see into his mind, would I flinch from the hatred that had brought him here in pursuit of Robert Falcon? Would I find the answer to his strange behavior toward me? There was a stubble of beard on his chin, and except for the gauntness of his face he looked very much as I had first seen him in Chengfu prison, when he had gently touched my face with his hand, driving away my fear.

Something stirred inside me, in a fierce awakening. Tears began to run down my cheeks. Scarcely aware of what I was doing, I knelt beside the bed, took his hand in my own and pressed my lips to it. I could not understand why I was crying until it came to me that in this moment, despite all anxiety, I was filled with a kind of happiness I had never known before. I simply knelt there, whispering, "Nick . . . dear Nick . . ."

Then Dr. Langdon came in. "Don't be afraid, Lucy child," he said softly. "That's a very healthy young man. I'm sure he'll make a good recovery now. He's been lucky, of course, but I fancy a young fellow as determined as Nick makes his own luck."

I rose from my knees and sat down. "I still can't understand how he got here so quickly. He left England only eight or nine days before Mr. Marsh and me, and we came by destroyer, much faster than any ordinary ship."

Dr. Langdon smiled. "Nick didn't come by ship. He came most of the way by rail. The new Trans-Siberian Railway isn't completed yet, but it runs five thousand miles across Russia as far as Sretensk, and then river steamers connect with the railway line running down to Vladivostok. He came on from there in a Russian troopship, claiming he was a war correspondent and paying a few bribes."

"But Chang Li told us that the Englishman was called Falcon."

"Using the name of some fellow who was out here before was a precaution. You see, our old friend Huang Kung, the Mandarin of Chengfu, has sent most of his troops to help in the attack on Peking. He hasn't troubled much about this little mission so far, except to send forty or fifty Boxers. But think, Lucy—suppose he had caught Chang Li and heard that Nicholas Sabine was alive, and here at the mission? He'd scrape together every soldier in Chengfu and send them against us."

Dr. Langdon took an empty pipe from his pocket, looked at it wistfully, then put it away again. "Run along to the kitchen for breakfast, Lucy. You'll be swamped by children, of course. They're longing to see you."

Later that day I was allotted my particular duties. For certain hours I would look after Nick, and for others I would be on watch. If an attack came, I was to go to the kitchen door with Mr. Marsh's pistol and guard it as best I could. In an attack the men must remain in the upper rooms, firing down from vantage points with their rifles.

All that day Mr. Marsh seemed to be everywhere, giving his instructions with brisk confidence. When dusk came he went over the wall and set up strings at knee height, with jangling tins on them to give warning of any approach at night. I was in the kitchen when he returned from his sortie.

"I didn't have enough string to set a trip line on the north side," he said thoughtfully. "I know they never attack there, but it worries me that I don't know why."

"I think it's the portrait of Nick that Robert Falcon drew on the north wall," I said. "They take it as the picture of a foreign-devil demon, so it frightens them. The Boxers are very superstitious."

At that moment Dr. Langdon came into the kitchen, smiling. "Nick's awake, Lucy, and he's asking for you."

Mr. Marsh squeezed my shoulder gently. "You've saved him, Lucy. Give him my love. I'll come up myself in a minute or two."

The lopsided smile was on Nick's lips as I entered his room. "So it really was you last night," he whispered. "I thought I was dreaming again. Foolish little monkey, following me out here."

I bent to kiss his cheek. "How are you feeling, Nick?"

"Not too bad." I sat down and took his hand in mine. He turned his head away. "Don't be too kind, Lucy. It only makes everything harder. . . . Oh Lord, I'm so damn weak, I can't even hold my tongue."

"Why should you? Say whatever you want to me. Please."

He turned his head to look at me again. "Ah, Lucy, that would never do." Anxiety came into his eyes. "Doctor Langdon said my father is here. I must talk to him, Lucy. There are things to be done, for when those Boxer madmen attack again."

"Don't worry. Your father—" I broke off. "Ah, here he is now."

Mr. Marsh came to stand beside the bed. "Hello, Nick. It seems Lucy did a good job of surgery on you."

"Yes . . . Doctor Langdon told me. Listen, Father, I got some gunpowder last night. You have to make bombs with it. You'll need to compress the powder in tin cans, with bits of iron. And you'll need some sort of fuse. I haven't worked that out yet."

"I mixed some powder with a little sand, Nick, to make it burn more slowly, then filled a straw with it and set it in a hole in the tin. It worked very well. They took heavy losses in an attack today."

Nick stared from sunken eyes. "What else have you done, Father?"

"Rearranged some firing points, set trip wires, mined the gate . . ." Without wasting words, Mr. Marsh explained all that he had done, and his reasons. As he ended his account he smiled. "Don't look so surprised, Nick. I fought in fourteen campaigns, you know."

Nick lay silent for a minute, then said slowly, "I've been a fool. I'm sorry, Father."

Mr. Marsh shook his head. "Don't apologize to me, Nick. I'll always feel I failed your mother and you. Perhaps it's late to start being friends, but . . . could we try?"

I felt Nick's hand tighten feebly on my own. "We might even find it easy," he said.

"I'm very glad," Mr. Marsh said simply. "I'll leave you with Lucy now. Before I've finished with those Boxers they'll wish they'd never been born." He moved away, brisk and erect as a man half his age.

After a long silence I said, "Nick dear, will it tire you if I talk?"

"No." He smiled faintly. "I like listening to you."

"I want to ask a favor, Nick. I know why you came here. You said in your note you were going to pay off an old score. But *please* forget your enmity for Robert Falcon. It frightens me to think what might happen."

"Wait, Lucy." Nick was staring at me. "Did you think I followed Falcon to China? That I planned to do him some mischief?"

"I knew you meant to stop him getting the emeralds somehow, and I was afraid of . . . how it might end."

He began to laugh, then winced with pain and stopped. "But I didn't care about the emeralds. I haven't even looked behind that bronze shield. He can have them. The score I came to pay was one I owed to Dr. Langdon. . . . Didn't you read the newspaper that morning I left? The small paragraph by the correspondent on his way to Peking? He wrote that he'd spoken with an American doctor in Chengfu who was going to a nearby mission to help the people there. The doctor said the troubles would come to a head any day, and the massacres would begin. If the American and European governments didn't send relief quickly it would be too late for foreigners all over North China. They'd be dead."

I felt light-headed with relief. "That's why you came?"

"I had to, Lucy. I owed Dr. Langdon my life. I couldn't sit comfortably in England while he and everybody here were slaughtered. So I came to give a hand."

I found myself laughing and crying at the same time. Clutching his hand I said, "Oh Nick, Nick, I've been such a fool."

He closed his eyes. "I'd never harm Robert Falcon. I know you love him."

"Love him?" I caught my breath. "What do you mean, Nick?"

He opened his eyes and gave me a tired smile. "That's the first time you've ever pretended with me, Lucy. I know you love him because I saw you in his arms one night in November in the light of the bonfires. You're Lucy, without an ounce of deceit in your whole body. You wouldn't put your arms round a man and kiss him if you didn't mean it."

Shocked, I said, "Nick, please listen to me. I was alone, and unhappy, and with no friends. Robert began to call on me. He was very patient with a girl in a strange land. On the night of the bonfires he came out of the darkness to where I was standing alone. He took me in his arms and kissed me. It was my first kiss, and from a man who had been kind to me.

"Yes, I did kiss him back, and later I wondered if I loved him. When you don't know what it feels like to be in love, Nick, you wonder. . . . After I moved to Moonrakers he began to court me again, but we kissed only that one time." My hands were locked tightly together. "I'm not making excuses, Nick. I'm just saying that you shouldn't think I love him just because you saw us in that one moment—" I broke off, startled. "Then it *was* you I saw just afterward! You *were* there!"

He nodded. "Yes, I'd just come back. I knew from Dr. Langdon that you'd gone to live with the Greshams and I went straight to High Coppice to find you. The whole family was busy with the fireworks in the valley. I went down, and I saw you with Robert." He stirred restlessly. "After that . . . I don't quite know what happened for a while. I remember wandering about in the smoke. I didn't see you again. I didn't know you'd seen me. It must have been very frightening for you. I'm sorry."

"It doesn't matter now. Go on, Nick."

"Well . . . then I went away. Nobody knew I'd come back from China. I went over to Normandy with the idea of buying a fishing boat and doing some smuggling." He smiled wryly. "But that sort of thing didn't entertain me anymore. So I came back for you."

I wanted to ask him why he had returned for me, but another question came suddenly to my mind, and I blurted it out. "Nick, do you know Chislehurst Caves?"

He looked at me blankly. "I know *of* the caves, but I've never been in them. Of course, Robert Falcon knows them well—he obtained permission to explore them a few years ago. He wanted to publish a pamphlet about them. Why do you ask, Lucy?"

"After I saw you that night I fell down a slope and banged my head on a rock. While I was unconscious someone carried me into the caves and left me there. It was only by a miracle that I found my way out. Oh Nick—sometimes I've thought it was you."

I had to restrain Nick as he tried to sit up. "God Almighty, that was Falcon," he said savagely.

"It can't have been! Why should he do such a thing only a few minutes after kissing me?"

He lay back. "Why? Because he's Robert Falcon. I can't explain how his mind works—I can only tell you that at times he's capable of anything. When he came to you in the valley it might have been touch and go whether he courted you, hoping to make you his wife, or did away with you. And when he found you lying unconscious later . . ." Nick shook his head grimly. "Falcon will do anything to get what he wants. He's never been sound of mind. And only Moonrakers matters to him. Did Mrs. Falcon never warn you?"

"Well, yes, she did. I thought . . . But Nick, *why* would he want to do away with me?"

"Probably because he thought that with you dead, Moonrakers would be safe for a little longer. You see, he knew I'd married you, even before he returned home from China. He was stunned that day when I arrived at Moonrakers to collect you—but he was only surprised to see me alive, not to learn I was your husband."

"You mean he knew all the time? But how?"

"Simple enough. He came to Chengfu. If you're making inquiries in a foreign city, the best place to start is with one of your own countrymen. Mr. Tattersall was an obvious choice, and he blabbed to Falcon that he'd married us. I know, because Tattersall spoke of it later to Dr. Langdon."

"Why then did he ask me to be his wife?"

Nick's brow was creased in thought. "It would make sense, Lucy. If he'd decided that I was dead, the safest way to keep Moonrakers was to let you inherit it, but to be sure that you married him."

I sat there remembering the mingled sorrow and happiness I had known with Nick during our weeks in the little Chelsea house. I knew now that I loved him; I had felt it in that moment when I knelt and kissed his hand as he lay unconscious on the bed. I was sure, too, that what I felt for him now had been there before, held back by the fear that he did not want me.

I said, "Nick dear, may I tell you what I truly feel? I love you. I know it's immodest for an English girl to say that, but I'm not modest. I grew up in a different world. You don't have to love me back, Nick. Nobody can help how they feel, and it's not good to pretend. When this is all over you can—"

"Wait, Lucy . . . Do you know what you're saying?"

"Yes. Don't worry, Nick." I wiped his face with a cool cloth.

"Worry?" He flinched with pain for a moment. "It's your turn to listen

now, Lucy, while I tell you a story. It's about a man who lived hard and enjoyed it, a selfish man with little thought or tolerance for others. He did whatever took his fancy, and be damned to everybody." Nick took my hand. "And then . . . then there came a day when he was going to die. In prison he met a girl, different from anybody he'd ever known. Like Cinderella's slipper, she was made of crystal—he could see all the way through her, and he saw nothing but courage and love and unselfishness."

"No, Nick, please! I'm not like that. I'm not—"

"Hush now, and listen. This man married the girl for his own reasons, believing he was to die. But he didn't. A brave old doctor saved him. In hiding, he lay abed for several weeks, getting his strength back. And he had a lot of time to think about this girl, time to realize how rare she was. He fell in love with her, Lucy. When he went home he saw this girl, and knew that he'd made a great discovery. He knew at last what it was to love."

Nick touched my fingers to his lips. "But she was in love with another man, or so he thought, because he saw her in his arms. So he went away rather than spoil her happiness. He wasn't quite so selfish now, because he loved her. But he worried, for he knew the other man well, knew that behind any mask of friendship there was a mind obsessed. So in the end this clever fool became so anxious about the girl he loved that he decided to claim her as his wife after all—to save her from danger."

I started to speak, but Nick lifted a warning finger. "Truth to tell, he realized now very clearly that he wasn't nearly good enough for this girl. So he took her to his house, but they didn't really live together because he loved her too much and thought it would make her unhappy."

"Dearest Nick, why didn't you tell me? I was so sad you didn't want me."

"Sad?" He drew in a shaky breath. "But let me finish, Lucy. This fellow thought that if he kept his wife away from the dangerous man she was in love with, she might forget. He kept away from her himself as much as he could, and tried to make her see that she was a person in her own right. But sometimes he'd be really selfish again, and then he'd take her out to dine, or to the theater, and glory in having her beside him."

I began to cry. Nick put his hand gently to my cheek. "And then he'd pull himself together, and leave her alone again, because he didn't dare to be with her. He never even dreamed that she might come to love him."

"You speak as if I were so special, Nick, and I'm not. I get angry and scared and unreasonable, and I tell lies and I've been a thief. You don't know what my page in the Recording Angel's book is like."

Now the sparkle of wicked laughter was back in his weary eyes. "That's good. I wouldn't want you *too* perfect. Will you marry me, Lucy Sabine? Properly? This time meaning every word we say?"

"Yes. Yes, please, Nick. I'd like that so much."

"Then you'd better be immodest again, and kiss me."

I bent over him and rested my mouth on his dry lips. He put his good arm about me and held me. After a few seconds I felt the arm trembling, and gently straightened up. He lay back on the pillows, looking at me with a tenderness I had never thought to see in those dark, wicked eyes.

"Never change," he said.

THE SIEGE AT the mission continued for another eight days, with three attacks by the Boxers driven back by bombs and rifle fire. Throughout those days I was only half aware of the dangerous situation, for Nick and I were living in a sunlit world of our own. I performed all my duties knowing that soon I would be with him again. Knowing that he loved me.

His wound healed well. It was a joy to feel the growing strength in him when he held my hand or put his arm about me. We talked of plans for the future, and of small things remembered from the past. I had never experienced such happiness.

"I know you loved Moonrakers," he said one day as I was changing the dressing on his chest, "but I've no wish to turn the Falcons out now, if they can't pay, and it's the last thing you'd want. Besides, you have a moonraker of your own now, sweetheart. Only a half-blind fool who didn't know the moon from a cheese could have failed to see how unhappy I made you in Chelsea. And I thought I was being unselfish, leaving you alone."

"I wasn't unhappy all the time, Nick dear. Only when I thought you didn't like me."

"Well, all that's over now. For better or for worse you're a moonraker's bride. . . . Lucy, where do you want to live?"

"Anywhere with you, Nick. Houses aren't important. It's the people in them who make them what they are. I love our little house in Chelsea."

"That's fine for now, but it won't be big enough for a family. How many children do you want, Lucy?"

"Keep still, Nick. I can't kiss you while I'm doing this. Four would be nice."

"I'll make a note of it. I've a disgusting knack of making money, so we could have a farm perhaps. Or we could travel awhile before we settle down."

On another day Mr. Marsh came into the room while I was with Nick and dropped a small leather bag on the bed. It was almost black with age. He said, "Since you've been so preoccupied, Lucy, I've just looked myself behind the bronze shield in your old room. It was held in only by dried mud, whitewashed over several times."

Nick picked up the bag. "So the emeralds *were* there?"

"Look for yourself."

The bag held thirty-six large uncut stones. In this state they looked like greenish pebbles, but Nick seemed to recognize them for the gems they were. He examined one of them closely, then gave a low whistle. "To the naked eye, this one looks flawless, and that's rare for emeralds. Ten or fifteen carats, at least, and it isn't the largest. There's a vast fortune here, Lucy."

Mr. Marsh said, "What will you do with them, Nick?"

"Ask Lucy that. She found them. But in my privileged position as her husband, I venture to advise that she retain a quarter of their value for herself, for you, for the mission and for Dr. Langdon—we never want to think of him scratching around for a few coins again. The other three quarters to be shared equally between the Greshams and the Falcons."

THE SIEGE OF the mission did not end dramatically. It simply petered out. One morning a young Chinese woman walked up the hill and called to us from beyond the wall. I went out to speak to her through the gates.

"Is it truly you, Lu-tsi? In the village we thought you had gone to the land of the foreign devils."

"I came back. Why have the Boxers let you come?"

"They went away in the night. A message came from Chengfu. Foreign-devil soldiers have taken Peking, and the Empress has ordered the Boxers to disperse, under pain of death."

"Is this true?"

"I swear it. We of Tsin Kai-feng hated the Boxers, but we were afraid to speak against them until they had gone."

I said good-by and ran back into the mission to break the wonderful news. In my foolish joy I thought that all troubles and dangers were behind us now. I had forgotten the first reason that brought me back to China.

Next day a party of American soldiers arrived by way of Chengfu, to collect foreign survivors and take them to Tientsin, where they could remain until peace terms had been arranged. Mr. and Mrs. Fenshaw gathered the children together and set off with the soldiers. The American lieutenant said that he and his men would be returning in six or seven days, and would take us to Tientsin then, for Dr. Langdon had suggested that Nick should not make the journey yet. Dr. Langdon himself would not be going with them, as he intended to return to his practice in Chengfu. He left three days later, riding in the mule cart of one of the villagers.

I would not leave Nick, of course, and Mr. Marsh would not leave either of us. Yu-lan too remained, because a poor farmer in the village had asked if his son could have her as a wife. Yu-lan was eager, and Mrs. Fenshaw had agreed.

It seemed strangely quiet in the mission with just the four of us. One afternoon I went down to the village to find some material for repairing Nick's badly torn jacket. He was still unsteady on his legs, but he had insisted on getting dressed. I left him sitting on the edge of the bed, wearing trousers, boots and shirt.

I was in the village for half an hour or more. As I climbed back up the hill I saw a horse tethered at the mission gate. It was lathered, as if it had been ridden hard, and I wondered who the rider could be.

The door of the mission stood open. As I entered my heart jumped. Mr. Marsh lay sprawled on the floor, an ugly blue lump above one temple, a trickle of blood running down his face. I knelt over him, fear pounding within me. To my relief, he was still breathing. Then a new fear brought me to my feet and I ran for the stairs, crying, "Nick! Nick!"

As I raced along the passage to the bedroom I heard his voice lifted in a shout. "No, Lucy! Go back! Run!"

I burst into the room and stopped short. Robert Falcon said, "You didn't think she'd run, did you, Nick?"

He stood against the wall, a pistol in his hand. Nick was sitting on the bed, his face like stone. I ran to him, and he reached out an arm to draw me beside him, never taking his eyes from Robert Falcon.

Robert smiled. "My luck's turned at last. For two weeks I've been fretting in Tientsin, desperate to get here as soon as the war ended. And then, on my way, I met those soldiers with the mission people. So I knew you were here, and Lucy with you. Dear little Lucy, who found the answer to the riddle but didn't tell me. . . . I thought you'd won, Sabine, but you haven't. It's my turn at last." There was something in his smile that made me sick with terror. "My turn," he repeated, moving from the wall toward the foot of the bed. "Give me the emeralds."

Nick slid his free hand under the pillow behind him and drew out the ancient leather bag. "They're all here." His voice was flat. He threw the bag, and it fell at Robert's feet. "You're welcome, Falcon. You were going to get your fair share anyway."

Robert shook his gold-haloed head, still smiling that eerie smile. "Winner takes all, Sabine."

"Then take them and go."

"Leaving you alive? I'd never feel safe, old friend. No, Sabine, your luck has run out. It's journey's end for you."

"So be it. Let Lucy go. Now."

"Leaving her alive to tell the tale? That would never do. And your father will have to go too, if he isn't dead already. I hit him on the head." He looked at me, his face suddenly melancholy. "I don't want to kill you, Lucy, but I have to. You understand, don't you?"

I said, my voice wavering, "No, Robert, I don't understand. Please put down the pistol. You're overwrought—"

"Stop that," he snapped furiously. "If you don't understand, it's because you're a fool. I should have done away with you in the caves that night, but I couldn't bring myself to. I don't know how you found your way out, but it taught me a lesson. I won't make *that* mistake again."

I felt that the longer he talked, the more chance there was that this fit of madness might pass. "Why did you leave me in the caves to die, Robert?"

He stared at me with angry impatience. "What else could I do? I was ready to marry you, by God! I'm a Falcon, yet I was ready to marry an orphanage girl, to save Moonrakers. But then the Greshams forbade me to call on you, so I had to get rid of you. But you escaped, and when you came to live at Moonrakers I could think again of marrying you."

I had no hope that Mr. Marsh might come to our aid. The brutal blow on his head would hold him unconscious for far longer than I could expect to keep Robert talking. I could only pray that some word of mine might pierce the cloud of unreason about Robert's mind. I said, "You were very kind to me, Robert. Didn't you feel anything for me at all?"

He looked irritated. "For you? The only thing I feel for is Moonrakers. Oh, you're pretty enough—I never *wanted* to do away with you. I don't want to now." His eyes glittered and a muscle twitched in one cheek. "But I'm going to settle the score with Sabine, so you have to go too. Surely any fool can see that!" The pistol came up. "You first, Sabine," he said.

When the shot came the sound of it struck me with a force so terrible that it was as if I had taken the bullet in my own body. I gave a dreadful sob, and looked at Nick. He had not moved. He was staring toward Robert in unbelief; incredibly the bullet must have missed him.

I turned my gaze to Robert, a wild appeal on my lips, but I did not speak, for I saw that his hand had fallen to his side, and the pistol was slipping from his limp fingers. He swayed, staring at Nick with astonished blue eyes. Then his legs began to crumple. The light went out of his eyes, leaving them empty, and he fell back.

Then I saw that Yu-lan stood in the doorway behind him. She was clutching Mr. Marsh's pistol in both hands, a wisp of smoke coiling from the barrel. Her voice trembled as she spoke. "I had to, Lu-tsi. This one has killed Mr. Marsh. I saw it happen, but he did not see me. I ran to get the pistol. When I found it I came up quietly. I heard him say he would kill you. I had to stop him, Lu-tsi."

From a dry throat I said, "You saved us all, Yu-lan. Don't be afraid. And Mr. Marsh is not dead."

Nick rose painfully from the bed, his face colorless, and took the pistol from her shaking hands. "Poor devil," he said, "his mind was gone. . . . We shall not forget, Yu-lan."

"Nick—" I took his arm. "Lie down. You look awful."

"I don't wonder." He braced himself. "But I can't lie down yet, Lucy.

There's my father to see to. And this. . . ." He looked at the form on the floor.

"Yu-lan and I can manage, Nick. Don't worry. We've managed a lot of things alone before."

He swayed, and I helped him to the bed. "You've managed too much alone." His voice was breathless, but his eyes were angry. "This is the last time you'll ever have to manage alone. I promise you that, Lucy."

WE SAILED FROM Tientsin a month later. By then Mr. Marsh was fully recovered from the concussion he had suffered after Robert Falcon's brutal and unexpected attack on him, and Nick was almost himself again. That was a wonderful voyage. Nick and I had a cabin with two bunks, but I slept in his arms. It was cramped and hot, but we did not care. To be together, and safe, was all that mattered.

We came home to England after the last leaves had fallen, and renewed our marriage vows in a small church in Chelsea. Edmund Gresham came to the wedding, as did Mr. and Mrs. Falcon, bringing Matthew, who sulked a little when I kissed him, because he was jealous of Nick.

We told the Falcons a lie about Robert's death, for we said that he had been with us during the siege at Tsin Kai-feng and had lost his life defending the gates against a Boxer attack. He lay buried now in the English cemetery of Chengfu.

Mrs. Falcon looked at me, her beautiful eyes heavy with grief, and said quietly, "Robert was a strange boy, and . . . well, it's kind of you to tell us he died bravely. That's how we shall remember him."

Another guest at our small wedding was Lord Shipley, who demanded of Mr. Marsh to be invited. He threatened Nick: "Make sure you're damn good to that child, Sabine, you hear me? Treat her like a queen or by God I'll have you dropped in the Thames one dark night and marry her myself. She's worth ten of you."

"More like twenty, sir." The devils danced in Nick's eyes. "And if you were thirty years younger, sir, I'd call you to account for sending her to Peking."

"Quite agree. But I couldn't stop her, boy. She was coming to find you anyway. And they damn well saved the day there, she and Marsh between them."

The fortune from the emeralds we shared as Nick had suggested. We received a rather stilted letter of thanks from Mr. Gresham. The Falcons were reluctant to take their share, for they had now decided to leave Moonrakers and move to Cornwall; but I pleaded with them and they accepted in the end. Nick sent money for Dr. Langdon and the mission through a bank, and included five hundred pounds of his own money for Yu-lan, which in China would make her rich for life.

It seems that when fortune smiles she brooks no half-measures. Two months after our wedding a letter came for me by the late post. We had been to the theater and dined out that evening, so it was not until we returned to our Chelsea home at midnight that we found the letter, which bore the stamp of the War Ministry.

I could scarcely wait to take off my evening cloak before reading the letter, and then I gasped. "It's an official letter from Lord Shipley, and there's a draft on the Treasury for . . . for a thousand pounds. He says it's for 'invaluable services rendered to Her Majesty's Armed Forces.' Then he says your father is being sent a similar sum! Oh Nick, what shall I do with it all?"

He laughed delightedly. "It's a miserable sum. Less than the cost of a few salvos from a battleship." Then he reached down, put an arm under my knees and lifted me to hold me cradled. "Do with it, Lucy? Perhaps you could have your eyes altered so that they aren't all round and ugly, like foreign devils' eyes."

"Nick, stop teasing and put me down."

"No. You're much too beautiful. If I put you down, somebody might steal you." He kissed me, and began to carry me upstairs.

I said, "I'm so pleased about your father, Nick."

"Yes. He could have retired already, of course, but he'll go on working, being a servant."

"A father to be proud of?"

"Yes, Lucy. And what will you go on being?"

"Me? I'll just go on being your immodest, loving wife, please Nick." We were on the landing now. "What about you?"

He pushed open the bedroom door with his foot and carried me in. "That's easy, sweetheart." He kissed me again, very gently. "Just never change, and I'll go on being the luckiest man in the world."

The Golden Unicorn

A CONDENSATION OF THE NOVEL BY

Phyllis A. Whitney

ILLUSTRATED BY DENNIS LUZAK

Successful New York journalist Courtney Marsh has beauty and fame, but lacks the one thing she wants most: a sense of who she really is. Adopted as a baby, she has recently lost the only parents she has ever known in a train accident. Armed with just two clues as to her identity—a faded newspaper clipping and a small gold unicorn—Courtney is led to a dark-shingled mansion on Long Island. There she finds a family whose secrets haunt them and a terrifying legend foretelling death on the night of a unicorn moon.

Phyllis A. Whitney is the author of many popular novels of romantic suspense, including *Thunder Heights* and *Vermilion.*

CHAPTER ONE

EXCEPT FOR THE MUMBLING of the television set, the living room of my New York apartment seemed utterly still and empty, without life. My presence hardly mattered. I had dressed for bed in my new gown with its matching blue robe—but there was no one to see, and I had a strange feeling that nothing about me or the room had any reality. I felt as empty as the apartment—emotionally drained. The loss I had suffered two months ago in July, as well as what had happened to me this afternoon, was having a delayed effect.

If I was honest, what had happened today wasn't even terribly important. Tomorrow I would be on my way to East Hampton and my search would go on. But for now I was numb with discouragement.

On the screen the talk-show host was putting on his best now-I-am-about-to-present expression and I tried to focus my attention. "I want you to meet a young woman who has enjoyed an amazing success," he was saying. "I'm sure you've read her interviews in *National Weekly*, and you know what lively and penetrating pieces she writes. I want you to welcome Miss Courtney Marsh."

The audience applauded and the girl came out. Don't swing your arms when you walk, I thought. She was slim, her blond hair fell to her shoulders, and she was smartly dressed in a dark red sheath that hinted at a good figure. She moved with poise, shook hands with the host with grace, and sat down. She answered questions in a clear voice without self-consciousness, speaking modestly of her surprising success.

"You're still in your twenties, aren't you?" Hal Winser said. "How did you become such a whiz so soon? How come people tell you so much in your interviews?"

"I've always been interested in people," she told him smoothly. "I like to find out what makes them tick."

"But now you specialize in women—not even famous women. Why?"

"I suppose I've become aware of a great many outstanding women in the arts and the professions today. Most are working quietly without a great deal of recognition. I try to give them a little of the credit they deserve."

"Did your parents encourage you when you were young?" he asked, with the easy familiarity of his breed.

I left my chair and turned off the set with a sharp click. I didn't want to hear any glib talk about Courtney Marsh and her parents.

I was Courtney Marsh. Yet I could hardly recall the taping of that show a few weeks ago. It had lost all reality. I sometimes wondered what reality there had ever been for me.

Without warning, memory whipped back to fifth grade. I had been adopted when I was two months old, and my adoptive parents had never kept this fact from me. No one had ever made anything of it until that day in school in a small Connecticut town. I could still hear the poisonous boy who had sat next to me. "My mom says you don't have any mother and father. My mom says you aren't real."

I had run away from school before classes were dismissed that day. I had run all the way home to Gwen Marsh's arms, and she had consoled me. "Of course you're real," she had said. "You're the realest thing in our lives. We *are* your mother and father, even though you weren't born to us."

I switched off the memory as sharply as I'd turned off the set. The only thing I knew for sure was that I was not the natural child of Gwen and Leon Marsh. But they'd done the very best for me they could, and I had loved them both dearly. Now they too were lost to me, in that dreadful accident. Their loss had brought everything to a climax in my life.

I felt terribly alone. The girl I had just seen on television wasn't real. She didn't know how to be a person in her own right, how to be a woman a man could love. Of course I had friends. I had Jim, who had brought me home this afternoon—if I wanted to call him. But apathy persisted.

The phone rang as I stared at it. My "Hello" wasn't exactly welcoming.

"Courtney, hon, you were terrific on Hal Winser's interview! You showed *him*." That was Jim's voice. "You couldn't have looked more elegant and sure of yourself. I liked the way you turned his snide questions about professional women back on him without being rude—really great!"

"I couldn't watch," I said.

There was a small silence. "Darling, don't let what happened this afternoon get you down."

"Good night, Jim," I said. I put the phone aside and looked about the room as though I were seeing it for the first time. Antique Persian rugs, an elaborate stereo, original oils and name lithographs on the walls. To whom did this room belong? What was that person trying to prove? A sophisticated taste and good blood—all acquired and superficial?

I turned my back on it, went into the bedroom, and got into bed. I wasn't Jim Healy's darling. Courtney Marsh wasn't anybody's darling. How could she be, with a great part of her vital identity missing? "Go to sleep and stop being a fool," I told myself. "You're at the top of your profession, and you're only twenty-five. What on earth do you want?" I answered my own critical self: "Not all that much. Just to know who I am."

This afternoon I had tried—and once more failed. I went through the scene again in my mind. The lawyer was already on guard when I walked into his office. I'd had to give my identity in order to make the appointment, and he must have looked up my name in his files. "I believe it was your firm that handled the details when I was adopted nearly twenty-five years ago, Mr. Pierce," I began abruptly.

The guarded look moved from me to a folder on the desk before him, and he nodded. "My late father handled the case, Miss Marsh. Has the adoption worked out well for you?"

"It has gone very well," I said. "But that doesn't mean I haven't a right to know who I am."

He was shaking his head before I'd finished the sentence. "I'm sorry, but these matters are legally sealed—and very sensibly so, in order to protect all the parties concerned."

I couldn't help the bitterness that crept into my voice. "Yes, I've been to the agencies where such records are kept. They wouldn't give me anything. But I was told that your firm had handled the case, and I knew you weren't bound by the same rules."

His expression was not entirely without sympathy, but I could see that he didn't mean to give an inch. "Perhaps not. But we are governed by a responsibility to those concerned. Gwen and Leon Marsh adopted you and gave you a good home. Have you considered the pain you may bring them by asking such questions?"

I swallowed hard and tried to keep my voice steady. "They both died just two months ago in a train crash in Italy."

He looked shocked. "I'm very sorry. I can understand that this loss has left you with an emptiness you want to fill. But you have to remember that your mother gave you away. To speak bluntly, she's not likely to want you back in her life now."

"I don't want to make trouble for her. I probably wouldn't even let her know who I am. It's only my identity I'm seeking."

He shuffled the papers on his desk impatiently. "You think now that you'd be silent. But if you found your mother, sooner or later you'd be driven to identify yourself. It would be wiser to accept the end of the road in this office and stop fighting something that can't be changed."

"It's not the end of the road," I cried. "I know where my mother lived. Her home was on Long Island. In East Hampton."

He was suddenly alert. "What makes you think that?"

"When I was going through Leon's things after the crash, I found a letter to him from an elderly aunt. It asked how the little girl from East Hampton was doing. Won't you even confirm this small detail?"

He shook his head, his expression again guarded.

"It doesn't matter." I stood up. "I'm going to East Hampton tomorrow."

"Without a single lead to follow? That's pretty foolish, isn't it?" He rose from his desk and came around to stand beside me, his manner softening a little. "I'm sorry I can't help you, Miss Marsh."

Jim was waiting for me in the outer office. "You notice I'm not asking questions," he said when we were alone in the elevator. "Your face is a mile long. Let's go over to Bruno's."

I couldn't bear to talk while we walked the two blocks, and I let him rattle on, trying to cheer me. He found us a booth and ordered coffee for me and a whiskey sour for himself.

"Courtney, why don't you give this up?" Jim said. "You're just banging your head against a stone wall. I don't like to see you hurt."

I found myself studying his broad, good-natured face in the dim light of the booth. Jim and I worked together at the *National Weekly*, where he was an assistant editor. I respected his intelligence and integrity, and he had taught me a lot about my job. But I wasn't in love with him. I hadn't ever been really in love with anyone.

"Listen," I said. "I'm an adult. I *do* have a right to know who I am."

He reached across the table and took my hand. "What have you got to go on? You haven't any leads."

Around my neck, hidden beneath the collar of my blouse, I wore a pendant on a fine gold chain, and now I reached back and opened the clasp. "I have this," I said, and held up the chain so that the golden unicorn dangled from it—a tiny, perfect thing, its front legs prancing, the slender golden horn protruding from the forehead, the etched eyes somehow wise and knowing. "It was around my neck when Gwen and Leon brought me home. It was a—a memento from someone. Someone who must have cared a little to leave such a precious thing with me."

"But it gives you no information of any kind."

"Perhaps it does. There's something else." I opened my handbag and took out a yellowed clipping and spread it open on the table. "When I went through their bank deposit box after Gwen and Leon died, I found this."

Jim bent over it, studying a hazy reproduction of a painting by an artist named Judith Rhodes. It showed a beach with a long stretch of sand—a night scene with a full moon sailing an empty sky above the dark ocean.

Jim looked up at me, puzzled. "So what?"

"Read the penciled words on the margin," I said.

He turned the clipping sideways and read, " 'Is this the unicorn in our Courtney's life?' " He shook his head. "Who wrote this? What unicorn?"

"It's Gwen's handwriting. Look at the shadow on the moon."

It was there when he searched—the outline of cloud in the unmistakable shape of a unicorn. "It's not much to go on," he said. "Who is Judith Rhodes?"

"When I found that clipping I took it to an art gallery on Fifty-seventh Street. The owner was enthusiastic. He knew her work well, though she's something of a recluse. She doesn't exhibit often and doesn't care to sell many of her paintings. He told me that the Rhodeses are an old, wealthy family in East Hampton. That might tie in with that letter I found asking about the little girl from there. Judith Rhodes's husband is in banking—plenty of money—and when she does have a show he brings in the paintings and sees to everything. She never comes in herself."

Jim shook his head. "So—what's the connection?"

"The man at the gallery told me she makes rather a thing of including unicorns in her pictures. There must have been some connection in Gwen's mind because she wrote those words in the margin of the clipping. Anyway, I'm going to East Hampton."

"Blindly, without any more of a lead than this? Are you pinning some wild hope on having this Judith Rhodes turn out to be your mother?"

"No, what sort of reporter do you think I am? There's not enough evidence to lead to that. I only want to find out why there's a unicorn in my life. Besides, Judith Rhodes is an artist of unusual talent, one of those women I like to interview. I wrote to her, and her husband, Herndon Rhodes, answered. He is keen on the idea, and he's sold it to her, which is unusual. So I'm to go out there to get the material for my piece. And Jim—I'm not coming back to the office."

He looked startled. I folded the clipping carefully and put it back in my bag. "Today I turned in my resignation," I told him. "I'll free-lance a bit if they want me to, but after this piece I'm on my own."

"But why, Courtney—why?"

"I want to write a book based on my articles. I even have a publisher who's interested."

"They'd give you time off from the magazine if you asked."

"I don't want time off. I want to get away, burn my bridges. Oh, Jim—don't you see? I've got to find out how to be *me*."

Jim brought me home, and all the way I sat numbly, letting New York slip by the cab windows without being conscious of it. Now, alone in my apartment, I thought again how much I needed to know where I had come from. I finally fell asleep, wondering about my mother, a mother I knew absolutely nothing about.

CHAPTER TWO

THE NEXT MORNING I made the long drive out toward the eastern tip of Long Island in my Volvo, and when I turned into the village of East Hampton, I immediately liked its air of rural tranquillity, its old houses and unique windmills. Drowsing in the center, where the road divided, lay the Town Pond and the Old South Burying Ground. On either side were houses of historical vintage, their shingles a silvered brown.

The Rhodeses wouldn't expect me until early afternoon, so I parked, planning to ask a few careful questions and have lunch before I drove to their house. As I walked down Main Street, I found myself wondering if I could have been born here. Was there a house in this town where I had slept in my crib until I was nearly two months old? Something in me quickened at the thought.

I liked the casual, informally dressed people who moved in the warm sunshine of early September without the urgency of New Yorkers. I stopped in a dress shop to look around, and mentioned to the woman behind the counter that I was here to do an interview with Judith Rhodes. She seemed oddly startled. "Oh? Then you'll be going up to The Shingles?"

I knew the name of the house from the stationery on which Herndon Rhodes had written me. "Yes. Is it one of those houses on the ocean?"

She nodded. "It's on the dunes, but it's not a summer house. Old Ethan Rhodes built for the year round, and the family has always lived there."

I asked to see a yellow-and-brown scarf displayed in a glass case. I bought it to go with the pants suit I was wearing. Then the woman went on, "Once when I was a little girl the Rhodeses opened the house to visitors for the regular summer tour. It's a spooky old place. But they haven't been a part of our tour for many years now."

"Why is that?" I asked directly.

"Perhaps it was all those deaths, coming so close together as they did. Even all that long ago. Anyway, they don't entertain much anymore."

It wasn't wise to ask too many questions of one person, so I knotted the scarf about my throat—hiding the golden pendant—thanked her, and went outside again.

A restaurant displayed an attractive interior through long windows, and I entered. Bay scallops were in season on Long Island so I ordered some. The young waitress was friendly. "The Shingles? Oh, wow! Hardly anybody gets inside that house. I have a girlfriend who works there as a maid sometimes. She says there's a woman they shut up in the attic who paints pictures all the time—though my friend has never seen her."

This was fantasy. It was interesting, though, that mentioning The Shingles could bring so curious a response. When I'd finished my meal I left and turned down a cross street, and found a well-stocked bookstore where I could buy a map and ask directions. The woman in charge had seen me on television the night before and was friendly and helpful—and much less lugubrious than the others. Apparently members of the Rhodes family often dropped in, and she spoke of having borrowed paintings of Judith Rhodes's occasionally to hang in the store. "Herndon Rhodes comes in for books frequently. You'll like him."

"How many are there in the family?" I asked casually.

"There's Stacia, to begin with. She's the daughter of Herndon and Judith, and she lives at the house with her husband, Evan Faulkner. There's John, Herndon's older brother. He does a lot of traveling, though he's at home right now. He was in here yesterday." There was approval in her slight smile, as though John Rhodes was someone she liked.

"Is there a Nan Kemble too?" I asked. "Herndon Rhodes mentioned her in his letter. I'm to stop at her gatehouse shop when I arrive."

"Yes, of course. You'll like Nan—but she's not really a Rhodes. Her sister Alice was married to John, but Alice has been dead a long time."

I shook my head in bewilderment and spread my map on the counter. "You've given me more names than I can handle, I'm afraid. Will you show me how to find The Shingles?"

"That's Ethan Lane, right there," she said, pointing a pencil at the map. "Ethan Rhodes built the house back in the mid-1800s. The lane is a dead end and it runs right into Rhodes property. There are several ways to find it." She marked a few arrows on the map and I thanked her and went back to my car.

The road I took lost me in a maze of wide lanes, green-gold in sunlight. It was going to be a late fall, and only a few trees had begun to turn. Now and then I glimpsed enormous lawns leading to white mansions, most of them built in a much earlier day. Yet in the midst of all this luxury there would appear an unexpected potato field. Potatoes and summer people—these were the main businesses of this South Fork of Long Island.

I paid no attention to directions now, content to wander and catch the flavor of the place. The lanes enchanted me—Maidstone, Asparagus, Lily Pond Lane. The latter would take me in the right direction, and I followed it idly. There were no other cars, no one on foot, no sidewalks. Some of the summer houses were already shuttered up for the season.

The sign came up without warning: ETHAN LANE. I drove along it slowly, green hedges shutting me in as the lane curved and narrowed. Ahead rose two crumbling stone gateposts. There was no sign, but I knew this was the place. Beyond the gate I could see the dark shingles of the old gatehouse. I drove through and parked my car in a small clearing beyond.

Oaks and maples that must once have given the area a parklike aspect now shut out the sun, and the air felt dank and chill. I could smell the sea, though it was not in sight. The gravel drive disappeared among the trees, and there was no main house in view. The gatehouse had a slanting roof that overhung the front door, where a sign said simply THE DITTY BOX. I wondered how customers ever found their way to so remote a spot.

I opened the door to step inside, then paused in the doorway. Two women near a flight of stairs at the rear of the shop arrested my attention. One was a blond girl of about my own age, while the other woman, who stood facing her in some moment of crisis, was probably in her mid-forties. The girl had been crying, and one cheek was puffy and bruised. But her eyes sparked fury. "He struck me, Nan! Evan's an absolute brute and you've got to talk to him. He won't listen to anyone else."

As I pushed the door fully open, a bell jangled over my head, and both women turned surprised looks in my direction. The girl put a hand to her swollen cheek and ran upstairs out of sight, leaving the other woman to come toward me through the shop.

Casual brown slacks and yellow sweater suited her small, lean frame. Thick, iron-gray hair was worn in a straight and uncompromising bob, with long bangs down her forehead. Beneath them gray eyes appraised me as she crossed the shop. Her eyes were large and candid, truly beautiful.

I smiled at her. "Miss Kemble? I'm Courtney Marsh. Mr. Rhodes wrote that I was to stop in and let you know when I arrived."

She walked briskly toward me, holding out her hand. Her clasp was strong and firm. "Of course," she said. "I recognize you from the television show last night. Did you have any trouble finding us?"

"No trouble at all. I stopped in the village for lunch and a map, and then I drove around for a while."

We were indulging in a polite circling of words, but I had the feeling that her real attention was not upon me, but upon that tearful girl upstairs. I looked about the shop. On a nearby shelf there was a graceful model of a clipper ship. Near it stood a ship's wheel. Scrimshaw was displayed in a glass case, and occupying a corner was a battered ship's figurehead of Davy Crockett, his hair long under his coonskin cap. "The Ditty Box!" I said. "Now I understand."

She smiled at me, her intelligent features warming. "Yes—ditty boxes were what sailors kept their small possessions in on a voyage. I specialize in nautical antiques."

"What a marvelous idea!" I said.

"Now, I'd better phone the house and have someone come to take you up," she told me. "I'll phone Herndon too, as he wants to come home from the bank. We all watched you on that program last night." She moved toward the telephone on her desk.

"What did you think of the interview?" I asked.

"Squirmy," she said, without hesitation. "I can't stand Hal Winser. I wouldn't have been watching if Herndon hadn't insisted, and if I hadn't read your articles. I'm glad you didn't let him put you down."

I was pleased that she hadn't indulged in empty flattery. " 'Squirmy' is the right word. I couldn't watch it."

She smiled again and picked up the phone, letting Herndon Rhodes know that I had arrived. Then she phoned the house.

"Evan Faulkner—Stacia's husband—will come for you," she told me when she got off. "You saw her just now at the back of the shop. She was a bit upset. Why don't you sit over here and have a cup of coffee?"

I accepted mine black, as she took her own, and I sat and looked around the shop again. Apparently this big pine-paneled room had once been the gatehouse living room.

"I think you'd better be somewhat prepared," Nan Kemble said. "I can't go into details, because it's a family matter, but something unpleasant has happened up at the house. It's caused a lot of surface tension. I don't know what's behind it, but it needn't affect your story about Judith."

"Thank you for warning me," I said. "Is there anything you want to tell me about Judith Rhodes that will help me talk with her?"

She nodded toward an opposite wall. "Have you seen her paintings? That's one over there."

I walked to the wall to study the picture more closely. It was a beach scene, with drifting mists. A strange globe—something that was neither moon nor sun—sailed a sky of pale Persian blue. I looked closer and saw that it was a small, floating face. Not a child's face—more the face of a doll, with staring, glassy eyes. For some reason it chilled me.

"Why the floating face?" I asked, coming back to my chair.

Nan Kemble shrugged. "You don't ask Judith why. I'm not sure she knows. She paints what she sees, and imagines. I suppose genius has its own reasons."

"You regard her as a genius?"

"That's a large word. But yes—I think I do."

"That's why I'm here—because an expert in New York used that word. But I'm also interested in the woman behind the painter."

"I know. That's what you do best. But I'll warn you—Judith won't be easy. She goes her own way. She doesn't trouble about the world very much. Perhaps she lives in that fantasy country of sand and ocean and sky that she likes to paint." Nan picked up her cup and stirred the sugarless coffee vigorously. I sensed caution settling in. "You might as well know that I sided with Judith against your coming here. I argued with Herndon about it. I think you may stir up old pain that needs to be forgotten."

"I'll be careful. I assure you I don't want to hurt anyone."

"That's not good enough. You won't know quicksand when you see it. The wisest, kindest thing you can do is go straight back to New York."

"I'm sorry," I said. "I can't do that."

She sipped her coffee, apparently resigned to the fact that I was not to be discouraged. "Have you seen other work of Judith's around New York?" she asked more conversationally.

"Unfortunately, no. All I've seen is a reproduction in a newspaper of another beach scene with the shadow of a unicorn on the moon."

Nan nodded. "That's one of her best. You'll see it hanging in the living room at The Shingles."

"But why a unicorn?"

"She often uses it. There's some sort of Rhodes legend. Get one of them to tell you about it. . . . I wonder what can be keeping Evan? He should be here by now."

"If I'm holding you from your work—" I began, but she had turned her head and was looking toward the rear of the shop. I turned too and saw Stacia Faulkner coming down the stairs.

She had washed away her tears and recovered herself, so that she held her head high, daring anyone to notice the purpling skin below her left eye. Her blond hair was as fair as my own, though she wore it shorter, and her eyes were as deeply blue. She looked slim and attractive in lime-green slacks and a hemp-colored shirt. We were of nearly the same build, average in height and fairly small-boned, but her lips seemed thinner, and perhaps a little petulant. I was seeking a resemblance between myself and this girl who was nearly my own age. What might she be—a cousin, a sister?

Nan introduced us. Stacia gave me a cool, firm clasp and released my hand immediately. "Your timing couldn't be worse," she told me frankly. "My mother's in a terribly upset state—"

Nan broke in. "Miss Marsh knows there's been an upheaval."

Stacia waved an airy hand, on which I caught a shine of sapphire. "And a good thing, don't you think? Isn't it high time someone kicked up a fuss? Three people died, and no one ever looked into it."

"That's ancient history, and there was nothing to look into," Nan said calmly. "Two were accidents and one was a natural death. But I don't think your father will want Miss Marsh troubled with all this past unhappiness."

"Sorry! I forgot what a loyal member of the clan you are, even if only through your sister's marriage. We can't have all the family skeletons paraded for publication, though it might be interesting, at that."

I was beginning to dislike Stacia Faulkner and take sides with Nan, even though family skeletons were exactly what I wanted to know more about.

Turning to me, Stacia said, "Can I take you up to the house?"

"Evan will be here any minute," Nan told her. "I've already phoned."

"If Evan's coming, I'll get out of the way—fast!"

She caught up a jacket from a chair, waved a hand at both of us, and started for the door with a lithe, swift movement that reminded me of some jungle cat. But she was already too late. The door opened just before she reached it, and Evan Faulkner walked into the room.

I found myself staring at this man whom I was prepared to dislike, since he was the author of the bruise on Stacia's cheek. He was probably around thirty-five—a tall, strongly built man, though rather on the lean side, with tanned skin and dark hair, and eyes the color of gray ice as he looked at his wife. With a hand clapped to her cheek, Stacia ducked past him and out the door without a word.

"What's the matter with her?" he asked directly of Nan.

"That isn't hard to figure, is it? You needn't play that rough." She turned apologetically to me. "The skeletons seem to be falling out of all our closets today, Courtney. I'm sorry, Evan. It's none of my business."

A dark flush had swept up lean cheeks to stain his forehead, but it was caused by anger, not embarrassment, and I saw that those cold eyes could spark hotly. He was a man I would not want to make angry. But he kept whatever he was feeling well under control and came across the shop to me, holding out his hand. "Miss Marsh?" he said formally. "I'm Evan Faulkner. Would you like to go up to the house now?"

I stood up, feeling thoroughly uncomfortable over my plunge into the middle of a family quarrel. "Thank you," I said stiffly. "My car is outside."

"We'll go up in mine," he told me. "Asher can come for your car and bags later."

Nan put out her hand to me. "Come and see me again. I owe you some quieter hospitality."

"I'd like to," I said. "I want to see your shop when there's more time."

Evan Faulkner held the door and I went out to his battered gray station wagon and got in. We started along the gravel driveway, winding between thick undergrowth on either side. My sense of being thoroughly uncomfortable continued. As we came around a curve, he broke the silence for the first time, braking the car and startling me. "This is the best spot to catch your first glimpse of The Shingles," he said.

The house that lifted three stories into the air atop its high dune was anything but beautiful. Impressive, yes, with a great and brooding dignity as it raised shingled walls and tall brick chimneys against the blue sky. But its color was an oppressive dark umber, shading into ebony in the shadows. It had stood there since the last century, braving the storms that had burst over it, riding like a ship into the very teeth of the gales and high seas that must have hurled themselves upon it. The Shingles seemed a modest name for so overpowering a structure. There was a faint prickling at the back of my neck. Had I been born in that house? Had I belonged to it in those early months before I was adopted?

I became aware that Evan Faulkner was studying me. I turned my head to meet his look and felt an odd sense of disquiet go through me. He was weighing and measuring me, and I sensed dismissal as clearly as though he had spoken. I thought I knew why. "I suppose you saw that dreadful television program last night?"

"Dreadful? I thought you were in control every minute," he said coolly.

When I spoke, I knew my resentment was showing. "You sound as though you don't approve of women being in control."

He didn't rise to the foolish bait, but started the car up the slope that led to the house. I saw now why everyone spoke of going "up" to The Shingles. We were climbing the line of dunes that ridged the southern shore along the ocean. In the vicinity of the house some order had been brought to the wild tangle of beach vegetation, and the gravel drive rose to end at a brick parking area before a long garage.

As we came to a stop Evan Faulkner said, "We go that way." A brick walk mounted toward steps that rose steeply, ending in a sheltered alcove. Into this was set a massive front door. We got out of the car, and had just reached the door's double panels when one side opened. An old man stood peering out at us. "This is William Asher, who has looked after the Rhodeses for many years," Evan Faulkner said. "Asher, will you take Miss Marsh to her room and then see that her bags and car are brought up from the gatehouse?" The old man bowed and mumbled a greeting.

I gave Evan Faulkner my best smile and said, "Thank you." He nodded and went off down a long hallway. He wasn't going to bother about me further, now that he could pass the burden along.

The thin, bony figure of William Asher mounted the stairs ahead of me. When we reached the second floor I could discern the layout of the house. A long, rather narrow hall ran its width, with all the bedrooms facing the ocean, and a series of closets and storage rooms on the land side. Asher paused before a door and opened it for me. "In here, Miss Marsh. I'll fetch your bags. My wife takes charge of this part of the house. Please ring the bell by the door to call her if there's anything you want."

I thanked him and he went off, leaving me to step into a room that shimmered with sea light. Two white-curtained windows, both open, looked out upon a tremendous view, and I walked over to them. Below me, I saw that wooden steps descended over the barrier dune in a steep pitch from house to beach. White sand stretched in either direction as far as I could see, and the lacy surf of Judith's painting scalloped its edge, flowing up and then receding. There was little wind and the sea made a flat, endless plain clear to the horizon. Far out on the water the white wings of a sailboat hung limp, and I heard the distant throb of a motor.

I breathed deeply of salt air, feeling an unexpected joy—as though I had come to a place where I belonged. I smiled at my own imaginings. I already

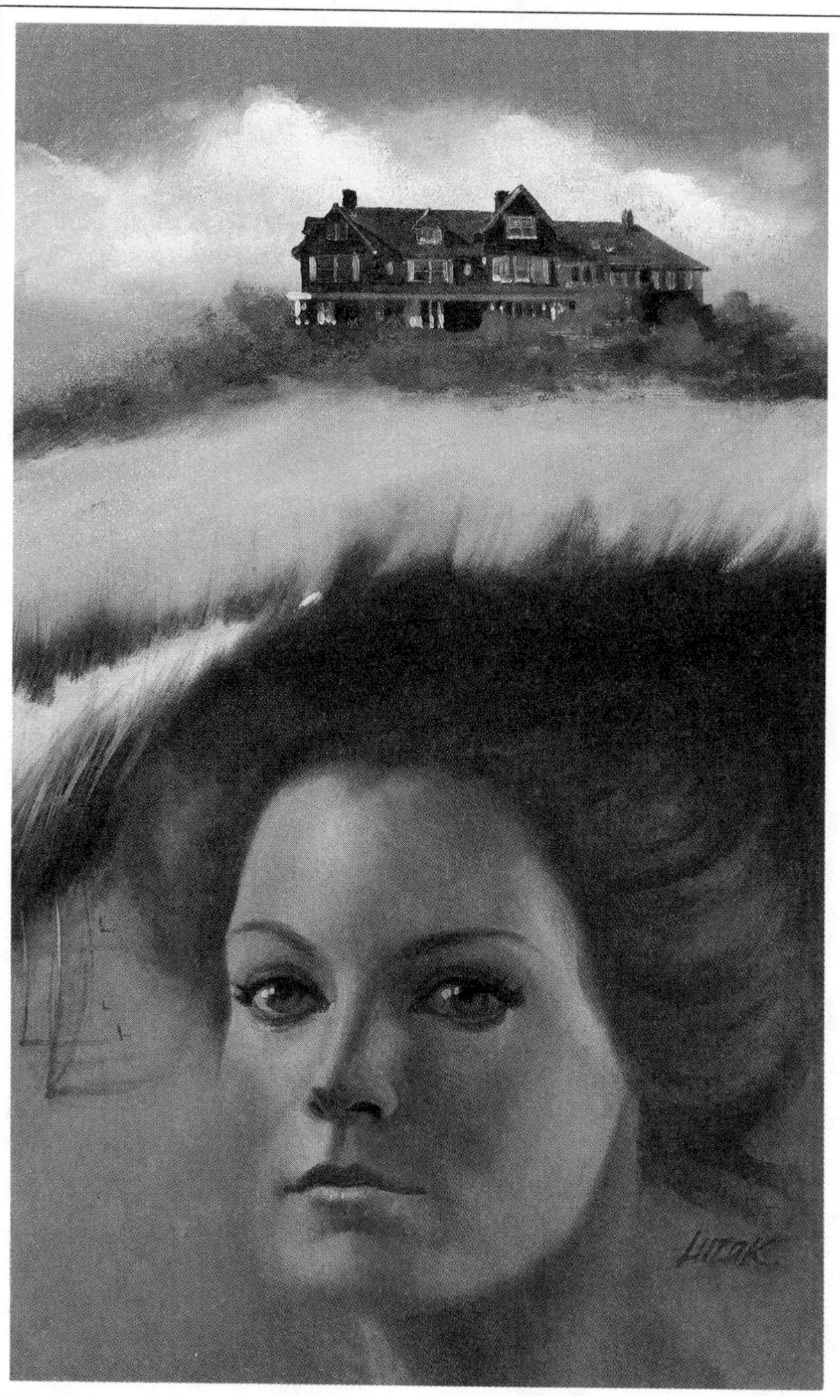

knew there was something far from reassuring about the dark, massive house. But at least I could escape it when I pleased and walk the beach—as someone else was doing now.

The man on the sand was not young, in his fifties perhaps, as I judged by his silver-gray hair. But, dressed in white shorts and a gray pullover sweater, he was jogging along the water's edge with the vigor of a man much younger. As he came even with the house, he ran lightly up the wooden steps. Halting beneath my window, he stood looking up at me. "Hello, Courtney Marsh," he said. "I'm John Rhodes. I've been looking forward to your arrival."

As I smiled and returned his greeting, I remembered what the woman in the bookstore had told me. John was Herndon's older brother, and he had been the husband of Nan Kemble's sister, Alice—the one who had died.

"I was envying you your run on the sand," I said. "There have never been enough beaches in my life."

"At this time of the year it's all yours to enjoy." He gave a generous wave of his hand and disappeared inside the house. I liked him, I decided.

A knock on the door signaled Asher with my bags and a message. "Mr. Herndon has phoned," he said, as he set down my cases and coat. "He would like to see you downstairs in half an hour, if that is convenient."

"I'll be there," I assured him, and when he'd gone I unpacked a few things and hung them in the good-sized closet. Now I had time to admire my room, which was simply furnished and quite charming. A walnut lowboy with brass pulls served as a dressing table, with a gilt-framed mirror above it. In a corner stood a gold-upholstered wing chair, and there was a great braided oval rug of mottled green and yellow. The spool bed wore a handsome quilt in a warm yellow fan design. Charming though the room might be, however, I had no desire to sit down and wait out my half hour. John Rhodes had invited me to enjoy the beach—so why not?

In the corridor, as I neared the stairs, a woman came up from the floor below. "I'm Mrs. Asher," she said. "If there is anything you want, Miss Marsh—" She was younger than her husband and might have been faintly pretty if she had released her hair, now pulled back in a brown knob.

"There's nothing, thank you, I'm very comfortable," I said, and went on down the stairs. They ended in a short hallway separating living room from dining room. Another, longer hall opened off it, running the width of the house at the back and paralleling the upstairs corridor. I could see an outside door at the far end, and I started toward it.

On the way, I glanced through an open door upon a dark-paneled library with old books lining the shelves, and a long table in the middle, heaped with boxes and papers, as though some sort of work was in progress. A library collection could be a good source of family information, I thought, and noted the room as a place to visit another time. I walked to the far door and went down steps to a grassy terrace that disappeared around the ocean side of the house. I walked along the terrace to a flagged section above the water, where beach furniture had been invitingly set, sheltered by a green-striped awning. As I moved into the open, I found that the wind was rising, bringing with it the soft roar of the surf just below.

I turned to look up at the broad façade that towered above me with its dark, weathered brown shingles. At a high window a curtain moved, and I knew that someone looked down at me—not openly as I had looked down at John Rhodes, but wanting to watch without being seen. A hand touched the curtain. I caught the flash of a sapphire ring and remembered that I had seen such a ring on Stacia's finger. No matter. What did I care if she chose to peer at me from behind a curtain?

They were all rather strange in this family—even Nan Kemble and Evan Faulkner, who were not blood-related. I found myself wondering about Evan. What was his work? And what strains had he been under that drove him into striking his wife so brutally?

Behind me something snuffled ominously. I whirled about, startled—and froze. The largest Great Dane I had ever seen watched me from a few feet away, his cropped, pointed ears held high and alert. He was black-masked, and his coat was a mottled white and blue-black, his skull and chest massive, his neck muscular. The dark eyes stared at me suspiciously and there was no wagging of his thin tail, which had the curve of a saber.

"Hello, boy," I said cautiously, not moving a finger.

His answer was a deep growl, then a sudden bark that shook me with fright. The dog was moving closer, tensing his body as if to spring. "Help me, someone! Please call the dog!"

A door off the terrace was flung open and a woman came running across the flagstones. "Tudor!" she called. "Stay, boy. It's all right—stay!" The dog halted his relentless approach and the long tail began to wag at the appearance of his mistress.

It was in this way, with a total lack of formality and without introduction, at a time when I could hardly have been more distraught, or she more in control of the situation—it was in this way that I met Judith Rhodes.

CHAPTER THREE

I STOOD WELL BACK from the Great Dane as she knelt beside him. I was trembling to my fingertips, not only because of the dog but also because this was the woman I had come to confront and I had no idea what place she might have in my life. I waited for her to speak.

She wore a cotton peasant dress, flowing to the ground in bright patchwork squares, belted at the waist and with a square neck. Her hair was black and straight and very long. It fell about her, covering her back where she knelt crooning over the dog, slipping down in silky strands that touched the terrace stones. I couldn't see her face until, having quieted the dog, she looked up at me and I met the brilliant green of her eyes.

She must have been as old as Nan Kemble, since she had a daughter nearly my age, yet there was an agelessness about her and a serenity that took me by surprise. If there had been some eccentricity evident, the shyness of a recluse, even a touch of derangement, I would not have been surprised. But when she rose to her sandaled feet, one hand resting on the dog's brass-studded collar, there was only a lovely calm worn as gracefully as she wore her patchwork gown.

"I'm sorry," she said. "I didn't know you were out here, or I'd never have let Tudor come onto the terrace."

I realized that introductions weren't necessary, and she went on, her voice low and resonant. "You needn't be afraid of him. A few years ago my brother-in-law John brought him home from Germany for Stacia, but somehow he attached himself to me."

She studied me thoughtfully. "You aren't in the least like the girl I saw on television last night," she stated. "I think you'll be all right—so tomorrow morning we'll begin." And that was all. With her hand still resting on the dog's collar, guiding him, she moved along the terrace.

I had no need to seek for resemblance here. There was no fairness of coloring about Judith Rhodes, and her bones were far more prominent than mine or Stacia's. Which meant nothing, of course. I had spoken not a single word, and she was already out of sight around the far end of the house, leaving me gaping after her. No wonder she had said I wasn't like the Courtney Marsh she had seen on television—I was a shaking lump of flesh, without poise, without a voice.

Asher came out of the house. "Mr. Herndon is waiting for you in the living room," he announced. "If you will come in, please."

"Of course," I said, recovering myself.

Though I had played at times with the thought of Judith Rhodes being my mother, I'd had no fantasies about her husband. With a baby that had been given away, anyone could be the father. He was standing near a fire in a big brick fireplace in the living room. He came toward me, hand outstretched. "I'm glad you've come, Miss Marsh," he said.

His hair was completely gray, and the face beneath seemed worn and faintly sad. He was a big man, though not as tall as Evan Faulkner, and he looked older than the older brother I'd seen jogging on the beach.

"I'm happy that you were willing to let me come," I said. "I've just met your wife on the terrace—and I think I've been accepted."

"That was quick," he said. "I really haven't been sure what would happen when you arrived. She's doing this to please me, you know. Last night she decided she wasn't going to like you."

I smiled at him. "I don't blame her. I saw some of the program myself, and I didn't like that girl either. Perhaps I redeemed myself with Mrs. Rhodes just now by practically being eaten by her dog. I was so scared I couldn't even open my mouth, and that may have reassured her."

He smiled. "I'm sorry about Tudor, but delighted if you got past Judith's guard." As he seated me near the fire I had an opportunity to study him. For a seemingly quiet, self-controlled man, a banker, there were surprising touches to his dress. A vest of red plaid, and a tie only a shade less bright, gave him a flamboyance that hardly matched his subdued manner.

But the place interested me even more than the man, and I looked about the big, high-ceilinged room. It was windowed along the water side, letting in a rippling light from the ocean as well as brightness from the sky. The original dark woodwork had been covered with creamy-pale paint, and unlike the exterior of the house, which seemed gloomy with age, this room shone with a bright aura of wealth and elegance. It was not a room through which one would run with wet bathing suits and sandy feet, and it was large enough to dwarf the grand piano that stood beside rear windows. Two great Chinese rugs covered the floor, and on the mantel handsome Chinese porcelains gleamed in blue and white.

But the most arresting feature of the room was the large oil painting I had seen before in the newspaper. The golden moon with its unicorn shadow shed an unearthly light over the beach. In the foreground an ancient figurehead—perhaps from a clipper ship—sat atilt in the sand, turning the sad, weathered face of a woman toward the sea.

The picture drew me, and I left my chair to stand before it. Its mood was sadly haunting, as had been that of the other beach scene hanging in Nan's shop. Judith's work had a dreaming emptiness that the imagination could easily people with wraiths. "Judith Rhodes must be one of the finer painters in this country," I said. "That scene is real, and yet it's surreal at the same time. It has a mood I won't easily shake off."

"Perhaps that's the mood of this house," Herndon said, coming to stand behind me. "The Rhodeses are a haunted lot, I'm afraid. Maybe it has complemented something rare in Judith's talent. I'd like her to be recognized to a far greater extent than she is, especially since . . ." He paused, then went on. "Especially since we may not have The Shingles too much longer—and then I don't know what will happen to Judith's painting."

His words startled me. "But the house has always belonged to your family, hasn't it?"

"Even so." He shrugged unhappily, and I knew that whatever might be bringing about a change, he would not tell me now.

"I'd like to know a little more about the family," I said.

"We can start with my great-grandfather, Ethan Rhodes, who built this house. He was a whaler—he had a fleet of ships, one of which he captained. He lived originally in Sag Harbor, which was a great whaling center in the old days. When he retired he built this house on the dunes, before any of the summer places went up. Ethan's sons scattered round the country. The eldest, Brian, stayed in this house. He was a sailor too. His son Lawrence was my father, but he turned to the law for his career."

"Are Lawrence and his wife dead—your father and mother?"

"Yes. My mother died about thirty years ago, my father five years later."

"You and John are their only sons?"

"That's right. I married Judith, of course, and John married Alice Kemble. She died shortly before our father did."

I remembered the woman I'd talked to in the dress shop. "All those deaths, coming so close together," she had said. And Stacia had mentioned three deaths. Who else had died? The deaths had all occurred close to the time of my birth. "Have there been other children in the family besides Stacia?" I asked tentatively.

"No—none."

Had he replied too quickly? So far everyone I'd met seemed quick to turn away from certain questions. I threw out another tentative hook. "Miss Kemble mentioned that I have come at a bad time—that something disturbing has happened to upset all of you. I'm sorry if I'm a burden."

"Let's sit down," he said. "There. . . . The afternoon is getting on—would you like something to drink?"

"No, thank you," I said, and waited.

He went on, choosing his words carefully. "Nan Kemble shouldn't have worried you with this. What happened was nothing more than a malicious trick played by some irresponsible person."

"I understand," I said. I gave my attention again to the painting. "Can you tell me about the unicorn on the moon?"

He seemed glad to turn to history. "Ethan's wife, my great-grandmother Hesther, had a superstition about unicorns. She had been given a little gold one by a visiting potentate. Unicorns are supposed to bring good luck, but Hesther devised her own legend when she claimed to have seen a cloud shadow like a unicorn drift across the moon. That was the night Ethan's father died. Afterward she always said that a unicorn on the moon could mean either disaster or good fortune for a Rhodes. Hesther's gold unicorn became a sort of talisman against any possible threat."

"What happened to it?" I asked, and held my breath.

"Unfortunately, I don't know. Trinkets have a way of disappearing over the years. I asked Judith to look for it once, because I thought it should be given to Stacia, but she couldn't find it." He suddenly looked weary, as though he carried some inner burden.

"Perhaps I'll go upstairs and change for dinner," I said, wanting to let him escape the strain of talking to me.

He stood up as I rose. His mouth wore a grim look that was disturbing to see in the face of a man who seemed kindly and considerate.

In my room I stood once more at the window, gazing out toward those ceaseless waves rolling in on the beach. There was a surging of uncertainty in me, like those waves. My own tides were swollen with unanswered questions, and with temptations to believe when there was no proof. Yet there *was* the unicorn. Now I knew it belonged here. Did that make me a Rhodes? There was so little to go on, especially since there seemed to be no missing child on the family tree.

In the bathroom I ran a hot tub and sprinkled in the fragrant mauve salts I found in a cabinet. When I felt rested and refreshed and some of those throbbing questions had been quieted, I dressed for dinner. I had no idea what was customary in this house, but my St. Laurent print chemise should be suitable, with its red roses scattered to the long hemline and a decorous ribbon tie at the throat. But I could not wear my unicorn, since it would show above the neck of the dress and this was not yet the time to reveal it. I folded chain and pendant into a tissue and tucked them into the drawer of the lowboy dressing table where I had put my cosmetics.

I braced myself before I went downstairs, as though some sort of battle lay ahead of me. In this coming dinner encounter, I must watch and listen, and try to find the right questions to ask without in any way betraying the true reason for my asking.

When I reached the living room, I found the three men talking before the fire, glasses in hand. Herndon looked grimmer than ever, Evan angry, and even John had lost his cheerful air. They all turned and looked at me. I knew that I was anything but welcome at that moment. It was John who smiled and came toward me. He was a tall man, with a handsome, rather saturnine look and flyaway eyebrows that could be cocked mockingly. There was an ease about him that the other two lacked. "We'll be glad for your company at the table tonight, Courtney Marsh," he said. "Stacia and Judith are having their meals upstairs. Judith often does so, and Stacia isn't feeling well. So we need you badly."

His light touch was exactly right. I accepted the glass of wine he brought me, accepted his compliment about my dress, and recognized that he was not ignorant on the subject of fashion. John Rhodes was more cosmopolitan than anyone else in this house.

In the dining room John seated me at the table's foot, opposite Herndon. Candles had been lighted in crystal holders down the length of the table, and old linen damask shone in a patina of pale light. Asher served us. I gathered that he and his wife lived in the house, while the cook and housemaids went home at night.

Unlike the living room, the dining room still had the original dark woodwork, rich with the dignity of another century. Again the ceiling was enormously high, and the windows on the ocean side correspondingly tall, with burgundy draperies pulled across against the night. Above the low mahogany paneling, raspberry wallpaper rose to a plate rail, where Spode, Sevres, and Meissen plates were on display. The sideboard too was mahogany, and huge, with a well-polished Georgian silver service set upon its top. In a corner stood an impressive glass cabinet filled with china and crystal.

John was the only one who made much of an effort at conversation. We found that we had mutual friends in New York, and it was easy to slip into small talk with him. Herndon appeared lost in a world of his own. Once he roused himself and nodded toward the portrait of a woman that hung over the sideboard. "You were asking about members of the Rhodes family, Miss Marsh. That is a portrait of Alice Rhodes."

"It was painted just after we were married," John said. "I never thought it a very good likeness."

I glanced up at the portrait, and the brown eyes of the girl who had posed for it seemed to meet mine quizzically. She wore a pale blue dress, with a touch of pink at the throat, and there was a pink rose in her brown hair. One cheek dimpled in a smile, and the portrait seemed to suggest that she might burst into laughter at any moment.

"I can remember her like that when she was very young," Herndon said. "But it's true that she was never a 'sweet Alice.' She was much more of a person than that."

"She was still young when she died," John said bleakly.

I wanted to ask how she had died, but this wasn't the time. Apparently John Rhodes had never married again.

Strangely enough, however, it was not Herndon and John who held my most interested attention, but Evan Faulkner, who was not a Rhodes at all. I discovered that he was a marine biologist and I tried to draw him out about his work at the Ocean Science Laboratory in Montauk. But his resentment of me, somehow begun when he had seen me on television, seemed to have deepened. His answers were in monosyllables. I had given up trying to talk to him and was lost in my own thoughts when I realized that he had asked me a question and I hadn't been listening. I was forced to apologize. "I'm sorry. I didn't hear what you asked."

His dark eyes regarded me steadily. "I was wondering whether you would put anything about the Rhodes family history into your article."

"It depends on how things fit in," I said. "I don't like to discard anything until I'm sure it doesn't belong."

"The Rhodeses have an interesting history," Evan said. "I'm trying to preserve it by cataloging the family's books and papers and captains' logs. If you've any interest, Miss Marsh, stop in the library sometime and I'll show you some of the materials on whaling."

Evan Faulkner had made a civilized offer and I thanked him for it. But if I went to the library to learn more about the Rhodeses and the past, it would be for reasons he could not suspect.

We had nearly finished the meal when Asher came into the room, clearly agitated. He carried a salver on which lay a plain envelope and placed it before Herndon. "It's another one, sir," Asher said. "I just found it."

Herndon ripped open the envelope and unfolded the single sheet of cheap, lined paper. He looked up at Asher. "Where was it?"

"Someone pushed it under the front door, sir," Asher said. "I was going through the hall and I saw it. I don't know how long it was there. No one was about when I looked outside."

"If there are any more, bring them to me at once," Herndon told him.

"Of course, sir." Asher bowed his gray head and went off.

"Well, what's in it?" John demanded. "What does it say this time?"

Herndon tapped the sheet before him. "There's just one word. Letters cut out of a newspaper again and pasted on ruled paper. They spell Anabel with a question mark added. That's all."

Evan said, "That could refer to the boat, of course."

"Not coming on the heels of the last note. I don't think so."

Herndon glanced in my direction. "I'm sorry, Miss Marsh. You might as well know that someone is sending anonymous notes which arrive at our door without anyone seeing who brings them. Probably it's no more than malicious mischief."

"Mischief from someone who knows a remarkable lot about the family," Evan said. "You should show them to the police."

"No!" Coming from the quiet banker, the word was unexpectedly explosive. "I won't have Judith troubled. She had to know about the first one because she was present when it came, but I would prefer it if you don't mention that there's been another one. Not any of you."

Evan was watching me, and when I caught his look it seemed a challenge. "You understand, Miss Marsh, that this affair is off the record as far as you are concerned." He spoke coldly.

"Of course," I agreed.

John's smile was reassuring. "I don't think we need worry about Courtney. And let's dispense with this 'Miss Marsh' formality. She is going to be part of the family for the time being and undoubtedly treated to our innermost secrets. So let's relax with her a little. I know her writing and she doesn't do hatchet jobs."

"Thank you, John," I said.

"In any case," he went on, "we all know that Judith did everything she could at the time in question. What happened wasn't her fault."

Evan took the note from Herndon and examined it carefully. "Is there anything—well—in doubt about that time when she died?" he asked. "Anything someone who disliked the Rhodes family could make something of? The first note referred to Alice."

"There has always been gossip," Herndon said. "But it had no base. What happened was a double tragedy, but simple enough in each case."

"Then you've nothing to worry about," Evan assured him.

Herndon pushed back his chair, closing the subject without further comment, and we left the table.

I excused myself on the score of being tired. I had had enough of uncomfortable undercurrents for one day, and I wanted to spend the rest of the evening alone. I ran up the stairs quickly and hurried down the hall to my room. I pushed my door open, and there, stretched upon the patchwork quilt on the bed, was Stacia Faulkner, her arms behind her head and her bruised cheek clearly in view.

"Hello," she said. "I hope you don't mind my waiting for you here."

I was not pleased to find myself with a visitor—particularly not Stacia. On the other hand she might tell me more about this curious household, in which some sort of as-yet-hidden crisis seemed to be approaching. "I don't mind," I said, and dropped into the wing chair.

Stacia raised herself on an elbow, regarding me with large, luminous blue eyes. "That's a beautiful dress." Her tone was almost wistful, and I wondered why. Beautiful gowns would hardly be a rarity to this girl. "But it's lost in a place like this," she went on. "Wasted."

"You didn't seek me out to talk about dresses," I said.

"No—you're right. What do you think of us so far?"

"I don't know enough about you to think much of anything."

"I'll bet that's not true!" she challenged. "I think you're already liking and disliking, taking sides. And perhaps wrongly."

"I'm open to suggestions." Stacia was nearly my age, yet sometimes she seemed younger, more vulnerable than I would have expected.

"I can tell you one thing," she said. "Uncle John is the only real human being in this house."

"Are you discounting your father and mother?"

"Judith doesn't care about anything but her painting, and my father doesn't care about anything except her."

Behind her words lay resentment and pain—perhaps the pain of a child who had been neglected. Unexpected pity for her stirred in me. "I like your uncle too," I said. "By the way, I don't really know what he does."

"He's mainly a parasite—like me. I suppose he has a touch of genius, but he doesn't work at it hard enough. I was born too late to know, but I understand that Grandfather Lawrence was enormously proud of the boat Uncle John designed—the *Anabel*. It's still in the marina over in Sag Harbor, and I've gone sailing in it a few times. Grandfather was ready to build a small shipyard, to try to revive shipbuilding here on Long Island—and let Uncle John design and build boats."

"Who was Anabel?" I asked.

Stacia sat up on the bed and crossed her long legs in their green slacks. "It's a Kemble family name. I gather that the boat was already built and Aunt Alice had named it before little Anabel was born. The poor thing wasn't around long. Have you heard about the baby who died?"

I sat very still, all too aware of the sudden thumping of my heart. "No, I haven't. Whose baby was it?"

Restlessly, she left her perch on the bed and went to a window to part draperies that had been drawn against sky and ocean. She said over her shoulder, "I'm talking out of turn. I keep forgetting you're a reporter. Ask Judith to tell you—she knows everything about this family, and she was the one who found Aunt Alice when she died. If you're going to do an honest piece about my mother, you'd better learn the right questions to ask. Everything's going to be pulled down before long anyway, so a little more upheaval won't matter. We'll be leaving this house soon, and that will destroy Judith. I don't think she can work anywhere else."

"Why must she leave the house?"

"Because it will be sold. Whether they like it or not, it will be sold!"

"Who will sell it? I shouldn't think your—"

"That's another question you can ask her." Stacia left her place at the window and threw herself on the bed again. "If it wasn't for Nan and John, I might have run away years ago. Nan's never tried to order me around, and she never scolds me."

"I liked Nan Kemble when I met her this afternoon," I said. But it wasn't Nan I wanted to talk about. "I don't suppose you remember your grandfather—Lawrence Rhodes?"

"No. He died before I was born. Yet sometimes I think he's closer to me than those of my family who are living. Maybe I'm like him. I'd have made a good pirate."

"I thought Lawrence's field was the law."

"It was. Dry stuff—trusts and wills and estates. Not much room for pirating there. But he was a pirate, just the same. Captain Yellowbeard, whose word was law. He ruled them all, and he would cut down anyone who disobeyed him. The good name of the family mattered more than anything else. When a Rhodes didn't measure up, he was banished—or destroyed."

"When did Lawrence die? What happened?"

"He died only two or three months after Alice and the baby. A heart attack. Judith was with him. Isn't that a strange thing about my mother? She was always there when someone died—Alice, the baby, Lawrence. Oh, not that she had anything to do with causing anyone to die. The Rhodes name wouldn't stand for that. Close the ranks, shut out the press, save the family! Now Judith paints melancholy pictures of sea and sand, and floats severed heads across her scenes."

"I don't think I like what you're telling me," I said quietly. "Even if you dislike your mother, you mustn't try to prejudice me."

Abruptly, disconcertingly, Stacia dissolved into tears. She turned on her stomach and wept long, heaving sobs like a child. "I don't dislike her!" she wailed. "I love her. I've always wished I could be beautiful and talented and have people love me so much they would give up their lives for me."

The outburst seemed utterly childish and forlorn, yet I wondered if there was a woman's calculation behind it. What did she want of me—and why? I went into the bathroom and brought back a dampened washcloth. "Let me wipe your face. You mustn't cry like that." As I touched her a curious feeling came over me, an emotion I had never experienced before—as though I touched someone dear to me who was of my own blood. A sister, perhaps? But the feeling was only fleeting. Stacia herself took care of that.

As she reached up to hold the cold cloth against her puffy cheek, the heaving sobs stopped abruptly. "Go look in the top drawer of the dressing table," she said. "I left something there to shock you. But you've been more decent than I deserve, so you'd better look now, while I'm here."

Uneasily, I went to the lowboy and opened the drawer. This was where I had placed my golden unicorn. I looked for it first and found it, still wrapped in its tissue. Farther back in the drawer my fingers touched something small and cold and round. I drew out the china head of an old-fashioned doll, one with round cheeks tinted rosy and soulless eyes that clicked open as I held it up. I stared at it with repugnance and set it down.

"Spooked you, didn't I?" said Stacia. "But it's a kindness, really. It will help prepare you when you walk into Mother's studio tomorrow."

"What do you mean?"

"You'll see." Stacia pushed herself up from the bed, her body again limber as a cat's, and slipped past me out the door. When it closed behind her, I turned back to see the staring eyes of the doll's head fixed blankly upon me. Hastily I thrust it into another drawer, away from the unicorn.

My feeling was one of odd disorientation. So much had been hurled at me, yet all of it had amounted to nothing more than fog. Only one truth had emerged. There *had* been a baby. A baby named Anabel. And that was the name, complete with question mark, that had been written on the note so recently delivered to Herndon Rhodes. Was it possible that I had been that baby?

BY THE NEXT MORNING, MY SPIRITS had risen and I was looking forward to the day. No one here knew who I was. I could reject this family and go back to New York anytime I chose. Even if evidence was given me that I was a Rhodes, I could take it or leave it.

I dressed in white slacks and a turquoise shirt, and brushed my hair till it shone. The morning was beautiful, and when I went downstairs to breakfast bright sunlight was pouring in at the tall dining-room windows. Stacia, John, and Herndon—this morning his vest was green—were already at the table. Someone said Evan had eaten early and was working in the library.

Stacia, seeming subdued, greeted me briefly. John ate with a hearty appetite, finished first, then gave me a smile and a nod and left the table. I suspected that of them all he was the one who most savored the creature comforts. I wondered what he would do when The Shingles was sold.

"Judith will be ready for you around ten," Herndon told me. "Her studio is on the top floor, in the attic. And, Courtney—don't worry if she doesn't talk to you easily at first. She's rather shy with visitors and it may take a while to get her to relax."

"That's my job," I said. "Most people are self-conscious at first."

"I'm calling on several of our bank branches in the area this morning," he went on. "But if you need to reach me, ring up the number in East Hampton. They'll know where I am."

From her corner of the table, Stacia looked up. "Did anyone hear the weather report on the radio? There's a hurricane starting up the coast from the Caribbean. I hope it comes this way! I love storms." She gave her father a sly smile, excused herself, and left the table in the direction of the living room. In a few moments stormy music from the piano broke out, filling the house.

"She's very good," I said. "What is that composition?"

"It's her own," replied Herndon. "And she is good. She could have taken it up professionally if she had wanted to, but discipline has never been something she has welcomed, not even from herself."

He waited at the table until I had finished my toast and coffee, then went off to one of his banks. I thanked Asher for serving me and wandered down the long rear hall toward the far end of the house. The library door stood open, and I paused to look in.

Evan Faulkner sat at the long table, pencil in hand, writing in a ledger before him. He did not look up as I stood in the doorway, and I could study him for a moment. Something about the dark, bent head, the strongly carved profile, aroused a curious ambivalence in me.

As I stood there unseen a telephone on the table rang. Evan lifted the receiver, and when he spoke, the chill note I had heard before was in his voice. "Hello. . . . No, you may not speak with her. I've left word that any call from you is to be transferred to me. . . . If you keep on your present course, Olive, you will end up on the wrong side of the law. . . . Don't bother making threats—do what you like. . . . What did you say? . . . Hello? . . . Olive? . . ."

Apparently the speaker had hung up, and I realized tardily that I was eavesdropping. I turned away and saw that I was not alone. A little way down the hall William Asher had come within hearing, and looked thoroughly upset. When he noted my attention he disappeared into the dining room. Turning back to the study, I asked, "May I come in?"

Evan regarded me without welcome, rising reluctantly from his place at the table. His eyes seemed to hold me off, and I wondered whether it was because he disliked reporters in general or me in particular. "Last night," I reminded him, "you said you would tell me something about Ethan Rhodes and the great whaling days of Long Island."

"Do you know anything about whaling?"

"Very little, I'm afraid. What fascinates you most about it?"

"The whales themselves. And of course the men who hunted them. It's a dramatic story. The great whaling days lasted only a short time, but they were filled with drama and tragedy—both human and animal."

His eyes had brightened, and his voice came alive as he went on. "I want to see these old books and papers preserved. Whalers were the country's early explorers and geographers and sociologists. Ships setting out from Sag Harbor helped chart waterways we knew nothing about and brought us knowledge of faraway places and people."

"What will happen to all these records?" I asked.

"I'm trying to pull them together into some sort of order. Then they'll go to a museum, where they can be available to researchers. I need to finish before the house is sold."

"Why is The Shingles being sold?"

"Do you mind if I get back to work?" he asked coolly as he pulled out his chair at the table. "You can look around, if you like, and ask any questions about these things that occur to you."

"Thank you," I said, equally cool. "But it's the Rhodeses I want to know about. From Ethan on down. Why is everyone being mysterious about what is going to happen to this house?"

His smile was scarcely friendly. "You don't give up, do you? Perhaps the reason no one pins anything down for you is because no one is sure what will happen. At this moment, no one really owns the house."

"How can that be?"

"Herndon Rhodes, who isn't the oldest son, was the one in whose care Lawrence entrusted it. But it is only held in trust, and his responsibility will come to an end in a few weeks. Then we'll all find out what's going to happen. There's been talk of selling—you might say a threat of selling."

I was still hopelessly in the dark. "But by whom?"

"By my wife, Stacia. On her twenty-fifth birthday."

A faint chill seemed to trace itself down my spine. What happened to the house meant nothing to me, since I had no real kinship with any of these people. Yet a few steps more, the answers to a few more questions, and I could be plunged into the vortex—into an involvement I might not want.

I dropped my questioning and Evan turned back to his work. I took books from a shelf, riffled through them, put them back. Next to the fireplace was a wall space where several pictures hung. One was a yellowed photograph of a sailing vessel called the *Hesther.*

"Did this ship belong to Ethan Rhodes?" I asked.

Evan glanced toward the picture. "Yes. Hesther, of course, was the name of Ethan's wife. That was one of his last ships."

"And this picture?" It was of a graceful sloop, its sails filled with wind.

He answered with slightly more warmth in his voice. "That one was built more recently. John designed and built her before his father died. She's a real beauty. The *Anabel.*"

Anabel. The name that had also been given to a baby.

I wandered back to the table and looked over Evan's shoulder. He had put his ledger aside and appeared to be checking a box of assorted oddments against a faded, handwritten list. "Do you want to help?" he asked abruptly.

For Evan Faulkner this was almost amiable. I pulled up a chair to sit down, and he pushed the box toward me. "I'll read the list and you can look for the matching item."

I bent over the box and plucked out a blackened bit of tubular silver. "I think this is a toothpick holder," I said. "Silver."

He checked it against the list he had found in the box, and read the next item. "Sugar tongs."

We went through the box, which seemed to contain little of real value, checking off item after item—a garnet pin, a small ivory elephant, a miniature ivory carving of a sailing vessel. Then Evan exclaimed, "Here's a mention of something the family has looked for a long time! A gold pendant in the shape of a unicorn."

For a moment I couldn't breathe. "Does the list give any description?"

"It says that the initial *R* has been scratched onto one hoof. Is the unicorn there?"

"It isn't," I said. I didn't need to look. I knew very well that the golden pendant was upstairs in my room. I had never noticed an *R,* but if there was such a marking, then any last doubt would be gone.

"Too bad," Evan said. "Herndon always wondered what became of Hesther's unicorn. He wanted it for Stacia."

I pushed my chair back from the table. "If you don't mind—I think I'm getting a headache. I'd better go and take an aspirin before ten o'clock, when I'm to visit Mrs. Rhodes."

"Of course," he said, as though he hadn't expected much of me. There was no need to take aspirin—my head was fine—but I couldn't wait a moment longer to take out my golden unicorn and examine its hoofs.

While I was out, my room had been made up. I went into it and closed the door, then pulled open the drawer and took the folded tissue in my hand. It felt light, with nothing lumpy in the center, and I knew before I spread the paper open that the unicorn was no longer there.

CHAPTER FOUR

MINUTES TICKED BY WHILE I stood before the open drawer with the wad of tissue in my hand. Stacia could have seen the pendant last night when she put the doll's head in my drawer. Had she taken it away as something she felt I had no right to? And what was I to do about it now? It might be better to say nothing, just wait and see what developed. But the unicorn was mine! Someone long ago had wanted me to have it, and I meant to get it back. For now, I was forced to let the matter drift and wait for Stacia to make her next move.

In the meantime, I felt increasingly uneasy. Perhaps fearful would be too strong a word, but fear was there at the back of my mind, senseless, yet pervading my consciousness. There was a climate here that suited the growth of hidden motives like mushrooms sprouting in a cellar. Let me get my interview and go away, I thought. I didn't really want Judith or Alice for my mother, or Herndon or John Rhodes for my father. At least I would have no trouble now in interviewing Judith. I was a reporter, a writer, and she was my subject—no more and no less.

At ten I picked up my notebook and walked into the hall, seeking the stairs to the attic. They didn't rise from the top of the main staircase, and as I walked down the hall looking for them, Mrs. Asher came out of a bedroom. I asked her about the stairs.

"They're right down there at the end of the hall, ma'am," she said, and would have scurried out of sight if I hadn't stopped her.

"Have you worked for the Rhodeses a long time?" I asked.

"No, ma'am. I've only been here for a few years—since I married William." She waited for no more and ducked back into the bedroom. So this was a late marriage for William, I thought.

At the end of the hall the narrow stairs climbed steeply. There was a square landing at the top, with a closed door straight ahead. I tapped on the panel and Judith's voice called to me to come in. I opened the door.

The woman at the easel sat on a high stool facing me, and I could not see the canvas she was working on. Her complete focus on what she was doing enabled me to study her openly. She wore a rust-colored smock over light twill pants, and her long black hair was caught at the back of her neck with a rust-red velvet bow. She sat on her perch with a brush in one hand, palette in the other, a slight frown of concentration between dark brows. Her face was a long and beautiful oval, with those great green eyes, and lips so perfectly formed that she needed no lipstick to enhance them.

"Do you mind if I look around?" I asked.

"As you please. I'll work a little while longer, and then we'll talk."

Overhead, the studio roof rose in the high, beamed peak of a cathedral ceiling. At the northern exposure a large glass window had been set into the slanting roof, throwing full daylight into the room—an artist's necessity, and evidence that this large room had been remodeled in every detail for the woman at the easel. Dividers had been set about here and there, to bring the spaces in a bit closer, and on these, framed canvases had been hung, while other paintings were stacked in corners.

As I started toward the nearest partition, there was a movement beyond Judith's easel. Tudor eased himself to his feet, curled his lip, and growled. "Be quiet, Tudor. This is a friend," Judith said. The dog sat back on his great haunches, his look fixed upon me.

Following the side of the room farthest from the dog, I stood before the first partition and gazed at the four paintings mounted upon it. One looked out on a stormy sea, with waves crashing high over wet black rocks, and a small round face floating on the stormy surface. The other three were beach scenes, one of which again had that strange signature of a disembodied doll's face. Along the sand of the fourth painting, a golden unicorn pranced at the water's edge. "Your husband was telling me about the unicorn legend," I said. "It must appeal to you."

She slipped down from her stool with a smooth movement and began to clean her brushes. "I'm not sure 'appeal' is the right word. Perhaps 'haunt' would be a better one."

"Do you think there's anything to the legend?"

"I don't know. There have been Rhodeses who claimed to see the unicorn moon before they died. Sara, Lawrence's wife, was one of them. And of course Hesther, who started it all."

"What about Lawrence Rhodes?" I asked. "Did he see it too?"

She gave me a startled look as she put her brushes aside. "Yes, he saw it. There was a full moon that night shining into the living room downstairs. He told me he had seen the unicorn—that he was going to die."

I waited, hoping for more, but that was all she meant to tell me. "Let's sit down," she said, "where we can be comfortable."

At a short distance down the attic, East Indian prayer rugs made an island, with a sofa, chairs, and central coffee table arranged upon them. She led the way to this oasis, and as I moved past her easel I looked at the picture she was working on. Again there was a stormy sea, this time with a small boat, and once more a doll's face floated in the sky.

She waited for me to take my place on the flowered couch, and then seated herself, seeming completely poised and untroubled.

"Why do you paint dolls' heads into your pictures?" I asked.

"*I* can answer that!" Stacia Faulkner sauntered into the studio, her hands set jauntily in jeans pockets.

"Good morning, Stacia." Judith Rhodes spoke quietly.

"What do you think of this, Mother?" Stacia asked, displaying her bruised cheek. "What do you think of a man who beats his wife?"

Her mother glanced at me, noting my presence as a captive audience.

"We don't have to be proper with Courtney," Stacia went on. "She knows. Everyone knows by now that Evan struck me." Though Stacia's words and behavior were outrageous, Judith still said nothing. Wide green eyes regarded her daughter without expression.

Stacia was looking at me so intently that I could almost feel the thought of my golden unicorn burning between us. I was sure she had it, and I wondered what it meant to her.

"Come," she said to me. "I want to show you something." She went to a cabinet just under the slant of the roof, knelt, and pulled out a drawer. I followed her and looked in. Tumbled helter-skelter were two or three dozen dolls' heads, from every type of doll possible—wax, china, wood, plastic, some with hair, some without, staring up at me with blue or brown eyes, or with no eyes at all, just empty sockets. I felt a horrid fascination at the sight.

Stacia stood up and waved a proud hand at the collection. "They're all mine. Or were mine as a child. As I decapitated my dolls, Mother brought the heads up here. There's a doll graveyard out in the woods, where all the bodies are buried."

I stared at her in disbelief. "You mean you broke all the dolls?"

"Right! It was fun to smash them. It upset people."

I walked back to the sofa and sat down. Judith said nothing, only looked down at her hands. Stacia closed the drawer with a vigor that set the heads rolling and clattering—then they were all quiet again, staring at nothing in the dark. "Go ahead with your interview," Stacia said, coming over and dropping down on the sofa beside me. "I'd like to listen."

She made my hackles rise. "I never work with an audience," I told her.

"Let her stay if she wants to," Judith said, raising neither her voice nor her eyes.

Stacia settled back with an air of triumph. There was nothing more I could do. "Have you always liked to paint?" I asked Judith.

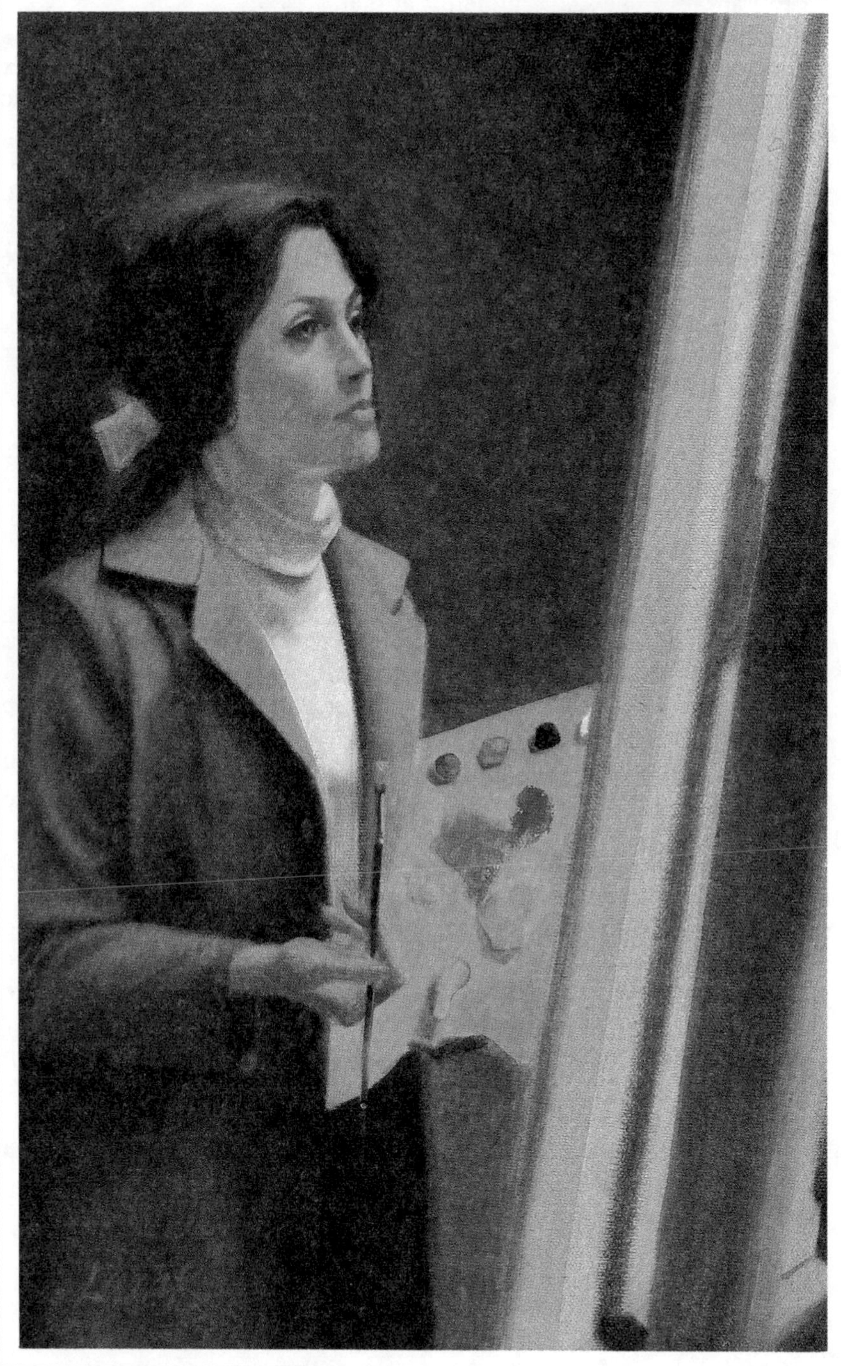

"Not always," she said, and left it at that.

"Not until all those people began to die," Stacia put in.

Judith gave her daughter a long, intense look that made the younger woman drop her own gaze. "I began painting in my early twenties," she said, "trying to escape from much that was tormenting me. It helped."

"And you could hide in it when other people needed you," Stacia added. "Dad always said you mustn't be disturbed, so I let you alone and took to breaking up my dolls. If it hadn't been for Uncle John—"

"I expect I wasn't always a good mother," Judith agreed, her composure showing no crack. "I'm sorry," she said softly. "I've always been sorry. But there wasn't anything else I could do. I had to paint. But I don't think any of this can be interesting to Miss Marsh."

"Do you know what an encouragement you are to other women?" I asked. "So many of us grow up thinking we can't achieve anything."

"I'm afraid I'm not a feminist," she replied. "I've never suffered from being a woman."

"Because Dad was such an angel to you!" Stacia cried. "He protected you, gave you everything. Except the one thing you wanted most."

Judith's eyes were downcast again. "What do you think I wanted most?" she asked her daughter.

Stacia sprang up and circled the sofa. "What you really wanted was freedom from guilt, wasn't it, my darling mother?"

I don't know what might have happened next if there hadn't been a tap on the door. Judith called, "Come in."

A maid entered carrying an envelope, which she handed to Judith. "I found this near the front door," she said. "Mr. Asher isn't about, so I brought it up to you. Your name is on it, Mrs. Rhodes."

"Thank you." Judith took the envelope and stared at it while the maid went away, then she slit the envelope flap with a forefinger. From where I sat I could see the uneven pasting of cutout letters across the single lined sheet. Judith read silently and leaned back in her chair, letting page and envelope float to the floor. Stacia pounced on the letter and read aloud, " 'What did you do to Alice's baby?' "

My breath quickening, I watched Judith, who seemed so quiet, so frozen, that I wondered if she was going to faint. I bent toward her. "Are you all right, Mrs. Rhodes?"

For an instant she did not move, and then she raised her head to look at me blankly, as though she had forgotten who I was. When she spoke, she was not addressing either of us. "Who is doing this to me?"

"You look ill," Stacia said. "You shouldn't let an anonymous letter get to you like this. You haven't anything to hide. It really was an accident, wasn't it—when Alice's baby drowned?"

I wasn't sure whether Judith heard her words, but they were ringing through my mind. *Alice's baby.* Had these words anything to do with me?

Stacia dropped the letter and moved toward the door. "I don't think I'll stay around, Mother," she said. "I'll leave you to Courtney Marsh."

She went out of the room and I heard her clatter down the stairs.

Judith raised her head. She listened for a moment, then picked up the letter and reached calmly for a packet of matches on the coffee table. She lit one, touched it to the corner of the note, and held the paper while a small blaze flared up. When it burned close to her fingers she dropped the paper into an ashtray and watched it blacken. Only then did she look at me. "There was no letter," she said.

Her look held my own, and though I gave her no verbal promise, she must have read something in my eyes that reassured her. "You might as well know the truth," she said. "It wasn't Evan who struck my daughter. I did. She drove me too far, and I slapped her, quite hard."

I found myself wondering what might lie seething under all this calm she turned to the world. "I can't say I blame you," I told her. "Stacia seems to ask for it."

"An eldritch child, born of a witch," she said lightly, and suddenly her laughter floated through the great echoing room. It was a shocking outburst, checking all the sympathy I had been ready to bestow on Judith Rhodes. I felt thoroughly shaken. If I had been unsure of my identity before I came to this house, now I was totally torn and confused about it. All I wanted at that moment was to escape.

I stood up and walked the length of the studio, past Tudor, who raised his head watchfully, past the easel with its scene of a boat in a storm, and went downstairs to the dining room. There, over the great dark sideboard, hung the portrait of Alice Kemble Rhodes in her summery blue dress. I stared up at the smiling face in the picture. The large, beautiful eyes looked familiar, and I realized they were like her sister Nan's eyes.

Was she my mother?

There seemed to be something around her neck. Yes—a gold chain, and against the hollow of her throat a tiny pendant vaguely in the shape of a unicorn. So now I knew. This girl had surely been my mother. Something terrible had happened—a death she could not have sought at that young age—and she had left a baby that others must have given away. My mother would have wanted me, since I had stayed with her for at least two months after my birth. But now, if I had found her, I had also lost her, for she had died a long time ago—leaving John as my father.

All my life I had been warned, "Don't try to find out who you are, Courtney. You may uncover horrors that you're better off not knowing. Let the door stay closed." But a door that has begun to open has a momentum of its own. I knew very well that I must walk through, that I wanted to walk through, no matter what it cost me.

So absorbed was I in my thoughts that I didn't hear Asher come into the room until he stood at my elbow. I turned and saw that he carried a tray of silverware, which he wanted to store in the sideboard. I stepped aside, wondering about this old man who ran the house for Judith and Herndon. I asked him the same question I'd asked his wife. "Have you been with the family a long time?"

He answered me guardedly. "I came here when I was a young man to work for Mr. and Mrs. Lawrence Rhodes," he said.

"That's a long time. I suppose you remember Alice Rhodes?"

"Yes, of course, Miss Marsh."

I asked my next question without warning. "How did she die?"

With a start he dropped the tray of silver on the sideboard, so that the pieces rang against each other. He recovered in a moment and answered me quietly. "She died out near Montauk, where the Kemble family has a cottage. She went swimming alone one morning and was drowned. Mrs. Judith found her on the beach."

"And the baby—what happened to her after her mother died?"

"She was lost in an accident at sea only a few days later. It was very sad—especially for Mr. John, who had a double loss, and for Mr. Lawrence, who had been so happy over having an heir."

The old man began to sort the silver carefully into its flannel containers. I thanked him and went away, only a little more informed than before.

An urge to escape this house, with all its secrets and its alarming deaths, had seized me. One death hadn't happened, if I had been that baby, Anabel. But the deception was disturbing. Why had someone gone to so much trouble to cover up?

I fetched a jacket and let myself out the front door, with no word to anyone. Thick fog was beginning to blow in from the sea. I walked into the mist gratefully, wanting only to let it close about me. Perhaps then I would be free from that dark, towering house that held so many ominous secrets.

MY WAY LAY downhill. Mist cut off the tops of the old trees and I found myself hurrying, wanting to put The Shingles behind me. When the gatehouse emerged from the fog, I could see a warm glow at the windows. For a moment I was tempted to stop and talk to Nan Kemble. I had liked her at our first meeting. Perhaps she was even my aunt. But I really didn't want to talk to anyone at the moment. I needed to be alone.

The old iron gates stood open between crumbling stone posts, and I slipped through into Ethan Lane, myself a ghost in the enveloping mist. It was as though I were walking through one of Judith's strange landscapes. I would hardly have been surprised to see a doll's face peering at me from within the thick hedge, or to have a unicorn come prancing along.

The road widened, and I realized that I had left Ethan Lane for one of those town lanes that were less private, though still bordered by high hedges of untamed privet, grown impenetrable with intertwined branches thick as my arm. There was no sidewalk, and I wandered down the middle of the road, my thoughts still tied to all those back at the house.

The sound of a car coming toward me was deadened by the fog, and I was not aware how close it was until I saw its lights shining through the mist. It was coming fast and I realized that the driver would not see me in time to swerve. I sprang aside, and the fenders scraped by with hardly an inch of space to spare. Leaning against the hedge, I took deep breaths to steady myself.

Behind me, the car braked, and I could hear it turning. The driver was coming back to make sure I was not hurt. I stepped out, expecting him to stop. Instead, the two orange eyes of the fog lights were coming straight at me with a sudden spurt of speed. This time I didn't leap aside in time. A fender grazed my thigh, and I was thrown against the hedge, where I lay propped and stunned. I didn't see the driver crouched at the wheel, but I was aware of the circular emblem on the hood. The car was a Mercedes.

Down the lane it was backing, turning, squealing in haste. There was no doubting the intent of the driver now. I scrambled to my feet and ran beside the hedge, trying desperately to find a way through. The privet was thick as a jungle and all of fifteen feet high, with no driveways to offer an escape.

The car was coming back more slowly this time, more deliberately. What was happening was mad, insane, impossible, but there was no time to wonder why. If I was found dead or dreadfully injured in this lane, the authorities could only put it down to a hit-and-run driver and my assailant would never be caught. But where could I turn—how could I escape?

Then I heard the sound of another car coming from the opposite direction, saw another set of lights bearing upon me. I sprang away from the hedge, waving my arms frantically. The driver braked in front of me. The Mercedes accelerated, swung past us, and disappeared up the lane. I leaned over the hood of the car that had rescued me, gasping with fright and relief.

A man got out and came around to me. "Courtney!" he cried, and I looked up into John Rhodes's reassuring face. "What made you jump out like that?"

I pushed myself up from the hood and clung to him. He held me gently, until I could talk. "There was a car. That other car that drove away! It was a Mercedes."

"A Mercedes? What about it?"

"It was dark blue, I think. I couldn't see the driver, but he tried to run me down. He tried to kill me!"

The fog swirled around us. "You're shivering," John said. "Come and get into my car and I'll take you back to the house. You've had a shock."

I let him put me into the front seat. He found a blanket in the back seat, wrapped it around me, and held me for a little with my head against his shoulder, not speaking, not questioning, just letting me recover. Slowly my shivering quieted. Yet I wanted to lean against him. I wanted this—from my father? Could it be? Had the feeling I so longed for come to me at last? John Rhodes holding his daughter in his arms? But even if that was true, he couldn't know I was his daughter. I was only a stranger in need. I raised my head and sat up. "I'm all right now. Thank you."

"I'll drive you home. You've had a nasty fright. But you must realize that it's very hard to see in a fog like this. I was almost upon you before I saw you. It may have been the same with the other driver."

"That hardly explains why he turned around twice and *tried* to run me down. It was deliberate. If you hadn't come along I might have been killed."

As we rode following the curving lanes I could sense his disbelief. I could hardly blame him. What had happened was so unlikely that I hardly believed it myself—except that there was a throbbing in my thigh where I had been struck.

We drove through the gateway without slowing and climbed the driveway to the house, halting before the garage. A sudden thought seized me. The moment the car stopped I got out and went toward the open doors of the low building. John came with me. Along with several other cars, there was a dark blue Mercedes inside. "Look!" I said, and put my hand on the hood. The car was warm. "Whose car is this?" I demanded.

"It belongs to Judith. But we all use it from time to time. There's always a key out here."

"Someone drove it," I said. "Someone who tried to kill me."

"I'll find out who may have had this car out in the last half hour," he said, touching my elbow and turning me toward the house. "But you mustn't let something accidental go to your head. I assure you no one in this family goes in for murder."

Limping a little, I went with him silently up the steep steps to the house, and he let me in the front door. "Mrs. Asher has had training as a nurse," he said. "I can send her up. Unless you'd like a doctor?"

"I don't think it's anything." I turned to him, suddenly wanting to recover that brief feeling I'd had toward him in the car. "Thank you for coming along when you did."

His look was kind, but also a little puzzled, and I knew he did not believe my account of what had happened. Nor could he be aware of the emotion that moved me.

I walked upstairs slowly to my room, meeting no one, for which I was grateful. I got out of my dust-stained white slacks and examined the bruise on my leg. It was sore and swollen, and it would be uncomfortable for a few days—but it was only a flesh bruise, with no real damage done. I wrung out a cold cloth to press against it and lay down on the bed, waiting for the throbbing to subside. There was, however, no quieting the thoughts that whirled through my mind.

It was hard to believe that the driver of a random Mercedes had tried to strike me down. I tried to fit the identities of those who lived in this house into the driver's seat of that murderous car, but no one seemed to belong. Not Judith. Not Herndon. And John had been driving a different car when the first one sped away. Once more a twinge of feeling surged up in me. I was glad he was out of it. It had not been Evan—I was sure about that. Not Nan, of course. Stacia? Perhaps. I could imagine her trying almost anything. But why?

The wet cloth on my leg had grown warm, but the bruise wasn't hurting as much. I got up to dress and went to stand at the window, looking out upon a calm blue sea. As swiftly as it had come, the mist had disappeared, and the sun-drenched beach invited me with its sense of peace. I went downstairs and let myself out the door at the end of the house. I crossed the terrace to the wooden steps that led down over the dune—steps weathered by rain and sun and salt air so they creaked beneath my feet. When I left them, I walked with my heels sliding in loose sand until I reached the water's edge, where dampness offered better footing.

Farther west, toward the city, the barrier of Fire Island sheltered the land, but here the shore was fully exposed to any storms that might come pounding up the coast from the hurricane belt. However, today, with sun sparkling on clear water, it was hard to imagine a hurricane blowing up from the Caribbean, or a blue car hurtling out of the mist with murderous intent.

I followed the damp sand, with white-fringed waves curling in to reach for my feet and gulls swooping overhead. I saw no one, heard no one. However, the pain in my leg resumed, and before long I turned back. A real tramp along the beach would not be comfortable today. Before I reached the flight of wooden steps, something I hadn't noticed before caught my attention. At the foot of the dune, in a matting of beach grass and partly buried in sand, stood a ship's figurehead, gray and weathered. It had a woman's face, with hair blowing back and eyes staring wide, lips pressed into a haunting smile.

"She came from the *Hesther*," a voice said behind me.

I turned to face Evan Faulkner. "From Ethan Rhodes's ship, the one I saw a picture of in the library?" I asked.

"Yes. In her day she carried cargo and passengers around the Horn to San Francisco. The figurehead really belongs in a museum, but Judith wants it here."

I looked again at the splitting wood of the weathered face and wondered what those staring eyes might have seen in all that sailing of the seas. "I've been thinking how much she knows and keeps to herself," I said.

"John told me what happened to you." There were scowl lines between the brows of Evan's dark eyes. "We've checked with everyone in the house and no one admits to taking out the car."

"But the hood of the car was warm!" I cried. "It *had* been taken out." My thigh was throbbing. Abruptly I sat down on the steps and pulled my knees up under my chin.

"Are you hurt, Courtney?"

"Just shaken," I said. "I can't imagine who would want to harm me."

"It might be better if you returned to New York as soon as you can," Evan said. "I don't like what's happening here."

I felt my resistance hardening. "That's what Nan Kemble told me. She mentioned quicksand and said I wouldn't know it when I saw it."

"An apt way of putting it. I don't think an outsider is welcome here at the moment."

I pressed on. "The anonymous letters are a part of it, aren't they?"

His stiffness toward me was increasing. "That's no concern of yours."

"But this—this family history, spat, whatever it is—isn't what I want to write about," I protested. "I only want to write about Judith as an artist." I could see that he didn't believe me, and in a moment he would turn away. I spoke quickly, impulsively. "Judith told me that it was she who struck Stacia. I—I'm sorry."

"Sorry for what?"

An unfamiliar warmth was rising in my cheeks. I'd never thought myself the blushing type. "I suppose for misjudging you."

"You haven't misjudged me."

I wasn't sure what he meant—only that he was throwing my feeble apology back in my face. I pushed myself up from the steps and started toward the house, but at that moment Stacia came out, her hair bleached pale in the sunlight. She had changed to denim shorts and a light blue pullover, and her legs were brown and graceful as she moved. She came to where we stood and slipped a proprietary hand through her husband's arm. "I'm sorry about what's happened, Courtney," she said. "Are you all right?"

"I had a bad fright, but no real damage was done."

"You poor thing!" She looked at me appealingly. "Who on earth would want to hurt you?"

Evan removed her hand and she dropped it to her side, aware perhaps of a rebuff. There was sudden angry passion in the look she turned upon her husband, and I could see the answer to it in Evan's eyes—whether dislike or an angry sort of love I couldn't tell. I didn't want to remain in the company of those two a moment longer. There was some strong, unhappy bond between them.

Without another word, I went past them, up the steps, and entered the house. When I reached my room I went to the dressing table, where I had put my notepad and pen. Now was the time to set down the impressions I had gained this morning about Judith. Reaching in the drawer, my hand touched the tissue where the pendant had been hidden, and I stiffened. Something hard lay within the folds. I snatched up the paper and opened it to reveal a gleaming golden shine. The unicorn pendant had been returned. The sense of danger that had begun to haunt me deepened.

Carefully I turned the pendant about in my fingers. On the bottom of one tiny prancing foot I could just make out a crudely scratched *R*. There was no longer the slightest room for doubt. I fastened the clasp at the front of my neck, letting the pendant hang concealed by my collar at the back. I would wear it always from now on. With this precious keepsake, I would take no more chances. It was proof of who I was. Of *me*.

If only there were someone to whom I could turn. Someone who would talk to me honestly. At least I could put a lot of it down on paper. I sat at the room's small desk with my pad before me, and managed to fill three pages with helter-skelter impressions—not just of Judith, but of all of them. Even of Evan Faulkner, to whom my thoughts kept returning in half-resentful, half-curious fascination. When words ceased to tumble out, I slipped into a light coat and picked up my handbag. I knew where I was going and to whom I could talk.

Outside I hurried down to the garage, where my Volvo was parked. I had no taste at the moment for walking alone down any lane. I backed the car around and followed the driveway to Nan's gatehouse shop.

CHAPTER FIVE

LAMPS BURNED PLEASANTLY around the main room of the crowded shop, and there was a delicious odor of savory cooking somewhere at the back. Nan was nowhere in view, and in spite of the tinkling peal of the brass bell, no one appeared from upstairs. On a nearby glass case a sheet of paper had been placed conspicuously. I picked it up and read:

> I've had to go to town—will be back shortly. Make yourself at home. That's minestrone cooking on the stove—you're welcome to stay to lunch, whoever you are.
>
> Nan Kemble

I smiled at this informal greeting to any customer who might wander into her unlocked shop, and decided to await her return. My nose led me to the small living area that opened through an arched partition at the rear—a room that at one end held a tiny kitchen, complete with stove, sink, and cupboard, plus a pot of soup cooking slowly. At the other end of the partitioned area I found a comfortable armchair, a well-worn couch, and a large bookcase that contained an assortment of mystery novels, old classics, and modern nonfiction. Opposite the chair stood a television set on which had been placed a bowl of yellow chrysanthemums.

From the shop came a tinkle of the doorbell and I went to the archway in the partition to greet Nan—and perhaps invite myself to lunch. But it was Judith Rhodes, who had come into The Ditty Box and stood reading Nan's note. I stepped back, just out of sight, not wanting to face her. She was wearing corduroy slacks and a brown suede jacket with brass buttons. Her long hair cascaded down her back in a fall of black satin. I must let her know I am here, I thought. But then she did so curious a thing that I halted in the very act of stepping through the arch.

Having read the note, she went directly to a row of built-in cupboards and knelt to open a lower drawer. She drew out a large carton, which she carried to a nearby table. Hurrying, she began to scrabble through the contents. A set of notebooks interested her most, and she picked up one after another and riffled through the pages. Each time, after a brief examination, she set the book aside and picked up another. Soon she had a pile of them on the table beside her.

When the bell sounded again, she paused with a notebook in her hands and looked at the door. Nan walked into the shop with a grocery bag in her arms. There was a moment of silence, and I could almost sense a crackling of antipathy while each waited for the other to speak.

Nan gave in first. "Hello, Judith," she said. "Are you looking for something?"

The answer came without confusion or effort at concealment. "Yes—I want to see those old diaries Alice used to keep. I can't find them."

Setting the bag on a counter, Nan answered calmly, "She never kept a diary. Exactly what is it you're looking for?"

"I'd like to find the last book she wrote in before she died."

"Because you think there might be an answer in it to these letters you've been receiving?"

"Yes."

Nan took off the denim jacket she wore and came toward the other woman. "Alice never kept a diary. She used to write stories constantly, as you know—stories for children. That's what fills those books. There never was a diary."

"I don't believe you," Judith said with quiet authority.

It was time for me to betray my presence before this turned into a quarrel, and I coughed apologetically. Both women turned to stare at me. "I've been waiting for you to return," I said to Nan.

She smiled stiffly. "I'll be with you in a moment, Courtney."

Judith ignored me. If it disturbed her to find that I had been in the shop all along, she didn't show it. She piled the notebooks back into the box and slid it into place in the cupboard drawer. "Thanks, Nan," she said, without the slightest apology. Then she turned to me, smiling. "I'm glad you weren't hurt by that car, Courtney. Please come back and we'll talk when we can be alone. Stacia was no help to us today." She waved casually and walked unhurriedly out of the shop.

Nan watched her go with astonishment. "Would you believe," she said, "that I haven't seen Judith Rhodes for three months? And then she just walks in and out like that?"

"You warned me she'd be hard to interview," I said. "That's why I came to see you. Also because I need to talk to someone who isn't a Rhodes."

"I know how you feel. Alice and I used to have attacks like that. We never really belonged to the clan. Why don't you stay to lunch?"

I nodded toward the note she had left near the door. "I've already accepted your invitation."

Nan carried the shopping bag out to the kitchen and I followed, already feeling a little less strange than I had at The Shingles. While she was putting apples and oranges and a carton of eggs away in the refrigerator, Nan observed, "You're limping. What happened? What did Judith mean about your not being hurt by a car?"

"That's one of the things I want to talk to you about. Someone in a dark blue Mercedes tried to run me down when I went for a walk in the fog this morning. John Rhodes drove by just in time. If he hadn't rescued me . . ." I faltered to a stop.

Nan was staring at me, openmouthed. After a moment she said, "Sit down, Courtney," and pushed me toward the armchair. When I'd dropped into it, she lifted the cover of the soup pot and stirred the contents with a spoon. "I hope you're hungry—I've made a lot. I never know who may drop in."

"It really happened," I told her. "I can show you the bruise."

"I believe you. I suppose you know there's a Mercedes at the house?"

"Yes. John and I went into the garage and found the hood warm. I'm sure it was the same car that struck me."

With neat, economical moves, she opened a gateleg table, spread it with a green cloth, and set out soup bowls and dark brown bread. "Have you any notion of who might have been driving the car?" she asked.

"None. I couldn't see the person at the wheel. I can't think of any good motive for someone to try to injure me."

As she began to ladle out the steaming soup, I found that I was hungrier than I'd been since my arrival. The delicious soup was thick with vegetables, the bread crusty and filling. Nan made no speculations about what had happened to me. I let the matter of the car drop, as there were other things I wanted to know.

I began hesitantly. "Several people have mentioned Alice's baby—the child who died in an accident. Can you tell me about her?"

Nan swallowed a mouthful of minestrone. "Does it matter? It was such an unhappy time. I don't like to talk about it."

"I can't work in the dark," I said. "It's the past that's made Judith the way she is now—perhaps made her an artist. But I don't even know the right questions to ask. Was the child born in East Hampton?"

"No. Alice ran away to Europe when she knew the baby was coming. Anabel was born in Switzerland."

This surprised me. "Ran away? Why? I should have thought old Lawrence Rhodes would have wanted his grandchild born here."

"He didn't know the baby was coming. Alice had quarreled with him over a new will he was drawing up. She wouldn't stay around to have the baby taken into his hands when it was born. So she and John went abroad. They took me with them to help. But before we got to Switzerland Lawrence sent for John to come home. Of course his father still didn't know about the baby, but John had to do as Lawrence wished. Everyone always did. I stayed on to help my sister as best I could."

"You and Alice must have been very close."

"Not always. I think our best and happiest time together was at the end of that trip, in Grindelwald. I'll always remember that little valley, with the great Jungfrau rearing up behind it."

Switzerland! Had I been born in Switzerland in the shadow of the Jungfrau? "How did the baby come to be left with Judith?" I asked carefully.

"That part was horrible! We brought Anabel home and Lawrence was told of her birth. But we didn't go to The Shingles. When Alice went there she wanted to be in a better bargaining position. She meant to use her baby to get what she and John deserved from the old man—some real standing in the family. You see, it had always been Herndon he trusted—never John—and that wasn't fair. So we went first to our mother's cottage out near Montauk, a comfortable house on the water. Mother welcomed us, and it seemed a safe harbor. It wasn't, of course."

Nan's voice had altered as she spoke, tightening as though she held back some strong emotion.

"Were you there when Alice died? And when the baby"—I couldn't help my hesitation over the word—"when the baby died?"

"No! I wasn't there! None of it would have happened if I'd stayed. But I'd been with Alice for months, trying to make things easier for her, and by that time I couldn't approve of some of the things she was doing. So I went to San Francisco for a while. Unfortunately, only Alice had my address, and it wasn't until Judith answered a letter I'd written Alice that I learned my sister had drowned. That was the first I knew the baby had died too. So I came back—though there wasn't much to come home to. My mother was ill and she needed me—" Nan broke off for a moment and then went on. "Alice had left me something in her will, and Herndon fixed it with old Lawrence so that I could have this gatehouse to start my shop. In a few months Lawrence was dead as well. Tyrants do eventually die!"

Her words had poured forth. Yet somehow I had the feeling that she wasn't telling me all she knew about Alice's death. I put forth another question. "It was Judith who found your sister on the beach that day?"

She pushed her soup bowl away. "Yes—when it was too late. Alice was a very good swimmer, but nevertheless she drowned."

"How did Judith happen to be out at Montauk?"

"John told me afterward. They were all there, except the old man. He had sent Judith, Herndon, and John to Montauk to bring his granddaughter home, and he also wanted them to watch each other. He never trusted anyone and always liked to set them against one another whenever he could. At the time Alice died, the baby was sick with a cold. So Judith stayed there, while Herndon and John brought Alice's body home."

The whole account had made me feel a little ill. To Lawrence Rhodes, I—if I really had been that baby—had only represented another pawn in his game of power. Even to Alice, my mother, I had been a counter to use in the play against Lawrence.

When I spoke there was resentment in my voice, but Nan, lost in her own thoughts, didn't notice. "What happened to the baby?" I asked.

She seemed to shake herself in an effort to return to the present, and she stared at me for a moment before she dipped into the past again. "The baby's cold got worse, and Judith panicked. She felt she had to get Anabel to a doctor quickly. My mother's doctor was just across the cove from our cottage. All the Rhodeses used to take to boats as easily as to their cars, and Judith thought nothing of wrapping the baby well and taking her across the small stretch of water. The doctor said nothing much was wrong, gave Judith a prescription, and sent her home. On the way back a sudden squall blew up and the boat capsized. The Coast Guard rescued Judith, but"—Nan's voice broke—"the baby was lost."

I could have told her that it might all be a lie. Anabel—if I was Anabel—had never been lost from a capsized boat. "What happened after that?"

She swallowed hard and steadied her voice. "Old Lawrence was wild, of course. I don't know what he'd have done to Judith if she hadn't been able to tell him that she too was pregnant, and there would still be that Rhodes heir he wanted. Herndon returned to Montauk to bring Judith home, and from that day to this she's never gone out in a boat again. She seldom even walks on the beach. She only paints it—endlessly. The beach and the sea.

Obviously she's ridden with guilt. But you've asked enough questions, Courtney. I haven't talked about these things for years, and I hadn't meant to talk about them now."

Nan rose and brought cheese and fruit to the table. We finished eating, though not without strain. The easiness between us had been lost. When the meal was over, Nan showed me about the shop, speaking with affectionate pride of her treasures, though I suspected that her intent was to hold me off and stem any further questions. She came with me to the door, but she didn't ask me to visit her again. "When will you be leaving East Hampton?"

"I'm not sure. I really haven't accomplished much in my one talk with Judith. I'm going to try again this afternoon, since she seems more amiable toward me now."

"Good luck," Nan said dryly. "But don't stay around too long. Or take any more walks by yourself."

I went back to my car and got into the driver's seat. Someone had been there ahead of me. On the passenger's side lay the head of a doll with long black hair, its eyes peacefully closed. As I picked it up the eyelids clicked open to reveal emptiness behind. The hollows where eyes should have looked out seemed more horrid than staring blue glass. Then I saw an envelope on the floor. I picked it up and took out the single sheet of notepaper. It bore The Shingles imprint at the head, and beneath the few handwritten lines was signed Stacia's name. I read the words:

> I thought you might like this one, Courtney. Judith had the wig especially made from her own hair because she was foolish enough to think I might have fun combing it in different styles—the way she used to comb hers. Imagine!

The silky black hair clung insinuatingly to my fingers, as though it still carried living electricity. I set the thing down on the seat and started the car. It was necessary to have a talk with Stacia Faulkner, a private talk. I wanted to know if she had been the driver of that Mercedes.

BACK AT THE house I went upstairs, the doll's head bulging a pocket of my slacks. At the north end of the corridor, the door to the room Asher said was Stacia's stood closed, but I could hear a radio, and I tapped on the panel. The sound was switched off and Stacia called to me to enter.

She was sitting near a window when I opened the door, one hand on a notebook in her lap, and she looked around at me with a smile. "Do come in, Courtney. Have you heard the news on the radio? The weather report says that our hurricane has started in toward the Florida coast."

With the door firmly closed behind me, I stood looking about the cheerful room. Storms of an outdoor nature had no interest for me at the moment, only the inner storms that filled this house.

The room was large, and a bit more fussy than I'd have expected. A flowered satin flounce decorated the top of the four-poster bed, with a satin quilt to match. Stacia sat reclining on a flowered chaise longue. Narrow bookshelves had been set against the wall on either side of a white fireplace, and on the floor were fringed cotton rugs woven in multicolored stripes. It was hardly a man's room, and I saw nothing in the few clothes strewn about that might have belonged to Evan.

Stacia gestured toward a gingham-covered chair, but I took the doll's head from my pocket. "This is your property, I believe?"

She nodded brightly. "So you found it? Eerie, isn't it—that black hair coming from Judith's own head?"

For a moment I said nothing, trying to hold back an impulse to hurl words at her in anger. When I could manage to speak quietly, I went on. "What are you trying to do, Stacia? Do you really think I can be frightened by childish pranks?"

"I don't know yet," she told me frankly. "Breaking points are different for everyone." She laughed, with a touch of hysteria in her voice.

"Why should you want to break me?"

Her eyelids drooped lazily, so that long blond lashes lay upon her cheeks. "I think we both know the answer to that."

"You found the unicorn pendant, didn't you?" I said. "Why did you take it away?"

"I wanted to make sure it was the right one." She smiled at me—a triangular smile, like a cat's. "Why did you come here, Courtney?"

"I had the mistaken idea that I wanted to learn about my forebears."

"Maybe you *are* Alice's mysteriously lost baby. I always did think there was something fishy about that story. Odd to think we may be cousins. For you it must seem strange to come suddenly into a whole nest of relatives. What are you going to do with a family like this?"

I attacked in earnest. "Nothing serious enough to cause you to run me down in a car."

She lay very still, her eyes closed and the tiny smile gone from her lips. When she opened her eyes I saw venom in her look. "What do you expect me to say to an outrageous accusation like that?"

"I expect you to lie," I told her calmly. "The way you did about Evan striking you."

With a swift movement she sat up, and the notebook fell to the floor. "Listen to me, and listen carefully. On my twenty-fifth birthday, which is only a few weeks off, my grandfather's will goes into effect. I will inherit this house and all the family treasures and most of the money. He was mad at the whole family when he drew up that will—so I profit. And I don't mean to keep The Shingles for one moment longer than I have to. I'm already making plans to sell it—sell everything in it that isn't personally owned by the others. Then I'm going to buy anything my heart desires and have the most marvelous time in the world."

She leaned over to pick up the notebook, and I noticed that it matched the ones Judith had been rummaging through in Nan's shop. With an abrupt gesture she held it out to me. "Here—you can have this. A heritage from your mother. Alice used to write stories, and Nan gave me this book of them. Maybe you'd like it. I don't care for fairy stories."

I took the book from her. "What does Evan think of your plans?"

"He'll try to stop me, of course. But he won't succeed. In the end he'll do what I want him to do. He always does. We're tied together, Evan and I. Remember that, Miss Anabel Rhodes!"

"That isn't my name. I'm Courtney Marsh, and I expect to go on being Courtney Marsh."

She stared at me. "I don't believe you. You'll want to get your hands on some of that money—perhaps all of it, if you can!"

"How could I possibly? Your grandfather left a will, didn't he? He thought I was dead. I don't come into it at all. And I don't want to."

She thought about that for a moment and frowned. "I suppose that's true. But there is something else you want here, isn't there?"

I stared at her blankly. "I don't know what you're talking about."

"What about John? What about your father? Did you know that our saintly, beautiful Judith was in love with him at one time—her own husband's brother?"

Judith and John? I pushed the thought away. "I don't believe you," I said. "Anyway, I don't want to know any more. I have an interview to do, and then I'm going away. Whatever you do with your inheritance is no concern of mine. I just want you to stop your tricks."

Her sudden laughter chilled me. But when I started for the door, she left the chaise longue and stopped me with a quick hand on my arm. "Wait, Cousin Courtney. Wait till I show you one more part of your heritage." Her fingers tightened upon my arm, propelling me across the room to a portrait on the wall opposite the ocean. I was caught at once by the intensity of the blue eyes that looked out at me.

"Our grandfather Lawrence," Stacia said softly in my ear. "Old Yellow-beard. That was his sailing outfit, when he wasn't in his law office."

The man in the picture wore a brass-buttoned jacket and a captain's cap, and the lower part of his face was covered by a thick yellow beard. His mouth was grim-lipped, and he had the look of someone who liked to get his own way. Could I possibly be related to this man, whose cruel grip upon this family was becoming more and more evident to me?

But I had heard all I wanted to hear, and I started again for the door. Stacia came with me to let me out. "I hope everything is clear now between us," she said.

I had no answer to that. I didn't even know what she meant. I had come to have something out with her, but I wasn't at all sure I had succeeded. "I hope *you're* convinced that there's nothing here I want," I said. "I'll be leaving soon."

"But you can always come back, can't you?" she said softly as she closed the door behind me with a sharp click.

I carried the notebook that she'd given me back to my room and put it in a drawer. I would look at it later, perhaps read some of the stories, try to find some means of reaching through to the woman who might be my mother. Now it was time to return to the studio and take advantage of Judith's invitation to talk with her again.

I could hear voices as I reached the landing, and the door to the studio stood open. There were three people in the big room—Judith was sitting in the prayer-rug area, with John and Herndon standing nearby. They all stared at me as I reached the door. When I hesitated, Herndon started toward me, making a visible effort to control his emotions. "I'm sorry, Courtney, but I'm afraid this isn't the time—"

I was already turning away when Judith broke in, her voice quiet and controlled. "Come in, Courtney. Come and listen to this fascinating discussion. You may have an idea for us. We've been talking about Stacia. Perhaps you know by this time that her grandfather's will is going to put this house into her possession in a very short time. She's announced that she plans to sell it. We've been trying to find a way to stop her."

"This isn't anything I can have an opinion about."

"You're right," Herndon said restlessly, "and I think we'd better break up this hopeless conference right now."

"It's not hopeless," Judith said. "Before I will move away from this house, I'll walk into the ocean and never come back."

"I don't want to hear any more about your walking into the ocean, Judith," Herndon said harshly. "I'll see to it that you don't have to move from this house. Stacia will be stopped in this—I promise."

I had never heard this forceful note from Herndon before, and I knew he would go to some lengths to spare Judith so painful a move.

"Courtney can't possibly help in what is a private family problem," he went on. "I'm sorry we tried to involve you, Courtney."

I turned in the doorway, and John followed me out of the room, waving a hand at Judith. "We'll discuss this later," he said. We went down the attic stairs. "Get your coat," he told me. "I want to show you something. You might as well use this time to improve your background knowledge of the clan."

There was nothing else I wanted to do, and John Rhodes interested me a great deal. I wanted very much to get to know him better. After all, if I was Alice's child, he was my father.

CHAPTER SIX

JOHN'S CAR WAS LOW and small and maroon, with a bullet nose that suggested speed. I had ridden in it when he'd rescued me, but I hadn't noticed it then. His mastery and enjoyment of the swift-moving car was evident. I was aware of an exuberance in him. It was easy to see how attractive he must have been in his youth—and was still, for that matter.

"You must be thoroughly tired of The Shingles by this time," he said as we drove through the lanes in the direction of town.

"I don't know whether 'tired' is the word," I said. "I've felt disturbed by the house and the family, perhaps. Especially after today's events."

"Where I'm taking you, we'll have a chance to talk," he told me. "Peacefully." We turned down Main Street and drove beneath tall elms to the Old South Burying Ground, where he pulled up to the curb and parked. "It's a good place to be alone," John said. "Come."

He took my hand with natural ease, and we crossed the road and climbed a slope to where a stile led over the fence that enclosed the cemetery. For a time we wandered inside, no longer hand in hand, but still comfortable together. I was glad to be with him, just as a friend. I tried not to think about who he might be.

Now and then I bent to read dates and inscriptions. Some of the stones went back to the 1600s, others were so badly worn that the markings were effaced. Old trees of cedar and yew hung their limbs protectively above the graves. Yew to prevail against the powers of evil, I had read somewhere. John's goal was a stone of granite engraved with the name ETHAN RHODES. "You've been seeing the worst side of the Rhodeses, Courtney. Ethan was the good side. I wanted you to see that he really existed."

Unexpected tears came into my eyes as I studied the inscription with long-ago dates, and I blinked rapidly, not wanting John to see. I'd had no sense of relationship to Grandfather Lawrence, but I felt something for old Captain Ethan. My great-great-grandfather. "Are other Rhodeses buried here?" I asked.

"Only Ethan's wife, Hesther. Hers is the grave beside her husband's. This old graveyard hasn't been used for a long time."

A little way from where Ethan and Hesther lay, a green aisle ran between the stones, and I found a place in the sun and sat down upon the grass. "Do you mind?" I asked John. "I'd like to stay here quietly for a while."

He nodded and wandered off among the stones. I was glad he had the perception to let me stay alone. Now I could give myself over to emotion—

as though, strangely, I had at last come home. Sitting here in this quiet, lonely spot, I began to feel calmer and less disturbed than at any time since I had come to The Shingles. A gull's feather lay on the grass near me and I picked it up to brush it softly through my fingers.

John's step was soundless on the soft grassy cushion and I didn't hear him come back until he stood beside me. Now I could look up without tears into his blue, sardonic gaze. He dropped down and sat cross-legged beside me, relaxed. When he spoke he was not looking at me, but staring off toward the treetops, where a redbird was singing. "Are you wearing the pendant?" he asked softly.

Involuntarily my hand flew to my throat to touch the chain. Now I could guess why he had shown me Ethan's grave and watched for my reaction.

He held out his hand. "May I see it again?"

"Again?"

"Stacia brought it to me when she took it from your room. She wanted to know what it meant."

I reached back, released the clasp, and gave him the unicorn. Holding it by the chain, he watched the tiny golden creature swing in the sunlight. "This has been in the Rhodes family for a long time, Courtney. May I ask how it came into your possession?"

There was no point in holding back the truth. "It was around my neck when my adoptive parents received me."

"Did they know who your real parents were?"

"I don't think they knew for sure. They died in a train accident a few months ago, and among their papers I found a clipping—a reproduction of Judith's painting of the unicorn moon. There were words written in the margin that asked whether this was the unicorn in my life."

He gave back the pendant. "So you came here to find out?"

"That was part of the reason. I *am* going to write about Judith. But I've always wanted to know my own family. I thought I might find them here."

"And have you?"

"How am I to know? Do *you* know? Do you think I am Alice's child?"

His blue eyes studied me. When he spoke he formed his words carefully, without emotion. "It's quite possible that I am your father."

My breath was coming raggedly and I felt shaken. People had always said to me, "What if you do find your parents and they reject you?" Was this the moment of possible acceptance—or painful rejection?

"Don't look like that," he said. "We're guessing, aren't we? But if I am to have a daughter, I can't imagine one I'd rather have."

The words were serious enough, but his tone was light, and I had the feeling that John Rhodes would hardly sweep me into his arms as a long-lost daughter. It was probably too late in any case for me to come into his life as a daughter, and over this I felt a twinge of regret. "Why did it happen?" I asked. "If I was the baby who was supposed to be lost at sea, why did Judith give me away? And why wasn't it found out . . . what she did?"

"Lawrence—my father—was still powerful when it all happened, and he managed to take hold, sick though he was. The story of the accident was accepted—two unfortunate accidents which occurred close together."

I looked at him and saw in his face the dregs of an old anger left over from that tragic time. The damage the old man had done reached down through the generations, even to me.

"I was—still am—the eldest son," John said, and I sensed the depth of meaning in his words. Others had said that it was always Herndon old Lawrence had placed first, and at the time of Alice's death and the supposed death of the child, it was likely that little consideration had been given to John's loss. Even Herndon would have been more concerned with protecting Judith than with his brother's suffering. I could believe in that suffering now, no matter what tales Stacia concocted about an affair between him and Judith.

"Couldn't *you* get any of the answers?" I asked.

"My father was only interested in closing ranks and avoiding any hint of scandal. He didn't want any of us to dig beneath the surface. He and I had our last quarrel and I went away. I didn't come back until after he died."

"Did you and Alice want a baby?"

His look seemed far away, as though he searched some distant horizon. "We wanted one a great deal—Alice as much as I. For that little time she was a happy mother. And I was just beginning to feel like a father."

Instead, he had lost both his wife and child. Sympathy stirred in me, but nothing more. He was too distant, too far out of my reach. But as long as he was not rebuffing me, I had to know more. "What about the selling of the house? Do *you* want this to happen?"

"Perhaps it might be for the best. It's become too much of a shrine—a temple for Judith's talent. It might be a lot better for her as a painter to leave and never come back. She needs to test herself in the world."

"What will happen to you?"

He turned his head to smile at me. "I can drift with the wind if I have to. I'll make a landing somewhere. I'm still a pretty good designer of boats, you know."

"I've heard about the *Anabel*," I said. "Why was it given that name?"

"Alice chose it."

"And then she named the baby Anabel. Why was she so attached to that particular name?"

He regarded me thoughtfully. "It was a name that had some meaning for her—a family name. This has been quite a quizzing, hasn't it, Courtney?"

"I'm sorry. You're the only one willing to answer all my questions."

"No, not all your questions. Not yet. Shall we go back now?"

He stood up and held out his hand. I let him pull me to my feet. "Just one more question," I said. "When you rescued me from that car, did you know then who I was?"

He shook his head. "Stacia showed me the pendant just after that."

His clasp was warm, but an awkwardness had grown between us. It seemed as though he was telling me not to come too close. Neither of us had much to say as we drove back to the house. When we reached the garage, Stacia was waiting there.

"Where have you been?" she demanded of John.

She slipped her hand into the crook of his arm in the same possessive gesture she had made toward Evan—as though she was warning me away from property that belonged to her. "I want to talk to you," she said to John. "Let's go for a walk on the beach."

"Of course," he agreed. "Thank you for your company, Courtney." The words were formally courteous, the manner hardly that of a father.

I watched as they went down the steps and around the house, then I walked inside and went up to my room. For all the questions I had managed to ask, nothing had been resolved, and I seemed no nearer to discovery than before. All that had happened was that a few more possibilities had surfaced.

Remembering Alice's notebook that Stacia had given me, I took it from its drawer and sat down in an armchair to look through it. I expected no startling discoveries, and I found none. The stories were all for children, handwritten in a flowing script, and most of them were fantasy, telling of sprites and elves, kings and princesses and handsome princes.

As I turned the pages, I found that the tales seemed increasingly to be written for younger and younger children. Tiny pencil illustrations near the end were directed toward a very young child. The inference seemed clear. Alice, looking toward the arrival of her own baby, had been thinking of the time when her own child would be old enough to hear the stories read aloud. For the first time, I felt a pang of hurt as I thought of Alice. She had, indeed, been looking forward to being a mother. If I was the child she had held in her arms, she had known me—and I her—for so very short a time.

However, if this was the book that Judith had been seeking in Nan's shop, there was no apparent reason why she had wanted it. Judith had spoken of a diary, and this, certainly, was no journal of daily affairs. When I came to the end of the stories, there were no blank pages—Alice had filled the book completely. I was about to set it aside when I noticed snips of paper clinging to the inner spine, as though pages had been torn away. Stacia must have taken them out before giving me the book. Unless someone else had torn out those pages—perhaps Alice herself?

When a tap came on my door, I opened it and found Mrs. Asher there.

"If you please, ma'am, Mrs. Rhodes would like to see you in her studio."

"I'll go right up," I told her.

The door to Judith's studio was closed. When I knocked, she came to open it, shutting it after me and shooting the bolt. "There," she said, "now no one can disturb us. I'm glad you could come, Courtney. This is a good time to talk." I followed her across the attic and we found places for ourselves in the small oasis in the middle of the vast room. "Now then," she went on when we were comfortable, "ask me anything you wish about my work."

Such openness, so unexpected a welcome, took me aback. Had John or Stacia told her about me? Fortunately, I had questions in my notepad to fall back on, jotted down before I had left New York. "Why do you prefer sea and beach scenes?" I asked, though the answer was obvious.

She waved a graceful hand at the dormer window. "That's what is out there—sand and ocean. Their variety is infinite. The sky changes, the water changes, things come in from the sea."

"What things?"

"Driftwood, fish, all sorts of things—we had a dolphin once, although the poor creature died before we could return it to the sea. But I painted it first." She rose, went to a stack of canvases leaning against a wall, sorted through them, then brought one back and placed it across the arms of a chair. The shining creature lay half in the water in its last moments of life. Above, a single gull with outspread wings dipped inquisitively. For once there was no fantasy—no dolls' heads, no unicorns.

"You should have this one on display," I said.

"It's too sad," she told me, and picked it up to return it to its place against the wall. I realized for the first time how expressive her face could be, how her every emotion was visible when she relaxed her guard.

An interview must sometimes progress by prodding, by a treading on sensitive areas—otherwise the real person doesn't come through. "Someone has mentioned that after Alice's death you seldom walked the beach anymore," I ventured.

She raised her head and her calm green gaze regarded me. "Yes, you're right. The dolphin wasn't my first meeting with death on a beach. I might as well admit that Alice's death didn't seem as tragic to me as the dolphin's. There—have I shocked you?"

"I don't know anything about your relationship with Alice."

"I disliked her intensely. In some ways she was like Lawrence Rhodes. She liked nothing better than to bend other people to her will. There were times when she was downright unkind to Nan. No, I couldn't be sorry when Alice died, except in a general sort of way, as one must regret any death."

Those charming little children's stories I had dipped into did not seem to fit with the picture Judith was giving me of a ruthless, dominating woman.

But at one time Judith was supposed to have been in love with John, and she might have been prejudiced against his wife.

I left my place and went over to where the easel stood with her current canvas upon it—the boat scene on a stormy sea. When I got close to it, I stopped with a gasp of astonishment. The unfinished painting had been covered by defacing slashes of blue.

"Why?" I said. "Who did this?"

She shook her head at me, laughing softly. "No—it's not what you think. Stacia hasn't been up here messing around. I just got upset and vented my own annoyance. It's a picture I've never been able to finish, though I've tried it again and again."

It was disturbing to see that her serenity could break apart in so destructive a manner. I had to seek the reason. "Does this scene represent the time when Alice's baby was . . . lost at sea?" I asked carefully.

"Yes. But as I say, I've never been able to finish it."

"Why not?"

"Because it's a lie," she said quietly. "The baby wasn't lost at sea."

I sat down opposite her, unable to speak, waiting for her to go on. But she had nothing more to add. "Why did you tell me this now?" I asked.

"Because the time has nearly come to tell the true story."

It was difficult to keep my voice steady. "What is the true story?"

She shook her head. "It's not quite time yet."

Someone rapped at the door and Judith turned alertly. "That's Evan," she said, and bent toward me. "He's come for you, Courtney. We're going to stop Stacia! Between you and me and Evan, we're going to make certain that she never sells this house!" She flew down the long room to the door and let Evan in. He looked at once to where I was sitting, his attitude questioning. "I've told her everything!" Judith cried. "And she's going to help. Run along, Courtney, and don't worry, everything will be fine!"

I rose in bewilderment and started toward the door. "I haven't the faintest idea what she's talking about," I told Evan.

His sigh bespoke exasperation as he shook his head at Judith. "Is this a railroading job you've done on Courtney?"

Judith slipped an arm about me as though we were old friends. "Of course not. You *must* help us, Courtney. You must help us save The Shingles. You can do it so easily, and think what a good story it will make. Much more dramatic than anything you could write about Judith Rhodes the painter."

"We need to go now," Evan said to me. "We have an appointment and the time is short. Come and you can decide later what you want to do."

I was too much the reporter to refuse this opportunity, even if the means had been a bit high-handed. I stepped back from Judith's touch. "We'll talk again," I promised her dryly, and followed Evan out.

In the garage area, I saw Tudor lying in the afternoon sun, secured at the end of a sturdy chain. The dog stood up when we appeared, but recognizing Evan, he offered no outburst. "It's not far," Evan said, after we'd settled into the front seat of his station wagon. "I'm glad you're willing to come." He turned the car onto the driveway, then added, "I'll give you a little background. The woman we're going to see moved away a long time ago. She has come back to stir up trouble. Her name is Olive. Olive Asher. She is William Asher's ex-wife and she used to live with him at The Shingles. She's staying now with a friend from the old days."

My interest quickened, and I felt suddenly eager for the encounter. The name Olive had been tantalizing me ever since I had overheard Evan's telephone conversation in the library. "You should give me some sort of clue," I protested. "What is she up to?"

"We haven't all the answers yet," he replied, and I knew he wasn't going to tell me any more just then.

By this time we were following Montauk Highway, running east through little towns that bordered the ocean. In one such village we turned off onto a narrow country road that ran between potato fields. Evan drew the car up before a small cottage with a rose trellis over the porch. The woman who answered his ring had an air of uneasiness about her. She wore dark slacks and a gray shirt over a figure that bulged in the wrong places. Her gray hair had the fuzzy look of a too-tight permanent.

Olive Asher gave me a suspicious look, but when Evan walked past her into the house and I followed, she pulled the door shut and waved us into a small sitting room. "My friend is out for a little while," she said. "We have to finish before she returns, because she doesn't know anything."

"Then let's get to the point," Evan said, leaning an elbow on the mantel over a small fireplace. "Mrs. Rhodes has asked me to tell you not to annoy her anymore with phone calls."

"Annoy her?" The dumpy little woman stood in the middle of the floor with spite in her eyes. "She's got it coming! For a long time she made it worth my while to keep still. But now she's stopped sending what she owes me, and I'm not going to stand for it."

"What do you plan to do?"

"Talk—that's what! Maybe I'll go to Mr. Herndon. Could be I'll go to the police."

Evan regarded her with distaste. "Admitting that you were an accessory in a kidnapping?"

She refused to be cowed. "You're bluffing. She doesn't want all this coming out in the open. The police would still be interested, what with all this money coming to Mrs. Judith's daughter—when it doesn't belong to her at all."

"Who do you think it belongs to?"

"Why, to that baby of Mrs. Alice's and Mr. John's. The one I helped Mrs. Judith smuggle away to New York."

Evan looked at me. "I hope you're listening to all this, Miss Marsh."

I managed to nod. "I'm listening."

"Good," he said, "because I know you'll want to write the details into your story."

Until now, Olive Asher had ignored me, but at his words she swung around and stared at me balefully. "What has she got to do with it?"

"She's a reporter, and she will be writing it all up in an article she's doing for a national magazine. So you see it won't be necessary to pay for secrecy anymore. If there's any further annoyance from you, *we'll* be the ones to tell the police. They don't look kindly on blackmail."

Olive dropped into a chair. "What are you talking about? Mrs. Judith never wanted any of this to be known."

"That's not true any longer," Evan said. "She wants it all to be known. She wants to find out what has happened to that baby. She wants to find the woman she is now and bring her here."

"But then *her* daughter won't inherit."

"Exactly. The girl who should inherit Lawrence Rhodes's fortune is Alice and John's daughter—Anabel Rhodes. We're going to find her and see that justice is done."

Olive sat in a heap and turned her head from side to side in bewilderment. "I don't understand—I don't understand."

"There's another thing I've been asked to tell you," Evan said. "Stop sending anonymous letters to the house."

"Letters? Why would I write letters? I've been phoning since I got here."

"I see." Evan turned back to me. "Miss Marsh, would you like to ask Olive any questions?"

Words were tumbling around in my mind and my legs were not too certain under me, but I managed to reply, "No, I haven't any questions." This wasn't true, but I couldn't ask them with Evan present.

We left Olive where she was and returned to the car. "Judith won't have any more trouble with her," Evan said as we got in.

As he started the car I looked around carefully, noting the number of the house and the street sign—I had to come back to this place alone to talk with Olive Asher. As we drove toward the highway my mouth was so dry it was hard to speak. "Why are you mixing in this?" I asked at last.

"I'd like to stop Stacia and see the house is kept in Herndon's hands. For Judith's sake."

"How can you want to help her when she's done this vicious thing?"

"How do you know it was vicious? What if it was for the child's own safety?"

"But you haven't found this imaginary heiress yet. Suppose she wants to sell the house herself?"

"Just going to the authorities with the facts will cause any payment to Stacia to be postponed. That will give us time to find Anabel Rhodes. And it's likely she'd sell to Judith and Herndon out of gratitude. Stacia only wants to injure."

I could think of nothing more to say, and we were silent most of the way back to The Shingles. As we turned into Ethan Lane, Evan spoke. "It will be up to you as to how much of this you'll want to publish. Mainly, you were a threat to hold over Olive's head."

"I can see that Judith will hope I won't publish," I said. "But *why* did she do such a thing?"

"That's a question she won't answer, except in hints. There's the obvious reason—she knew she was going to have Herndon's baby and she wanted her own child to inherit. But I have a feeling it's something more complex than that."

"What will Herndon say?"

"He'll be upset. But he'll back Judith in the end. He always does."

We had reached the house, and the afternoon shadows were lengthening. I felt cold and my leg was aching. When Evan stopped the car, I sat for a few minutes without moving. Should I tell him the whole thing right now?

He didn't open the car door at once, and I became aware that he was looking at me strangely, as he'd done once or twice this afternoon, and the harshness he so often showed me was gone. "What's troubling you, Courtney?"

"I don't know what I want anymore," I told him. "It's just that everything I was doing in New York seems to have become meaningless. But I don't know what I can put in its place."

"You're on the road to finding out, I think," he said. Then he touched my hand—a light, reassuring touch, and I was all too aware of him close beside me. I wondered what would happen if I turned my own hand and clung to his. But I neither turned it nor drew it away.

"We'll talk again, Courtney." I heard the promise in his words. But the time was not ripe for either of us. Whatever current had leapt so unexpectedly between us had come too soon.

He left the car and came around to my door. As I got out Tudor growled. Evan spoke to him and he subsided. When Evan started up to the house, I left him and walked around to the front terrace. To go inside, to face any of them right now, was the last thing I wanted. I hurried toward the wooden steps and down to the beach.

It was a relief to find the long stretch of sand empty, to have it to myself. The sky had begun to gray with coming evening and soon it would be dinnertime. But I wanted to stop the churning inside me. I must take one bit at a time, I told myself as I walked briskly, ignoring the twinges in my leg. The curling waves soothed and quieted me.

But I couldn't escape for long. Sooner or later I had to think. I was Alice and John's daughter and Stacia's cousin, and both Stacia and John knew it and were keeping silent. I didn't want to be Anabel Rhodes. Judith meant to use that child—a child grown into a woman—to stop Stacia from coming into Lawrence's money. I didn't want to be Judith's pawn.

In the meantime, what about Stacia? What did Stacia mean to do?

Suddenly, and without the slightest doubt, I knew Stacia was my enemy. There was something unbridled in her character, something disturbingly unbalanced. She would never permit the money to come to me, if she could help it. I shivered, thinking of the times I had been alone with her. I must go away, return to New York, where I could be safe until I could decide what to do.

But first I would go back to see Olive Asher. Perhaps she could tell me more about my mother. In all this, there was only one comfort—Alice had wanted her baby daughter, had loved her, no matter what anyone might say.

I turned and walked back toward the steps.

As QUICKLY AS I could after dinner, I went up to my room and put on my coat. Then I walked to the far end of the hall, where a flight of back stairs let me slip out of the house without being seen. As I walked through the darkness, my way guided only by lights from the house, music came floating out from the living-room windows. Stacia was at the piano again, playing one of her disturbingly dissonant compositions.

The garage area was quiet, with a single light burning over the central door. Tudor stood up restlessly as I appeared, but he neither barked nor strained at his chain. He simply watched as I got in my car.

Uneasy about facing Olive alone, I decided to ask Nan to go with me. I could trust her more than the others, I knew, and she was tied into this through her sister. I needn't tell her anything, and I didn't think she'd ask. In her shop, lights were burning downstairs as I pulled up beside the door. For once, however, the door was locked, and though I pounded the brass knocker no one answered. It was my bad luck to find Nan out, but that wasn't going to stop me.

I found my way to the house I had visited earlier. However, it was not Olive who opened the door, but a tall, rather gaunt woman, whom I took to be Olive's friend. She stood in the doorway, not inviting me in. "Olive's gone," she told me curtly. "She's been called away."

"Is she coming back?" I asked.

The woman shook her head. "She had a telephone call a little while ago. She packed up right away and a car came to take her to the train."

I tried to sound casual. "Do you happen to know who was in the car?"

"It was none of my business, was it?" She regarded me disapprovingly.

Discouragement engulfed me as I drove back to The Shingles. It didn't matter, really, that I had learned nothing from Olive. All that mattered now was that I leave tomorrow and make it my business never to see any of the Rhodes family again.

Lights still burned downstairs in Nan's shop when I went through the stone gateway, but I didn't stop. As the car swung around a turn, my headlights lit the driveway ahead to shine on two people walking in the dark with only a flashlight to guide them. It was Nan Kemble and Herndon Rhodes. He drew her quickly to one side and I leaned out the window to greet them, though I didn't stop.

I heard Nan's voice call after me as I continued on up to the garage area. I parked my car where it would be out of the way, turned off the ignition, and opened the door. Across the brick paving Tudor stirred and growled. I was thankful indeed that he was chained.

I began to walk past him, ready to give him a wide berth. But I had taken only a few steps before he began to bark furiously, leaping against his chain. He had been willing to let me leave, but was unwilling to have me return. Suddenly I knew the dog had changed his position. He was no longer chained. Then I heard the click of his feet on brick, coming fast. I screamed just as his weight struck me full in the back. I was thrown to my knees and he was upon me, worrying my body like a rag. I felt his breath, the wetness of his tongue—and then pain in my arm. I tried to fight him off with my other hand, but he was a thousand times stronger than I. I might have fainted from the hurt and left my face and throat unguarded, but distant voices roused me. Soon someone pulled Tudor off me, someone else was struggling to restrain him, and I was picked up in Evan's arms and carried into the house. There was a sofa in the hall, and he laid me upon it gently. Behind him, Judith's voice was calling for Helen Asher. In the background I could hear John's angry voice. "That chain was snapped! I just had a look at it and one of the links was damaged."

"You'll be all right now, Courtney," Evan said, smoothing the hair back from my forehead. His sympathy and the touch of his hand almost made me forget the pain in my arm. I was dimly aware of faces looking down at me. They were all there, even Stacia and Nan and Herndon.

Judith said, "It's probably not bad. I think her coat protected her. Helen, help me get her out of it."

Drawing my arm through the sleeve was painful, but my blouse had short sleeves and they didn't bother with that. I remembered my unicorn, thankful I had hung it out of sight at the back of my neck. Evan held me while they worked, and I found comfort in leaning against him and letting everything go.

"I'll let you take care of her, Helen, while I phone the doctor," Judith said. "Tudor's a healthy dog, but they'll want to treat the wound and give her tetanus shots, or whatever." She must have caught my look because she bent toward me. "Courtney, I wouldn't have had this happen for anything. I thought Tudor was safe out there."

Beyond her Stacia said, "He's a guard dog. You can't blame him. That's what he's there for."

"Who put the chain on him?" John asked, still sounding angry.

"I did," Herndon said. "It was in perfectly good shape. I examined every link to make sure. Nan and I heard the dog barking, Courtney, but we couldn't get here quickly enough."

At his shoulder Nan regarded me anxiously. I made a feeble effort to smile at them. "You came in time. Evan came in time."

Judith came back as Mrs. Asher finished working on my arm. "Dr. Grant will see you at his house. Will you take her, please, Herndon?"

"I'll go along," Nan said.

I could walk now, and Herndon helped me down the steps. Nan insisted that I lie down in the back seat of the car with my head in her lap, while Herndon drove. She steadied me so that the movement of the car wouldn't jar my arm, and when I went into the doctor's office, she came with me.

The wound was not serious, the doctor said. I would have a sore arm for a few days, and I'd better not drive. When I'd been properly disinfected, bandaged, and given a booster shot, Nan walked me back to the car, where Herndon waited. I sat up in the front seat, turning to look at Nan. "I tried to catch you this evening," I said, "but you must have been out. I'd hoped you might come with me when I went to see Olive Asher."

There was a brief silence in the car and then Nan spoke to Herndon. "Did you know Olive was back in town?"

"Of course," Herndon said. "We all knew. Asher recognized her voice on the phone. Why did you want to see her, Courtney?"

"Evan took me there this afternoon, but I thought there was more she might talk about. So after dinner I drove back."

Herndon turned his head briefly to glance at me. "Did you think she might be of help in writing about Judith?"

"I didn't know, but I wanted to find out."

"And what did you learn?"

"Nothing. She was gone—someone must have bribed her to leave town."

It seemed to me that the man beside me relaxed a little, and Nan's gasp was soft, half suppressed. "Never mind." She sighed. "It was all over and done with years ago. You don't want to know any more—in this case it's better to be an ostrich. I recommend the example to you, Courtney."

"I don't need the example," I assured her. "I'll probably go back to New York tomorrow."

"You can't drive with your arm in that condition," Herndon said.

"I think I had better go. Twice now someone has tried to kill me."

In the back seat Nan was very still, offering no argument. After a long silence, she spoke. "Why should anyone want to hurt you, Courtney?"

"Reasons aren't necessary. The fact of two attacks is enough for me."

When we reached the gatehouse, Herndon stopped the car and opened the door for Nan. "I'll phone tomorrow, Courtney," she said. "Come see me before you go back to New York."

We waited until Nan had used her key to go inside, then drove up to the house. As we reached the parking area, I threw a quick look around, but Tudor must have been fastened up somewhere else.

John and Judith came from the living room to meet us, but Evan wasn't around, and Stacia did not appear. Herndon assured them that my arm would be fine, and that all I needed was a good night's sleep.

Judith came upstairs with me, and I noted in surprise that a cot had been set outside my door. Inside the room Helen Asher was turning down my bed. "Helen will sleep beside your door tonight, Courtney," Judith said. "You may need something during the night."

I thanked her, refused an offer of help to get into my nightgown, and waited until both women were gone from my room. What a lovely family I had inherited, I thought, as I began to undress gingerly. I could feel homesick now for my *real* parents, who had adopted and loved me. How foolish I had been to come on this quest.

The pain capsules I'd been given by the doctor helped me to drop into a deep sleep. But at some time in the middle of the night I came wide awake. My arm had begun to throb and I slipped out of bed and went into the bathroom for a drink of water. Then I walked to a window, pulled back the draperies, and opened it.

Moonlight fell brightly upon beach and ocean, and the emptiness stretched for miles. But on the sand a shadow moved. Someone else who could not sleep was down there looking out across the ocean. The figure was too far away for me to tell whether it was a man or a woman.

Before I returned to bed, I crossed to my door and put my hand on the knob. I would open it just enough to make sure that my guardian still slept in the hall outside. I turned the knob, and through the narrow crack I could make out the sleeping form of Helen Asher on the cot, dimly lighted by a hall sconce.

As I started to close the door it suddenly resisted my touch and a slim hand came through the crack. Stacia stood there, blocking the door's closing. Her short, fair hair was tousled and she wore pajamas and a pink silk robe. The brightness of her eyes held me, and the smile on her lips that was only the mockery of a smile.

I was once more afraid.

CHAPTER SEVEN

"AREN'T YOU GOING TO invite me in?" Stacia asked.

My throat seemed to close and I couldn't even call out to Helen. I was more afraid of Stacia than I'd been of the dog—if that was possible—because here was evil undisguised.

"How silly of Mother to put Helen outside your door," she said lightly. "We all know she sleeps like the dead. Come on, Courtney—don't stand there staring. I want to talk to you."

The impression of evil faded a little in the face of her commonplace words. With difficulty I managed to speak. "What can we possibly talk about?"

"I should think quite a lot, cousin dear."

This time I challenged her. "For instance, that you tried to run me down in your mother's Mercedes? That you smashed a link of Tudor's chain, when you knew I would be coming back to the garage after dark?"

"Oh, come on, Courtney! What a vivid imagination you have. All I want to know is why you went streaking off to see Olive Asher tonight."

My first wave of frightened reaction was subsiding, but nevertheless I pushed past Stacia, out of the door, and bent over Helen Asher. "Wake up!" I said, and shook her by the shoulder.

She started under my hand and blinked in dismay to find us looking down at her. "Mrs. Judith said no one was to bother Miss Marsh tonight. You shouldn't be up here, Mrs. Faulkner," she said.

"Go back to sleep, Helen," Stacia said calmly. "I'm not going to hurt your patient."

Now that Helen was awake, I wasn't afraid anymore. "Just stay awake," I told her. I followed Stacia into the bedroom, leaving the door open a crack and turning on all the lights. Stacia flung herself into a chair and curled her legs beneath her, while I sat on the bed and pulled the covers over my legs. "All right," I said, my voice low. "What do you want?"

"I've told you. What did Olive Asher have to say?"

"Nothing. Someone had already gotten her out of town." I reminded myself that I was dealing with an irrationality that must go clear back to Stacia's childhood and all those venomously destroyed dolls. I tried to speak calmly. "What difference does it make now?"

" 'Those who are strong are the ones who are armed,' " she went on sententiously. "Your mother said that. It was in one of those dear little fairy tales she used to write."

"Why did you tear the pages from the back of her book?"

Her smile mocked me. "Those pages were just a little too revealing. I couldn't have them fall into her darling daughter's hands."

"What have you done with them?"

"Nothing drastic. They're in a safe place, where no one will think to look."

"Listen to me," I said. "Please pay attention. I'm going back to New York as soon as I can. I can't think of anything I want less to be than a long-lost heiress. I'll make a bargain with you. If you let Judith and Herndon keep this house, I'll never step into your lives again."

She smiled at me as sweetly as ever. "I'll think about it."

I hunched up my knees and hugged them with my good arm. "What does Lawrence Rhodes's will say that makes you think I might be the heir? Didn't he leave everything to you?"

"I don't suppose there's any secret about it now. Grandfather didn't want to leave everything to either of his sons, because he was angry with both of them. When he drew up his will he named no names. He didn't know that Alice was having a baby in Switzerland. So all he set down was that the first grandchild was to be his heir when she or he reached the age of twenty-five. When he did know about Alice's baby, I gather he was pleased, but he didn't change the wording. It referred to any child who happened to get born first in the family. So then, of course, when dear little Anabel disappeared, *I* became the first. I mean to stay first, Courtney. That's what I came here to tell you."

"You're welcome to the place," I said. "But if you're going to turn Judith out of this house, then perhaps I'd better hang on for a while. With a bodyguard around, of course."

She jumped up like the nervous little cat she was, and prowled the room. I hugged my knees and waited. At length she stopped opposite my bed, regarding me with wide blue eyes. "How can I trust you? How can I believe you mean what you say?"

Before I could answer, a woman's scream reached us through my open window—a sound shrill with terror. I was out of bed in a flash, but Stacia was ahead of me and we leaned out the window together. There had been only one scream, and then a flutter of small cries.

In the moonlight we could make out figures below, one of them lying prone on the terrace. Stacia turned from the window and ran toward the door. I caught up my robe, pulling it on as I went after her down the hall, past Helen Asher's empty cot.

When I ran through the living room and out onto the terrace, Stacia was well ahead of me. Asher was already there, wrapped in a woolly bathrobe, with a flashlight in his hand, while his wife knelt beside the limp figure silent on the stones.

Stacia dropped beside Helen Asher. "Uncle John!" she cried. "Uncle John, what's happened to you?"

Judith materialized beside us, wearing a long dark gown, her black hair hanging loose down her back. "What is it?" she demanded. "I heard someone scream. What's happened to John?"

"There's a lump on the back of his head, Mrs. Judith," Helen answered. "Somebody's struck him down from behind."

I moved to where I could see the side of John's white, cold face, and something stirred in me unexpectedly. This was my father.

Down the terrace, wooden steps creaked and Evan Faulkner came from the direction of the beach. He was dressed in slacks and a pullover, as though he'd been up for a long time. Judith told him quickly what had happened. Then she asked the others, "Who reached him first?"

"I did, madam," Asher said. "I don't know how long he was lying there. I went upstairs at once for my wife. When she saw him on the stones she screamed. After that, everyone came."

As if the voices speaking above him finally penetrated his consciousness, John moaned softly and put a hand to his head.

"Let's take him inside," Evan said.

He and Asher managed to get John up and to a couch in the living room. Stacia remained by his side, murmuring softly and now and then casting a deadly look around at the rest of us, as though we must be to blame. When John insisted upon sitting up, she knelt beside him to hold his hand, and he reached out somewhat shakily to touch her hair. As he would never touch mine, I thought, unexpectedly sad.

Evan bent to examine the lump at the back of John's head and then turned to Judith. "A blow like that could have killed him."

"Did you see who struck you, John?" Judith asked.

He started to shake his head, then groaned. "No, I didn't see a thing. I came out on the terrace around twelve because I couldn't sleep. I was sitting there, smoking, when something hit me. I don't remember anything else."

"I know why you were struck, Uncle John," Stacia said.

We all stared at her. "What are you talking about?" Evan demanded.

She gave him a spiteful look. "Someone tried to kill him because he knows about that time when Alice died. Doesn't he, Judith? He knows why Alice died by drowning that time out in Montauk!"

Even under such circumstances, Judith managed to look unruffled—a tall figure in her dark gown. She regarded her daughter for a quiet moment before she spoke. "Yes, Stacia. I believe he does know. Perhaps it would be wiser if he would tell what he knows and be rid of the secret."

John moaned again, concerned only with the racking pain in his skull.

"Where is Herndon?" Judith asked. "His bed was empty. He must have stayed up late, or wandered off somewhere because he couldn't sleep."

Evan went out to the terrace to look around. Judith busied herself getting aspirin for John, finding a blanket to throw over him, sending

Helen for a pillow and warm water to bathe the wound. Stacia remained where she was, kneeling on the floor, clinging to John's hand.

I had dropped into a chair in a far corner of the room, feeling even more shaken than I'd been earlier. There *was* evil abroad in this house—not merely in the person of Stacia, but somewhere else as well.

Before Evan came back from his search, Herndon walked in, like Evan fully dressed, even to his usual bright vest. The news about John seemed to strike him like a blow and he bent over his brother. I had never seen any affection between the two, but now when the older brother opened his eyes, Herndon spoke to him gently. "You must have some notion about what happened, John," he said. "We need to know who did this."

John looked up at Herndon. "If I knew, would I say?" he asked.

Herndon stepped back from the couch and walked gravely over to Judith. "Shall we call the police?"

"No! Certainly not." Judith was positive. "He needs a doctor, not the police. You know what a scandal there would be."

Old Lawrence Rhodes had trained them well, I thought, to close ranks and protect the family.

Evan came back from his search outside and saw Herndon in the room, but neither he nor the others asked where Herndon had been, or why he had gone out walking at such an hour. After all, Evan had been out too. Restless men walked abroad at night, I guessed. Both were married, both had wives beneath this roof, yet they walked abroad lonely by moonlight.

"I think you should all go to bed," Herndon told us. "I'll light the fire and stay here with John tonight."

Once more John opened his eyes. "Play for me, Stacia. Something gentle. Perhaps it will help me fall asleep." Stacia jumped to her feet and walked to the piano. She ran her fingers over the keys. The last thing I wanted tonight was to hear Stacia's playing.

I left my chair and went quickly through the door toward the stairs. As I reached the landing, Evan came up behind me. "I'll see you to your room," he told me. "You're looking rocky—and with good reason."

I gave up trying to be strong and invulnerable and leaned on his arm as we went up the stairs. "I'll have to stay another day," I said. "I won't be able to drive home tomorrow."

"I'll drive you to New York whenever you want to go. Do you have anyone to stay with you there?"

I shook my head. "There's no one now."

"I don't think you should be alone trying to take care of yourself," Evan said. "Not for a few days, at least. But I know you want to get away from this house for a while. . . . Why not come with me for a sail tomorrow?"

"With this?" I touched my bandaged arm.

"You won't have to do a thing. I know an empty beach we can sail to, where you can lie on the sand in the sun, and not be afraid. You have been afraid, haven't you?"

"Of course. I seem to have become a target."

His look hardened. "That will stop. You're not to be left alone again. I shall tell Judith that. Will you come with me tomorrow?"

He was once more as he'd been when we were together in his car, and when we reached my door I smiled my gratitude. I needed to be alone with Evan away from the house, where I could talk to him. He was the one person I could trust and I was going to tell him everything. "There's nothing I'd like better," I said.

He put a hand gently against my cheek, cupping it for just an instant. It was the lightest of caresses—but it *was* a caress, and I didn't move away. Then, as quickly, he stepped back and waited until I'd entered my room.

When he'd gone, I turned out all the lamps but one, and got into bed. I put my hand against the cheek Evan had touched. What would happen when we were alone tomorrow? What did I want to happen, and what still lay between Evan and Stacia? Was I heading straight for a greater hurt than I'd ever known?

When I awakened the next morning, the sun was long up and the scent of frizzling bacon drifted through the house. I thought first, not of my arm and the dog's attack, not of John lying on the terrace, but of the fact that I was going sailing with Evan Faulkner. I dressed and went downstairs to the kitchen, where Asher and his wife were having breakfast.

"Have you seen Mr. Faulkner this morning?" I asked.

"Yes, miss," Asher replied. "He is working in the library. And he has already asked Mrs. Judith about taking out the *Anabel*."

I went to the dining room, and was eating hot buttered toast, heaped with East Hampton's specialty, beach plum jam, when Judith came into the room. She sat down at the table near me.

"How is your arm, Courtney? Would you like me to drive you to the doctor's before you go sailing with Evan?"

"It's feeling better, thank you," I said. "I'll wait and see him tomorrow, when he'll need to change the bandage."

She played idly with a silver saltshaker, her fingers not quite so relaxed as her bearing. "It's a long time since I've been out in the *Anabel*," she went on. "Years ago, John used to take me sometimes. Herndon never cared much for sailing."

"How is John this morning?" I asked.

"Nothing keeps John down. He's up and around as though nothing occurred."

"What does he say about what happened last night?"

She regarded me brightly. "I'm afraid Helen led us into jumping to a wrong conclusion. This morning John says he must have fallen and struck his head on the flagstones. He says he'd been drinking all evening." Which meant she wasn't going to tell me anything, that the ranks were firmly closed. She pushed back from the table and rose.

"I expect it's safer to believe that," I said. "Even though he was lying face down. Just as it's safer to believe that it was an accident when a car tried to run me down, and another accident when Tudor broke his chain."

"All accidents—of course, my dear. What else could they possibly be?" Judith gave me her slight, lovely smile and walked out of the room.

THE DRIVE TO Sag Harbor in Evan's car was pleasant, and when we reached it we parked and walked along the streets so he could show me the lovely old houses. Evan knew the history of the town, and he relished the stories he had to tell. Finally we walked down to the harbor, and Evan pointed out the *Anabel* anchored out in the water.

When we were aboard, Evan helped me into the cockpit, where I was able to sit comfortably and rest my arm. I had tied my hair back from my face with a red scarf to match my sweater, and I felt free—ready to run with the wind like the boat itself.

We used the engine to get out into the bay, and then Evan tied the tiller so he could set the sails. With the noisy vibrations of the motor stopped and water slapping against the *Anabel*, I felt lulled and enchantingly relaxed. As we glided swiftly across the water I watched the man who handled this lovely winged thing so skillfully. He seemed more natural than I had ever seen him. He too had needed this escape.

We talked very little. Islands and land, inlets and houses along the shore, seemed remote and unreal. There was only the sun and the sea and our *Anabel*. Eventually we dropped anchor off an empty beach. "There were visitors here during the summer," Evan said, "but there'll be no one around now."

We got into the dinghy we'd towed behind us and rowed into shallow water, where Evan jumped out barefoot and pulled the small boat farther onto the sand. I took off my shoes, rolled up my slacks, and then jumped down into Evan's arms. He steadied me, released me, and walked beside me along clean, damp sand that felt firm and cool beneath my feet.

Evan made a small cache of our possessions, our lunch and the jackets we didn't need, piled on the sand. For a while we walked along the beach together, not talking at first, but hand in hand—as if that were the only proper way to walk a beach. It was all so beautiful, so utterly peaceful. Yet it wasn't possible for me to relax. I knew I must let myself go and tell Evan everything. How to start was the problem. Perhaps there would be a way if I got Evan to talk a little first, and I began tentatively, "You grew up around here, didn't you? What was it like?"

"It was wonderful. I could be outdoors all the time—summer and winter. My father was what they called a naturalist then. He knew all about ecology before the word became so common."

"And your mother?"

"She was a social science teacher in our local high school. She's retired now and lives with a sister out in Colorado. My father died when I was ten, but he taught me a great deal before that time."

"You were lucky," I said.

Something in my tone caught his attention. He led the way up the beach to dry sand and we dropped down on it together. "What does that mean?" he asked. "That I was lucky? What about you?"

It was easy now. "I was adopted when I was about two months old and taken to live in a small town in Connecticut. I meant that you were lucky to have your own real parents. But I couldn't have had a better mother and father, and I loved them very much."

He caught the past tense. "What happened?"

"They died last July. In a train crash in Italy."

"I'm sorry." His hand reached for mine. "I remember what it was like when my father died, without warning, of a heart attack."

"I've been floundering ever since."

"That's not exactly the impression you give."

"I'm good at bluffing," I said. It was time to open up the whole subject, yet I still wasn't ready. Instead, I asked a question I hadn't meant to ask—at least not yet. "Have you always known Stacia?"

The peaceful spell was gone, and I had banished it. Evan picked up a bit of broken shell and tossed it in one hand. "As you must have noticed, there's no marriage left between Stacia and me. When I've finished this effort to preserve the Rhodes collection, and done what I can to save the house for Judith and Herndon, I'll go out to Montauk to live near the lab."

"Does Stacia know?"

"She knows, but she hasn't accepted it yet. She never lets go of anything she thinks belongs to her."

"Has she always been like that—I mean, the way she seems to be now?"

"Judith says she has, but yet—"

His voice gentled, and I knew he was looking back to the Stacia he had known in the beginning. How beautiful and desirable she must have been. I had seen the occasional flashes that sparked between them, and I wondered if a man like Evan ever got over a woman like Stacia.

"We won't talk about her," he said, suddenly curt. "It's over. I just wanted you to know."

"Thank you," I said, and my own voice was so low I could hardly hear the words. In spite of his tone, I had to acknowledge this tentative reaching out between us. This was a strong man who had been bitterly hurt.

"I've tried to talk to Judith and Herndon," he went on. "Judith accepts what's irrevocable. She's even encouraged me to break away. Herndon turns back from reality, never willing to face anything."

I knew so much less about any of these people than Evan did. "Of course I can't know Herndon as you do," I said, "but I sense a greater complexity than that. I don't think Judith has given him as much as he has given her."

"That's true enough. But when it comes to a talent like Judith's, perhaps it's right for her to take whatever she can to nurture it."

"Do you really believe that?" I asked.

"I've taught myself to believe it."

"That doesn't make it true. Though I used to think that too. Ambition was the law I lived by, the thing that drove me. I couldn't understand compromise. But I was always searching for something more."

"Searching for what, Courtney?"

"For my family—my natural parents. Do you know what it's like—not ever knowing, looking into faces you pass on the street and wondering if this one, or perhaps that one, is related to you?"

"I suppose I've never thought about it," he said gently.

I went on, trying to make him understand. "Adopted children haven't any *past*. The things most children grow up with—stories about Grandpa Bob and Aunt Judy and all the rest—aren't really ours. The relatives we hear about, we didn't come from *them*."

"Yes," he said. "Yes, I'm beginning to see."

"It's all taken for granted with those who have families. But not with me, or the others like me. From the time we're children we ache to know. We think the answers will give us everything. And by the time we find out, we may be left adrift again and unable to go back to what we had before. That's what's happened to me."

"You have found out then?"

I turned to meet his eyes. "Yes, I've found out. That's why I came to East Hampton."

Realization dawned in him slowly. "The Rhodeses? Do you mean—are you the baby Judith gave away?"

I answered him starkly. "Yes, I am. I can't find any reason to doubt it. Evan, how long have you known that the baby didn't die?"

He found it difficult to speak. "I didn't know until yesterday, when Judith sent us out to talk to Olive Asher. I'd believed, along with everyone else, that the story of the baby's drowning was true. But Judith didn't tell me that *you*—"

"I'm not sure she knows. About me, that is."

He went on as though I hadn't spoken. "That *you* are Anabel. And Stacia is your cousin. Which makes John and Alice—" He seemed too stunned to go on.

"Yes to all of that," I said. "I've wanted to tell you. But somehow there

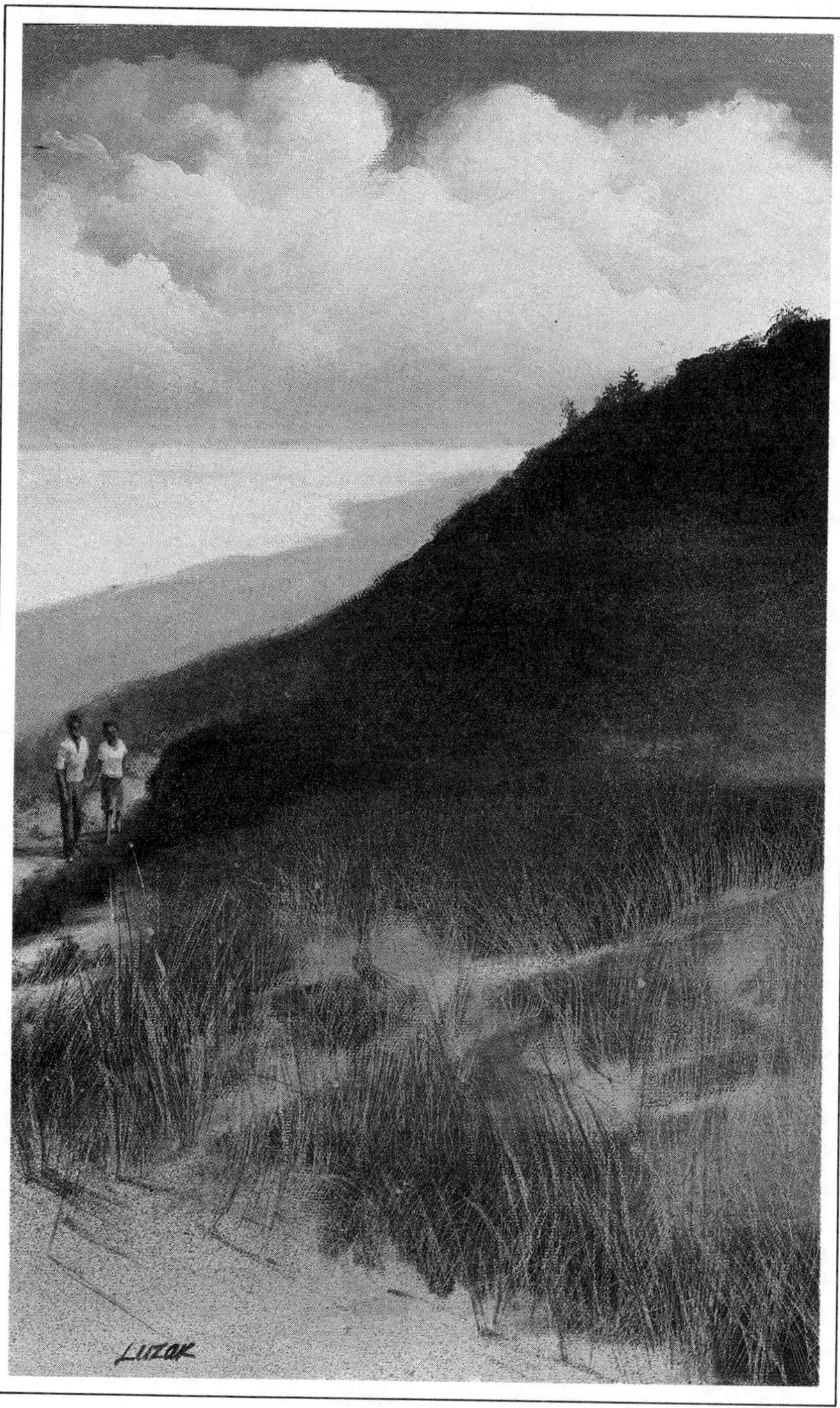
LUZAK

was never the right time or opportunity." The air around us seemed to stir, as if somewhere out on the clear waters of the bay a storm was brewing, sweeping inland, sending a cold breath ahead.

"I see," he said, and now the chill was in his voice. "So you are the heiress Judith wants to use to defeat Stacia. What proof do you have?"

I drew the little unicorn from about my neck and showed it to him. I told him of the leads I'd found, and of the way everything seemed to add up.

"So you came to The Shingles to spy on us, to see if we would suit you."

The lash of his words made me angry. "What else could I do? How could I know ahead of time if any of my leads were true? Please try to understand."

"I am trying. But taking advantage of people who are hospitable and innocent has always been something I've detested." He stood up abruptly. "Let's eat that lunch and start for home."

We retraced our steps in the damp sand to where we'd left our things, and I could feel tears of anger and frustration starting, though I blinked them back indignantly. When we reached our possessions, I opened the lunch box with fingers that shook a little, spread the cloth that had been enclosed, set out food and the thermos of coffee.

"Who else knows about this?" he asked, picking up a sandwich.

"Stacia and John know. Stacia found the unicorn in my room and showed it to John yesterday. Whether anyone else knows, I haven't been able to tell. Anyway, Stacia doesn't believe I mean it when I say I only want to go back to New York and never see any of the Rhodeses again."

"It doesn't really matter what she believes, does it? Once Judith institutes her search for the lost Anabel, the trail will lead to you—if that's who you are. And you can't sidestep an inheritance. So you're probably quite safe."

I could hardly swallow for the anger that rose in me. "I would hate to be like you! I'd hate never to trust or believe in anyone! I'd hate not to know honesty when I see it!"

"Honesty? You?" His laughter seemed to crack around the edges. "I was right in my first estimation of you when I watched that television show. You've lived up to everything I thought about you then."

I started to cry. But I tried not to let him see. I jumped up and began busily to collect the things we would take home with us, folded the trash into a paper bag, packed away the uneaten food. And all the while tears wet my cheeks and I had to rub them away surreptitiously so as not to be reduced to complete humiliation. Of course he saw anyway, and ignored them—for which at least I was grateful. Yet strangely, even in my anger, I understood something of why he reacted as he did. Stacia had left her mark on him. He would never easily trust a woman again.

There was no comradeship between us when we returned to the *Anabel*.

My tears, at least, were spent, but something fresh, a newborn part of me, had been wrenched away.

No, not wrenched away. If only it could be! This deep new pain was something I would have to live with from now on. Here, beside him in the *Anabel*, I knew what loving would be like when I'd have to love alone. At every turn I would think of him. Almost anything at all would remind me of my loss, and my self-sufficient life in an empty apartment would never again satisfy me. Work might become an anesthetic, numbing me as time passed. The moment I could handle a steering wheel I would leave, because here the reality of Evan's presence and the knowledge of how he despised me would be too much to bear.

The afternoon was graying by the time we reached Evan's car and drove back to The Shingles. Only bare courtesies had been exchanged between us. But he did give me a warning before I got out of the car. "Be careful," he told me. "If I'd known earlier what I do now, I'd have urged you to go back to New York today. You must leave tomorrow at the latest. I can drive you in your own car, and return by train."

"That won't be necessary," I said, wanting only to be away from him. "I'll leave the minute I can drive myself." Before he could say anything more, I got out and ran up to my room, where I busied myself with whatever came to hand, trying to ignore the double hurt tormenting me. The physical soreness of my arm was the lesser of the two. I took Alice's notebook from the drawer and sat down near a window. As I opened it to the flyleaf, the name Alice Kemble Rhodes confronted me in strong handwriting. My mother's writing. I touched the page where her hand had rested, seeking. I closed my eyes, but Alice Rhodes remained a misty figure.

I began to read the stories again, this time more carefully. When I got to the eighth story—the one that came just before pages had been torn out—I realized it was different. I sensed that the writer had been trying to say something through the indirection of fiction. This tale was about the Princess Anabel, granddaughter of the Great King. A princess who would one day come into a magnificent heritage, providing she found the answer to three questions that her grandfather had put to her. Young Anabel lacked the answers, it seemed, but her mother, the Princess Royal, was very wise, and she could tell her daughter all she must do to please the king.

I knew there must be allegory here, knew that Alice had been playing with bits of truth mixed into her make-believe. However, before I could discover what had been intended, the story stopped abruptly—with the rest of the pages torn out. At least I had come upon the name Anabel again, a name that had had significance for Alice. I must find out more about it. The best person to tell me was Alice's sister, Nan.

I wanted to take no walks alone, but I could surely drive as far as the gatehouse. I returned the notebook to its drawer and left my room.

CHAPTER EIGHT

THE AFTERNOON HAD DARKENED still more, though the garage lights had not yet been turned on, and the area was shadowy. Just as I was about to get into my car, I caught a movement near the shrubbery that grew beside the steps, and Stacia stepped out. Walking beside her, his leash in her hand, was Tudor, massive in his Great Dane's dignity—and totally alarming to me. "Don't worry," Stacia said as she approached. "He's always obedient. See—he isn't even growling at you."

"Just take him away," I said.

"Are you all that fearful? When I'm right here holding on to him?"

I asked the old question of her again. "Was it you who smashed the link in his chain so he could break loose?"

She smiled at me sweetly, her blue eyes wide. "What if it was?"

"And it *was* you who drove the Mercedes and tried to run me down?"

"Not really," she said. "Oh, I was driving the car all right, but I wouldn't have hit you. I'd have braked in time. Honestly, Courtney, I only wanted to frighten you away. Did you enjoy your day of sailing with Evan?"

I heard the note of spite in her voice, but I managed to answer quietly. "It was a lovely day for a sail, and the *Anabel* is a beautiful boat."

"Isn't she though? I've sailed her myself a good many times. But I don't want you to go sailing in her again. You'd better remember that Evan is mine." She was coming into the open now, admitting to her own dangerous tricks and ready to threaten me further.

"When I leave here," I said, "I don't expect to see any of you ever again."

"I hope that's true. But I didn't come find you for chitchat. Judith asked me to give you a message. She'd like you to come to her studio as soon as you can. You've been neglecting the job you came here for, haven't you, Courtney?" She waited for no answer, but turned Tudor around and walked down the drive, the dog moving proudly at her side.

I would have to postpone my visit with Nan. Judith's summons had to be respected.

When I reached the attic she was working at her easel. I paused in the doorway. "Stacia said you wanted me."

Her smile of greeting seemed melancholy. "Yes, I thought we might continue if you have any questions you'd like to ask. I understand that you'll be leaving us soon." She motioned to a chair she had placed nearby.

I sat down, and noticed that the chair had been placed so I couldn't see the canvas on her easel. I shifted to a better vantage point in order to watch her at work. The sight of her new painting chilled me. In the center of the canvas floated a large head with staring blue eyes and a mouth fixed in a smile as set as concrete. The face was Stacia's. A Stacia-doll. The effect was eerie and disturbing.

"What do you think?" she asked, glancing around at me.

"I—don't know. What are you planning for the background?"

"More heads! A hundred more dolls' heads—watching her! The way all of us watch her now—because she's about to affect our lives. Unless you can stop her, Courtney."

"I?"

"Are you wearing your little golden unicorn now, Courtney?"

So she knew, and I could only wonder how long she had known.

"Alice put it around your neck soon after you were born. She wanted it to be yours. I felt superstitious about taking it off. I never thought it would identify you. John told me how Stacia brought it to him after you came. You've played quite a deception on us, haven't you, Courtney? All this pretense of wanting to write about me—"

"Why did you do it?" I broke in. "Why did you give me away?"

"It isn't necessary to go into that old story. Let it be forgotten." She bent toward her canvas, putting a touch more crimson on one cheek of the Stacia-doll.

I wouldn't be dismissed like that. "Forgotten! How can you say that?"

"It seemed the only thing to do at the time," Judith said, her real attention on the canvas.

"So your own unborn baby could be Lawrence's heir?"

She turned toward me without resentment, paintbrush in hand. "There were other reasons, but I suppose that was the main one. But giving you away wasn't good for us in the long run—not when you consider Stacia as she is now." Bright green eyes regarded me calmly. "Stacia poisons everything she touches. She destroys. But you are going to stop her, aren't you, Courtney?"

"I'm not going to do anything!" I said sharply. "All I want is to go away and never see any of you again."

"Do you know"—she spoke lightly, turning back to her canvas—"you could have been my daughter instead of Alice's. That is, if I had married John, if I had left Herndon." Another head was taking shape beneath her quick brush—a small one floating beyond the large central face.

A sick revulsion shook me. I didn't want any of them. My search had come to nothing and I wished I had never made it, leaving undisturbed the memory of Gwen and Leon, whom I loved and who had loved me.

"Do you think I haven't suffered over the years?" she went on quietly. "Suffered for all those things I couldn't tell anyone? Only Olive Asher knew, because I had to have her help."

"And she's been blackmailing you all this time?"

"I never thought of it that way. I gave her small sums out of gratitude, and she was satisfied—until I stopped."

"Mind if I come in?" asked a voice from the doorway, and John Rhodes walked into the room.

"Come in," Judith said. "Perhaps you'd like to sit beside your daughter and watch me while I paint?"

John raised an eyebrow. "It's all out in the open now?"

I nodded. "How are you feeling?"

"Never better. But I may have been mistaken about falling." He looked straight at Judith. "It seems that a weapon has turned up in the shrubbery along the terrace—a long wrench from the garage. Evan seems to be sure that it's what struck me down. Though which one of my affectionate family used it, there's no telling."

He walked around me and stood where he could see the canvas. "That's an ugly thing," he said. "Don't finish it, Judith."

"Why not? I have an ugly child!" Without warning, her serenity cracked like splitting silk and she whirled to fling her paintbrush across the studio. Then she ran to the little oasis of furniture and threw herself on the couch, her head on her arms, sobbing convulsively.

I made a move to go to her, but John put his hand on my arm. "Let her cry. She's been bottling everything up for too many years. Let it all spill out."

"I can't take on what Judith wants. I don't want it—not at all."

"Nevertheless it's inevitable, my dear."

"Whose side are you on?" I demanded. "What is it *you* want?"

"I don't think I've ever found that out for sure," he said. "And as for whose side I'm on—always my own, young Courtney. You'll have to accept that."

I stayed where I was, aware of the touch of his hand on my arm, while I looked up into the sadness in his eyes. *My father*, I thought. Startling myself as greatly as I startled him, I kissed his cheek lightly, then ran toward the door, away from the sound of Judith's sobbing.

On the way to my room I met Stacia. She was carrying a cardboard carton. "See what I have, Courtney." She smiled sweetly.

Reluctantly I looked into the box and saw all the little heads staring up at me, rattling against each other as she shook the box. "What are you doing with those?" I asked.

"My mother isn't going to need these anymore when she moves away from this house. So I mean to give them a proper burial. Perhaps a burial at sea." She laughed lightly and started past me.

More than a little distressed, I went to my room and lay down on the bed, wanting only to close my eyes and shut everything away. After a little while the hurt in my arm seemed to surmount everything else, and I got up to take some capsules. I wouldn't go down to dinner, I decided. I couldn't face any of them at the table. Tomorrow I would leave—somehow. I put on my nightgown and got into bed. Rain beat at the windows and whispered a lullaby. I touched the unicorn at my throat. In spite of everything, it was comforting to know that it had been my mother's hands that placed it about my neck. When I fell asleep, my pillow was damp beneath my cheek.

Awakening to a gray morning, I got stiffly out of bed to look from a window. It was no longer raining, but fog had come in from the ocean and drifted in wisps that obscured the beach.

When I went down to breakfast, they were all there at the table except Stacia, who was apparently sleeping late. Judith smiled at me with a forced cheeriness and I mumbled a "Good morning" in response. Evan gave me one quick glance, then seemed to dismiss my existence. I fought back the stab of pain. John and Herndon were engaged in some interfamily argument and paid me little attention. I was glad enough not to be noticed until I'd finished my first cup of coffee. Then I made my announcement. "I'm going home today," I said.

They all looked at me. "But your arm, Courtney," Judith said. "You can't possibly drive."

"I'll take a train. I don't need my car in the city. If you don't mind, I'll leave it here until I can come back for it."

Then Herndon spoke. "Apparently I have been the last to be told who you are, Courtney. I wish you had come to me with the truth at once, so that you could have been given a happier welcome."

"I've had quite enough welcome in this house," I told him stiffly. "All I want is to go home."

"But there are legal matters to take care of," he went on, "and a final identification to be made. You really must stay for a few days more."

"You don't seem to understand," I said. "I don't want Stacia's inheritance. I'm not Anabel Rhodes. I'm Courtney Marsh. If you think I'm going to cooperate with you in any way, you're mistaken."

"I don't think you have much choice," John put in quietly. "Stay and see it through. It will be harder if you run away."

"In any case," Herndon said, "you exist and you *are* here now, Courtney. You can't change the circumstances."

Only Evan was not a Rhodes, and I turned to him in pleading. No matter how much he disliked me, he was the only one who could help me now. He was stirring his coffee, but he must have sensed my silent entreaty. "I'll drive you back to the city, Courtney. But not until this afternoon. I have to go out to the lab this morning for something that's just come up."

"I won't be here when you get back," I said. "Not even if I have to take a taxi to New York!"

"Then come with me to Montauk," he said, suddenly fixing me with a look down the table, his eyes dark with determination. "Stay at the lab with me for the morning, and this afternoon I'll drive you back to the city."

I was caught. I wanted to get away from Evan Faulkner, more than any of the others. Yet I wanted to be with him too. While I was being pulled by my own ambivalence, Judith spoke up cheerfully. "I know what! We'll all go with you, Evan. I haven't been out to the Point on a picnic for years. It will be lovely!"

We stared at her in astonishment. This was Judith Rhodes, the recluse, speaking. Judith, who seldom left the shelter of The Shingles. What was she up to now? Why was she suddenly determined that Evan and I shouldn't go out to Montauk alone?

Herndon looked pleased over the suggestion. "A good idea. Since it's Saturday, I can go with you. Perhaps you can do some sketching, Judith."

"I'm tired of sketching, tired of painting. I just want a change!"

Herndon reached out to touch her hand. "Then you shall have it."

"Are we taking Stacia along?" I asked.

"No," said Herndon firmly. "Let her sleep this morning."

There was no telling whether Evan was pleased or not by this intrusion on his plans, but he offered no objection. As soon as Judith finished her breakfast, she went out to the kitchen to supervise the hurried preparation of a lunch to take along. Thus the die was cast and the steps begun that would lead to an ending we never expected.

While I was dressing in warmer slacks and a sweater, and binding my hair back with a flowing green scarf that left its ends trailing down my back—while I was doing all these ordinary and prosaic things, something new and determined came to life in me. I too began to make a plan.

From the first there had been an air of suppressing the truth about what had happened on the beach in Montauk. The cottage must still be there. Perhaps I could get Evan to take me to it from the Point. What I could possibly find in this house on an empty stretch of beach, I had no idea. Nothing would be left to tell me anything of my mother's death—yet there was in me a new urgency to see both the beach and the house.

FALL IS OFTEN the best of all seasons on Long Island, and September had been living up to the pattern until yesterday's rain and this morning's fog. There were hurricane warnings, but the storm was still far south off the Carolinas and there was hope that it would lose itself at sea.

No one talked as we set out now, and the atmosphere inside the car was hardly the gay one of a family household starting off on a picnic. Because he had put me there, I was in the front seat beside Evan, with the other three in back. I stole a guarded sidewise look at Evan, memorizing details against the time when he wouldn't be beside me ever again.

There was an end-of-the-world look about the far tip of Long Island. The country around was still a little wild, and the town of Montauk had the appearance of being set down in the midst of a sandy wilderness of scrub growth. Evan turned down a side road, where we checked in with the guard at the gates of the New York Ocean Science Laboratory. The area was located on Fort Pond Bay, and had its own pier, a seaplane hangar, helicopter pad, and numerous long, low buildings set out rather bleakly on the sandy earth like a government installation, which it once had been.

Evan and I got out, and the others followed. As we walked toward a smaller building that stood apart from the rest, Judith hung back. "I don't like the smell of fish," she said, and the other two stayed behind with her.

I followed Evan inside, into a long room that did indeed smell strongly of fish. With an absorbed interest that I'd never seen before, he began pointing out various lobsters in their glass tanks. "This little girl is special," he said, designating one lobster in a tank alone. "You can see that she's molted. Her old shell is completely gone and we've given her a hollow pipe to crawl into for protection. In the ocean this would be a dangerous time, since a lobster can easily be attacked before its new shell hardens."

Evan walked on. "We're working on a way to farm lobsters on a large scale—a good food shouldn't be an expensive luxury for the few."

He was on his own ground, at home and thoroughly involved, and my understanding of him began to expand. Outdoors again, we crossed a wide road and entered another building, where there was a huge model showing tides and currents. The scope of the laboratory was vast. Biological and physical sciences of the sea, aquaculture programs, studies of shoreline erosion—the list was endless, the promise enormous. And I could see that Evan was playing an active, creative role in much that was going on.

Inside the building that housed the auditorium, we walked along an empty corridor, with the place to ourselves since it was Saturday. I became aware that Evan was watching me and looked up to meet his eyes. "I made some pretty strong accusations when we last talked, Courtney," he said. "I've been regretting them. I've had too much experience in distrusting and judging harshly, and I'm not sure I'll ever get over being that way. But that's no excuse for the things I said."

I didn't want apologies from him. "It doesn't matter. I understand."

"I wonder if you do. I'd like you to understand—about Stacia, for one thing."

Stacia was someone I didn't want to understand. I took abrupt refuge in the proposal I'd been waiting to make. "Evan, that house—the one that used to be owned by Nan Kemble's mother—isn't it located somewhere around here?"

He halted our progress down the corridor, regarding me intently. "Yes—that's right."

"I'd like to go there," I said hurriedly. "Will you take me, Evan?"

"Why do you want to visit that place?"

"After today I have to forget everything connected with the Rhodeses and the Kembles. This is my last chance."

"It's occupied, you know," he said. "And don't be surprised if the others oppose your doing this. Perhaps you'd better not say anything ahead of time. We'll try after lunch."

He left me to go into an office on the errand that had brought him here, and I sat on a bench in the corridor to wait. Soon he returned, and we walked back to the car. I saw that Judith was resting in the back seat, while Herndon and John paced the road nearby, their heads bent in earnest conversation. What were they plotting? I wondered suspiciously.

"Let's go out to the lighthouse at the Point and have our lunch," Judith suggested as we reached the car. No one objected, and Evan took the road east out of town. The land rolled on either hand in low hills to the dunes, overgrown with pines and grasses.

The red sandstone lighthouse at Montauk Point is one of the most photographed and painted scenes on Long Island. It has stood for nearly two hundred years, and the foghorn still marks land and danger for the seafarer. At the Point, we left the car and walked toward the tower rising before us in grace and strength. The earlier fog had lifted and the sea was dotted with small fishing boats. In the far distance, Block Island was visible. Evan pointed out these things to me, and his mood continued friendly, though impersonal.

When we'd found a place to sit not far from the tower, Judith began to unpack our lunch, with Herndon helping her. This was hardly a happy outing, and I wondered again why Judith had put this plan together so impulsively. Evan and I sat on a grassy patch, apart from the others, and though Judith glanced doubtfully our way now and then, no one said anything.

As we ate I tried to put a few more thoughts into words—just for Evan's ear. "I suppose nothing ever matches what we imagine ahead of time. Such stories I used to build up as a child! All about accidental meetings where I would find my real parents, even my grandparents, and we would know and love each other instantly." Evan nodded. Though his eyes were on a distant fishing boat, I sensed his understanding.

"And now I've found that my mother is dead, and I'll never be close to my father," I went on. "Stacia is more his daughter than I could ever be. Blood doesn't keep people from being strangers."

"Nor does marriage, Courtney." Evan stirred beside me. "Will you listen if I try to tell you something?"

I found myself stiffening, fearful of hurt. But I said, "I'll listen."

"I did love her, you know. I wanted a marriage that would last, and I didn't realize that she would never change, never grow. Perhaps it was my fault that I was able to have so little effect on her. There's still feeling between us. Rage, I'm sure, something close to hatred at times—nothing I'm proud of. Whatever it is, it's not love."

There was nothing for me to say, and I dared not speak.

"Do you know what I see when I look at you, Courtney?"

I shook my head, not meeting his eyes.

"I see a young woman with an appealing vulnerability, with a mind of her own, with talent. A woman with a longing to love and to be loved. A woman who would, I think, be loyal and truthful, and generous, if ever she loved. A woman I have become very fond of. I'm not sure I'm ready to love again, Courtney, but if we were alone and in a different place, I know I'd want you in my arms. Would you come, Courtney?"

I looked at him then, through tears that I couldn't hold back. "I'd come," I said.

He held out his hand and I put my own in his. His clasp was warm and I could return it—as though it were a kiss, an embrace. A beginning had been made between us.

"If we're to stop at that cottage on the way back, we'd better leave now," he said, releasing my hand. "It's on the north shore of Montauk and off the main road."

I packed up our things and got to my feet. Evan stood up beside me. "Courtney," he said, "when you get back to New York—what then?"

"I resigned from my job, but I think they'll take me on again."

"Why did you resign?"

"I didn't want that sort of life anymore. I was going to work on a book. I meant to free-lance and live away from the city. But it's no use. I have to go back to work at a job so I can forget what has happened to me here."

Judith called to us then, and there was no more time left to explain. We picked up our things, and when we returned to the car, Judith gave us a brief, curious glance.

Evan drove fast on the way back, not slowing until we came to a side road and turned north to follow it. Judith stirred in the back seat. "Where are you going, Evan?" Her voice was suddenly sharp.

"Courtney wants to visit the Kemble cottage."

"No!" The cry was explosive. "No, I won't allow her to go there! Turn back, Evan."

Evan kept on his way, deaf to her words.

I looked around at Judith. "Why don't you want me to see this place?"

"It's—it's a place with terrible memories. I don't want to go there, and I should think you, of all people, would want to avoid it, Courtney."

"It's where my mother died, isn't it? Why shouldn't I see it?"

"I think we should go back," Herndon put in quietly. "If Judith doesn't want this—"

John made a derisive sound. "She's not that fragile. And what does it matter at this late date?"

Judith turned to him with an urgency that seemed all the more disturbing because it was uncharacteristic. "But there's the possibility—" she began.

"Don't," John said. "Let what will happen, happen. It doesn't matter now. And sooner or later Courtney will have to know."

Judith sank back in her seat and it was alarming to see that she could appear so terrified of the place. What had she been hiding all these years? What had really happened there?

Before long, Evan turned off onto a narrow, sandy road running toward the water, and we drew up before an old-fashioned Victorian structure with a wide veranda and much gingerbread carving. As Evan and I left the car I saw a mailbox out in front that bore the name Kemble. The sight startled me; surely there were no Kembles living here now!

When I stopped at the sight of the box, Evan held out his hand. "Come along," he said. "This may be a test for you. You wanted to see this place, so you'd better face whatever it holds."

We went up the steps together, but I stopped Evan before he rang the bell. "Wait—let me look around a little."

I walked toward the sharp angle of the veranda to the side stretch that overlooked the water, and came to a halt. A woman sat with her back to us—a woman in a wheelchair. I could see by her profile that she was old—perhaps near eighty, with hair gone completely white and cut short. She sat wrapped in a voluminous gray shawl, staring out at the water.

Evan stood back, letting me do as I chose, now that I was here. I stepped around to be within the line of her eyes and spoke to her gently. "Hello," I said. "I'm Courtney Marsh, and I've been visiting the Rhodeses in East Hampton. I believe my mother, Alice Kemble, lived in this house at one time, and I wanted to see it before I go back to New York."

Her gaze remained fixed on some distant horizon and she made no response. Was she blind, deaf? I glanced at Evan, questioning.

"I'd better ring the bell," he said.

But I had to know, and while he went to the door, I bent to the old woman in the chair, putting my hand lightly on her arm. "Can you see me? Can you hear me?" Her look did not quicken and she gave no sign that she could feel my touch or hear my words. A sense of something like fright was creeping through me.

In response to Evan's ring, a plump woman in a nurse's uniform opened the door, and regarded him with surprise.

"I'm Evan Faulkner," he introduced himself. "And this is Courtney Marsh. We're from The Shingles. We were in the area and thought we'd like to stop in and see how Mrs. Kemble is doing."

"Of course," the woman said. "I'm Miss Dickson, her nurse." She came out to us and spoke softly to the old woman. "Now then, Anabel, do you think you could give the young lady a nice smile?"

I put my hand on the veranda rail to steady myself. Anabel! Anabel Kemble—for whom I had been named, my grandmother.

"It's one of her bad days," Miss Dickson said. "If I'd known you were coming I'd have tried to get her ready. But usually only her daughter, Miss Nan Kemble, comes to see her."

I dropped on my knees and took her thin hands in mine, pressing them gently. "I would have come sooner if I'd realized you were here. You are my grandmother Anabel. Can you understand that? I'm Alice's daughter. I'm your grandchild." My words seemed to penetrate the distance in which she lived. She began to turn her head slightly from side to side. "No," she said, and the word was so faint I could hardly hear it. "Baby—baby."

I pressed her hands. "I'm grown up now, Grandmother."

Weakly she tried to draw her hands from mine, rejecting me, but I didn't let them go. Miss Dickson looked thoroughly startled when I looked up at her. "How long has she been like this?" I asked.

"I don't know exactly. For close to twenty-five years, I suppose. I haven't been with her all that time—just the last three years. She's very good, you know. Sometimes she seems to listen to me. And she eats quite nicely. Not very much—but she does eat."

I could feel the tears on my cheeks. All the emotion that would not come before was rushing through me now. Anabel! Alice had named a boat for her mother, named her baby for her. Used the name in a story. She and this feeble woman in the wheelchair had once been close.

Down the veranda there were sounds, and I saw that Judith had not been able to remain in the car. She and the two men came up the steps and across to where I knelt before the wheelchair. Looking up into the old lady's face, I saw something stir in her eyes. Her thin, wrinkled lips moved as if to whisper. Her fingers moved like a fluttering bird in mine and I pressed them reassuringly. Again fragile lips moved, and there was a whisper of sound. I bent to catch it. "No! Wicked, wicked!" she whispered, and then sighed as though the effort to speak was too much for her. She closed her eyes and leaned back against the cushions in her chair.

Miss Dickson came to her aid at once. "She's not used to visitors, Miss Marsh. I think you'd better go now."

Judith fled down the steps and Herndon and John went after her.

I had no further desire to walk the beach where my mother had died, or to enter the house that had known her presence. Evan took my arm. "I'm sorry," he said to the nurse, and then led me back to the car.

Judith stood beside it, waiting for us, angry now. "You see what you've done, Courtney? That poor thing deserves to be left alone. We never come to see her because the sight of us only upsets her. I blame you, Evan."

Her indignation left him unruffled. "Maybe Courtney should know all that remains to be known about her family."

He opened the car door and I got into the front seat, feeling thoroughly shaken, with tears still wet on my cheeks. The others sat in back again, and Herndon was trying to calm Judith, while John remained quiet.

The drive back to East Hampton seemed quicker than the trip out, in spite of the accompanying silence. "Wicked," she had said. But she had stared at all three of them, and which one she meant I couldn't tell—or even if she meant all three.

Reaching The Shingles, we got out of the car rather stiffly, as though we'd been on a far longer journey than to Montauk, and Herndon took Judith into the house at once. John climbed the steps with me, ahead of Evan. "I'm sorry, Courtney. If I had known what was going to happen, I might have warned you. But we never thought you needed to know about her. Her life is over, and it could only hurt you to see her. Nan gives her the best of care. There's nothing the rest of us can do."

My bags were packed and waiting for me up in my room. I held out my hand. "I'll say good-by now. I wish—I wish I could have met you sooner."

He pressed my hand lightly and then let it go. "I almost wish that too, Courtney," he said. "Almost. But it was probably too late a long time ago. Good-by, Courtney."

Evan had a few things to do before he would be ready for the trip to New York, and he asked me if I could kill a half hour before we left. I assured him that I could. He and John went into the house, but I wanted to be under that roof for as little time left me as possible. I walked around to the terrace above the beach and down the wooden steps to the sand. Mists were gathering once more over the water, and the figurehead from the *Hesther* wore a wispy veil. With her staring, weatherbeaten face, she looked like some ghostly being. I fled from her down to the water's edge and walked with my hands thrust into my jacket pockets in the afternoon chill.

At first the beach lay smooth and undisturbed, but now I noticed that footprints had materialized suddenly in my path, indentations in the damp sand. They moved ahead of me along the beach, evidence that someone had walked along the dry sand above before descending to the water's edge. But I could see no one and there were no returning prints. Something small had been tossed upon the beach a few steps farther along, and I walked toward it and looked down. A china doll's head lay on the sand.

So Stacia had come here for her "sea burial," I thought, and walked on, wondering if these were her footprints. Mist concealed the distance, but the stretch ahead was empty until I came upon the next little face on the sand, and then there were two more heads, and a few feet later there was a fifth. A feeling of eerie horror grew in me as I came upon head after head lying along the beach.

Whose footsteps were these that seemed to follow the line of heads? I wondered. I dropped upon one knee and stared more closely. The footprints had been made by someone wearing shoes—either a man's shoes or the flat-heeled sport shoes that might be worn by a woman, perhaps even sandals. It was a small foot for a man, but maybe a little large for a woman? I wasn't sure.

A big patch of light brown seaweed lay ahead and I walked on to see if more heads had been caught in its wet meshes. Fog seemed to close in suddenly around me, so that when I looked back I could no longer see The Shingles. The beach was safe enough when it was visible to all—but not with fog shutting out the world. And not with Stacia perhaps walking the sand ahead of me, and lost to my sight in mist.

She *was* there ahead of me, but no longer walking. I paused beside the clump of seaweed and looked down, feeling my stomach churn. It was not seaweed, but the old tan raincoat Stacia sometimes wore, and she was still wearing it. She lay face down, her blond hair wet and filled with shiny grains of sand. Her bare legs and feet protruded below the wet hem of the coat. Nearby lay the carton of dolls' heads.

I bent and touched her. She was cold, and unbreathing. She had not died in the last few hours. The footprints did not match her small, bare feet, and they must have been made earlier this afternoon. They stopped at this point, moved about a little, then mounted the damp edge of sand and vanished into the dry sand. Someone knew. Someone else had stood here looking down upon her, and had raised no outcry.

Frantically, I began to run—back along the beach, avoiding the footprints, avoiding the dolls' heads. Gasping, I reached the steps that led up the dune to The Shingles. Only then did I catch my breath enough to scream for someone to come.

CHAPTER NINE

EVAN REACHED ME FIRST as I climbed to the terrace, and Herndon and John came out of the house after him. The Ashers looked from windows at the far end, and then William Asher rushed outside, with Helen behind him. There was no Judith. The moment Evan understood me he ran down to the beach and disappeared in the fog, with John and Herndon after him. "The footprints!" I shouted after them. "You mustn't destroy the footprints!" I ran to the top of the steps, but was too late. The three would run along the firm sand, and whatever those prints might mean was already being lost.

"I—I'll call the doctor, Miss Marsh," Asher said, managing to rouse himself from his own state of shock, but looking gray.

"Yes—and call the police," I told him.

When he went into the house, his wife looked after him anxiously. "He's been sick since early this afternoon," she said. "He ought to be in bed."

I had no time to sympathize over William Asher. "Make a big pot of coffee," I directed. "Make it right away."

She hurried toward the kitchen, and I walked into the living room, where I stood before the fire that had been built against the damp mists of late afternoon. Flames crackled as cheerily as though death did not exist, but Stacia would never run along the beach again, never warm her hands at this fire or any other. Drowned? Drowned like Alice? But she hadn't been swimming in that cold water, and she hadn't been wearing a bathing suit.

Where was Judith? Someone must tell her. Or did she already know? Still feeling shaky, I held tight to the railing as I climbed the stairs to Judith's studio and knocked on the door. There was no answer, and I walked in to find it empty. Her painting things had been put away, and the canvas of the Stacia-doll had been removed from the easel.

I returned to the second floor and went to Judith and Herndon's room. The door stood open and there was no one there.

I now seemed to be moving without my mind's volition, as though some urgent instinct governed my actions. I simply followed the instinct out to my car, got in, and started it up. There was no hurry and I didn't rush the Volvo toward the gates, but drove slowly because something in me had already decided where I was going and what I would find. When I reached Nan's shop, I parked the car and sat for a moment, trying to think what I must say. But my mind had turned blank.

The bell jingled as I went into The Ditty Box. There was no one in the front of the shop. As I walked toward the archway at the rear, I saw Judith and Nan drinking tea in the little back room. They both looked up as I approached. Nan's expression was questioning and almost tentative, so that I wondered what Judith had been telling her. "Hello," she said. "Will you have some tea with us, Courtney?"

"Stacia is dead," I told them. I hadn't meant to break it like that, but I no longer seemed able to think a moment ahead of my own actions.

Judith didn't seem to react—she only set her cup down and stared at me. Nan gulped a swallow of tea and choked.

"I went for a walk on the beach," I said, "and I found her. I think she's been dead for a long time."

Nan put both hands to her face and sat without moving. Judith seemed frozen, without expression—frighteningly like one of those immobile dolls that she painted.

Then with an effort Nan reached out to touch me. "Let's go up to the house," she said. She turned to Judith. "Are you able to? Or would you rather I brought Herndon here?"

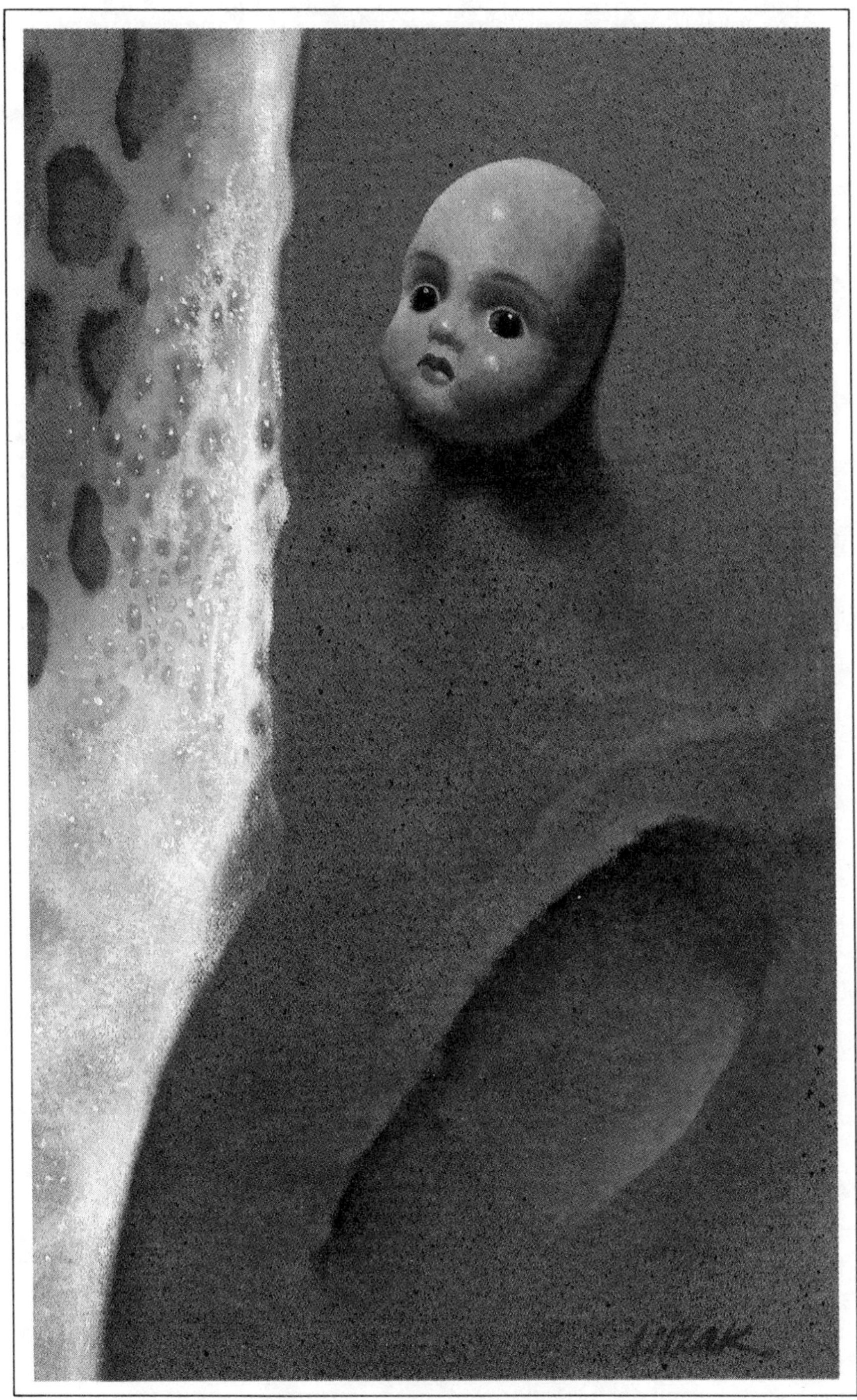

As though puppet strings had been pulled, Judith rose quite steadily, staring at us with that blank frozen look.

"Asher has called the doctor," I told them. "And probably the police."

The word appeared to jolt Judith, and she looked at me as though she were seeing me for the first time. "The police?" she said.

"It has to be that way," Nan assured her. "Until they know how she died. Are you sure, Courtney, sure that—"

"I'm very sure," I said. "Can I drive you back to the house, Judith?"

"You'd better," Nan said. "I'll close up the shop and follow in my car."

Judith walked beside me to the door. "I don't have to leave The Shingles now," she said. "It will belong to us." She turned her head to look at me. "It *will* belong to us, won't it, Courtney?"

Her words and dull, emotionless tone shocked me. "I'm sure I don't want it!" I cried. "I don't want anything."

When I drove up to the garage, Herndon came running down the steps. He pulled open the door on Judith's side and helped her out. Clearly he expected her to collapse in his arms, but she did nothing of the kind.

"When she was little I loved her," she said quietly. "But I haven't been able to love her for a long time."

Herndon's words shocked me still more. "She won't ever hurt you again," he said.

Evan was on the phone in the library when we went into the house. Judith sat down in a chair by the living-room fire, poker-erect, her expression set, her eyes dry. Nan and I stayed near the door, waiting for Evan to tell us what to do, or how we could help. "Why didn't you bring her up to the house?" Judith asked.

"Evan said this was a matter for the police," Herndon answered, "and we shouldn't move her. He's talking to them on the phone now."

Then Evan came into the room, looking grim. "They'll be here soon."

"How did she—how did she die?" Nan spoke from behind me. I looked around and saw that she was crying.

It was Evan who answered. "We don't know for sure. Drowning, probably. But ordinarily a drowning doesn't happen in shallow water and the body doesn't surface until later—if ever."

"It's like Alice!" Nan cried. "It's like Alice all over again!" She turned and ran out of the room.

"There were footsteps on the damp sand at the water's edge," I said, speaking to Evan.

He nodded. "Of course. You walked along that stretch both ways, didn't you? I saw your prints."

"There was another set. I took care not to step on them."

"Another set? They're gone now—with the three of us tramping back and forth. What did they look like?"

"Made by shoes or sandals. A small man. Perhaps even a woman. They stopped near Stacia. Whoever it was must have gone up the beach, because the prints didn't return the same way. With the tide coming in they wouldn't be there long anyway."

"I'd better have a look," Evan said. "When the police come, bring them down, Herndon." He went out through the terrace door.

In my confusion only one question emerged, a question almost irrelevant now. What had Stacia done with those pages she had torn from Alice's notebook? Perhaps looking for them would give me some purpose. They might even hold the answer to her death. No one noticed as I went upstairs and down the long hall to Stacia's room. The door was closed. I opened it softly, stepped inside, and stood frozen, gasping in astonishment.

Across the room Nan appeared to be searching a handbag of Stacia's, while tears rolled openly down her cheeks. But it was the state of the room itself that caused my startled gasp. Someone had torn the room apart in a desperate search. Clothes had been strewn about, the contents of the closet emptied, and Stacia's possessions spilled from drawers onto the floor. The scene was one of utter chaos.

Nan made a disclaiming gesture in my direction. "Courtney, I didn't do this. Believe me, I didn't."

She was here for a purpose—as I was. "What were you looking for?" I asked.

"I wanted to find the notebook in which my sister wrote her last stories. Stacia hinted to me that it had told her something."

"I have the book," I said. "But Stacia tore out the final pages. Besides, wasn't that book in your hands for years? Didn't you read what was in it?"

"I used to read Alice's stories when we were young. But after she died, I couldn't bear to. When her things were packed up, John gave me the notebooks, and I put them away. It was only recently that I took out the last one and gave it to Stacia. I thought she ought to read some of her aunt's stories. I'm afraid it was a mistake."

"Why a mistake?"

"That's when the anonymous letters began. Stacia was sending them. She admitted as much to me. She wanted to torment her mother."

"I wanted those pages too," I said. "I thought they might contain something I needed to know. Because Alice Rhodes was my mother. You know that now, don't you, Nan? Judith must have told you."

For an instant her look warmed, but she didn't move. "Yes, Judith told me. Just a little while ago. I'm sorry. We all believed you dead. Judith fooled us all."

"I don't want to talk about it now. I only want to read Alice's words. I think you're right that they told Stacia something. Perhaps they told her something that led to her death."

"Yes," Nan said. "I'm afraid of that too."

The sound of the doorbell reached us, followed by a chatter of voices. We stood listening to the tramping through the house as the voices moved out to the terrace. "Perhaps we'd better not be found here with the room in this condition," Nan said. "I didn't do this and I don't want to be blamed."

Nan and I left and I went down the hall to my own room. There I stood at the window, watching the men on the beach as the fog thinned out. They were all gathered around Stacia, some kneeling, some standing. She would never attack me again, I thought. Yet there was no release in this. It wasn't Stacia who should have been most feared. There was still another—someone who remained hidden. The one who had caused her death, and who might be watching even now, ready to strike out again.

Someone passed the door of my room and I went to look out. Helen Asher was carrying a tea tray to the servants' quarters. As I followed her, she glanced over her shoulder. "William's very sick," she said. "I thought this might help settle him a little."

Something I'd not thought of occurred to me, and when she turned the knob, I stepped to the doorway behind her. Asher lay on the bed, still clothed, with a blanket thrown over him. "I brought you some tea, William," his wife said, and set the tray beside the bed.

He had seen me at the door and he paid no attention to Helen. "I'm sorry, Miss Marsh," he said. "Please tell them I'll be all right. I know they need me now. I'm just under the weather after what happened today."

"May I come in?" I asked, and Helen nodded reluctantly.

Asher's shoes lay on the floor beside the bed. I picked one up and turned it over. Grains of sand clung to the narrow sole. "You were down on the beach today, weren't you?" I said. "Did you find her, Asher? Were those your prints I saw on the sand?"

He turned his face away and said, "Miss Stacia didn't come down for breakfast, and Helen said she wasn't in her room this morning when she went to make it up. So when lunchtime came, I went along the beach to see if I could find her anywhere. She often liked a morning run. First I saw all those dolls' heads, and then—I found her."

"Why didn't you tell anyone?" I asked.

"I was—frightened. I thought they might think that I—I mean I just wanted somebody else to find her."

"No one will blame you," I told him. "But I think Mr. Faulkner had better know about this. Will you talk to him if I send him up here later?"

"I'll talk to him," he said, with a sigh of relief.

It was a long while, however, before I could send Evan up to Asher. The police kept him busy, and I didn't want to present Asher's role to them unless Evan thought it necessary. Evan was taking charge, rather than Herndon, whose only concern now seemed to be for his wife.

It was after dinner before Evan could be told, and he went at once to Asher's room. I waited for him. When he came out, he spoke to me briefly. "There's no real point in involving the old man," he said. "She was dead long before he found her, and he seems to be afraid of something."

"Everyone's afraid of something," I said. "Or of *someone*. I am too."

Evan gave me a dark look and went away. That lovely moment out at Montauk seemed never to have been.

Nothing specific came out in the days that followed. Stacia's funeral was a sad affair, with few people from outside attending. It was found that she had indeed died by drowning, but no one could explain how it could have happened. The odd set of footprints I'd seen had been obliterated in a mass of trodden sand when the three men had first run down the beach. Asher was questioned by the police, but only in a general way. No one guessed that he had found her first, and the fact really did not matter. Stacia's room, with its strewn possessions, was shortly discovered, but no one admitted knowing anything about that either.

And there were a few new developments. The police had to be told my identity, and since I was instructed not to leave East Hampton, I had to remain at The Shingles while everything spilled out into the papers. There were phone calls from New York—from my friends, and from the office. Jim Healy called me and wanted to talk, but I had no heart for talking.

A small matter that hardly attracted my attention at the time was the radio news that the hurricane that had been creeping up the coast had blown out to sea. Long Island breathed more easily for the moment, but the hurricane season was not over and we didn't know then of a new "disturbance" stirring down in the Caribbean.

DURING THOSE DAYS that moved toward September's end, nothing surfaced to give us the answer to Stacia's death. The investigation continued and I was requested to remain in East Hampton.

There was now a string of Rhodes lawyers that I had to see. With Herndon supervising I moved through all the discussions and arrangements in a dazed state. Papers were signed because I was told to sign them. Only now and then did my old self protest. I did manage to sign over The Shingles to Herndon, and he was quietly grateful for that and insisted upon payment. Gradually I began to accept the fact that I was going to be a very rich woman. A rich woman who had nothing at all that she wanted.

Both Herndon and John were about the house as usual, with Herndon going off to his banks, John disappearing into his own pursuits. I held them off when they made any gesture of friendship, since I could trust no one and was only marking time until I could escape for good. I didn't visit Nan again and she never came to The Shingles after that first tragic day.

I was trying not to think of Evan at all. I saw him as a driven man in whom Stacia's death had brought about a terrible change. I caught him looking at me darkly in odd moments, but he spoke to me only when others were present—as though he was afraid I might bring up that past moment between us when he had spoken tentatively of love.

One gray afternoon Herndon came home early from work and sought me out. "Come for a walk with me," he said, and I lacked the will to refuse.

He took me, not to the beach, where neither of us wanted to walk, but along the empty driveway that lay between The Ditty Box and The Shingles. There had been an early frost, and red and yellow leaves were drifting to the ground. It felt like rain, and there was a wind rising.

"I wanted to talk with you, Courtney," he said.

"It seems to me we've done nothing but talk in the last week or two," I told him.

"I know. I *do* know that you hate all this, but you need to come out of your apathy."

"Nothing seems to matter anymore," I said.

"Evan matters."

I looked in surprise at the man who walked beside me, and saw to my distress how much older he had grown since Stacia's death. The little touches of colorful flamboyance in his dress were gone. Perhaps I'd never given enough thought to Herndon, who had also been a victim in all that had happened over the years.

Now he had spoken to me of Evan. This was a matter I couldn't talk about with anyone, couldn't even face in the silence of my own mind. What had barely begun was already over, destroyed by Stacia as surely as though she still lived. "He's not my affair," I said.

"He's very much your affair. I'm fond of Evan, and I don't want to see him hurt again."

"Hurt—Evan? What are you talking about?"

"Let your heart tell you," Herndon said.

No right words would come to me. So often I seemed to have guessed wrong about Herndon, not giving him enough credit for sensitivity toward others. "I don't think Evan needs anyone," I told him.

Quite gently Herndon took my hand and slipped it through the crook of his arm, patting it lightly. "I must seem hard and distant to you, but that's not what I want to be. You're my niece, Courtney, and perhaps there's still affection to give in this unhappy family."

I felt unexpectedly touched by his words. How strange to have a gentle sense of affection come to me from this surprising source. "Thank you," I said, and let my fingers press lightly against his arm.

Perhaps there might have been more, but we heard a car coming behind us and stepped aside. It was the Mercedes and Judith was at the wheel. I'd hardly seen her since Stacia's death, but she looked strong and purposeful now as she leaned toward us in the open window, braking the car. "Will you come with me, Herndon?" she asked. "I've an errand to do, and I need you."

He asked no questions of this woman who almost never had errands away from the house, but gave me an apologetic look. "I'm sorry, Courtney. We'll talk again." He went around the car and got into the seat beside Judith. I stood back to let them pass. With a pang of loss, I watched the Mercedes disappear down the curving drive in the direction of the gatehouse.

I walked back to the house alone, sadness breaking through my apathy.

THE NEXT DAY was Saturday, though I had forgotten the day of the week until after lunch, when I went idly down the hall to the library. Evan was there, working on the Rhodes family records. Before I could escape, he looked up and saw me. "I'm sorry," I said. "I won't interrupt."

He rose from his chair. "Come in, Courtney. Come and sit down." There was nothing kindly in his tone, and his words commanded me without sympathy. But I sat in the chair he pulled out, and looked down at my hands because I couldn't meet the anger in his dark eyes. Why should he be angry with me, and why should I sit here and listen? But I stayed.

"I've made up my mind about you several times over," he told me, "and each time you've turned out to be someone else. Now I don't know you at all. You've become a zombie." He sat down beside me. "What has taken the life out of you, Courtney?"

"It went out of me when I stood on the beach and looked down at Stacia," I said. "I didn't like her, and she tried to injure me and others too, but she didn't deserve what happened. And now I find I belong to a family that has been trained to such self-protection that murder is being hidden. Who is it? My father? My uncle? My aunt? They're all guilty because each of them is protecting the other—and I can't bear it."

His tone gentled when he spoke again. "Yes—I feel that way too. I can't rest. I can't be my own man until this thing is cleared up. I owe this to Stacia. She believed that someone had killed Alice, and I think she was pursuing that trail in her own willful way. If she discovered the truth, that may have brought about her own death. So now a double murderer must be exposed."

"Have you said this to the police?"

"I can't go to them with surmises. The worst of it is that the Rhodeses are all close to me and have been for years. Yet what happened when Alice died is being repeated—the secrecy, the concealment. And that can't go on."

"Do you think they all know who killed Stacia?" I asked.

"I can't tell. They've been trained all their lives—trained by old Lawrence himself—to protect their own. Even Nan Kemble hasn't escaped."

"Yes, I've seen that. I feel sick about being related to such a family."

He went on as though he mused aloud. "I have to blame myself for a great deal. Stacia was very young when I married her. Seventeen. Very gay and young and beautiful."

Something in me hardened. "There were already the dolls."

"But I should have been wise enough to change her. I should have tried harder."

"Do people ever change?"

"Perhaps not. I would have needed to change too—and that was something I couldn't manage. Can't manage. Just as you can't manage to be anything else but what you are, Courtney. So go back to New York and take up your life again. Be a writer, be a success. Don't let this money affect you."

"I don't have any money that I haven't earned," I told him. "I'm going to set up trust funds where they're needed. I don't want any Rhodes money. And as soon as all this quiets down, I'll close my apartment in New York and go away to write my book." All this poured out of me in a surprising flow, and an enormous sense of relief swept through me.

"Where will you go?"

"I don't know yet. Not East Hampton."

"What about Montauk? It's quiet out there—at the end of the world."

I couldn't look at him. There was never any telling how much or how little he meant. And I didn't want only a little.

He changed the subject. "I suppose some sort of investigation about you has been made," he said, "so that it's settled that you really are Anabel Rhodes?"

"Yes—there's no escape for me there. The lawyer's files in New York have been opened. Someone has even dug up my Swiss birth certificate, and there are prints to identify me. I was born to Alice and John Rhodes. It's all down in black and white."

"But it doesn't really matter, does it?"

His words startled me. "What do you mean?"

"Blood doesn't matter all that much. You grew up in a different environment. You were lucky enough to escape this house before it could affect you."

I sat quietly, considering. "Blood still matters," I said.

The look he'd turned upon me had softened. "Remember about Montauk," he said. I nodded, not trusting myself to speak as I rose and started for the door. He came with me, and before I reached it his hand was on my arm. "You said you would come—when the time was right. Is this the time?"

That desperate something inside was warning me that not to feel was to be safe, not to feel was to avoid future wounding. And all the while a warming tide of emotion was rising in me, and would not be denied.

I went into his arms and for a moment he held me close, with his cheek against my hair. Then he tilted my chin with one finger and looked at me—as though he must know the very shape of my face, the color of my eyes, the trembling of my lips—and his very look was a caress. When he kissed me the old fears died. I knew who I was now, I knew what I wanted. I knew that running away from love would bring me nothing, even though staying would mean taking the risk I'd always been afraid to take.

Raising his head and denying the hunger in us both, he held me at arm's length for a moment. "That's only a beginning," he told me, and I heard the promise in his words.

"I know," I said. "I understand. There is still the matter of Stacia to be settled. And no one left but you to do it."

"Yes. A debt to pay."

"Be careful, then. I'll come to Montauk," I told him, and left the room.

It was already afternoon, but there was still time to push toward the thing I must do. I went to the telephone in the hall and called the police chief. I told him that I wanted to go back to New York. "It's all right, Miss Marsh. You can leave anytime you want to. We're not going to hold any of you in East Hampton any longer."

I gave a small whoop of relief when I hung up. Then instead of going to my room to pack, I followed the back flight of stairs up to the attic. Judith was at her easel when I reached the studio, and she looked as though she had been working feverishly for some time. "I came to say good-by," I told her. "The police aren't restricting us anymore."

"You sound glad, Courtney."

"I'm practically delirious."

With her palette hooked over her thumb and her paintbrush in hand, she took a few steps toward me, almost conciliatory. "We've given you a bad time, haven't we? And I'm sorry. Herndon's been scolding me."

She continued to look at me, her face calm and expressionless. In a moment she would return to her own imaginary world, and it would be hard to draw her out again.

"I was talking to Evan a little while ago," I said, "about people changing. Have you been changed, Judith, by what has happened?"

The attic was still, except for a spatter of rain against high dormer windows. A storm was beginning.

She nodded gravely. "Yes, I've changed, a marvelous, wonderful, blessed change! I can be quiet now. I can work."

The brightness of her smile startled me, and I must have looked shocked, because she shook her head in reproach. "Don't be so conventional, Courtney. Don't condemn me because I'm relieved to know that

Stacia is gone. She has damaged all our lives, including Evan's, and she would have damaged yours. But now I can work again. I feel free for the first time in years."

I turned my back and walked toward the door, feeling sickened.

"Wait," she called after me. "You must understand why I took the action I did with you—if you'd grown up here, you might have been in danger. Don't you see that?"

"What danger?"

She started to speak and then shrugged. "Perhaps it's better if you never know. But come—before you leave, you must look at what I'm painting."

It would probably upset me further to go back and look at this new canvas, but I was drawn in spite of myself.

"You see?" she said. "Perhaps I have a talent for portraiture after all. Perhaps I don't need to paint beaches anymore."

The head on the canvas was indeed a portrait—and not the head of a doll. She had painted Stacia in a likeness immediately recognizable, yet with something added. Faintly discernible behind the beauty of blue eyes and perfect features was the underlying skull, with hollow eye sockets in eerie counterpoint.

"It's been good therapy for me to paint that, Courtney. I won't go on painting like this, of course, but she was my child and it was something I needed to say about her—death beneath life. I'd like to paint you, Courtney. Won't you stay and pose for me?"

I fled down the room and out the door in haste to be away from the sight of that terrible portrait. This time I ran directly to my room, where I pulled my bags out of the closet and flung my clothes in a heap on the bed. With the rain slashing ever more loudly against the windows and the sound of a muffled roar from the sea, I tossed the clothes helter-skelter into my suitcase. Driving to New York in a storm would be unpleasant, but it would have to be done.

The suitcase filled, I removed the remaining contents of drawers and bathroom shelves and dumped everything on the bed. Then I unzipped my flight bag and began to thrust into it bottles and jars, toothbrush and cosmetic case. When I tried to shove my comb and brush into a side pocket of the case, they stuck because something was already there. Impatiently, I jerked out a wad of paper, dropped it into the wastebasket, and returned to my packing.

But then I thought I might have thrown out some of my own notes, and I fished the wad out of the basket. Handwriting across the sheets arrested my attention, and I felt a shock of recognition. So this was where Stacia had hidden the torn pages—here in my own baggage. My cousin had left me a legacy after all. I'd packed more neatly the last time, before the trip to Montauk, and hadn't touched the side pocket.

I forgot that the afternoon was getting on, and that I faced a long drive in stormy weather to New York. I flipped on the lamp beside the armchair, dropped into it, and began to smooth the rumpled pages out upon my knees. Now I would be given the answers. Now I would know.

Alice's last story had never been finished—that little allegory about the Princess Anabel. Instead, swiftly scrawled sentences changed to personal statements as my mother had poured out her thoughts in diary form.

> They're all here now—John, Judith, Herndon. Lawrence has sent his troops to bring me home. But this time I have the power to bargain—now that I can give him the heir he craves. Now I can make him pay for all the humiliation he has made us suffer.
>
> I've told John there will be no divorce and he knows I won't give in. He's a fool, of course. Judith has had her fling, and she has already gone back to Herndon. John hasn't faced that yet. He doesn't know what I know—that Judith is already carrying Herndon's child. For safety, mine has been born out of the country. Judith's a little afraid of me now, but she's too late—because I have my baby first. The first Rhodes heir, a darling little girl I've named Anabel to spite them all. She'll be a Kemble, not a Rhodes.
>
> I've told Herndon about John and Judith. He will forgive her, but I wanted to make sure he knew the truth. John he will never forgive. And of course none of them will forgive me. They all hate me now. But I'm the strong one—I'm the one who will win. Money, power, and eventually a heritage of wealth for my Anabel, who will have everything Lawrence wouldn't give John and me.
>
> All this is being set down as a precaution. If anything happens to me, perhaps Anabel will read it one day.

I paused, feeling as sick as when I had seen that painting of Judith's upstairs. Alice had been no better than the rest of them. There was still more and I forced myself to read on. She had scrawled dates in the margins of her entries, and this one was two days later.

> I'm glad Olive Asher is here with me. In the morning, when it's warm enough, I like to go for a swim, and Olive stays at a window, or sometimes comes down to the beach with me, bringing Anabel. Today the baby has a cold, so Olive will remain here with her while I swim. But she will still look out a window from time to time and watch.

Here I turned to a new sheet and came upon a hole—a tiny oblong that had been deliberately cut in the paper. Before she had hidden these pages in my bag, Stacia must have deleted a name with scissors—the one name that mattered most. Alice's words went on after the blank.

> ____ is down on the beach this morning. But I'm not afraid. I'm a better swimmer than any of them—and Olive will look out from her window. So I'll have my dip as usual. Let any of them threaten me, if they dare! Good-by, my little Anabel—I'll come back to you soon.

But she had not come back. Strong swimmer or no, Alice had died in the water. Revulsion was like a gripped fist just under my ribs, and I didn't know whether it would ever go away. All my life long I would remember this moment of revelation, and wish it had never come to me. Because now, staring at Alice's words traced across the paper in my hands, I knew the truth—just as Stacia had known whose name belonged in that slot. I knew who had been down on the beach that morning when Alice had gone swimming, and who had followed Stacia along the sand when she had carried that box of dolls' heads down to the water's edge.

It was time to act. Flight first, for my own safety—though there seemed no danger for me unless my knowledge was discovered. I would leave, nevertheless, and go back to New York. I would get Evan to come to me there, so I could tell him the terrible truth.

The storm sounded louder now, howling and rattling the windows. But I ignored it. I folded the notebook pages carefully and returned them to the side pocket of the flight bag. I zippered the case shut and managed with some difficulty to pack the rest of my belongings in the suitcase. I pulled on my coat and tied on a rain bonnet, then picked up my bags and went into the hall.

Judith was coming down the attic stairs. "You're not leaving in this storm?" she called.

I could hardly bear to look at her. I merely said I was, and went on quickly. The storm battered the house with a force that shook the walls, and I stood at the front door for a moment, bracing myself to face what waited for me outside. Then I reached out and pulled open the door.

CHAPTER TEN

THE ROAR AND THRUST of the storm hurled itself upon me. Tree branches thrashed as the wind howled through them, and rain slashed in horizontal sheets, blinding and soaking me as I stood in the doorway.

Judith cried out behind me, and at the same instant Herndon came running up the steps to push me back into the house and slam the door behind him. He saw my bags as he stood shaking rain from his slicker, wiping it from his face. "Where do you think you're going, Courtney?" he demanded. "You can't possibly go out there now."

"I'm going back to New York," I told him. "And I *am* leaving now."

"Don't be absurd," he said. "There's a hurricane out there. The edge hit New York and it's coming east. You'd have to drive straight into it."

I made a last effort to escape and my voice rose shrilly. "But I must go! I don't want to stay in this house any longer."

"It was all I could do to get home," Herndon said, taking the bags firmly from my hands and setting them down near the wall. Drawn by the sound of my voice, John came to the living-room door and quietly said that Herndon was right.

There was nothing to do but give in. Above me on the stairs, Judith spoke to her husband. "While you're still wet, will you bring Tudor inside? He can't be left outdoors in this."

"I'll get him," Herndon said. "Where's Asher? We've got to shutter the house."

They forgot me then. Herndon went outside, and Evan came out of the library to help. I left my bags in the hall, feeling useless in this emergency. Back in my room I waited while the wind roared and shook the house. When the afternoon grew dark, I turned on lights. When the lights went out, I sat in darkness. I heard shingles clattering on the roof, but I didn't care. It was not the assault on the house that frightened me. A storm—even a hurricane—was nothing compared with the tumult of anxiety that churned inside me.

A lull came in the storm, perhaps the eye—that space of time at the center before we met the winds hurtling in the opposite direction. I peered out the window at a cloud-torn sky. Miraculously, there was a glimpse of moon—a moon still full, though slightly on the wane. It wavered before my eyes, vanished behind clouds, emerged again with a shadow across it. I stared, unbelieving, as the form of a unicorn took shape for an instant, then shredded into blown strips as the bright sphere vanished. The Rhodes unicorn moon!

All track of time was lost to me, and I didn't know the hour until Helen Asher came upstairs with a flashlight to fetch me. "It's late. You'd better come downstairs now, miss," she said. "The cook's gone home, but William and I have put together a cold meal."

I didn't want to go. I didn't want to sit at the table, knowing what I did—knowing that perhaps two of those I sat with knew very well what the third had done. I was afraid, too, lest by some sign I didn't intend I should give away my knowledge. I didn't want to remember the unicorn moon.

There was no help for me, however. Downstairs there were candles in the dining room, sending wavering shadows up the walls as gusts swept through the room—in spite of shuttered windows. The storm was in full voice again. As I sat down at the table, Evan regarded me sternly. "Herndon says you were trying to leave in this storm, Courtney. What idiocy! Wait until it's over and I'll drive you in."

I hoped it wouldn't be too late for me by then. But that was foolish, of course. No one knew. Stacia had hidden Alice's words well, though someone had searched her room for them.

Just as we finished a meal of cold meats and fruits, Asher came in to report that the phones were out, and Evan rose from the table. "If the phones are gone, I'm going down to the gatehouse. Nan shouldn't be alone through all this if she can't call for help."

I wanted to cry out to Evan not to leave, that I needed him too, but of course I couldn't. He was right to go to Nan. A feeling that what would be would be was growing in me, as though all my life had been building toward this moment. I knew now that I couldn't run away from it. My destiny lay under this roof. I was a Rhodes by blood and a Kemble too, and there must be no more secrecy. As soon as Evan came back, I would tell him what I knew, show him Alice's pages. But until that moment I could only mark time.

When the others rose from the table, I rose with them. I went into the hall and picked up my bags to carry them back to my room. I'd borrowed a flashlight from Asher, and I would light some candles and wait for the hurricane to pass. In the meantime, I would have my flight bag with its contents in my possession, where I could watch it.

Herndon and Judith went to their room, and I went to the door of mine. Looking down the dark hall, I could see them sitting before a fire, Judith talking animatedly. I wondered what she was telling her husband. I entered my room and set some candles about. They cast an eerie glow, and more than once I winced as wind slammed against the house and set the shadows quivering. To reassure myself, I opened the zipper bag and felt in the side pocket for Alice's pages. Suddenly everything crashed in upon me. The pages were gone!

When I had been downstairs, I must have revealed my fright, my urgency to escape, so that one person had been alerted—and had looked into that flight bag standing in the hallway. Now it was known that I knew. I could not trust any of those three—not the one who was guilty, or the two who had kept silent all these years, and were keeping silent still.

I must not stay here alone. No matter how fierce the storm, I must try to reach Nan's shop, where Evan was. With shaking hands I pulled on my coat again and tied the plastic hood over my head. Then I opened the door cautiously and used my flashlight in the hall. Herndon and Judith's door was closed, and the storm hid any noises I might make on the stairs.

I was thankful to find the lower hall empty. Candlelight illumined the doorway to the living room, and a flicker of firelight made the shadows move. I turned off my flash and crept softly toward the outside door. I had my hand on the doorknob when a soft radiance fell about me and I turned, startled, to see John standing in the living-room doorway holding up a hurricane lamp in one hand.

"Courtney!" he said in surprise. "You're not going to attempt the storm again, are you? I can't let you do that, you know."

A sense of my own helplessness swept through me. "I suppose it is hopeless to go out there," I said, and turned back to the stairs.

He came to me and took my arm gently. "I need your company tonight, Courtney. Perhaps this will be our last chance to talk. Come and sit with me before the fire."

In his face I could read the truth as he held the lantern high, and I knew that he knew what I had learned tonight. Hastily I cast a look down the hall toward where the Ashers had been sitting in the kitchen. John shook his head. "They'll never hear you if you call, my dear. No one will hear."

His hand on my arm propelled me, and I found myself walking into that beautiful, comfortable room that held no comfort for me now. The shutters had been closed against the storm, but gusts forced their way in, and not even the fire on the hearth could offer much warmth while that cold fury crashed outdoors.

Tudor lay upon the hearth rug, and when he saw me he raised his great body instantly into a guard position. Involuntarily, I drew back. John patted my arm. "You needn't fear Tudor tonight, Courtney. He will obey my orders."

He led me into the room and seated me in a chair near the fire, much too close to the dog. "Sit," he told Tudor. "Stay," and the animal relaxed into a sitting posture, though still alert.

"It's really too bad that you had to find those pages from Alice's notebook," John went on conversationally. "I searched for them in Stacia's room, but you must already have had them. It *is* too bad. You and I could have got on very well. Now that I've read those pages, I understand what Stacia believed she held over me. It was clever of her to cut out my name, but not clever enough."

Something new had come into his voice—a hinting of anger long suppressed. I tried to talk to him calmly. "You're right," I said. "She wasn't clever enough. The pattern of the names was there. A long cut could have meant either Judith or Herndon, but a short one could only mean John. Or Nan, but she had gone away."

"Nan!" He laughed unpleasantly. "May I ask what it was you had planned to do?"

I couldn't miss the past tense, or that quiver of rising anger in his voice. "What does it matter? I hadn't really decided. After all, I would be acting against my own father."

He smiled at me, falsely gentle. "If only I could have trusted you, Courtney. But I found I couldn't even trust Stacia. After all I'd done for her . . ." Anger was in the open now—blazing in his eyes as he looked at me.

"I can understand about Alice," I said. "But not why you had to hurt Stacia. Weren't you two of a kind and on the same side?"

His smile stiffened, froze on his mouth. "Not exactly. Perhaps we both wanted money, but Stacia was like her grandfather—my father. She was power-hungry. And after she had read those pages she came to the mistaken conclusion that she had power over all of us. Especially me. That was where she made her mistake."

"What do you mean? She loved you, surely?"

"I think not. She could play that game while I was useful to her, but when I refused to go along with what she wanted—which was to get rid of you—she was against me. Who else would have struck me down that night on the terrace, when she believed I meant her harm? I had to deal with her. And I did." For the moment anger had died, and there was only cold, unbelievably treacherous fact in his statement.

I found that I was shivering. "What about Alice?"

He had no reluctance about telling me everything now. "Olive Asher saw me with Alice that day on the beach, and she told Judith. Judith was still half in love with me then, and even though she'd found it sensible to return to Herndon, she kept what she knew to herself and paid Olive off, sent her away. I was stupid enough to think Judith might turn to me after Alice's death, but she didn't."

His rage rising again, shattering the guise of sanity, he went on, "Judith will have to pay for what she did, because I will inherit as the older son. I will have the money and the power, and I can make them all grovel."

My terror grew. What he meant, of course, was that with me gone he would inherit. I wanted to close my eyes, to shut out the terrible look in his face, somehow shut out the seething hatred in his voice.

The new, dreadful voice went on. "A few months after Alice was out of the way, it became apparent that Judith was going to have Herndon's baby. She then told my father the truth about what Olive had seen on the beach, and the shock killed him. She has never tried to tell anyone else, and she's been a little afraid of me ever since. But I would never hurt Judith—not physically. I'm very fond of her, really. It's just that she owes me a debt from long ago—and she'll have to pay it now. In full."

"She must have told Herndon," I said flatly.

"No, strangely enough. Alice had seen to it that he learned about the affair between Judith and me, but he never let her know that he knew. He forgave Judith, and he couldn't be rid of me. My father's will stipulated that I was to live here as long as I wished, until the new heir inherited. But Herndon never knew that it was I down there on the beach that morning. That's one of the priceless jokes Judith managed to play on herself."

He laughed softly again, and I shivered at the sound. "My loyal brother has believed all these years that Judith was behind Alice's death because Alice threatened her with exposure of our affair. He has given his life to protecting her. I don't know but what he might even have protected me, being a good Rhodes."

"But Stacia loved you. She—" My words came out weakly. I broke off.

"Stacia was jealous and angry and bitter! Stacia loved Stacia. She became dangerous when she started sending those anonymous letters to stir everyone up again about Alice and Alice's baby. And she began to guess that from my viewpoint it might be much better for me if I made peace with you, as your father. You would have been more generous toward me, since you're far more loving than Stacia. We quarreled about a number of things that last day of her life. In the end she actually taunted me with exposure. So what could I do?"

"What did you do?" I asked faintly.

"The same thing I did with Alice. There are pressure points that can make a person quickly unconscious. The water took care of the rest. It was very simple."

So calm, so clear, so reasonable. The sickness in me was growing. I didn't know what he meant to do with me, but I knew it would be terrible. And the most terrible thing of all—the thing that kept beating at me—was the fact that John Rhodes was my father.

As though he had read my thoughts, he spoke to me with that dreadful, seemingly gentle note in his voice. "I've really liked you, Courtney, and I never wanted to hurt you. If it will comfort you, you might as well know that you are not my daughter."

I could only stare at him blankly. "But then—then who—"

"No! It's too long a story. There isn't time. Do you know what I saw tonight, Courtney? I saw the moon—"

"I saw it too," I said with a sense of fatalism. "The unicorn moon."

"You know the legend, don't you?"

"That when a Rhodes sees the unicorn moon it can mean either great good fortune or utter disaster. But perhaps I'm not a Rhodes?"

His smile gave me no answer. "Tonight I think that moon will carry out both prophecies—one for you, and one for me. It shouldn't be difficult for you to figure out which will be for which."

"John," I managed, "you can't get away with another accident."

He regarded me calmly. "I can get away with anything I choose. No one has ever known the man I am. I've hidden from all of them—behind the cheerful, unambitious playboy! I've taken their beastly treatment, but now it's my turn.

"Come outside with me, Courtney," he said as he picked up an oilcloth slicker from another chair. He pulled it on, buttoning it high, and turning up the collar. When he bent to fasten a lower button, I sprang from the chair and hurled myself toward the door, forgetting the dog. Tudor snarled, but he was still obedient to the command to stay that had been given him. John caught me and pulled me back with a jerk that wrenched my still-tender arm. I cried out in pain, but he did not let me go. It was all in the open now—the rage gone out of hand.

"Don't try that again," he said. "You'll excite the dog."

Tudor was on his feet, watching me, alert for the slightest command.

John directed me in a voice turned low and deadly. "We'll go out through the terrace door. Come, Tudor—guard." The dog was beside me at once, huge and menacing. John flung open the door to the terrace, letting in a roar of wind. He pushed me ahead of him into wild darkness and closed the door after the dog came through.

Outside the pitch-black night screamed with sound, and cold rain slashed our faces. Wet sand stung my eyes, as the wind tore and whipped my hair into a wet tangle. All around us there was a howling, as though demons had risen from the ocean and been let loose on the land.

John knew his way instinctively, and he was pushing me out from the terrace to stand on the rim of the high dune. The beach must have vanished as waves boomed across it and broke against the dune, sending spray into the air, eroding the embankment and carrying sand back into the sea. The undertow would be treacherous tonight.

John's voice sounded close to my ear, so the wind couldn't snatch his words away. "We can't risk the steps in the dark. Dig in your heels as you go down the dune. Slide with the sand."

I shouted back at him. "No! I won't go down."

"Tudor!" John cried, and the dog pressed against me. He was so close that I could hear the growl in his throat, and I knew that I might feel his teeth in another moment.

"You have a choice," John shouted in my ear. "The water or the dog."

There was a madness in him that I was powerless to oppose. If I went down the dune the waves would snatch me away, drag me out to sea in the undertow—where I would drown, as I was supposed to have drowned twenty-five years ago. And John would concoct some story that would leave him free of guilt. But if I stayed, Tudor would gladly obey any order of John's. I would be driven into the sea in either case.

As my heels dug into the sand, I felt it slide beneath me, taking me down a few feet. The water was close now. I fell backward from the force of the wind, sliding farther down the sand, so that water came over my ankles and up my legs. I lost my shoes and my wounded arm had gone numb, but I managed to thrust myself to my feet, and stood in the surge of water that came up the dune. John had slid along beside me. "Go down, Courtney! Go all the way!"

Water would be better than the dog. Perhaps I could stay afloat and make my way up some dune farther along the beach. Darkness was the one thing in my favor. The moment I was away from John's touch, he couldn't see me. I took another step into the sea and was promptly knocked down by a wave, submerged, with water in my mouth and the deadly suction drawing me out. I came up choking, pulled up by John.

"Go out farther," he shouted. "Let the water take you. It will be easy that way."

I flung myself away from him, away from the dog. Another wave battered me down, but I came up choking farther along the beach, and John wasn't grasping me now. If I could manage the struggle against waves and wind until I came to a place where I could climb up the next dune, out of sight in the darkness, I might escape. I could hear him shouting behind me, coming nearer, and knew that he was in the water too, pursuing me—to make sure of what he wanted to happen.

My hands were stiffening in the bitter cold and I struggled in water up to my knees, trying to stay on feet I couldn't feel. John shouted again, but he must be floundering too. I rose and fell, choking, my lungs burning, my eyes afire, fighting against that fatal suction that tried to pull me out to sea.

Then without warning a blaze of light shone directly into my face, and I heard voices through the crash of wind and water. A hand grasped my tender arm so that I cried out in pain—and was engulfed by darkness.

Before I opened my eyes, I heard the crackle and felt the warmth of a roaring fire. Well wrapped in blankets, my wet clothes gone and a warm nightdress on my body, I lay on something soft drawn close to the fire. There was no more sea, no wind, no icy water sucking me down. As my eyes began to focus, I saw that this was the hearth where Tudor had lain earlier in the evening, but he wasn't there now. And I was warm again, warm and safe. My hand felt for the pendant and it was still there at my throat. Whatever had happened, I hadn't lost it.

"She's coming to," a voice said.

My eyes blurred and then cleared as I looked up into Nan's face, and saw Evan beside her. Behind them I could see Judith, unmoving as a statue, her face white. "John," I said. "He's out there. And the dog. He tried to—"

Nan bent over me. "Hush, Courtney. We know. The men have been searching. We think he's been lost in the water. Tudor came in by himself."

"But how—how did you find me? How—"

This time Evan leaned toward me. "No more talk now." He picked me up, blankets and all, and carried me upstairs. When I'd been tucked into bed Evan stood beside me for a moment longer, looking down into my face. Drowsily I murmured something sweet and foolish. He leaned down and kissed me, then he went away. I was vaguely aware of candlelight, of Nan sitting in a chair across the room, of the lessening storm sounds outside. And then I was asleep.

Dawn pressed at the window when I next opened my eyes. Nan was asleep in the chair. The moment I stirred she awakened, and as she came over to me I felt new energy surge through my body, while my mind brimmed with unanswered questions. "You should have gone to bed," I told her.

"I wanted to stay," she said. "How do you feel?"

"Wonderful! Free again. But how did they find me in time?"

She moved about the room, stretching her arms over her head, wriggling her shoulders back to life, and then drew the chair closer to my bed and sat down. "Judith talked to Herndon last night. She told him the truth—as far as she knew it—about John. What Olive Asher had told her—that he was guilty of Alice's death. And probably of Stacia's. Herndon went through the storm to fetch Evan back to the house, and I returned with them. Herndon didn't know you were in any danger then, but he wanted to confront John, and he didn't want to do it alone. Luckily Asher was also uneasy. John thought he'd seen the unicorn moon, and he told Asher, so the old man stayed alert for anything that might happen.

"Asher was listening in the hall, and he heard some of what John said to you. When he realized that John meant to take you outside, bringing the dog with him, he was frightened. He knew he couldn't stand against John alone. It was sheer luck that brought the three of us back in time. Asher told us where John had taken you—"

"He's not my father," I broke in. "Oh, Nan, he's not my father!"

She was silent, watching me. When she spoke at last it was in a cold, remote way. "You weren't Alice's baby either, Courtney. You were named after your real mother—Anabel. That was a little whimsy of Alice's because it was a name I never liked, even though it was our mother's too. I never used it, but it's my name."

It seemed an eon before I could speak. At the window the light grew brighter with the new day. "Please tell me," I managed at last.

Hesitantly, she began to speak, and then the words poured out—as though the pressure of release was too much to resist. Yet she still spoke without feeling, with nothing I could reach out to.

"There are no good excuses for what I did. I was young and I was pregnant and I had no husband. It was a situation made for Alice's machinations. The one thing she wanted more than anything else was an heir to satisfy old Lawrence and make certain of her own power in the family. She had given up hope of having a baby—even if John had given her one, it might not have been in time to provide that *firstborn* heir. So she promised me a home and a mother and father for my child—something I couldn't give. She promised that the baby would be raised as a Rhodes, with all the care and benefit that implied. And I didn't know the Rhodeses then as well as I do now. Worst of all, she threatened to ruin your father if I didn't do as she wanted."

"Who was my father?"

Nan went on as though I hadn't spoken. "I went abroad with Alice and we fooled old Lawrence completely. My sister and I looked a lot alike in those days, and it was simple to switch passports when we went into Switzerland. So you were safely born to Alice and John Rhodes."

Nan paused, and for a moment the room was very still. Then she went on. "After I saw you, I wasn't sure anymore. When we came home to the cottage in Montauk, where our mother was staying, I began to fight against Alice's plan. When Lawrence learned about the baby, he sent Herndon, Judith, and John out to the cottage to bring Alice and the baby home. When I told her I was going to tell the truth and keep you, no matter what, she told me again just what she could do to your father if I didn't take myself off and do it quickly. On the other hand, if I behaved, I could come back to East Hampton later and be a loving aunt to my own child—so the little girl wouldn't have to grow up without knowing me. Alice and I fought bitterly, but she was older and stronger-willed, so she won and I went away. If only I'd stayed a little longer—"

Her voice broke, but she controlled her emotion quickly and continued. "You know the rest. Olive saw John and Alice down on the beach, and I think she told our mother. Mother went to pieces, and she's never been right since. I didn't learn of Alice's death and that of my little Anabel until some time later, and then I came straight home."

"Judith told me she gave me away partly for my own safety. But why wouldn't I have been useful to John—presumably as his child?"

"You could have been. But since he knew you weren't Alice's child or his, he was afraid of what might happen when I came back to town. Lawrence would never have forgiven our tricking him. In any case, when I returned you were supposedly dead, and Herndon had gone back to Judith, as I always knew he would."

"Herndon?"

"Yes. While Judith had her brief fling with John, Herndon was left hurt and terribly wounded, and I'd always loved him. For a little while he turned to me. He's the decent one of the lot, Courtney. He's the one Lawrence trusted, and if he weren't so bewitched by Judith . . ." She blinked hard, then said firmly, "Of course he never knew that Alice's baby was mine—and his."

I closed my eyes and turned my head away from her. Even in the last words Alice had written in her notebook, she had carried on the lie that I was her child.

Nan's cold, clear voice continued. "You owe me nothing but contempt, Courtney. Ever since Judith told me the truth about you and I knew what even she didn't know—that you were *my* daughter—I've been trying to find some way to ease this story in the telling. But there wasn't any easy way. I've never forgiven myself, and I'll never ask—or want—anything of you. It's too late."

When I heard her leave her chair and walk to the door, I turned my head. "Nan," I said, "wait." Suddenly I could understand. Her remoteness toward me was a defense, because she couldn't bear to be hurt any more and she didn't expect anything from me except rejection for what she had done. I was out of bed in a moment, running across the floor in bare feet and nightgown. "I've come through all the years of my life to find you," I cried. "You can't go away from me now!"

The tears she had held back brimmed her eyes, spilled down her cheeks, yet she was afraid to reach out to me. So I put my arms about her and held her close, with my own wet cheek against hers.

There were years to be bridged, both a mother and a father to become acquainted with—yet the human heart could span all this in an instant, and with my cheek against Nan's, I knew I had come to the end of my search.

When we'd cried a little and laughed a little and could stop hugging each other, she said, "Herndon still doesn't know. I'm fond of him, Courtney, but there aren't going to be any more secrets. I can give him the gift of you now, when he needs it most. And Judith—well, Judith will have to accept the past. She has her painting, and I know he'll stand by her."

But there was someone else I had to tell before we told Herndon. I must talk to Evan now, and I wanted to see him quickly.

Outside, when I reached the terrace, the view was one of devastation. Grass and foliage were flattened, and everything bore scars of the storm. The wooden steps had been broken and partly washed away. Evan was climbing the altered bank, and when he saw me he came quickly to my side. "How are you, Courtney?"

"I have to tell you something," I said. "Will you listen, please?"

He listened gravely, not touching me, and I knew he was glad about Nan. As I talked I looked down the sandy bank and saw that the old figurehead had been shifted by the storm. Hesther no longer stared off toward far horizons, but with her sand-beaten face turned inland, she seemed to be watching me with an air of wise understanding. *So another Rhodes has come home,* she seemed to be saying. I touched the shining surface of my golden unicorn and knew the bond was there.

But now there had been enough of talking. "Hold me," I said to Evan. "Just hold me and tell me a lot of foolish things I need to hear."

His tenderness was healing and I knew that all my searching was over. I had come home indeed—at last.

Kirkland Revels

Kirkland Revels

A CONDENSATION OF THE NOVEL BY

Victoria Holt

ILLUSTRATED BY ANNE YVONNE GILBERT

Kirkland Revels—a joyful name for a magnificent manor house on the English moors. But Catherine, who comes there as the bride of Gabriel Rockwell, is to find little joy at her husband's ancestral home. Next to it are the ruins of an ancient abbey. Once inhabited by a self-sufficient community of monks, it is now, centuries later, crumbling, isolated, brooding.

At first Cathy is fascinated by the place and enjoys her solitary strolls there—until she senses that her every movement is being watched. Unknown to the others in the family, a sinister presence is among them . . . hiding in shadowy corners, passing silently under stone archways. Terror strikes as first Gabriel, then Cathy, becomes its prey.

Victoria Holt, whose work has made her name synonymous with that of the gothic thriller, also writes novels as Philippa Carr and Jean Plaidy.

CHAPTER ONE

I MET GABRIEL AND Friday on the same day, and strangely enough I lost them together, so that thereafter I was never able to think of one without the other. My life became a part of theirs because they both began by arousing some protective instinct in me; all my life up to that time I had been protecting myself and I think I felt gratified to find others in need of protection. I had never before had a lover, never before had a dog; when these two appeared it was natural enough that I should welcome them.

I remember the day perfectly. It was spring, and there was a fresh wind blowing over the moors. I had ridden away from Glen House after luncheon with the feeling that I was escaping. This feeling had been with me since I returned home from school in Dijon. My home was a somber place. How could it be otherwise when it was dominated by someone who was no longer there? I had decided on my return that I would never live in the past. I was nineteen and I was determined to live in the present—the past forgotten, the future left to unfold itself.

Thinking back, I realize now that I was a ready victim for the fate that was awaiting me.

Six weeks before it happened, I had come home from the school I had attended for the past four years. I had not been home in all that time, for I lived in Yorkshire and it was a long and expensive journey halfway across France and England, and my education was costly enough. I had expected my father would be at Harrogate to meet my carriage, and had hoped my uncle would be. But that was ridiculous, for if Uncle Dick had been home he would have come all the way to Dijon for me.

It was Jemmy Bell, my father's stableman, who was waiting for me with the trap. He whistled when he saw the size of my trunk. Then he grinned.

"Looks like you've grown into a right grand young lady, Miss Cathy." He was looking incredulously at my bottle-green velvet traveling coat with the leg-o'-mutton sleeves, and the straw hat that was tilted over my eyes and decorated with a wreath of daisies. He did not often see such fashionable clothes in our village.

"How is my father?" I asked. "I expected him to meet me."

Jemmy thrust out his lower lip and shook his head. "A martyr to gout, Miss Cathy. He can't abide the jolting. Besides . . ."

"Besides what?" I asked sharply.

"Well . . ." Jemmy hesitated. "He's just coming out of one of his bad turns."

I was conscious of a little tug of fear remembering those bad turns, which had descended upon the house with a certain regularity. When they were with us we tiptoed about the place and spoke in whispers. As for my father, he would disappear from view, and when he reappeared he was paler than usual; he did not seem to hear when he was spoken to; he frightened me. While I had been away, I had forgotten the bad turns.

My father had no profession. He was what was known as a gentleman. He had come down from Oxford with honors, had taught for a while, and a keen interest in archaeology had taken him to Greece and Egypt. After he had married, my mother traveled with him, but when I was about to be born they settled in Yorkshire, he intending to write works on archaeology and philosophy. He was also something of an artist, and Uncle Dick used to say that the trouble with my father was that he was too talented, whereas he, Uncle Dick, having no talents at all, had become a sailor.

As we set off in the trap I said to Jemmy, "My uncle is not at home?"

Jemmy shook his head. " 'Tis more than six months since we've seen him. Happen it'll be eighteen more afore we do."

I nodded. Uncle Dick was a sea captain and he had written to me that he was off to the other side of the world. I felt depressed; I should have felt so much happier if he had been at home to welcome me. But now the time for dreaming was over. I had to face my home as it was—not what I wished it to be.

We went on, driving through lanes that were sometimes so narrow that the foliage threatened to snatch my hat from my head. Soon this scenery would change; the neat fields and narrow lanes would give way to the wilder country and I should smell the open moors. I thought of them with a burst of pleasure and Jemmy must have noticed my expression brighten, for he said, "Not long now, Miss Cathy."

And there was our village—Glengreen: a few houses clustered around the church; the inn; the green and the cottages. On we went past the church to the white gates, then up the drive and there was Glen House, smaller than I had remembered it, with the venetian blinds drawn to shut out the light. As I got out of the trap, Fanny, who must have heard us arrive, came out to greet me.

She was a round tub of a Yorkshire woman who should have been jolly, but was not. Perhaps years in our house had made her dour. She looked at me critically and said, "You've got thin while you've been away."

I smiled. It was an unusual greeting from someone who had not seen me in four years and who had been the only "mother" I could really remember. Yet it was what I expected. Fanny had never petted me; she would have felt it "daft," as she would call it, to show affection. She prided herself on plain speaking. Studying my clothes, she said, "Yon's what you wear over there, is it?"

I nodded coolly. "Is my father at home?"

"Why, Cathy . . ." It was his voice and he was coming down the staircase to the hall. He looked pale, and I thought to myself, seeing him with the eyes of an adult for the first time, He looks bewildered, as though he did not quite belong in this house, or to this time.

"Father!"

We embraced, but although he endeavored to show some warmth, I was aware that it did not come from the heart. I had a strange feeling that he had been happy to be rid of me, that he was not pleased to have me home. If only Uncle Dick had been there to greet me, how different my homecoming would have been.

BEFORE I HAD been home five minutes the gloomy house closed in on me. I went to my room on the top floor and opened the blinds; light flooded the room. Then I opened the window. As I looked out on the moor I felt myself tingling with pleasure. I remembered how I had exulted in riding there on my pony. When Uncle Dick was home we would ride together, galloping across the moors with the wind in our faces. Tomorrow, I thought, I'll ride out onto the moors . . . this time alone.

How often had I wished that Uncle Dick had been my father!

My uncle lived with us between voyages; it was he who had come to see me at school, lifting me in his arms as he used to when I was a child. He had taken me out and bought me new clothes because he had imagined that some of the other girls were more elegantly clad than I. Dear Uncle Dick! He had seen that I had a very good allowance, and it was because of him that I had a trunk full of clothes in the latest Parisian styles.

I studied my reflection at the dressing table before I got into bed that night. The light from the candles softened my face so that it seemed—though not beautiful nor even pretty—arresting. My eyes were green, my hair black and straight; it felt heavy about my shoulders when I loosened it. If I could wear it so, instead of in two plaits wound about my head, how much more attractive I should be. I thought then that what happens to us leaves its mark upon our faces. Mine was the face of one who had had to do battle. I had been fighting all my life. I looked back over my childhood and I saw a sturdy child with defiant eyes who had subconsciously wanted—despite the exuberant affection of my uncle—the gentle love of a parent.

Although it was long before I slept, I eventually dozed, to be awakened by a voice, and I was not sure in that moment whether I really heard it or dreamed it. "Cathy!" it said in anguish. "Cathy, come back."

I was startled—not because I had heard my name, but because of all the sadness and yearning with which it was spoken. My heart was pounding. I sat up in bed, listening. Someone *had* called my name. I got out of bed and leaned out the window. Immediately below was the open window of my father's room. I felt sobered because I knew what I had heard was him calling out in his sleep. And he called for Cathy.

My mother had been Catherine too. I remembered her vaguely—not as a person but as a presence. Or did I imagine it? I seemed to remember being held tightly in her arms, so tightly that I cried out because I could not breathe. Then it was over, and I never saw her again.

Was that the reason for my father's sadness? Did he, after all those years, still dream of the dead? Perhaps my homecoming had revived old griefs that would have been best forgotten.

HOW LONG WERE the days; how silent the house! As the weeks passed I was finding the house more and more intolerable, and spent a good deal of time out of doors, riding. Ours was a household of people whose lives belonged to the past. I felt rebellion stirring in me. I did not belong here.

One day Fanny said to me, "Your father's going off today." Her face was tightly shut, without expression; I could not tell whether she disapproved of my father's going or not. But I knew she held some secret.

There had always been those times when he went away and did not come home until the next day; and when he did come back we still did not see him because he shut himself away in his room and had his meals taken up to him on a tray. He would eventually emerge looking ravaged, and then he was more silent than ever. I said to Fanny, "So he still goes . . . away?"

"Regular," Fanny answered. "Once in t'month."

I kept thinking about this all day, and wondering. Then it came to me. My father was not very old—perhaps forty. I decided that he had a mistress whom he visited regularly, only to arrive home filled with remorse because he still loved my mother and believed he had desecrated her memory.

He returned the following evening and the pattern was as I remembered it. I did not see him come in; I only knew that he was in his room, that trays were taken up to him. When he did appear the next day he looked so desolate that I longed to comfort him. And so at dinner that evening I said, "Father, are you ill?"

"Ill?" His brows were drawn together in dismay. "Why should you think that I am ill?"

"Because you look so pale and tired. I wondered if there's anything I can do to help. I'm not a child anymore, you know."

"I'm not ill," he said, without looking at me.

"Look here, Father," I said boldly, "I feel something is wrong. I might be able to help."

At that point he looked at me, impatience giving way to coolness. "My dear child," he murmured, "you are imaginative." He picked up his knife and fork then and I understood. It was a curt dismissal. I had rarely felt so alone as I did at that moment. It was as though I were trapped in the web of my childhood, and life would go on in the same dismal way forever.

And then the day arrived when Gabriel Rockwell and Friday came into my life.

I had ridden out onto the moors as usual and had galloped over the peaty ground to the rough road when I saw the Gypsy woman and the dog. The animal was in pitiful condition, thin and pathetic-looking, and about his neck was a rope acting as a lead. I pulled up beside the woman and said, "Why don't you carry him? He's too weak to walk."

"And what's that to you?" she demanded, and I was aware of her sharp beady eyes beneath a tangle of graying black hair. Then her expression changed. She had noticed my smart riding habit, my well-cared-for horse, and I saw cupidity in her face. I was gentry, and gentry were for fleecing. She said, "It's not a bite that's passed me lips, lady, this day and last. And that's the gospel truth."

She did not look as though she were starving, but the dog undoubtedly was. He was a little mongrel with a touch of terrier, and I was drawn to him. "It's the dog who looks hungry, and the rope's hurting him," I said, on impulse adding, "I'll buy him. I'll give you a shilling."

"A shilling! Why, lady, I couldn't bear to part with him. Companion of me sorrows, that's what he's been." She stooped to the dog, and the way in which he cowered betrayed the true state of affairs, so that I was doubly determined to get him. I felt in my pockets for money. To my dismay I discovered that I had come out without any.

She was watching me intently; so was the dog, and I fancied that his terrier eyes were imploring me to rescue him.

I began, "Look here, I've come out without money. . . ."

Even as I spoke her lips curled in disbelief. She gave a vicious jerk at the rope around the dog's neck and he let out a piteous yelp.

And it was then that Gabriel appeared. He was galloping across the moor on a black horse, and he was very elegant, fair-haired and wearing a well-cut dark coat and breeches. Afterward I realized it was a strange thing to do—to stop a stranger and ask him to lend me a shilling to buy a dog. But there he was, like a knight in shining armor. There was a brooding melancholy about his delicate features that immediately interested me, although this was not so apparent on our first meeting as it was to become later.

I called to him as he came onto the road: "Stop a moment, please."

He pulled up. "Is anything wrong?" he asked.

"Yes. This dog is starving," I said.

He looked from me to the dog and the Gypsy, summing up the situation as he did so. "Poor little fellow," he said. "He's in a bad way."

"I want to buy him," I explained, "and I've come out without money."

"Look here," whined the woman, "I ain't selling him. Not for no shilling, like the lady offered."

I looked pleadingly at the young man, who smiled as he dismounted. He said to the Gypsy, "Here's two shillings for the dog."

The woman could not hide her delight. She held out a dirty hand for the money that, with a fastidious gesture, he dropped into her palm. Then he took the rope from her. The dog made a little whimpering sound that I felt to be pleasure.

"Thank you," I cried. "Oh, thank you." I picked up the dog, who made a feeble attempt to wag his tail.

I was drawn to the young man because I knew that he cared as much about the dog's fate as I did. But I was torn between two desires: I wanted to learn more about him, to know what could have produced that melancholy I saw; at the same time I wanted to take the dog home and feed him.

"I must be going," I said.

He nodded. "I'll carry him," he replied, and helped me to mount. Then he mounted and, taking the little creature from me, tucked him under his arm. "Which way?" he asked.

I showed him, and in twenty minutes we reached Glengreen, scarcely speaking on the way. At the gates of Glen House we paused. "He's really yours," I said. "You paid for him."

"Then I make a gift of him to you." His eyes smiled into mine and from that moment the dog became a bond between us. "But I shall want to know whether he lives or not," he said. "May I call and ask . . . tomorrow?"

"If you wish."

"And for whom shall I ask?"

"For Miss Corder . . . Catherine Corder."

"Thank you, Miss Corder. Gabriel Rockwell will call tomorrow."

FANNY WAS HORRIFIED by the presence of the dog. "Happen we'll be finding dog's hair in t'soup and fleas in our beds."

I said nothing. At intervals all through the rest of the day and once in the night I fed the dog myself, on bread and milk in small quantities. I found a basket for his bed and took it to my bedroom. He lay in it too weak to move, but his eyes told me that he knew I was his friend. I wondered what to call him. Then I remembered that I had found him on a Friday and I thought, He'll be my dog Friday. And from then he had his name.

By the morning he was on the way to recovery. Now I waited for the coming of Gabriel. It was three o'clock, and I was in my room, when I heard the sound of his horse's hoofs below. I hurried down to meet him at the steps. He swept off his hat in a manner that I knew would be called daft by Fanny, but I thought it elegant and the height of courtesy.

"So you came!" I burst out. "Dog Friday will recover. I've christened him after the day on which he was found."

"I'm glad you were able to save him," he said.

"*You* did that," I said, and he looked pleased.

I led him inside and the house seemed brighter for his presence. In the drawing room, I rang for tea. While we waited I said, "I trust you did not have to ride far, Mr. Rockwell?"

"From the Black Hart Inn in Tomblersbury."

I knew this was a small village some five or six miles away. "And where is your home?"

"On the outskirts of the village of Kirkland Moorside. The house is called Kirkland Revels."

"Kirkland Revels! That sounds joyous."

The expression that flitted across his face was enough to tell me that my remark had made him uncomfortable. Perhaps he was not happy in his home life. Was that the reason for that moodiness of his? I said quickly, "Kirkland Moorside—is that far from here?"

"Some thirty miles perhaps."

"And you are on holiday in this district, and you were taking a ride on the moors when—"

"When our little adventure occurred. You cannot be more glad than I am that it happened."

I felt reassured that the temporary awkwardness was past and I said, "If you will excuse me, I will bring Friday down."

When I returned with Friday my father was there, and Gabriel was telling him how we had acquired the dog. My father was listening attentively and I was pleased that he showed an interest. At sight of Gabriel, Friday, in his basket, made an effort to rise, and Gabriel, with his long, elegant fingers, gently stroked the dog's ear.

"It is not a bad idea to have a dog in the house," said my father, standing beside us to look down into the basket.

As we stood there together I reflected that this was my happiest afternoon since I had returned from France. I now had something in the house that I could love. I had Friday. I did not think at this stage I had Gabriel too. That came later.

DURING THE NEXT FEW WEEKS Gabriel called regularly at Glen House, and at the end of that first week Friday was fully restored to health. He proved to be the faithful sort, wanting to be not only my companion but my defender as well, and he followed me everywhere. I talked to him continuously. The house had changed; my life had changed because of him.

Then there was Gabriel. Although he had said that soon he would be going home, he continued to stay at the Black Hart. I wondered why. There was a lot I could not quite understand about him, but that air of mystery about him enthralled me. There were times when he talked freely about himself, but even at such times I had the impression he was holding back something, some dark secret perhaps, or something he did not entirely understand himself.

We had become great friends, but I did not ask him any questions about his home even though I longed to know more. There was something unusual about Gabriel, and that should have warned me not to allow myself to become too deeply involved. But my father seemed to like him—or at least he made no protests about his constant visits—and I had been so lonely that I longed for a friend of my own age. So I refused to see any danger signals and we continued to meet.

We liked to ride onto the moors, tether our horses and stretch ourselves out in the shelter of a boulder, looking up at the sky, while we talked in a dreamy, desultory way. Again and again I sensed he was on the verge of confiding some secret to me, but could not quite bring himself to do so.

It was three weeks after we met that Gabriel seemed to come to a decision, and the day he began to talk to me about his home marked a change in our relationship. We were lying stretched out on the moor and he pulled up handfuls of grass as he talked.

"I wonder what you would think of Kirkland Revels," he said.

"I am sure I should find it attractive. It's very old, is it not? Old houses have always been enormously interesting to me."

There was a faraway look in his eyes. Then he began to speak: "The Revels was built in the sixteenth century, when the king dissolved the monasteries. It was then that Kirkland Abbey and its lands were given to my ancestors. They took stones from the abbey and with them built the house. Because it was used as a house in which to make merry it was called Kirkland Revels. . . . I must have had very merry ancestors." He laughed mirthlessly.

"So the stones which built your house were once those of an ancient abbey!"

"Yes, and there's still much of the old abbey in existence," he continued. "When I stand on my balcony I can look across to those gray and ancient arches and it is easy to imagine that they are not merely ruins. You can almost see the monks in their habits moving silently among the stones. You will see what I mean when . . ." He stopped, and I saw a slow smile curve his delicate lips.

I am forthright and had never been able to hedge, so I said, "Are you suggesting that I shall see it?"

The smile expanded. "I have been a guest in your home. I should like you to be one in mine." Then it came bursting out: "Miss Corder, I shall have to go home soon."

"You don't want to, do you, Mr. Rockwell?"

"I believe we are great friends. I feel we are," he said.

"We have known each other but three weeks," I reminded him.

"But the circumstances were exceptional. Please call me Gabriel."

I hesitated, then I laughed. "What's in a name? Our friendship cannot be greater or less, whatever I call you. What were you saying, Gabriel?"

"Catherine!" He almost whispered my name as he leaned on his elbow to look at me. "You are right, I don't want to go back. And the reason is that it would mean saying good-by to you. These have been the happiest weeks of my life."

"Perhaps we should meet again."

"When?" he asked almost angrily. "How do we know what time is left to us?"

"How strangely you talk, as if you thought that one . . . or both . . . of us might die tomorrow."

There was a faint flush in his cheeks that seemed to make his eyes burn brightly. "Who can say when death shall come?"

"How morbid you have grown. I am nineteen. You have told me that you are twenty-three. People of our ages do not talk of dying."

"*One* evidently does. Catherine, will you marry me?"

I was shocked by this unexpected outburst and I said, "How can you speak of marriage after such a short acquaintance?"

"It does not seem short. We have met every day. I know that you are all I want, and that is enough for me."

I was silent. In spite of our great friendship I had not considered marriage with Gabriel. I should be desolate if he went away, but when I thought of marriage he seemed almost like a stranger. There was so little I knew about him; I had never met any of his family. Indeed when they, or his home, briefly intruded into our conversation I was immediately conscious of Gabriel's withdrawing from me. In view of all this I thought it very strange that he should suddenly suggest marriage.

He went on: "Catherine, what is your answer?"

"It is no, Gabriel. There is so much we do not know about each other."

"You mean there is so much you do not know about me."

"Perhaps that is what I mean."

"But what do you want to know? We love horses, we love dogs, we find pleasure in each other's company. I can laugh and be happy with you. I could never be completely happy with anyone else, never laugh so freely."

"It seems a flimsy structure on which to base a marriage."

"You feel I have spoken too soon, Catherine?"

I knew then how desolate I should be if he went away, and I said quickly, "Yes, that is it. This is too soon. . . ."

"At least," he said, "I do not have to fear a rival. Do not say no, Catherine. Think of how much I want this to be, and try to want it a little yourself."

I stood up. I was no longer in the mood to stay on the moors. He made no protest, so we rode back and said good-by.

When I reached the stables Friday was waiting there for me. He always knew when I went riding and never failed to be in the stableyard watching for my return. I lifted him in my arms and hugged him. I was growing more and more fond of him every day, and my affection for him enhanced my feelings for Gabriel.

As I turned into the house it occurred to me how very much I needed to escape from here. Now a way was being offered me. If I refused to take it, might I not be regretful for the rest of my life? I wondered what marriage with Gabriel would be like. I was already beginning to believe it was a state I could contemplate without abhorrence.

MAY WAS UPON us now and the days were warm and sunny; it was a joy to escape to the moors. With each day I was withdrawing farther and farther from those at Glen House and feeling closer and closer to Gabriel. We talked of ourselves, yet there was a feverishness about Gabriel as though he were looking over his shoulder at some pursuer, while being desperately conscious of passing time. He was willing enough now to tell me about his home. Perhaps he had already convinced himself that I would marry him and that it would be not only his home but mine.

In my imagination it was a hazy gray edifice of ancient stones. There was a balcony, I knew, and I could picture the scene from that balcony, for Gabriel described it to me many times: the river that wound through meadows and past woods; then a quarter mile from the house those magnificent ruins; and across a wooden bridge, beyond the river, the wild moorland country. I also learned by degrees that Gabriel, like myself, had known no mother; she had been advanced in years when he was born and had not survived. Our motherlessness was a further bond between us.

He had a sister, fifteen years older than himself, a widow with a seventeen-year-old son—his father was now very old. "Ruth, my sister, rules the household," he told me, "and will do so until I marry. Then of course my wife will do that, because I am the only son and the Revels will one day be mine."

"When you speak of the Revels you do so in a tone of reverence," I said. "And yet you are not eager to return."

He took no notice of my observation, but murmured as though to himself, "It ought to have been Simon. . . ."

"Who is Simon?"

"Simon Redvers. A sort of cousin. A Rockwell through his grandmother, who is my father's sister. You won't like him very much. But then you'll rarely meet. There isn't much communication between the Revels and his home, Kelly Grange."

He was talking as though there was no doubt that I would marry him and that one day his house would be my home.

Sometimes I wondered if there was not some subtlety in Gabriel. He painted pictures in my mind, so that gradually his home and family came alive for me; I became caught up in his life. I knew that if he went away I should be desperately lonely.

And one sunny day, as we sat on the moor against a boulder with Friday crouched before us on the grass, Gabriel said to me, "There's something I haven't told you, Catherine."

I felt relieved, because I knew he was going to tell me something that he'd been trying to for a long time.

"I want you to say you'll marry me," he went on, "but so far you haven't. You don't dislike me—you're happy in my company, Catherine?"

"Of course," I said. "If you go away . . ."

"You'd miss me, Catherine, but not as much as I should miss you. I want you to come back with me. I love you. I never want to leave you again." He moved closer to me and put his arm about me. "But, Catherine, there are things you should know. I cannot be happy without you and . . . there cannot be much time left to me."

I drew away. "What do you mean?" I demanded sharply.

He looked straight ahead and said, "I cannot live more than a few years. I have received my sentence of death."

I was angry, for I could not bear to hear his talk of dying. "Stop being dramatic," I commanded, "and tell me exactly what all this means."

"It's perfectly simple. I have a weak heart—it is a family complaint. I had an elder brother who died young. My mother died at my birth, of the same heart condition. I could die tomorrow, or next year. It would not be a great many years, Catherine."

I stood up. I yearned to comfort him, but I was so overcome by my emotions that I could not speak. I started to walk quickly and Gabriel fell into step beside me. We were both silent, and Friday kept running ahead to look back at us anxiously, his eyes imploring us to be gay.

That night I scarcely slept at all. I could think of nothing but Gabriel and his need of me. I kept seeing those melancholy eyes and hearing him say,

"I could die tomorrow," and remembering how at times he could be happy. And I could make him happy for what time was left to him—I alone. How could I turn away from someone who needed me so much? Perhaps I was not in love; perhaps pity was at the root of my feelings for Gabriel. But by the morning I had made up my mind.

THE BANNS WERE read in the village church and Gabriel went back to Kirkland Revels, I presumed to inform his family, while I prepared for my wedding. When Gabriel had formally asked for my hand, my father, looking worried, had hesitated, and I knew that he was wishing that Uncle Dick were here to consult. He reminded Gabriel of my youth and the short time we had known each other, but I assured him that I had quite made up my mind. After a while Father said that he supposed I must have my way.

Three days before our marriage was to take place, Gabriel came back and put up at our village inn. When he called at Glen House I hurried to the sitting room where he awaited me, and as soon as I opened the door he strode toward me and we embraced. He looked excited, younger; some of the strain had gone from him. I took his face in my hands and kissed it. I wanted to look after him, to make what life was left to him completely happy. I was not passionately in love with him; passion was something I knew nothing about at that time. Yet I loved him nonetheless, and when he held me, I knew that the kind of love I had for him was what he wanted.

I withdrew from his arms and made him sit down on the couch. I wanted to hear what his family's reactions were to the news and how many were coming to the wedding. "Well, you see," he said slowly, "my father is too infirm to make the journey. As for the others . . ." He shrugged.

"Gabriel!" I cried. "Do you mean none of them is coming?"

"Well, you see, my aunt Sarah, like Father, is too old to travel. . . ."

"But there's your sister and her son."

He looked uneasy. "Oh, darling," he said, "what does it matter? It's not *their* wedding, is it?"

"But not to come! Does that mean they don't approve?"

"Of course they approve. But the ceremony itself is not important."

I tried to hide my uneasiness. It was very strange. No members of his family at the wedding! But I told myself that I must not expect Gabriel's relatives to behave conventionally, any more than Gabriel himself did.

"Happen they think you're not good enough for 'em," was Fanny's verdict. But I was not going to let Fanny see how the behavior of Gabriel's family disturbed me, so I merely shrugged my shoulders. All in good time I should discover for myself what they thought of the marriage.

And so I was married to Gabriel in our village church on a day in June about two months after we first met. I wore a white dress made rather hurriedly by our village seamstress, and I had a white veil and a wreath of

orange blossoms. There were very few guests at the reception, which was held in the drawing room at Glen House: the vicar and his wife, the doctor and his, and that was all.

Immediately afterward, Gabriel and I left for a week's holiday on the coast in Scarborough. I felt when we were alone together in our train compartment that we were like any bride and groom despite the unconventional manner of our marrying. When Gabriel held my hand I knew I had never seen him look so peaceful. Friday was with us, traveling in a loosely woven closed basket, and I too felt relaxed. And so we reached our hotel.

During those first days of our honeymoon, I felt my love for Gabriel growing because he needed me so desperately to lift him out of the dark moods that could quickly descend upon him; there was a wonderful gratification in being so important to another human being. I would let nothing stand in the way of his happiness for the years that were left to us.

CHAPTER TWO

DURING THE LAST DAY of the honeymoon we had both been on edge. Gabriel had been silent and—although I would not admit this—I had been a little nervous about facing the Rockwell family. Friday sensed our mood and lost some of his exuberance. The journey homeward was a long one because we had to change trains, and the afternoon was over by the time we reached Keighley, the station nearest Kirkland Moorside.

A carriage was waiting for us—rather a grand one—and when the coachman saw me I fancied he was startled. Surely he had not heard of Gabriel's wedding, for why else should he be surprised when a bridegroom arrived with his bride? Gabriel helped me into the carriage while the coachman dealt with our luggage, taking covert looks at me as he did so.

Dusk had fallen, so it was in the half-light that I first saw my new home.

We had passed over the moors, which were wild and eerie in this light, and we were coming near the hamlet of Kirkland Moorside when Gabriel leaned toward me. "Now you should be able to see Kelly Grange—my cousin Simon's place."

I strained my eyes and thought I saw the faint outlines of a house away to the right. Then we went over a bridge and I caught my first glimpse of the abbey. I saw the ancient Norman tower with walls clustered about it, and it was impossible to see at this distance that it was a mere shell. It looked grand yet forbidding.

We were driving along a road bordered by massive oaks; then suddenly we were in the clear and there before me was the house. I caught my breath, for it was beautiful. I was struck by its size. It looked like a massive oblong of stone. I later learned that it was built around a courtyard and that, although it was of Tudor origin, it had been restored through the subsequent centuries. The windows were mullioned and about them were fantastic carvings of devils and angels, pitchforks and harps, scrolls and Tudor roses. This was indeed a historic baronial hall. I thought then how small Glen House must have seemed to Gabriel.

About a dozen worn stone steps led to a great stone portico carved in a way similar to the windows. There was a heavy oak door decorated with finely wrought iron, and even as I began to mount the steps the door opened and I met the first member of my new family. She was very fair, a woman in her late thirties whose resemblance to Gabriel told me at once that she was his widowed sister, Ruth Grantley.

She looked at me appraisingly a moment, then said, "How do you do? You must forgive us if we're surprised. We only heard this morning. Gabriel, it *was* perverse of you to be so secretive."

She took my hands and smiled, but what struck me was her coldness. "Come along in," she said. "I'm afraid you'll find us unprepared."

I looked at Gabriel questioningly. What could have been the point in not telling her?

We stepped from a passageway into the hall, in which a log fire was blazing. I immediately felt the air of antiquity about the place. The walls were hung with tapestries that doubtless had been worked by members of this family centuries ago, and in the center of the hall was a refectory table with utensils of brass and pewter. "Well?" said Ruth as I looked around me.

"It's so . . . exciting to be here," I said.

She seemed a little gratified. She turned to Gabriel. "Gabriel, why all this secrecy?" Then, turning to me, "He seems to have no reason for keeping us in the dark until this morning."

"I wanted to surprise you all," said Gabriel. "Catherine," he went on, "you'll be tired. You'd like to go to our room."

"Of course you would," put in Ruth. "And meet the family later. We're all very eager to know you." Friday, in his basket, barked suddenly and she said, "A dog too? So you are fond of animals, Catherine?"

"Yes, very. I'm sure everyone will be fond of Friday." I was aware of a movement above me and I looked up quickly to a gallery high in the wall.

"That's the minstrels' gallery," Gabriel explained. "We use it for the musicians when we have a ball."

"We adhere to old customs here, Catherine," said Ruth, in a voice suggesting that I couldn't possibly understand the traditions of a family such as theirs.

A dignified manservant whom Gabriel addressed as William appeared, to handle our luggage. He mounted the stairs with my trunk. Gabriel took my arm and we followed. Ruth came after us and I could feel her eyes on my back, taking in every detail. I was never more pleased with Uncle Dick, for my smart traveling costume of dark blue gabardine gave me confidence.

It was a wide staircase of great beauty. At the top of the first flight was a door, and Gabriel said, "That's the door to the minstrels' gallery." I hoped he would throw it open and that I should see whether someone was there, because I was certain that I had seen a movement and wondered what member of the household had preferred to hide there to take a glimpse of me instead of coming down to welcome me. But he did not.

"My rooms," Gabriel told me, "are at the top of the house. It's a long climb."

We had reached the third floor when a young man appeared. He was tall and slim, and very like Ruth. He had cried, "Are they here yet, Mother? What's she—" before he saw us. He stopped, laughing at himself, not in the least embarrassed, while his eyes went to me.

"This is Luke, my nephew," said Gabriel.

"My son," murmured Ruth.

"I am delighted to meet you," I said, and held out my hand.

He took it and bowed over it so that a lock of his long fair hair fell over his face. "The delight then is mutual," he said. "It's amusing to have a wedding in the family." He was very like his mother, and Gabriel too: the same rather prominent, aristocratic features, the delicate fairness, the almost languid air. "What do you think of the house?" he asked.

"She has been in it less than ten minutes," his mother reminded him.

"Tomorrow I will take you on a tour," he promised. He bowed once more and stood aside for us to pass, then joined the end of the procession up to the fourth-floor rooms that I gathered had always been Gabriel's.

"Here we are," said Gabriel when we'd reached the top floor of the house. I heard Friday in his basket on my arm then; he whimpered faintly as though he sensed my mood and knew I felt that I was resented here. I was in an extraordinary position. I was eventually to be the mistress of this house, and yesterday no one in it had been aware of my existence. No wonder I was resented.

I shook off the uneasy feeling and followed Gabriel down a corridor until we came to a door, which he threw open. I gave a gasp of pleasure, for I was standing on the threshold of a charming room. Heavy red damask curtains hung at the windows; a fire was burning in a big open fireplace. On the beautifully carved white marble mantelpiece were candles in gleaming silver candlesticks, which threw a soft light about the room. I saw the four-poster bed with curtains to match those at the windows, the tallboy, the chairs with tapestry backs worked in gold and red. On a table was a bowl of red roses.

Gabriel looked at them and flushed. "Thank you, Ruth," he said.

"I'm going to leave you now," she told us. "I'll have hot water sent up.

Could you be ready to dine in three quarters of an hour?" When I said we could, she and Luke left us.

As the door closed Gabriel and I looked at each other in silence. Then Gabriel said, "What's wrong, Catherine?"

I could not restrain my resentment. "Why on earth didn't you tell them you were getting married!"

He looked distressed. "Well, I didn't want any fuss—"

"Fuss!" I interrupted. "But I thought you went back to tell them."

"So I did."

"And you found you couldn't when it came to the point?"

"There might have been opposition. I didn't want that."

"You mean they wouldn't have thought me worthy to marry into their family?"

"Good heavens, no!" Gabriel caught me by the shoulders, but I freed myself impatiently. "They'll be delighted, once they know you. They don't like change though. You know what families are."

"No," I retorted, "I don't. Explain why there has to be this mystery."

He looked very unhappy. "But there is no mystery. It's simply that I didn't tell them. I wanted to marry you as quickly as possible so that we could make the most of all the time that's left."

When he spoke like that my anger disappeared. The desire to make him happy enveloped me.

I vaguely sensed that he was afraid of something in this house, and that he wanted an ally. I was to be that ally. I knew because, although I had been in Kirkland Revels less than half an hour, I was catching that fear.

"Friday's still in his basket," I said.

"I'll take him outside." He opened the basket and Friday jumped out, barking his pleasure to be free. There was a knock and I turned sharply, for the sound did not come from the door by which we had entered. I noticed then that there were two doors in this room.

A voice in a broad Yorkshire accent said, "Hot water, master."

The door was shut before I had a chance to see the owner of the voice.

"That's the old powder closet," said Gabriel, indicating the door. "I use it for my ablutions. You'll find it useful."

He fastened the leash on the dog. "You don't want to lose yourself on your first evening, Friday," he said. And when he had gone I went into the powder closet. There I saw the hip bath, the cans of hot water, soap and towels. A big mirror in an ornate gilded frame was fixed to the wall, and attached to this frame were two gilded candlesticks in which candles burned.

In the mirror my eyes appeared to be more green than usual, and I found that they quickly strayed from my reflection and were looking over my shoulder, probing the shadowy corners of the room. Old houses in twilight . . . was it possible that in such places the presence of those long dead lingered? I took off my costume and began to wash the stain of travel from my person. Tomorrow, in daylight, I should laugh at my fancies.

THERE WERE SIX of us that night at dinner. This was the family. Ruth and her son, Luke, I had already met. I now encountered Gabriel's father, Sir Matthew Rockwell, and his aunt, Miss Sarah Rockwell; they both seemed very old, being in their eighties.

Because Sir Matthew was obviously pleased to see me, I began to feel happier. He was tall but stooped; his hair was white, his face quite ruddy, and his blue eyes bright—one might say jaunty. "Gabriel's lucky to have such a beautiful wife," he said flatteringly. He kept my hand in his, then kissed it lingeringly. Not too old for gallantry, I guessed. He gave the impression that he had enjoyed life and hoped the young members of his family would follow his example.

"You must sit beside me," he said. "I want to look at you and hear what you think of your new family." So I sat beside him at the dinner table and every now and then he would lean toward me and pat my hand.

Aunt Sarah was quite different, although I recognized the Rockwell features and fairness. Her blue eyes were vacant and she had an air of strain, as though she could not quite catch up with what was going on about her. I imagined her to be even older than her brother.

"Sarah," shouted Sir Matthew, "this is my new daughter, Catherine."

Sarah nodded and gave him a smile that was sweet in its innocence. "Are you interested in tapestry, dear?" she asked.

"I admire it, but I don't excel at it," I said.

"I must show Claire my tapestries. She'd like to see them," she went on.

There was a brief silence. Then Ruth said quietly, "This is Catherine, Aunt. Not Claire." And to me: "Claire was Gabriel's mother."

Ruth said that before the end of the week there would be a dinner party to celebrate our marriage. "There are certain people who will be most eager to meet you," she said.

"Whom do you propose to ask?" Gabriel put in quickly.

"Well . . . Simon, I suppose. After all, he's part of the family. We shall have to ask Hagar too, but I doubt she'll come. And I thought the vicar and his wife, and of course the Smiths."

Sir Matthew nodded. Then he turned to me. "We want you to feel at home, my dear, without delay."

I thanked him. I felt then that they were doing their best to make me welcome.

When the meal was over, Gabriel came to my side and remarked that I looked tired. "No doubt it has been a busy day," murmured Ruth. "We shall all understand if you retire early."

I said good night to my new family and Gabriel and I climbed to our room at the top of the house. Friday came out of his basket to greet us as we entered. It was clear that he too was finding it difficult to adjust to his new surroundings.

"Before we retire," Gabriel said, "I want to show you the view from the balcony. Come now."

He put his arm about me and we went out into the corridor, to the end, where he opened a door and we stepped onto the balcony. The moon was high and its light shone on the scene about us. I saw the abbey ruins, like a great ghost of its former self. I saw the dark river winding through the grassland, and the black hump of a bridge, and beyond, away in the distance, the shadowy outline of the moor.

"It's beautiful," I breathed.

"Every night I come here. This view has held a fascination for me since I was a child." He looked down suddenly. "Two of my ancestors—the only two suicides in our history—threw themselves over parapets, though not this one. There are three others in the house."

I felt a shiver run along my spine as I too looked down into the dimness below. "Come along in," I said. "I'm tired." And when we entered the room I felt my fear returning.

In the days that followed I tried to make myself a pleasant addition to the family. I wanted Ruth to know that I had no intention of ousting her from her position as mistress of the house, that I considered she had more right to be the chatelaine of Kirkland Revels than I had. She told me of the dinner party she was planning, and I replied that she must go ahead with her plans, for I had come from a very small household and had done no housekeeping. This seemed to please her and I felt happy.

I had never stayed in such a large or ancient house. The furniture had been there for centuries, and at times the present seemed to merge into the past; this was how the house had looked when other footsteps had been heard, other figures had made these long shadows on the walls. I enjoyed the house in the daytime, but the habit of looking furtively over my shoulder when I was alone, especially at dusk, persisted.

On that first morning, Gabriel was with his father; I guessed there were matters concerning the estate that had to be discussed, and I planned to take Friday for a walk, for I was eager to explore the abbey ruins. But on my way downstairs I met Luke. He grinned at me and stooped to have a friendly word with Friday. Then he asked, "Have you seen the house yet?"

"Not all of it," I said.

"I'll take you on a conducted tour. You ought to know it. You'll get lost if you don't."

I was anxious to be friends, so I accepted his invitation. I had had no idea of the size of the house. I reckoned there must be at least a hundred rooms. Each of the four parts that enclosed the courtyard was like a house in itself, and it was easy to get lost.

"The story goes," Luke told me, "that one of our ancestors married four wives and kept them in separate parts of the house, and for a long time none of them knew of the existence of the other three."

"It sounds like Bluebeard."

"Perhaps the original Bluebeard was a Rockwell. There are dark secrets in our history, Catherine. You've no idea the family you've married into!"

His light eyes regarded me with amusement not untinged with cynicism, and I was reminded of Gabriel's decision not to tell the family that he was going to marry me. Of course they regarded me as a fortune hunter, for not only would Gabriel inherit this house but also the means to live in it, and a title as well, when his father died.

"I'm beginning to learn," I told him.

I went through those rooms in a state of bewilderment—there were so many, and all had the high windows, the lofty ceilings often decorated with exquisite carving, the paneled walls. I saw the other three balconies so like ours; I examined the massive stone pillars that supported them and the faces of gargoyles that grimaced at me from everywhere.

When we reached the picture gallery Luke took me around, explaining who the subjects of the portraits were. There was the first Sir Luke, who had built the place, a fierce-looking gentleman in armor. There were Thomas, Mark, John, several Matthews and another Luke. "We always have Biblical names," he said. "Always Matthew, Mark, Luke and John, Simon, any you can think of, even down to the Angel Gabriel. Now that's Sir Luke . . . he died young. He jumped off the balcony in the west wing."

I stared at the young man in the picture.

"And that," Luke went on, "is John who, about a hundred years after, decided he'd die the same way. He jumped off the balcony in the north wing. Strange, isn't it? Oh, and here's your father-in-law himself."

A younger Sir Matthew looked back at me, his flowing cravat and green velvet jacket the essence of elegance. I judged him to have been something of a rake in his day. Beside him was his wife, Claire, Gabriel's mother, who had died at his birth. She was beautiful in a frail way. And there was a picture of Gabriel himself, looking young and innocent.

"You'll be beside him," said Luke. "Captured like the rest and held prisoner on canvas, so that in two hundred years the new lady of the house will come to look at you and wonder about you."

I shivered, and was conscious of a great desire to escape from Luke, to get out of the house, because the talk of suicides oppressed me. "Friday is impatient for his walk," I said. "It is very good of you to have taken so much trouble to show me everything."

"But I have not shown you *everything!* There is a great deal more for you to see."

"I shall enjoy it more another time," I replied firmly.

He bowed his head. "When it will be my pleasure to continue our tour."

I went down the stairs and made my way to the abbey. As Friday and I approached the ancient piles I was struck with wonder. I could have believed that this was not a ruin, for the great tower was intact and so was the wall facing me; it was not until I came close that I realized there was no roof but the sky.

The abbey had been vast. Here, I told myself, must have been the cloister, here the nave, here the monks' dormitory. I wondered from what part of the abbey the stones had been taken to build the house. I wanted to learn something of the history of the house and family to which I now belonged. There was so much I did not know about my own husband. Naturally he was moody; he was a young man afflicted with a disease of the heart that threatened his life. But I would make him happy. Moreover I would not accept the inevitability of his early death as he seemed to. I would take such good care of him that he would live on.

Friday's barking startled me out of my daydream. I called, "Friday! Friday!" As he did not come to me, I went to look for him.

I found him in the hands of a strange man; he was struggling, and if he had not been held so expertly, he would have bitten the hands that imprisoned him. "Friday," I called again. Then the man turned to look at me. He was of medium height and I was struck by his brilliant dark eyes and olive complexion.

He released the dog and, taking off his hat, bowed. Friday, barking furiously, stood between me and the stranger as though to protect me.

"So the dog is yours, madam?" said the man.

"Yes, what happened? He's usually so friendly."

"He was a little annoyed with me. He didn't understand that I probably saved his life." The man pointed to what I now saw was a well. "He was perilously perched on the edge, looking down. If he had decided to explore further, that would have been the end of him."

"Then I have to thank you."

"I should put him on a lead if you bring him here again. You will come here again, won't you? I can see this place intrigues you."

"Surely everyone would be interested."

"Some more than others. May I introduce myself? I believe I know you. You are Mrs. Gabriel Rockwell, are you not?"

"But how did you know?"

He spread his hands and smiled; it was a warm, friendly smile. "A simple deduction. I knew you had arrived and, as I know almost everyone in these parts, I put two and two together and tried a guess."

"Your guess was correct."

"Then welcome to our community. My name is Deverel Smith. As a doctor and an old friend of the family I am at the Revels almost every day. Sir Matthew and Miss Rockwell both need my services. In fact I was going to call there today. Shall we walk back together?"

We did so, and he made me feel that I had found a new friend. He talked familiarly of the family, and told me that he had been invited to dine at the house on Saturday. "My daughter and I," he added.

I was astonished that he should have a daughter old enough to be invited to a dinner party, for he looked to be somewhere in his mid-thirties. He saw my surprise, and I liked him no less because he appeared to be pleased by it. He said, "I have a seventeen-year-old daughter. She enjoys parties. My wife is not well enough to attend them."

"I shall look forward to meeting your daughter on Saturday."

"Damaris is looking forward to meeting you." He smiled.

"Damaris! That is an unusual name."

"You like it? It's from the Bible. A brief mention, but it's there."

We went into the Revels together. The doctor sent one of the servants to tell Ruth he had arrived, and I went up to my room.

I WORE A gown of white chiffon and lace, very simple, on the night of the dinner party. I had no qualms about the dress because I knew it would appear elegant in any company. I put my hair up in a coronet, a style that Gabriel liked; then I waited for him to come in and dress.

As he did not come, I went out onto the balcony to see if he was on the grounds. He was nowhere in sight, but I heard voices coming up from the porch. A deep masculine voice was saying, "So I gather, Ruth, you have not taken to our little bride?"

I felt the hot color rush into my cheeks.

"It's early yet," answered Ruth.

There was a laugh. "I've no doubt she found our Gabriel easy prey," the voice went on. "Why did you let him stray so far from home? He was bound to find some little fortune hunter sooner or later."

I stood still, furiously angry. Then the man who had been speaking stepped away from the house a little, and I saw him. His hair was light brown. He was very tall and deeply bronzed. There was a resemblance to the Rockwells, but a faint one. Whoever he was, I hated him.

I was trembling as I went back to our bedroom. Gabriel was there. "I forgot the time," he said. "I shall have to dress quickly."

It was on the tip of my tongue to tell him what I had heard, but I changed my mind. No, I would fight my own battles; I should have to teach this relative, whoever he was, a lesson. Gabriel dressed, and when we went down I met my enemy.

He was Simon Redvers, the cousin. Gabriel introduced me. His light brown eyes were cynical, and when he took my hand, they looked straight into mine and I knew exactly what he was thinking. His mouth was smiling slightly, but not his eyes. I knew my own were flashing with anger, for I could not get the sound of his words out of my ears.

"How do you do?" he said.

"I am well, thank you," I answered.

"I suppose I should congratulate you."

"Pray do not, unless you wish to."

He seemed faintly amused. Just then Dr. Smith and his daughter arrived. The doctor came over and greeted me warmly. I was pleased to turn my attention to him, but the girl who accompanied him immediately claimed it and, I imagine, that of everyone in the room.

Damaris Smith was one of the loveliest creatures I had ever seen. She was slim and lissome, of medium height, with olive skin. Her hair was smooth and silky with that blackness that has a sheen of blue in it, like a bird's wing. Her eyes were black and languorous; the shape of her face was a perfect oval; her lips were delicately formed yet sensuous; her nose was almost aquiline, giving dignity as well as beauty. There was silence as she entered—the silence that was homage to her beauty.

I asked myself, Why did Gabriel marry me when there was such a goddess on his very doorstep? Her effect on Luke was that he was less nonchalant than usual, and Sir Matthew's admiration was apparent. But he admired all women, it seemed, and during dinner he divided his attention between myself and Damaris.

Damaris herself I did not understand; she was a quiet person who had a smile for everyone. The first impression she gave was merely that of an innocent girl; I don't know what made me feel that that smooth, rather expressionless perfection was a mask.

The dinner was in honor of Gabriel and myself, and our health was drunk. Apart from the family, the Smiths and Simon Redvers, there were the vicar Cartwright and his wife and two other local people.

Simon Redvers, who was sitting next to me at the table, asked what I thought of the countryside and how it compared with that part from which I had come. I answered that when not at school I had lived as close to the moor as they did, so that the change was not very great. I believe that a note of asperity came into my voice when I addressed the man, that he noticed it, and it amused him. He said, "You must have your portrait painted so that it can be added to those in the gallery."

"There's plenty of time for that."

"You'll make a good subject. Proud . . . strong . . . determined."

"So you read character?"

"When it is there for me to see."

"I had no idea that I had such a legible face."

He laughed. "It's unusual in one so young. But don't you agree that as one grows older fate . . . life . . . whatever you call it, is like a mischievous artist, gradually etching lines of betrayal?" He gazed along the table; I refused to follow his gaze.

"I believe what you say to be true, but is it not a little impertinent to test the theory on the present company?"

"You'll find me a blunt Yorkshireman. They're not noted for tact."

I saw a smile touch his lips; I thought it rather a brutal smile. But there was great virility there. His personality dominated the company in its masculine way as Damaris' beauty did in the feminine.

Simon enjoyed baiting me because I was a worthy opponent. At least I had the satisfaction of knowing that; even if he did consider me a fortune hunter, he did not find me a simpering one. I said impulsively, "You are Gabriel's cousin, are you not? Yet how unlike him you are!"

He gave me a cool, appraising smile. I was telling him that I did not like him, and he was retaliating by implying that I would not have caught him as I had caught Gabriel. As if I should have wanted to! As if there had been any "catching" in our marriage!

Sir Matthew leaned forward and patted my arm. "Don't listen to my nephew. He's annoyed because he's a Rockwell on the distaff side and the Revels is not for him. The Redvers family were always jealous of the Revels. Simon's grandfather married one of my sisters but she wouldn't stay away from the Revels. She was always coming back from Kelly Grange and bringing first her son, then her grandson. Don't see you here so often now, Simon."

"I must remedy that," said Simon, smiling ironically at me. Sir Matthew chuckled deeply.

After dinner the ladies retired to the drawing room and I tried to get to know Damaris, but it was not easy; she was pleasant, but so reserved that she made little effort to help with the conversation, and I decided that a blank mind lay behind that lovely face. I was pleased when the men joined us; and when Simon Redvers kept at Damaris' side—rather to the chagrin of Luke—I was glad and gave myself up to conversation with the vicar, who told me how the grounds of the Revels were used for the annual church garden party, and that he and his wife were hoping to do a miracle play or a pageant in the abbey ruins for next year's Midsummer Night's Eve. He hoped that I would support their endeavors.

It was shortly after dinner that Sir Matthew was taken ill. He lay back in his chair, his face a deeper red than usual. Dr. Smith was immediately at his side, and with the help of Simon and Luke took him to his room. The incident naturally broke up the party, but when Dr. Smith rejoined us he assured us that Sir Matthew would be about again in a day or so.

When Gabriel and I retired to our room he put his arm about me and told me that I had been a success and he was proud of me.

"I'm not sure that I was very popular with everybody," I said.

"Who could fail to be charmed?"

"That cousin of yours for one."

"Oh, Simon! He is a born cynic. He is jealous. He'd throw away Kelly Grange for the Revels any day."

"I don't understand why his desire for the Revels should affect his attitude toward me."

"Perhaps he's jealous of me for more reasons than one."

"How absurd!"

At that moment Friday began barking furiously and leaping at the door as though he would break it down. Gabriel turned pale. "Someone's out there," he whispered.

"It's evidently someone Friday doesn't like," I said.

The dog continued to bark frenziedly. I picked him up, opened the door and called, "Who's there?" There was no answer, but Friday was struggling to get out of my arms.

"Something has disturbed him," I said. "I'm going to put him on his lead. I don't want him jumping over the balcony." I slipped the lead on; when I set him down he tugged at it with all his might. He dragged me down the corridor, but before we reached the door to the balcony he leaped at a door to the left of it. I tried this and it opened easily. It was a large empty cupboard, and Friday ran into it and began sniffing around. Then we went out onto the balcony; there was no one there either. "You see, Friday," I said, "it's nothing."

When I returned with him to the bedroom I saw how pale Gabriel still was, and a terrible thought came to me then: He was afraid of what was out there and he let me go alone. Was the man I had married a coward? I discarded the thought almost as soon as it entered my head. "Much ado about nothing," I said to him lightly.

Friday appeared to have satisfied himself; when I took him off the lead, he leaped into his basket and curled up there. As I prepared for bed I wondered what Gabriel had been so disturbed about. The balcony seemed to hold a morbid attraction for him. Had he thought it was a ghost prowling out there? In a house like this fancies came easily.

IT WAS LATE the next afternoon when I discovered that Friday was missing. I remembered then that I had not seen him since the morning. It had been a busy day, for the guests of the previous night had all paid duty calls to give conventional thanks. I saw Simon Redvers ride up on a magnificent gray horse, and I decided to stay in my room until he had left. Then Dr. Smith and Damaris came by—the doctor to see how Sir Matthew was after his attack. With all the guests arriving it seemed like a continuation of the party. So it wasn't until dinner was over that evening and there was still no sign of Friday that I really became alarmed. Was it possible he was lost? I slipped on a light coat, intending to ask Gabriel to come with me to look for him, but I could not find my husband and so went out alone.

I kept calling Friday's name, straining my ears for an answering bark. There was none. I found myself wandering toward the abbey. It had been a glorious day and the red sky was a sign of a fine day to follow.

It was an uncanny experience to stand among those ruins at sunset. Here a community of monks had lived long ago, and I could almost believe that I was moving back in time—that the half-walls would become walls in their entirety, that a roof would appear to shut out the blood-red sky.

Then suddenly fear came to me. I felt that I was not alone; that through those narrow slits in the walls, which had once been windows, eyes watched me. I imagined that somewhere, not far distant, I heard a stone dislodged and, following that, a footstep. "Who's there?" I called, and the hollow sound of my own voice startled me. I felt my heart hammering.

I walked about. There was nothing but those piles of stones, those half-walls. I began to call Friday again. I noticed that it was getting darker. The sunset afterglow was disappearing and soon full darkness would descend upon me . . . and the abbey. I tried to leave by the way I thought I had come, but after a few minutes I realized that I was in a section of those vast ruins I had not visited before. I was lost in a maze of stone while with every passing second the last light was fading. I blundered on. My one thought, my great desire, was to escape from Kirkland Abbey.

At length I did escape; in a panic of fear I came out on the far side of the abbey. The ruins were now between me and the house, but nothing would have induced me to go back the way I had come. I found a road and, guessing my direction, I hurried on, now and then breaking into a run.

As I came to a clump of trees through which the road wound, a figure emerged and for a moment I knew terror. Then it took on a familiar shape and a voice I knew said, "Hello! Have you got the devil at your heels?"

At the note of mockery in that voice, annoyance swamped my fear. "I lost my way, Mr. Redvers. But I think I'm on the right road now."

He laughed. "You are, but I can show you a shortcut—"

"Doesn't this road lead to the house?"

"Eventually. But if you cut through the trees you come out about half a mile nearer. Will you allow me to escort you?"

"Thank you," I said stiffly, and we set off side by side.

"How did you come to be out alone at this hour?" he asked.

I told him that I was anxious about finding my dog.

"You shouldn't wander too far alone," he reproved.

I did not answer him; we had come through the trees and I saw the house. In five minutes we were there. Gabriel, Ruth, Luke and Dr. Smith were all on the grounds looking for me. Gabriel was so anxious that he was almost angry with me, for the first time. I breathlessly explained that I had been looking for Friday, had gotten lost among the ruins and met Simon Redvers on the way back.

"You shouldn't have gone out alone at dusk," said Dr. Smith gently.

"I know," I said, smiling with relief because I was so happy to be back. I turned to Simon. "Thank you, Mr. Redvers."

He bowed ironically. "Such a pleasure," he murmured.

"Has Friday come home?" I asked Gabriel. He shook his head.

"He'll turn up tomorrow," Luke put in.

Gabriel slipped his arm through mine. "There's nothing else we can do tonight. And you look exhausted. Come along in."

They all seemed to be watching us. I turned and said good night. There was an echoing answer as Gabriel drew me into the house.

"I've never seen you look so white and tired," he told me.

"I thought I should never get back."

He laughed and put his arm about me. He said suddenly, "Wasn't that honeymoon of ours wonderful! But it was very short—we ought to have a longer one. I've often thought I'd like to go to Greece."

"The isles of Greece, the isles of Greece! Where burning Sappho loved and sang," I recited, and my voice had a high pitch to it. Although I was worried about Friday I was very relieved to be safe, which seemed unaccountably foolish.

"You go to our room," said Gabriel, "and I'll go to the kitchen and tell them to bring you some hot milk. It'll make you sleep."

I went on up to bed, thinking how gentle he was, how considerate. So exhausted was I that I was almost asleep when Gabriel entered the room. He sat by the bed and talked excitedly about our trip to Greece. Soon a servant came in with my milk on a tray. I did not really want it but I drank it to please Gabriel, and in a few minutes I fell into a deep sleep.

I WAS AWAKENED by a banging on my door. I sat up in bed to find Ruth standing in the room. Her eyes were enormous, her face the color of white paper. "Catherine," she was saying. "Wake up! Wake up, *please!*" And I knew something terrible had happened.

I looked for Gabriel but there was no sign of him.

"It's Gabriel," said Ruth. "You must prepare yourself for a shock."

"What . . . has happened?" I asked with the greatest difficulty.

"He is dead," she said. "Gabriel has killed himself."

I did not believe her. I felt as though I were struggling out of a fantastic world of dreams. Gabriel . . . dead? It wasn't possible. Why, only a short while ago he had sat by my bed, talking of our trip to Greece.

"You'll have to know," she said, looking at me steadily; and was it with a hint of accusation in her eyes? "He threw himself over the parapet of the balcony. One of the grooms has just found him."

I stumbled out of bed, trembling. One thought kept hammering in my brain: *This is not true. Gabriel did not kill himself.*

CHAPTER THREE

I DO NOT CLEARLY remember the sequence of the events of that day, but I can recall the numbness that took possession of me, the certainty that something inevitable had taken place, something that had threatened me from the moment I entered the house.

I do remember keeping to my bed that first morning, at Ruth's insistence. And I know that sometime in the afternoon I joined the family in the winter parlor—one of the smaller rooms on the second floor. Sir Matthew, Aunt Sarah, Ruth, Luke and Simon Redvers were there, and I was conscious of the gaze of everyone as I entered.

"Come here, my dear child," said Sir Matthew, and I sat down beside him. "This is a terrible shock to us and especially to you."

Luke stood at the window. "It was exactly like the others," he said. "He must have remembered them. He must have been planning—"

I said sharply, "If you mean he committed suicide, I don't believe it!"

Aunt Sarah came over and, taking a chair on the other side of me, placed her hand over mine. "What do *you* believe happened?" she asked, and her blue eyes were bright and eager with curiosity.

"I don't know," I cried. "I only know he didn't kill himself."

"My dear Catherine," said Ruth, "you're overwrought. We all have the utmost sympathy for you, but . . . you knew him such a short time. He is one of *us* . . . all his life he has belonged to us. . . ."

Her voice broke, but I did not believe she was sincerely sorry. And I thought, The house will pass to Luke now. Are you pleased about that, Ruth?

"Last night Gabriel talked about the holiday we should have," I insisted. "He spoke of our going to Greece. Why should he talk of that if he was planning to . . . ?"

Simon spoke then. His voice seemed to come from a long distance. "We do not always say that which is in our minds."

There was a knock on the door and William announced Dr. Smith. When the doctor entered, his eyes were sympathetic and it was to my side that he came. "I cannot express my grief," he murmured, laying his hand on my shoulder. "And I am concerned for you."

"Please don't be," I replied. "I shall be all right."

"I'm going to give you a sedative for tonight," he said. "Then when you wake up there'll be a night between you and all this."

Aunt Sarah spoke suddenly in a high, rather querulous voice: "She doesn't believe he killed himself, Doctor."

"No, no . . ." soothed the doctor. "It's hard to credit it. Poor Gabriel." I said nothing and he went on. "If you have not been out today, Mrs. Rockwell, a little walk in the grounds would do you good. I should be glad to accompany you." It was clear that he had something to say to me alone, and I rose at once.

"You should wear your cloak," Ruth put in. "There's a chill in the air."

A chill in the air, I thought; and a chill in my heart. What would happen next? My life seemed suspended between Glen House and Kirkland Revels, and the future was like a thick fog about me.

When a servant came with my cloak, Simon took it and wrapped it around me. I looked over my shoulder at him and tried to read what was in his eyes, but that was impossible. I was glad to escape from that room.

The doctor did not speak until we had left the house and were walking in the direction of the abbey. "My dear Mrs. Rockwell," he said, "I suggested this walk because I could see that you wished to get away from the house. You feel bewildered, do you not?"

"Yes," I said. "But there is one thing of which I am certain."

"You think it impossible that Gabriel killed himself?"

"Yes, I do."

"Because you were happy together?"

"We were happy together."

"I think it may have been because Gabriel *was* happy with you that he found life intolerable. You know his health was precarious?"

"He told me about his heart before we married."

"It was a family weakness. I had a conversation with him only yesterday about it. I am wondering now whether this had something to do with the tragedy. May I be frank with you? You are very young but you are a married woman, and I am afraid I must speak."

"Please do."

"Thank you," he said. "I was struck from the first by your good sense and I rejoiced that Gabriel had chosen so wisely. Yesterday Gabriel came to me and asked me some questions about . . . his married life."

I felt my cheeks flush and said, "Pray tell me what you mean."

"He asked me if the state of his heart made it dangerous for him to indulge in marital relations."

"Oh!" My voice sounded faint and I could not bring myself to look at the doctor. We had reached the ruins and I stared up at the Norman tower. "And what was your answer?"

"I told him that in my opinion he would take a considerable risk if such relations did occur."

"I see." He was trying to read my thoughts, but I would not look at him. What had happened between me and Gabriel should, I decided, be our secret.

"He was a normal young man, apart from this weakness of the heart. He was proud. I realized when I warned him that I had given him a shock—but I did not understand then how deeply it had affected him."

"And you think that this . . . warning . . . decided him?"

"It seems logical. What is your opinion, Mrs. Rockwell?"

I touched a fragment of broken wall, and my voice was as cold as the stones when I said, "I do not think that what you told my husband made him wish to end his life. Now do you mind if we turn back? It seems to have grown colder."

"Forgive me. I should not have brought you out. I just did not like to think that any words of mine . . . But I'm afraid I've behaved brutally to you, discussing this indelicate matter when—"

"No, you have been kind to me. But I am shocked . . . and I cannot believe that only this time yesterday . . ."

"Time will pass, believe me. You are so young. You have your life before you. You will go away from here—at least I suppose you will."

"I do not know what I shall do. I have not thought about it. But thank you, Dr. Smith. I shall remember your kindness."

We walked back in silence, and as we approached the house I looked up at the balcony and shivered. When I went inside a feeling of desolation came over me, and I hurried to the servants' hall to ask about Friday. No one had seen him. I went through the house calling him, but there was no response.

So I had lost Gabriel and Friday . . . together.

THERE WAS AN inquest, at which Dr. Smith testified that Gabriel had been suffering from a weakness of the heart that depressed him. The verdict, given without demur, was that he had taken his life while temporarily insane. Why, I kept asking myself, was everyone so certain that Gabriel had killed himself? How else could he have fallen? By accident? Was that possible? It must be; it was the only reasonable explanation.

My father came to Gabriel's funeral and I was pleased. I believed that he would offer me comfort, but when I saw him he was as remote as ever. He sought an opportunity to speak to me but I was conscious all the time that to him it was a painful duty.

"What are your plans, Catherine?" he asked.

"Plans?" I echoed blankly. I had not considered my future. I had lost the only two who had loved me and I could think of nothing but my loss.

My father seemed impatient. "Yes, yes. You'll have to decide what to do now. I suppose you could stay here or come back to Glen House. . . ."

I had never felt quite so lonely in my whole life. "I have made no plans so far," I said stonily.

"Perhaps it's early yet," he replied in his weary voice. "But if you should want to come back, you must of course."

I turned away from him; I could not trust myself to speak.

My father left immediately after the funeral, saying that he had a long journey ahead of him and adding that he would expect to hear from me what my plans were for the future. Had he shown me in some small way that he really wanted me to come home, I should have been eager to go back with him.

I was drawn to Sir Matthew, who had lost all his jauntiness since the tragedy. He was very kind to me and made me sit beside him when all the mourners who were not members of the family had gone. "How do you feel, my dear," he asked me, "in this house full of strangers?"

"I feel only an emptiness now," I told him.

He nodded. "If you wish to stay here," he said, "you would always be welcome. This was Gabriel's home and you were Gabriel's wife. If you want to go away, I shall understand, but I should be very sorry."

"You are kind to me," I said, and his words brought the tears to my eyes that, till now, I had not been able to shed.

Simon was standing beside me. "But you will go away from here. What is there here for you? It is so dull in the country, is it not?"

"I came from the country," I said, and I was glad that Luke walked over to us and began to talk of other matters. But I thought I detected a certain glitter in Luke's eyes. He was, after all, the new heir. Was his grief for Gabriel rather superficial? Frightening notions were creeping into my mind. I did not really believe that Gabriel had had an accident. I did not believe that he had killed himself. But what else was there to believe?

When Gabriel's will was read I learned that he had left me comfortably off. Although not rich, I now had an income that would make me independent. This was a surprise because, although I had known that Kirkland Revels would pass to Gabriel on his father's death, together with an income adequate for its upkeep, I had not realized that he had so much money of his own.

A week passed and I was still at the Revels. I knew the family were waiting for me to come to a decision as to whether I was going to stay, and I found it difficult to make up my mind. I thought of Glen House: those dark rooms, Fanny's pursed lips, my father's "bad turns." No, I was not eager to return; yet I was not sure that I wanted to stay at the Revels. I lingered on because Sir Matthew clearly wanted me to stay, and so did Aunt Sarah. Dr. Smith, who was at the house every day now, was invariably kind and solicitous, giving me the comfort I so desperately needed. It seemed that he alone understood my grief and loneliness.

I walked each day and my footsteps always seemed to lead me to the abbey. I had found in the Revels library an old plan of the abbey as it must have been before the 1530s and the Dissolution, and it took my mind from morbid thoughts to attempt to reconstruct those ruins. I was able to identify certain landmarks, and I was excited when I came upon what must have been the monks' chapel, the gatehouse, the kitchens.

One day returning from my walk I took a new route and consequently arrived at the back of the Revels instead of the front, so I entered through a door I had not hitherto used. I was in the east wing—a part of the house with which I was not yet familiar. I mounted the stairs to the fourth floor, knowing that there were communicating corridors between the wings and thinking I should easily find my way to my own apartments. But this was not so, for I found myself in a maze of corridors, not sure which door communicated with the south wing. I hesitated, afraid I might walk into someone's private room.

At length I knocked at several doors, and at one a voice said, "Come in." I entered, and Aunt Sarah was standing so close to the door that she startled me and I jumped back. She laughed and put out a thin hand to clutch my sleeve. "Come," she said. "I'd been expecting you, my dear."

She ran around me as I entered—she seemed more nimble than she was when with the rest of the family—and quickly shut the door. "I know—you've come to see my tapestries. That's it, isn't it?"

"I should greatly enjoy seeing your tapestries," I told her. "Actually I lost myself. I came in by the east door. I have never done that before."

She shook a finger at me as though I were a naughty child. "Ah, it's easy to lose your way, when you don't know. You must sit down."

I was not sorry to do so; I was quite tired from my walk.

She said, "It was sad about the little dog. He and Gabriel went together. Two of them . . . lost. That is sad."

I was surprised that she remembered Friday. I knew at times her mind flitted from past to present in a disconcerting manner, but there were also occasions when she was capable of unexpected clarity.

I noticed in fascination that the walls of this large room were hung with tapestries, all beautifully worked in bright colors. She chuckled with pleasure. "That's all my own work. You see what a large space they cover . . . but there is so much more to be done. Come closer, my dear." She took my hand. "I will tell you all about them."

"They're exquisite," I said.

"You like them? Claire, you didn't work hard enough at yours."

I said gently, "Aunt Sarah, I am not Claire. I am Catherine."

"So you have come to see my tapestries, Catherine. It is time you did."

She came closer to me and peered into my face. "You will figure in one of my tapestries. I shall know when the time has come."

"I?" I asked, bewildered.

"Here. Look. Do you recognize this?"

"It's the house."

She laughed gleefully and pulled me away from the tapestry and toward a cupboard, which she opened. There were stacks of canvases and skein upon skein of silks of all colors. She stroked them lovingly. "I sit here and I stitch and stitch. I stitch what I see."

"That one of the house, it's so real," I told her. "That is the exact color of the stones. And the people—why, I recognize them."

"Yes," she said. "There is my brother and my sister Hagar, and there is my niece Ruth, Gabriel and myself and . . ."

"They are all looking at the house," I said.

"Yes." She nodded excitedly. "We are. . . . Perhaps you should be there now. But I do not think you are looking at the house. I see a great deal," she went on. "I watch. I saw you come—"

"You were in the minstrels' gallery."

She nodded. "From there you see so much . . . and are not always seen. Here is the wedding of Matthew and Claire."

I was looking at a picture of the church at Kirkland Moorside and a bride and groom, the latter recognizable as Sir Matthew. It was astonishing how she had managed to convey a likeness with those tiny stitches. She was undoubtedly an artist.

"And over here is Ruth's marriage," she was saying. "He was killed in a hunting accident."

I walked around the room and saw scenes from the life of Kirkland Revels, and I realized that here on these walls was Rockwell history as seen through the eyes of this strange woman. I saw Ruth's husband being carried on a stretcher from the hunting field, and then the mourners about his bed. And in between each scene was a picture of the house and those recognizable figures gazing at it. I said, "I believe that is Simon Redvers, among those who look at the house."

She nodded. "Simon looks at the house too, because it could be his one day—if Luke were to die as Gabriel died." She was studying me intently and from the pocket of her gown she took a notebook, and while I watched she sketched a figure. She managed to suggest myself by a few deft strokes of her pencil.

"You are very clever," I said.

She looked at me sharply and asked, "How did Gabriel die? *You* said he did not kill himself."

"I do not know how. I only sense within me that he could not have done it."

"We must discover how it happened. I must know for my picture. I shall soon want to start it. You must tell me."

I felt stifled suddenly by the room and by the effort of trying to catch at her innuendos, and I asked her for directions to my wing of the house.

She insisted on accompanying me and at my door I thanked her, and told her I had enjoyed seeing the tapestries. Her face lighted up; then she put her fingers to her lips. "We must find out. Don't forget. There's the picture to do." Then she smiled conspiratorially and went quietly away.

It was a few days later when I made my decision.

I was still using the rooms in which I had lived with Gabriel and I found little peace in them. I was sleeping badly—something that had never happened to me before—and though outwardly calm enough, inwardly I was beset by misgivings. Not only had I lost my husband but I had to accept the possibility that he had killed himself. Furthermore there was no one at the house with whom I could make a real friendship. Each day I asked myself, Why do you stay here? and the answer was, Where would you go if you left?

I was wandering among the abbey ruins one golden afternoon, calling Friday as I did now and then, when I was startled by the unmistakable sound of footsteps, and Simon Redvers emerged from the cloister. "So you still hope to find your dog," he said as he came toward me. "Don't you think that if he were here he would lose no time in coming home?"

"I suppose so. It is rather foolish of me."

"It is strange," he mused, "that he should have disappeared the day before . . ." I nodded. Then abruptly he said, "I congratulate you on your serenity, Mrs. Catherine. So many women in your position would have been hysterical—but then I suppose with you it was different."

"Different?"

He smiled, and I was aware that there was no real warmth in that smile. He shrugged and went on almost brutally, "You and Gabriel—well, it was no *grande passion*, was it? At least on your side." I was so angry that I was unable to speak. "Marriages of convenience," he continued in an insolent tone, "are as one would expect them to be—convenient. It was a pity though that Gabriel took his life before the death of his father . . . from your point of view of course."

"I . . . I do not understand you," I said.

"I am sure you do. Had he died after Sir Matthew, so much of what he inherited from his father would have been yours . . . Lady Rockwell instead of plain Mrs. . . . and there would have been other compensations. It must have been a great blow to you, and yet you are the perfectly composed yet sorrowing widow."

"I think you are trying to insult me!"

He laughed, but his eyes flashed angrily. "I looked on him as my brother," he said. "I could see what you had done to him. He thought you were perfect. He should have enjoyed his illusion for a little longer. He would not have lived very many years."

"What are you talking about?"

"Do you think that I could accept his death just like that? Do you think I believe that he killed himself because of his weak heart? He had known about that for years. Why did he marry and then do this thing? Gabriel was a sensitive man. If he discovered you had married him not for love . . . he would think life was no longer worth living, and so . . ."

"This is monstrous! You seem to think that he found me in the gutter, that he lifted me out of squalor. You are quite mistaken. I knew nothing of his father's precious house and title when I married him. He told me none of these things."

"Why did you marry him? For *love?*" He seized me suddenly by the shoulders and put his face close to mine. "You were not in love with Gabriel. Were you? Answer me."

"How dare you!" I cried. "Take your hands off me at once!"

He obeyed and laughed. "At least I've shaken you out of your serenity," he said. "No, you were never what I should call in love with Gabriel."

"It may be," I answered curtly, "that your knowledge of such an emotion is slight. People who love themselves so deeply, as you evidently do, rarely understand the affection which some are able to give to others."

Trembling with rage, I turned and hurried toward the house.

So he was suggesting I had married Gabriel for money and that Gabriel's discovery of this had driven him to take his life. Why had I married Gabriel? I kept asking myself. No, it was not for love but for pity's sake, and perhaps because I longed to escape from the gloom of Glen House. In that moment I wanted nothing so much as to put the abbey, the Revels and the whole Rockwell family behind me forever. Simon Redvers had done this to me, and I could not help wondering whether he had whispered his suspicions to the others and they believed him.

As I entered the house I saw Ruth; she had come from the garden and carried a basket full of red roses like those she had put in our room on our return from the honeymoon. How pleased Gabriel had been with them. I thought of his pale delicate face flushed with pleasure, and I could not bear to remember Simon's hideous insinuation.

"Ruth," I said on impulse, "I've been thinking about my future. I don't think I should stay here indefinitely."

She looked at the roses instead of at me. "You know you always have a home here, if you wish it."

"Yes, I know. But here there is this unhappy memory. I shall leave and go back to my father's house while I make my plans."

JEMMY BELL WAS AT THE STATION to meet me, and we drove to Glen House. I could almost believe that I had dozed on the journey home from school and had imagined all that had happened between then and now, it was so like that other occasion.

Fanny met me at the door. "Still thin as a rake" was her greeting, and her lips were tight. I knew she was thinking, Well, I didn't hope for much from that marriage.

My father was in the hall, and he embraced me, a little less absentmindedly than usual. "My poor child," he said, "this has been terrible for you. But you're home now. We'll look after you."

Fanny cut in with: "Warming pan's in your bed. There's been mist in the air lately."

I realized that I was receiving an unusually warm welcome.

When I went up to my room, I stood at the window looking out on the moor, and was poignantly reminded of Gabriel and Friday. Why had I thought I could forget in Glen House more easily than at Kirkland Revels?

I slipped into the familiar pattern. Two melancholy weeks passed before, at last, I made up my mind to rearrange my life. I was after all a young widow with some means. I could set up a house, engage a few servants and live a completely different life from that which I had lived with my father or my husband. I wished then that I had some real friend to advise me. If Uncle Dick had been at home I would have been able to confide in him.

I was considering what form my new life should take when a possibility occurred to me that excited me and made me feel that all my half-formed plans would be cast aside if this was indeed true. I told no one of my suspicions, but several weeks later I visited our doctor.

When he completed his examination he was smiling at me. "There is no doubt," he said. "You are going to have a child."

How can I express my emotions? All the rest of that day I hugged my secret to myself. My own child! My whole life was changed. I no longer brooded on the past. I believed that this was the consolation Gabriel was giving to me, and that nothing had been in vain.

It was when I was alone in my room that I remembered that if this child was a boy he would be the heir of Kirkland Revels. Never mind, I told myself. There is no need for him to look to that inheritance. The Rockwells need never know that he is born. Let Luke take everything. What do I care?

But the thought tormented me. I did care. If I had a son I was going to call him Gabriel, and everything that I could give him must be his.

Next day during luncheon I told my father the news. He was startled and then pleased and excited. "You are happier now," he said. "God bless you." He advised me to inform the Rockwell family immediately.

I caught his excitement, and I went at once to my room and wrote to Ruth. It was not an easy letter to write because I could well imagine the consternation the news would cause her.

Dear Ruth,

I am writing to tell you that I am going to have a child. My doctor has just assured me that there is no doubt of this, and I thought I should let the family know that there will shortly be a new member of it.

I hope Sir Matthew has completely recovered from his attack. I am sure he will be delighted to hear that he is to have another grandchild.

I am in excellent health and I hope you are the same. I send my very best wishes to all.

Your sister-in-law,
Catherine Rockwell

Ruth's reply came within two days.

Dear Catherine,

We are surprised and delighted by your news. Sir Matthew says that you must come at once to the Revels because it is unthinkable that his grandchild should be born anywhere but here. Please do not refuse his request. He will be most unhappy if you do, and it is an old tradition with us that our children should be born in the house.

Please let me know by return mail when I may expect you. I will have everything ready for you.

Your sister-in-law,
Ruth

There was also a letter from Sir Matthew. The handwriting was shaky but the welcome was indeed warm. He had missed me, he said, and there was nothing that could have delighted him more at this sad time than my news. I must not disappoint him. I must come back to Kirkland Revels.

I knew he was right. I had to go back.

RUTH AND LUKE came to Keighley Station to meet me. They greeted me with outward pleasure, and Ruth made solicitous inquiries about my health while we drove to the house. But Luke had lost a little of his breeziness. How did it feel, I wondered, to think yourself heir to something you must always have coveted, only to find an intruder might be on the way?

I was filled with emotion as we left the moors and, crossing the old bridge, I caught a glimpse of the abbey ruins and the Revels itself.

We reached the house and went through the portico, and I felt that the faces of the devils looked smug and evil, as though they were saying, "Did you think you had escaped us?" But I felt strong now. I had someone to love, to protect, and because of that someone the emptiness had gone from life and I was ready to be happy again.

CHAPTER FOUR

WHEN I ENTERED THE house Sir Matthew and Sarah were waiting. They both embraced me, and handled me with such care that I might have been a piece of porcelain; it made me smile. Ruth showed me a room on the second floor of the south wing, saying, "You won't want too many stairs."

The room was almost a replica of that which I had shared with Gabriel, and I saw from the windows the same view of the abbey. "It is very pleasant," I said.

My bed was a four-poster, with blue silk curtains about it that matched curtains of blue damask at the windows. There was an enormous fireplace, a wardrobe and several chairs, besides an oak chest over which hung a brass warming pan. There was a bowl of red roses, put there, I guessed, by Ruth. I smiled at her. "Thank you," I said.

She inclined her head in acknowledgment, but I was sure her welcome could not be wholehearted because of what the birth of a son to me would mean to Luke. She adored Luke, and now that I was to be a mother myself I understood how ambitious one could become on behalf of one's children, and I felt no resentment against Ruth even if she did toward me.

One of the maids came in with tea; she bobbed a curtsy to me and set the tray on a table. I thanked her.

"Mary Jane will be your personal maid," Ruth said.

I was pleased. Mary Jane was a tall, fresh-faced young woman who I was sure would be conscientious. Because I showed my pleasure she allowed me to see hers, and I believed I had a friend in the house.

Ruth said, "I expect you'll want to unpack. Mary Jane will help you."

She left, and I watched Mary Jane kneeling by my trunk, taking out my clothes. "I shall have to buy some new clothes soon," I said. "These will not fit me."

Mary Jane smiled. She was about my height, and it occurred to me that she might like some of my clothes when I grew too large for them.

"You look pleased, Mary Jane."

"It's t'news, madam. And I'm right glad to see you back."

"It'll be a long time to wait," I said.

"Yes, madam. My sister Etty—her husband works up at Kelly Grange—she's expecting. Hers will be born in five months' time. Time was, our Etty got terrible scared, but her husband asked the doctor to see her and he's been wonderful."

"Dr. Smith?"

"Oh, aye. He's kind. Don't care nowt whether you be gentry or poor folk."

"We are fortunate to have such a good doctor."

After dinner that first evening we were all assembled in a sitting room when Dr. Smith was announced.

"Bring him up," said Ruth, and as the door closed on the servant she said to me, "He comes at all times. He's so attentive."

"He fusses too much," grumbled Sir Matthew. "I'm all right now."

As Dr. Smith came into the room he was, I was sure, looking for me. "I'm so pleased to see you, Mrs. Rockwell," he said.

"You know why she's returned, eh?" Sir Matthew asked.

"Indeed I do. I prophesy that by the end of the week there won't be one person in the village who doesn't know it. I can assure you that it makes me very happy. We must take great care of Mrs. Rockwell."

The doctor came over to me and took my hand in his. There was a magnetism about this man, which now struck me forcibly. He was outstandingly handsome in his dark way, and I knew that he was capable of deep feeling.

"I know you are so fond of riding," he said, "but I don't think I should indulge in it too frequently, not after this month."

"I won't," I promised.

"You'll be a good and sensible young lady, I am sure of that."

"Have you been visiting Worstwhistle today?" asked Ruth.

"I have," said the doctor.

Ruth turned to me. "Dr. Smith gives his services free, not only to patients who cannot afford to pay, but to this . . . hospital."

"Oh come," cried the doctor, laughing. "Don't make a saint of me. Someone has to look in on those people now and then. And don't forget, if I have poor patients here I also have rich ones. I fleece the rich to help the poor."

"A regular Robin Hood," said Luke.

Dr. Smith turned to Sir Matthew. "Well, sir," he said, "since I am here, I'm going to have a look at you."

"If you think it necessary," said Sir Matthew rather testily, "but first you must join us in a toast. I'm going to have some of my best champagne brought up from the cellars. Luke, ring the bell."

Luke did so. The wine was brought, the glasses filled. Sir Matthew lifted his glass and cried, "To my grandson!" He put his arm about me while we all drank.

Very soon after that the doctor went with Sir Matthew to his room and I went to mine. Mary Jane was there turning down the bed for me. I said good night to her, but as she went to the door I called, "By the way, Mary Jane, do you know a place called Worstwhistle?"

She stopped short and stared at me. "Why yes, madam. It's some ten miles on the way to Harrogate. . . . It's the place where mad people go."

NEXT DAY AUNT SARAH INSISTED ON showing me the nursery. "Right under the eaves," she murmured, as she led the way up a short flight of stairs in her section of the house. "The schoolroom, the day nursery, the night nursery, Nanny's quarters and those of the undernursemaid." She opened a door and said in a hushed voice, "This is the schoolroom."

I saw a large room with three windows, all fitted with window seats. I found my eyes fixed on these windows, which had bars across them in accordance with nursery tradition. My child would be safe up here.

Close to one window was a large table covered with cuts and scratches; it must have been used by many generations of Rockwells. "Look," cried Sarah, "can you read that?" I leaned forward and saw the name Hagar Rockwell carved there with a penknife.

"She always put her name on everything." Sarah laughed gleefully. "If you went through this house peering into cupboards and such places, you would see her name. Our father said she ought to have been the boy instead of Matthew. She used to bully us all, especially Matthew. She was annoyed with him for being the boy. Of course if she had been the boy, she would be master here now, wouldn't she? And Simon would be . . ."

"Hagar is Simon Redvers' grandmother?" I asked.

Sarah nodded. "She thinks the world of him." She came close to me. "She'd like to see him here . . . but she won't now, will she? There's the child, and there's Luke too . . . both before Simon. The child first. . . . Are you going to call him Gabriel?"

I was astonished and I wondered how she had guessed my thoughts. "It may not be a boy," I said.

She merely nodded as though there was no doubt of it. "Little Gabriel will take big Gabriel's place," she said. "Nobody can stop him, can they?"

"If the child is a boy he will take his father's place."

"Our father liked to take Hagar round the estate with him. He was sorry when she married John Redvers. Then the trouble started with Matthew, trouble about women. He was sent home from Oxford. There was a young woman there. I remember that day. She came here to see Father. I watched them from where they couldn't see me."

"From the minstrels' gallery?" I said, and she giggled.

I looked at the watch pinned to my bodice and saw that it was four o'clock. "It's teatime," I told her. "How quickly the time passes when one is interested! I am going down to tea." She did not answer me.

IT WAS SOME days later when Ruth came to my room with a letter. "One of the servants from Kelly Grange brought this over for you," she said.

The message was formal; almost a command. "If Mrs. Gabriel Rockwell will call at Kelly Grange on Friday at 3:30 Mrs. Hagar Rockwell-Redvers will be pleased to receive her."

Because I had already crossed swords with Mrs. Hagar Redvers' grandson, I was prepared to do so with her. I flushed faintly with annoyance. I passed the invitation to Ruth.

"A royal command. It's characteristic of my aunt Hagar," she said with a smile. "I really believe she's of the opinion that she is head of the family. She wants to inspect you."

"I have no intention of being inspected," I retorted rather sharply.

Ruth shrugged. "The servant's waiting. My aunt will expect a reply."

"She shall have that," I answered, and I sat down at my writing table and wrote, "Mrs. Gabriel Rockwell regrets that she is unable to call on Mrs. Hagar Rockwell-Redvers at Kelly Grange on Friday at 3:30."

Ruth took the note. She was clearly amused.

Early the following week I was on the front lawn when Simon Redvers rode up to the house. He leaped from his horse, lifted his hat to greet me, shouted to one of the grooms as though he were master of the house, then said to me, "Mrs. Catherine, may I say that it is a great pleasure to see you here again?" He looked more arrogant than ever.

I tried to look as dignified as possible. "You may say it if you wish."

"You are still angry with me."

"I have not forgotten certain remarks you made to me before I left."

"I am sorry about that. I have come to apologize."

"Indeed!"

"I wish to ask your pardon for certain unmannerly remarks I made at our last meeting. I have come to offer my congratulations, and to wish you good health and happiness."

"So you have changed your mind concerning me?"

"I hope I shall not do that, because I always admired you. But may I explain my feelings? Let us say that I was angered by the loss of one who was as my brother. I am the type who loses control of his tongue in anger."

"Then let us say no more of the incident."

"You are gracious beyond my deserts. Now I am going to ask a favor of you. Not for myself," he added hastily, "but for my grandmother. She has asked you to visit her."

"It was scarcely a request."

He laughed. "You must forgive her methods. She is used to authority. It is a great grief to her that she has not seen you, and it would give her much pleasure if you would pass over the manner of her asking and remember that she is almost ninety and rarely able to leave the house."

"Did she send you to give this second command?"

"She has no idea that I have come. She was hurt by your refusal of her invitation. Will you allow me to take you there tomorrow?"

I hesitated. "Oh come," he urged. "Remember she is old, she is lonely, she is greatly interested in the family. Please say yes."

He suddenly seemed attractive: his eyes, screwed up against the sunlight, had lost their boldness; his teeth looked very white against his sun-bronzed skin. As I looked at him I found myself relenting.

"'Very well. I will come."

"Oh thanks," he cried, and his face was creased in smiles. He's really fond of that old grandmother, I thought; and I almost liked him because he was fond of someone other than himself. "You'll like her," he went on exuberantly. "And she can't fail to like you. I shall call for you tomorrow at two o'clock."

He did not wait for any more. He was shouting to the groom for his horse and seemed to have forgotten me. Yet I liked him for it, and liking him, I was prepared not to dislike his grandmother.

THE NEXT DAY Simon arrived in a phaeton drawn by two of the handsomest horses I had ever seen. I sat beside him during the journey, which was under two miles. "I could have walked," I said to him.

"And deprived me of the pleasure of taking you?" The mocking note was back in his voice, but the antagonism between us had lessened; we could no longer hate each other so wholeheartedly.

We drove through a pair of massive wrought-iron gates, then along an avenue of chestnut trees. Soon we had drawn up before the front porch. Kelly Grange was a gray stone manor house that I guessed to be less than a hundred years old—quite modern when compared with the Revels.

"There! What do you think of the Grange? A pale shadow, eh, of the Revels."

"It's very attractive," I said.

"It has its points. Kelly Grange can offer more comfort than the Revels, I assure you. Wait until the winter and compare them. Our great fires keep the house warm. There are many drafty spots in the Revels."

The door was opened by a parlormaid as we alighted from the phaeton. We went into a tiled hall from which rose a wide staircase. The house was built around this hall, and standing in it one could look up to the roof.

Simon asked me to wait and mounted the stairs to the gallery to knock at a door. In a moment he beckoned and I went up. He stood aside for me to pass and said with some ceremony, "Mrs. Gabriel Rockwell!"

I entered. It was a room crowded with heavy furniture; thick plush curtains as well as lace ones were held back by ornate brass fittings. There was a long table in the center of the room as well as several occasional tables; there was a horsehair sofa, a grandfather clock, many chairs, cabinets containing china, an epergne filled with white and red roses.

But all this I took in at a glance, for it was the woman in the high-back chair who demanded my attention.

This was Hagar Redvers, the autocrat of the schoolroom, who had remained an autocrat all her life. It was evident that she was tall, although she was sitting down; her back was very straight; her chair was no soft and comfortable one, but had a hard back of carved wood. Her white hair was piled high on her head and on it was a white lace cap. There were garnets in her ears, and her dress of lavender satin had a high lace collar held in place by a garnet brooch. A gold-topped ebony stick leaned against her chair. Her eyes were bright blue; another version of Gabriel's eyes, but with none of Gabriel's gentleness. Her hands, resting on the carved wooden arms of the chair, must have been beautiful in her youth; they were still shapely, and I saw garnets and diamonds there.

Conscious of a faint hostility, I held my head high and said, perhaps a bit haughtily, "Good afternoon, Mrs. Rockwell-Redvers." I coolly took the hand she had extended as though she were a queen and I a subject.

"It was good of you to come this afternoon," she said. "I had hoped you would come before."

"It was your grandson who suggested that I come this afternoon."

"Ah!" Her lips twitched a little, I fancied with amusement. "You are no doubt thirsty after your drive," she said, her keen eyes seeming to search through mine into my mind. She turned to Simon. "Ring the bell, grandson."

Simon immediately obeyed. The parlormaid appeared, and the old lady said, "Dawson, tea . . . please." Then: "Simon, you will not wish to join us. We will excuse you."

Simon said, "Very well. I'll leave the two of you to become acquainted."

We did not speak until the door closed on him; then she said, "I had hoped to see you when you were at the Revels previously. I was unable at that time to visit you and I did not invite you because I felt certain that Gabriel would bring you here in due course. I am sure he would have done so had he lived. He was always conscious of his duty to the family."

"I am sure he would."

"I am glad that you are not one of those stupid modern girls who faint when any difficulty presents itself."

"How can you know that on such a short acquaintance?" I asked.

"My eyes are as sharp as they were at twenty. Moreover Simon told me how admirably calm you were during that distressing time. I am sure you are not one of those foolish people who say, We must not talk of this or that. Things exist whether we talk of them or not, so why pretend they don't by never mentioning them. Do you agree?"

"I think that may be true."

"I was pleased when I heard you had married Gabriel. He was always rather unstable. So many of the family are, I'm afraid. No backbone, that's the trouble."

I looked at her erect figure and I permitted myself a little joke. "You evidently do not suffer from that complaint."

She seemed pleased. "What do you think of the Revels?" she asked.

"I find the house fascinating."

"Ah. It is a wonderful place. There are not so many like it left in England. That's why it is important that it should be in good hands. An estate like that needs constant attention if it is to remain in good repair. My father was very capable. Matthew could have done better, but there was always some woman. That's bad. As for Gabriel, he was a pleasant creature but weak. That was why I was gratified when I heard he had married a strong young woman."

The tea arrived and my hostess said to me, "Would you care to take charge of the tea tray? I suffer from rheumatism and my joints are a little stiff today."

I went to the table on which the tray had been set. On it were a silver teapot, kettle, creamer and sugar bowl, and small sandwiches and cakes. I had the feeling that I was being set this task to ascertain if I could perform an important social activity with grace. Really, I thought, she is an impossible old woman; and yet I liked her.

I asked how she took her tea and carried her cup over to her and set it on a table by her chair. Then I offered her the sandwiches and cakes.

She ate heartily and talked as though there was so much to say that she feared she would never say half of what she wanted to. She encouraged me to talk too, and I told her how Gabriel and I had met when we had rescued Friday.

"Then you heard who he was. That must have been pleasant for you."

"Heard who he was?"

"That he was an extremely eligible young man, heir to a baronetcy, and that in due course the Revels would be his."

Here it was again—the suggestion that I had married Gabriel for money and position. My anger would not be controlled. "Nothing of the sort," I said sharply. "Gabriel and I decided to be married before we knew a great deal about each other's worldly position."

"Then you surprise me. I thought you were a sensible young woman."

"I never thought it necessarily sensible to marry for money. Marriage to an incompatible person can be most unpleasant, even if that person is a rich one." She laughed and I could see that she was enjoying our encounter. She had made up her mind that she liked me; what shocked me was that she would have liked me equally well if I had been a fortune hunter.

"And now you are carrying the heir. If your child is a boy, that will be the end of Ruth's hopes for Luke." She sounded triumphant. "Luke," she went on, "will be another Matthew—he is very like his grandfather. . . . The doctor's beautiful daughter often visits the house, I hear."

There was a brief silence and then she returned to the subject of my coming child. "I am certain the baby will be a boy. I shall pray for it." She spoke as though even the Deity must obey her commands, and I smiled. "If it were a girl," she went on, "and Luke were to die—"

I interrupted in a startled way: "Why should he?"

"Some of the members of our family enjoy longevity—others die young. My brother's two sons were extremely delicate in health. Gabriel, had he not died in the manner he did, could not have lived many more years. His brother died at an early age. I fancy I see signs of the same delicacy in Luke."

I looked at her and I thought I detected a gleam of hope in her eyes. Luke and my unborn child, if it is a boy, I thought, will stand between Simon and the Revels. If Simon was the master of the Revels, then she would return to spend her last days there.

I said quickly, as though I feared she would read my thoughts, "And your son, was he also delicate?"

"Indeed no. Simon's father was killed fighting for his queen and country in the Crimea. Simon never knew him—and the shock killed his mother. *She* was a delicate creature." A faint scorn came into her voice. "It was not a marriage of my making." Then she said, more gently than I had heard her speak before, "But they left me my grandson."

We were both surprised when Simon arrived to take me back to the Revels. The two hours or so I had spent with Hagar Redvers had been stimulating. She said, "You will come and see me again." Then her eyes twinkled and she added, "I hope." And it was as though she recognized in me one who could not be commanded. I knew she liked me for it.

I said I would come again with pleasure.

When Simon took me home we did not say very much, but I could see that he was rather pleased by the way things had gone.

DURING THE NEXT weeks I walked a little and rested a good deal, lying on my bed in the afternoons reading the novels of Mr. Dickens and the Brontë sisters. I visited Hagar twice more. We seemed to grow even closer and I knew I had a friend in her.

I tried to take an interest in the life of the neighborhood. I had tea at the vicarage; I went to church and sat in the Rockwell pew. I felt that I was settling in as I had not begun to do while Gabriel was with me.

We did no entertaining because of our being in mourning, but close friends of the family visited us now and then. Damaris Smith came, and I could see that Luke was in love with her, but I was not at all sure of her feelings for him. I wondered idly whether Damaris had any feelings. I had noticed that even with her father she seemed unresponsive sometimes.

The doctor was often at the house, to keep an eye on Sir Matthew and Sarah, he said; not forgetting Mrs. Rockwell, he added, smiling at me. He said I was not to walk too far and must rest whenever I felt so inclined.

One day when I had gone for my morning walk, I was about a mile from the house when the doctor's brougham pulled up beside me. "You've tired yourself," he said. "Please get in. I'm going to give you a lift back."

I obeyed, but protested that I was not in the least tired, that in fact he looked much more tired than I.

"I've been up to Worstwhistle," he said. "That always tires me."

Worstwhistle! How good he was to give his services to those people with their poor clouded minds. "You are very good to go there," I told him. "I have heard how you comfort these people, not only with your medical skill but with your kindness."

"Ha!" He laughed suddenly. "I have a great deal to be thankful for. I'll tell you a secret about myself. Forty years ago I was an orphan—a penniless orphan. But life was good to me. As I grew up it became the dream of my life to heal the sick. I had no hope of attaining my ambition until I caught the notice of a rich man. He educated me, he helped me to realize my ambition. Whenever I see a beggar or a criminal I say, There but for the grace of that rich man go I. Then I give myself to my patients."

"I did not know . . ." I began.

"And now you think less of me because I am not quite a gentleman."

"I think you are a very great gentleman," I said fiercely.

We had reached the Revels. "Then will you do me a favor?" he asked.

"If it is in my power."

"Take great care of yourself . . . even greater care."

It was two weeks later, in mid-September, that my peaceful existence was shattered and the horror and doubts began.

I had passed the day pleasantly. I had been along to the church with Ruth, Luke and Damaris to take flowers to decorate it for the harvest festival. Later we had tea at the vicarage and then walked home at a leisurely pace. It was an atmosphere of absolute peace—the last I was to know for a long time.

I tried afterward to recall that evening in detail, but on looking back it seemed like many other evenings. I had gone to bed early, as was now my custom. And of one thing I was certain—that the curtains around my bed had not been drawn. I always insisted on this, which shocked Mary Jane as much as did my sleeping with the windows open, for she was certain the night air was unhealthy.

I blew out my candles and lay in bed for some time looking at the windows. The moon was nearly full; it flooded my room with soft light.

I slept. And . . . suddenly I was awake and in great fear, though for some seconds I did not know why. I was aware of a cold draft and the room was filled with moonlight. But that was not all. Someone was there . . . someone was standing at the foot of my bed watching me.

I started up. If ever I had known fear in my life I knew it then.

It was a figure in a black cloak and cowl—a monk; over the face was a mask such as those worn by torturers in the chambers of the Inquisition. There were slits for the eyes, and though it was not possible to see those eyes I believed they watched me intently.

The figure moved as I looked. Then it was gone. It could be no apparition, for I was not the sort of person to see apparitions. Someone had been in my room. I turned my head to follow it but could see nothing. So dazed was I, so shocked, that it was a second or so before I realized that the curtain on one side of my bed had been drawn so that the door and that part of the room that led to it were shut off from my view.

Still numb with shock and terror, I could not move until suddenly the sound of a door quietly closing brought me back to reality. I stumbled out of bed and hurried to the door, calling, "Who was that? Who was that?"

There was no sign of anyone in the corridor. I ran to the stairway. The moonlight, falling through the windows there, threw shadows all about me. I felt suddenly alone with evil and I was terrified. I began to shout: "Come quickly! There is someone in the house."

I heard a door open; then Ruth's voice: "Catherine, is that you?"

"Yes, yes . . . come quickly. . . ."

It seemed a long time before Ruth started down the stairs, holding a small lamp. "What happened?" she cried.

"There was something in my room, standing at the foot of my bed."

"My dear, you have had a nightmare."

"I was awake, I tell you. I woke up and saw it." I felt frustrated and angry with her, for what can be more exasperating than the inability to convince people that you have seen something with your eyes and not with your imagination? "It was not a dream," I said emphatically. "There was someone in my room. I did not imagine it."

Luke appeared on the landing above us. "What's the commotion?" he asked, yawning.

"Catherine has been . . . upset."

"There was someone in my room. Someone dressed as a monk."

I saw Ruth and Luke exchange glances, and I knew they were thinking that I was obsessed with the abbey—the victim of one of those vivid nightmares that seem a part of reality.

"It was not a dream," I insisted fervently. "Someone came into my room. Perhaps it was meant to be a joke. . . ."

"A dangerous joke—on a woman in your condition. But you should go back to bed," Ruth added gently, and she led me back to my room.

"You see," I said, "the curtain is drawn at the side of the bed. It was not like that when I went to sleep."

"Mary Jane must have done it."

"I told her not to. Why should she come back after I had said good night to her, to draw a curtain which I had expressly asked should not be drawn?"

"Come, lie down," Ruth said. She drew back the bed curtain and sat by the side of the bed. "I don't like to leave you while you are so upset."

I was ashamed to ask her to stay, and yet I felt afraid. "I am so sorry to have disturbed you like this," I said. "Please go back to your room. I shall lock the door when you have gone. That way I shall feel safe."

"If you can only feel safe like that, you must. But Catherine, who in this place would do such a thing? You must have been dreaming. . . . Well, I'll say good night if you're sure . . ."

"I am all right now."

When she had gone I locked the door and went back to bed, turning the question over and over in my mind. Who had done this, and why? It was no practical joke. Someone had meant to terrify me because of the precious burden I carried. One prospective master of the Revels had died violently; was something being plotted against another?

That was the beginning of my period of terror.

CHAPTER FIVE

I AWOKE SOON AFTER six o'clock the next morning, rose and unlocked my door; then I returned to bed and fell asleep, to be awakened by Mary Jane at my bedside with a breakfast tray. I started out of a deep sleep, remembering the horror of the previous night, and stammered, "Oh—oh thank you, Mary Jane."

She propped me up with pillows and helped me on with my bed jacket. Then she placed the tray on my knees. "Is there anything else, madam?"

She was unlike herself, almost anxious to get out of the room. As she went I thought, Good heavens, has she heard already?

I sat sipping my tea. I could not eat. The whole thing had come back to me vividly now; I found that my eyes kept straying to the foot of my bed. I put aside the tray and thought, There must be a logical explanation of my horrific adventure, and I must find it.

There was a knock on my door and Ruth entered. "Good morning, Catherine." She looked at me anxiously. "How are you feeling this morning?"

"A little weary," I said. "I'm sorry I made such a fuss last night."

"It doesn't matter. You were really frightened. The best thing we can do now is to try to forget it. I think Deverel Smith ought to give you something to make you sleep tonight. You'll feel all the better for it."

I could see it was useless to argue with her. She had made up her mind that I had been the victim of a nightmare, and nothing would change it.

It suddenly occurred to me how servants talk and that the story would soon reach the ears of Hagar and Simon Redvers. The idea of their hearing a version other than my own disturbed me, so I decided to walk over to Kelly Grange in the afternoon to tell Hagar exactly what had happened.

It was three o'clock when I arrived; Hagar was again sitting in her high-back chair and I took her hand and kissed it as I had seen Simon do—a concession to our friendship.

"It is good of you to call," she said. "But you don't look well."

"I did not sleep well last night, and I wanted to tell you what happened before you heard it from another quarter. I wanted you to hear my version."

"Please tell me."

So I told her what had occurred, omitting nothing.

She listened. Then she nodded almost judicially. "It is quite clear," she said, "that someone in the house is trying to alarm you. Perhaps trying to ruin your hopes of producing a child."

"This seems a strange way to go about that. And who . . . ?"

"It may be the beginning of a series of alarms. I think we must be on our guard against that."

There was a tap on the door and Simon entered. "Dawson told me that Mrs. Catherine was here. Have you any objection to my joining you?"

"I have none," said his grandmother. "Have you, Catherine?"

I hesitated, then looked at him. I had never seen anyone so vital, anyone who radiated so much common sense. "I have no objection to his hearing what has happened," I said.

"Then we'll tell him," said Hagar, and proceeded to do so. Never once did she say, "Catherine thinks she saw," or "Catherine believed it was," but always "Catherine saw" and "it was." How grateful I was for that.

Simon listened intently, and when she had finished he said, "Someone in the house is playing tricks."

"Exactly!" cried Hagar triumphantly. "And why so?"

"I imagine it concerns the heir who will soon make his appearance."

Hagar said, "If it was someone in the house, it must have been either Ruth, Luke, Matthew or Sarah. Did you see them all afterward, Catherine?"

"Not Matthew, nor Sarah," I said. "But I cannot imagine either of them running about the house in the night dressed up as a monk."

Simon leaned toward me. "The Rockwell family are all a little crazy where the Revels is concerned." He smiled at Hagar. "Everyone," he added. "I wouldn't trust any one of them. They're all living in the past half the time. Who could help it in that old mausoleum? Anyone who lives there for any length of time is likely to get strange ideas."

"And you think I have!"

"Not you. You're not a Rockwell simply because you married one. You're a forthright Yorkshire woman who'll blow a blast of common sense into the stuffy old place."

"I'm glad you don't think I imagined all this. They are all pretending I did. They call it a nightmare."

"Naturally the trickster would want that put about."

"I shall be prepared for him next time. I can lock my door tonight."

"He won't play the same game twice, but he may try something else."

"I'm ready for tea," said Hagar, changing the subject. "We will have it together. Then, Simon, you must drive Catherine back to the Revels."

Once again I presided over tea. I felt almost normal now; the comfort I drew from these two astonished and delighted me. They believed in me; they refused to treat me as a hysterical subject; they gave me the courage I needed to be alone in my room that night, and that was wonderful.

Simon brought me back at five o'clock. As I watched him drive off and turned to go into the house, in which the first shadows of evening were beginning to fall, I felt my courage begin to ebb.

Matthew, Luke and Ruth seemed to watch me rather furtively through dinner. Afterward Dr. Smith and Damaris called to take wine with us. I was sure Ruth had sent for him, telling him what had happened, for when Damaris and Luke were whispering together, Ruth drew Sir Matthew aside—Aunt Sarah had already retired—and the doctor said to me, "I hear there was a little trouble last night. Mrs. Grantley thought she ought to tell me."

"It was nothing," I said quickly.

"Ah, you have recovered from it," he said. "A nightmare, was it?"

"If it had been merely a nightmare I should not have left my room and awakened others."

"Could you tell me all about it?"

So once more that day I told the story. He listened gravely, and made no comment but to say, "You may not sleep very well tonight. Would you like a sleeping draft? I have one here with me."

"It's unnecessary."

"There's no harm in having it at hand. Then if you can't sleep . . ."

I took the small bottle and slipped it into the pocket of my gown. "You are very attentive, Dr. Smith. Thank you."

"I am anxious to look after you."

When I retired that night I put the sleeping draft by my bed. Then I searched my room and locked the door. I went to bed, but I did not sleep as readily as I had believed I should. I would doze and then start out of my sleep, my gaze going immediately to the foot of my bed.

I was by no means a hysteric, but I had received a violent shock and even the calmest of people cannot expect to recover immediately. The clock was striking midnight when I took Dr. Smith's draft. Almost at once I sank into a deep and restful sleep.

WITHIN A FEW days I had completely recovered from my shock, but I was still watchful. Nothing else of a similar nature had happened, but I was no less determined to discover who had been disguised as a monk.

Gabriel and Friday were still in my thoughts during the weeks that followed. I was still hoping that one day Friday would come back to me. I simply could not bear to think that he was dead. But there was one matter that surprised me: although I remembered so vividly the occasion of my meeting with Gabriel, I had to concentrate to remember exactly what he looked like. I reproached myself for this because it seemed disloyal; and yet, deep in my heart, I knew that although we had been husband and wife, Gabriel and I had been in some respects almost strangers.

Now I carried his child, and I believed that when I held my baby in my arms I should be happy. Already I loved my child in a way that made the feeling I had had for Gabriel seem shallow by comparison. I longed for the spring as I never had before because my baby would be born in March. This was November. There were to be many dark days between me and that happy time.

One afternoon I had walked over to Kelly Grange to see Hagar, and Simon had driven me back. My feelings toward him had undergone a change, and this was a result of my friendship with his grandmother. When I was with her the conversation invariably turned to Simon. I was reminded again and again of his many virtues, and I believed I understood him better now. He was blunt to the point of tactlessness; there was a hardness in his nature that I imagined no one but his grandmother had ever penetrated; he liked undertaking difficult tasks and proving that they weren't difficult—all part of his arrogance, of course, but admirable in its way.

When we returned to the Revels that afternoon, I said good-by to him and went straight up to my room. It was growing late and darkness would soon descend. There were shadows on the stairs and in my room, and as I opened the door I felt that horrible sense of evil that I had experienced when I awoke and saw the monk. It was only a slight but reminiscent matter that aroused these feelings: the curtains were closed about my bed.

I walked straight to them and drew them back, half expecting to see the monk there. But of course I saw nothing. I looked hastily around the room. No one was there. I rang the bell and Mary Jane soon appeared.

"Why did you draw the curtains about my bed?" I demanded.

Mary Jane stared at the bed. "But madam, I didn't. . . ."

"Who else would have done that?"

"But madam, the curtains are *not* drawn about your bed."

"What are you suggesting? That I imagined they were? I have just drawn them back." I looked at her fiercely and she recoiled from me.

"I—I did nowt to 'em. You've always said you didn't want them drawn."

"You must have drawn them. Who else would have been here?" I asked.

"No one else, madam. I always do your room myself. But I didn't touch them, madam."

"You did," I answered unreasonably. "You may go now."

She went, her face stricken. I stood staring at the door, trembling. I was thinking of it all again, that sudden waking in the night . . . that awful apparition. Then I realized I had become angry because I was afraid; but I had no right to turn that anger against Mary Jane. I felt contrite and went at once to the bell. Mary Jane came immediately in answer, but her bright smile was missing.

"Mary Jane," I said, "I'm sorry. I know that if you had drawn the curtains, you would have said so. I'm afraid I was overwrought."

She looked at me and said, "Oh madam, it's of no account."

"It is, Mary Jane," I insisted. "It was unjust, and I hate injustice. Go and bring the candles. It's grown dark."

By the time she came back with the candles I had decided to be frank with her. I said, "Mary Jane . . . when I saw those bed curtains drawn I was reminded of that occasion . . ."

"I remember, madam."

"And I feared someone was playing another trick. So I wanted it to have been you who drew them. That would have been such a comforting explanation."

"But it wasn't, madam. I couldn't say it was if it wasn't."

"Of course you couldn't. So I'm left wondering who did it—and why."

"Anyone could have, madam. You don't lock the door during the day."

"Yes, anybody could have done it. Perhaps I'm too sensitive due to my condition." Then I added, "Well, Mary Jane, I've a dress here I thought might do for you. I can't get into it anymore. I'd like you to have it."

I brought out a dark green gabardine dress trimmed with red-and-green tartan, and Mary Jane's eyes glistened at the sight of it. "Why, thank you, madam, it's grand. It's sure to fit."

When she had gone I felt that some of her pleasure remained behind her. I caught a glimpse of my reflection in the looking glass. I looked young, and my green eyes were brilliant. But even as I looked I found I was peering beyond my own reflection; I was trying to probe the shadows in the room. I was expecting some shape to materialize behind me.

Fear had come back.

It was only a few days later that I discovered that the warming pan was missing from my bedroom. It usually hung on the wall over the oak chest.

When Mary Jane brought my breakfast tray to me I said, "Why, Mary Jane, what have you done with the warming pan?"

She set down my tray and looked around. Her astonishment was obvious. "Oh, madam, it's gone! But I didn't take it away."

"Then I wonder who— I'll ask Mrs. Grantley. She might know what has happened to it. I rather liked it there. It was so bright and shining."

I ate my breakfast without giving much thought to the warming pan. At that stage I did not realize that it had any connection with the strange things that were happening to me. It was that afternoon before I again thought of it. I was having tea with Ruth, and she was talking about Christmas in the old days and how different it was now—particularly this year, when we were living so quietly because of Gabriel's death.

"It was rather gay," she told me. "We used to take a wagon out to bring the Yule log home, and there was the holly to gather too. We usually had several people staying in the house at Christmas. This time it can't possibly be more than family. I suppose Aunt Hagar will come over from Kelly Grange with Simon. They generally do, and stay two nights."

I felt rather pleased at the prospect of Christmas, and wondered when I could go into Harrogate or Keighley to buy some presents.

"I must tell the maids to air Aunt Hagar's bed thoroughly," Ruth was saying. "Last time she declared we were putting her into damp sheets."

That reminded me. "By the way," I said, "what has happened to the warming pan that was in my room?" She looked puzzled and I explained. "It's no longer there, and Mary Jane doesn't know what has become of it."

"The warming pan in your room?"

"I thought perhaps you'd given orders for someone to remove it."

She shook her head. "It must have been one of the servants," she said. "I'll find out. You may be needing it when the weather turns."

THE NEXT EVENING when I went to the dining room for dinner I found Matthew, Sarah and Luke waiting there, but Ruth was absent.

"Not like her to be late," said Sir Matthew.

"Ruth has a great deal to do about Christmas," Sarah put in. "She's worried about Hagar, who'll be having her nose into every corner and telling us that the place is not kept as it was when Father was alive."

"Hagar's an interfering busybody and always was," growled Matthew.

Ruth came in then, looking slightly flushed. "Of all the ridiculous things . . ." she began. "I went into Gabriel's old room and noticed something under the coverlet there. What do you think it was?"

I felt the color rushing to my cheeks, because I knew.

"The warming pan from your room!" She was looking straight at me, quizzical and intent. "Whoever could have put it there?"

"How—how extraordinary!" I heard myself stammer.

"Well, we've found it. That's where it was all the time." She turned to the others. "Catherine had missed the warming pan from her room. She thought I'd told one of the servants to remove it. Who on earth could have put it into the bed there?"

"We ought to find out," I said sharply.

"I asked the servants. They clearly knew nothing about it."

I heard my voice rise unnaturally. "Someone must have put it there."

Ruth shrugged her shoulders.

"But we must find out," I insisted. "It's someone playing these tricks. Don't you see? It's the same sort of thing as the curtains being drawn."

"Curtains?"

I was annoyed with myself because that matter had been known only to Mary Jane and myself. Now I should have to explain. I did so briefly.

"Someone must have been rather absentminded," said Luke lightly.

"I don't think it was absentmindedness," I retorted.

"But, Catherine," put in Ruth patiently, "why should anyone want to pull your bed curtains about your bed or remove the warming pan?"

"That's what *I* should like to know. *Why?*"

"You *are* getting excited, my dear."

"I want to know why these strange things are happening."

"The duckling is getting cold," said Sir Matthew. He came to me and slipped his arm through mine. "Never mind about the warming pan, my dear. We shall know why it was moved . . . all in good time."

"Yes," said Luke, "all in good time." And he kept his eyes on my face as he spoke, and I could see speculation there.

We sat down at the table, but my appetite had deserted me. I kept asking myself what the purpose was behind these strange happenings that seemed in some way to be directed toward me.

I was going to find out. I must find out.

BEFORE THE MONTH was out we were invited to the vicarage to discuss plans for the imminent "Bring and Buy" sale, the latest fund-raising venture.

"Mrs. Cartwright always gets the wind in her sail at such times," said Luke. "This is nothing to the June garden fete or her hideous pageants."

"Her qualities make her an excellent wife for the vicar," said Ruth.

Mrs. Cartwright was a large, somewhat florid woman with a powerful personality. One morning she assembled a group of us in her drawing room, where coffee was being served by a maid, and in her booming voice told us of the need for speed. The sale must be in time to give people opportunities to buy their Christmas presents. "So please ransack your attics, and any little *objet d'art* will be appreciated. Remember it is for the good of the church, and the roof does need attention. Has anyone any suggestions?"

When the details of the meeting had all been settled she came and sat with me. "It is wonderful to see you looking so well and to know that there is to be an addition to the family. I know that Sir Matthew is delighted. It is a comfort to him in the circumstances. . . ." She was one of those women who carry the whole of a conversation for the sheer joy of talking. "Of course at the moment you are feeling less energetic than you will after . . . But I'm so pleased that you have come. You are going to be such a help to us later, I know, with the pageant. I do want to do a pageant in the ruins this summer. It must be historical, with such a setting. Last time we went back to before the Dissolution."

"You have had one before?"

"Five years ago was the last. The costumes were excellent."

"How did you find the costumes?"

"We were lent some from the Revels and we made others. It was most effective. People said that on that day it was as though the abbey were no longer a ruin."

I tried to keep the note of excitement out of my voice. "So some of the players were dressed as monks."

"Indeed yes. Many of them. And those costumes were so easy to make . . . just a black robe and a cowl really. But each person had to play several parts. You know, a monk in one scene was a Cavalier in another. It was necessary because we hadn't enough players. But in the end nearly everyone took part. I even tried to get Dr. Smith."

"Did you succeed?"

"No. It was his day for going to . . . that institution."

"And his daughter?"

"She was the little Prince Charles. She looked wonderful in velvet breeches with her long hair. I shall never forget her. Everyone was splendid. Even Mr. Redvers—and no one could say acting was in his line."

"Oh, what part did he play?"

"He was merely a monk. But he did join in."

"How . . . interesting."

Ruth was trying to catch my eye, and I rose. We said good-by to Mrs. Cartwright and started for home. As we walked I found it difficult to make conversation. I kept saying to myself, Somebody who played the part of a monk in the pageant five years ago had a monk's costume that still exists today. The person who came into my bedroom used it.

Simon had had a monk's costume, but who in our household had played a monk? It could only have been Ruth or Luke. Sir Matthew and Aunt Sarah would have been too old.

I said to Ruth, "Mrs. Cartwright was talking to me about the last pageant. Did you play a part in it?"

"You don't know Mrs. Cartwright very well if you think she would let any of us escape. I played the king's wife, Queen Henrietta Maria."

"Just that part and no other?"

"It was an important part."

"I only asked because Mrs. Cartwright said that some people played several roles since she was short of players."

"Those would be the people who had small parts."

"What about Luke?"

"He was well to the fore. He was in and out of everything."

"Did he play one of the monks?"

"Why, yes, he did. And a Roundhead, and several other parts as well."

Luke! I thought; and I remembered that it had been some time before he had appeared on that night; he had plenty of time to take off the robe and put on a dressing gown. And the bed curtains and the warming pan? Why not? He was the one who would have had every opportunity. My doubt was becoming almost a certainty. Luke was trying to terrify me; he was trying to kill my child before it was born. Obviously Luke was the one who had most to gain from the death of my child.

The house was now in view and my eyes went, as they always did, to that south parapet from which Gabriel had fallen. There was something different about it. I stared and Ruth was staring too. "What is it?" she said, and she quickened her pace.

There was something dark on the parapet; from this distance it looked as though someone was leaning over it.

"Gabriel!" I think I must have said it aloud because Ruth at my elbow said, "Nonsense! It can't be. But what . . . but who?"

I began to run; Ruth was beside me restraining me and I could hear my breath coming in great gasps. "Someone's there," I panted.

Now I saw that whoever was there was wearing a cloak, and the hood of the cloak and part of the cloak itself were hanging over the parapet. It was impossible to see the rest.

"She'll fall. Who is it? What does it mean?" cried Ruth as she ran ahead of me into the house. I followed as quickly as I could.

Luke appeared in the corridor. He stared after his mother, then turned to look at me, laboring up behind.

"What on earth's happened?" he asked.

"There's someone on Gabriel's parapet," I cried.

He started up the stairs ahead of me. Ruth appeared at the top and there was a grim smile about her lips. She was holding something in her hand. I recognized it as a blue cloak that belonged to me—a long winter cloak with a hood attached to it.

"It's mine," I gasped.

"Why did you hang it over the parapet like that?" she demanded.

"I . . . But I did no such thing."

She and Luke exchanged glances. Then she murmured, "It was made to look exactly like someone leaning over . . . about to fall. It gave me quite a shock when I saw it."

"Who did it? Who is doing all these silly cruel things?" I cried.

They were both looking at me as though certain doubts they had had concerning me were being confirmed.

CHAPTER SIX

I HAD TO FIND out the meaning of these strange happenings. I thought of going to see the Redverses and telling them everything, but I was growing so distrustful of everyone that I was not even sure of Hagar. As for Simon, he had taken my view of the monk incident, but what would he think of the bed curtains, warming pan and cloak? Besides, he had worn a monk's robe in the pageant, yet had not mentioned it to me when I told him of my experience. It seemed ridiculous to suspect Simon, for how could he possibly have been in the house at the time? And yet I had to remind myself that he was next in succession to Luke. It was alarming to feel that I could trust no one, but that was exactly how I did feel.

So when I called to see Hagar the next day I said nothing of the cloak incident. Instead I kept the conversation on everyday matters and asked her if I could do any Christmas shopping for her when I went into one of the nearby towns. She pondered this and eventually made a list of things to get. While we were discussing it, Simon came in.

"If you'd like to go to Knaresborough," he said, "I can take you. I have to drive in one day soon on business."

I hesitated. I did not really believe he would have tried to frighten me, and yet I reminded myself he had not liked me in the beginning; it was only because of my friendship with his grandmother that we were brought together. It seemed reasonable not to place him outside suspicion.

My hesitation amused him. It had not occurred to him that I suspected him of villainy, only that I feared to offend the proprieties. He said with a grin, "Luke and Damaris might like to come with us. If they'll come, perhaps you would deign to."

"That would be very pleasant," I replied. And it was eventually arranged that when he went to Knaresborough he should take Luke, Damaris and myself with him.

The day was warm for early December. We left soon after nine in the morning and planned to be back by dark. As we sat in the carriage, Luke and Simon seemed to be in high spirits and I found myself catching them.

It occurred to me that whenever I was away from the house I recaptured my old common sense. I ceased to believe that there was anything to fear. I could believe, as I listened to Luke's bright conversation, that he had played these tricks on me to tease me. How foolish I had been to be afraid. I had merely been the victim of youthful high spirits. That was my mood as we drove into Knaresborough.

We stopped at an inn for some light refreshment and afterward separated, Simon to do the business that had brought him here, Luke, Damaris and I to shop, having arranged to meet later back at the inn.

Very soon I had lost Luke and Damaris, who, I presumed, had wandered off to be alone together. I made the purchases on Hagar's list and a few for myself, and then, as I had almost an hour to spare, I decided to explore the town, which was one of the most charming in the area.

There were few people about on that bright December afternoon, and as I looked at the gleaming river Nidd, at the steep streets of houses with their red roofs, and the ruined castle with its fine old keep, I felt invigorated. I was making my way to the riverbank when I heard a voice behind me calling, "Mrs. Catherine!" Turning, I saw Simon.

"Finished your shopping? There is almost an hour before our rendezvous. What do you propose to do?"

"I was going to wander along the riverbank."

"Let's do it together," he said, and took my parcels.

As he walked beside me two things struck me—one was the strength that radiated from him, the other was the loneliness of the riverbank.

"I know what you want to do," he said. "You want to try your luck at the well."

"What well?"

"Haven't you heard of the famous Knaresborough Well?" He clicked his tongue mockingly. "Your education has been neglected."

I laughed. "I should like to see it."

"And wish? If you hold your hand in the water, then wish and let your hand dry, you will get your wish."

"Yes. I should like to wish."

"And will you tell me if it comes true?"

"Yes."

"But don't tell me what you have wished until it comes true. That is one of the conditions. It has to be a secret between you and the powers of darkness . . . or light, I'm not sure which. There's the well now. Water seeps from the soil through the sides of the well. You must let it drip onto your hands and wish. Will you go first or shall I?"

"You go first."

He leaned over the deep well and I watched the water drip onto his hand. Then he turned to me. "Now it's your turn."

He was standing close to me as I took off my glove and leaned over the well. I was conscious of the silence all about us. We were alone in this spot;

only Simon Redvers knew I was here. As the cold water dripped onto my hand he was immediately behind me, and there came to me then a moment of panic. In my mind's eye I saw him not as he had been a few seconds before, but wrapped in a monk's robe. Not Simon, I was saying to myself. *It must not be Simon.* And so vehement was my thought that I forgot any other wish.

I could feel the warmth of his body, so close was he, and I held my breath. I was certain then that something was about to happen to me. I swung around and he stepped back a pace.

"Don't forget," he said. "It's got to dry. I can guess what you wished."

"Can you?"

"Not a difficult task. You whispered to yourself, 'I wish for a boy.' "

As he spoke a man appeared close by. I had not noticed his approach, but perhaps Simon had. He gathered up my parcels, then took my arm in a possessive manner and drew me away from the well and toward the street. I held my damp hand out before me to dry as we walked along.

Luke and Damaris were waiting at the inn for us and we had a quick cup of tea and then started home. It was dusk when we reached Kirkland Moorside. Simon dropped Damaris at the doctor's house and then drove Luke and myself on to the Revels.

I went up to my room feeling dejected. It was because of these new suspicions that had come to me. I was fighting them, but they would not be dismissed. Why had I felt frightened at the side of the well? Had Simon been planning something that the casual arrival of a stranger had prevented? Why should I care whether it was Luke or Simon?

But I did care. It was then that I began to suspect the nature of my feelings for this man. I had no tenderness for him, but I felt more alive in his company than I did in that of any other person. I cherished his opinion of my good sense, and each time I saw him I slipped more and more under the spell of his personality. Now that he loomed so large in my life I began to understand what my feelings for Gabriel had been.

I had loved Gabriel without being in love with him; I had married him because I could give him comfort and he could provide me with an escape from a melancholy home. Although I had lost him, I could still look to the future with hope. Simon and the child had helped to do that for me.

It had been a cry from the heart that I had wished at the well: *It must not be Simon.*

I HAD NOW become aware of a change in the behavior of everyone at the Revels toward me. I intercepted exchanged glances; even Sir Matthew seemed watchful. I was to discover the meaning of this through Sarah, and the discovery was more alarming than anything that had gone before.

I went to her apartments one day and found her mending the lace on the family christening robe. "I'm glad you've come," she greeted me. "You used to be interested in my tapestries."

"I still am," I assured her. "I think they're lovely. What have you done on them lately?"

She giggled and put aside the robe; standing up, she took my hand. Then she paused and her face puckered. "I'm keeping it a secret until it's finished," she whispered.

"Then I mustn't pry. When will it be finished?"

I thought she was going to burst into tears. "How can I finish it when I don't know!" she said. "It's *you!* I don't know where to put you."

"You don't know where to put me?" I repeated, puzzled.

"I've got Gabriel . . . and the dog. He was a dear little dog, Friday."

"Aunt Sarah, what do you know about Friday?"

"Poor Friday. Such a faithful little dog. I suppose that was why . . ."

"What about Friday, Aunt Sarah? Please tell me."

She looked at me with a certain concern. "He was your dog," she said. "You should know."

"Aunt Sarah," I said impulsively, "show me the tapestry."

A light of mischief came into her eyes. "But it isn't finished, and I didn't want to show it to anyone until it is. Until I know . . ."

"Please," I wheedled, "do show me."

"Well, perhaps you," she said. "No one else." She went to the cupboard and brought out a canvas, an oil study for her tapestry. She held it up. Depicted on it was the south façade of the house, and on the stones in front of it was Gabriel's body. Lying beside him was my dog Friday, his little body stiff in death. It was so vivid that I felt a sudden nausea as I gazed at it. I stammered, "It looks so—so real."

"Oh, it's real enough . . . in a way," she said dreamily. "I saw Gabriel lying there, and that was how he looked."

"And Friday?" I cried. "You saw him too?"

She seemed to be trying to remember. "He was a faithful dog," she said. "He died for his faithfulness."

"Did you see him dead, as you saw Gabriel?"

Again that puckered look came into her face. "It's there on the picture," she said at length.

"But he's lying there beside Gabriel. It wasn't like that."

"Wasn't it?" she asked. "They took him away, didn't they?"

"Who took him away? Please . . . please tell me, Aunt Sarah. It's very important."

"I—I can't remember. . . ." Then her face brightened. "I know, Catherine. It was the monk."

She looked so innocent that I knew she would have helped if she could. I could not understand how much she had discovered. I was sure that she lived in two worlds—that of reality and that of the imagination—and that the two became intermingled so that she could not be sure which was which.

I turned my attention again to the picture and now I noticed that it took up only one half of the canvas. The rest was blank.

She read my thoughts immediately. "The rest is for you," she said; and in that moment she was like a seer from whom the future, of which the rest of us were utterly ignorant, was separated only by a semitransparent veil.

As I did not speak, she came close to me and gripped my arm. "I can't finish," she went on peevishly. "I don't know where to put *you* . . . that's why. You don't know. I don't know. But the monk knows. . . ." She sighed. "Oh dear, we shall have to wait. Such a nuisance. I can't start another until I finish this one."

She went to the cupboard and put the canvas away. Then she peered into my face. "You don't look well," she said. "Come and sit beside me. We are friends, aren't we? I felt it from the first. As soon as you came I said, 'I like Catherine. She understands me.' Now I suppose they say that's why—"

"Aunt Sarah, do tell me what you mean. Why should you and I understand each other better than other people in the house?"

"They always said I am in my second childhood."

A wild fear came to me. "And what do they say about me?"

She was silent for a while, then she said, "I've always liked the minstrels' gallery."

I felt impatient in my eagerness to discover what was going on in her muddled mind; then I saw that she *was* telling me and that the minstrels' gallery was connected with her discovery.

"You were in the minstrels' gallery," I said quickly, "and you overheard someone talking. You heard something about me?"

Glancing over her shoulder, she nodded, then shook her head. "I don't think we're going to have many Christmas decorations this year. It's all because of Gabriel. Perhaps there'll be a bit of holly."

I felt frustrated but I knew that I must not frighten her. She had heard something that she was afraid to repeat because she knew she should not, and if she thought I was trying to find out she would be on her guard. I forced myself to be calm and said, "Never mind. Next Christmas . . ."

"But who knows what'll have happened to us by next Christmas, to me . . . to *you?*"

"I may well be here, Aunt Sarah, and my baby with me. If it's a boy they'll want it brought up here, won't they?"

"They might take him away from you. They might put you . . ."

I pretended not to have noticed that. I said, "I should not want to be separated from my child. Nobody could do that, Aunt Sarah."

"They could . . . if the doctor said so."

"Did the doctor say so?" I asked.

"Oh yes. He was telling Ruth. He thought it might be necessary . . . if you got worse. And it might be a good idea before the baby was born."

"You were in the minstrels' gallery."

"They were in the hall. They didn't see me up there."

"Did the doctor say I was ill?"

"He said 'mentally unbalanced.' He said something about it being a common thing to have hallucinations—and to do strange things and then think other people did them." Her lips trembled. "Oh, Catherine," she whispered, "I've liked your being here. I don't want you to go to Worstwhistle."

The words sounded like the tolling of a funeral bell, my own funeral. If I was not careful, they would bury me alive.

I could no longer remain in that room. I said, "Aunt Sarah, I'm supposed to be resting. You will excuse me if I go now?"

I did not wait for her to answer. I stooped and kissed her cheek. Then I walked sedately to the door and, when I had closed it, ran to my own room, shut the door and stood leaning against it. I felt like an animal who sees the bars of a cage closing about him. I had to escape before I was completely shut in. But how?

I very quickly made up my mind as to what I would do. I would go see Dr. Smith and ask him what he meant by talking of me in such a way to Ruth. I knew they were saying, "She is mad." The words beat in my brain like the notes of a drum. They were saying that I had hallucinations, that I had imagined I had seen someone in my room; and then that I had begun to do strange things—silly, unreasoning things—and imagined that someone else did them. I had to prove to Dr. Smith that they were wrong.

I put on my blue cloak and made my way to the doctor's house. It was a tall, narrow house and the venetian blinds at the windows reminded me of Glen House. The door was opened by a gray-haired maid in a starched cap and apron. "Good afternoon," I said. "Is the doctor at home?"

"Please come in," she answered. I stepped into a dark hall. "I'm afraid he is not at home at the moment. Perhaps I can give him a message. Could I have your name, please?"

"I am Mrs. Rockwell."

"Oh!" The maid looked startled. "It may be an hour before the doctor is here, I'm afraid."

"I will wait for him. Is Miss Smith at home?"

"She also is out, madam."

"Then perhaps I could see Mrs. Smith."

The maid looked somewhat taken aback; then she said, "I will tell her you are here."

She went away and in a few minutes returned to say that Mrs. Smith would be pleased to see me. I followed the maid up a flight of stairs to a small room. The blinds were drawn and there was a fire burning in the grate. Near the fire was a sofa on which lay a woman. She was very pale and thin, but I knew at once that she was Damaris' mother, for the remains of great beauty were there. "Mrs. Rockwell of Kirkland Revels," she said as I came in. "How good of you to come to see me."

I took her hand; it was cold and clammy. I said, "As a matter of fact I came to see the doctor. As he is not in, I asked if you could see me."

"I'm glad you did."

"How are you today?"

"Always the same, thank you. That is . . . as you see me now. I can only walk about this room and then only on my good days. The stairs are beyond me."

Ruth had once told me Mrs. Smith was a hypochondriac and a great trial to the doctor. But what I saw on her face was real suffering.

"I have heard you are going to have a child," she said.

"I suppose the doctor told you."

"Oh no. He does not talk about his patients. My daughter told me."

"I have seen a great deal of her. She is so often at the Revels."

The woman's face softened. "Oh yes. Damaris is very fond of everyone at the Revels."

"And they of her. She is very charming."

"There is only one fault that can be found with her. She should have been a boy."

"Oh, do you think so? I hope for a boy but I shan't really mind if my child is a girl."

"No, I didn't mind—one doesn't oneself."

I was talking desperately to keep my mind off my own plight, and not really thinking much about her or her affairs, but I said, "So it was the doctor who cared."

"Most ambitious men want sons, to see themselves reproduced. It's a tragedy when they are disappointed. Please tell me, is anything wrong?"

"Why do you ask?"

"I thought you looked as though it might be so."

"I . . . I want to consult the doctor."

"Of course. I'm sure he won't be long."

Let him come soon, I was praying. I must speak to him. Nobody, I told myself fiercely, is going to tell me I'm going out of my mind. I must make him understand.

"Did you want to see him so very urgently?" she asked.

"Yes, I did."

"I remember when I was having my children I was continually anxious."

"I didn't know you had more than one, Mrs. Smith."

"There is only Damaris living. I have made many attempts to have a son. Unfortunately I did not succeed. I lost them in the early stages of pregnancy. My last, born four years ago . . . born dead . . . was a boy. Since then, I have never been well."

Worried as I was about my own problem, I felt a bond between us.

"I was very upset when I heard of your tragedy," she said.

"Thank you."

"Gabriel was a charming person. It is hard to believe—"

"It is impossible to believe what they said of him," I heard myself reply vehemently.

"Ah! I am glad you do not believe it. I wonder you don't go back to your family . . . to have your child."

I was puzzled by her statement. I noticed that there was a little color in her cheeks and the thin white hands were trembling. She was excited about something and I fancied she was wondering whether to confide in me. But just at that moment Damaris came in.

"Mother!" she cried, and her face looked different because the masklike quality had left it. She seemed younger—a lovely, vital girl. I knew in that moment that she was very fond of the invalid. Her face changed as her gaze fell on me. "But Mrs. Rockwell! What . . . ?"

"I called on the doctor," I said, "and as I had to wait I thought I'd make use of the opportunity to see your mother."

"Oh, but . . ."

"Why, have I done something I shouldn't? I'm sorry. Are you not allowed to receive visitors?"

"It is the state of her health. My father is very careful of her." Damaris went to her mother and laid a hand on her brow.

"I'm all right, my darling," said Mrs. Smith.

"Would you like me to go?" I asked.

"Please no," said Mrs. Smith quickly, but Damaris was looking doubtful. "Sit down, Damaris," she went on, and turning to me: "My daughter is overanxious on my behalf."

"And I expect the doctor is," I said.

"Oh yes . . . yes!" Damaris put in.

"I know he must be because he is so kind to all his patients. I hear his praises sung wherever I go."

Mrs. Smith lay back, her eyes closed, and Damaris said, "Yes, yes. It is so. They rely on him."

"I hope he will soon be back," I said.

Damaris sat down near her mother and began to talk. I had never heard her talk so much before. She talked of our trip to Knaresborough, of the church sale and other activities. It was thus that the doctor found us.

I heard his footsteps on the stairs and then the door was flung open. He was smiling, but it was a different kind of smile from that which I usually saw on his face, and I knew that he was disturbed. "Mrs. Rockwell," he cried. "Why, this is a surprise."

"I decided to make the acquaintance of Mrs. Smith while I was waiting."

He took my hand and held it firmly in his for a few seconds. I had a notion that he was seeking to control himself. Then he went to his wife and laid a hand on her brow. "You are far too excited, my dear," he said. "Has she been exciting herself?" He was looking at Damaris and I could not see his face clearly.

"No, Father." Damaris' voice sounded faint, as though she were a little girl and not very sure of herself.

He turned to me. "Forgive me, Mrs. Rockwell. I was concerned on two counts. On yours and that of my wife. You have come to see me. You have something to tell me?"

"Yes," I said. "I want to speak to you. I think it is important."

"Very well," he said. "Will you come to my consulting room?"

"Yes, please," I said, and I rose and went to Mrs. Smith's couch. I took the cold hand in mine and I wondered about her as I said good-by. She had changed with the coming of her husband, but I was not sure in what way; it was as though a shutter had been drawn over her expression.

I said good-by to Damaris, and the doctor led the way down to his consulting room. As he gave me a chair at the side of the rolltop desk and took his own chair I felt my spirits rise a little. He looked so benign that I could not believe he would do anything but help me. "Now," he said, "what is the trouble?"

"Strange things have been happening to me. You know about them."

"Yes," he admitted. "Some you yourself have told me. I have heard of the rest through other sources."

"You know then that I saw a monk in my bedroom," I said.

"I know that you thought you saw that."

"So you don't believe me."

He lifted a hand. "Let us say at this stage that I know that you saw it—if that comforts you."

"I don't want comfort, Doctor. I want people to accept what I say as truth."

"That is not always easy. But remember I'm here to help you."

"Then," I went on, "there were the incidents of the bed curtains, the warming pan, the cloak over the parapet. Do you believe I fancied them all—that they did not really happen outside my imagination?"

"Let us review this with calm, Mrs. Rockwell," he said. "I am a doctor and I have had experience of many strange cases. I know I can talk to you frankly and intelligently."

"So you do not think I am mad?"

"Do not use such a word. There is no need to."

"I am not afraid of words . . . any more than I am afraid of people who dress up as monks and play tricks on me."

He was silent for a few seconds, then he said, "You are going through a difficult time. Your body is undergoing changes. Sometimes when this happens the personalities of women change. You have heard that they have odd fancies for things to which they previously have been indifferent—"

"This is no odd fancy!" I cried. "I am here because I know you have been discussing me with Mrs. Grantley and that you have both decided that I'm . . . mentally unbalanced."

"You overheard this!" I could see that he was taken aback.

I had no intention of betraying Aunt Sarah, so I said, "I know you have been discussing this together. You don't deny it."

"No, that would be foolish of me, wouldn't it?" he said slowly.

"So you have decided that I'm crazy. What are you planning to do . . . send me to Worstwhistle?"

He stared at me, but he could not disguise the fact that the thought had been in his mind. Stricken with panic, I started up, but he laid his hand on my shoulder and gently forced me back into my seat. "You have misunderstood," he said, speaking softly. "This is a painful matter to me. I am very fond of the family at the Revels and their tragedies affect me deeply. Please believe that there is no question of your going to Worstwhistle . . . at this stage."

I took him up at once. "Then at what stage?"

"Please, please, be calm. Very good work is done at . . . that place. You know I am a regular visitor there. You have been overwrought for some weeks. You could not hide this from me."

"I have been overwrought because someone is trying to make me appear hysterical. And how dare you talk to me of that place!"

"I only want to help you."

"The best way in which you could do that would be to find out who dressed up as a monk and came to my bedroom. If you could find that person, I should be in no need of help."

He looked at me sadly and shook his head. "Mrs. Rockwell . . . Catherine . . . I wish you would trust me. More than anything I want to be your friend. You can't doubt that, can you? I want you to confide your troubles to me as you might to your own father. I want to protect you."

"So you think someone *is* threatening me?"

"Something is. It may be heredity. It may be . . ."

"I don't understand you."

"Perhaps I have said too much."

"No one is saying quite enough. If I knew everything that was in the minds of these people about me, I should be able to show you all that you have misjudged me when you think me . . . unbalanced."

"But you believe now that I want to help you. You do, I hope, look on me as a friend as well as a doctor?"

His eyes were gentle and I saw the anxiety in them. I was deeply moved. "You are very kind," I said.

A look of pleasure touched his features. He leaned forward and patted my hand. Then he was suddenly very serious. "Catherine," he said, "I have convinced you, haven't I, that I have your welfare at heart? I want you to know too that I owe a great debt to the Rockwell family. You may remember I told you that I began my life as an unwanted child, and that it was a rich man who gave me my opportunity to do the work I longed to do. That man was a Rockwell—Sir Matthew, in fact. So you see I can never forget the debt of gratitude I owe to him and to the family."

"I see," I murmured.

"He wants his grandson to be born strong and healthy. I long to make that possible. My dear Catherine, you must place yourself in my hands. You must let me take care of you. And there is one fact of which I believe you are ignorant, and I am now turning over in my mind whether or not I should tell you this."

"You must tell me. You must."

He hesitated, as though seeking the right words. Then suddenly they came rushing out. "Catherine, you know that I have for some years made a habit of visiting Worstwhistle."

"Yes, yes."

"I am in a very trusted position there and I have access to the records of patients. A close relative of yours is in that institution, Catherine. I do not think you know of this—in fact I am sure you do not. Your mother has been a patient at Worstwhistle for the last seventeen years."

I stared at him. It seemed to me that this room with its rolltop desk, this man with the gentle eyes, were dissolving and in their place was a house made dark by an atmosphere of brooding tragedy. I heard a voice crying in the night: "Cathy . . . come back, Cathy." And I saw him, my tragic father, going off each month and coming back dispirited, sad, melancholic.

"Yes," the doctor went on, "I fear it is so. I am told that your father is devoted to his wife, that he pays regular visits to the institution. Sometimes, Catherine, she knows who he is. Sometimes she does not know. At Worstwhistle all that can be done for her is done, but she will never leave the place. Catherine, do you see what I mean? Sometimes the seed is passed on. I am only telling you this so you will put yourself in my hands. Believe me, Catherine."

I found that I had buried my face in my hands and that I was praying. I was crying, "Oh, God, let me have dreamed this. Let this not be true."

He had risen and was standing by my chair, his arm about my shoulders. "We'll fight it, Catherine," he said. "We'll fight it together."

Perhaps the word "fight" helped me. It was a lifelong habit of mine to fight for what I wanted. I would not accept this theory that I was the victim of delusions. My voice sounded firm as I said, "I know someone is determined to harm me and my child."

Suppose it was true that my mother was in that place. I was certain that, whatever had happened to my mother, I had not inherited her insanity. I faced him and said, "Nothing will convince me that I imagined these things which have happened to me since I came to the Revels."

He nodded. "Well, then, my dear," he said, "the thing for us to do is to find out who is behind this—but now you are exhausted. You should go home and rest."

I was aware how weary I was, and I said, "I should like to be at home in my room—alone to rest and think of all this."

"That is wise. Will you allow Damaris to walk back with you? I would drive you back but I have another patient to see."

"That is not necessary."

"You said you would take my advice, and this news of your mother has been a great shock. Please, Catherine, do as I say."

"Very well. If Damaris has no objections."

"She will be delighted. Wait here and I will go and fetch her."

I was not sure how long I remained alone. I kept going over it in my mind, my father's leaving Glen House and not returning until the following day. He must have stayed a night near the institution . . . perhaps after seeing her he had to compose himself before returning home. So this was the reason for that house of gloom; this was why I had felt the need to escape from it.

Damaris came into the room with her father. I thought she looked sullen and reluctant to accompany me, so I began to protest that I was in no need of companionship.

But the doctor said determinedly, "Damaris would like a walk." He smiled at me as though everything were normal and he had not almost shattered my belief in myself.

"Are you ready?" asked Damaris.

"Yes, I am ready."

The doctor shook my hand gravely, and Damaris and I set out together.

"How cold it is!" she said. "Let's go through the copse. It's a little longer but we shall escape the wind."

I was walking as though in my sleep. I did not notice where we went. I could only go over and over in my mind what the doctor had told me, and the more I thought of it the more likely it seemed.

We stopped, for Damaris said she had a stone in her boot. She sat on a fallen tree trunk, removed the boot and shook it. She grew red trying to do the buttons up again. "Oh dear, these wretched buttons," she said.

"Let me help."

"No, I can do them myself." She struggled for a little while longer before she got the boot buttoned, and we were off again.

I was surprised when I found that we had come out of the trees on the far side of the abbey, and that it was necessary to walk through the ruins to reach the Revels.

"I know," said Damaris, "that this is a favorite spot of yours."

"It was," I amended. "It is some time since I have been here."

The afternoon light was beginning to fade. It seemed even darker in the ruins because of the shadows cast by those piles of stones.

We were in the heart of the abbey when I saw the monk. He was passing through what was left of the arcade; silently and swiftly he went, and he was exactly as he had been at the foot of my bed. I cried out, "Damaris! There! Look!"

The figure paused at the sound of my voice and beckoned to us. Then it turned away. Now it disappeared behind one of the buttresses; now it was visible again as it moved between one buttress and the next. I watched it, fascinated, horrified, unable for a moment to move. Then I exclaimed, "Quick! We must catch him."

Damaris clung to my arm, holding me back.

"But there is no time to waste. We'll lose him. We know he's somewhere in the abbey. We've got to find him."

Damaris said, "Please, Catherine . . . I'm frightened."

"So am I. But we've got to find him." I went stumbling toward the arcade, but she was dragging me back.

"Come home," she implored. "Come home at once."

I turned to face her. "You've seen it," I cried triumphantly. "So now you can tell them. You've seen it!" I realized we could not catch him, but that was not so important now. Someone else had seen him and I was vindicated. "Oh, Damaris," I said, "how thankful I am that it happened—that you saw."

She turned her beautiful, blank face toward me and her words made me feel as though I had suddenly been plunged into icy water: "What did you see, Catherine?"

"Damaris . . . what do you mean?"

"You were very excited. You could see something, couldn't you?"

"But do you mean to say you didn't?"

"There wasn't anything there, Catherine. There was nothing."

I turned on her, choking with rage and anguish. I believe I took her arm and shook her. "You're lying," I cried. "You're pretending."

She shook her head as though she was going to burst into tears. "No, Catherine, no. I didn't see anything. There wasn't anything."

I said coldly, "So you are involved in this, are you?"

"What, Catherine, what?" she asked piteously.

"Why did you take me to the abbey? Because you knew it would be there. So that you could say that you saw nothing. So that you could tell them I am mad!" She was clutching at my arm but I threw her off. "I don't need your help," I said. "I don't want your help. Go away. At least I've proved that you are his accomplice."

I stumbled on alone.

I entered the house; it seemed quiet and repelling. I went to my room and I lay on my bed until darkness came. Mary Jane came to ask if I wished to have dinner sent up to me; but I said I was not hungry, only very tired. I sent her away and I locked the door.

That was my darkest hour.

Then I took a dose of the doctor's sedative and fell into merciful sleep.

CHAPTER SEVEN

THERE IS SOME SPECIAL quality that develops in a woman who is to have a child; already the fierce instinct is with her. She will protect that child with all the power of which she is capable, and as her determination to do so increases, so it seems does that power.

I awoke next morning refreshed after the unbroken sleep that the doctor's sedative had given me. The events of the previous day came rushing back to my mind; but I was going to fight this thing that was threatening to destroy me—not only for myself but for the sake of one who was more precious to me. I tried to review the situation clearly and work out what must be done. I knew what I had seen. There must be an explanation somewhere. Damaris was clearly involved in the plot against me. And if she was hoping someday to be Luke's wife, it was reasonable to suppose that she would work with him. Was it possible that these two young people could plot so diabolical a scheme?

The first thing that occurred to me was that I might go back to my father's house. I rejected that idea almost at once. I should have to give a reason. I should have to say, "Someone at the Revels is trying to drive me to madness. Therefore I am running away." Furthermore I did not think I could endure the solemnity, the morbid atmosphere of my father's house.

I made my decision. I could never know peace of mind again until I had solved this mystery; therefore I could not run away. I was going to intensify my search for my persecutor. I must now make a practical plan, and I decided that I would go to Hagar and take her into my confidence. When I had bathed and dressed, I set out immediately for Kelly Grange.

It was about half past ten when I arrived there, and I went straight to

Hagar and told her what the doctor had told me. She listened gravely, and when I had finished she sent for Simon so that he might hear my story. Remembering my suspicions of him, I was a little anxious, but as soon as he entered the room they vanished, and I was ashamed that I had ever entertained them. That was the effect he was beginning to have on me. Hagar then said she had to go to her room to rest and think about what I had told her. She left me with words of reassurance.

Simon was practical, as he always would be. "It's all such nonsense. You're as sane as I am."

I said vehemently, "I am, Simon, I am."

He took my hands then and, to my astonishment—for I had not until this moment thought him capable of such a gesture—he kissed them. Then he pressed my hand so tightly that I winced. "Inside the monk's robe was a real person, and I'd wring his neck if I could find him," he said. "Catherine, I'm with you in this."

I knew a moment of great happiness. I felt the strength of him flowing into my body, and I was grateful, so grateful that I wondered whether such gratitude must be love. "Do you mean it?" I said.

"Heart and soul," he answered. "Nobody shall take you where you don't want to go. Now your first step," he went on, "is to write to your father. You must ask him for the truth about your mother. But mind you, whatever the truth, you're not to be downhearted. I've always admired you for your sharp wits and your courage."

"I don't feel very courageous now."

"You are going to be. Yes," he repeated, "you are going to be, and I will help you." He looked at me intently, and I read in his looks the knowledge that he wished me to share. He and I were about to embark on a new and exciting relationship. We were two of a kind. He recognized that, as I did now. I knew what he was telling me, and I wanted so much to listen.

He pressed my hand again, brought it halfway to his lips, then smiled and went on: "If we could only catch the monk in the act, that is all we should need to prove our case. It's my opinion that he's found some place in which to hide himself. We must try to discover it. Next week the Christmas festivities will begin, and my grandmother and I will spend two nights in the house. That may give us a chance to discover something."

"I wish it were this week."

"It will soon come," he said gently.

"And if they try anything in the meantime . . . ?"

He was silent for a few seconds, then he said, "If you should see the monk again, tell no one. I believe he wants you to talk of what you've seen, but do not give him that satisfaction. Continue to lock your door at night so that you can't be startled from your sleep. In the meantime you will hear from your father—and you are not going to be distressed, whatever he has to tell you. I never did believe that we relied on our ancestors for what we are. We are in command of our own fates."

"I'll remember that, Simon."

"All right. When you go back to the Revels how are you going to feel?"

"I don't know, except that it won't be so good as I feel here."

"No," he said. "You're going to be afraid. You're going to hurry in, turning to see if you are being pursued. You're going to throw open the door of your room, and look anxiously about you to see if he's there. Then you're going to lock him out, but you won't lock out your fear because it's there in your mind, and with the darkness your fear will grow stronger."

"You are right of course."

"Catherine, there is nothing to fear. There is never anything to fear. Fear is like a cage which prevents our escaping, but *we* make the bars of the cage ourselves. We ourselves have the power to break those bars."

"You are telling me *I* have nothing to fear!"

"Nothing has really harmed you, has it? You've only been frightened."

"How can I know that it never will?"

"The motive, at least, is becoming clear. Your own life is not in danger. This person's motive is to reduce you to such a state of fear that your chances of producing a healthy child are endangered. In view of Gabriel's death, it has to appear natural."

"And Gabriel's death . . ." I began.

"I am beginning to think that was the first act in the drama."

"And Friday?" I murmured, remembering then the night before Gabriel's death, when Friday had insisted on going into the corridor. I told Simon of this. "There was someone there. Waiting. Except for Friday, Gabriel might have died that night. And then Friday disappeared."

"We don't know how it happened," he said. "Let us concern ourselves with what lies ahead of us. If we can catch our monk in his robe, then we can demand an explanation, and I have no doubt that we shall learn what part he played in Gabriel's death."

"We must find him, Simon."

"We must. But if you see him again, do not try to seize him. Heaven knows what he might do. If there's anything in our conjectures about Gabriel, we may be dealing with a murderer. You must do as I say."

"I will, Simon."

"And remember," he added, drawing me to him and kissing me lightly on the cheek, "you are not alone. We're fighting this . . . together."

We left and he drove me back to the Revels. I trusted Simon. I no longer felt alone and that was a great comfort.

I wrote to my father and I believed that I should have the truth from him in a few days' time, because he would understand my need to know quickly; and when I had posted the letter I felt strengthened.

CHRISTMAS WAS TWO DAYS AWAY. The servants had decorated the hall with branches of holly, and there was mistletoe too. I had seen the dignified William seize Mary Jane and give her a resounding kiss under the pearly berries. Mary Jane responded good-humoredly; it was all part of the fun of Christmas. Then I received the letter from my father. With wildly beating heart I hurried to my bedroom, and took the precaution of locking the door before I opened the envelope.

My dear Catherine,

I was startled and shocked to receive your letter. I understand your feelings, and before you read any further, I want to assure you that the Catherine Corder who is now in Worstwhistle is *not* your mother, although she is my wife.

My wife and I were devoted to each other, and two years after our marriage we had a child—a daughter named Catherine. But this was not you. My wife adored our daughter and spent her time in the nursery supervising everything concerned with her. We had a nurse of course. She came highly recommended and was fond of children and efficient—when she was not under the influence of gin.

One day when my wife and I had been visiting friends, the nurse took advantage of our absence and became intoxicated; and while in this state she decided to bathe the baby. She put our child into a bath of scalding water. There was only one consolation—death must have been almost instantaneous.

My dear Catherine, you who are about to become a mother will understand the grief which overtook my wife. She blamed herself for leaving the child in the nurse's care. I shared her grief, but hers did not grow less as time passed. She continued to mourn, to accuse herself. She would pace through the house wildly sobbing, wildly laughing. I was alarmed and saw the urgent need to pacify her. And then your uncle Dick had an idea.

I know how fond you are of your uncle Dick. He has always been so good to you. That is natural, Catherine, when the relationship between you is known. He, Catherine, is your father.

It is difficult to explain this to you. I wish he were here so that he could do it himself. He was not a bachelor as you thought. His wife—your mother—was French. He met her when he was in port for a spell at Marseille and they were married there. They were ideally suited and they deeply regretted your father's long absences. Strangely enough, tragedy hit both our families in the same year. Your mother died when you were born, and that was not more than two months after we had lost our child.

Dick brought you to us because he wanted a settled home for you; he and I also believed that having a child to care for would help to comfort my wife. You even had the same name as our child. You were Catherine too. . . .

I put the letter down for a few seconds. I was seeing it all so clearly. I thought of the woman who had held me so tightly and then disappeared from my memory; of the man whom I had known as my father, living through those weary years, never forgetting the happiness he had shared with the woman in Worstwhistle, calling for her return—not as she was now, but as she had been.

I was filled with pity for him, for her; and I wished that I had been more tolerant of that gloomy house with its drawn blinds and the sunlight shut out. I picked up the letter.

> Dick thought that you would feel more secure with us than with him. It was no life for a motherless child, he said, with a father who was constantly away. So we let you believe that you were my daughter, and in the beginning I was sure your aunt would think of you as her own more readily that way.
>
> If only it had worked! For a while we thought it would. But the shock had been too much for her to bear and it was necessary to send her away. When she had left we moved to Glen House. It seemed better to cut ourselves off from old associations, and there we were not far from her place of asylum. . . .

How I wished I had known! Perhaps then I should have been able to do something to comfort him.

But the past was over and I was happy on that December morning because I was delivered of my fears. Now I would set to work to discover who in this house was my enemy, and I would go to it with such a will that I could not fail.

My baby would be born in the early spring, and I would never for a minute be parted from my child. Uncle Dick—I should never be able to call him my father; he would always be Uncle Dick to me—Uncle Dick would come home. I would watch over my child, and Simon would be there, and our relationship would develop as such relationships should, gradually budding, flowering, bearing fruit.

Yes, I was happy on that day.

IT WAS AFTER luncheon the next day when Mary Jane came to me in a state of excitement. "It's my sister Etty, madam. Her time's come. We hadn't thought it would be till the new year."

"You want to go and see her, don't you, Mary Jane?"

"Oh well, madam . . . me mother's gone over there."

"Look, you go along to Kelly Grange and see how she's getting on. You may be able to help. Just a moment," I continued. It was a bitingly cold day and I took from my wardrobe my heaviest cloak. It was the blue one that had been hung across the parapet. I put it about Mary Jane and pulled the hood over her head. "This will keep out the wind," I said, "and the cold can't penetrate. I don't want you catching cold, Mary Jane."

"Oh, madam . . . thank you." Her gratitude was indeed sincere. She went on rather shyly, "I'm so pleased, madam, because you've seemed so much better this last day or so."

I laughed. "I am better. Much better," I told her. "Go on now. And don't worry about getting back. Stay for the night if they want you."

It was dusk when she returned. She came straight up to my room, and I saw at once that she was deeply disturbed. "Is it Etty . . . ?" I began.

She shook her head. "The baby was born before I got there, madam. A lovely girl. Our Etty's all right."

"What's wrong then?"

"It was when I was coming home. I came round by the abbey. And I saw it, madam. It gave me a turn. You see, it was nearly dark—"

"You saw . . . what?" I cried.

"*It*, madam. The monk. It looked at me and it beckoned."

"Oh, Mary Jane, how wonderful! What *did* you do?"

"I stood for a second or two staring. I was struck all of a heap. Then I ran. It didn't follow me from the arches. I thought it was going to."

I put my arms about her and hugged her. "Oh, Mary Jane, I only needed this." She looked at me in some astonishment, and I stood back to gaze at her. She was about my height and the cloak was all-enveloping. She had been mistaken for me because she was wearing my cloak—the well-known blue cloak that had been put over the parapet.

I decided then that I would take Mary Jane into my confidence. She was loyal; there was a bond between us; I knew that she looked upon me as the kindest mistress she had ever had.

"Mary Jane," I said, "what did you think it was? A ghost?"

"Well, madam, I don't rightly believe in such things."

"Nor do I. I believe that what is inside that monk's robe is no ghost."

"But how did it get into your bedroom, madam?"

"That's what I'm going to find out."

"And did it draw the curtains and take the warming pan away?"

"I believe it did. Mary Jane, for the time being will you please say nothing to anyone of what you have seen? Our monk thinks it was I hurrying home through the abbey ruins. He has no idea it was you. I want to keep him in ignorance for a while. Will you do this?"

"I always want to do as you say, madam."

CHRISTMAS MORNING DAWNED bright and frosty. I lay in bed happily reading my letters and greetings. There was one from the man whom I still thought of as my father. He sent me Christmas greetings and hoped that his previous letter had not upset me. A letter from my real father told me that he hoped to be home in the spring.

As I lay in bed my thoughts went back—as indeed they often did—to the identity of my persecutor, and I went over the various monk incidents in detail. The monk had appeared in my room, sped along the second-floor corridor when I hurried after him, and disappeared. Was there some secret hiding place in the minstrels' gallery? The monk had been seen not only in the house but in the abbey ruins. What if there was some connecting passage between the abbey and the house?

I remembered the old plan of the abbey that I had seen in the library when I first came to the Revels; it might show where such a passage could be. I did possess two vital clues. There was the arcade in the ruins where the monk had been seen twice—by Damaris and me, and by Mary Jane. I would study the plan very closely at that spot. And there was the minstrels' gallery in the house.

I was so excited I slipped on a robe and hurried down to the library. I had little difficulty in finding the plan, and I brought it back to my room, where I got into bed again and studied it. The plan was headed "Kirkland Abbey" with the date 1520, and as I looked at it, it was as though the place came alive under my eyes. There it was—a series of buildings that housed a community that had no need of outside resources, one that was completely self-supporting. Beginning with the central Norman tower, I traced the principal features with my finger: the north and south transepts, the sanctuary, the chapter house, the monks' dormitory. And the arcade, with its buttresses, where I had seen the monk, led to the dining hall, to the bakehouses and malthouse. Then my eyes fell on the words "entrance to the cellars."

If there were cellars beneath the abbey, there would almost certainly be tunnels connecting them with other underground chambers. Such a labyrinth, I knew, was a feature of abbeys of the period. I noticed with rising excitement that the cellars were on the side of the ruins nearest the Revels.

I got up and dressed. The family would be ready for church early. We must all be in our pew on Christmas morning. Yet I was longing to look for those cellars in the abbey, and I wanted to do it when no one could follow me there. If only I could make some excuse for not going to church, for about two hours there would be no one to surprise me.

I went down to the hall. I should have liked to go to church with the family; I felt a need of the peace that the service would give me. But I had a more imperative need—the protection of my child—and I decided to practice a little deception. As Matthew and Sarah were stepping into the carriage I stood very still for a moment, putting my hands to my body.

Ruth said sharply, "What's wrong?"

"It's nothing, but I really don't think I shall go with you. The doctor said I should be very careful not to overtax myself."

"I'll stay behind with you," Ruth told me. "You should go to bed at once."

"No, you must not miss the Christmas service," I insisted. "Mary Jane will help me. She is very good and understands perfectly."

Ruth hesitated. Then she said, "Well, if you insist . . ."

She sent for Mary Jane, who came hurrying out. "Mrs. Rockwell doesn't feel well," Ruth said. "Take her to her room and look after her."

"Yes, madam," said Mary Jane.

Ruth, satisfied, got into the carriage, and in a few seconds they were driving away, while Mary Jane and I went up to my room.

When we were there I said, "We are going out, Mary Jane."

"But madam . . ."

I knew I had to take Mary Jane into my confidence again. "I feel quite well," I said. "I should have liked to join the church party, but there is something else I have to do. We are going to the abbey."

I made her wrap herself in the blue cloak, and I myself wore another of dark brown. Then we set out. I was anxious that we should lose no time; we had to be back in the house before the others returned.

"I have been looking at a plan of the abbey," I told Mary Jane. "We have seen the monk near one spot in the ruins, and that spot is close by the entrance to the cellars. What we have to do is find out if there is some means of getting from the abbey ruins into the house. Everything points to the fact that there is a secret entrance."

She nodded. "It wouldn't surprise me, madam. Why, this house is full of odd nooks and crannies."

Reaching the ruins, we went along the arcade from buttress to buttress as I had seen the monk do; and we came to what I knew to be the bakehouses and malthouse. We saw the remains of a spiral staircase, which I was sure must lead to the cellars.

Warily I descended the stairs ahead of Mary Jane, and at the bottom we came to two passages, both leading in the direction of the Revels. These had evidently been tunnels, and I felt disappointed because they, like the nave and transepts, had only the sky for their roofs. However, we each walked along one of these, a half-wall dividing us, and when we had gone about fifty yards they merged into one and we were in what could easily have been a dwelling place. There were several large chambers, the remains of brick walls showing us where they had been divided. I suspected that this was where valuables were hidden in time of war. There must be some link from here to the house. We had to find it.

We crossed these chambers and that seemed like the end of the ruins. The Revels was close now, and I knew that the part of it that contained the minstrels' gallery was opposite us. I was excited yet exasperated, for it appeared that we could go no farther.

Mary Jane looked at me helplessly, as though to ask what next. But I knew that we must return to the house to be back by the time the church party returned. "We'll have to go now," I said, "but we'll come again."

Mary Jane in her disappointment kicked at some large stones that were propped against a crumbling wall. There was a hollow sound, but the significance of this did not occur to me until later as my mind was on the conjectures that might arise if it was found that I had feigned indisposition in order to visit the ruins. "Another time," I said. "We must go now."

THAT AFTERNOON HAGAR and Simon came to the Revels, and a little later Simon and I had an opportunity to talk together alone. The older members of the family were in their rooms resting. I did not know where Ruth and Luke were. Ruth had said that as I felt too unwell for church that morning I ought to rest before tea. I said I would do this, but I was restless in my room and I came out after ten minutes and went along to the winter parlor, where Simon was sitting thoughtfully by the fire.

He rose with a delighted expression when I entered the room. "You've been looking radiant since we arrived," he said. "The change is remarkable. I'm sure something good has happened. You've discovered something?"

I told him about the letter and Mary Jane's adventure with the monk, and I was thrilled to see the way he received the news of my parentage. His face creased into a smile and then he began to laugh. "There couldn't be better news for you, could there, Catherine?" he said. "As for me"—he leaned toward me and looked into my face—"if you came from a line of raving lunatics I should still say you are the sanest woman I've ever met."

I laughed with him. I was very happy there in the winter parlor . . . the two of us sitting by the fire; and I thought, If I were not a widow, this might be considered a little improper.

On impulse I told him how I had avoided church to explore the ruins.

"The deceit of a woman!" he mocked me. "Now tell me," he went on, "what have you discovered?"

"Nothing for certain, but I believe it very possible that some connecting passage exists between the abbey and the house."

"Why are you so sure?"

"Because of the way in which the monk appeared both in the house and in the abbey ruins. He would have to keep his costume somewhere. Then he disappeared so neatly on the first night I saw him. I have a suspicion that the way into this hiding place is in the minstrels' gallery."

"Good God, what are we waiting for?" asked Simon.

Together we made our way to the minstrels' gallery. It had always seemed an uncanny place, and on this afternoon it was dismal and eerie. It had no window, and the only light came from the balcony overlooking the hall below. Heavy curtains hung on either side of the balcony. The idea was for the musicians who played there to be heard but not seen.

The back wall was hung with tapestries that had clearly not been moved for years. Simon went around tapping the wall, but he could only do so through the tapestries, which was not very helpful. At one spot he found that the tapestry could be pulled aside, and my excitement was great when behind this we discovered a door. He opened it, but it was only an empty cupboard that smelled damp and musty.

Somewhat discouraged, we returned to the winter parlor.

DINNER THAT EVENING was to be served in the hall. For centuries Christmas dinner had been eaten there. The long refectory table had been dressed with taste. At intervals candles burned in candlesticks of pewter, shining on gleaming cutlery and glass, and sprigs of holly were strewn on the huge lace tablecloth. It would be impossible not to be festive at such a table. Candles burned in their sconces on the walls and I had never seen the hall so brightly lighted. As I descended the stairs, wearing a loose tea gown of mole-colored velvet with ruffles of lace at the neck and sleeves, I thought, This is how the hall must have looked a hundred years ago.

It was the custom, Ruth had told me, to exchange gifts at dinner, and I saw that brightly colored packages were piled up at various places on the table. There were only seven of us to dine, although after dinner several people would call on us, as Sir Matthew had said, to take wine. I knew that among these people would be Dr. Smith and Damaris, and Mr. and Mrs. Cartwright and some members of their family.

Ruth was already there. "Ah," she said as I came down, "are you feeling better?"

"I am feeling very well, thank you."

"I'm so glad. It would have been unfortunate if you had not been well tonight. But if you should grow tired before everyone leaves, you must slip away. I'll make your excuses."

"Thank you, Ruth."

She pressed my hand; it was the first time I had felt any warmth from her. The Christmas spirit, I told myself.

Hagar was the next to enter. I watched her sweep down the staircase, and although she had to walk with the aid of a stick she made a magnificent entrance. She was dressed in a velvet gown of heliotrope, a shade becoming to her white hair, and wore an emerald necklace, earrings, and a ring with a huge square-cut stone. I had never seen anyone with as much dignity as Hagar; I felt that everyone must be a little in awe of her, and I was glad that she and I had become such friends. She put her cool cheek against mine and said, "Well, Catherine, it is pleasant to have you here with us. Isn't Simon down yet?" She shook her head in affectionate exasperation. "I am sure he is dressing under protest."

"Simon never did like dressing up," said Ruth. "I remember he once said that no occasion was worth all the trouble."

"He has his opinions about such matters," agreed Hagar. "And here's Matthew. Matthew, how are you?"

Sir Matthew was coming down the stairs and I saw Aunt Sarah behind him. She had put on a gown with rather extreme décolletage. It was of blue satin decorated with ribbons and lace, and it had the effect of making her appear very young—but perhaps that was the excitement one sensed in her. Her eyes went to the table. "Oh, the presents!" she cried. "Always the most fascinating part, don't you think, Hagar?"

"You never will grow up, Sarah," said Hagar.

But Sarah had turned to me. "You like the presents, don't you, Catherine. You and I have a lot in common, haven't we?"

Simon descended the stairs then. It was the first time I had seen him dressed for the evening, and I thought that he looked very distinguished.

"Ha!" cried Hagar. "So you have succumbed to custom, grandson."

Simon took her hand and kissed it, and I watched the contented smile at her lips. "There are times," he said, "when there is no alternative but to succumb."

Once Luke had arrived, we sat down at the table. While William and the maids began to serve us, we looked at our presents. Sarah squealed with delight like a child; the rest of us opened our gifts decorously and murmured conventional thanks to one another.

There was one present beside my place that held a certain significance. The card bore the inscription "A Happy Christmas from Hagar and Simon Rockwell-Redvers" in Hagar's bold handwriting. When I opened the box I stared in amazement, for it contained a ring. It was some family heirloom, I guessed—a ruby set in a circle of diamonds. I lifted it out of the case and looked from Simon to Hagar. Simon was watching me intently; Hagar was giving me the special smile she usually reserved for Simon.

"But this—this is too . . ." I stammered. I was aware that the attention of all at the table was on me and the ring.

"It has been in the family for generations," said Simon. "The Redvers family, that is."

"Slip it on your finger," said Hagar. "I want to see if it fits."

It was too small for the middle finger of my right hand, on which I tried it first, but it fitted perfectly on the third finger.

"It looks becoming, does it not?" Hagar asked, glaring around at the others as though daring them to contradict her.

"It is such a beautiful ring," Ruth murmured.

"The Redvers seal of approbation, Catherine," said Luke.

I knew that there was a significance about this of which everyone else at the table was aware, though I was not . . . entirely. But I did know it was a very valuable present and that in giving it to me Simon and Hagar were proclaiming their affection for me; perhaps they meant to tell my persecutor that he had to deal not only with me but with them also. "How can I thank you?" I said, looking at Hagar, for I could not look at Simon then.

"By wearing it," Simon answered.

"It's a talisman," cried Luke. "Did you know, Catherine, that while you wear that ring nothing can harm you? It's the old family tradition. The genie of the ring will protect you from the powers of evil."

"Then it's doubly precious," I said lightly. "Since it not only preserves me from evil but is so decorative. I am so grateful to you for giving me such a lovely present."

Because I was afraid that I might betray the emotion this gift aroused in me, I said no more and hastily turned to my soup. By the time the turkey had been eaten and the Christmas pudding brought in, I was conscious of a quiet peaceful pleasure. The pudding was magnificent with its wreath of holly around the base and the sprig stuck jauntily into the top. William poured the brandy over it and Sir Matthew set it alight.

Sarah was staring at the flaming pudding. "Last night," she said in a hollow voice, "I lay in bed thinking of all the Christmases of my life. The first one I remembered was when I was three. I went right through them all until I reached last Christmas. Do you remember how we drank the toasts afterward? There was a special one to Gabriel after his escape."

There was a silence of some seconds, which I broke by asking, "What escape was that?"

"Gabriel's," said Sarah. "He might have been killed." She put her hand to her lips. "Just think if he had . . . he would never have met Catherine. You wouldn't be here with us today, Catherine, if he had died. You wouldn't be going to . . ."

"Gabriel never told me about this accident," I said.

"It was hardly worth mentioning," said Ruth sharply. "One of the walls in the ruins collapsed. He was close by and there was a slight injury to his foot—a matter of bruises."

"But," cried Sarah, her blue eyes flashing almost angrily because, I thought, Ruth was trying to make light of something that she felt important, "just by chance he saw what was about to happen. He was able to escape in time. If he hadn't seen it, he would have been killed."

"Let's talk of something cheerful," said Luke. "It didn't happen. So that's that."

"William," said Ruth, "Mr. Redvers' glass is empty."

I was thinking of Gabriel, of the fear he had seemed to have of his home. Was the falling of the wall really an accident? Did Gabriel know that someone in the Revels was trying to kill him? Was that why he had married me—so there would be two of us to fight the evil that threatened? Had that evil caught up with him? If so, it meant that someone wanted his inheritance. That person must have been horrified when, after murdering Gabriel—and I was convinced now that he *had* been murdered—he found there was another who might step into Gabriel's shoes: my child.

I found myself looking at Luke. With his long fair hair falling about his pale face I thought he looked like a cross between an angel and a satyr. He reminded me of the figures that were carved on the stonework of the house. There was a satanic gleam in his eyes as they met mine. It was almost as though he read my thoughts and was amused by them.

The meal over, the table was quickly cleared by the servants, and we were ready to receive our guests. Dr. Smith and Damaris were the first arrivals, and I wondered what the doctor's wife thought of being left alone on Christmas Day. Then the Cartwrights came with several members of their family. There was no dancing and the guests were conducted to one of the drawing rooms; even the conversation was quiet. On this day everyone was remembering Gabriel, because it was due to his death that the traditional entertaining had not taken place.

I found an opportunity to thank Hagar privately for the ring. She smiled and said, "We wanted you to have it . . . both of us."

Then Simon was standing beside us, and I turned to him. "I was thanking your grandmother for this magnificent ring."

He took my hand and held it for a few moments, regarding the ring with a smile of satisfaction.

Ruth joined us. "Catherine," she said, "if you want to slip away to your room, I should do so. You mustn't tire yourself."

I did feel then so moved by new emotions that I wanted to go to my room, for there was a great deal I had to think about. Moreover I knew I should be resting. "I think I will," I said.

I said good night to Hagar, and she drew me to her and kissed my cheek. Then I gave my hand to Simon. To my astonishment he bent down swiftly and kissed it. I could feel his kiss hard and warm on my skin. Flushing faintly, I hoped Ruth had not noticed. Quietly I slipped away.

I was too excited to sleep. I lighted the candles and lay down on my bed, turning the ring round and round on my finger, going over everything that had happened, right from the first. I was conscious of an urgency. Time was short. This mystery should be solved, and quickly. If I could find that secret way into the house . . . if I could find the monk's robe . . .

I realized that we had not really examined the minstrels' gallery thoroughly enough. We had found the cupboard but had not looked behind all the tapestries.

I rose from my bed—I had not undressed—then went quietly along to the gallery and closed the door behind me. It was so dark and gloomy that I told myself I had been foolish to hope to discover anything in this poor light. I leaned over the balcony, looking down on the candlelit hall. As I stood there the door opened behind me, and I turned. A shape loomed on the threshold. For a moment I thought it was the monk, and a shudder of fear ran through me.

But this was no monk. It was a man in ordinary evening dress, and when he whispered, "Why . . . Catherine!" I recognized the voice of Dr. Smith. He went on speaking very quietly. "What are you doing here?"

"I couldn't sleep."

He came into the gallery and we stood side by side near the balcony. He put his fingers to his lips. "There is someone down there," he whispered.

I was surprised that he should consider that a matter for secrecy as there were so many guests in the house, and was about to say so when he seized my arm and drew me closer to the balcony. Then I heard the voices.

"Damaris! We're alone at last." The sound of that voice gave me a pain that was almost physical. It was not only the words but the tone in which they were spoken that was so significant. For it was both tender and passionate, and only rarely had I heard that timbre in the voice. It was Simon who was speaking.

Then Damaris: "I am afraid. My father would not be pleased."

"In these matters, Damaris, we do not please our fathers but ourselves."

"But tonight he is here. Perhaps he is watching us now."

Simon laughed, and as they moved from immediately below the balcony toward the center of the hall, I could see that he had his arm about her.

I turned away, not wanting to look. I was afraid they might be aware of us. My humiliation would have been complete if Simon knew that I had looked on at his flirtation with Damaris, and I moved toward the door of the gallery. The doctor was still beside me, and together we went out. He seemed preoccupied, scarcely aware of me, and I had no doubt that he was very worried about his daughter.

"I shall forbid her to see that . . . philanderer!" he said.

I clasped my hands together and touched the ring that but a short time ago had seemed to have such significance.

"Perhaps it would be useless to forbid her," I suggested.

"She would have to obey me," he retorted, and I saw the veins prominent at his temples. I had never known him so agitated; it seemed to mark the depth of his affection for her.

"He is overbearing," I said, my own voice angry. "I believe he would always find a way of getting what he wanted."

"I am sorry," said the doctor. "I am forgetting you. You should be resting. What made you come to the gallery?"

"I couldn't sleep. I was too excited, I suppose. What made *you* come to the gallery?"

"I knew they were down there together."

"I see. And you would frown on a match between them?"

"A match! He would not offer her marriage. The old lady has other plans for him. He'll marry *her* choice and it won't be my daughter. Besides, she is for Luke."

"Is she? She did not seem to think so tonight."

"Luke is devoted to her. If only they were older they would be married by now. It would be a tragedy if she were ruined by this—"

"You do not think very highly of his honor."

"His honor! You have not been here long enough to know his reputation in the neighborhood. But I am keeping you and it grows late. I shall take Damaris home immediately. Good night, Catherine."

I went to my room. I was so upset that I forgot to lock my door. But there were no midnight visitors, and I was alone with my emotions. That night I learned their true nature, and I blamed myself for allowing them to become so strong, disguised as they were by the semblance of dislike. I learned that hatred grows out of the strength of one's own emotions; and that when a woman comes close to hating a man she should be watchful, for it means that her feelings are deeply engaged.

He is a cheat, I told myself, a philanderer who amuses himself with any female who is handy. I happened to be at hand. What a fool I am, and how we hate those who make us aware of our own folly. Hate and love. There are times when the two can run side by side.

CHAPTER EIGHT

I DID NOT SLEEP well that night and it must have been near morning when I was awakened by Mary Jane. It was dark and she was carrying a lighted candle. I sat up in bed. "Mary Jane!" I said. "What is the time?"

"It's six o'clock, madam."

"But why . . . ?"

"I wanted to tell you yesterday, but with all the Christmas preparations I didn't get a chance. I found it—while we were getting the hall ready!"

I cried, "Mary Jane, you have found the way out of the house?"

"I think so, madam. It is in the minstrels' gallery—in the cupboard. There are two floorboards there with a gap between them, enough to get your fingers in. I gripped one of the boards and it lifted up easy. Then I saw the great black space below, so I got a candle and looked down. There are some stairs leading down. I thought I'd come straight to you to tell you. But then William was calling and I had to go to the kitchens to help and I didn't get another chance."

I was excited, for this was the proof I needed. "We must look into this at once," I said. "And we must move quickly. I'll put my cloak on over my nightgown."

The house was very quiet and even my slippered tread seemed noisy. But we reached the gallery with no one appearing. Mary Jane very gently shut the door behind us, and I held the candle while she opened the cupboard and showed me the floorboards. She knelt and lifted one of these up, and I leaned over the opening, holding the candle.

I could see the flight of steps. I longed to go down, but there was a short drop to the top step and I dared not trust myself to do that. But Mary Jane was lithe and slim. "You go through," I said, "and I'll hand you the candle. Just tell me what you see down there."

She had turned a little pale, but she lowered herself through the aperture and, when she was standing on the steps, took the candle.

She said, "It seems like a big room down there. It's very cold."

I warned her to be careful, adding, "Just have a quick look round. Then we'll try to find the way in from the abbey side."

I heard her voice as she descended the steps: "I'll do that, madam. I'll just have a quick look."

My heart was beating madly. I wanted to be down there with her, but I dared not risk slipping on those stone steps. I glanced over my shoulder. I could not rid myself of the feeling that someone was watching us. But there was no one there; there was no sound at all in that silent house.

I heard a sudden call from Mary Jane. "I've found something, madam."

"Come back now, Mary Jane. Bring what you've found—if you can."

She appeared on the steps and I breathed more freely. She was holding the candle in one hand and something under her arm. She handed a bundle up to me and I knew at once that it was the monk's robe. She quickly scrambled back through the aperture and replaced the floorboard exactly as it had been. We took the robe back to my room.

"Shouldn't we tell someone?" she asked. "Shouldn't we show them the robe?"

The day before, I should have told Simon. But I could no longer trust him, and if I could not trust Simon, I trusted nobody. "We will say nothing of this for the moment," I said. "We have the evidence here. I will lock it in my wardrobe."

"And then, madam?"

I wondered what my persecutor would do when he discovered his robe was missing. Perhaps he would think there was need for prompt action.

"Mary Jane, you will be missed if you stay here much longer. I will go back to bed. Bring my breakfast in the ordinary way. I want to think what I ought to do next."

"Yes, madam," she said. And she left me.

I stayed in my room all day, giving fatigue as my excuse, but joined the family at dinner. Simon, sitting next to me, appeared anxious on my behalf, and although I had told myself that I would give no sign of my changed feelings toward him, I could not help a coolness creeping into my manner.

"I am disappointed," he told me, "that I've had no opportunity of being with you today. I had planned that we should take a drive together—you, my grandmother and myself. She too was disappointed."

"You should have made up a party with the others."

"You know that would not have been the same thing at all."

"Perhaps Damaris would have accompanied you."

He laughed, and lowered his voice. "I have something to tell you later about that." I looked at him interrogatively. "Because," he added, "you obviously noticed. It is often necessary to go by devious ways to reach a certain goal."

"You are talking in riddles."

"Which is not inappropriate. We have a riddle to solve."

I turned away and engaged Sir Matthew in a lengthy conversation. To Simon's exasperation, I left the company soon after dinner.

I had not been in my room more than five minutes when there was a knock on the door and Sarah entered. She smiled at me conspiratorially and whispered as though to excuse the intrusion, "Well, you were interested. That's why . . ."

"What do you mean?" I asked.

"I've started to fill it in," she said. She was watching me and her face seemed suddenly full of knowledge.

My thoughts went to her half-finished tapestry. "Can I see it?"

"Of course. That's why I came. Will you come with me?"

I went eagerly, and when we were in the corridor she put her fingers to her lips. "I don't want anyone to hear us," she said, and led the way to her tapestry room. She was now as excited as a child with a new toy. She lighted several candles, then ran to the cupboard and took out the canvas.

I picked up a candle and held it close to the picture. On one side were the dead bodies of Gabriel and Friday; on the other, a faint pencil drawing had been added. This was of another building, and the effect was that of looking through barred windows into a room like a prison cell. In that cell was the outline of a woman holding something in her arms. I felt a thrill of horror as I realized this was meant to be a baby.

"I suppose that figure is myself," I said.

She nodded. "You see, the baby is born."

"But we seem to be in a sort of prison."

"I think it would feel like being in prison . . . that place."

I understood. "The doctor made a mistake," I exclaimed. "There is no need to think of that anymore."

She shook her head petulantly. "But it's here," she insisted. "It's here in the picture."

I knew she moved quietly about the house, listening from secret places. Yet I was foolish to allow myself to be upset by a vague idea that circulated in her wandering mind.

"In a prison," she murmured, "there has to be a jailer. I can see him. He's all in black, but he has his back to me and his hood makes it impossible to recognize him."

"The monk!" I said, my apprehension increasing.

She came up to me and looked into my face. "The monk is very near you, Catherine. The monk is waiting for you, waiting to catch you."

"You know who it is!" I accused her.

"It's a lovely night," she answered. "The stars are wonderful . . . and, Catherine, the view is beautiful from the balcony."

I drew away from her. "I think I should go." I went to the door but she caught my robe and clung to it. I began to shiver, but not with cold.

"The candle," she said. "You'll need one. Take mine." She thrust a lighted candle into my hand. I grasped it and, disengaging myself, hurried off along the corridor, half expecting her to pursue me.

I was breathless when I reached the sanctuary of my room, and my apprehension remained with me. I could not dismiss Sarah's ramblings from my mind because I was certain that there was some meaning hidden within them. How I longed to confide in someone that night.

THE NEXT MORNING Simon and Hagar left Kirkland Revels. I said good-by warmly to Hagar, coolly to Simon. He was aware of my changed attitude and it seemed to amuse him. I thought, Can he really be as cynical as that?

When they had gone I went to my room to formulate some plan. I knew that I must act quickly, because it might be that already the robe had been missed. I still clung to the belief that Luke was my enemy, and I was trying to come to some decision when I noticed an envelope had been pushed under the door. I opened the door, hoping to find someone hurrying away, but there was no one there.

I shut my door and slit the envelope. There was a single sheet of paper inside, and on it was written in a shaky handwriting, "Go back to your old home without delay. You are in imminent danger."

I stared at it. I did not know the handwriting; the letter was unsigned. What did it mean? Was it yet another trick? But there was something tangible about a piece of paper. No one could say I had imagined this.

I went to my window and looked out. Then my heart began to hammer wildly, because I saw someone hurrying away and I recognized her—Damaris! I was certain it was she who had come quietly into the house and left that note under my door. But why?

I suspected Damaris of plotting against me, but I would not let myself believe that she was working with Simon. I had seen them together Christmas night, and what had been implied by their words had shocked me deeply. Yet I couldn't believe this of Simon. My common sense might insist I do, but my ridiculous feminine emotions refused to be convinced.

Someone had sent Damaris to put that note under my door. Was it Luke? He could have done it himself. Dr. Smith? Then I remembered that occasion when I had called at Dr. Smith's house. I thought of his sick wife. The shaky handwriting might be that of a sick woman, a woman who was in some stress.

I put the paper into my pocket, wrapped myself in my heavy cloak and went out. There was a bitterly cold wind blowing but I was impervious to the weather. I hurried away from the house, looking back only once to see if I was being followed. I could see no one, but I felt that from every window eyes might be watching me.

The doctor's house seemed more gloomy than it had before. The maid let me in and said, "The doctor is not at home, Mrs. Rockwell."

"I have come to see Mrs. Smith. Please tell her that I am very eager to see her on a matter of importance."

In a few moments the maid returned and led me to the room I had visited before. I was astonished to see Damaris there. She was standing by Mrs. Smith's chair as if clinging to her mother for protection.

Mrs. Smith looked even more emaciated than when I had last seen her; her eyes were enormous and they seemed to burn with some deep purpose. She said in a quiet voice, "Good morning, Mrs. Rockwell. It was good of you to call." I went forward and took the hand she extended; and then the door shut on the maid and we three were alone.

"Why did you come here?" she asked quickly. "This is the last place you should come to." I took the sheet of paper from my pocket and held it out to her. "Have you shown this to anyone else?" she asked.

"To no one. But I believe you wrote it and sent it to me. I saw Damaris leaving the house."

There was silence. Then I cried, "You did write it, didn't you?"

Damaris put her arm about her mother. "You must not be disturbed," she said. She looked at me almost defiantly. "You are making her ill."

I answered, "I think she can help me to find out who has been trying to make *me* ill."

"You must not fret, my darling," said Mrs. Smith to Damaris. "It was unwise of her to come here, but she is here now and I must do what I can."

"Will you tell me this," I asked. "Did you write that note?"

She nodded. "I did it because I know that if you wish to give birth to a child that will live, you must get away now. If you do not, it will be too late."

"How can I know that I can trust you?"

"What could I possibly gain by warning you?"

"Don't you see that I'm in the dark?"

"Yes, I do. You are headstrong. You will not take my advice and go. You want to solve mysteries. You are too bold, Mrs. Rockwell."

"Tell me what you know," I said. "You owe that to me."

"Mother," gasped Damaris, and the mask dropped from her lovely face. I knew that she was terrified.

I took Mrs. Smith's thin, clammy hand. "You must tell me," I said. "You know you must tell me."

"And if I can convince you that you and your child are in great danger, will you go to your father's house today?"

"If I think that necessary, I will."

"Mother," said Damaris, "you must not . . . You dare not."

"You are afraid still, Damaris?" Mrs. Smith said.

"So are you, Mother. We both are—we always have been."

"Yes, I am afraid. But I am thinking of the child . . . and of her. We cannot stand by and see that happen to her, can we, Damaris?"

I was beside myself with impatience, but still Mrs. Smith hesitated. Then, bracing herself as for a mighty effort, she began.

"I married against my family's wishes. You may think my story has nothing to do with this. I am merely trying to tell you how I happen to know . . ."

"Yes, yes," I cried.

She plucked at the blanket that was wrapped about her knees. "I had a small fortune of my own. As you know, when a woman marries, her fortune becomes her husband's. He needed the fortune . . . so he married me. I had a great opinion of him. He was the dedicated doctor and I wanted to work with him. I wanted to help him . . . his patients loved him so. But you see there were two doctors. There was the doctor who went among his friends and patients—such a charming man, so solicitous of others. And there was the doctor at home. They were two different men. He liked to play his part but we couldn't expect him to act all the time."

Damaris murmured, "You must not. . . . When he hears . . ."

"You see," went on Mrs. Smith, "he believed himself to be not quite mortal. He had done brilliantly at his work and from such humble beginnings. I admired that—at the start. But he soon tired of playing the part for me. When Damaris was born, he was very angry that she was not a boy. He wanted a son, to be exactly like himself—which in his eyes meant perfect. Damaris quickly learned to understand him. Do you remember, Damaris, how you would be playing, happily forgetful? Then we would hear his step in the hall, and you would come to me and cower beside me."

"He ill-treated you?" I asked.

"Not physically. That is not his way. But he came to hate me. Why should he do otherwise? He had wanted my money and that was now his, and when after many attempts I had failed to give him a son, I was of little use to him. Those years of sadness and terror—I cannot think how I lived through them."

"So it is Dr. Smith who has tried to destroy me. Why . . . why?"

"I will tell you that too. I met his foster mother. She lives not far from here in a little cottage on the moors. He was brought to her as a baby, the son of a Gypsy girl who had forsaken her people for a while to work in the kitchens at the Revels. The girl was married to a Gypsy named Smith, but when her baby was born she did not want the child and she deserted him. Sir Matthew had taken an interest in the girl. I do not know if he was ever her lover, but that was what Deverel always believed—that he was the son of Sir Matthew. Do you begin to understand now?"

"I begin to see some light," I said.

"And when Sir Matthew had him educated and trained as a doctor he was certain of this. He married me, and our daughter was called Damaris because the Rockwells had always chosen names from the Bible for their children. But it was a son he wanted. He wanted to see a son of his in the Revels. And so . . ." She turned to Damaris, who was crying quietly. "I must tell her this," she soothed. "I should have told her before. But you know how we have always feared his anger."

"Please go on," I pleaded.

"After several miscarriages I was warned not to have any more children. But he wanted a son. I tried again. The child was born dead and I . . . well, I have been an invalid ever since. I think that he would have rid himself of me if it had not been for Damaris. You see, he does not know how far she would betray him if he attempted to destroy me." She put out a hand and stroked her daughter's hair.

"It was four years ago that I became an invalid. Before that I was not strong but I was able to take part in the life of the neighborhood. I played a part in the pageant—only one of the monks, it was true. I still had my robe though. Until a few months ago."

I caught my breath and said, "So it is yours, that robe?"

"Yes, it is mine. I had kept it. I am a little sentimental about such things. It was a reminder to me of the days when I was not an invalid."

"But Damaris helped him," I said accusingly. "She swore at the ruins that she had seen nothing."

"I had to," the girl whispered with a sob in her voice. "He told me what I had to do. We always obeyed him. We dared do nothing else. I was to take you to the ruins—not too quickly, to give him time to get there before us. And then, when he appeared, I was to pretend I saw nothing. There is a way from the ruins into the house. He discovered it when he was a boy. So he appeared to you in the house as well."

Now that I had the vital facts, events began to fall into place. I was filled with a wild exultation, and the reason was that the wish I had made at the Knaresborough Well had come true. It was not Simon.

"Why . . . *why?*" I demanded.

"He was determined to live in the Revels one day. He saw that the way to get there was through Damaris. She was to marry Luke."

"But how could he be sure of that?"

"My daughter has a rare beauty. Luke is not unaware of it. They were thrown together always. If not, my husband would have found some way of insisting on that marriage. He discovered the secrets in people's lives and used them when he found it expedient. He would have uncovered something which Sir Matthew would not want known—or Mrs. Grantley. The marriage would have taken place.

"He was not unduly concerned about Gabriel, who was delicate—he himself diagnosed that weak heart. But when Gabriel married he became a menace. My husband feared what actually did happen—that you might have a child. He was determined that Gabriel must die. So Gabriel . . . died."

"It is not difficult to imagine how," I said grimly. And I pictured it. Did he lure Gabriel onto the balcony, or did Gabriel go there as he had made a habit of doing? The night before, Friday had heard someone in the corridor, but there was no Friday this night to warn him of a sinister presence, for Friday had already been killed. And then as Gabriel stood there, a stealthy movement from behind, a hand over his mouth and his body lifted and sent hurtling over the balcony.

Mrs. Smith said, "We are wasting time. There is nothing more I can do for you. Go at once to your old home. There you will be safe."

"You know that he plans something?"

"We know he is angry. He does not take us into his confidence, but we know something has happened recently to anger him."

I knew what that was. He had discovered that the robe had been removed. He was planning some immediate action against me. I knew I had to act promptly. I could not see how he could harm me now, because I had so much evidence against him, but I did not doubt that he was diabolically clever.

"Go at once," pleaded his wife. "He may return here at any moment. If he found you, if he knew what we had told you . . ."

"Yes," I agreed. "I will go at once. How can I thank you for—"

"Don't waste time in thanking us. Please go. He *must* not see you leave this house."

So I went. I was in a state of great excitement. I knew now what I should do. I was not going to Glen House. I was going to Kelly Grange. But first I would return to the Revels, because I was determined to take the monk's robe with me. I was not going to allow anyone in the future to believe that I had suffered from hallucinations.

As I walked I thought back. Now that I knew who my enemy was, it was easy to understand how he had been in a position to act as he did; how easy it was for him to slip in and out of the house, pull the curtains about my bed, remove the warming pan and put my cloak over the balcony. He could come by the secret entry and if he was seen, on the stairs, in the hall, he would always have a plausible answer. He had been worried about Sir Matthew, Sarah, myself, and had dropped in to see that all was well.

And Simon? I had to face the truth. I now believed that Damaris regarded her father's determination to marry her to Luke with repulsion, and what I had originally thought was an affection between her and Luke was merely Damaris' desire to please a father whom she feared, and Luke's natural interest in an attractive girl. But with Simon, it would be different; I did not believe that any woman could be completely indifferent to the virile charm of Simon Redvers.

I must not think of Simon. But Hagar was my friend. I could rely on her. So I would get the monk's robe and go at once to Kelly Grange. Those were my plans as I entered the Revels.

I RANG MY bell, and Mary Jane came to my room. "I am going at once to Kelly Grange," I said. "Pack some things that I shall need. I will send for you and them. But I propose to go on immediately on foot."

"Yes, madam," said Mary Jane, her eyes wide with surprise.

"Something has happened," I told her. "I cannot stop to explain now. But I am going to leave this house at once."

As I spoke I heard the sound of carriage wheels, and I went to the window. I saw Dr. Smith alight and I felt myself tremble.

"I should be gone," I said. Seizing the monk's robe from the wardrobe, I hurried out of the room, leaving a bewildered Mary Jane staring after me, and went along the corridor to the stairway. Then I heard the doctor's voice; he was in the hall talking to Ruth. "Is she at home?"

"Yes, I saw her come in only a few minutes ago."

"That is fortunate. I will go and get her now."

"What if she . . . ?"

"She will know nothing until I have her safely there."

My heart began to hammer uncertainly. He was already starting up the stairs. I slipped down the corridor into the minstrels' gallery, thinking that I might hide there while he went to my room. Then I should run out of the house and to Kelly Grange. But Ruth had remained in the hall and I wondered how to get past her. Would she tell the doctor that I had run out of the house? If so, how long would it take him to catch up with me?

I quietly shut the door of the gallery and I immediately thought of the cupboard. If I could escape by way of the secret tunnel . . .

But even as I went toward the cupboard, the door of the gallery opened and he was standing there. "Hello, Catherine," he said.

He was smiling the benign smile that had deluded me in the past. I could say nothing for the moment; my voice was lost in my constricted throat.

"I came to call on you, and I saw you come in here when I got to the top of the stairs."

"Good morning," I said, and I felt that my voice sounded calmer than I had thought possible.

He stepped into the gallery and shut the door. When I glanced over the balcony I could see Ruth standing below.

"It's a fine morning," he went on. "I wanted you to come for a little drive with me."

"Thank you. I was just going out for a walk."

"You are doing too much walking. A drive will do you good."

"Thank you, but I do not wish to go."

He came toward me and took my wrist; he held it tenderly yet firmly. "I am going to insist today, because you are looking a little pale."

"No, Dr. Smith," I said. "I do not wish to go for a drive."

"But, my dear Catherine"—his face was close to mine and his gentle manner seemed more horrible than violence—"you are coming with me."

I tried to walk past him, but he held me firmly and said, "My dear, you must allow me to decide what is good for you." He took the robe from me and threw it on the floor.

I was filled with sudden panic. I called, "Ruth! Help me."

When she opened the door of the minstrels' gallery, I thanked God that she was at hand. He was still holding me in a grip so firm that I could not extricate myself.

"I am afraid," he said, "that she is going to give us a little trouble."

"Catherine," said Ruth, "obey the doctor. He knows what's best."

"He knows what is best! Look at this robe. He is the one who has been playing those tricks on me."

"I fear," said the doctor, "that her condition is more advanced than I believed. It is a mistake to delay too long in these matters. It has happened before in my experience."

"What diabolical plan have you in mind now?" I demanded.

"It is the persecution mania," murmured the doctor to Ruth. "Believing that they are alone against the whole world." He turned to me. "Catherine, you must trust me. Have I not always been your friend?"

I was truly frightened now, because I began to see what he planned to do with me, and that Ruth either believed him or pretended to, and that I was alone with them, and friendless. "Dr. Smith," I said, "I know too much. It was you who decided that my child should never be born. You killed Gabriel and you were determined to kill anyone who stood between Luke's inheriting the Revels—"

"You see," he said sadly, "how far advanced it is."

"I found the robe, and I know too that you believe you belong here. I know it all. Do not think you can deceive me anymore."

He had seized me firmly in his arms. I smelled a whiff of what might have been chloroform as something was pressed over my mouth. I felt as though everything was slipping away from me, and his voice seemed very faint, as though it were a long way off: "I hoped to avoid this. It is the only way when they are obstreperous."

Then I slipped away . . . into darkness.

I HAVE HEARD it said that the mind is more powerful than the body. I believe that to be so. I knew he was going to take me to Worstwhistle. My mind commanded my body to reject the chloroform even as it was pressed over my mouth. So it was that, half-conscious in his jolting carriage, I summoned all my willpower to fight the terrible drowsiness.

The swaying of the vehicle was helpful; the clop-clop of the horse's hoofs seemed to say, "Doom is at hand. Fight it. Fight it with all your might. There is still time. But once you enter that building it will not be easy to come out."

"You should not struggle, Catherine," said the doctor gently.

I tried to speak but the effect of the drug was claiming me.

"Close your eyes," he murmured. "There is nothing for you to fear. I shall come and see you every day. I shall be there when your child is born."

Subconsciously I knew that this had been his plan all along, to get me to Worstwhistle before my child was born, to attend to me there and to make sure, if my child was a boy, that he did not live.

Fight as I would, I could only remain in this half-awake state. And I reserved my remaining strength for the moment when the carriage wheels should stop and he would call strong men to help him bring another reluctant victim to that grim prison.

THE CARRIAGE HAD drawn up. We had arrived. I felt sick and dizzy, and still only half-conscious.

"Why, my dear Catherine," he said, and he put his arm about me; and once more I felt his gentle touch to be more hurtful than a blow. "You are unwell. Never mind. This is the end of the journey. Now you shall know peace. No more fancies, no more visions. Here you shall be cared for."

"I . . . am not going . . . in there." I seemed to drawl the words.

He was smiling. "Leave this to me, my dear," he whispered.

There was the sound of running footsteps and I felt a man take my arm. I heard a voice: "She knows where she's going, this one. . . ."

Then the doctor's voice: "They have their lucid moments. Sometimes it's a pity."

I tried to scream, but I could not. My legs were buckling under me. I was being dragged forward. I saw a great iron door swing open. "No," I sobbed. But they were so many, and I was so weak against them.

I heard the clatter of a horse's hoofs. Then the doctor said sharply, "Quickly! Get the patient inside." And there was suddenly a note of fear in his voice.

Then my whole being seemed to come alive again, and I realized that what seemed to make the blood run hot in my veins was hope. A voice I knew well, a voice I loved, was shouting, "What the devil's all this!"

And there he was—the man whom I had failed to dismiss from my thoughts although I had tried—striding toward me; and I knew that he had come to save me from my enemies.

"Simon," I sobbed, and as I fell I felt his arms about me.

I ceased to fight the lassitude then; I accepted the darkness. I was no longer alone.

AND SO I was saved from Worstwhistle on that terrible day. Mary Jane had left the house with all speed while I was struggling in the minstrels' gallery, and had gone to Kelly Grange. She had overheard what the doctor had said about taking me away, and she knew enough to guess where.

Simon had gone straight to Worstwhistle, and although I was not able to see how he fought for my freedom, I knew it had happened. He had faced Deverel Smith and accused him of the murder of Gabriel. He had threatened the superintendent of the asylum with the loss of his post if he dared take me in merely on Dr. Smith's word. I could imagine the power of him as he fought for my freedom and the life of my child.

Of course he won. Simon must always win. He is invincible when he has determined on what he would have. I have grown to learn that, and I would not have it otherwise.

He took me to Kelly Grange, where Hagar was waiting for me, and I stayed there until my child was born. That happened prematurely, which was not to be wondered at, but my Gabriel soon picked up and became a strong little boy. We doted on him, Hagar and I; and I think Simon did too, but he had decided to make a man of the boy and he rarely showed the softer side of his feelings.

But there were other happenings before the birth of Gabriel.

I often think of Deverel Smith, of his belief in himself, and I am sure he saw himself as godlike, powerful beyond other men, of greater cunning. He believed that he was Sir Matthew's son and that no one should stand between him and his inheritance. He killed Gabriel to open the way for Luke, and when Luke had married Damaris he would have come to live at the Revels. In his subtle, sinister way he would have been the real master there, because he would have used blackmail in order to dominate those about him.

That was his delight—to dominate. Ruth told me, much later, that he had discovered an indiscretion of hers. She had had a love affair after the death of her husband that could have created a distressing scandal if it had become known. Smith was aware of it and in exchange for his silence he exacted her support and an outward show of friendship.

I have often wondered what would have happened in that household but for Simon. I should have been out of the way—I do not care to think even now of what my future would have been. But there at the Revels, I imagined the doctor the master, holding his gentle but evil sway over them all. . . . Yet it was not to be so. How he must have hated Simon; but Simon could return hate with hate. *He* would have no mercy and Deverel Smith knew it. When he stood facing Simon at the portals of Worstwhistle he must have realized that at last he faced an adversary stronger than himself.

So he died—as he had lived—dramatically. While Simon was summoning a carriage to take me to Kelly Grange, Deverel Smith returned to the Revels. He went to the top of the east wing, to the only balcony in the house from which a Rockwell had not fallen to his death, and he threw himself over in a last defiant gesture, as though to prove to the world what he had always sought to prove to himself—that he was of the family, and Kirkland Revels meant to him all that it ever could to any Rockwell.

THERE IS LITTLE else to say. Mrs. Smith, whose health improved after her husband's death, went away with Damaris. I heard later that Damaris made a brilliant marriage in London. Luke went up to Oxford and there collected several bad debts and became involved in some trouble with a young woman. That was all part of growing up, said Sir Matthew, who had done it all before him. Ruth changed too. Her manner to me grew warmer and she was contrite because of her readiness to play the doctor's game, even though she was ignorant of his wicked motives.

Sarah remained, as always, my good friend. Gleefully she told me she had completed the picture. I was there, with the baby, but I was in my own room at Kirkland Revels, not in a cell. She had wanted to warn me because she knew I was in imminent danger, but she had not realized that the monk and the doctor were one and the same, and this had baffled her. How happy she was now that the danger was past.

Simon told me that he had begun to suspect the doctor, whose motive might be to prevent my bearing a living child so that Luke should inherit and marry Damaris. But he wished to confirm his suspicions. "For that reason," he explained, "I paid attention to Damaris. I knew she was not as interested in Luke as she pretended to be and I wanted to see the effect on her father if someone else began paying court to her."

"It sounds as good a reason as the other," I told him.

"What other?" he wanted to know.

"That she happens to be one of the most attractive women either of us can ever have seen."

He grinned at that and seemed pleased, and now that I know him well I understand that it was my jealousy that pleased him far more than Damaris' charms.

It was Simon who, after Deverel Smith's death, discovered the way into the secret chamber from the abbey side. Mary Jane and I had come near to finding it on that Christmas morning. Had we removed the stones that, in her exasperation, Mary Jane had kicked, we should have disclosed the passageway to the chamber where she later found the robe.

Years later, while exploring the tunnels, I discovered a hidden recess and came on Friday's grave. I guessed then that Deverel Smith had poisoned him and buried him in this spot. There was nothing left but his bones.

One day shortly after my Gabriel was born, Simon stood looking at him, and I saw the regret in his face. I said, "What is it, Simon?"

Then he looked straight at me and said, "He's a grand chap, but there's one thing wrong with him. He ought to be mine."

That was his proposal of marriage, and as I lay there with the child, I experienced the happiest moment of my life.

All that spring and summer we made our plans. Because my son Gabriel would one day be master of Kirkland Revels, he should be brought up between the Revels and Kelly Grange, and this would mean that to some extent the two estates would be as one.

Uncle Dick came home and it was wonderful to accept the close relationship between us. He gave me away when, the following Christmas, I married Simon. And as we came down the aisle together after the ceremony I thought, And that is the end of the beginning.

Then I wondered what the future would hold for us and if in the years ahead we should weather the storms that must surely beset two such personalities as ours. Life perhaps would not always be calm between us. We were both headstrong, and neither of us meek.

But as we came out into the Christmas sunshine, my spirits were lifted. I knew there was nothing to fear, for there was love between us, and it is love that casts out fear.

Wings of the Falcon

Wings of the Falcon

A CONDENSATION OF THE NOVEL BY

Barbara Michaels

ILLUSTRATED BY ALAN LEE

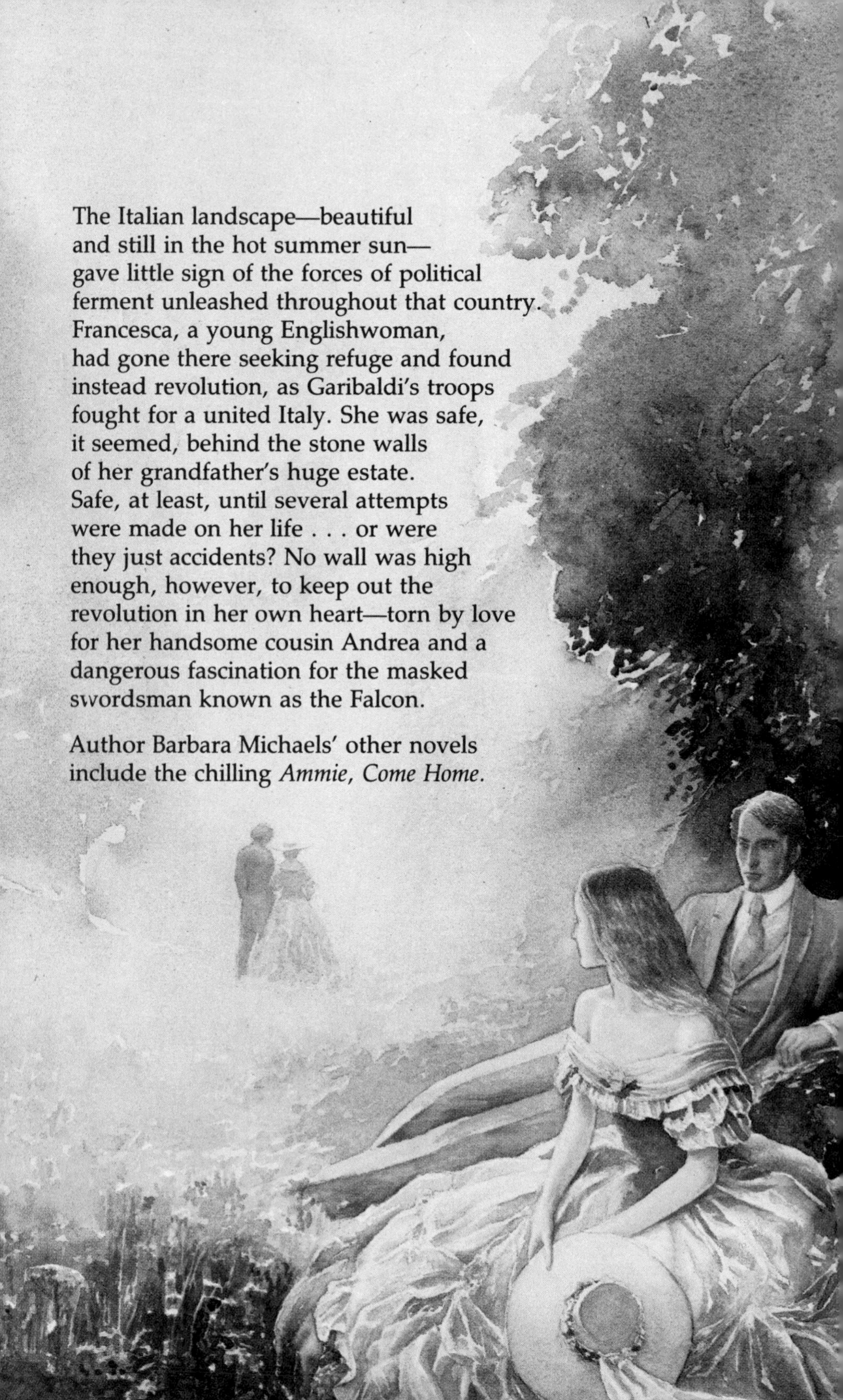

The Italian landscape—beautiful and still in the hot summer sun—gave little sign of the forces of political ferment unleashed throughout that country. Francesca, a young Englishwoman, had gone there seeking refuge and found instead revolution, as Garibaldi's troops fought for a united Italy. She was safe, it seemed, behind the stone walls of her grandfather's huge estate. Safe, at least, until several attempts were made on her life . . . or were they just accidents? No wall was high enough, however, to keep out the revolution in her own heart—torn by love for her handsome cousin Andrea and a dangerous fascination for the masked swordsman known as the Falcon.

Author Barbara Michaels' other novels include the chilling *Ammie, Come Home*.

CHAPTER ONE

Authors who write in the first person cannot expect their readers to be seriously concerned about the survival of the main character. A heroine who can describe her trials and tribulations in carefully chosen phrases obviously lived through those trials without serious damage. Yet I remember being absolutely breathless with suspense when the madwoman entered Miss Jane Eyre's chamber and rent her wedding veil asunder.

Some of the experiences that befell me, at a certain period of my life, were as distressing and almost as improbable as any of my favorite heroine's adventures. Even now, a good many years later, a reminiscent shiver passes through me as I remember Lord Shelton and that dreadful moment when he held me helpless in his grasp, his breath hot on my averted face and his hands tearing at my gown.

I anticipate. It is necessary to explain how I found myself in such a predicament, and to do so I must relate some of my family history.

My father was an artist—not a very good one, I fear. His father was able to leave him a small sum of money, enough to keep him in relative comfort for several years while he traveled on the Continent, ending finally in that artists' mecca, Rome. To a young man of romantic tastes and ardent spirits, the old capital of the Caesars had many attractions beyond its artistic treasures—the companionship of other struggling young artists, the wine and laughter and song in the soft Italian nights.

Father was a remarkably good-looking man, even when he was dying of consumption. The pallor of his complexion was refined by soft dark hair and lustrous black eyes framed by lashes so long and thick that any woman would have envied them. I can imagine how handsome he was at twenty, when he met my mother, and I can understand how he won her heart so quickly. Her family did not find it so easy to understand, for she was the daughter of a noble Italian house.

A romantic accident threw my parents together. The carriage in which my mother was traveling to Rome was delayed by bad weather, and in the darkness was set upon by bandits. Father happened upon the moonlit scene just as the miscreants were dragging the lady from the carriage. As his horse came thundering down upon them, the bandits thought him the leader of a troop of defenders, so that there was time for him to lift my mother's fainting form into the saddle and escape.

It was not until they reached an inn a few miles away that he first saw the face of the girl he had saved. I resemble her only in my coloring; I am fair-haired and blue-eyed—Italians of the northern regions are often fair. My features, however, are more like those of my father, who would never allow that any woman could equal my mother's beauty.

The circumstances of their first meeting were romantic enough to dazzle any young man. My mother was in a dead faint when he carried her into the inn and placed her near the hearth. The firelight turned her tumbled ringlets to red gold, and this gleaming halo framed a countenance of pure perfection. As he knelt beside her, supporting her head upon his arm, her lashes fluttered and lifted. The first thing she saw was his handsome face, the first thing she felt was the strength of his arm around her.

The authorities were notified of the attack upon the carriage, and Prince Tarconti was informed that his daughter was safe, but not before the lovers had had time to converse for hours in a language more eloquent than Father's fluent if ungrammatical Italian. It is no wonder they fell in love at that first meeting. What is wonderful is that their love should have won out over all obstacles, for the practical difficulties were great. For one thing, it was virtually impossible for them to be married in a country where Protestants were not even allowed to hold church services.

My parents' romantic history was my favorite bedtime story in childhood, and if my mother was the saint to whom I addressed my childish prayers, a certain Count Ugo Fosilini was the villain of my youthful nightmares. Distantly related, he was the suitor destined for Francesca Tarconti by her father; she had been on her way to visit his parents in Rome when fate intervened. It was natural that he should be the emissary sent by Prince Tarconti to recover his daughter. As soon as Count Ugo set eyes on my father, he knew he had a rival. Too arrogant to challenge a man whom he considered his social inferior, he hired assassins, of whom there were plenty to be found in Rome. My father was saved only through the devotion of his friends, who assisted in the couple's eventual escape from Italy.

They were married in London. At first the young couple lived obscurely, fearing retaliation, but in the end they learned, through acquaintances in Italy, that Prince Tarconti had disinherited his daughter and forbidden her name to be pronounced in his hearing. To her family she was as good as dead. And alas, in a short time she was. She died at my birth; and when Father wrote to Italy to announce the two events, he received no reply.

The succeeding years—fifteen of them—may be passed over quickly. They were not good years for him, but I did not know that until it was too late. I played with expensive toys and wore pretty dresses without wondering where the money came from, or why Father was so often absent from home. He continued to paint and, I assumed, to sell his paintings. It was not until one winter night, when he collapsed in a fit of uncontrollable coughing as he bent to kiss me good night, that I realized he was ill.

I was too young to understand the ominous portent of the attack. He was quick to reassure me; and the action of a lady of his acquaintance, in sending him to the south of France, undoubtedly did prolong his life. I remained in England, in boarding school. I did not realize that my school fees were payment for my father's services, nor that the term "patroness" was a euphemism for her real role in his life. She was not the first of his patrons—nor the last. I understand that now. I do not judge him. I still believe he did it primarily for me, to give me the comfort and security he could supply in no other way.

After the incident I have mentioned, his health seemed to improve. But I saw very little of him and couldn't understand why he had to keep me from him. He even managed to delude the innocent ladies who ran the boarding school in Yorkshire. The dear old Misses Smith adored my father and always hovered over him when he came on his rare visits, accepting him as the gentleman of means he pretended to be.

Yet I ought to have sensed the increasing desperation under his smiling manner. And he had good reason to be desperate that winter before my eighteenth birthday, but I would never have guessed it when he came to fetch me for the Christmas holidays. He had never looked more handsome, and the dear ladies fluttered about him, offering him wine and seed cake.

I sat demurely, my hands folded in my lap, while my future was discussed. With beaming pride the ladies told him that my education was complete. I was the star student, accomplished in all forms of needlework. My skill on pianoforte and harp was praised, my knowledge of French commended.

I think it was only in recent weeks that my father had begun to face the truth about his condition. Now he was being forced to face another unpalatable truth. My schooldays were almost over. I must leave school for . . . where? That was the problem now, and it must have seemed to him that everything was collapsing at once.

But my father was an accomplished actor, and he carried off the visit in style. We took our places in the handsome traveling coach, well wrapped in furs and robes against the chill of winter, although I was too happy to care about the weather. I had not seen him for almost a year. I did most of the talking, babbling on while Father listened with a smile. As the afternoon drew on, I finally fell asleep.

I woke with a start. The shadows of early evening filled the coach. Father was bending over me. In the dimness his face shone with a pearly pallor, causing me alarm. "What is it?" I cried.

He realized that he had frightened me. He took my hand in his and smiled. "Don't be upset. I was studying your face. You are so like . . . When she died, something in me died too. But you are a young woman now, and what in heaven's name am I to do with you?"

"Why can't I stay with you, Father?"

He let out a groan and buried his face in his hands. Now thoroughly frightened, I tugged at his fingers. "What is it? Are you ill, are you in pain?"

A long shudder passed through his body. Then he lowered his hands and smiled. His voice was calm when he said, "It is only a little pain, my darling. Of course you must stay with me. We will not be parted again, until . . . Francesca, you remember my stories of your mother's family?"

"Of course. What cruel people they must have been."

"I should not have given you that impression," he said slowly. "I was wrong. I, of all people, should have understood their grief at losing her. Your grandfather—"

"He was cruel," I said firmly.

Father shook his head vigorously. "He did what any father would have done. He was not unkind to her, Francesca. She loved him."

"She loved you more," I said.

"Yes."

He relapsed into silence after that. I thought he was remembering the past. I know now that he was struggling with a cruel decision. That night, after our supper in the inn where we broke our journey, he called for paper and ink and sat up late, writing. I remember the shadows the candlelight cast across his face. The hollows in his eye sockets and sunken cheeks became shapes of darkness, like the stark modeling of a tragic mask.

THE HOLIDAYS WERE sheer delight. We had lodgings in a fine old house in Leicester, maintained by a genteel elderly widow. Like most women, she fell genteelly in love with Father, and we made merry together, decking the house with Christmas boughs and holly. Father's gifts to me surpassed even his usual extravagance—a new pelisse, trimmed with ermine and silver buttons, a tiny muff of gray squirrel, a necklace, books, music for the pianoforte . . . too many to be recalled. I went reluctantly back to school, cheered only by Father's promise that he would come for me soon.

I expected to finish out the term, but to my surprise and delight early in April Father appeared without advance warning. He was handsomer than ever, with a fine rosy flush on his cheeks, but he was terribly thin. He admitted cheerfully that he had been ill and was still plagued by a slight cough. But fine weather would soon set him up.

I accepted this facile good cheer, because I wanted to believe it. My trunks, hastily packed, were loaded onto the carriage. The Misses Smith embraced me, weeping. I wept too, and sobbed as I bade farewell to my school friends. Little did I know that they, the daughters of small merchants and prosperous tradesmen, had far more hopeful futures than I.

Father had taken a house in Richmond, outside London. It was a tiny box of a place, but it had a lovely garden. We led a retired life. Though sometimes I would hear him coughing at night, Father seemed quite gay. I had a small talent for drawing and, with his help, made considerable progress. One afternoon I came back to the house after finishing a sketch of the garden with its beds of daffodils. Upon entering the house, I had no warning of guests until I approached the parlor door and heard voices. Such was my haste, and my stupid innocence, that I never thought to knock.

I heard one sentence before they were aware of my presence in the doorway. "But surely you did not think you could elude me forever—"

A cry from my father made the speaker break off and turn on his heel in a quick, violent movement. He did not look like a man who could move so fast. He was tall and heavily built; not fat, but with a flabbiness of face and body that suggested self-indulgence. I was immediately struck by his attire, with its small, peculiar touches of almost feminine elegance—gloves of pearl-gray satin, a stickpin that was a single huge opal, and a cloak lined with sea-green satin. His appearance filled me with instinctive repugnance. Perhaps it was his eyes, of a gray so pale that they seemed to blend with the unhealthy pallor of his cheeks.

My father, who had stood paralyzed during these few seconds, now moved as if to approach me. The other man did not turn, but one arm shot out to bar Father's way. "Why, Allen," he said in a mocking tone. "I understand now the incentive for your—er—actions of late. No effort is too great to keep this pearl snug in its little casket, eh? Will you introduce me? No? Then . . ." He made me a courtly bow and addressed me directly. "I am Lord Shelton, my dear. Allen hasn't mentioned me? How ungrateful! His oldest and dearest friend—the patron who appreciates his talents so generously."

I made him a curtsy and said, "How do you do, sir. I have been at school—you must excuse my ignorance of my father's business affairs. I hope in future to be closer to him."

Lord Shelton chuckled softly. "Father," he said between chuckles. "Why, Allen, I would never have supposed you had a child of . . . What are you, my dear—fifteen or sixteen?"

"Almost eighteen," I said.

"Such a great age! Yes, a lovely age—so tender, so untouched. . . . But, Allen, I must scold you for concealing this charming young lady. I would like to be of service to her, as I am of service to her father. The three of us should get on famously together, don't you think?"

From my father came a horrible, choking gasp. He fell forward, clutching at Shelton's outstretched arm. His lordship was quick to act. Lowering Father's limp body to the floor, he bellowed for the servants. They came running and dragged me forcibly from my father. He was still choking, and from his lips issued a bright crimson stream.

He died three days later, unconscious almost to the end. I was with him; so was Lord Shelton. There was no way of keeping him out of the house; indeed, I had no desire to do so, for during those three dreadful days he managed everything.

The night Father died I knelt by the bed holding his limp hand, praying for some last word from him. His lordship sat at the foot of the bed.

They say that the souls of the dying go out with the tide, or with the turn from night to day. It was dawn when my father's eyes opened.

"Francesca," he said. A faint smile played about his lips. Then, with horrifying abruptness, he sat bolt upright. His eyes turned wildly, focusing finally on the man who sat at the foot of the bed. His lordship rose to his feet. My father pointed, his finger quivering. In a strong voice he cried, "It is a dead man who speaks to you, Shelton. As you act toward my defenseless child, may God requite you in kind. Remember!"

He fell back on the pillow. With a steady hand I closed my father's staring eyes. I rose; like a sleepwalker I passed his lordship. I was able to reach my own room, and my bed, before unconsciousness claimed me.

I PASSED THE next few days in the same trancelike state. I don't think I would have moved at all if the housemaid had not told me what to do. Her name was Bessie, and I attributed her care for me to genuine kindness. "You must eat something, Miss Fran. See the nice soup the cook has made for you." "No, Miss Fran, you must not wear that dress. It is not respectful to your poor papa to wear colors. Here is a new black frock his lordship ordered for you."

His lordship was often mentioned. He had ordered the funeral arrangements and selected the coffin. He paid the bills too, although I did not know it. But he did not come near me until the day after the funeral.

The services were short and simple, and I stood in tearless calm by the grave, his lordship beside me. But when the first clods struck hollow on the coffin, I felt an echoing blow in my heart. That night I finally wept.

Later I lay staring into the darkness. I was alone. What was to become of me? For the first time I thought about money, which I had not had to think about until then.

It brings a wry smile to my lips now to recall that I saw his lordship as my best hope. Had he not promised to be of assistance to me? And was he not, by his own claim, my father's friend? I even interpreted Father's dying speech as an appeal to a trusted comrade. I was glad, therefore, on the following evening when his lordship was announced.

I was sitting in the parlor with my embroidery; the last gentle light of sunset was fading in the west. I rose to greet him, and despite my feelings of gratitude I did not care for the way his narrow gray eyes moved over me. I was wearing the black dress he had ordered for me; I was suddenly conscious of the way it clung to the contours of bosom and waist.

"Your lordship." I made him a curtsy. "I am glad you have come. I wanted to thank you—"

"There is no need for that." He advanced a few steps into the room, then turned to Bessie and said, "You may go now."

When the door had closed after Bessie, I had a panicky feeling of abandonment. I told myself I was behaving foolishly. . . . But his look was so odd! I started to sit down and then, though I could not have said why, I decided to remain standing.

"You have been so kind," I said. "I am glad to be able to thank—"

"Your father was my friend, and after all, what other choice is there? I am doing a kindness." He looked squarely at me, and a light came to his eyes. "A kindness," he repeated as if to himself. "Yes, it would be a crime to let such beauty fade, in a factory or on the streets. Someone will enjoy it. Why not I? I have the best right. . . ."

He began advancing toward me, his face flushed, his tongue darting in and out like that of a serpent, moistening his lips. I backed away. He stopped, and his eyes narrowed cunningly.

"Wouldn't you like rubies and emeralds, my love? And pretty clothes—gowns of satin and silk instead of that ugly black; fine lace around those pretty white shoulders of yours. . . ." With one of those quick, serpentine movements so unexpected from a man of his bulk, he darted forward and caught me in his arms.

No man had ever held me in that way before. His gross, flabby body against mine sickened me. I struggled and tried to scream, but only a faint cry came from my straining throat. He laughed, pressing me closer to him. "Don't waste your breath calling for Bessie. She's too busy counting the gold I have given her. It is my money that has paid her wages all along."

I stopped struggling for a moment as the sense of his words penetrated my mind. He struck, as a snake might; I turned my head to avoid his lips and felt them hot and wet against my neck. He continued to mumble, between kisses, saying horrible things that hurt even more than his grasp.

"Paid her wages—and everything else. . . . How do you think Allen got his money? You owe me, little love, you must pay your father's debts. . . ."

The dreadful monologue went on and on. I felt my senses falter, but when his clawing hand closed on the collar of my dress and ripped it down over my shoulders, the cool air struck my bare flesh like a dash of ice water. I revived; I struggled again, and tried again to scream. The sound was muffled by his lordship's mouth closing over mine. His touch filled me with such loathing that I summoned up enough strength to bite him. He swore and freed my mouth long enough for me to give one last despairing cry.

I do not believe that miracles occur in this modern age, at least not to unworthy persons like myself. What happened was not a miracle; it was surprising only in its timing. I had one final glimpse of his lordship's face looming over me; I closed my eyes, knowing that I was lost, praying for unconsciousness. Then suddenly I felt myself falling, and landed on the carpet in a sitting position. Momentarily I expected to feel Lord Shelton's arms grasping me again. When nothing happened, I dared to open my eyes.

I will never forget my first sight of *him*. Under the circumstances any man would have looked like an avenging hero to me; and he was so handsome! Tall and broad-shouldered, his hair a mass of clustering golden ringlets, his features strong. . . . He towered over me. His face was set in a scowl and his strong brown hands held Lord Shelton by the throat. He shook him as a terrier might shake a rat; then, with a gesture of contempt, he flung his limp body against a chair, which collapsed under the weight.

Then my rescuer turned to me. He dropped to one knee. His eyes were blue; they blazed like pools of deep water with sunlight in their depths. My hands flew to my breast in an effort to gather the rags of my dress around me. The young man averted his eyes. "Are you hurt?" he asked in a deep, reverberant baritone. "If he has harmed you, I will kill him."

"No," I croaked. "No, you mustn't kill him, he didn't . . . You will only get into trouble."

"Bah," said my hero vigorously. "Who cares for that? This *cretino,* this vandal, has dared to touch you. . . . Do you allow—may I have the honor to carry you to your room? Then I will return to deal with this creature."

As he gathered me gently into his arms I let my head fall against his chest. He rose effortlessly to his feet and turned to his lordship, who was crawling toward the door. "He glides, like the serpent he is," remarked my hero with satisfaction. "Old rascal, I would challenge you if you were worthy of the honor, but those of my race do not fight with low persons."

His lordship gathered himself together and staggered to his feet. "Your race?" he sneered. "I am Lord Shelton, and you have no right—"

"I have the best right," said the strange young man. "I am the Conte Andrea del Baldino Tarconti. My grandfather is Prince Tarconti. I am this lady's cousin, her natural protector. And since you claim to have a few drops of gentle blood, I may trouble myself to kill you after all, my lord."

CHAPTER TWO

To CALL MY COUSIN Andrea impetuous is to do him no more than justice. I soon learned that immediate, vigorous action was habitual to him; he was enthusiastic, forthright, direct.

When I awakened the morning after his dramatic appearance, it was because of Andrea's hearty voice outside my door. He was expostulating loudly with someone. Finally the door opened and Bessie peeked in. "Miss?" she quavered. "Are you ready to get up, miss?"

"Yes," I said shortly; I had not forgiven her for her part in my betrayal. Andrea had reduced her to tears and howls of repentance the previous night when he heard what she had done. He had proposed flinging her out into the night, but it was obvious that I could not remain in the house without an attendant, so he had allowed her to stay.

When I came out of my bedchamber, wrapped in a respectable dressing gown, Andrea took one look at me, blushed deeply, and looked elsewhere. Even when we were seated at the breakfast table, he found it hard to look directly at me. As the meal progressed, however, he grew more at ease, and finally he said naïvely, "In England, a young lady may appear in her nightclothes without impropriety, is it so?"

I stopped eating, a forkful of food halfway to my lips, and contemplated the ample folds of my dressing gown in some dismay. Father and I had always breakfasted so. "It is not my night attire, really," I said. "Surely, since you are a member of the family . . . a cousin . . ."

"A half cousin only," said Andrea. "Your mother and my father were only half brother and sister."

"I know little of the family," I said, and looked at Andrea. He was even more handsome than I remembered. His fair hair was a little longer than an Englishman might have worn it, but he was clean-shaven.

"What did you mean, we are half cousins?" I said.

"But it is very simple. Our grandfather married twice. My father and your mother were children of different mothers. My grandmother was an English lady—that is why I speak English so well."

"Ah, I see. Your grandmother taught you."

"Not my grandmother, she died before I was born. Her sister, who came to Italy when Grandmother married into the family, was my teacher—if it is teaching to shout a word very loudly and then strike, very hard, when the young pupil does not understand."

"She sounds horrid," I said indignantly.

"She *is* horrid," said Andrea, smiling broadly. "She is—how do you say it?—a typical English old maid. Our parents died of fever when my brother and I were infants, and so Aunt Rhoda had the task of bringing us up."

"I am so confused! You mention a brother. . . ."

"Did not your mother speak of the family? But no, her resentment—"

"She died when I was born," I said. "And she was not resentful. It was my grandfather who refused to forgive her, or acknowledge her existence."

Andrea flung his head back and laughed heartily, displaying a set of splendid white teeth. "Yes, he would do that. He is a horrible old man. But he is mellowing. I think he will receive you kindly."

"You *think* so? Didn't he send you? I didn't even ask how you happened to appear so miraculously. It was like an answer to a prayer."

My cousin's keen blue eyes softened. "Perhaps it was. Who knows? But, of course, I forget that you did not know of your father's letter. . . . It was a fine letter. He wrote that he was dying, that you would be left alone, and he suggested that you might have need of protection. How he knew this . . . But I distress you. Forgive me."

I had bowed my head, remembering the night in the inn when Father had sat writing, his face set and tired. It must have hurt him to be forced to appeal to the cruel old man, but what an eloquent letter it must have been, to overcome my grandfather's long-held anger. I said as much to Andrea, and was faintly amused to see my cousin look uncomfortable.

"That is not quite how it was." Andrea sighed deeply. "I think I must explain about the family. You should know about them if you are to live with them."

"But what if I am not welcome?"

"Of course you are welcome. Besides, where else can you go? Now, there is Grandfather, of course. He is . . . ah, but it is impossible to describe him. Only stand up to him and you will get along. Then there is Aunt Rhoda. She is our great-aunt, really, but we call her 'Aunt.' I have told you about her. She and Grandfather fight constantly."

"Your brother," I said. "Is he older or younger than you?"

"We are twins. He is the heir, however—he was born first. He is not strong, poor Stefano, but he is very clever. He reads a great deal. It is he you must thank for my coming. I have the strength in the family, but Stefano has the brains."

I had already conceived a girlish admiration for my cousin. Now, suddenly, I liked him too, liked him very much. His modesty and good nature were irresistible. "I will look forward to meeting your brother and thanking him," I said. "But I can never forget that it was you who—"

"No, no, you must not thank me, what else could I do? Only what any gentleman would do." He flung his napkin down and bounded to his feet. "We have talked enough. Time is passing. We must leave this house as soon as possible."

"But—" I began.

"No buts!" His hands braced on the table, he leaned toward me. His face was serious. "Cousin, I do not think you should stay in this house. . . . I have many things to arrange—you will forgive me if I leave you? You shall be packing while I am gone, so that we can be away from here by nightfall. Do not worry," he added kindly, while I gaped. "Stefano has planned it all. He told me what I must do."

"Wait," I cried, for he was already striding briskly toward the door. "Cousin— I am ashamed to confess it, but I am afraid. What if his lordship should return?"

"His lordship? Ah, the villain of last night." Andrea turned. The sunlight pouring into the breakfast room changed his golden curls into a shining halo. "I have taken care of him, there is nothing to fear. I was out early this morning. And I did it myself," he added, with obvious satisfaction. "Stefano did not instruct me."

"Did what?" I gasped. I think I knew the answer before he spoke.

"Killed him," said Andrea calmly. "These meetings always take place at dawn. Hurry with your packing, little cousin."

By the time I had recovered from my shock he was gone, so I did the only thing I could do—I began packing.

As the day wore on and Andrea did not return, I began to be frightened for him. There were laws against dueling. He was a stranger, and his lordship was a peer of the realm, with powerful friends. When the doorbell finally rang, late in the afternoon, I flew to answer it. My disappointment was extreme when I saw not my cousin but a stranger—an elderly woman, stout and gray-haired, who stared at me through gold pince-nez.

"I am Miss Perkins. Alberta Perkins," she said. "May I come in? I was sent by Count Tarconti."

I nodded. "Where is the count?" I asked, leading the way to the parlor.

"His letter will explain." She withdrew an envelope from her large handbag and handed it to me. I ripped it open.

> Dear Cousin,
>
> Here is Miss Perkins, your companion, who will bring you to us in Italy. She is highly recommended. Forgive me that I do not escort you, but friends have told me that your stupid English law [*the word stupid had been scored out, but I could still read it*] makes it necessary for me to leave without delay or risk prison. I will greet you on the happy day of your arrival.
>
> Your devoted cousin,
> Andrea

I looked at Miss Perkins, studying her with more attention. She was—well, ugly. She was short and stout, with square shoulders and a massive bosom. Her clothing was quite severe except for one item—her bonnet, tied under her chin with ribbons of bright crimson matching the feathers attached, somewhat insecurely, on the left side. I liked that bonnet, recognizing in it a hidden romantic streak. Her eyes too had a mild, benevolent expression, and her voice was beautiful—a soft, deep contralto. I smiled tentatively at her and she responded with a beaming grin.

"Please sit down," I said. "And forgive my inattention. Would you care for refreshment? A cup of tea, perhaps?" Within five minutes we were chatting like old friends. One thing we had in common from the start was our amazement at Andrea. Apparently he had simply walked into the employment bureau where she had come to apply for a new position and had hired her on the spot. "I am a judge of character, madam," he said, "and I saw at once you are someone to be trusted. I am entrusting to your care my beloved young cousin."

I could not help laughing as she repeated this characteristic speech.

"I would judge him to be somewhat impetuous," she said.

"He certainly is that," I admitted. "Miss Perkins, I think it is only fair to you to tell you why Andrea found it necessary to depart with such haste."

"He told me why," Miss Perkins said. "And if his version of the story is accurate . . . Well, my dear, you have had a difficult time, but that is over and done with. You must start thinking about the future."

Different as they were in other ways, Andrea and Miss Perkins had one quality in common. When they acted, they acted with dispatch. Miss Perkins moved me out of the house that very evening to respectable lodgings, and we remained there for three days, until we found passage on a steamer going to Civitavecchia, the port north of Rome.

It was with indescribable emotion that I stood on the deck of the ship and watched the roofs of London fade into a black smudge on the horizon. My old life was over. What would the new one bring? I felt a qualm. Then I looked to my right, where Miss Perkins stood, her big hands clutching the rail and her crimson plume blowing bravely in the breeze, and I had a feeling that things were going to work out after all.

I HAD IMMEDIATE cause to be grateful for Miss Perkins' presence. As soon as we entered the Channel, I became horribly seasick. She had not a moment's discomfort. In between tending to me she made frequent expeditions onto the deck, from which she would return with animated accounts of the conversations she had had with other travelers, the sailors, and even with the captain. She was insatiably curious. Finally I was persuaded to drag my miserable body on deck. There, as she had suggested, the air did me good, and it was not long before I was over my discomfort.

I became, however, prey to other worries as the voyage went on. To say that I was going to my mother's family sounded well enough, and yet it was like entrusting myself to utter strangers. As for the country to which I was traveling, I knew nothing of it. Miss Perkins did her best to remedy my ignorance, but the Italian peninsula contained a confusion of kingdoms and states. There was no Italian nation. Yet, according to Miss Perkins, the dream of unity had animated patriots for half a century. It was from this amazing woman, who seemed to know something about every subject under the sun, that I first heard the name of Garibaldi—and of Pius IX, called Pio Nono by his subjects, who was not only the reigning pope, but the temporal monarch of the country in which my grandfather's estates were situated.

Miss Perkins had a habit of rubbing her nose vigorously when she was agitated. When she mentioned Pio Nono, the gesture became almost violent. "They called him *il papa liberale* when he first assumed the papacy," she said, "but if Italy is to become unified, the pope must give up his temporal powers, and he refuses to do so. He rules now in a most tyrannical manner. There is no such thing as freedom of speech or of the press, and as for freedom of religion—"

She would have gone on, her indignation rising, if I had not interrupted.

"I don't understand what you mean by temporal ruler. Is the pope a king, then, with his own army?"

"Exactly. The Papal States lie directly across the center of the peninsula, between Piedmont in the north and the Kingdom of the Two Sicilies in the south. The pope has French and Austrian troops to help him keep Italy divided."

"There are three countries in Italy, then," I said.

"There are more than three, but these are the most important. Piedmont is ruled by Victor Emmanuel, the hope of the liberals. He would rule constitutionally, with legal safeguards. Francis the Second, the king of Naples and Sicily—for that is what is meant by the Two Sicilies—is a tyrant even worse than the pope."

"I had no idea you were such a fiery revolutionary, Miss P.," I said. "You have spoken of this man Garibaldi with great enthusiasm. Are you one of his disciples?"

"We have mutual friends," said Miss Perkins primly.

By the time we landed I knew more about modern Italian politics than I wanted to know. But Miss Perkins also lectured me on Roman history. She fairly bubbled with excitement at the prospect of seeing the land of Julius Caesar and Brutus. I could not share her raptures. As the moment of confrontation approached, I became increasingly nervous. What if Grandfather refused to receive me? What if Andrea was not there to support me?

When we steamed into the harbor of Civitavecchia on a bright spring morning, Miss Perkins could hardly contain herself. "Precisely as it was in imperial times!" she exclaimed.

But the town itself, with its filthy streets and inns, dampened even Miss Perkins' enthusiasm. Unfortunately it was necessary for us to spend the night there. So we sought out an inn, where we might hope to hire a carriage and driver. We were received by the host without much show of courtesy until Miss Perkins mentioned our destination. The Tarconti name wrought a miraculous change; we were shown to the best chamber the place afforded, and with a deep bow the host begged our indulgence while he went to see what could be done for us in the way of transportation. It was not long before he returned with good news. He had found a coach and a driver who knew the road, and we might set out first thing in the morning.

We were up early the next day and joined the other guests awaiting transportation in the inn parlor. After conversing with one of them, Miss Perkins let out a cry of excitement. *"È vero?"* she demanded eagerly. "Is it true?" The gentleman nodded and handed her the newspaper he had been reading, as if this would verify his statement.

"What is it?" I asked curiously.

"Garibaldi has landed in Sicily!" exclaimed Miss Perkins. "He sailed a few days ago secretly from Genoa, with a thousand volunteers."

At this point the host returned to tell us our carriage was ready. It was a shabby equipage, but after inspecting it closely Miss Perkins pronounced it sound. We had just taken our places within the carriage when a pair of riders with wide-brimmed hats and ferocious mustaches came quietly out of the stables and took up positions behind the coach. They looked like the bandits in the wild tales some of the girls at school had read surreptitiously.

Miss Perkins put her head out the window and shouted for the host. They exchanged words; then Miss Perkins withdrew into the coach and looked doubtfully at me. "He says they have been hired to protect us. The roads are infested with robbers."

"Oh, dear," I exclaimed, "they may be robbers themselves." The fierce aspects of the two men frightened me.

"There would be no sense in that," Miss Perkins said. "If the host meant to set thieves on us, he would keep them out of sight until we were in the countryside. I think we may proceed."

Soon we were out of the city, and after a time we left the coast and headed inland toward a range of undulating hills. The scenery grew wilder and more rugged, and as the sun sank lower we had fine views of hillsides covered with dark foliage, shining in the westering rays.

We stopped for the night at a village called Palo, where the inn had been recommended. It was a simple place, but clean, and the food was good.

The sun was barely above the horizon when I awoke the next morning. Miss Perkins was not in the bed. I had come to rely on her so much that at first I was panic-stricken by her absence, but I forced myself to be calm. I dressed quickly and went out in search of her.

I found her in the courtyard, sitting on a block of wood, talking animatedly to one of our guards, who wore a loose shirt with a scarlet sash tied tightly around his slim waist. I stood listening for a moment unnoticed, then moved forward, and the guard caught sight of me. He gave a start and Miss Perkins turned. "Ah, good morning, Francesca. A beautiful morning, is it not? I have been chatting with this young man. Antonio is his name."

Antonio's broad-brimmed hat was already in his hand. He swept it toward the ground in a low bow. When he straightened, I saw that his eyes were big and brown and gentle, and that he was much younger than I had thought. He smiled shyly at me, said something in Italian, and began to back away. As he turned I saw something that made me gasp. But not until he had gone into the inn did I exclaim to Miss Perkins, "Did my eyes deceive me?"

"They did not. He has lost his right hand. That is the punishment Pio Nono's mercenaries deal out to rebels. If Antonio's family had not had influence, he would have been executed." Seeing my stricken face, Miss Perkins added, "You are not in England, Francesca. Life has many perils, and it is better to be prepared for them."

"You are right," I said, remembering Lord Shelton. "I suppose Antonio has trained himself to use his left hand."

"Yes, doesn't he do beautifully? I had quite a good talk with him. He told me that your grandfather's estates are situated in the old kingdom of the Etruscans. I do hope there are tombs on your grandfather's land. He may allow me to do some digging. Only imagine, dear Francesca, the thrill of discovering a princess's tomb, like the one found recently."

"Tell me about it," I said with affectionate resignation.

She did, and at some length, during our journey that day in the coach. My initial prejudice soon gave way to interest, for what girl could resist the allurement of buried treasures, rich jewels, and mystery? But as the day waned, so did my enthusiasm. Even Miss Perkins eventually fell silent, and after we had dined on a basket of food we both dozed off.

I was awakened with a shock as the carriage gave a violent lurch and stopped, so suddenly that I was thrown from my seat. Dizzy with sleep, I heard the rapid pounding of horses' hoofs mingled with shouts and curses and the explosions of firearms. Before I had time to recover my wits, the carriage door was wrenched open.

Miss Perkins, her bonnet askew but her courage high, blocked my view. "How dare you?" she demanded indignantly. "What is the meaning of—"

The speech ended in a gasp as a man unceremoniously pulled her out of the carriage. Now seriously alarmed, I followed. Poor Miss Perkins, blinking and rumpled, was held by the ruffian who had removed her from the carriage. His crimson jacket, dirty white breeches, and tall plumed hat matched the costume worn by half a dozen other men who surrounded the carriage. All carried muskets, one of which was leveled at our driver.

The fact that the men were soldiers did not reassure me. I had never seen more villainous faces. "Let go of her at once," I cried.

The man did so, but as his eyes swept over me I realized that he had not been responding to my order; he had simply found a new interest.

At that moment another of the soldiers called out—in French—and a man on horseback appeared, obviously an officer.

"Thank heaven," said Miss Perkins. At once she spoke to the officer, whose uniform, in contrast to those of his men, was a model of military neatness. "Your assistance, sir, if you please! Or does the Holy Father allow his soldiers to molest helpless Englishwomen?"

Leaning forward, the officer inspected us with insolent deliberation. "You travel, madame, through a troubled country at a troubled time. You must expect some slight inconvenience. We are on the track of a dangerous criminal, and even now some of my men pursue two suspicious characters who were following your carriage. They fled at the sight of us."

"Yet I have heard that the sight of papal soldiers is not always welcome," said Miss Perkins. "Even to the innocent."

The officer's lips tightened. "I advise you not to be so free with your tongue, madame."

I thought this very good advice. I couldn't imagine why Miss Perkins was being so belligerent; yet my anxious ear seemed to detect a note of uncertainty in her speech. Then there was a clatter of approaching hoofbeats and several other soldiers rode up. It was not necessary for them to report failure; they had no prisoners. I heard Miss Perkins give a soft sigh.

The officer turned back to us. "It is necessary, madame, for me to ask you the identity of the two men who rode with you."

"I have no idea," said Miss Perkins calmly. "I was unaware that we had any such escort."

The officer was not stupid. When he asked the question, he watched me, not Miss Perkins, for the surprise that my face betrayed at her answer.

"Indeed," he said softly, his eyes still on me. "Then I fear, madame, that you must come with us."

"Impossible," said Miss Perkins angrily. "We are already late."

"It is no use arguing with me, madame. Get into the carriage."

I looked at Miss Perkins, making no attempt to conceal my alarm. She nodded to me and said clearly, "Perhaps, sir, you will send a messenger to Prince Tarconti, telling him that you are holding his granddaughter a prisoner and that she will, therefore, be delayed."

"This young lady is the granddaughter of Prince Tarconti?" The officer dismounted quickly and came toward us. "Why did you not say so at once?"

"You gave me no opportunity, sir," said Miss Perkins.

"But then— You will accept my apologies, madame? My apologies, and my escort. The roads are dangerous. I would not have any relation of the prince in danger through my negligence."

"Certainly, sir," said Miss Perkins graciously. "Would you care to join us in the carriage?"

The officer accepted the invitation with alacrity. His name, he informed us, was Captain Raoul de Merode. He was not a bad-looking man, and when he removed his helmet, his face was softened by thick brown hair. But I was not misled by his smile. He had been ready enough to be rude—perhaps worse than rude—to two undefended women when he thought them unimportant. I knew Miss Perkins was no more deceived by his present courtesy than I. She had some hidden motive behind her actions, but what it was I could not guess.

One thing she certainly wanted was information. She leaned forward and asked, "Who is this dangerous criminal you are pursuing, Captain? A murderer—a brigand?"

"One might call him a brigand. Or a traitor. He is quite a famous character in these parts. You would not have heard of him, being strangers here. They call him Il Falcone."

If Miss Perkins had ever heard the name, she was too clever to betray the fact. "The Falcon," she translated, unnecessarily. "How very romantic!"

"Childish," de Merode corrected, with a snap of his even white teeth. "These rebels are like that—like spoiled children who don't know what is good for them. But the games they play are sinister, dangerous games, and one day they will be punished as they deserve. They are men of the so-called educated classes, who have read too much and thought too little."

"Is this Falcon person an educated man, then?" Miss Perkins inquired.

"I don't know who he is or what he is. If I did . . ."

I could not contain my curiosity. "Do you mean that this man's identity is unknown? How can that be?"

"He is an elusive creature," de Merode said. "And he commands a certain loyalty. We have caught and—er—questioned several of his men. They died without divulging his name."

I felt a sudden chill. "They—died?" I repeated.

The captain's eyes turned to me. "They were executed, mademoiselle. The price of treason is death—even in your country."

Miss Perkins asked, "Does this man have his own army?"

De Merode's thin lips curled. "They are not soldiers, they are bandits. They hide behind rocks and pick off my men as we ride. They encourage the peasants to resist taxation. They plaster the walls with inflammatory posters. Wherever there is trouble in this province, you may be sure the Falcon is behind it."

"Tell us about him," said Miss Perkins persuasively.

"The man himself? I wish I could. We have no consistent description of him. Sometimes his hair is gray, sometimes black, sometimes he is bearded, sometimes he has a patch over one eye. But he rides so well he must be young. He is always well mounted. A man with access to horses of such quality, and so many of them, must be a man of wealth. And if the proclamations issued in his name are written by him, he is well educated."

"Young, rich, well educated," Miss Perkins repeated. "Forgive me, Captain, but you paint a portrait irresistible to females. Don't tell me that he is also handsome, or we will lose our hearts to your rebel."

"I would advise you not to say such things," said de Merode sharply. "Anyone who is suspected of assisting Il Falcone is subject to arrest. That is why—forgive me—I was suspicious of you. One of the men who was following you looked like a certain Antonio Cadorna, who is known to be one of the Falcon's lieutenants. But there is no more loyal subject of His Holiness than Prince Tarconti."

"Indeed," said Miss Perkins thoughtfully. Thereafter she lapsed into silence, broken by ostentatious yawns. These eventually had their effect. The captain excused himself and resumed his place on horseback.

"Miss Perkins," I exclaimed as we started up again. "What on earth—"

"Shsh." Miss Perkins gestured toward the carriage window. One of the soldiers was riding close by. She said aloud, "Sit next to me, my dear, and try to sleep. We still have some distance to go."

I obeyed. We could then converse in soft tones without being overheard. "Are these ruffians really soldiers?" I whispered.

"Pio Nono has enlisted an army of crusaders, as he calls them, from all the Catholic countries of Europe. Some of them are honest fanatics, but many are only unemployed scoundrels who enjoy violence for its own sake. This young captain is one of the fanatics."

"And the Falcon—I have never heard such a wild tale! Why did you deny knowing Antonio?"

"Because he warned me that he and his friend were wanted by the authorities. They accompanied us in order to protect us from ordinary bandits, but they knew they were no match against so many armed men."

"But why should they bother to protect us?"

"I'm not sure," Miss Perkins said. "But the rebels hope for aid from England—they know they have English sympathy for their cause, since they are fighting for freedom. Your grandfather seems to be an important person. They may think you can influence him."

"He sounds like a man whom it would be hard to influence," I whispered. "A hard man."

"We must not judge him. . . . I liked Antonio. I convinced him that I sympathized with his cause, so he was ready to confide in me—up to a point. He certainly did not tell me he was one of the Falcon's men."

"Then you had heard of this mysterious adventurer?"

"Oh, yes. Il Falcone is not one of the well-known heroes of Italian liberation, yet in his own way he is famous enough. But don't be misled by the romantic trappings," said Miss Perkins dryly. "If what I have heard of that young man is correct, he is a very shrewd person indeed. No revolution can succeed without the peasants' support, and they are wretchedly poor and downtrodden. By playing the role of an Italian Robin Hood, our friend the Falcon hopes to win them over."

"I think it is very exciting," I said.

Miss Perkins was silent for a long time, then said, "Exciting? To me it is noble and terrible and pitiful. They are so young, these boys like Antonio, with their brave mustaches and their shining courage. . . . But I have seen so many noble causes fail, Francesca. The race is not always to the swift, and virtue does not always triumph."

This time when she fell silent I had no wish to pursue the subject.

CHAPTER THREE

I FELL ASLEEP, AND when I awoke, the interior of the coach was dusky with twilight. I was stiff and aching from travel, and I was now close to the meeting I had dreaded for days—with the unknown people who would decide my fate.

"Ah, you are awake," Miss Perkins said as I stretched my cramped limbs and yawned. "I was about to rouse you. We are almost there."

"Oh, dear," I said. "I do hope Andrea is there to welcome us."

"I daresay we will manage somehow even if he is not. What interesting country this is! I noticed several mounds that may be Etruscan tombs."

I sat up and tried to straighten my clothing and smooth my hair. It was impossible to see anything out the window now, for trees lined the narrow road so closely that their branches scraped the sides of the coach.

"Where is our escort?" I asked.

"They left us a few miles back—when Captain de Merode was satisfied that we were really going toward the Castello Tarconti. He promised, however, to call on us soon."

The carriage lurched into, and out of, a deep hole. Then Miss Perkins let out an exclamation. "Look, Francesca."

Through the window on her side of the coach I saw a view that made me catch my breath. The trees and shrubs had vanished; we were traveling along the edge of a deep ravine. How far down the cleft descended I could not tell. The sun's rays, striking through a break in the western hills, cast a strange and brilliant light. Then I realized that Miss Perkins had been looking not at the ravine but at what lay beyond, on the crest of the hill.

Only my nervous apprehension made Castello Tarconti appear ominous as it sprawled across the hilltop. With the rich light of evening gilding its stone and plastered walls, it really was quite an attractive sight; the outline of the chimneys and quaint turrets against the sky had considerable charm. As I was to learn, it was even larger than it appeared—with a jumble of additions from different centuries. For the princes of Tarconti, this was their ancient family seat. It had grown into a great château, surrounded by extensive gardens and provided with every modern comfort.

Neither of us spoke further as the carriage strained up the last steep approach and passed under a sculptured arch into a long avenue lined with towering cypresses. We rolled along a graveled surface much smoother than the road and emerged from the lines of trees into a broad park with fountains and flower beds.

The house, immediately before us, was staggering in its sheer size. At each end were towers topped by turreted spires. A great staircase mounted superbly to a terrace whose balustrades were adorned with flowering plants in pots—roses, orange trees, gardenias and geraniums, all in bloom, perfuming the dying day. The carriage turned to the left and passed through a gateway into a walled courtyard, where we descended and stood looking about us.

The neatly paved stone courtyard was clean and well kept. Shrubs and flowers fringed the perimeter and grew about the edges of a small fountain. The doorway of the house was surmounted by a carved stone crest, presumably that of the Tarcontis, but badly worn by time and weather.

Interesting as these features were, they were overshadowed by the strange collection of objects that littered the courtyard. Broken columns and headless statues stood all about. In a spot of honor near the front steps, sheltered under an awning, was the strangest object of all: a great stone box, carved all over with reliefs and surmounted by the semireclining statue of a man. He was raised on his elbow, and his loose robe had fallen away from one shoulder. In his hand he held a cup, lifted as if in salute.

Miss Perkins let out a cry of delight. "It is an Etruscan sarcophagus!"

"Do you suppose he is the only one who is going to greet us?" I said coolly, trying to hide my real feelings—which, had I displayed them, would have made me scramble back into the shelter of the carriage. I might have done it, had not the door of the house swung open and a person come trotting down the steps.

It was a stout, elderly servant who wore a peasant costume—a white apron brightly embroidered, a laced bodice, and a high, fluttering cap. She came straight to me, dropped a stiff curtsy, and broke into a flood of speech. I understood only enough to believe that my arrival had been expected, and we followed her into the house.

Tired and worried though I was, my first impression of the place was not unpleasant. The servant escorted us through the entrance hall, with its broad flight of curving stairs, and into a handsome drawing room. It was a room of considerable grandeur, with large windows and light-painted paneling. There were paintings on the ceilings and on the paneled walls, and fine carpets covered the floor. A pianoforte of rosewood stood in a bay formed by the curved windows. Before the fireplace, like a throne, stood a big red velvet chair. The servant indicated the person who was sitting in this chair and immediately withdrew, closing the door behind her.

For some time no one spoke. I realized that the person who had received us was deliberately silent in order to increase our discomfort. We stood there weary and travel-stained, like beggars come to ask a favor. It was a lady who sat there, and she was as typically English as the servant had been typically Italian. We were in the presence of Andrea's Aunt Rhoda.

She was extremely thin, and she seemed tall. Her face was long and narrow, her hair gray. Her eyes were gray too, almost colorless. She wore a gown of heavy black wool, with hoops puffing out her skirts. Her hands were so long and thin and white they looked liked naked bone.

"Good evening, Aunt Rhoda," I said.

The lady, who had been staring curiously at poor Miss Perkins, turned her icy gaze on me. "I am not your aunt," she said. "You may address me as Miss Rhoda."

I bowed my head without replying. I was beginning to be angry. She might at least ask us to take seats!

Like a subaltern making his report, Miss Perkins introduced herself and explained how she had come to be employed by Andrea.

"Only last week did we learn of your coming," said Miss Rhoda. "I have had rooms prepared for you. I detain you now because it is necessary that you understand the basis on which you are to be received here."

"Then," I said, "perhaps you will allow Miss Perkins to sit down. We have had a tiring journey."

Miss Rhoda looked at me, if not with warmth, with more interest than she had hitherto displayed. "She may sit. You, miss, will remain standing before your elders. And I suggest that you do not adopt that tone with me. Your status is not so secure that you can afford to be insolent."

"What is my status?" I inquired. Miss Perkins did not sit down. She shifted a little closer to me, and I was conscious of her approval and support. I knew I could not allow Miss Rhoda to bully me or she would continue to make my life miserable. After all, she had less standing in the family than I. She was not even related by blood.

"That of a dependent," said Miss Rhoda bluntly. "You have a certain moral claim, no doubt, but it was not that consideration that prompted the prince to receive you here. I pointed out to him that his family honor demanded that you be rescued from the disgrace and infamy into which you would descend without his charity. Your father—"

"My late father," I interrupted.

I could say no more. I knew if Miss Rhoda spoke disparagingly of my

father I would cry. I did not want to cry in front of her. As I was to learn, she was hard, but she had a strong sense of propriety.

She nodded grudgingly. "We will say no more of that. I only mean to warn you that your grandfather does not wish to see you. Do not expect from him affection or kindness. He means to support you and shelter you, but that is all." Miss Rhoda rose. She towered over us. "Follow me."

She swept toward the door, but the surprises of the day were not yet over. As we crossed the entrance hall a man came into sight around the curve of the stairs. Preoccupied with his private thoughts, he did not catch sight of us until almost at the bottom of the flight. He recoiled, so suddenly he had to catch with both hands at the railing to keep from falling, and there he remained, staring.

He was elderly, but not fragile as I had expected him to be. His figure was still broad-shouldered and vigorous, his gray hair thick. His features were marked by harsh lines of pride and temper, and his mouth was thin-lipped. Yet there was something in the expression of his eyes—some vague wildness—that did not fit the general impression of severity.

After Miss Rhoda's warning I would not have been surprised to see him turn his back in silent disdain, or to hear an angry tirade. Instead, incredulously, I beheld the stern face soften. It took on a look of radiant joy.

"Larthia!" he whispered. His voice was that of a man welcoming back to life a loved one whom he has given up for dead.

THE ROOM THAT had been prepared for me was not good enough, my grandfather declared. Only one of the grand state apartments would suffice. Miss Rhoda's furious objections were brushed aside, but my own insistence that I would prefer the smaller, cozier room persuaded Grandfather to leave matters as they had been arranged. Another advantage was that Miss Perkins' room was next to mine. They were not quite servants' rooms, not quite. But it was clear that Miss Rhoda was not anxious to see me comfortably settled. It was grotesquely comical to see her and Grandfather shouting at one another, for she did not use a word of Italian and he answered only in that language. Yet they seemed to understand each other well enough. Finally she withdrew. My grandfather followed her out, after summoning an army of servants to assist us. He was oddly formal, almost shy, with me. There were no warm embraces, yet the affectionate smiles and glances he gave me were a welcome I had not hoped to receive.

At last Miss Perkins and I were alone. She dropped into a chair, her feet extended, and I followed her example. "Imagine, Miss Rhoda daring to tell me that Grandfather didn't want to have me here," I said. "She must have known I would see him sooner or later."

"Precisely why I suspect she was not lying," said Miss Perkins.

"But nothing could have been fonder than his treatment," I protested.

"Yes. Therefore we must conclude that between the time he gave her her orders and the moment when he saw you something happened to change his attitude. I observed that he addressed you by the name Larthia."

"Name? I thought it was an Italian word for welcome."

"No, I know the language fairly well. It was not your mother's name?"

"Her name was also Francesca."

"Most peculiar. It's a name I've heard before. But where?"

"I don't know it. Nor do I really care. I am limp with relief, Miss Perkins. I confess I was very much afraid of how we would be received."

"I know you were." Miss Perkins smiled at me. "Now, I suggest we make use of those basins of hot water the servants have provided. The prince said he would see us at dinner, and we mustn't be late."

I agreed, and Miss Perkins retired to her own room. I was no longer tired. The joy of finding that I was welcomed had restored all my energy.

The room was on the third floor, so the view was splendid. The castle grounds descended in a series of terraced gardens to the valley below. On the left, half hidden behind trees, was a small, ornate building. Its roof was like that of a miniature castle, with battlements and a tiny tower. As I peered through the gathering darkness, a light sprang up in one of its windows. So the little house was inhabited. I wondered by whom. It was the sort of place that might have belonged to a knight in a romance.

A knock on the door tore me from my musings, and a maid arrived to help me unpack and dress. Teresa was a pretty child, with coal-black hair and a rounded figure. She would not allow me to do anything for myself, even brush my hair. When I started to pin it up, she objected, and indicated by gestures that I should allow it to flow loose down my back. I shook my head. I had not worn my hair so casually since I was a child.

Miss Perkins, who had joined us, said, "Do as she says, Francesca. She would not make such a suggestion on purely aesthetic grounds. It could have been requested by someone who has a right to do so."

"Do you think Grandfather . . ."

"We will soon find out," said Miss Perkins, for Teresa was indicating that we should follow her.

The room into which Teresa ushered us was a pleasant chamber on the ground floor. It had French doors that stood wide open, admitting perfumed breezes from the gardens. Darkness was almost complete, but the room was brilliantly lighted with dozens of wax candles. Two men sat on either side of a low table, where a chessboard was set out.

My grandfather rose quickly to his feet as we entered. His clothing was that of an earlier, more colorful era—knee breeches of brown velvet and a matching coat trimmed with gold braid. He frowned slightly at the sight of my somber black dress with its simple white lace collar; but his frown turned to a smile as he touched my hair, and I knew it had been by his orders that I was wearing it loose. His hand resting gently on my shoulder, he turned me to face the other man, who had not risen from his chair.

In the first moment I was misled by his curling fair hair, but my start of joyful recognition was premature. This must be Stefano, Andrea's brother. His features were like Andrea's, but his face was thinner, and the expression of his eyes lacked Andrea's cheerful candor. His fashionable white-and-black evening garb contrasted with Grandfather's more flamboyant suit. He was balancing a slim black stick between his hands, and as I returned his critical stare with interest he lowered this to the floor and started painfully to rise. With embarrassment, I realized he was lame. Without the aid of the stick he would not have been able to stand.

Stefano greeted Miss Perkins courteously in English. Then he turned a satirical eye upon me. "My dear Miss Perkins, are you sure you and Andrea found the right young lady? This infant doesn't look old enough to be out of the schoolroom. What on earth am I to call her? Miss—"

"Francesca will do nicely," I interrupted. I had felt sorry for his infirmity, but his sarcastic manner of speaking about me was irritating.

His thin smile broadened. "I see you have a mind of your own, Francesca. But pray be seated, and you too, Miss Perkins. There are several matters to be explained. From now on regard me merely as a translator. The sentiments I express will be those of His Excellency. He understands English—better, I sometimes think, than any of us realize. . . ."

He turned his sardonic smile on the old gentleman, who glowered at him. "In any event," Stefano went on, "he refuses to speak the language. It is his way of annoying Miss Rhoda. So I am here. First, I must tell you that initially he was opposed to your coming. When your father's letter arrived he was unbearable for several days. It was Andrea who persuaded him to behave sensibly. Andrea is the favorite here."

"I had hoped Andrea would be here," I said.

"Oh, he has gone off on some jaunt or other," Stefano replied. "He is quite a gay blade, my handsome, athletic brother. . . . But he was here long enough to tell us of the unfortunate situation in which he discovered you."

The tone and the implication were cruel. I felt tears of shame and vexation rise to my eyes. Grandfather burst into a torrent of agitated Italian and even shook a fist under his grandson's nose. Stefano laughed.

"The prince says I must apologize. But perhaps we should abandon that subject. Andrea, in short, insisted that you come here, and the prince agreed so long as you kept out of his way. Is it clear now to whom you owe your reception?"

I nodded. Again Andrea had been my good angel. It was like his modesty to have given so much of the credit to his brother.

Stefano continued to watch me with the same fixed smile. His mouth was a contradiction: the lower lip was full, a sign of passion and sensuality, while the upper lip was narrowly cut. If the laws of physiognomy were true, his was a nature in which the emotions warred with the intellect; and his sour, cynical look showed that resentment had overcome both.

"Very well," he said after a moment or two. "The next question is this: Why did our esteemed ancestor change his attitude toward you? I am myself in the dark as to this, but I am to inform you that you are his dear granddaughter and the beloved daughter of the house. However, I fear Miss Rhoda is not well disposed toward you, Francesca. She dislikes almost everyone, and—"

Here he was again interrupted by Grandfather, who had been listening with increasing signs of impatience. I had suspected that we were getting quite a few of Stefano's personal opinions. "I am relieved of my duties," Stefano said with mock distress. "We are to go in to the others now. . . . What?" He glanced toward the prince. "Oh, yes, I am to assure you of his affection. You are to come to him with any difficulties, and you are to tell him you understand what I have told you."

I turned to the old gentleman, who was leaning forward in his chair watching me with affectionate anxiety. Words seemed too flat, so I smiled and put my hand on his. He clasped it tightly, then raised it to his lips.

"A touching moment," said the dry voice I was learning to dislike.

A footman appeared and opened the door. Imagine my surprise when I saw that Stefano was offering Miss Perkins his arm in a most gentlemanlike fashion. He walked with a perceptible limp, but more nimbly than I had expected, though he leaned heavily on his cane.

As we walked side by side along the hall, Grandfather smiled down at me and patted my hand. With his affection to support me I was not afraid of meeting the other residents of the castle, but if Miss Rhoda was an example of what I had to expect I was not looking forward to it.

Then the footman opened a pair of doors at the far end of the corridor and stood back. There were several people in the great drawing room. Miss Rhoda I knew. The other two were strangers. My eyes fixed themselves on one of them. She was the most beautiful girl I had ever seen.

CHAPTER FOUR

GIRLS KNOW WHEN THEY are pretty. I knew I was not ugly, and I confess that I had a fairly good opinion of myself when I walked into the drawing room that night. But this girl! A mass of coal-black hair, shining in the candlelight; great black eyes, soft as velvet, framed by feathery lashes and brows that might have been shaped by the brush of a master; a mouth . . .

Well, in my jealousy I thought her mouth a little too small, a little petulant, but it was a perfectly shaped Cupid's bow.

As we entered she rose. She bent in a curtsy that displayed the grace of her movements and the abundance of her flowing locks.

The older ladies had to be presented first. Miss Rhoda wore a magnificent gown of plum-colored velvet, but a Gorgon would have looked less grim. The other older lady wore mourning that was extreme—not a touch of white or of color lightened the somber black of her gown. From her widow's cap hung a heavy black veil that framed her pure-white hair. Her face was gentle and almost as pale as her pearly hair, without a trace of color in lips or cheeks, but her eyes though sunken were as bright and black as jet beads. She was a striking study in moonlight and shadow, and I could see that once she must have been as lovely as the dark girl—her daughter. When I realized what name Grandfather had said, I started. The lady of pearl and jet smiled faintly. "It is a pleasure to meet you, signorina," she murmured.

"Contessa." I made a rather clumsy curtsy and turned to meet her daughter. I could not say the name. I knew it well from my father's stories of the past. Count Fosilini, the pursuer of my mother, the cruel rival of my father. . . . Could these two be his widow and daughter? The two families had been friendly, distantly connected, if I remembered correctly. This was a shock I had not expected in all my worst forebodings.

Then I told myself firmly that I was being foolish. The old rivalry was far in the past. Neither of the Fosilini ladies showed any signs of recalling it. The younger countess smiled in a very friendly manner and indicated a chair near her own, which I took. She leaned toward me and said softly in French, "I hope you will be happy here, mademoiselle. It will be a pleasure for me to have a young lady of my own age to talk to."

"You are very kind," I said, returning her smile. "If we are to be friends, as I hope, you must call me Francesca."

"Ah, a good Italian name! Mine is Galiana."

"How nicely you embroider," I said admiringly, leaning forward to examine the design of flowers on which Galiana was working.

"Thank you, but I will never embroider as well as my mother. That is the second altar cloth she is making for the chapel."

Then I realized that the contessa had been watching us. She smiled sweetly and turned her embroidery frame so that I could see it. "It is lovely," I said respectfully. I was groping for some means of continuing the conversation when a servant announced that the meal was served.

Just at that moment I was conscious of a strange sensation, like an insect sting squarely between my shoulder blades. I had risen; now I turned, and met the intent stare of a woman who had appeared as if by magic behind the chairs on which Galiana and I had been sitting.

She was short and squat, with a broad peasant face and coarse features. Her thick eyebrows grew together in a single bar. She was clad all in rusty black, and her expression, as she stared at me . . .

I decided I must have been mistaken about her inimical look. As soon as I turned, her black eyes lowered submissively. She moved with stealth to the contessa's embroidery frame and workbag, which she picked up.

Grandfather had offered his arm to the contessa, while Stefano escorted his aunt. That left Galiana and me and Miss Perkins to go in together. I whispered to Galiana, "Who is that woman over there?"

"Oh, Bianca," said Galiana indifferently. "She is the contessa's maid. She is mute and very stupid. But she adores my mother—she would do anything for her."

"One of the contessa's charities?" said Miss Perkins.

"My mother is a saint," Galiana said seriously. "She would have entered a convent after Father's death, if it had not been for me. As it is—"

But here she was forced to stop. We had entered the dining salon and were shown to our places. I sat next to Grandfather. Conversation was general and rather stilted, but there was one lively exchange, when Miss Perkins described our encounter with Captain de Merode. She censored the account considerably, but even in its abridged version the story produced shocked exclamations. Grandfather was indignant until I explained that the captain had been quite courteous after he learned who I was.

"Ah," Grandfather said, somewhat mollified. "Then it is excusable. I will speak to the captain, all the same. He comes here often."

The rest of the meal passed in comparative silence, and finally we returned to the drawing room. Before long the fatigues of the day caught up with me. A yawn that I was unable to suppress drew Grandfather's attention, and he immediately dismissed us. Each person stood before the prince to bid him good night. The ladies curtsied and Stefano bowed formally. Grandfather acknowledged these gestures with as much condescension as a reigning monarch, but after I had curtsied he took me by the shoulders and kissed me gently on the brow.

The next days were so busy that I needed all my strength to keep up with Grandfather's plans for me. He had the energy of a young man and the arrogance of an emperor. He was also a busy man. The life of a leisured dilettante was not to his taste, and much of his wealth came from business enterprises that he himself controlled. But he spent considerable time on my concerns. First and foremost was the refurbishing of the apartment he had selected for me. It had been my mother's, and because it had not been touched since the day of her elopement, the rooms—bedroom, sitting room, and several smaller chambers—were to be completely redecorated.

I also had to have an entire new wardrobe. Among the battalions of servants was a resident seamstress, who was immediately set to work. It was during this long and, I must confess, enjoyable procedure that I became better acquainted with Galiana. I couldn't help liking her. Her dark, somber beauty did not match her personality, which was cheerful and gay.

"From the first I knew we should be friends," she told me. "You cannot know how good it is to have another girl here when I come."

"Then you and your mother don't live here?" I asked. We were rummaging among the fabrics in a storeroom.

"Live here?" she replied. "No, we have a house over the mountain. But we stay here much of the time, since our roof leaks."

I smiled. "But why don't you have the roof mended?"

Galiana opened her big black eyes even wider. "But there is no money. My father was not a sensible man. He spent it all—all. I am glad your mother did not marry him, for then I would not be here, eh? Perhaps I would have been you! Ah, but that is funny, is it not? I would be you, and you—you would not exist."

The oddest chill ran through me when she said that. For a moment I almost fancied that the merry black eyes had lost their sparkle and were regarding me with cold dislike. But the next moment she was laughing as she draped herself in a piece of gold brocade, pretending to be Cleopatra.

One bright afternoon a week or so after we arrived I went out into the courtyard looking for amusement, and there I found Miss Perkins seated on a fallen column and staring solemnly at the great sarcophagus with its statue of a reclining Etruscan.

"Did you know that His Excellency your grandfather excavated that object himself? There is an entire Etruscan cemetery not far from here. I do hope I shall have time to see it before I leave."

"Leave?" I stared at her. "But, Miss Perkins—"

"Well, my dear, I was hired to bring you here and I have done it." She turned her cheerful smile on me.

I was conscious, all at once, of the deep lines in her face. No longer young, far from prepossessing in appearance, eccentric in her habits—I could see that she might not easily find another position. Impulsively I threw my arms around her. "Miss P., please stay. There is a great deal more for you to do. I need you. Please don't leave me alone."

"But, Francesca, you are not alone. You have a whole new family, and you are the pet."

"But I would like you to stay," I mumbled. "Unless you have duties in England."

"No, I am quite independent."

"Oh, splendid. I will ask Grandfather now." And leaving her staring after me, I ran up the steps and into the house. I did have the courtesy to knock before I entered the library, and as soon as he saw me Grandfather gave me a beaming smile.

Stefano, who was seated beside the desk, did not look so pleased. "How charming," he exclaimed as I stood with Grandfather's arm around me. "Curls flying, frills and ribbons fluttering, the fresh young face flushed—we must have your portrait taken in just that pose, cousin."

Grandfather's right hand moved in one of those eloquent Italian gestures and Stefano subsided. It was a curious relationship. Grandfather regarded Stefano with a mixture of respect for his cool intelligence and contempt for his physical weakness. Stefano served as a useful adviser to Grandfather in business matters. The two of them spent long hours in the library. The discussions were not always amicable, but Grandfather was the only one who shouted. Stefano never lost his temper, he only incited other people to lose theirs.

I was determined not to let him incite me, so I ignored him and plunged into my speech. I knew some Italian by then, but in my excitement I forgot what little I knew. Grandfather always seemed to understand me anyway. "It is about Miss Perkins," I exclaimed. "I would like her to stay here. Couldn't she be my governess or companion, or something like that?"

For once Grandfather didn't understand. He turned a bewildered look on Stefano, who was watching me with his familiar narrow smile. He translated what I had said and added in English, "What a high-handed young person you are, Francesca."

Grandfather waved him to silence. "You may have anything you wish, child," he said. "If you want her to stay, it is settled."

"Grazie!" I stood on tiptoe and kissed his cheek.

He patted me on the head. Courteous as he was, I could see he was anxious to get back to his work. Before I could take my leave, Stefano spoke again. "One more question, cousin. Why are you so anxious to have Miss Perkins remain? She can't be of any use to you."

"It is just barely conceivable that I might be of use to her," I replied sharply. "She is not young. I don't suppose she is rich—"

"Ah, it is sheer benevolence on your part, then." Stefano nodded. "What a beautiful thing to see."

That was the day when I realized how thoroughly I disliked him.

It was also the day when we received a formal call from Captain de Merode. We ladies were sitting in the main drawing room. This was a penance I paid daily, unless I could think of some excuse for not joining in the teatime ritual insisted upon by Miss Rhoda. I must say that she had trained the servants well, and I found the delicious little sandwiches and cakes some compensation for the dull conversation. Usually the gentlemen did not join us for tea, but on this particular afternoon Grandfather and Stefano were both present when the captain was announced.

Grandfather rose, and I could see that he was honestly pleased to see the young man. De Merode was in dress uniform and looked quite handsome.

His spurs, sword, and decorations shone brilliantly, his boots had been polished to a mirror finish, and his helmet, which he held under one arm, had a lovely white egret plume. He bowed over the hand of each lady, leaving mine till last. There was design in that, I thought, when his warm lips lingered on my fingers instead of brushing the air above them.

Grandfather—who could speak adequate French when he had to—immediately took de Merode to task for his rudeness, but his smiling manner showed that he was prepared to forgive.

"My dear prince—have pity!" De Merode covered his eyes with his hand in mock repentance. "Credit me only with too much zeal in my profession. We have been on duty day and night this past week."

"Ah." Grandfather leaned forward. "Then that wretched mountebank has in fact appeared again?"

"You mustn't refer to our hero so rudely, Prince." De Merode smiled meaningfully at me. "I believe the ladies find him very romantic."

"Oh, certainly we do," Galiana exclaimed.

"Galiana." The poor girl jumped at the sound of her mother's soft voice. "You should pray for his soul and deplore his actions."

"Yes, Mama," Galiana muttered, lowering her eyes.

"What has he done now?" I asked.

"Rescued his printing press," said the captain. "An informer enabled us to locate the abandoned hut in which the machine had been concealed. Unfortunately we arrived too late. It was gone."

"But most of the peasants can't read," Grandfather protested. "How stupid these revolutionaries are, to waste print on such animals."

Stefano coughed gently. "The gentry can read. It is they, one supposes, whom your bird of prey wishes to convert."

"Precisely," de Merode agreed grudgingly. He introduced another sensitive topic. "I had hoped to greet Count Andrea," he said, accepting a sandwich from an offered tray. "Where is he?"

"You know Andrea," Stefano said casually. "Always the gadabout. Actually, he has been in Rome on family business."

"Really? That's strange. A friend mentioned to me that he had seen the count a few weeks ago in Genoa."

The name struck the assemblage like a cannonball. The blood rushed into Grandfather's cheeks, Stefano's eyes narrowed, Miss Rhoda made a sudden movement, and Galiana let out a little squeal.

Thanks to Miss Perkins' interminable lectures, I knew why they had reacted as they did. From that northern port, in the darkness of night only two weeks before, the Thousand had set forth with Garibaldi for the liberation of Sicily. That the volunteers had had some military success we all knew, for Grandfather subscribed to the official Roman newspaper. Even the papal press was forced to admit that Garibaldi's ragged forces were making amazing headway against the trained troops of King Francis of the Two Sicilies.

"But surely," I said, "it is possible to visit Genoa for innocent reasons. Your zeal carries you too far, Captain."

The captain, of course, made quick disclaimers, and the conversation turned to harmless topics. When de Merode took his departure he bowed gracefully over my hand, but this time I did not let it linger in his. This tight-lipped fanatic, as Miss Perkins had called him, had no interest in me as a woman. He cared only for the cause in whose name he was willing to commit acts of horrible cruelty. But why had he come to visit us? Unless . . .

Knowing Andrea's ardent temperament, I could imagine him taking up the cause of liberation, even though it was anathema to Grandfather. Had not Miss Perkins said that some young aristocrats followed Garibaldi? But surely Andrea wouldn't be so foolish! Life was pleasant here in the castle; would he risk losing all that for a hopeless cause? Nor was that all he stood to lose. I had not forgotten young Antonio.

I FOUND THE captain's visit even more disturbing in retrospect. Thoughts of Andrea wounded, lying in pain on the dusty plains of Sicily, haunted me. The weather did not help my mood. Wind and rain brought unseasonable cold, and darkness set in early. My little room, once so cozy, seemed cramped and shabby. When Teresa had finished dressing me for supper, it occurred to me that I would see how the repairs in my new rooms were progressing. I was anxious to move into them.

Snatching up a candle, I set out along the corridor—all gloomy in the half-light, melancholy with the sound of the wind moaning at the windows. The rooms themselves, unlighted and desolate and a long way from finished, only increased my gloom. A gust of air from an uncurtained window lifted a corner of a dust sheet, and I started nervously. Imagine, then, my horror when I heard the sound of footsteps approaching. There was no reason for anyone to come here at this time of night. I had worked myself into a panic when I saw a familiar form in the doorway.

"Grandfather." I gave a nervous little laugh. "You frightened me."

He was pale; the candle he held trembled violently. He said nothing, only stared at me with a wild, haggard look. Then I realized why he looked so. The doorway of the sitting room was visible from his own room. Seeing a flickering shadow of light in a room uninhabited since his adored daughter left, he had thought . . .

"I came to see how the work is going," I explained, taking his arm. "Come, let us go—it is dark here, and cold." He yielded to the pressure of my hand as a child might.

Once out of the room, he recovered some of his spirits. Suddenly he said, "Your gown. It is not right."

Puzzled, I looked down at my frock. I had allowed myself to be persuaded to relax the mourning rules just a little and was wearing a dress of gleaming white satin with an overskirt of black lace.

Grandfather touched my jet mourning brooch. "Jewels," he said slowly. "A princess should wear jewels. Come. I will give you the ones that are yours. I have wanted so long to see you wear them. For me, *carissima?*"

It was impossible to refuse him. We strolled arm in arm to the library, and there he seated me in a chair while he went to the Raphael Madonna that hung between the windows. Behind it was a wall safe, from which Grandfather withdrew a box almost a foot square, and began to open it.

I caught a great solemn flash of gold as Grandfather put the first ornament around my neck. I had no opportunity to examine it before he came toward me with the next—a large golden brooch. Then came a bracelet several inches wide, carved all over with tiny figures of crouching animals; other armlets of sheet gold; gold filigree earrings so heavy they dragged at my earlobes.

"Please, Grandfather. . . ."

"One more." And on my brow he placed a diadem of twisted gold wires.

I knew the jewels were not family treasures but the ornaments of an ancient Etruscan lady, excavated no doubt from one of the tombs on his property. The chill I felt from them was not solely physical; it was eerie to reflect that the last warm flesh they had touched was now dust.

Grandfather's strange mood had lightened as he took out the jewels; now, standing back to admire the effect, he smiled and said something in which I recognized the word "mirror."

There was a tall, gilt-framed mirror on the wall, the silvering of the glass somewhat worn. Perhaps it was this quality, or the dim light of the candles, but the sight of myself in the muddy surface made me start back.

The necklace was my favorite. The chain was composed of half a dozen tiny individual chains woven into an intricate web. From it hung loops of even finer chain, and a series of flower pendants, each covered with the minute balls of gold, tinier than grains of sand, that were a distinctive sign of Etruscan goldwork. It was quite lovely. I touched it gently and said aloud, "This must have been her favorite. Oh, Grandfather, may I wear this tonight, just this one? I promise I will take the greatest care of it."

Grandfather understood my request, but I did not find it so easy to understand his answer. He wanted me to wear the entire set of jewels to dinner! I expostulated, but Grandfather did not brook argument. So we started down the hall, my hand on his arm.

Our entrance into the drawing room was sensational. Miss Perkins exclaimed in amazement and Miss Rhoda let out a snort. Grandfather took my hand and stepped back, displaying me. I curtsied carefully so as not to disturb the weight that dangled from me. While Galiana fluttered over, I looked at the others. The contessa might have been in another room; she had not lifted her eyes from her embroidery. As for Stefano . . .

I had not expected we would see him that evening, but there he was, with that black stick balanced in his fingers, looking me over with a cool stare. Well schooled as his face was, I thought I detected an even more fiery emotion than usual in his blazing blue eyes, and I made him a mocking little bow. As the heir he probably would not like to think that Grandfather would give me objects of such value.

A servant came to announce supper; I swept in on Grandfather's arm, feeling like a queen. It wasn't easy to eat, since a jangle of gold accompanied every movement I made. And throughout the meal, whenever I turned to Miss Perkins, I found her watching me with a puzzled frown.

THERE WAS RAIN in the night, but morning dawned clear and bright. By noon the sun had dried all but the deepest puddles, and I decided to go out. Bored, I wandered into the gardens in search of amusement. They were so extensive that I had not yet explored them completely. I was in no mood to do so that morning—fountains and flowers are not exciting enough for restless youth—but in lieu of anything better to do I went on.

Passing along a tunnel of vines, I suddenly found myself in an open area bathed in sunlight. All around were flowers growing in delightful profusion, their spicy perfume filling the air. Before me were the walls and turrets of a little house, which I recognized as the one whose fantastic roof I had seen from my bedroom window that first night. It was quite charming. Leaded windows broke the austere lines of the stone façade. An octagonal tower at the left front corner had a quaint little carved balcony. My curiosity aroused, I ascended the steps to the front door. But before I reached it, the door opened and a man came out.

The fairy-tale look of the place had me half convinced that it was unoccupied. I fell back with a cry of surprise. Stefano—for it was he—also started violently. "What are you doing here?" he demanded.

"I was unaware that this was forbidden territory," I replied, recovering myself. "Even Bluebeard warned his wife not to intrude on the chamber of horrors. If you wish to be undisturbed, you might have said so."

"I am saying so now," Stefano replied in a tone of haughty irony.

"So this is where you hide like a cross old hermit," I said. "It is a pretty little cell, cousin. Aren't you going to invite me in?"

"No. But don't sulk, cousin, it spoils the shape of that charming mouth. I am not discriminating against you in particular. No one comes here without an invitation from me."

"Not even Grandfather?"

"Not even he. There is nothing to see," he added, shifting his weight carefully from one foot to the other. "Only bachelor's quarters, austere and extremely untidy." Stefano smiled. "I'll give you a proper tour some other time, Francesca. At my convenience."

"But I'm bored now," I said.

"Then you are a young woman with few resources. Read, embroider, sketch, ride. . . . The prince has given you the gentlest mare in his stables."

"I can't ride alone. Why don't you come with me?"

Stefano's smile vanished; his face grew dark with anger. "Oh, well done, cousin. However, lest you think your triumph too complete, I must tell you that I did remount the horse that threw me—two years ago, after my bones had healed in the inadequate fashion you see. But I ride, in my own clumsy way, privately. I certainly do not intend to give you the pleasure of jeering at me." And with a lurch that almost threw him off balance, he plunged into the house and slammed the door.

The echoes were still reverberating as I ran down the flowery path. Tears of shame and anger clouded my vision. I had assumed that Stefano had been crippled for years, perhaps since birth. That was bad enough, but for a man to be struck down in the full flush of his youthful vigor was certainly tragic. How he must rage against such a cruel fate.

I went into the yew garden, where a gardener was delicately clipping the bushes, which had been shaped into fantastic animals. It was precise, exacting work, and very boring to watch. I wandered on toward the stables. Though I had no intention of riding that day, I thought I might pay a social call on Stella, the little mare that had been assigned to my use.

I was delighted when I found Grandfather in the stableyard, booted and spurred, watching his favorite steed being saddled. "Where are you going, Grandfather?" I asked eagerly. "May I come with you?"

His stern face lightened at the sight of me, but he shook his head. "I am going to the tombs."

"The tombs from which my lovely jewelry came? But I want to see them. You promised you would take me one day. Why not now?"

"It is bad country," Grandfather said slowly. "Rough and wild. Your pretty dress . . ."

"I'll change into an old dress. Please wait for me!" And since he said no more, I turned impetuously and ran quickly back to the house.

I put on one of the muslin dresses that had been dyed black, and found a bonnet and gloves. The library doors opened as I passed them and Miss Perkins appeared, a great thick book open in one hand. "Where are you off to?" she asked, seeing my outdoor attire. "Don't go far, Francesca."

"It's all right, I'm going with Grandfather." I paused before a mirror to adjust my bonnet. "He is taking me to see the tombs."

"The Etruscan tombs? Oh, Francesca, I don't think—"

I had turned away, my skirts flaring, and now she caught my arm. I turned in some surprise and saw that her face mirrored the urgency of her tight grasp. "Wait, child, I must talk to you. I have just found something—"

"Excuse me, Miss Perkins, but I really must run. As soon as I get back you can show me your great discovery." I ran away, laughing, leaving her standing with her hand outstretched in a frustrated appeal.

The horses were saddled when I reached the stableyard. Grandfather said nothing, only swung into the saddle and turned the horse's head toward the gate. Clumsily I followed suit. He seemed to be in a bad mood.

Conversation would have been difficult in any case. There was a trail of sorts, but one shaded from the sun by olives and firs, and so narrow and overgrown and rocky that we had to go single file. Then we began to descend. Before long I started wishing I had not come. The slope was so steep in places that I closed my eyes and clutched the pommel with both hands. When at last the track leveled out, I saw that we were riding slowly through a green twilight. The trees here were evergreens, in whose perpetual shade the ground was damp and slippery. It was a strange, haunted place.

The end of the ravine opened up into a wider, less overgrown area, and I began to see the gaping, square holes that opened into ancient tombs. I ventured to urge my horse into a faster walk until I was beside Grandfather.

"Those are tombs, are they not?" I asked in my careful Italian.

He turned his head. From under his frowning gray eyebrows his eyes contemplated me blankly, as if I had interrupted some train of thought. "Yes," he said. "The tombs of peasants. It is not here, the place we seek."

As we went on I was amazed at the extent of the ancient cemetery. There were tombs of all types. In some places I could see the scars of digging, but vegetation had covered all but the most recent holes. It was not a place to visit alone. The concealed shafts were like traps into which one might easily tumble. The atmosphere was uncanny too. It was so still. No bird sang, no small animals rustled through the coarse grass. I remembered something Stefano had said to Miss Perkins the previous night at dinner. The peasants thought this was a haunted place, sacred to the dead.

To the right of the rough path rose the biggest mound I had yet seen. It must have been thirty feet high. Around its base was a circle of masonry, big, roughly hewn blocks like a stone girdle.

"Is that it?" I asked. "The tomb of the jewels?"

"Sì, sì. La tomba della principessa." Grandfather dismounted and came around to help me down. For a moment he stood looking about with a puzzled air, as if he could not remember the way. Then, taking my hand, he struck off toward the mound. We had gone halfway around its circumference before he stopped. Grandfather pushed into the thick bushes at the base of the mound, tramping down weeds and thrusting branches aside.

"Here," he said. He had torn away some of the underbrush. There, in the slope of the bank, the blocks of the surrounding stonework had been cut out to form an entrance in the shape of a Gothic arch. A single monolith filled the opening. So precisely had it been cut to fit the rounded sides that one could scarcely see the crack between door and frame.

I watched, fascinated, as Grandfather tugged at the stone. The stone must be balanced in some clever fashion, I realized, or he could never have hoped to move its hundreds of pounds—perhaps even tons. He found a catch of some kind, and the heavy block began to move. Without speaking or looking at me, he stepped through the opening. When I peered inside, I saw him standing at the top of a flight of stone steps. On a shelf inside the entrance he found a box of candles and lighted one. "Come," he said.

I hesitated. The candlelight was feeble; I could see nothing beyond the stairs. From the pitch-blackness came a breath of clammily cold air.

"Avanti," Grandfather repeated, beginning to descend. His voice came back, echoing hollowly. With a shiver I picked up my skirts and followed.

At the foot of the stairs was a chamber some thirty feet long, but very narrow. The candle burned blue in the dank air. I would have retreated then and there, but Grandfather stalked on, holding his inadequate light high like an ancient priest. At the far end was a doorway. It had been filled with blocks of masonry, but these now lay broken and tumbled. Grandfather stepped over the blocks and passed into the inner chamber. I followed.

This far chamber was also the last; there was no other exit. It was a little smaller than the first and had a steeply vaulted ceiling smeared with lichen and mold. At the very end was a low stone platform.

When I understood the function of this rude bier, I felt a chill. The purpose for the structure had been funereal.

"Here is where she lay," Grandfather said, his eyes fixed on the low platform. His hand was trembling. The candlelight flickered wildly across the stained ceiling. "Here . . ." And then he said something else I didn't understand. He began to back away, as if he were retreating from the presence of a monarch, or from something he was afraid to turn his back on. I took one step after him, and then his shaking hand lost its grip on the candle, which fell to the floor, extinguished.

I cried out. When the echoes of the scream died, I heard Grandfather stumbling over the loose stones around the inner doorway. I was afraid to move for fear of falling or touching the foul slime that covered the walls and floors. Naturally I assumed he was going to get another light. I could see part of the tomb entrance—a square of brightness against the black of the interior. Grandfather's body blotted out much of the light as he climbed the stairs. And then—then . . . the light disappeared. I stared into blackness, unable to believe what had happened, although the dull, grating thud of the closing door confirmed the evidence of my eyes.

I don't know how long I stood there, waiting . . . how long it was before the truth dawned on me.

I didn't really believe it. Instead, I began making my slow, careful way back toward that closed slab of stone, moving an inch at a time, sliding first one foot and then the other along the slippery floor. Strain my eyes as I might, I could not see even a crack of light. Those ancient artisans had known their business. Yet there was light in that dreadful place—patches of lichen that glowed with a faint greenish pallor, like the ectoplasm produced by mediums.

When I reached the steps, my knees collapsed completely. But it was better to crawl up the stairs; they were steep and slippery. I crouched on the topmost step with my palms flat against the unyielding surface of the slab. I thought for a moment that it moved slightly, but that was an illusion. It was my arms that gave way. I rose, and a curious lethargy seized me.

Leaning against the stone, I suddenly remembered what Grandfather had said just before he dropped the candle. "Here is where she lay. . . ." But the Italian word for "she" is *lei,* and that is also the word for the formal "you." One would use the formal version when addressing royalty—a princess. . . . With that realization other clues fell into place. My entombment had not been an accident. If he had dislodged the slab by some ill-judged movement, he would by now have opened it again.

I realized that I was being overcome by some miasmic atmosphere in that long-sealed place. I seemed to feel the door move again, and knew this time that my senses must be deceiving me.

The door swung open.

Sunlight blinded me. A rush of warm, sweet air filled my straining lungs. For a moment I stood swaying on the threshold. I thought that this was a dream, for before me—his white shirt dirt-smeared and torn, his eyes wide with horror, his fair hair curling damply—was Andrea. With a long sigh of relief I fell forward into his outstretched arms.

CHAPTER FIVE

"YOU WERE NEVER IN serious danger, you know." How he knew I was awake I could not imagine. I lay still, my eyes closed, sensuously enjoying the touch of the sun on my upturned face. There was something soft under my head. I did not need to open my eyes to know that it was not after all Andrea, but Stefano, who had released me. I had made that error once before—stupidly, for the brothers were not that much alike. Certainly Stefano's cool ironic tones were unmistakable.

I opened my eyes. He was sitting on a rock a few feet away. The soft bundle of cloth under my head must be his coat. He was in his shirt sleeves. Perspiration streaked his face and his bare throat.

"If I was not in danger, why are you so pale?" I inquired.

"Exhaustion," Stefano replied coldly. "The exertion of moving the stone was strenuous, for a cripple."

"I can't imagine how you did it," I murmured, letting my eyes linger on the breadth of shoulder displayed by his wetly clinging shirt.

Stefano smiled. "Because my leg is injured does not mean all my muscles are atrophied. Can you stand?"

"No."

"I can lift you," Stefano said, "but I cannot carry you any distance. So unless you wish to remain here all day . . ."

"Oh, stop baiting me!" I turned my head so he wouldn't see me crying. Now that the danger was over, I felt drained of all strength.

After a moment Stefano spoke in a gentler voice. "I know it must have been frightening, cousin. You are no coward, I'll say that for you—I expected to find you screaming, or in a swoon. Rest awhile, but Miss Perkins will be pacing the floor until she sees you safe and sound."

"Then Miss Perkins sent you? Or did you know he would do this?"

"In God's name, how can you suggest such a thing?" Stefano demanded, in a rough voice quite unlike his usual smooth tones. "It was an accident."

I raised myself on one elbow and looked earnestly at him. "Stefano, you must tell me the truth."

He studied me thoughtfully, then nodded. "It all began here, five years ago, when he excavated this particular tomb. It is a very old one, dating back to the early days of the Etruscan kingdom—the seventh or eighth century before Christ. Many of the other tombs had been robbed, but this was untouched—the rich treasure was still here, including the jewels you wore the other night. Also—there were the bodies of the dead.

"Those in the outer chamber were mere heaps of dust. But the inner chamber had been sealed. Only a few of the bravest of Grandfather's people had entered the tomb with him and now they fled, screaming of curses and vampires. So he took up chisel and hammer himself and attacked the wall. His imagination had been fired by the fine things in the outer chamber. As soon as one block had been removed, he thrust his head and one hand, holding a candle, into the aperture.

"The air in such places is usually bad, but the candle flared up and the scent that reached his nostrils was not noxious. It was dry and strangely, spicily perfumed. As the candle flame leaped, he saw—her.

"She was lying on the stone bier at the far end of the chamber. She was all gold, from her glittering gown and jewels to the golden hair streaming over her shoulders and down her ivory arms and breast. Her face was pale and unmarred. The prince stood transfixed, and as he watched, her pure perfection suddenly crumbled. She fell into dust before his very eyes.

"It must have been an appalling sight—he fell into a swoon after that dreadful vision. A courageous attendant, venturing into the tomb in search of his master, found him lying on the floor, cold and still as a dead man. He was ill for days, but as soon as he could move he insisted on returning to the tomb. We helped him demolish the wall, Andrea and I. There was nothing on the slab—only the eerie suggestion of a vanished form, outlined by the positions of the jewels that had fallen from it."

"I don't believe it," I muttered. "Such things don't happen. He must have been dreaming. He was ill. He saw the jewelry—fallen, as you saw it—and collapsed. In his delirium he imagined the rest."

"That is what I myself believe," Stefano said. "But it doesn't matter, does it? What matters is what *he* believes. And he believes he saw her—the Etruscan princess, the ancestress of our race.

"There is one more thing," he said slowly. "In the inner chamber we found some silver cosmetic jars. They were inscribed with a name."

"And the name was—"

"Larthia."

"So," I said. "It *was* Miss Perkins who sent you in search of me."

"Yes. She had only a vague foreboding, but when she told me he had called you by that name . . . You have the golden hair, the family blood. Such a fancy might explain his sudden reversal of feeling toward you. He has had . . . odd spells since the discovery. They don't last long, they are infrequent, but . . . I thought he looked strange last night, when he had decked you out in his treasure. And so I came. I—I met the prince between here and the castle. When I asked him where you were, he looked surprised and said he had not seen you since breakfast."

"You saved my life," I said.

"Don't thank me, thank your Miss Perkins. She told me she had been haunted by that name since you came. She spent the morning in the library looking for the reference."

I sat up. My head spun for a moment, but soon I was able to get to my feet. I felt exhausted.

Stefano also rose and helped me into the saddle, not without difficulty. His horse was cropping the grass nearby, but he made no move to approach it. "Ride on," he said curtly.

I started to object, and then I understood. He did not want me to see him struggling to mount. So I turned the mare's head and set her into a walk. After an interval Stefano came up beside me, and, as the trail narrowed, he went ahead. We did not speak again.

I WAS NOT so resilient or so brave as I had thought. For some time I had horrible dreams of being pursued through underground passages by invisible horrors. I said nothing to Galiana about the experience. In fact, no one knew about it except Stefano—who never again referred to it—and Miss

Perkins, who brushed aside my emotional thanks with gruff embarrassment. Grandfather behaved as if no such thing had happened, and when several days later he made a casual remark about taking me to see the cemetery, "which you have not yet seen," I realized that the episode had been wiped from his mind. Strangely, I was not uneasy with him.

I had in any case plenty to occupy my mind, and before long the incident faded in my thoughts except for occasional dreams. The work on my new rooms proceeded apace, and dressmakers from Florence arrived with cartloads of lovely fabrics for my wardrobe. Galiana and I reveled in a rainbow assortment of India muslins, silver lace, flame-colored taffeta.

I had become fond of Galiana. Some of her traits annoyed me, however. One of the most annoying was the way she behaved toward Stefano. It would not be quite accurate to say she flirted with him, for she seemed a little in awe of him, but she hung on his words with a breathless attention I found disgusting. One evening she chose a seat on a footstool next to his chair and never took her big black eyes off his face as he discussed antiquities with Miss Perkins. Stefano left early that evening, and next morning, as Galiana and I were preparing to go out, I said, "I didn't realize you were so interested in ancient history, Galiana."

"I am not." Galiana giggled with a sweet, high-pitched little laugh.

"Then it must be Stefano who interests you," I went on.

"But he is the heir," Galiana said calmly. "One day he will be Prince Tarconti. Stefano is not as handsome as Andrea, but he will do quite well."

I found this mercenary and cold-blooded, but had to admit it was the accepted attitude regarding marriage, one shared by some of the girls at my school. Galiana hummed to herself as she studied her reflection in the mirror. I felt a stab of jealousy run through me. My new riding costume was finished and I had thought I looked rather well. The dashing cut of the jacket set off my slim figure quite nicely, but next to Galiana's delicious plumpness I looked like a child.

Feeling a little out of sorts, I turned from the mirror. "Let's go," I said. "The sky is clouding over. I don't want to be caught in the rain."

We were going to the village. It was not far away, and I couldn't see why we were not allowed to go alone, but whenever I rode out, a groom in the Tarconti livery followed at a discreet distance. This was not only a question of propriety, but also of safety. A trip to the village was a treat only because we got out so seldom. According to Galiana, it had little to offer, but the one shop of importance had ribbons and buttons, sufficient excuse for two bored girls to seek it out.

The sun had gone behind the clouds by the time we reached the town, making it look even more somber than it ordinarily appeared. The houses were of dull gray stone. There were no trees and no flowers, not even window boxes, such as I had seen in other Italian towns. The church, dedicated to Saint Sebastian, had a façade of the same gray stone. There was a café, with rusty iron chairs set out on the stone paving. When we came into sight the chairs were pushed back, conversation stopped, and the patrons—roughly dressed, bearded men—stared at us as hard as they could.

The shop was dimly lit and filthy. I found Signor Carpaccio, the owner, unpleasantly obsequious. We bought several yards of lilac twill, just to be buying something, and Galiana found a crude little statue of Saint Sebastian for her mother. When we came out the clouds had thickened, and we made haste to remount. Galiana set her horse into a canter at once and I followed, with the groom behind me. We were almost out of the town when a child darted out of an alley, right under my horse's feet.

I jerked on the reins and dismounted as quickly as I could. The child lay still, facedown in the dirt. Whether boy or girl I couldn't tell, as it wore the loose robe-shirt all tiny children wore.

I should not have moved it, Miss Perkins told me later, but, frightened, I caught the little thing up and lifted it onto my lap. Its bones felt as fragile as a bird's under my hands; its face was pale beneath a coating of dirt, and its eyes were closed. My heart gave a great leap and seemed to stop. Then the eyes opened. "Thank God," I cried. "Are you hurt, child?"

The groom, a stocky young fellow named Piero, was now beside me. After he had passed his hands over the child's body and limbs, he smiled reassuringly and spoke slowly. I caught the word *"bene."* The child continued to lie in my lap, staring up at me with great velvety eyes.

Galiana had not dismounted. "Come along, Francesca," she said impatiently. "It will rain any moment. We will be soaked."

"But the child—" I began.

"You heard Piero say it is not hurt. Put it down and hurry."

Angrily I gathered the child into my arms and stood up. It weighed nothing at all. I was looking around, wondering where its home was, when the door of a nearby house opened and a woman ran out, her lined face anxious. She limped as she ran. The small face came alive at the sight of her. Stretching out two bony little arms, the child cried, *"Mamma."*

The woman took the child, pressed it to her bosom, and wrapped her shawl around its bare legs. I had expected her to rail at me; instead she snatched at my hand and tried to kiss it. I fumbled in my purse and pressed a coin into her hand.

"Francesca, do come!" cried Galiana. "Peasant children are just like animals, my dear. They aren't easily hurt." Tossing her head, she rode away.

The woman with the child was retreating, bowing with every step. I looked helplessly at Piero. Smiling, he held his hands for me to mount.

I made no attempt to catch up with Galiana immediately. I was puzzled and shocked by her attitude and felt quite unfriendly toward her. But she reined up, and waited for me with an angelic smile on her pretty face.

"I have just thought of something very amusing," she said. "Did you hear what the woman said to you when she was mumbling over your hand? She called you by the name these ignorant people give to the harvest goddess. They have a festival in the autumn, and the girl who plays the goddess must bleach her hair yellow if it is not that shade already. I suppose they confuse her with His Excellency's princess—the one he found in the tomb with all her jewels."

I jerked on the reins so hard that Stella stopped. "What?"

"You must have heard of the princess," Galiana said. "That's why the villagers won't go near the old tombs. Well, you have yellow hair, like hers."

"How strange," I said. "I don't think I want to be taken for a goddess."

"It's your own fault," Galiana replied, "getting involved with these people. You'd better take a bath as soon as we get back, Francesca. They all have fleas, you know. And you look a fright, all covered with dust."

I lifted my chin in my most dignified manner and said nothing.

WHEN I NEXT rode to the village Miss Perkins was with me, and I felt as if I were seeing it through new eyes.

Galiana insisted on coming. Miss Perkins didn't mind. "There is no harm in the girl," she said after I had indignantly described Galiana's callous behavior toward the child. "She is the product of her class, Francesca—she has never been taught to think of others. You mustn't blame her. Perhaps you can help educate her."

I had to admit that Galiana was not beyond hope. She came with us even though she knew my reason for going was to inquire after the child.

We stopped in front of the house and Piero went to knock at the door. In a moment the child's mother came running out and tried to kiss my hand, which I hastily pulled away. With Miss Perkins to interpret, I found that the child had taken no harm. It was even then at play in the piazza. So, after giving the woman a few coins, we rode that way.

Miss Perkins surveyed the mean little street through which we were riding and shook her head. "This country is ripe for a revolution. Look about you. There is no school in this town, no hospital, not even a doctor. Do you know how old the child's mother is? Thirty-one! She looks sixty. She is badly crippled with rheumatism—the result of malnutrition and living in damp, filthy old houses. Those houses belong to your grandfather, Francesca. How long has it been, I wonder, since he repaired any of them? Yet he is considered a kindly lord in comparison to others in the province."

I was too shocked to answer. By the time we reached the piazza Miss Perkins had forgotten her libertarian sentiments, and the face she turned to me was beaming with admiration. "What a beautiful old town!" she exclaimed. "Look at the stonework on that balcony, Francesca. The church cannot be later than the fourteenth century. See the shape of the Gothic arches in the rose window."

When she had finished pointing out the beauties of the piazza, it looked quite different to me. The sun was shining brightly and the fine weather had brought the townspeople out. Women filled great jars at the fountain. A group of children sat in the dirt playing some sort of game. I saw my small acquaintance among them, but did not go to him (Miss Perkins had ascertained that he was a boy and named Giovanni), fearing it might alarm him. Galiana was already before Signor Carpaccio's shop, calling to us. Miss Perkins paid no attention and rode across the piazza toward the church. I followed her; Galiana did so reluctantly.

Miss Perkins slipped out of the saddle and climbed the steps of the church, her head tilted back as she contemplated the carved Gothic window. Then she turned and peered nearsightedly at one of the yellowed placards fastened to the façade. "Ha—but what is this?" she exclaimed.

"It is a notice of taxes," Galiana said.

"So I see." Miss Perkins adjusted her pince-nez.

Galiana sighed impatiently. Miss Perkins proceeded to read all the notices while we fidgeted. Finally she walked toward the door. We were about to follow when there was a shift of movement all over the piazza. For a second everything froze. The next moment the piazza was empty. The women and children had gone, the villagers had melted away.

The troop of soldiers came into the piazza two abreast. They carried long muskets with bayonets attached. Behind them came the cavalry—a dozen or more mounted men—and Captain de Merode.

"What miserable-looking soldiers they are," I said, for these slouching rascals looked like scarecrows.

Miss Perkins shook her head. "These men may be dirty, but their bayonets are freshly polished. . . . Look at their faces—their eyes. The peasants call them *lupi*—wolves."

The captain lifted his hand and the little troop came to a ragged stop around the curving steps of the church. De Merode dismounted with a jingle of sword belt and spurs. He swept off his helmet. "Ladies, what a pleasure to meet you here. I would not have thought this wretched hole had any amusement to offer you. And you, Mademoiselle . . . Parker? I was under the impression that you had returned to England."

"Were you?" Miss Perkins did not bother to correct his mistake about her name. "You do your spies less than justice, Captain. I am sure you know everything that goes on in this district."

The word was ill-chosen—deliberately, if I knew my Miss Perkins.

The captain scowled. "My spies"—he emphasized the word—"are less efficient than I could wish. I have not yet succeeded in cleaning out this viper's nest of traitors. Since you are here, however, you may watch."

Turning, de Merode snapped out an order. Two of his men came forward. One was carrying a roll of paper, the other a pot and a brush. Before long, the façade of the church bore a new notice. From where I stood I could see only one line of the printing—the number 10,000.

Miss Perkins scrutinized the notice. "So much money for the capture of one local rebel?"

De Merode said, "It is a small price to pay for peace in this province, but a large sum for a poor man." His voice carried across the quiet piazza. He spoke Italian, instead of his usual French.

"Larger than the thirty pieces of silver Judas earned. . . . You will excuse us, Captain. We have come to see the church."

She swept us before her through the heavy doors. The interior was so dark, after the sunlight of the piazza, that I stopped short. Then Miss Perkins caught my arm and drew me to the far side of the church.

"The reward," I said. "Was it for the Falcon?"

"Yes."

"But why did he make such a great show of putting up the notice?"

"I don't understand that myself," Miss Perkins admitted. "I think perhaps we should go back to the castle. I have an uneasy feeling."

But when this proposition was put to Galiana, she made a loud outcry, insisting on visiting the shop. Miss Perkins gave in, but I began to share her uneasiness as we crossed the square toward the shop. The mounted men had gone, but many of the foot soldiers were still there, relaxing like men released from duty.

At first the shop seemed deserted. After a moment Signor Carpaccio appeared from the back. He greeted us with his usual obsequiousness and ran to show Galiana a tray of trinkets newly arrived from Florence. While we were standing there, we heard a burst of coarse laughter from one of the soldiers at the café next door.

"I can't understand why they are still here," Miss Perkins said. "They are stationed at Parezzo."

Signor Carpaccio shrugged. "It is only this wretched outlaw, this Falcon. He has sworn to tear down a reward notice if one should be put up. The soldiers are waiting for him to come. But," he added quickly, "the villain will not dare appear. He will certainly be captured if he does."

"Of course he will appear," Miss Perkins snapped. "His reputation depends on keeping rash, stupid promises. Girls—come, we must go."

Galiana, her eyes sparkling, joined me in pleading for a delay. She was as anxious as I to catch a glimpse of the romantic bandit. Unlike myself, she seemed to believe he would appear soon. I could not believe any man, even a romantic bandit, would be so foolhardy. However, Miss Perkins was adamant. She herded us out into the piazza, where we found the mood had relaxed. Some fluttering skirts could be seen among the uniforms, and one bold-faced black-haired village girl started to sing. Miss Perkins urged us to mount, and we turned toward the narrow street that led to the castle.

We had almost reached it when a thunder of pounding hoofs was heard. A shot rang out. I tried to stop and turn around. The horses reared, and for a few seconds all was confusion. However, I saw him come.

Like a bullet from a pistol barrel, the great black stallion came plunging out of a narrow alleyway. Before the surprised soldiers could aim their weapons, the rider had reached the church steps. Swaying sideways in his saddle, he thrust at the newly affixed placard with his sword. The glue had not yet set; the paper pulled free and wrapped itself around the blade. The rider whirled it once around his head with an indescribable air of mockery and disappeared into another alleyway, as narrow as the first.

It transpired in far less time than it takes to tell it, yet I was left with an indelible memory of horse and rider. The bandit's clothing matched the ebony hue of his steed. Even his head was covered with a close-fitting black hood. The only touch of color was the blood-red sash tied around his waist—the scarlet badge of rebellion. I had never seen anything more vigorously alive than the man and his beautiful stallion.

I was still staring at the narrow alley into which the rider had vanished when something struck Stella on the flank. The mare might have bolted if Piero had not caught her bridle. I turned to see a jostling mass of horsemen filling the street behind me. The cavalry had been lying in ambush somewhere along that main thoroughfare—which, though narrow, was considerably wider than the other streets that led into the piazza. But the riders had been unable to follow the Falcon because of the impediment presented by our group. De Merode, his face livid with anger, was trying to lead his men through. It was he who had struck at Stella.

A few of the foot soldiers were already running in pursuit, but of course they had no hope of catching a rider—and such a rider!

We got ourselves straightened out finally, after considerable pushing and shouting. De Merode gave me a furious look before gathering his troops together and galloping off. I knew he must suspect us of deliberately barring his way, but I was quite willing to be the object of his mistrust rather than have him turn his attentions to the real conspirators—the girls who had been so friendly to his soldiers, distracting their attention and preventing them from reaching their weapons in time. I expressed this idea to Miss Perkins as we trotted along at a rapid pace.

"Quite right," she gasped. "The girl who sang . . . a signal—"

She broke off with a grunt as our horses, urged by Piero, went into a gallop. With growing amazement and indignation I asked myself, Had our romantic bandit had the cold-blooded effrontery to use us as a shield? The girl's song might well have been a signal; and if so, then the Falcon must have been lurking in the immediate vicinity, perhaps in one of the walled courtyards of the houses near the piazza. That would suggest that he lived in the town, or very close to it. Perhaps he had even known of our trip to the village while planning his strategy. If so, he must have spies in the very stronghold of his enemies—in the castle itself.

CHAPTER SIX

WE WERE LATE RETURNING, and the others were just sitting down to tea. Galiana was the first to enter, pushing past Miss Perkins in her anxiety to tell the exciting news. I thought Grandfather would have a fit. He turned an unbecoming shade of scarlet and rushed from the room. "My daughter," said the contessa, "you should not have told the prince."

"He would have heard of it sooner or later."

"It is certainly a most inappropriate time, however," sniffed Miss Rhoda. "He was already on the verge of a tantrum, after reading the newspaper. That bandit Garibaldi has captured Palermo."

Miss Perkins, her face aglow, read of her hero's exploits in the copy of *Monitore* that lay on a table. "All of Sicily must be in his hands by now," she muttered. "The newspaper is a week old."

"For heaven's sake, must we discuss politics?" said Miss Rhoda. "At least, Miss Perkins, I beg you to be silent in the presence of the prince."

However, Miss Perkins received support from Stefano at dinner that evening. He immediately talked about Garibaldi's success, with a sly sidelong look at Grandfather, and although the old gentleman fumed, it seemed to relieve his spleen to pound on the table and shout. Stefano egged him on; but Stefano didn't agree with Miss Perkins either. Like all moderates, he incurred the ire of extremists on both sides, and bore it with amused condescension.

The latest exploits of the Falcon amused Stefano even more. Galiana, always eager to gain his attention, described the incident in her breathless fashion, and he shook his head with a sneering smile. "The fellow is a clown. But how typically Italian. Conspiracy is in our blood. For the last fifty years the country has been crawling with secret societies, petty groups with poetical names, noble aims, and very little effect."

"Pardon me, cousin, if I object to your rhetorical style," I said heatedly. "But how can you speak so callously of a noble aim, however misguided?"

Stefano's fixed smile never left his face, but the look in his eyes indicated that I had touched him—probably evoked his contempt and annoyance.

At that point Miss Rhoda let out a loud "Hem!" and rose. The other ladies followed, leaving Stefano and Grandfather to resume arguing. The only one who was reluctant to depart was Miss Perkins.

I REMEMBER THE FOLLOWING THURSDAY for three reasons: it was Galiana's saint's day and we were to have a little party; one of my lovely new dresses was finished; and Andrea returned.

I was trying on the dress when he arrived, and he made such an uproar that all of us flew downstairs to see what was happening. We followed the sound of music—the grand piano, which was being played in great crashing chords. The music had a fine martial ring; and somehow I was not surprised when I ran into the room, with Galiana on my heels, to see my cousin seated at the instrument pounding away at a great rate. He bowed when he saw us, but did not rise. Instead he began to sing.

I needed no interpreter to understand his song. The ghosts of the martyrs were rising to join in the fight for Italy's freedom. Andrea fairly shouted the thrilling words, his golden curls tossing, his eyes shining. He ended with a mighty crash and bounded to his feet. He seized my hand and planted a hearty kiss upon it, then he turned to Galiana and caught her up in his arms. She shrieked with delight, her little feet dangling.

Still the same impetuous Andrea—but there were several significant differences. The blond mustache was new and so was the bronzed hue of his skin, but the most striking change was in his attire: the loose red shirt, the rakish bandanna at the throat. How well I knew them from Miss Perkins' descriptions! This was the costume worn by Garibaldi's Thousand—who had set sail from Genoa for the liberation of Sicily.

I was endeavoring to assimilate this startling new development when an outraged exclamation made me turn. Miss Rhoda stood in the doorway. Over her shoulder I saw the pale face of the contessa; her eyes were fixed on her daughter, still clasped in Andrea's red-shirted arms. And behind the contessa was her omnipresent shadow—the maid Bianca.

Andrea lowered Galiana to the floor as Miss Rhoda swept into the room and bore down on the young pair like a battleship. Grasping her hand, he pumped it so enthusiastically that her intended lecture turned into a series of stutters. His manner changed completely as he greeted the contessa; he took her hand gingerly, as if it would break, and raised it to his lips. Then, with obvious relief, he turned to me. "Cousin, it is good to see you. I am sorry I could not greet you on your arrival, but as you see, I had more pressing matters to attend to."

"I do see." I could not help smiling at the twinkle in his eyes. "But what a way to announce yourself, cousin. Is that the new anthem of Italy?"

"It may well be that. A stirring song, eh? We call it Garibaldi's Hymn." Then he asked, "Where is my grandfather?"

"Here!" Grandfather entered the room as he spoke. His face was set in a scowl that would have daunted most erring children, but not Andrea; he ran to greet him with outstretched arms. The old gentleman received him with an arm extended, not to embrace but to repel. He burst into speech. I caught references to the red shirt, and words like traitor and rebel. Then he turned and rushed out of the room. Andrea winked at us and followed.

They made it up, somehow, before dinner, which was a gala meal in honor of Galiana's saint's day. But Andrea was the center of attention. He had abandoned his red shirt in favor of formal evening attire, which was only to be expected. As for Grandfather, he glowered at Andrea from the head of the table, but the light in his eyes as he looked at this grandson gave him away. I suspected that in spite of his lack of sympathy with the cause he thought all the more of Andrea for fighting.

After dinner we had an evening of music. Both brothers played. I had heard Stefano once before and had admired his precise touch with Bach and Vivaldi. Andrea played with more bravado and less finesse; he sang a series of romantic ballads in a rousing baritone. It was all in good fun and I enjoyed it as such, but as the evening went on I wondered if Andrea was not becoming overexcited. His cheeks were so flushed he looked feverish.

The contessa was the first to depart—with Galiana, of course. Soon afterward we all said good night. It seemed that I had just fallen asleep when I was awakened by sounds outside my door. I heard Miss Perkins' voice, then quick footsteps moving away. I got up and slipped into a dressing gown.

Miss Perkins' door stood open. Her bed was not occupied. In alarm I went to the end of the corridor. I saw light at the bottom of the stairs, so I descended. The door of one of the family bedchambers was open and candlelight spilled out into the hall. The room was filled with people. As I peered in Miss Rhoda gave a sharp order: "Get out, all of you. I don't need any of you except the signora."

The signora was Miss Perkins, who was looking down at the bed with an expression of concern. I could not see the occupant until the servants obeyed the order to leave; as they came toward the door, I saw Andrea.

His eyes were half closed. On his brow and his bared breast were wet cloths; as I watched, Miss Rhoda removed one of these and replaced it with another. I caught a glimpse of Andrea's tanned body before the cloth was replaced, and at first I thought he must be wounded; there was a small reddish mark, roughly circular, just under the right collarbone.

When I moved aside to let the servants out, Miss Rhoda saw me. "This is no place for you, Francesca," she said sharply. "Go back to bed."

"Is he wounded?" I asked anxiously. "Can't I do something to help?"

"No, no, child. He isn't wounded, but he is feverish. Some illness he contracted in Sicily. He may be infectious, so don't come any closer."

With that I had to be content. I gave the handsome invalid one last look and reluctantly departed.

He was better the next day and on his feet again within the week, seemingly unhurt by his illness and as energetic as ever. Our quiet lives became full of activity as Andrea invented schemes for our amusement. He took me to task, in his quaintly humorous fashion, for being so lazy about my riding, and under his brisk tutelage I soon became a fairly competent horsewoman. Scarcely a day went by that we did not ride.

Sometimes Galiana accompanied us. More often her mother found reasons for her to remain at home. The girl's morose face on these occasions should have cast a slight shadow over my selfish pleasure, but I'm afraid it didn't. I wondered if the contessa suspected the two young people were becoming too attached to one another. Andrea was charming to Galiana, but he was charming to everyone.

Of course I fancied myself in love with him. Why not? He was a delightful companion: incredibly handsome, brave as a lion, romantic as a hero of legend. I yearned to see him again in his dashing red shirt, and I tried to question him about his adventures in Sicily. But on that subject Andrea's facile tongue failed him. He told me about Garibaldi—about the general's courage, his tenderness toward the wounded, his cheerful acceptance of danger and discomfort. But he would not talk about the fighting, and I finally came to realize that his memories were not the sort he could share with a young girl.

Being in love is great fun, however, and I had a wonderful time. Miss Perkins often accompanied us on our expeditions; even Stefano joined us when the activity was not too strenuous for him, and then Galiana usually made one of the party too. It was no pleasure to have Stefano along; whenever he came there was an argument, usually about politics.

It was a dangerous topic at that time, and in our house. Ever since Andrea's return I had been worried for fear the soldiers might arrest him. But when I expressed this worry, the others laughed at me, Andrea loudest of all.

Stefano was more explicit. "Andrea is protected by the outmoded feudal system he fought against in Sicily," he said with a mocking glance at his brother. "The Princes Tarconti are above the law—one might even say that, like ancient Roman tyrants, they *are* the law. And Andrea had sense enough to misbehave outside the borders of Umbria. Now, if he had chosen to lead a band of rebels against Pio Nono, he might be in serious trouble. Not even our grandfather's influence could protect him."

Andrea's eyes flashed. "I do not expect the prince or anyone else to answer for me," he exclaimed. "Nor will I subdue my conscience to his. You may make jokes, Stefano, but you know Italy *must* be unified."

We were sitting on the ground—or rather on a handsome rug spread on the grass—in the sunshine. Only Stefano sat upright, on a small chair that a servant had brought for him. He showed little emotion, but frowned slightly. "What a tiring fellow you are, Andrea," he said with an affected yawn. "Do try to control your zeal. You are boring Galiana and Francesca—"

"He doesn't bore me at all," I broke in. "And I agree with what he says. This country is still in the Dark Ages, it is ripe for revolution!"

"Cousin," said Stefano, speaking through his laughter, "the voice is yours but the words, I suspect, are those of Miss Perkins. Dear lady, you mustn't turn my little cousin into a revolutionary. Life is very pleasant here—why don't you both enjoy it and forget your radical ideas?"

That ended the argument for the day. But it did not end the subject. We received several newspapers, and Miss Perkins read them all. As the summer wore on she became more and more excited. Garibaldi had been proclaimed dictator of Sicily, and there were rumors that he planned to attack the mainland. Ironically, we were less well informed about what was happening in our own province than we were about events in Sicily. The reason for this was obvious: censorship ruled with an iron hand in the Papal States, so wild rumors flew about in lieu of facts.

Politics were not our sole concern, of course. Miss Perkins was almost as interested in antiquities, and one day, at her urging, we agreed to make an expedition to the Etruscan cemetery. I shrank from returning to the place, but Grandfather was eager to display it to Miss Perkins, and even the contessa agreed to go. The older ladies and Stefano took a roundabout route by carriage. The rest of us rode by the direct path; we reached the spot before the others, but agreed to wait for them before exploring the tombs.

It was a glorious morning, sunny and bright. Grandfather was in fine spirits. It was obvious that he had no recollection of having been here with me. I knew I had nothing to fear; Galiana and Andrea were with us, not to mention half a dozen servants. But I confess I felt a cold chill as I saw the high green mound that concealed the tomb of the princess.

The servants spread rugs on some flat rocks so that Galiana and I could sit without spoiling our dresses. Then they withdrew, and for a long time we sat in silence. In the warm pastoral stillness my nerves began to relax. It was quite a pretty place. Wildflowers bloomed everywhere; birds sang in the trees. Then a rustle in the underbrush made Galiana start. Andrea put his finger to his lips, smiling. A rabbit hopped out into the clearing.

It was the biggest, fattest, whitest rabbit I had ever seen, and the least timid. It hopped out onto the path and began to nibble at the grass. Galiana broke the spell by giggling. The rabbit gave her a sideways look and retreated, but not in a blur of motion. It bounced along in a leisurely fashion, as if it had just remembered a not very important engagement.

"How tame it is," I exclaimed. "Was it a pet at one time?"

"No," said Andrea. "All the rabbits here are wild, all are white, all are unconcerned about man. It is because they have never been hunted. The peasants think they are supernatural creatures—the souls of the old Etruscans, perhaps. Besides, the prince has a fondness for them."

Grandfather shrugged; he disliked being accused of sentimental weaknesses, though he had quite a few. "They are a curiosity," he said.

It was not long before we were joined by the rest of the party. They had come the last few yards on foot, leaving the carriage at the road. Miss Rhoda was being respectfully propelled along by two sturdy footmen, while the contessa leaned on the arm of her maid. Stefano brought up the rear; he obviously found progress both painful and difficult.

Since the tomb of the princess was the greatest attraction, we went there first. Miss Perkins was fascinated by the monolithic stone door.

"It is a curious structure," Grandfather said. "You see how carefully it is balanced. Once the trick of opening it is known, it can be moved by one man." He slipped his fingers into a crack that was in no way distinguished from other irregularities in the rock facing. "One pushes and *voilà!*"

And with that word the great slab slowly swung out. A breath of cool, dank air issued from the opening.

Stefano was watching me with his faint sardonic smile. He and Miss Perkins were the only ones who knew of my brief incarceration in this dreadful place. I might have concealed my agitation altogether if Grandfather had not, in all innocence, made a fatal gesture.

In our exploration of the tombs we had to manage without the help of servants. They were reluctant to come into the valley at all and would not go into the tombs. So when the door of the tomb swung open, Grandfather assumed the role of guide, lighting one of the candles and preparing to lead the way. It was then that he held out his hand to me. Suddenly I realized that I was unable to move. "No," I gasped. "No, I cannot—"

"Oh, that horrible dark hole!" said Galiana, putting her arm through mine. "We will stay here, Francesca. You brave gentlemen may descend into the dirt and the dark without us."

Thanks to her, my refusal was considered no more than a typical feminine weakness. The others tried to persuade us. Grandfather demonstrated several times that a wooden wedge inserted into the crevice prevented the stone catch from slipping into place; the door could thus be completely shut and still open from within. But in the end only Grandfather and Miss Perkins, assisted by Andrea, made the descent.

They stayed underground for quite some time. We could hear their voices, grotesquely distorted, and an occasional laugh from Andrea. When they finally emerged Miss Perkins was beaming, and she and Grandfather continued their discussion while we visited several other tombs. I found that I was able to enter these without a qualm.

Interesting as it all was, it was also a dirty, depressing experience. Even Miss Perkins had had enough when we emerged from the last tomb into the pleasant sunlight. The servants meanwhile had set out a magnificent repast, and after dining we were glad to sit for a while before going back to the castle.

The contessa decided to return to the carriage, where her embroidery was awaiting her attention. She and her maid went off, the slight form of the older lady leaning on the arm of the younger. They were both wearing their usual unrelieved black, but Bianca's rusty black skirts were like molting plumage; even the hoarse caw that was the poor creature's only mode of expression resembled the cry of a crow. After a while Miss Rhoda followed the contessa, declaring that she had had enough of picnics. But Miss Perkins was ready to explore again, and Grandfather, flattered by her interest, offered to show her another tomb at a little distance. So they went off. I looked about and realized that Galiana and Andrea were no longer with us. Even the servants had gone, after tidying up the remains of the banquet. Stefano and I were alone.

He had settled himself in the only patch of shade, under an overhanging rock ledge. It was too hot at this hour to sit in the sun, so I joined him, saying, "I wonder where Andrea and Galiana have gone."

Stefano, leaning against the rock with his eyes closed, said, "Leave them alone. They have few enough opportunities to be by themselves."

"Do you think they are—er—fond of one another?" I asked, conscious of a strange little pang.

Stefano opened his eyes and stared at me. "Are you jealous, cousin? I suppose that, like all the females who pass through Andrea's life, you fancy yourself in love with him."

"If I were, I certainly would not confess it to you," I replied angrily.

"Very wise of you," said Stefano, and closed his eyes again.

We sat in silence after that. I knew Stefano was not asleep, but I had no intention of arousing his biting tongue. After a while the heat and the quiet made me sleepy. I was beginning to doze when suddenly Stefano flung himself at me, knocking me off my rocky seat onto the ground and falling heavily upon me. A loud crash shook the air.

For a few seconds I was too dazed to move or cry out. The weight of Stefano's body robbed me of breath. Then he rolled to one side and I struggled to sit. The angry words I was about to say died on my lips as I saw the heap of tumbled rocks where we had been sitting. "Good heavens," I exclaimed, putting my hand to my stinging cheek. My fingers came away red.

"It is only a superficial cut," said Stefano. He was sitting up too, in a strange, twisted position. One leg was bent under him.

"You are quick to minimize other people's injuries," I snapped. Then, seeing his pallor, I repented my sharp tongue. "Are you hurt, Stefano?"

"How should I be hurt when you cushioned my fall so sweetly?"

I looked at the rocks, several of which were large enough to have dashed out my brains, and began to shiver. "What a miraculous escape! I must thank you again, Stefano. How were you able to move so quickly?"

"I happened to glance up and see the rock move." With a grimace he could not repress, Stefano tried to straighten his leg. "It was foolish of me to sit there. Such rockfalls are not infrequent."

"It was an accident, then?" I asked in a small voice.

Stefano's eyebrows lifted. "What else could it have been?"

By now the others had come running, alarmed by the crash. My injuries were slight, so I was not too distracted to notice that Galiana and Andrea returned together, nor too alarmed to wonder what they had been discussing to make Galiana's cheeks so rosy red and her eyes so bright.

CHAPTER SEVEN

STEFANO HAD SPRAINED HIS ankle. He retired to his lair, as I called it, and we saw nothing of him for several days. Our accident had one other consequence. The near fatality confirmed the servants' abhorrence of the valley of the tombs. To a man—and woman—they regarded it as an unlucky place and refused to enter it again.

Toward the end of that week, however, our social life was enlarged by a rare event. Stefano invited us all to supper.

He had been speaking the literal truth when he told me that no one visited him without a formal invitation. Andrea joked about his misanthropic tendencies. "He has traps set inside the garden wall," Andrea said solemnly. "Last year he caught two poachers and Aunt Rhoda. She limped for weeks. The last time I attempted to call on him, a bullet narrowly missed my head. I do not accuse, you understand, but—"

He broke off, throwing up his hands in pretended terror as his brother, who was listening to all this, fixed him with a cold stare. "Someone *will* shoot you if you continue to make such bad jokes," said Stefano. "I insist on privacy, it is true. I can enforce it only by being rude. If I did not, Aunt Rhoda would be bustling in every day to make sure the servants were cleaning properly, and all the bored inquisitive young ladies in the neighborhood would find pretexts to interrupt me." He smiled nastily at me.

"I can't imagine who would want to bother you," I said loftily.

"No? Unfortunately, cousin, not everyone has your delicacy. At any rate, I am giving you all a chance to exorcise your curiosity. I will show you over my domain and give you an excellent meal. Will you come?"

"Oh, certainly," said Andrea. "We must encourage your coming out of seclusion, Stefano. You are becoming very social."

In truth, we had seen a great deal of Stefano since his brother returned. I couldn't imagine why he spent so much time with us, for he didn't seem to enjoy himself.

I did look forward to seeing his house, and that evening I dressed with special care in a new rose taffeta gown. I had given up my mourning altogether, in deference to Grandfather's wishes. Also, he had given me my mother's jewels. Among them was a lovely seed-pearl set—bracelets, necklace, earrings, and ornaments for the hair. I decided to wear this.

Miss Perkins was the only one of the older people who was having supper with us. Stefano had insisted on her coming, since she had never seen his house. They got on well; she was one of the few people who were never disturbed by his sarcastic tongue. In fact, she made herself popular with everyone.

Miss Perkins and I joined Galiana and Andrea in the castle drawing room, where they waited under the watchful eyes of the contessa and Miss Rhoda. Galiana also had a new dress. The color was stunning on her—pale yellow-gold trimmed with bands of darker gold velvet.

The contessa was in unusually good spirits. With a warm smile she bade us enjoy ourselves, and she even patted Andrea affectionately on the arm as he bent to kiss her hand. Miss Rhoda grumbled, as she always did; this evening she predicted rain and remarked that my gown was cut too low.

It was a beautiful night as we set out across the gardens. Stefano met us at the door of the house. He wore immaculate evening dress, with bloodstone studs and amethyst cuff links. We went over the house before dining, and my expressions of admiration were quite sincere. Everything was in miniature, but in perfect taste. My favorite room was the library. It was a perfectly proportioned chamber, with a big hooded fireplace, the family arms above it. Wide French doors opened onto a terrace beautifully planted with rose bushes and gardenias, and the little courtyard beyond was enclosed by high brick walls hung with vines.

"Bluebeard's den," said Stefano, glancing at me. "You see, ladies, how harmlessly I occupy my time. I am working on a family history for the prince, and I amuse myself by writing on philosophical matters."

As we went through the other rooms we had evidence of other occupations. An easel and a model's throne showed his interest in painting, but he refused to show us his work, saying it was too amateurish. The grand piano in the drawing room was frequently used, as I knew from hearing him play. He even had a small chemical laboratory fitted up.

We dined on the terrace. It was an exquisite setting, with a tiny courtyard fountain tinkling. The food was excellent, as Stefano had promised. We had almost finished the meal, and the light was dying fast, when the peace of evening was broken by the sound of a gunshot.

"Poachers again," said Andrea calmly, as I turned a startled look on him. "I have told you, brother, that you must enforce the laws. We may sympathize with the poor devils' needing food, but they have no right—"

"It is not sympathy but lethargy that keeps me from enforcing the law," said Stefano, scowling. "The prince is strict enough about his rights. I am surprised that any of the peasants dare invade his grounds."

All evening Miss Perkins had nobly refrained from talking politics, but this reference to an outmoded feudal right was too much for her. "You aristocrats hunt for pleasure," she exclaimed indignantly. "At the same time you forbid starving men to hunt for food for their families, when you have deprived them of the means to earn an honest livelihood."

"Don't scold me, Miss Perkins," said Andrea. "I agree with you."

"And I do not," Stefano remarked with a smile. "But I won't argue with you, Miss Perkins. You are too clever for me."

He did argue, though, and the two of them went at it hammer and tongs, while Galiana yawned. But Andrea was conscious of her boredom, and as soon as possible he offered to escort her on a walk through the gardens.

When the moon rose in its silvery splendor, bathing the courtyard in pale light, Stefano finally ended the argument. "That was refreshing," he said. "But now I think we had better find Galiana and Andrea. Shame on you, Miss Perkins, for failing in your duties as chaperone."

"I could do with a walk myself," said Miss Perkins.

The young pair was not to be found in Stefano's small garden, so we went out into the grounds of the castle. As we passed into the rose garden another shot sounded. This one was much closer, and Stefano stopped with an angry exclamation. "I must put an end to this. Moonlight is tricky light to shoot by. The fool may injure someone."

He had scarcely finished speaking when something buzzed through the air—passing between us so closely that I felt the wind of it on my hair—followed by a third explosion. Miss Perkins dragged me to the ground. "Lie still," she said. "That was a bullet."

"But— Stefano—" I began, and then saw my cousin had disappeared.

Almost at once I heard him calling out, and the voices of the servants answering. Lights flared up and began to move through the darkened gardens. Before long he came back to us, accompanied by one of his grooms, who was carrying a lamp. He saw us sitting on the ground in an undignified jumble of skirts and hoops. "You can get up now," he said, gesturing to the footman, who extended a hand to help us.

"Oh, dear," Miss Perkins said, looking sadly at a tear in her skirt.

"Better your skirt than your scalp," said Stefano. "I think the danger is over. My people are searching the grounds, but the idiot who fired those shots will not linger when he realizes how close he came to murder." He turned to me. "Really, cousin, I begin to think you are bad luck for me. Have you perhaps stolen the crown jewels, or kidnapped the heir to the throne?"

A FEW DAYS later I began to wonder myself if someone had not mistaken me for the object of a family feud. Two accidents in one week might have been coincidence, but a third . . . ?

I had just a day or so before moved into my new rooms. The suite gleamed with fresh gold paint and smelled of varnish and beeswax. I had never lived in such luxury. The great canopied bed was draped with silk, and the dressing table held silver-handled brushes and heavy crystal bottles. However, the castle had a few inconveniences that I have not mentioned. Even Miss Rhoda's British housekeeping could not keep down all the mice, or the bats that hang about the eaves of such old places.

Mercifully, Teresa was with me, helping me dress for dinner, when my encounter with a bat occurred. The heavy draperies were pulled back from the open windows. But the light inner curtains had been drawn, since the light attracted moths and other insects. Teresa was brushing my hair when the curtain suddenly billowed out and I saw the flapping black shape behind the thin white fabric. "Oh, dear," I exclaimed, more annoyed than afraid. "Do chase it away, Teresa, before it—"

As I spoke, the bat came in through the opening in the curtains. It was enormous, much bigger than the others I had seen, and at once I realized that there was something wrong with it. Unlike those, this one seemed to be moved by a demonic energy. It flung itself across the room in a series of swooping loops and then darted straight at me.

With a shriek I fell to the floor, my arms over my head. Teresa's face had gone white. I could have excused her for fleeing; instead she ran toward me, swinging the hairbrush like a club, and the solid silver of the brush struck the creature down. It fell to the floor not three feet from me, but it was not dead; and I could have sworn that, crippled as it was, it tried to crawl toward me. I had one horrible, unforgettable view of its evil little face—the eyes glowing red, the fanged mouth open—before Teresa grabbed my shoulders and dragged me away.

Drawn by our screams, Galiana was the first to burst into the room. She fell back with the most earsplitting shriek of all as she saw the black horror flapping on the floor. Andrea was right behind her. He did not hesitate, snatching a poker from the fireplace and beating at the fallen animal.

I didn't faint, but I lost my powers of speech for a brief time. When I regained them, Miss Perkins was saying, "It is gone now. The count took it away. Francesca, did it touch you?"

"I don't think so," I said. "Why worry about that?"

Andrea returned at that moment and came to my side. He and Miss Perkins exchanged glances. "Tell her, if you think it wise," he said.

"The bat was rabid," Miss Perkins said. "If even a drop of its saliva had touched you . . ."

Andrea smiled reassuringly. "The danger is over, cousin. You were almost the victim of a rare and unusual accident. You will never see such a thing again in your lifetime, I am sure."

"Good God," I said faintly. "Teresa saved my life, then, with my brush. . . . Ask her, Miss Perkins, make sure she was not hurt. She is the one who took the risk."

Miss Perkins insisted on examining the girl, and could find no punctures. But then suddenly Teresa let out a shriek and fell back, her eyes staring.

The contessa had just come in, accompanied by Miss Rhoda and the ever-present Bianca. Andrea explained the situation and the contessa went in search of Galiana, who had returned to her room, overcome. Bianca followed her as a matter of course, and as they left I saw that Teresa had extended one hand in a strange gesture, her fingers rigid.

When we were alone, I asked Miss Perkins about this.

"It is simple enough," Miss Perkins said with a sigh. "Superstition, the curse of the uneducated. The gesture Teresa made was the ancient defense against the evil eye. Afflicted persons such as Bianca are often regarded by the ignorant as agents of the devil. I understand that the contessa actually saved the poor creature from persecution in her home village. It is no wonder that she regards the contessa as a saint."

"I still don't understand why Teresa made that gesture."

"I suspect that Teresa, like her ancestors, believes in a world which is infested by malevolent spirits. There is no such thing as accident. Therefore the rabid bat was a demon in animal form, a sort of witch's familiar. And Bianca is regarded as a witch. . . ."

"That is ridiculous," I said. "I must talk to Teresa. But I can't forget, Miss P., how brave she was in defending me."

"She deserves even more credit for facing what she believed to be an emissary of Satan," said Miss Perkins with a smile. "Thank God it turned out as it did. Now we can forget the incident and go down to supper."

We went down, but I did not quickly forget the incident. Of course it was impossible that any human agent could have sent the infected creature to attack me. All the same, three "accidents" . . . it was surely stretching coincidence rather far.

Some day I will probably tell my grandchildren that the mishap involving little Giovanni was the turning point in the development of my youthful character. It may be so. But I suspect the change was more gradual, the result of a series of incidents, each of which wrought a small alteration, until finally the accumulated influence exploded into my consciousness.

I well remember the day this occurred—a hot afternoon in August. I was drowsing over a book in the rose garden when the summons from the village reached me.

I had been to the village several times, driven by some vague impulse; I hesitate to call it kindness or charity, for charity should be more courageous. I crept there surreptitiously, fearing Galiana's mockery, bringing small baskets of food, worn-out clothing—stuff pilfered from the kitchens and storerooms of the castle. I spent most of my store on Giovanni and his family, since I had a particular interest in them, and also because of the mother's delicate health. So when one of Giovanni's innumerable brothers came running to me, gray-faced and incoherent in his alarm, I had a premonition of what had gone wrong.

As I was mounting my horse, however, I remembered Miss Perkins' skill in nursing and paused long enough to scribble a hasty note, which I gave to one of the stablemen. With Piero behind me and Giovanni's brother on his saddlebow, I galloped to the village.

Never before had the abysmal poverty of the house where Giovanni lived struck me so forcibly as when I entered the darkened chamber where the mother lay, with a group of silent women around her. As I knelt beside her she opened her sunken eyes and smiled feebly. But I had seen death before, and I saw it on the bloodless face.

I was helpless. I could only take the woman's gnarled hand in mine. That seemed to please her. She was beyond speech, but she tried to raise my hand to her lips. That gesture broke me down. I knelt, sobbing, with bowed head, while the woman died.

Miss Perkins found me there only minutes later. Her firm hands on my shoulders roused me and lifted me to my feet. She sent me out of the room. One of the hovering women had to go with me, I was so blinded by tears.

It was considerably later when Miss Perkins came out of the house. Her shoulders were bowed and she looked more than her actual age, but when she saw me she straightened up and tried to smile. "Come now, Francesca, tears accomplish nothing. You did your best for the poor soul."

"I could do nothing," I exclaimed angrily.

"You came when she called. Your presence gave her comfort. No one could have done more."

I covered my swollen eyes with my hand and heard myself saying, "It is not right. They shouldn't live this way. I want to do something, Miss Perkins. Show me how to help!"

"Splendid," Miss Perkins said in her most matter-of-fact voice. "If you really feel that way, then stop crying, wipe your eyes, and think how you can help that orphaned family."

So began my exercises in benevolence. As I had expected, Galiana was very much amused by it all. Grandfather made no objections; charity, after all, was a suitable occupation for a lady. He let me rummage through the cupboards and storerooms for food, and watched with a smile while I laboriously sewed smocks and shirts for the children.

On one of my visits to Giovanni's house, a strange thing happened. I had gone down with a basket of bread, fresh from the oven. I was greeted with the usual smiles, but as I entered I saw the figure of a man slip through a back door. For a moment he was silhouetted against the sunlight, and I had an impression of someone unusually tall, wearing a slouch hat pulled down low on his head. Inside, on the table, I saw a haunch of veal. I knew these people never saw meat unless they were given it, and I certainly had not brought this roast. Poaching did occur, but it was extremely dangerous and was usually limited to small game such as rabbits. They would never dare kill a calf.

I could not help connecting the unusual food with the mysterious visitor. A thrill ran through me. Surely I had seen that tall, agile figure before, a sword arm extended. . . . I needed no further evidence to be convinced that I had seen the Falcon on one of his errands of mercy.

I was learning a little sense, though, so I said nothing to the family. I sought Miss Perkins out as soon as I returned home and she listened to my story with interest, but with a twinkling eye.

"My dear child, you are hopelessly romantic. I know your hero is said to help the villagers whenever possible—he seems to have a special interest in this district. But surely he would send one of his men on such an errand."

"I suppose so," I said, disappointed. "He has been very quiet these last few weeks, hasn't he? Since Andrea came home, in fact."

Andrea's stay was about to end, however. According to Galiana, he had already remained longer than he usually did, finding the castle boring and going off frequently to seek amusement elsewhere.

"It is you he came to see," said Galiana, looking at me slyly. "I think he will marry you, eh?"

"Why should he?" I inquired.

"It would be most suitable. The two parts of the family united, the two pets of your grandfather. He would be happy to see it, I think."

"Would you be happy to see it?"

Galiana turned away, her face unusually sober. "He is not for me. I must marry an elder son. We have no money, it is for me to restore the family."

"That's silly," I said. "Andrea won't be a pauper. He will have quite enough to live comfortably. Do you . . . care for him, Galiana?"

"If I did, it would make no difference," said Galiana sullenly. "I must marry an elder son. But you—you too love him."

The betrayal in a simple three-letter word! And in fact her statement made me consider the question more seriously than I had done.

"I love him," I said thoughtfully. "Certainly I do. But do I love him as a cousin, as a kind friend—or as a man? I don't know, Galiana."

"Then you are a fool," said Galiana. "Sometimes I wish you had never come here. Sometimes I almost . . ." And as I stared at her in shocked surprise she burst into tears. "Oh, pay no attention to me, I never mean what I say," she sobbed. "I am not in love, I must marry—"

"I know," I said, putting my arms around her. "An eldest son. You are a bigger fool than I am, Galiana, if you really believe that."

Andrea left us the next day, to visit a friend whose villa was located near Lake Como. I was sorry to see him go, and yet it was almost a relief to have him out of the way for a while. We slipped back into our old quiet ways. Thus, when the blow finally fell, it came like a thunderclap out of a smiling blue sky—that unheralded thunder that was regarded by the Romans, and their Etruscan mentors, as a sign of the gods' displeasure.

CHAPTER EIGHT

ONE BREATHLESSLY HOT afternoon a week or so after Andrea's departure, we were having tea in the drawing room. The great doors burst open and Grandfather appeared, flushed and panting, waving a paper. At first he was too out of breath to speak, and I went to take his arm. "What is it, Grandfather? Is something wrong?"

"No, no, it is good news, excellent news." He waved the paper, his face aglow. "They have caught him! At last the rascal is behind bars!"

Miss Perkins made a queer gurgling sound and rose slowly to her feet. The others stared. It was Galiana who exclaimed, "Il Falcone? I don't believe it. Who is he, then, Your Excellency?"

"Most unfortunate," Grandfather said gruffly. "One of our best families. . . . It is the Cadorna boy—Antonio."

I caught Miss Perkins' glaring eyes in time to suppress my cry of distress. But Galiana did cry out. "Antonio? . . . Is he not a friend of Andrea?"

"I am afraid it is he," said Grandfather, ignoring the last question. "Yes, a fine old family. But the wretched boy deserves his fate."

"Oh, dear," said Miss Rhoda regretfully.

The contessa frowned at her. "I too regret the shame of a respectable family," she said. "But it is deserved. Will they execute him, Your Excellency? His family's prominence will not excuse him this time?"

"No. He is to be hanged in the square at Parezzo in two days. This letter, from Captain de Merode, informs me of the facts. Quite proper of him to notify me so promptly. He invites me to witness the execution." Grandfather spoke firmly, but he avoided our eyes. "I must go, it is fitting. As you know, I own the inn in Parezzo—we will have a fine view from the front balcony. You ladies can visit the shops. You will enjoy that, eh?"

The idea that we could be bribed by a shopping expedition into witnessing such a dreadful thing made me angry. I turned away. "No, I won't go," I said, and would have said more, but Miss Perkins caught my eye.

"I think we should all go," she said.

I knew her so well by then I could understand the way her mind was working. There were good reasons why we should go. "Very well," I said.

Grandfather smiled. He took my acquiescence for obedience and was relieved. "Excellent," he cried. "I will go tell Stefano the good news."

As soon as the doors had closed after him, Miss Rhoda rose to her feet, extremely agitated. "I don't understand this," she said. "I remember that boy. He was here for a visit a few years ago, at Andrea's invitation. He cannot be the bandit they are looking for."

"No, no." Miss Perkins was pacing up and down. "No, it is a trick—a trap. They mean to execute the young man, no doubt, but they hope to catch a bigger fish with him as bait."

"Good heavens," I exclaimed. "You have it, Miss P. The Falcon—the real Falcon—will not allow his friend to be murdered!"

Galiana's face glowed with excitement. "Il Falcone will come to his rescue," she cried. "Do you suppose he will ride into the piazza on a great black horse, as he did in the village? Only think, we will have a perfect view!"

I could endure no more. I ran from the room, out of the house, into the gardens. I needed air. As clearly as if I had seen it only the day before, the face of the young man came back to me—his soft brown eyes, the bravado of the big mustaches hiding his gentle mouth.

Antonio could not be the Falcon. I myself had seen the rebel leader rip the proclamation from the church door, his sword held in his right hand. Antonio had lost that hand. De Merode must know this as well as I did. The execution *was* a trap. Honor and affection for his friend would demand the Falcon make an attempt at rescue. De Merode would take every precaution, and we, as unwilling witnesses, might have to watch not one but two brave men die.

I was pacing up and down the terrace when Andrea came in sight on the path to the stables. His dusty riding boots and his perspiring face betrayed the haste with which he had traveled. He came to me with long, angry strides. "Is it true?" he demanded. "I heard the news yesterday and came straight back. Is it true about Antonio?"

"Yes," I said miserably. "Andrea, I'm so sorry."

"Others will be sorry," said Andrea, running into the house.

I stared after him. A new, monstrous suspicion had leaped into my mind. Was it possible . . . No, I told myself; it could not be. All the same, Andrea was not the man to stand idly by while a friend went to his death. Now I had a new fear to haunt me.

WE WERE TO leave early the next morning in order to be in Parezzo in good time. Later the same afternoon I went looking for Grandfather to ask about arrangements for the trip. When I reached the library I found the door slightly ajar. I was about to enter the room when I heard a voice I had not expected to hear—Miss Rhoda's; soon I heard Grandfather's low growl, and also Stefano's voice.

"He will be killed!" This was the comment by Miss Rhoda that reduced me to eavesdropping. "So ill-advised, so reckless—"

"It was certainly ill-advised of him to rush in here bellowing threats and curses," said Stefano's dry, drawling voice. "But very characteristic of Andrea, you must agree." Andrea must have gone straight from me to Grandfather and expressed himself with his usual vigor.

"He must be prevented from going," said Miss Rhoda.

Grandfather muttered something that I could not hear, and Stefano—infuriatingly—burst into a laugh. "Don't worry about your pet, Aunt Rhoda. The prince has given instructions to two of the larger footmen. How I look forward to watching Andrea trying to kick down his door! His comments should be amusing."

"Thank God," said Miss Rhoda with a sigh.

"What are you saying?" snarled Grandfather, venting his anger on Stefano. "You will not see or hear him. You are coming with us."

"Oh, no." Stefano shook his head. "I am not sufficiently depraved to enjoy the spectacle of a former acquaintance choking his life out at the end of a rope. Besides, I am needed here. You may lock Andrea in his room, Your Excellency, but I am the only person who can keep him there. Andrea is appallingly strong when he is in a rage. He is quite capable of battering the door down."

"Hmph," Grandfather grunted. "Very well. Suit yourself."

He turned to the window and stood there, his hands clasped behind his back. Stefano looked at the tall, unyielding figure, and for a moment his face had an expression I had never seen on it before. Then he shrugged and gave his cane an expert twirl, catching it in his hand. "Your commendation and thanks touch me deeply, Your Excellency."

"I approve of your plan, Stefano," Miss Rhoda said. "I count on you to keep Andrea here. Now, I will go and pack."

As she surged majestically toward the door I picked up my skirts and fled. Considering Grandfather's mood, it would be better for me not to talk to him; but my eavesdropping had relieved one worry. Andrea would be prevented from helping his friend. Did that mean, I wondered, that the mysterious Falcon would not make an appearance?

WE REACHED PAREZZO late the following afternoon after a hot, dusty ride. Parezzo was a city of medieval walls and towers, a grim reminder of the days when only the thickness of a man's walls protected him from the avarice and cruelty of his neighbors. On a high ridge above the town was an old fortress, now a state prison and military barracks.

We passed under a great stone archway whose fourteenth-century masonry was guarded by modern soldiers. A crowd of people eddied around the gate, where the soldiers were checking papers and identities. The Tarconti arms on the side of our coach were a sufficient passport; we were waved on without delay.

The horses stopped in front of the Albergo Tarconti, a big, rambling structure of which we had the entire second floor to ourselves. A large central chamber, handsomely decorated, overlooked the piazza and had a long stone balcony running its entire length. The piazza was beautiful. Of considerable size, it was virtually walled in by buildings of at least six stories in height. The cathedral was directly across from the inn. In the center of the piazza was a handsome fountain with a statue of Neptune, trident in hand and dolphins at his feet.

On this day, however, the broad steps before the cathedral were hidden by rows of wooden seats. Most were not more than planks on temporary supports, but in the center was a sort of loggia, with luxuriously cushioned chairs shaded by a striped canopy. This loggia was situated so that its occupants would have a direct view of the gallows.

It was almost finished. Workmen were hammering at the high crossbeam from which the rope would hang. . . .

After supper, which was served in the sitting room, the nervousness that afflicted us all became increasingly apparent. Grandfather pretended to read the paper, and the contessa stitched steadily at the altar cloth she was making. But the rest of us didn't trouble to conceal our feelings. It was not quite dark outside, but soon the situation—especially the rhythmic pounding of hammers—got on my nerves. I had just determined to go to my room when the landlord came to announce a visitor. I immediately sat down again, for it was Captain de Merode.

I had never seen him more impeccably turned out. He accepted a glass of wine and sat turning the crystal goblet slowly in his hands.

"Well," barked Grandfather. "How is it going, Captain?"

"*Très bien.* A pity that the young man must die, but he seems determined to end on the gallows. This is not his first offense."

"And is he really the Falcon?" Galiana asked.

"It seems so." De Merode sipped his wine.

"You know he is not," Miss Perkins exclaimed.

De Merode glanced at her. "I don't know anything of the sort, mademoiselle. Naturally he denies it, even under the most strenuous questioning."

"You have tortured him," I burst out.

Grandfather hurled the newspaper down. "Francesca, be quiet. It is sometimes necessary. . . . Whether the boy is or is not the man in question, he is a criminal deserving death. Captain, what measures have you taken to prevent a rescue?"

"We have the prisoner in the deepest cell of the fortress," said de Merode readily, "where he is guarded day and night by a dozen men."

The contessa raised her head. "His men must know the impossibility of rescue," she remarked. "The dangerous time, surely, is when the prisoner is removed to the place of execution."

"Your intelligence is admirable, Madame la Comtesse," said de Merode. "We know that, and have taken steps. May I say," he added, turning to Grandfather, "that I am honored to see you here, Your Excellency. But I am sorry not to see Count Stefano and Count Andrea. Are they, perhaps, abroad in the town?"

Grandfather stiffened. I was certain that de Merode knew quite well where my cousins were, but he accepted the prince's palpably false explanation that they were indisposed without the flicker of an eyelash.

"What a pity," he remarked. "I had hoped that Count Andrea in particular would attend." Then de Merode drained his glass and rose, adjusting his sword. "I must take my leave. There is much to do, as you can imagine. May I bid Your Excellency good evening? Ladies. . . ."

When he was gone I felt as if some oppressive presence had left the room.

WHEN I WENT out onto the balcony the next morning, the air was already uncomfortably warm, and Galiana was complaining about the heat. "It will be an oven by noon," she grumbled. "What a silly time for an execution! I thought dawn was the traditional hour."

"The captain wants the greatest possible degree of publicity," said Miss Perkins. "He has a good eye for drama, you must agree."

The scene was certainly lively and colorful. The viewing stands on the steps of the cathedral had been decked with tapestries and cushions. In stark contrast, the gallows was draped in black cloth. The stands were as yet unoccupied; presumably these favored seats were reserved for dignitaries. The troops were already in position and formed a continuous barricade around the piazza. The poorer spectators were beginning to congregate. One would have to come early for a good view.

I felt a little faint and turned away from the piazza. The servants had prepared breakfast. I watched Galiana bite into a roll thickly smeared with preserves, and for a moment I thought I would be sick.

Miss Perkins, who was watching me, remarked, "You must eat something, Francesca," and gave her head a little sideways twitch. I went to the serving table and took a roll. After a moment she joined me.

We stood with our backs to the others. Miss Perkins glanced around; then she reached into her ample bosom and produced a scrap of paper. Pantomiming silence with her finger to her lips, she showed it to me. There was a single line of writing—emphatic, spiky handwriting, clearly disguised. "Courage," it read. "He will not die." And down in the lower right-hand corner was a tiny hieroglyphic—a bird with a hooked beak.

"What does it mean?" I whispered. "Where does it come from?"

"I found it under my door this morning," Miss Perkins replied softly. "The meaning is clear, I think."

"Yes, yes, but . . ." Hope and astonishment closed my throat. "It is kindly meant, but why should he take the trouble to reassure you? Are you—"

"No." Her gray eyes were steady; I could not doubt her. "I was about to ask you the same question."

Encouraged by the note, though utterly bewildered by its import, I forced down some bread and tea and then took my chair, determined to miss nothing. My heart was pounding so hard I thought everyone must hear it, but no one was completely calm that day. Except perhaps the contessa, dressed in her usual black, looking icy cool despite the heat.

As the sun mounted higher the gaily bedecked stands began to fill up. As I had suspected, the occupants were persons of wealth and social position. One portly gentleman had a tricorne hat as large as that of Napoleon I, and rows of medals decorated the breast of his bright blue coat. There were even a few ladies among those present, carrying ruffled parasols to protect themselves against the sun. Behind the wall of soldiers the humbler townsfolk pushed and shoved for position. The central part of the piazza was kept clear. Beyond the spire of the cathedral, on the high promontory, the stone walls of the fortress could be seen. I looked at them, thinking of the young man who lay there, in the deepest dungeon. I shuddered to think of the torments he had endured.

As the morning wore on, the hopeful mood inspired in me by the note began to fade. The piazza was swarming with soldiers, all armed to the teeth. If the Falcon was contemplating a dramatic last-second rescue from the very foot of the gallows, he must be desperately foolhardy. There was no way out of the piazza. Mounted soldiers barred the exits into the narrow streets. Even the doors of the cathedral were guarded. No, perhaps instead he would attack the party while it was on its way to the place of execution, from the fortress.

There were six soldiers at the inn door, under our balcony. Galiana, leaning over the balustrade, was exchanging remarks with them. She straightened up and said, "Ah, but the captain is a clever fellow. Last night, he moved poor Antonio in secret from the fortress to the new barracks on the east of the town. The soldiers will bring him from there to the piazza."

She returned to her conversation with the soldiers. Miss Perkins and I stared at one another in consternation. "Even if the Falcon learns of the change in plan," she exclaimed, "he will be unable to arrange an ambush. Oh, dear, this is dreadful!"

The stands were completely filled. In the central box sat the local dignitaries, wearing formal clothes and top hats. The piazza was now a solid mass of people except for the open area in the middle.

Suddenly there was a disturbance under the arch at the opening of the Via della Stellata. The soldiers in the vicinity pushed ruthlessly at the crowd, until a small space had been cleared. In the midst of it two officers were struggling with a single figure, small and slight and dressed in the long dark habit and hood of a friar. As the soldiers roughly grasped the hood it fell back, and I, like the other watchers, let out a cry of surprise. The face was that of a handsome young lady. I caught only a glimpse of it, and its expression of anguish, before the uneven struggle was quickly ended and the slender figure was borne away.

"Santa Maria," Galiana said, "it is Elisabetta Condotti, Antonio's betrothed. At least she was betrothed to him before he became a revolutionary. She is supposed to be married next month to a rich banker in Florence. How foolish it was of her to do this."

"She hoped to see him one last time," I said softly. "Perhaps even to speak to him, or touch his sleeve. . . . And he would see her, and know that she had courage enough to be with him at the end." Miss Perkins looked at me curiously but said nothing.

Just then there was a stir among the crowd across the piazza, under a lichened stone archway, where the Via di Giustizia entered the square. The soldiers there were clearing the way.

"But surely it is not time," I exclaimed, turning to Miss Perkins.

"It is twenty past eleven. That cunning devil de Merode has thought of everything," she said. Unconsciously we had both risen to our feet. So had the others. Only Grandfather sat stolidly, staring straight ahead.

The soldiers had made a path into the center of the piazza. Through it came the procession. Two horsemen led it. Then I saw de Merode, his unsheathed sword in his hand, walking immediately behind the prisoner.

Antonio's head was bare. His arms were bound behind him, and he was dragged along between two soldiers. He was a pitiful sight. From the crowd came a low, sullen sound like the rumble of far-off thunder. It died as de Merode's voice cracked out an order and fifty bayonets rose to position.

The little procession approached the steps of the gallows in a quivering silence. The sunlight was so bright it hurt my eyes. The heated air distorted objects; they seemed to shimmer and sway. . . . No! It was not an error of vision; the stands before the cathedral really were swaying. Slowly the whole massive structure folded, as if a giant invisible knife had cut straight through the center. As it collapsed a great scream went up; dust and splinters flew into the air.

Before the dust had time to settle, another sound, not human this time, rent the shaken air—the roar of an explosion. A cloud of smoke rose behind the roofs of the town in the direction of the barracks. This second catastrophe, on the heels of the first, completed the demoralization of the crowd. There was no longer a cleared space in the piazza; it was jammed with screaming, struggling bodies.

Above the din one voice rose—that of de Merode, shouting orders. By sheer force of personality he had managed to keep a few of his men under control; they stood fast around the prisoner. The point of de Merode's sword was at Antonio's breast, announcing, as clearly as words, One move at rescue and I myself will perform the execution.

The piazza began to clear as the terrified spectators fled. The place was like a battlefield, with bayonets flashing, horses plunging out of control. There was no enemy to be seen, only utter confusion. Yet the sight was terrible. Those who had not been pinned under the debris were staggering or crawling away from the scene of the disaster. One person—the military gentleman I had noticed earlier—reeled across the square clutching his head. He had lost his tricorne hat, his blue coat was torn, and the crimson streams of blood on his face must have blinded him, for he plunged straight at the condemned man and his guard. . . .

Where was the guard? The soldiers had disappeared as if blown away by a magician's spell. It must have happened very quickly, for de Merode recognized that fact at about the same time I did. A great flash of light shone as his sword moved in the sun. It was crossed by another flash—the sword of the bloodstained man in uniform, who was staggering no longer. The padding that had disguised his body flung aside, he struck the captain's point away from the prisoner's breast. Antonio fell back and was caught by a man in dark clothing, who helped him onto a horse.

The piazza was a melee of struggling bodies. For every bright crimson uniform there were several dark-clad men, some of them masked, and a dozen miniature battles were going on. The soldiers were no match for opponents obviously acting in accordance with a brilliant plan. Speed was on the side of the attackers too. The fighting began and ended within a few minutes.

However, one struggle still went on, at the very foot of the gallows. De Merode's face was contorted in a wolflike snarl; his sword struck sparks every time it moved. The other man's face was obscured by blood, but it obviously did not affect his eyesight. Every stroke was neatly parried. Now that Antonio had been saved, the Falcon's design was to keep the captain occupied while his men made good their escape. But de Merode was no mean antagonist; the two were evenly matched. Soon the soldiers would get their wits together, and it would be a hundred to one. . . .

Suddenly Miss Perkins snatched up a potted geranium plant, lifted it high above her head, and threw it. The heavy pot came crashing down into the piazza. The sound made de Merode start. He recovered almost at once, but a fraction of a second too slowly to deflect his opponent's blade, and the thrust pierced his arm with force enough to fell him. His adversary snatched the bridle of a horse that was being held for him.

But instead of mounting, the Falcon paused and surveyed the piazza with a sweeping glance. His eyes narrowed. One of the fallen bodies, dressed in rough homespun, was moving. The Falcon reached it in a series of leaps. Bending, he swept the man up and flung him across his horse. Then he mounted and turned toward the Via della Stellata.

He was almost at the archway, and safety, when de Merode rose to a sitting position. His right arm hung limp; he held a pistol in his left hand, leveled it, and fired. He must have missed at such a distance. But his shot was a signal to the others. A rattle of musket fire burst out, and I saw one of the bullets strike the back of the blue coat of the mounted man. The impact of the shot flung him forward across the horse's neck. The startled animal bolted into the Via della Stellata, followed by a dozen men.

CHAPTER NINE

WE LEFT IMMEDIATELY FOR Castello Tarconti. Grandfather was like a man possessed; he barely gave us time to pack. He asked de Merode for an escort—and was met with a curt refusal. Every man was needed.

The Falcon had escaped, but only for the moment. His horse had been found running loose, its flanks horribly streaked with drying blood. No doubt the two men it had carried had found refuge in a stable or cellar in the city. The hundreds of hiding places in the old town would all be searched, and until the search was completed the town was sealed off.

When our coach reached the stone archway leading from the town, we found it guarded by an entire detachment of soldiers. We stopped and I saw Captain de Merode. His arm was in a neat white sling and he was paler than usual; otherwise one would not have known that he was injured. Grandfather's great black stallion stood next to the captain's horse, and the two men were talking together. Finally Grandfather shrugged and de Merode came toward us, saying, "Ladies, your pardon, but I must ask you to get out of the coach."

We got out and the soldiers practically tore the coach to pieces. But the transaction took less time than one might have expected, and in a few minutes we resumed our places.

What with the heat and the jolting, the ride was physically most uncomfortable. Darkness had fallen before we reached the castle. We went straight to our rooms, exhausted.

I found Teresa waiting in my beautiful new suite. Grandfather had sent one of the footmen galloping ahead to announce our imminent arrival. He had also carried the great news. I expected that Teresa would be overflowing with questions, but I found she knew as much about the affair as I did. We were on friendly terms; I thought she trusted me and liked me. But she had been taught to hold her tongue. That night, when I tried to get her to express her reactions to the events in Parezzo, she simply shook her head, and when

I asked her point blank, "Can he escape? *È possibile?*" she shrugged.

"Well, I hope he does," I exclaimed. Teresa stared at me, her face a well-schooled blank, and I added, "I will pray for him." For a moment then I thought the girl's black eyes softened.

That night I did pray, more fervently than I had ever prayed before.

I AWOKE THE next morning feeling wretched after a night troubled by visions of a hovering bird, now soaring high with beating wings, now plummeting earthward, its once-powerful wings limp in death.

The day was one of the hottest of the summer. Teresa laid out the coolest frock I owned, a thin pale green muslin, and I tied my hair back, looping the thick waves up off my neck and binding them with dark green ribbons.

There was no one in the breakfast room when I went down. Heat and anxiety had destroyed my appetite. I asked the steward whether he had seen Miss Perkins. He said she had breakfasted and left, he did not know where. I knew it was cooler inside the house than outdoors, but I wanted air, so I went into the gardens. There was no sign of Miss Perkins in the rose garden, which was usually one of her favorite spots. Increasingly hot and disgusted, I walked along the path that led to Stefano's retreat.

The flowers were drooping and dusty; the little house was shuttered against the heat. I leaned on the gate, staring at the closed door. By that time I would have talked even to Stefano, but I was afraid to risk a brusque denial. While I stood there, the door opened and Piero came out.

I said in my careful Italian, "Is *signor il conte* within? Can I—"

"He is within, signorina. He is not well today, he rests."

"I didn't want to see him anyway," I muttered, turning away.

I went back to the rose garden, and there at last I found Miss Perkins. She had been looking for me. She was trying to look cheerful, but I noticed the worry in her eyes. "Don't tell me there is bad news," I exclaimed. "Have they—have they captured him?"

"No, a message arrived this morning indicating that he has escaped from Parezzo. But the very fact that he is known to have left the town is cause for concern. De Merode cannot have searched every nook and cranny by this time, so he must have gotten word from an informer who knows the Falcon's every move."

"I think you are being too pessimistic," I said.

"I hope so," said Miss Perkins with a groan. "Oh, Francesca, how can a wounded man, weak from loss of blood, travel fast enough to elude a merciless pursuer like de Merode? I wish there were something I could do!"

"So do I," I whispered.

"Why?" We had been pacing slowly up and down the paths between the roses. Now she stopped and turned to face me. "Is it just a girl's romantic imagination that makes you so interested in this man?"

"No. Oh, I think any woman would respond to the sheer romance of the man, but I have seen how these people suffer from poverty, ignorance, and disease. They deserve better. This man is trying to help them."

"You have grown up a great deal in the last few months," she said.

"Yes, I have," I replied, trying to smile.

"Well, we must hope for the best," said Miss Perkins, beginning to walk again. "That is all women can do—wait and hope. Such a waste! We have more strength, more ardor, than men realize."

"Some men appreciate your abilities," I said. "Andrea once told me—" And then I came to a stop, my hand at my mouth. "Miss Perkins! I have been so distressed I forgot all about Andrea. Has he been released from his room? Piero said that Stefano is in his house, so I assume—"

"Yes, he is free. He went flying off in a perfect rage, according to the servants. By then it was too late for him to reach Parezzo in time for the execution, so I don't know where he has gone."

"That is a relief. Do you know, Miss Perkins, I was silly enough . . . For a while I actually wondered if Andrea might not be the Falcon."

"Did you?" said Miss Perkins thoughtfully. "Did you, indeed?"

For the remainder of the day I haunted a seldom-used chamber near the library, from where I could hear if a messenger arrived with the latest news for Grandfather. But the morning wore on without event, and after the midday meal we all scattered to our rooms for the afternoon rest. I lay down on my bed, but the heat was so great I could not sleep. When I arose after an hour or so, the sun still beat down outside.

My beautiful rooms oppressed me. I could not help contrasting them with the mean, stifling houses in the village. I thought of the man who might even now be lying in some such foul cellar on a bed of verminous straw—feverish, perhaps dying. . . . The picture was too vivid, too painful. I snatched up my straw hat and ran from the room. I had not visited my friends in the village lately. It might distract me from my painful thoughts to see how they were getting on.

The village looked like a city of the dead. The young groom who accompanied me had to pound on the door for some time before anyone answered. Finally the door opened a crack. I could see two eyes, wide with surprise or fear, then the door opened wide and I saw Alberto, Giovanni's older brother. "Signorina?" he said slowly.

"May I come in?" I held up the basket filled with food.

Instead of moving back, Alberto came out and closed the door. He spoke urgently. I caught only a few words, but his meaning was plain. He was telling me to go back to the castle.

I stared at him, offended and hurt. He had gestured toward the horizon, and there, it was true, I could see storm clouds beginning to darken the sky. But the storm was a long way off. There was no hurry.

Suddenly there was a stifled exclamation from my groom. I turned and saw that another man had joined him. They spoke together, and the groom's face turned gray. "Signorina," he said urgently, and tried to pull me toward my horse.

"What is happening?" I demanded, more indignant than frightened.

"Momento!" Alberto ran down the steps and caught the groom's arm. Another conference ensued, and then the stranger turned to me.

"Signorina—will you come with me?"

I started. He spoke not the local dialect but pure, elegant Tuscan. His dark face had a stubble of beard, but now I realized that his fine-boned face was not that of a peasant. I hesitated. And then, some distance away, I heard sounds. Voices were raised, some in alarm, others in command.

"The soldiers who search for the Falcon," said the stranger. "Will you come, signorina?"

"Where?" I asked.

"This way." I followed him into a narrow street until he stopped before a door half hidden in a deep archway. He knocked and the door opened.

It was the dark, evil-smelling cellar of my imagining. A single candle smoked and sputtered, giving barely enough light for me to see two men. Others may have been in the shadows. My eyes went straight to the man who was lying on a bed of straw in the corner. His shirt was open and rough bandages covered his breast. His head also seemed to be swathed in bandages.

I ran across the room and dropped to my knees beside him. As I did so, one of the guards struck out the candle.

"Stupido," I said angrily. "How can I see?"

The voice of my guide spoke close to my elbow. "Signorina, our leader has lived thus far only because few of us know who he is. Not even your family could save you if the enemy thought you could identify him."

The reasoning was convincing. There was only one flaw in the argument. I already knew the Falcon's real identity. Before the light was extinguished I had seen a mark on his bared chest—the same mark I had seen once before on the chest of my cousin Andrea.

"It doesn't matter," I said. "What matters is that we must get him out of here."

"But where? No place in the village is safe now."

"The castle. I will hide him in my rooms."

"Impossible! Some of the servants are with us, others are not. You could not get him to your rooms without being seen. Besides, the castle is probably being searched by now. A troop of men, headed by de Merode himself, was seen riding in that direction."

This news shook me to the core. Was de Merode already suspicious of Andrea? But Andrea's absence would prove nothing; only the capture of the Falcon would do that, and that I must prevent at any cost.

"He can be hidden somewhere in the hills," I said with urgency. "But first we must get him out of town. If he could ride—"

"I can ride, signorina. Or run, if I must," the man on the bed whispered. I had thought him unconscious. His voice was clearly disguised, a soft hissing. He went on, "Where is your groom? Your horses?"

His men were well trained. With a minimum of speech and the utmost speed, the plan the Falcon had hinted at was carried out. I stood biting my nails while the Falcon struggled into my groom's jacket and the plumed cap that was part of the Tarconti livery. We left by a passageway into a tiny piazza nearby, where the horses were waiting.

The sky was a queer, sullen gray. The dim light was a godsend, but my companion was a grotesque sight, for the jacket was far too small for him, and the disguise would pass muster only at a distance.

"I beg you, stay with him," his friend said, helping me to mount. "He can't go far alone. If I can, I will meet you outside the town—he knows the place—but if I should be caught . . . Promise you will not leave him!"

"I promise." I turned the horse's head to follow my "groom." There was not a soul to be seen. We went at a slow walk through the winding narrow streets. Finally we came out of the village onto a plateau where the ancient walls had once stood. We were halfway down a path that had been beaten through the weeds that covered the hillside, within a few yards of a grove of trees, when a shout behind us made me turn my head.

The soldiers' crimson coats stood out against the sober gray stone of the houses on the hill. I turned back and rode on at the same deliberate pace. My hands were wet with perspiration, and my shoulders hunched in anticipation of a bullet.

No shot came, of course. They must have known who I was, and they would not dare to fire. But they would report having seen me, and if de Merode learned that his quarry had escaped the trap of the village, he might put two and two together.

I dug my heel into my horse's side and came up beside the other rider. We were on level ground now, and under the shelter of the trees. He turned his head away and I thought, He doesn't know I have recognized him. I knew he still thought of me as his little cousin, too young and irresponsible to be trusted with this deadly knowledge. I would show him that I could keep a secret.

"Sir," I said primly. His eyes flashed with amusement, but he made no reply. I persisted. "You must find a hiding place. If those men report to their officer . . ."

He pointed. "You—" The extended finger stabbed emphatically. "You go there. I—" And his hand swung around.

"No, I have no intention of leaving you."

His eyes flashed again, but not with amusement. I stood my ground, my chin raised. After a moment he shook his head, muttered something under his breath, and rode on.

We must have proceeded for ten minutes, although it seemed much longer. We twisted through narrow ravines; we scraped through the brush. If the Falcon hoped to discourage me, he did not succeed. My dress was ripped by thorns, stained by berries. Insects bit me, perspiration poured down my face, but I pressed doggedly onward. I had not forgotten my promise. The injured man must have shelter from the elements as well as from his foes. But I had no idea where it was to be found.

We were riding through a narrow canyon when a man darted out from behind a rock. He was a middle-aged peasant, his long hair grizzled and his face half concealed by a bushy beard. He reported that the soldiers were coming. The horses were now a danger, we must leave them. He would return them to the castle stables. We must proceed on foot.

"But where?" I asked, dismounting.

The answer came—from the Falcon. "The tomb," he mumbled.

I looked around. Straight ahead, where the ravine widened out, a rounded hill loomed up against the stormy sky. Now I knew where I was. The familiar-looking valley ahead was the valley of the Etruscan tombs. "Come," I said, holding out my hand to him. "Hurry."

For a long moment he did not move. Then he slid slowly off the horse's back and fell into a crumpled heap at my feet.

Behind us in the ravine a man shouted—an enemy.

"Help me," I gasped to the peasant. I seized the fallen man roughly by one arm and tugged at him, but it was not until the peasant added his strength to mine that we succeeded in raising the Falcon to his feet. With him between us, we stumbled on to the mouth of the valley of the tombs.

As we paused, gasping for breath, with the weight of the half-conscious man dragging at us, there was a rustle of movement among the weeds. Something came out—something that shone with a pallid white light. . . .

I let out a sound that was half scream, half hysterical laugh. The spectral form was one of the big white rabbits. Unafraid, it sat up on its haunches, its paws folded demurely, and stared at us with great liquid eyes.

This diabolical vision was too much for my assistant, touching a layer of superstitious terror deeper than courage. He let out a shriek and fled.

I flung both arms around the limp body of the man whose sole support I now was. By a superhuman effort he managed to keep his feet, and we staggered on until we came near the mound of the princess.

Here a new difficulty arose. I could not remember where the door was, masked as it was by shrubs. The Falcon had one arm around my shoulders; as we stood there, it weighed more and more heavily till it pressed me to the ground. He had fainted at last. I huddled there in the grass, with my arms around him, and heard voices at the entrance to the valley.

Survival was the only idea in my mind, for myself and for the man whose head rested on my breast. His uneven breathing scorched my skin through the thin muslin of my dress. A jagged spear-length of lightning streaked across the sky. The unconscious man stirred, moaning. With the strength born of panic, I pressed his face against my breast, stifling his groans. In the abnormal stillness the slightest sound carried; our pursuers might have heard him, as I was able to hear them.

Dry branches crackled underfoot as the soldiers advanced. Another flash of lightning, brighter than the last, split the darkening sky apart. In its glare I saw the door.

The last five feet to sanctuary were the worst of the whole journey. Only the fact that the soldiers were making as much noise as we made kept them from hearing us. But finally my groping hands found the hidden catch and the door swung open. Our last burst of strength tumbled the two of us over the threshold. I placed the wooden wedge as Grandfather had shown, and pulled the door back into place.

CHAPTER TEN

TIME HAD NO MEANING in the stifling darkness. It might have been an hour later, or a century, before I forced the slab open once again.

The worst of the storm had passed, but rain was still falling steadily. I waited, listening, till I was sure the soldiers had gone. Then I crept out. I was careful to be sure the catch was wedged before I pushed the slab back into place, so that it could be opened from the inside—just in case.

I had not gone twenty feet before my soaked skirts were clinging to me, making every step an effort. I knew the way back to the castle, but this was the first time I had traversed it on foot. Running water turned every slope into a stream of mud. My fragile slippers gave no traction, and my hands were soon bleeding from the branches I grasped in order to pull myself up. It was a nightmare journey, and the need for haste made it seem even longer.

How long could an injured man survive in that dank, airless chamber without food or medical aid? He was safe from capture there, but he needed help and I was the only one who could bring it.

When I reached the lowest terrace of the gardens, the rain had stopped and a single star was visible in the night sky. I stood there swaying with fatigue, staring stupidly at it. Then I saw that the castle was illuminated like a building on a festal day, every window ablaze.

By a stroke of luck the man in the shadow of a tree moved, so that I saw the shape of his soldier's cap silhouetted against the sky before he saw me. I dropped down, my heart racing. The castle had been invaded and occupied. All very suavely and courteously, no doubt; de Merode could not arouse Grandfather's open hostility. His excuse would be that he wanted to protect the inhabitants against the dangerous criminal still at large. How much did he know? I wondered. How much was only suspicion?

Avoiding the graveled paths, I crawled on hands and knees through the wet grass. I had no plan in mind, only an instinctive need to avoid capture. I was shivering violently by then with terror and cold. My teeth began to chatter. I clapped my hand over my mouth to stop the sound, but it was too late. A dark form leaped over a wall and enveloped me in a crushing embrace.

"Signorina!" The whisper came just in time to stop me from screaming.

"Piero." I clung to him, gasping for breath.

He shook me. "Where is the Falcon? Quickly, signorina, tell me!"

"In the tomb," I whispered. "The tomb of the princess."

His hands left my shoulders and I dropped panting to the ground. Piero was gone as silently as he had come. It was done now. Either I had saved the Falcon or I had betrayed him, and only time would tell which.

I WALKED STRAIGHT to the house after Piero left, and I managed to reach the terrace before anyone saw me. Then two soldiers converged on me with shouts and brandished muskets. I let out a piercing shriek and sank to the ground. The pretended faint gave me time to think. Even after I had been "restored to consciousness," I continued to sob hysterically. As a footman carried me upstairs, Miss Perkins let out a cry of horror. She told me later she had never seen a more wretched-looking creature.

She and Teresa flew into action: warm clothing, brandy, medicines. As soon as I was tucked into bed, Grandfather burst in. "My child! What happened? Can she speak?" he demanded, turning to Miss Perkins, who tried to reassure him that my injuries were superficial.

"But I must know what has happened to her!"

"I think I can talk a little," I mumbled, trying both to look exhausted and to reassure Miss Perkins, by a meaningful glance, that I knew what I was doing. I held out a trembling hand to Grandfather. "Tell Captain de Merode," I whispered. "The Falcon captured me. . . . He made me go with him—as a hostage. He released me near the quarry, on the road to Parezzo. It took me so long to get here. I was afraid. . . ." I began to sob noisily.

Grandfather squeezed my hand. Then he ran out of the room, and I heard him talking to someone outside my door.

The place I had mentioned was as far to the north of the castle as the Etruscan cemetery was to the south. I had made my story as vague as possible, but if de Merode believed me he would send his men in the wrong direction and Piero would have a chance to reach his leader.

I had flung my arm over my face to conceal the fact that my sobs were not accompanied by tears. Now I saw Galiana standing at the foot of the bed. She was attracted by excitement as a moth is by light.

"Get her out," I hissed at Miss Perkins. "I must talk to you."

As soon as we were alone I started talking. Miss Perkins listened without interrupting; only an occasional sharp intake of breath betrayed the intensity of her interest. "Did I do right to tell Piero?" I asked finally. "I couldn't think, I was too upset. . . . If I have betrayed him . . ."

"No, no. An informer would have gone straight to the captain. I have long suspected that the Falcon has allies in the castle."

"But Miss Perkins, if we are wrong . . . He is injured and alone in that dreadful place."

Miss Perkins pressed me back against the pillow as I tried to rise, exclaiming, "It would be madness to try returning to the tomb, Francesca. You will be watched, be sure of that. Try to sleep now."

After she had gone I did try to rest, but it was impossible. Whenever I closed my eyes scenes of the past hours repeated themselves. I had to move about or lose my mind. I flung the covers back, went out, and began pacing in the sitting room. But I had not walked for long when a sound stopped me in my tracks. I stared dumbfounded as the door of the big painted armoire began to swing out—and was caught by four small white fingers.

The truth dawned on me, and it roused me to tigerish action. In a single bound I reached the armoire and flung the door wide. Galiana had retreated behind a row of dresses, but I dragged her out.

"You are hurting me," she exclaimed indignantly. "Let me go, Francesca!"

"I am tempted to strangle you," I said between clenched teeth. "How long have you been hiding in the armoire? What did you hear?"

Her chin began to quiver. "I was not in the armoire all the time, Francesca," she muttered. "I was listening at the door. I knew all along you were lying—I knew there was something you hadn't told. And I was right!"

"You couldn't have heard. We were whispering."

"Yes, but Miss Perkins has quite a loud voice when she is excited. She was most excited, wasn't she, when you proposed going back to the tomb?"

My heart sank. That speech would have told her all she needed to know.

Galiana was not the most intelligent of women, but she was quick at intrigue. She must have seen the consternation in my face—a tacit admission of the truth. "You see, I do know," she said triumphantly.

Again I was faced with a terrible decision. It was impossible to convince Galiana that she was mistaken. The circumstances were too damning. Still, I had to persuade this inveterate gossip to keep silent. But how? . . . There was only one appeal I could think of that might control her tongue.

"Galiana, it is Andrea," I said. And as she stared at me wide-eyed, I caught her little hands tightly in mine. "If de Merode finds out, Andrea will be hanged, as Antonio almost was. And this time there will be no

Falcon to rescue him. It is up to us—you and me—whether he lives or dies."

Galiana's eyes seemed to fill half her face. She had gone quite pale. "You are lying," she gasped. "It can't be."

"You needn't believe me," I said. "Tell de Merode, if you wish. I can't stop you. But if you do, Andrea's blood will be on your hands."

"No, no." Her hands twisted in mine. I held them fast.

"You will swear?" I asked. "Swear to keep silent?"

"It is true?" Her eyes searched my face. "Yes, I see you are not lying now. Francesca, I would die rather than see him in danger! Is he really in that horrible place? I must go to him, I must—"

"You must stay here and act a part, as you have never acted in your life! We must convince de Merode that we know nothing."

As I watched in breathless suspense, her lips tightened and she nodded. "I understand," she said. "I promise. Francesca, you do trust me, don't you? You know how I feel about . . ."

"I trust you," I said, wishing I were as sure as I sounded. We were two women who loved Andrea Tarconti, and who shared his deadly secret.

GALIANA STAYED WITH me that night and was still asleep when I got up the next morning. When she awoke I had my hands full calming her. Her resolution was unchanged, but her nerves had weakened.

We ate breakfast in my sitting room, and I was still encouraging her when we received a summons to appear downstairs. We found the rest of the family assembled in the library. De Merode stood by the fireplace.

It was obvious that no one had slept well the night before. Stefano's eyelids were heavy, his eyes dull. Grandfather looked even worse. He was wearing riding clothes, and I wondered where he had been so early in the morning. The contessa was seated in an armchair. She stretched out her hand to Galiana as soon as we entered, and the wretched girl ran to her and hid her face in the maternal lap.

I had read somewhere that the best defense is to attack, so I turned to de Merode and exclaimed angrily, "You see how you have affected us, Captain! We are all in a state of nervous excitement. Is this a courtroom or a meeting of the famous Inquisition?"

"Be calm, my child," Grandfather said. "The captain has assured us he will not take much of our time. He wishes to ask a few questions."

"I told everything I knew last night," I said.

"This is outrageous," Miss Rhoda added angrily. When I saw her shadowed eyes and the lines in her face, I wondered how much she knew.

De Merode ignored her. "What you told us was somewhat misleading. My men scoured the area you described. They found no traces."

"I don't suppose the man would wait there for you to find him," I retorted.

"No, indeed. He must have moved very quickly, for we did find certain signs in quite the opposite direction. Bloodstains."

"Bloodstains! But the rain—"

"They were in a sheltered spot. It struck me, you see, that this terrain contains a number of excellent hiding places, in the ancient tombs. And when I learned that one of those tombs has a heavy door, which cannot be moved unless one knows the secret . . ."

"So you forced the prince to show you," I said with a calm I certainly was not feeling. "You are insulting, Captain. Only members of the family know the secret of that door."

"But, mademoiselle, you malign me. There is no such thing as a secret from the servants of a great household. These people know everything that goes on. Obviously one of them is in league with the Falcon, for we found the bloodstains within the tomb."

I had not been absolutely sure till then that Andrea had made good his escape. By a supreme effort I kept my face and voice under control. It was imperative that I hold the captain's attention. I even managed, heaven knows how, to laugh. "Human blood, of course," I said sarcastically. "How clever you are, Captain, to be sure it was not that of a poor wounded animal. Once again, I have told you all I know. So if you will excuse me—"

"One moment!" De Merode's voice cracked like a whip. "You are quite right, mademoiselle, I have no proof of anything. I have only my suspicions, and my orders, which are to capture this brigand at all costs."

He turned to Grandfather. "Your Excellency is no doubt aware that Garibaldi is on the mainland, and if he takes Naples the Papal States will be next. Victor Emmanuel threatens our northern borders. If there should be uprisings here, he will need no further excuse to invade on the pretext of restoring order. The aim of the Falcon, and men like him, is to promote rebellions. I will stop at nothing—nothing!—to prevent this. The man must be found. When he is he will be shot, no matter who he is!"

"A neat summary, Captain," Stefano drawled. "But I fail to see why you are boring us with this information. Some of us know it already, and the ladies, I fear, are not interested in politics."

"Ah, but this matter of politics may concern them closely," said de Merode. "Where is Count Andrea?"

Galiana cried out, and Miss Rhoda exclaimed, "Do you dare suggest—"

"Count Andrea is a known revolutionary," de Merode said. "He is strong enough and clever enough to play the role of the Falcon. He is a friend of Antonio—"

But now he had gone too far. Grandfather rose to his full height and spoke in a voice that quivered with suppressed fury. "I too am acquainted with Antonio Cadorna, Captain. Do you accuse me of being the Falcon? I warn you, do not try me. Now I ask you to leave my house."

"I will go, Your Excellency. But if I find that any persons in this household are involved in any way with the Falcon, not even your influence can save them." He swung on his heel with a clash of spurs and strode out of the room.

Then Miss Rhoda—Miss Rhoda of all people—began to weep. "Why did you irritate him, you wretched girl?" she sobbed, glaring at me. "He is dangerous, horribly dangerous. How could you be so stupid?"

"Be silent," Grandfather shouted. "She was right! Too long have we endured the insolence of this creature. Francesca, I should not have allowed him to speak to you as he did. And if Stefano were half a man—"

Shame stopped him before he completed this unworthy speech, but the damage had been done. Stefano's lips curled in the expression I knew so well. "It is certainly a pity Andrea was not here instead of me," he agreed suavely. "He would have challenged de Merode and been neatly killed defending an arrogant, outspoken maiden like Francesca. It would have served her right if de Merode had turned her over his knee."

Grandfather was quivering with rage. "I only regret now that I did not assist this man who calls himself the Falcon. At least *he* is a man!" He went rushing out of the room, and the others followed, all but Stefano, who remained seated, balancing his stick across his hands.

"He didn't mean it," I said. "He is frightened and angry, or he would never have said it."

"Thank you for explaining the prince to me," said Stefano. "If you expect me to be equally noble—to say that I insulted you because I was distracted by worry—I am afraid you will be disappointed. I am not at all distracted, and I had excellent reasons for speaking as I did."

"Oh, you are impossible. You have no heart, no feelings!" I also rushed out, determined not to give Stefano the satisfaction of seeing me cry.

It was a terrible day. We were like a household waiting for news from the battlefield. I tried to find Galiana, but when I knocked at the door of the suite she and her mother occupied, Bianca would not let me in. I spent the rest of the day in my room, restlessly pacing the floor like a caged animal.

Miss Perkins finally came to me late that evening and insisted that I take a sedative to make me sleep. I agreed, on condition that she would do the same. "You look terrible," I said. "What have you been doing all day?"

"Worrying. There is still no news. But that is hopeful, I think."

"I need more than hope, I need facts. What of Piero? You don't suppose de Merode has arrested him?"

"Oh, no, Piero has been at his usual duties. I tried to question him, but he pretended he did not understand my Italian."

She looked so indignant I had to laugh feebly. Then the medicine began to take effect and I thought perhaps I could sleep. Miss Perkins stayed with me that night. I was in no mood to be alone.

One can become accustomed to anything, even to constant uncertainty. Two more days passed in the same way, and our nerves began to relax. I managed to catch up with Galiana, who swore she had not spoken. Of all of us she seemed the most affected. Stefano stayed sulking in his house, Miss Rhoda reverted to her usual cold control, and Grandfather refused to discuss the subject. He had enough to worry him in the political news. Garibaldi was advancing on Naples, and the peasants in Calabria were welcoming him with open arms. In our own area, de Merode's troops were arresting every stranger on suspicion of being a Piedmontese agent—more evidence of the captain's increasing mania.

In the midst of the furor Andrea came home.

We were sitting in the drawing room after dinner and I was at the pianoforte. Stefano had joined us for the first time in several days, but he had refused to play, so in an effort to relieve the gloomy atmosphere I had gone to the instrument myself. I was stumbling through a Verdi aria when the doors burst open and Andrea entered.

While the others stared he came straight to me, scooped me up in his arms, and kissed me soundly on both cheeks. "I salute the heroine of the day! You look quite healthy and blooming, cousin, for a young lady who has faced the mighty Falcon himself!"

It was all I could do not to throw my arms around his neck, I was so relieved to see him. He was blooming and healthy-looking too; apparently his injury had been less serious than I had supposed. Aware of the others, I said primly, "Andrea, I think you had better put me down."

My smile and my sparkling eyes belied my words. I knew Andrea understood my real feelings—some of them, at any rate. He obeyed with a smile and a wink. Then he went straight to Grandfather and kissed him. The prince was too moved to do anything but return the embrace heartily. Then Andrea made the rounds, greeting the others. But Stefano put Andrea off with the point of his stick, and remarked calmly, "Your exuberance is too much for an invalid like myself. Welcome home. You missed the excitement, but I see you have heard of Francesca's adventure."

"The province is ringing with it," Andrea exclaimed. "Such wild stories! You must tell me how it really was, cousin."

He stood with feet apart and hands on hips, his blue eyes twinkling. It was almost impossible for me to reconcile this vision of manly health with the fallen hero whose helpless head had rested on my breast. . . . And at that thought I began to blush so furiously that Andrea burst out laughing.

"Ah, I have offended her modesty. Forgive me, cousin. But you *are* famous—the report of your adventures has gone even to Florence."

"Then you were in Florence?" Stefano asked drily.

Andrea's eyes shifted. "And other places. . . ."

"Andrea, I must talk to you," Grandfather said. "Come to the library.

You too, Stefano. For once," he added irritably, "I would like to have a serious discussion without a pack of women interfering."

He stalked from the room. Andrea smiled and followed. Stefano pushed himself up out of his chair and limped after them.

"Well!" said Miss Rhoda indignantly.

I WAS UNABLE to speak to Andrea alone the next day, and in fact I felt flustered and embarrassed at the very idea. He had come to mean so much to me, yet I did not know whether he shared my feelings. I longed to be with him, and at the same time I was shy with him.

There was no need for me to warn him. Grandfather had told him of de Merode's hints. According to Miss Perkins, who knew everything that went on, Andrea had responded to this news with a shout of laughter and said he only wished he could claim the credit of being the Falcon.

So matters went for the next few days. I began to feel that an explosion was imminent, but did not know how and when it would occur. De Merode was fully occupied, for the entire province was seething like a volcano. Garibaldi had entered Naples in triumph. The Falcon had been seen in Parezzo. Andrea was home one moment, gone the next. . . .

The third evening after his return was cool; there was a fire in the fireplace when we retired for music after dinner. I was at the piano. Andrea and Galiana were sitting together on a sofa in a shadowy corner. I was painfully conscious of them, and amazed at how complaisant the contessa had become over their spending so much time together.

The contessa's maid sat behind her, but by now I had become as accustomed to Bianca as the others were. Stefano was moving aimlessly around the room, something he seldom did. Finally he came to me, where I sat idly fingering the keys, my short repertoire exhausted.

"Play something," I said. "Something loud. We are all too quiet."

He played the first Chopin ballade. I have heard it many times since then, but never as Stefano played it that night. The poignant, passionate chords of the theme pulsed in the warm air. The music ended in a plunging arpeggio. For a moment Stefano sat still, his head bowed, breathing quickly.

Then he rose. "Andrea," he said, making a beckoning gesture.

Andrea looked bewildered, but he obeyed the silent command, and the two brothers walked side by side across the room toward the contessa. They looked formidable as they came on, in silence, and the contessa's eyes widened. Then Stefano stepped to one side.

"Hold her," he said. "Quickly, Andrea, don't let her move." His hand darted out and snatched some small object Bianca was holding under the folds of her skirt. The woman gave her harsh, unearthly cry, and Andrea caught her arms as she snatched at the object Stefano had taken.

"Andrea, Stefano," the contessa exclaimed. "What are you doing?"

After that first instinctive gesture, Bianca did not move. Andrea's eyes grew wide as he stared at what Stefano had. Stefano's fingers hid the lower part. I could only see a rounded thing the size of a large marble, like a tiny doll's head. A lock of flaxen hair had been glued to it and crude features painted on. A sharp shining point protruded from its forehead.

"Good heavens," Miss Perkins exclaimed. "Do some still believe they can harm an enemy that way, by abusing a doll? Stefano, what person is this image meant to represent? Let me see it."

"No." Deliberately Stefano squeezed the body of the doll until its waxen substance oozed out between his clenched fingers. Bianca's eyes focused and she drew a long, quivering breath. "You see," Stefano addressed her in Italian. "It does not work, Bianca. The one you meant to harm is still alive and well, although I have crushed the image." Turning, he flung the mangled thing straight into the fire. A white flame shot up and quickly died.

As it died, so did the expression in Bianca's face. Galiana shrieked. The contessa put her hands up to her eyes. "Take her away," she moaned. "I tried to teach her of Christ and the Blessed Virgin, and behind my back she practices the arts of the devil. Take her away, I beg."

Miss Rhoda rang the bell and one of the footmen came in. Bianca moved obediently as he put a hand on her arm and drew her away. The contessa began to weep. Galiana and Miss Rhoda had to help her to her room.

When they had gone Miss Perkins said, "Stefano, how did you know?"

"I thought there might be some basis for the servants' gossip," Stefano answered. "When I saw her clutching something in her lap . . ."

"Who was it?" I asked. "Why didn't you let us see it?"

"You are too inquisitive," Stefano snapped. "What difference does it make? The image was too crude—I couldn't tell."

I twisted my hands nervously together. "Only three people have hair of that pale blond shade. You and Andrea—and I."

CHAPTER ELEVEN

THE INCIDENT CAST A pall over the household. As if in keeping with our mood, the weather the next day continued to be cool and windy. Rain threatened all forenoon. Andrea had left early in the morning for Parezzo.

"Was that wise?" I asked Miss Perkins. "If he encounters de Merode . . ."

"He can't hide in the castle all his life," she replied.

When I went to my rooms later, the note was waiting for me on the table beside the chaise longue. "Come to the tomb at once," it read. "There is desperate danger. Tell no one. Burn this." It was signed, "Il Falcone."

Instinctively my fingers closed over the note, crumpling it. My heart was beating fast and hard. Had Andrea met the soldiers—had he been wounded again? I did not stop to think twice. I paused only long enough to burn the note and to snatch up a hat and shawl.

I could not ride. The grooms would have wanted to know where I was going. I had to go on foot, and I was panting and disheveled when I scrambled down the last slope and ran toward the tomb of the princess. Imagine my consternation when I saw that the door was open. I was sure he had fallen unconscious within, unable to close the stone. I descended the steps, calling his name. Just as I reached the bottom the door closed.

The truth struck me in a single instant; my first emotion was not fear, but anger at my stupidity. I went back up the stairs and pushed at the door as hard as I could. It did not yield. Once again I had been deliberately imprisoned—and the ledge on which the candles were kept was bare.

I sat down on the top step with my back against the stone slab that would be my tombstone. Oh, there was a faint chance that someone would look for me here when my absence was noted, but the chance was not great.

Who could hate me so much? There was no doubt in my mind that I had been the victim of a series of attempts: the falling rock in this very valley, the bullet in the garden. But last night, when Bianca had been caught with her evil little doll, I had assumed it was she who was responsible for the other attempts. Why she hated me I did not know, unless in some twisted way she considered me a rival to Galiana's happiness.

But I realized that Bianca could not be responsible for this. She could neither read nor write. She could not have manufactured the false note. The identity of the villain, the motive for wanting me out of the way . . . I formed and discarded theory after theory, for none made any sense.

This sounds as if I behaved in a cool, sensible manner. But I was not sensible, I was paralyzed with hopelessness. There was no way I could get out by myself. All I could do was wait and pray that someone would think to look for me before I perished of exposure. As the cold began to seep into my bones, I huddled in my shawl and tried to remain calm. Eventually I fell into a sort of stupor; I was in danger of toppling down the stairs. So I crawled to the bottom and settled myself on the floor.

I had to believe that rescue would arrive eventually or I could not have kept my sanity. I recited all the poems I had been forced to learn by my dear old teachers. I did mathematical problems in my head. I repeated the capitals of the countries of Europe and the list of the kings of England. In a humiliatingly short time I had exhausted my entire stock of knowledge.

And I had solved the puzzle. It was so simple, really. De Merode had told the family he suspected the Falcon had been hiding in the tomb, but only two people, other than Piero, knew that I had been there with him and that any mention of the place would fetch me as neatly as a bait catches a fish. Miss Perkins I scorned to suspect. The other person was Galiana.

The facts fit only too well. Bianca might have carried out the other acts of violence, but the poor simple-witted creature could not have planned them. And how had she learned to hate me so? From Galiana, of course; Galiana, who loved Andrea and feared my influence with him. Perhaps the girl hated me for her father's sake. And I had thought she was fond of me.

Purgatory will be no novelty to me if ever I arrive there. The timelessness must be the worst of it; time without measure, not knowing when it will end. When a slit of light appeared at the head of the stairs, I could only stare, thinking that my mind had given way altogether. Then I staggered to my feet with a cry. They had found me after all. The sharp wind from outside felt like heaven in those airless depths. It fluttered the long veil of the woman who stood on the stairs.

Yes, she wore a veil, a black veil. She also carried a dagger in her right hand. It glittered in the dusky light. No rescue, then, but another threat. Why had she come back, hiding her face with one of her mother's veils?

The veiled figure leaned forward and with a sudden movement flung the veil back. A coronet of silvery hair gleamed like a tarnished nimbus. Slowly the woman descended the stairs. I retreated from the contessa.

With a sudden lunge she came at me. Backed against the wall, I threw out my hands against the threat of the dagger and felt a rope drop over my wrists; the noose tightened. I tugged at it, not believing what was happening.

"Stand still," she said sharply. "I need you alive. I acted too soon. I thought he would take my word, but that arrogant young fool wants evidence. So you must tell me how you knew. You didn't tell Galiana the truth. You are the only one who knows—the only one who can identify the Falcon."

At that moment I knew, as clearly as if a celestial voice had announced it from heaven, that I must be cleverer, quicker, stronger, than I had ever been in my life or I would die.

The contessa tugged impatiently at the rope. I pulled back. The noose around my wrists got tighter. A slip knot—of course. I could free myself of the rope easily enough. But she was between me and the stairs.

"Come," she insisted. *"Avanti.* The captain is waiting."

"No, wait," I said. "I will tell you. But first you must tell me why you are doing this." Then a blast of air funneled down the stairwell and lifted her veil around her like great black wings. She stared at me thoughtfully. I could see her features clearly now, and what I saw made me grow cold with terror. But the fear was not only for myself.

She said softly, "Yes, there is a reason. You should have seen it long ago. He must die, you understand. The other times he escaped somehow. But this time—"

"The other times? They were not accidents, then. But I thought I was the one they were aimed at."

Her exquisite old face was distorted, not by anger but by a furious contempt. "You? I would not soil my hands on you. In a sense you are to blame for his death. If he had not come to love you, I would not have to destroy him. But he will not marry my darling girl now. So he must die. I would have spared him if Galiana . . . It is better this way, she will be the Principessa Tarconti, my darling little girl. . . ."

Her voice trailed off in a crooning travesty of maternal love, but I had heard enough to confirm my worst fears. She knew about Andrea and she meant to betray him. The knowledge that I must overcome her gave me additional strength and cunning. I spoke sharply to her. "If you don't care about me, why did you trap me here to die?"

She spoke with a chilling indifference. "The opportunity arose, and the old man will be blamed. Oh, yes, it is safe, and I will shut you in again when you have told me. My darling will marry Andrea, he loves her, he always has."

She was wandering farther and farther from sense every moment, I thought. She couldn't even remember the name of the man she wanted for her daughter. I caught the rope and pulled sharply. Off balance, she stumbled toward me. One hard jerk freed my hands, and I struck at her arm with my clenched fist. The knife fell clattering to the floor.

I thought I had won then, but I had not reckoned with the strength of the insane. In an instant the frail old woman was transformed into a raging beast who used teeth and claws as an animal might. I turned my head to protect my eyes from her gouging nails. My only hope was to run.

I reached the stairs before her—only because she stopped to pick up the knife—and scrambled up them. When I reached the top, the full force of the wind hit me. Immediately I threw myself against the door to close it. But she had had sense enough to prop it open with a stone. My frantic push jammed it. I heard her on the stairs, so I ran, stumbling over rocks and thorny bushes, holding my flying skirts out of the way of my feet.

I did not dare look back. I had to watch each step for fear of falling, so uneven was the terrain. The darkening sky, boiling with rain clouds, was a fitting backdrop for that nightmarish flight.

Yet I reached the gardens of the castle without being caught, and there, in the shadow of the pines, I paused for an instant, my hands clasped over my aching ribs. No time! She was a ways behind me but coming on—a lean, dark figure against the gray landscape.

The castle was still some distance away—across the whole length of the gardens and up a steep slope—but I was not far from Stefano's house. Stumbling, I ran till I reached his gate. My goal was the library, whose French doors opened onto the terrace.

I burst through them and then clung to one of the bookcases, panting for breath. Stefano jumped up from behind his desk. He was in his shirt sleeves. Then Miss Perkins, who had been pacing around the room, turned and saw me and let out a shriek. I realized that my appearance must be alarming—my face white and scratched, my skirt torn.

"Francesca!" Miss Perkins exclaimed. "Good heavens, child, what has happened to you? The soldiers are here again searching for the Falcon, and they seem to think—"

"I know," I interrupted. "And so does the contessa. She knows that Andrea is the Falcon. She has gone mad, I think. She tried to kill me—"

My breath gave out, but there was no need for me to continue. Through the open door burst the madwoman. Without pausing, she rushed at me, knife held high. I couldn't move. It was Stefano who came between us. She struck him with the full weight of her body and he went staggering back, trying only to hold her off, whereas she was intent on murder.

Their bodies hit the wall with such violence that a picture fell with a crash of glass. Then, picking up a bookend, Miss Perkins hit the contessa on the back of the head. She collapsed unconscious. "Your belt, Francesca," Miss Perkins exclaimed, tugging at her own. "Seconds count now. Hurry, we must tie her up and hide her before the soldiers decide to search this place."

While she bound the contessa's hands, I fastened her ankles together with my belt, and then Miss Perkins gagged her with a strip of petticoat. When we had finished she dragged the contessa out to hide her.

It struck me then that Stefano was still standing against the wall where the contessa's rush had driven him, and I thought at first that the knife must have hit him after all. His face was as white as his shirt, his eyes were closed; his hands, pressing hard against the wall, were all that kept him on his feet. As I stared, thunderstruck, his head fell forward and he slid to the floor. I was kneeling at his side before I realized that he could not have been wounded in the brief struggle. I had watched the dagger with the intense concentration of fear. Never once had it come near his body.

I knew then, even before I saw the first crimson drops stain his white shirt. It was the first time I had seen him without a hood or the disguise of conscious playacting. Without its mocking smile, his face was dignified and gentle. I opened his shirt and saw what I expected to see—folds of bandaging, reddened by the reopened wound, and the birthmark he and his brother shared.

I was still staring, frozen with shock, when Miss Perkins returned.

"Stefano," I said numbly. "It was not Andrea. It was—"

"Of course it was Stefano," Miss Perkins snapped. "How could you have thought Andrea was the Falcon? He is a charming, handsome, quick-tempered fool. It is this boy who has risked his life and fortune for his dream of freedom, and if we don't act quickly he will be made to pay the full price. There is brandy in that cabinet. Fetch it—run!" As she spoke, her stubby, efficient fingers were working at the bandages.

When I returned with the brandy, Stefano's eyes were open.

"Francesca," Miss Perkins said, "support his head while I—"

"Francesca will do nothing of the kind," Stefano said. "Get her away, Miss P. Hide her—you know the secret room—"

"The contessa is already occupying it," Miss Perkins said calmly. "Francesca, do as you are told."

So I sat down on the floor and lifted Stefano's head onto my lap. As my hands touched his disheveled fair curls I wondered how I could have been so deceived, even with an actor of Stefano's skill deliberately misleading me. I had never been able to reconcile Andrea with the man I had held in my arms. If I had ever touched Stefano, even his hand . . .

Stefano started to speak, but Miss Perkins cut him short. "Don't waste your strength arguing," she said. "If de Merode comes here, you must be on your feet and seemingly uninjured. He already suspects you. The slightest sign of weakness—"

"Nonsense," Stefano interrupted. "He suspects Andrea."

"He is not such a fool. We haven't fathomed his real intentions yet, I feel sure. The time is critical. You know that better than I do."

"The crisis is closer than you think. I got word this morning. Parezzo must rise tomorrow at dawn, and I must be there."

"You aren't fit to go," Miss Perkins said.

"I am perfectly fit. That damned woman only jarred me." Stefano rolled his eyes up so that he was glaring straight into my face. "Francesca, if you aren't out of this room in thirty seconds . . ."

"Where is she supposed to go?" Miss Perkins demanded. "Hasn't she earned your trust by now? You aren't deceiving me, you know," she added cryptically. And a wave of color flooded into Stefano's pale cheeks. I did not understand its meaning, but I was fascinated by this new display of emotion from a man I had considered without feelings.

"You are the most frightful busybody," Stefano said with a resigned air. "Help me up, Francesca, if you please. I assure you, I am not as weak as you think. No real damage was done."

He struggled to his feet, leaning without reserve on my shoulder, and this demonstration of confidence pleased me more than I can say. I helped him to his chair, and noticed that he walked without any trace of a limp.

"Was it after your accident that you got the idea of using a counterfeit infirmity to conceal the identity of the Falcon?" I asked.

"I will tell you my life history another time," Stefano said. "At the moment we have a more immediate problem. Can't you do something about her appearance, Miss P.? Or de Merode may assume she has had another tête-à-tête with the Falcon and drag her off to prison."

So I made use of a basin and ewer in another room and straightened my hair. Though the situation was fraught with peril, I was filled with an emotion that was close to happiness. I returned to the room in time to hear

Stefano say, "In the next twenty-four hours the issue will be resolved. The uprising in Parezzo has been planned to coincide with risings in other cities. The papal mercenaries will fight, naturally, but there are not enough troops to handle a dozen different rebellions at once. That is why it is imperative that all the uprisings take place on schedule. By tomorrow morning de Merode will be riding hell-for-leather toward Parezzo, and thereafter he won't have the time or energy to worry about you here."

Miss Perkins' eyes were bright with excitement and admiration.

"But, Stefano, there is still tonight," I said. "I have felt for a long time that we are underestimating the captain. What if an informer has already told him?" I looked straight into his eyes. "What would happen to the rebellion if word got out that the Falcon had been arrested and shot?"

Miss Perkins struck the desk with her big fist. "She is right! That is why de Merode is here today. He knows, I tell you, or at least he suspects. He means to trap you. But how did he find out?"

"The contessa," I said. "Oh, heavens, and it is all my fault! I told Galiana that Andrea was the Falcon. But the contessa was not deceived. I don't know how she learned the truth—"

"I think I do," Miss Perkins broke in. "But there isn't time to explain now. And even if the contessa has been in touch with de Merode, he can't act without her testimony. Perhaps we are safe after all."

Just as she arrived at this comforting conclusion, there were sounds of a disturbance outside. Stefano struggled into his coat as the door of the library burst open. A footman came stumbling in; he tried to speak, but was stopped by a savage blow from the soldier who had followed him. Other soldiers crowded through the doorway. "The captain requires your presence in the castle, Count," their leader said. "And that of the ladies."

"Was it necessary to enforce your request so violently?" Stefano inquired. It cost him an effort to speak coolly; his eyes flashed as he gazed at his servant, whose face trickled blood.

"The man attempted to keep us out," said the soldier insolently.

Stefano rose, leaning heavily on his cane. "Yes, I think I had better have a word with the captain. But the ladies—"

"The captain said everyone."

The soldiers escorted us to the castle library, where two men stood guard with naked bayonets. The castle itself had been taken like an enemy fortress, as I realized the moment I saw Grandfather. His face had a strained, pinched look, and his eyes were fixed on his younger grandson.

Andrea stood between two soldiers, who held him by the arms. His hands were bound behind his back, but his head was high, his lips were curved in a cool smile. Never had he so closely resembled his brother.

Galiana ran to me. The tears were streaming down her cheeks. "He knows," she cried. "Francesca, he knows—but I did not speak, I swear—"

I put my arms around her. "Hush, Galiana," I murmured.

De Merode turned to face us. His burning eyes passed over me and Miss Perkins and looked directly at Stefano. "This is a most distressing situation, Count," he said. "I assumed you would wish to bid your brother farewell before we take him away."

"Where are you taking him?" Stefano asked.

"Back to Parezzo. The city is supposed to rise in rebellion tonight, and Count Andrea is the leader of the revolt. How it grieves me to inform—"

"He thinks I am the Falcon," Andrea interrupted.

"How very naïve of him," Stefano said.

"I don't mind." Andrea's voice was quite calm. "Let the captain concentrate his attentions on me—it will give the Falcon his chance to act. I am honored to serve, even in so small a role as this."

"Andrea, don't be so theatrical," Stefano said. "You are giving Captain de Merode the wrong impression. Captain, you are making a mistake."

"Am I?"

For a moment no one spoke. Then Stefano shrugged. "Very well, Captain. Take my brother to prison—"

"He is not going to prison," de Merode interrupted. "I have changed my mind. The Falcon deserves death." He turned to the soldiers. "Take the count into the courtyard and ready a firing squad."

It was a strangely quiet moment. Galiana's tears had stopped. As the guards led Andrea out, she exchanged a long look with him.

Then Grandfather rose and said, "I wish to be with my grandson when he dies."

De Merode nodded. "Escort the prince," he said to the soldier who stood by Grandfather's chair.

Miss Rhoda, who had been crumpled in her seat, sat up. "I, too."

Grandfather stopped. His elbow bent, he offered his old enemy his arm. She took it. The two walked slowly toward the door, allies at last, and very touching in their grief and dignity. At the door Grandfather turned and said to de Merode, "You know, of course, Captain, that I will spend my last ounce of strength to make sure you pay for this."

De Merode bowed and Grandfather went out. Then de Merode turned to Stefano. The moment had come for which all the rest had only been preliminary maneuvering. "Well, Count? The choice is yours. Your life or that of your brother. Will you let the innocent suffer for you?"

Galiana lifted her tearstained face from my shoulder. "What does he mean? Stefano, can you save him?"

"Oh, yes," de Merode said. "If Count Stefano chooses, his brother can be freed at once. Ask him now what he has done with your mother."

"My mother?" Galiana repeated.

"She is nowhere in the castle. I have searched. Ask him if he will sacrifice your mother and your lover—his own brother—to his insane ambition. You can help me, if you will."

Then Galiana drew herself up straight and said, "I don't understand. But I trust Stefano and Francesca, and I do not trust you, Captain. You are a cruel man. I know nothing, but if I did I would not tell you."

De Merode shrugged. This interview, the threat to Andrea and the anguish of his family, was part of the captain's revenge for the humiliation he had endured at the hands of his foe. The choice he was giving Stefano was no choice. The Falcon would die in any case. If Stefano remained silent and let the execution proceed, de Merode would kill him too. But he wanted a confession to show the board of inquiry.

"Well, Count?" he repeated.

Stefano had been leaning on his cane. Now he straightened up.

"You leave me no alternative," he said, and began to remove his coat.

"Stefano," I cried, trying to free myself of Galiana's clinging arms.

"Stand back," de Merode exclaimed, pulling out his sword.

Stefano laughed. "What, are you afraid of an unarmed man and a pack of women?"

"Of these women, yes," de Merode said grimly, looking first at Miss Perkins, then to me. "Spies! The old one is a member of a secret society in London. The young one has been a thorn in my side ever since—"

He broke off with a hiss of satisfaction, his eyes riveted on the bloodstains on Stefano's shirt as Stefano tossed his coat aside. "So I was right," de Merode breathed. "That wound will be all the evidence I need when I take your body to Rome—after displaying it in Parezzo."

"Aren't you afraid your firing squad will obliterate the evidence?" Stefano asked mildly.

"Do you think I am such a fool as to let you leave this room? You have too many tricks, Count."

Without warning de Merode lunged forward, the point of his sword directed at Stefano's breast. Stefano had been expecting the move. He took one great leap backward, landing on his toes with his knees bent, as the captain's blade ripped harmlessly through his shirtfront. He tugged at his cane. It came apart, displaying a length of shining steel.

De Merode swore aloud. "A sword-stick! I should have known. It won't save you, though."

I let go of Galiana and moved forward, but Miss Perkins caught my arm. "Stay out of the way, Francesca," she said. "Lock the door."

I did so, just in time. Shouts from outside were soon followed by blows against the door. The heavy panels would hold . . . long enough, so I turned to watch the life-and-death struggle.

If Stefano had been in good physical condition, I would not have feared for him. But wounded as he was, with a weapon that was surely inferior to the captain's heavy sword . . . I felt suffocated as I watched Stefano slowly retreat, his fragile blade bending under the violent strokes of his adversary.

In actual time, the duel lasted only a few minutes. De Merode defeated himself. His rage was so extreme he forgot caution, and when he stumbled over one of Grandfather's prized Persian rugs, Stefano ran him through.

The struggle had been short but violent. Stefano turned toward the French doors and flung them open. "This way," he panted, as the library door shuddered under the blows of the soldiers. "Quickly!"

Supporting Galiana, Miss Perkins and I obeyed. As I passed the fallen body I had a last glimpse of de Merode's face—the dark eyes glazed, the white lips still set in a snarl of rage.

When we returned to the library an hour later, de Merode's body had been removed. Stefano had signaled his supporters, who included most of the servants, and the castle was in our hands. Demoralized by the death of their leader, the soldiers were easily disarmed.

I will never forget the moment when Andrea, freed of his bonds, came striding into the library. He went straight to his brother and flung his arms around him. "Why did you not tell me?" he demanded, his eyes dimmed by tears. "Couldn't you trust me, Stefano?"

"You know it was not lack of trust," Stefano replied, trying to free himself. "Andrea, I am touched by your emotion, but if you aren't careful you will finish the job de Merode began. My ribs . . ."

Then silence fell as Grandfather came into the room. The stately old man tried to kneel to ask the forgiveness of the man he had misjudged. As Stefano bent to prevent this, I realized how hard it had been for him to appear as a weakling in the eyes of the old man he loved.

But time was passing, and Stefano was not the man to be distracted from what he considered his duty. A few hours later we stood on the terrace and watched the little band ride away to Parezzo and battle. We were all very brave. Grandfather stood straight as a soldier, and we women smiled till our jaws ached. Andrea, riding beside his brother, turned and waved the torch he was carrying in a flamboyant gesture of farewell. But Stefano did not turn, and as his tall, erect figure melted in the darkness of the long avenue I knew I might be seeing him for the last time.

Everyone knows what happened after that. On September 11 the Piedmontese troops crossed the frontier. In no time Umbria was part of the new kingdom of Italy, and only a small strip of territory around Rome itself was left to the rule of Pius IX. It was another ten years before Rome succumbed and the ancient capital became the capital of the new Italy, ending a bloody struggle for freedom that had taken almost half a century.

I fear we were less concerned with this in the next weeks than we were with our own selfish concerns. Galiana was lucky; Andrea was slightly wounded in the fighting at Parezzo and was forced to stay at home after that, alternately cursing his bad fortune and basking in Galiana's adoring care. I was not so fortunate. After the garrison at Parezzo surrendered, Stefano joined the troops of Victor Emmanuel. From time to time we would receive messages, or word of him; he was fighting with the gallantry we expected and surviving, that was all we knew. The suspense was well-nigh unendurable, particularly because I had no assurance that Stefano ever devoted a moment's thought to me, while I thought of nothing else. By the time a week had passed, I was convinced he cared nothing for me. He had never demonstrated any affection; quite the contrary, he had done nothing but sneer and joke at me since I came.

The only consolation I had during those weeks was the love of those around me. Galiana and Andrea, who were awaiting only the return of Stefano to make plans for their marriage, could not do enough for me. Andrea's love comforted Galiana during her mother's illness. The contessa's mind had given way altogether, and the doctors said she would not live long. It was she who had corrupted poor Bianca.

The object of her attacks had always been Stefano. Miss Perkins and I talked over the whole affair, and the first thing I did was take her to task for deceiving me. "After all our talk of spies, you were an English spy," I said, half jokingly.

"I thought surely you would wonder how Count Andrea found me so easily," Miss Perkins said, not at all abashed. "He told you the truth when he said Stefano had planned the entire business. He sent Andrea to certain parties in London, sympathizers with the Italian cause, who recommended me. But I assure you, Francesca, that I was not in Count Stefano's confidence, not until the very end."

"But you suspected him, not Andrea. I can't see how."

"The contessa did too. We older women were not misled by dashing adventures and brave speeches. When you told me—and the contessa, through Galiana—that you had identified the Falcon as Andrea, it was obvious that you based this on some physical characteristic. But it was equally obvious that Andrea was too heedless to maintain a disguise so long and plan his campaign so carefully. Stefano, on the other hand, was a perfect candidate—his habit of seclusion, his cool intelligence, his general character. The only thing against it was his physical disability, and there were hints enough, my dear, that that was put on. When he rescued you from the tomb, for instance, I began to suspect. But it was not until after you had helped him escape from the village that I was sure. I watched Stefano after that, and it was obvious to me that he was in considerable physical distress. I went to him and demanded to be allowed to help."

"But the contessa attacked him long before that," I expostulated.

"It was logical, in a mad way," Miss Perkins said, shaking her head. "The contessa was determined to see her daughter Princess Tarconti. Until you came, she was in a fair way of bringing it off. Afterward the contessa realized that Stefano would never marry Galiana. But if he were dead . . ."

"His brother would be Prince Tarconti in time," I said. "Yes, I see. She told me that, in her ravings, but I thought her mind was confused."

"It was confused," said Miss Perkins dryly. "Yet her methods probably would have succeeded. Andrea would have married Galiana in a moment. The contessa told Bianca what she wanted and the unfortunate woman proceeded to act whenever the opportunity arose. It was Stefano at whom the rockfall and the bullet were aimed. You happened to be with him on both occasions."

Suddenly I felt my eyes flooding with tears. "I'm sorry," I muttered, turning aside. "But it has been so long since he left, and he never said . . ."

"Jumping to conclusions is another fault of yours," said Miss Perkins unsympathetically. "You have been wrong fairly consistently, Francesca, but if you still think that young man is cold and unemotional . . ."

Well, I knew he was not unemotional. What I did not know was whether he had any emotional attachment to *me.*

On the afternoon Stefano came home I was in the rose garden, and I did not know of his arrival until I looked up from my book and saw him coming down the path from the castle. His sun-bleached hair formed a striking contrast to his tanned face, which was burned as brown as that of any peasant. I wondered how I could ever have thought Andrea was handsomer than he, and how I could have taken another man for him, even for an instant.

His long stride faltered when he saw me, and he came on more slowly.

Any woman will understand why I acted as I did. For weeks I had been in agony over him, thinking he might be killed in the fighting. Now I saw him safe—and in the reaction of relief I was absolutely furious with him. So when he stood before me, hat in hand, I said casually, "How nice to see you, Stefano. I do hope you enjoyed yourself."

It was the first time I had ever seen him at a loss for words. The dark blood rushed into his cheeks. "Men do enjoy fighting," I went on. "Don't they? You don't fight from a sense of duty, you love it! While we poor women sit at home and worry ourselves—"

Stefano put an end to this tirade, which was developing rather nicely, I thought, by picking me up off the bench and lifting me till my eyes were on a level with his, my feet dangling helplessly.

"Just like a man," I said, somewhat breathlessly. "When you are losing an argument, you resort to physical violence!"

"Oh, no," Stefano said. "The physical violence is only a preliminary. This is how I counter such arguments."

He kissed me. I felt as if my bones were melting.

It took me some time to recover. When I did, we were sitting on the bench, his arm around me, my head on his shoulder. "It was very presumptuous of you to do that," I murmured. "What made you suppose I would tolerate it?"

"I wouldn't have dared if I hadn't happened to meet Miss Perkins in the hall," Stefano said frankly. "She implied in her tactful fashion that you might not be violently opposed to the idea."

"She was kinder to you than to me," I said. "For days and days I have been trying to get her to reassure me as to how you felt about me."

"If you did not know, you were one of the few who didn't. Andrea taxed me with it weeks ago. Miss Perkins read my thoughts as if my head were made of glass. Even the contessa knew. Why do you suppose she abandoned her schemes for me to marry Galiana?"

"But how could I have known?" I exclaimed. "You were horrid to me."

"As you were to me."

"I have been in love with you for a long time. I can't imagine why you didn't notice."

"With me or with that mountebank the Falcon?" Stefano turned me in the circle of his arms and looked straight into my eyes. "I hope you did not fall in love with a myth, Francesca, for that person never really existed. I cannot tell you how glad I am to be done with him at last."

"I don't believe you," I said, half in jest, half in earnest. "The role you played here was the hard one. You had a wonderful time being the Falcon, don't tell me you didn't. He is a part of you, just as the sober scholar is a part. Don't cast him off altogether."

Stefano's eyes took on a reminiscent sparkle as I spoke, but he shook his head. "I am really a very dull fellow, my darling. And you are so young. God willing, you may have me on your hands for forty or fifty years. Do you think you can endure it?"

"I don't know how I can convince you," I said helplessly.

He put his arms around me and drew me close.

"Try," he said.

Lady of Mallow

Lady of Mallow

A CONDENSATION OF THE NOVEL BY

Dorothy Eden

ILLUSTRATED BY WARREN SMITH

It should have been me,
thought Sarah Mildmay angrily as the servants of Mallow Hall lined up to meet their new master and mistress. But instead Blane's wife, Amalie, was being welcomed as the new Lady Mallow and Sarah was just arriving there as governess.
Sarah was at Mallow on dangerous business—spying on the man who had recently turned up from the West Indies claiming to be the long-lost Blane Mallow.
She and Blane's cousin Ambrose, to whom she was secretly engaged, thought him a rank imposter. Sarah hoped to prove him so, but this tall, dark-haired stranger seemed so ruthless that even a small slip might be her last.

The late Dorothy Eden was born in New Zealand and lived for many years in London. Among her best-loved novels are *The Vines of Yarrabee* and *Ravenscroft.*

CHAPTER ONE

SARAH SHIVERED AND DREW her cloak more closely about her. The summerhouse had broken panes of glass in the windows, and the wind blew through in a cold stream. It was rapidly growing dark, and already lights were blooming in the windows of the house, visible through the leafless trees.

There was Lady Malvina's window, glowing boldly, with no curtains drawn. She would be nodding in front of an enormous fire, with her capacious skirts spread about her and her cap askew. In contrast, Amalie's windows showed a mere chink between the heavy curtains. Amalie, unlike her mother-in-law, seemed nervous of the darkness outside. Her thin, anxious face was seldom relaxed, and she was constantly watching her husband. Because she loved him too much? Because she was afraid he did not feel a similar affection for her? Whatever it was, the next window, Blane's, was in darkness, for Blane's restlessness kept him constantly on the move and seldom indoors.

At the far end of the third floor the nursery window was alight, because Titus, like his mother, Amalie, disliked the dark. She must go in soon, Sarah reflected, for he would be waiting for her. He was a high-strung little boy who got into fevers of apprehension if things went wrong. And he had that ridiculous fancy about a mouse lurking in the nursery cupboard, ready to spring when the candles were out. Sarah always made sure that he had a night-light.

If James Brodie didn't come soon she couldn't wait. The household would be preparing for the ball, and her absence would soon be noticed. She would have to scramble into her gown, making an even quicker change than Blane—who spent little time dressing for any occasion.

He was an unscrupulous impostor, Sarah thought angrily. But soon, when James Brodie appeared, she would be in possession of at least one piece of indisputable proof that would enable her to unmask him:

> Dear Miss Mildmay [Brodie had written],
> On instruktions from Mr. Ambrose Mallow, who I last seed in Trinidad, I have a packet to deliver to you. If you will communikate with me at the George and tell me where I can safely hand to you the said packet, it not to be trusted to the post, I will do my best to oblige.
> Your obed'nt servant,
> James Brodie

The wind was rising and rags of thundercloud, blacker than the approaching night, drifted across the sky. Sarah looked apprehensively into the darkness, and at last heard footsteps approaching.

"Mr. Brodie?" she started to call out eagerly. But before she could, a man's voice at the door exclaimed, "Amalie! What *are* you doing here?"

It was Blane. He strode forward and seized her roughly, swinging her around. "You!" he said with deep hostility, and the hard grip of his fingers on her arm held her there.

In a moment James Brodie would arrive with the letter from Ambrose that was too private and important to be entrusted to the post. It was too much to hope that Blane would respect its privacy. Already he was deeply suspicious of her. She had cleverly improvised reasons for other awkward situations, but it seemed as if this one would defeat her. She was lost. . . .

CHAPTER TWO

IT SEEMED MONTHS NOW since that day when she had paced restlessly about Aunt Adelaide's London drawing room, waiting impatiently for news from the court. News that either declared Blane Mallow the impostor they all believed him to be or confirmed his story as true.

Aunt Adelaide had lost patience with her. "For goodness' sake, child, you're driving me mad. Can't you keep still?"

"I'm sorry, Aunt Adelaide. I'm so nervous. The outcome of the case must surely be known by now."

"And none of your fidgeting will make any difference. Come away from that window and get out your embroidery."

Sarah was peering into the street. Already the fog was making it dark; the lamplighters had begun their rounds. "There's a cab now," she cried.

The sound of horses' hoofs approached and passed. It was not Ambrose. In any case, why should she think Ambrose would instantly come to her with the news? Indeed, the jury might not come to a decision until the next day, for there had been so much conflicting evidence. Never would Sarah forget Lady Malvina in the witness box, with her arrogant nose thrust forward, the cabbage roses on her bonnet nodding to her reiterated affirmatives. Nothing would shake her evidence. The black-browed adventurer in court was her son, her long-lost son Blane Mallow.

"Lady Malvina *must* have been telling lies," Sarah burst out. "She stood in the box and swore that impostor was her son. But Ambrose says Blane never had features like that, or that impudence. He was a gentleman."

"And this man is not?"

"Decidedly not. He was laughing all the time. At his mother—if she *is* his mother—at the judge, at Ambrose, at everybody. Oh, not openly. But you could see it in his eyes. And one dimple would come into his cheek—"

"That," said Aunt Adelaide, "doesn't make him not a gentleman."

Sarah shook her head with impatience. "He may have been a gentleman of a sort. Perhaps he has been in the company of gentlemen. But Blane Mallow I am sure he is not."

Aunt Adelaide gave her niece a shrewd glance. "Could it be, my dear, that you believe this because you have every reason to be prejudiced against him?"

Sarah gave an alarmed exclamation. "Aunt! You haven't told anybody about Ambrose and me?"

"Of course I haven't. Though secret engagements aren't to my liking."

"But it's all because of this wretched Blane Mallow that it has to be a secret! You know very well Ambrose can't afford to marry me if he doesn't inherit Mallow Hall. Under any other conditions he must marry an heiress. I can't encumber him with a penniless wife if he is poor himself."

"So all in all," Aunt Adelaide reflected, "it becomes very important to you that this man is denounced."

"I wish I could do it myself!" Sarah declared.

"I believe you would if you could," said the old lady, tapping her fan thoughtfully. "You have plenty of spirit."

"Thank you, dear Aunt Adelaide," Sarah said warmly. There was a deep bond between the two women. The older woman's astringency and humor appealed to Sarah, as Sarah's somewhat daring and rash behavior did to her aunt. The girl was born ahead of her time, Aunt Adelaide thought, but little harm that would do; the present generation of simpering, swooning young women was insufferable. She never remembered this excess of false modesty in her youth. But things had begun to change when Victoria had come to the throne, and even more when she had married her stiff-necked, dreary Albert. Now everything was pretense and disguise. The very table legs were concealed. No one had bodies.

Thank heavens Sarah was too honest for all this posing. She loved and frankly wanted Ambrose Mallow, and made a secret of it only because of this tiresome litigation as to the ownership of Mallow Hall. How extremely inconvenient it had been of Blane Mallow to arrive home after an absence of twenty years. It was so inconvenient as to be highly suspicious.

No one entirely believed he had come because of seeing the advertisements for him that had been printed in newspapers all over the globe. He couldn't have become conscience-stricken about his widowed mother. He was not the man, popular opinion declared, to have a conscience. On the other hand, he was definitely the type of man to be a seeker after easy reward. There was arrogance and confidence in every inch of him. But Lady Malvina's son? Heads were shaken skeptically.

The paradox was that Lady Malvina had identified him unhesitatingly and had swept aside his strange lapses of memory. As added proof, there was the little boy, Titus, the five-year-old child of this assumed impostor. The child was the living image of the very good portrait painted thirty years ago of Blane Mallow at the same age. In the light of this evidence of the return of the rightful heir, it seemed that Ambrose would lose Mallow Hall and poor Sarah would lose Ambrose.

"Did anybody recognize you in court?" Aunt Adelaide went on, eyeing Sarah sharply.

"Oh good gracious, no! I stayed at the back and wore my gray cloak, with the high collar drawn across my face. Even Ambrose didn't know I was there." She began to giggle. "I expect I was thought to be an unknown admirer of the claimant."

"I believe you enjoyed yourself, you shameless girl!"

"Indeed I should have if it hadn't been a matter touching myself so deeply. It was a most novel experience. And the wife, Aunt Adelaide! I wish you could have seen her, the deceitful thing. When the judge asked questions, it was all meekness. 'Yes, my lord.' 'No, my lord.' The wife is as guilty as he."

"If he is guilty."

"Oh, he is! There were so many questions he couldn't answer, obvious ones. They were excused because he once fell from his horse and had a bad concussion, giving him amnesia. But it was a too-convenient excuse. If it was not for his mother, who isn't to be swayed, he would have been in trouble long ago."

"And the child," Aunt Adelaide added.

Sarah frowned. "Yes. There is the child. It's strange about the child."

A LITTLE LATER Ambrose arrived. Flinging off his cloak, he came into Aunt Adelaide's drawing room. One look at his face told Sarah his news.

"He's won!" she whispered.

"Yes, he's won." Ambrose made belated greetings to Sarah's aunt, then threw himself angrily into a chair. In contrast to his cousin Blane, he was fair, with rather pale, thickly lashed eyes and a slight stature. He was fashionably dressed and had an elegance that Sarah found intensely pleasing. He belonged at Mallow Hall and would have been an ideal master. His life for the last ten years, when it seemed that Blane was surely dead, had been shaped to that end. True, he had continued his studies and become a lawyer, but only because he was an earnest young man with few frivolities. Indeed, falling in love with Sarah had so far been his only frivolity. Now it seemed that if he wished to live in suitable style, he must sacrifice Sarah and find a wife with money. It was an impossible position, and he was bitterly angry about it, doubly so because he was convinced that this fellow from the West Indies was an impostor. But how to unmask him?

"It was my aunt, Lady Malvina, who finally swayed the jury," he said. "She absolutely stuck to her story that this man is her son."

"She wanted him to be," Sarah said indignantly.

"Exactly. Now she can live at Mallow Hall and all her debts will be paid. She knows it would have been quite different if I—and you, my dear Sarah—had been the new owners."

"No one knows about me," Sarah said quickly. "You aren't bound to consider me." She went on, making herself speak the painful words. "I set you free, if you wish it."

"But I don't wish it, my love."

"You must marry an heiress," Sarah told Ambrose earnestly. "It's the only way. And I must make some sort of a future for myself."

"With me," said Ambrose firmly.

Sarah's face began to light up. Then sadly she turned away. "No, that can't be. There's no way."

"Yes, there's no way," Aunt Adelaide agreed. "Unless you're both content to live in obscurity—which neither of you would be. Ambrose has lived for years in the belief of inheriting a fortune. And you, Sarah, are not meek or self-sacrificing. You're strong-willed."

Ambrose appeared to be detached, looking into the distance, his eyes narrowed and thoughtful. He was so handsome, Sarah thought with a pang. A little austere, perhaps, but with all the signs of good breeding.

"There is a way out of this trouble," he said. "But you, Sarah," his eyes suddenly took her off guard by their intensity, "will have to help me."

"What can I do?"

"You can help prove this man an impostor."

"Why, nothing would give me greater satisfaction. But the judge and jury have made their decision."

"They've made it because of the weight of evidence this scoundrel has had months, perhaps years, to prepare. But there are too many things he forgets and conveniently attributes to his amnesia. My aunt Malvina helped him over the worst patches. So did the head groom, Soames, whom I never did trust. Can you explain Blane forgetting the day I locked him in one of the attic rooms? I left him there until long after dark and he came out as white as a sheet. It was the first time I'd seen him frightened."

"Why was he frightened?" Sarah asked.

"Because that was the room where, a long time ago, a maidservant named Bella hanged herself. They say that room has been haunted since."

Sarah had a brief recollection of the tall, black-haired man standing so straight and arrogant in the courtoom. Had those piercing black eyes ever held fear? She had a moment of complete incredulity that this could have been so. "Why did you do that to your cousin?" she inquired.

"The question doesn't seem to be why Ambrose did this curious thing to his cousin," said Aunt Adelaide, "but why his cousin shouldn't remember it. Did he flatly deny it had happened, Ambrose?"

"He cleverly evaded the question, saying that so many extraordinary things had happened to him since, a few hours in a presumably haunted room were trifling. But just for a moment he looked quite blank. Also, there were the names of servants he couldn't remember, classmates, the master who taught him Latin . . ."

"On the other hand," said Aunt Adelaide dryly, "he could describe Mallow Hall to the last detail."

"Oh, Lady Malvina could have coached him on that. He must have had other accomplices besides. The task ahead of us now, Sarah, is to unmask these people, to build up evidence—to succeed where the prosecuting counsel failed. Someone who lives with them must watch them day by day to catch them out in small things."

"And who is to carry out this extraordinary task?" inquired Aunt Adelaide. "Are you going to bribe the butler, or one of the maids?"

"One of the maids, yes. In other words, you, my dear Sarah."

"Me!" exclaimed Sarah in astonishment. "Spy?"

"It would be very simple. I know already that they want help with the little boy. The family intends to move down to Mallow Hall almost immediately. They think the country air will be better for the child, who isn't strong. Since he's too young for school, he's to have a governess. So that's how the idea came to me."

"That I should go?" cried Sarah. "But how am I to find out anything if they know of my connection with you? They'll be doubly on their guard."

"But they won't know of it, since we've kept our attachment a secret."

"She's been visiting the court every afternoon," Aunt Adelaide put in. "Mightn't she be recognized?"

"Sarah, you fool!" Ambrose exclaimed.

"But I would never be recognized. I was at the back among all those gaping people, and I kept the collar of my cloak around my face."

"But what on earth made you go there?"

"Because it was my future at stake as well as yours."

Ambrose's voice grew softer. "It was, of course. Though you could have trusted me to report the proceedings to you."

"I wanted to watch those people. They fascinated me in a repellent kind of way. They lied so smoothly."

"Then you didn't believe them?"

"Of course I didn't. Not even your aunt, Lady Malvina."

"She prefers a stranger at Mallow," Ambrose said bitterly. "She's always disliked me."

"She talks a great deal," Sarah said thoughtfully. "One could encourage her in that. Sooner or later she must say something significant."

"That's exactly what I mean. If you were in the house day after day, you must discover things."

"All this plotting isn't quite seemly," said Aunt Adelaide.

"Ah, Aunt, hush! I believe Ambrose is right." Sarah was growing enthusiastic. Since her father had died and left Sarah and her mother and sisters so poverty-stricken, life had seemed without zest. Then she had fallen in love with Ambrose, only to find that brilliant future also taken away from her, and her prospects once again bleak. This would be stimulating and perhaps a little dangerous. She would be able to pit her wits against that black-browed impostor, his sallow-faced wife and the garrulous Lady Malvina. Yes, Ambrose's idea was brilliant.

"Then you've recommended me to the new Lord Mallow?" she asked.

"Oh no, I've not been as indiscreet as that. You must appear to be a complete stranger. You know of the family only by reading about this celebrated case. You have taken a great interest in its outcome and congratulate them on its success. Knowing their child is five years old, you are sure they will be requiring a governess. The rest, Sarah, is up to you."

Sarah's aunt expressed shocked disapproval. "And what, Ambrose, may I ask, will you be doing while my niece belittles herself in this way?"

"I, dear Lady Adelaide, will be on my way to the Caribbean."

"But a deputation has already been there!" Sarah exclaimed.

"I'm aware of that. And I admit they discovered some superficial evidence. But this investigation requires a more dedicated interest."

"None of the cross-examination could shake Thomas Whitehouse's evidence," Sarah pointed out.

"Exactly. Yet this same Thomas Whitehouse has been remarkably elusive. Today, when I thought I had tracked him down, I found he had just sailed for Trinidad, no doubt with a fat fee in his pocket."

"Ambrose, you mean his evidence has been false? That he has not known Blane since he arrived as a boy in the West Indies twenty years ago?"

"I promise you I'll run him to earth in his own country. And not only that. I'll discover other evidence. There are things I mean to search for. Blane Mallow's tombstone, for instance."

"Heavens!" gasped Aunt Adelaide. "Do you think he's dead?"

"He could be. I don't know."

"But there's the little boy's extraordinary likeness to that portrait," Sarah said. "Everyone agreed on that."

For the first time Ambrose showed uncertainty. "I admit it's the strongest piece of evidence they have. But there must be an explanation, and I intend to find it. With your help, Sarah."

"I have no references," Sarah said. "No one is employed by respectable families without references."

"I won't comment on that word respectable," Ambrose said in a scathing voice. "But I'm sure your aunt will be happy to give you a reference."

"A forgery!" exclaimed Aunt Adelaide, scandalized.

"Is it a forgery to say that Miss Mildmay has been with you for the last eighteen months and is of the most pleasant disposition? Of course it isn't. Come, Sarah. Kiss me, and tell me that you're with me."

Sarah hesitated the merest second. Then she went happily to receive the brush of his lips on her cheek. It was such a little kiss. And there would be months, and the seas of the Caribbean, between them before she could be kissed properly, as a husband kisses his wife.

CHAPTER THREE

Outside the house in the fashionable area of South Kensington, another carriage drew up. It was dark now, and Lady Malvina, peering through the heavy curtains, could not see who alighted. It must be Blane. What a fine figure of a man he had become. Tall, handsome, a little swashbuckling. So different from his cousin, that disapproving dandy Ambrose.

She would never forget the moment when the news had been brought up to her that her long-lost son was waiting to see her. She had gone downstairs in the greatest trepidation, for she had almost completely forgotten what her wild young son had looked like twenty years ago. But when she set eyes on the little group waiting in the hall, she knew.

For there was the little boy.

Lady Malvina had taken a perfunctory look at the dark, slender young woman in the unsuitable, too-thin traveling cloak and spared not much more than a glance at the tall man at her side because the little dark-haired boy clutching his mother's hand was her baby all over again.

"Oh, my little darling! Come to me!" she exclaimed, reaching out her arms. The child shrank back. Lady Malvina did not realize what an alarming figure she must have made with her protuberant pale blue eyes and large, haughty nose, swooping down like this in a voluminous dark purple gown, her lace cap nodding on a tower of stiff gray curls.

"His name's Titus," said the man. "Have you nothing to say to me, Mama?"

"Titus!" she said happily. "You named him for his grandfather."

The boy cast a swift, unhappy glance at his mother. She quickly drew him to her, partially concealing his face in her skirts. "My husband decided on his name, ma'am," she said. "I confess I thought it an odd name for a little boy. But then my husband has talked incessantly about everything English for so long."

"Mama," said the tall dark man, "this is my wife, Amalie. Or, should I say"—he hesitated for a moment—"the new Lady Mallow."

An expression of triumph passed fleetingly over the young woman's face. Then her eyelids dropped and she curtsied demurely. Lady Malvina decided at once that she did not like her. A sly, ambitious miss. What was her background? Where had Blane picked her up?

Blane? At last, in her state of bemused excitement, she looked fully into the features of the tall man beside her.

Brilliant dark eyes, magnificent black brows, a nose as arrogant as her own, an expression of inscrutability and—could it be?—amusement. Skin burned dark with sea winds or tropical suns, a spare, strong body with a lazy grace. Was this the hot-tempered boy who had quarreled so violently with his father and run off to sea? She was too confused to decide, or to care about making a correct decision. She only knew she most urgently wanted her son home.

Everyone had said for years that Blane must be dead. His father had reiterated it with gloomy anger until the day of his own death a year ago. The legal machinery had been set in motion then to have Blane declared dead so that cold, ambitious Ambrose Mallow could inherit. Lady Malvina, for various reasons, had stubbornly refused to admit that this must happen. And now, like an answer from heaven, this handsome black-browed stranger stood in front of her.

Why should she hesitate to acknowledge him?

"Blane! My dearest son!" she cried. "Welcome home!"

Later, of course, there had been endless questions, for the trustees of the estate demanded proof that this man was indeed Blane Mallow. The small scar beneath his left ear, acquired after a fall from his horse, was not sufficient. Anyone, they said dourly, could have a scar. And against this were the man's random lapses of memory—his curious amnesia.

The trustees considered the estate too valuable for a decision to be lightly given. A claim had to be made and heard in court, a deputation sent to the West Indies and evidence sought there. For the purposes of the child Titus' succession, proof of the marriage to Amalie had to be produced. It all took time, and Lady Malvina was beside herself with impatience. Why couldn't they all go down to Mallow and live normally? This was her son and grandson. Surely that she should say so was sufficient.

The marriage to Amalie had taken place in a small Anglican church in Trinidad, and this was duly proved. Amalie was the daughter of a sea captain and a young Spanish woman. She was not all one would have desired, but she had a certain brittle handsomeness, and a wish, so far at least, to be the kind of English wife Lady Malvina would approve of. And her crowning achievement was producing the next heir to Mallow Hall, the little boy who was the image of his father as a child.

Now, peering out into the foggy gloom, Lady Malvina saw the tall figure of the man she had, for the past few months, been calling her son. Wheezing a little as her heart palpitated with excitement, she hurried to ring the bell. When the maid appeared she said eagerly, "Tell Lord Mallow I would like to see him at once."

Presently the young man strode in. "Well, Mama, thanks to you we won." He stood in front of her fireplace, tall, confident, full of triumph. If he was not her son, she thought confusedly, she would dearly like to have such a son. He made all his contemporaries look languid and anemic.

She was equal to the moment. For she too had her triumph. Now she could return to Mallow Hall. How soon, she wondered, could she tactfully request her son to pay her debts?

"Blane, my dear, I'm so happy! Not that I doubted for a moment. Truth must be acknowledged."

"It can also be twisted. My cousin Ambrose would have liked to do that."

"With his crafty legal mind! Have you told your wife?"

"Not yet."

"But you must. Bring her up here. We must have a celebration. Ask Tomkins to put some champagne on ice. We might give Titus a glass. It wouldn't hurt the child."

"No, it wouldn't, and he shares the celebration. After all, he's the heir."

Lady Malvina put her head to one side, studying Blane's splendid figure. He must have all the young women swooning. "Do you remember Maria?" she asked suddenly, at random.

"Maria?"

"The gamekeeper's daughter. With the fair curls."

She saw he did not remember. His eyes had gone blank.

"Although you were only fourteen, you wanted to marry her," she said slowly. "You loved her deeply, you said."

"Mama, if I remembered all the girls I've imagined myself in love with—"

She shook her head stubbornly. "One usually remembers the first. But it was before your accident. . . . Now, go and get Amalie."

He turned to obey, and had reached the door before she called to him.

He paused, standing there in the richly appointed room that had been built exactly to her late husband's requirements, with Italian marble for the fireplace, a gilded ceiling and woodwork of the finest mahogany. "What is it, Mama? You wanted to ask me something?"

"Are you—" Her voice was thick and uneasy. "Tell me, are you really my son?"

He came to kneel before her. He offered his face to the full glow of the gaslight. The nose was her own, surely . . . The boy she remembered had had dark eyes, but had they been of such intense, brilliant darkness as these? Had that unformed sixteen-year-old face given promise of this bony, splendid structure? It was absurd that a woman should bear a child in the greatest agony and then live to be unsure of his identity.

But if this was not Blane, who was it? And what did he want? A shiver of fear went over her. "We need a celebration," she said abruptly. "Titus must come, even if he's been put to bed. His grandmother needs him."

The man straightened slowly, then stooped to print a kiss on Lady Malvina's hot and fretted brow. "Thank you, Mama," he said gently, and left the room.

CHAPTER FOUR

SARAH DRESSED WITH THE greatest of care. She had to look like a gentlewoman, though an impoverished one. That was not difficult, for she had not had a new gown for two years, just before Papa had died. He had come back from Saint-Tropez in fine fettle, an infallible sign that he had been lucky at the tables. She and her sisters had been permitted to get new gowns, and Mama had had the drawing room done in a deep maroon wallpaper with a rich gilt design. But within a month Papa was dead of a chill, and they were all in mourning. And there was almost no money left.

The two eldest girls, Amelia and Charlotte, had gotten positions as companions to rich elderly ladies, and Sarah had been taken under Aunt Adelaide's wing. Aunt Adelaide had thought to find her a husband, but Sarah, after being annoyingly persnickety about several suitable young men, had chosen to fall in love with Ambrose Mallow, who was now as impecunious as herself.

It wasn't fair! Sarah told herself. The very thought of this turn of luck that had snatched away her and Ambrose's happy future made the color deepen indignantly in her cheeks.

She must remain calm. She could not present herself to the new Lady Mallow looking flushed and irresponsible. She must remember to keep her eyes lowered, and not to answer her ladyship as if she were an equal. Not only an equal, she thought indignantly, but a superior. For who was this woman straight from the West Indies? And that was where she would go back to very shortly, Sarah told herself vigorously.

Excitement made her impatient to hurry with her dressing and set out on the way. To make her unbidden visit even more plausible, she had cut out the newspaper gossip column reporting the result of the trial and slipped it into her reticule. It could be produced if the genuineness of her application was doubted.

"Lord Mallow," the piece informed her, "intends to travel to Mallow Hall, on the Kentish coast, early in the week. He says he is looking forward with greatest pleasure to displaying his childhood home to his wife and to his heir, Titus. Lord Mallow has not yet made plans for the education of his son, who is still too young for preparatory school. It seems likely a governess will be employed."

Sarah brushed her hair back and arranged it in a cluster of curls, displaying her ears and the line of her cheek. This made her look a little older and more responsible, she thought. Her face, so serious now in the little mirror on the dressing table, had no great beauty. Aunt Adelaide had told her her charm lay in animation, but added that her eyes, wide apart and of a curious smoky blue, were most distinctive. A little less color in her cheeks might have been desirable, as it was more fashionable to be pale.

From her modest wardrobe she took her bottle-green merino day dress, and wore over it the gray felt cloak trimmed with black velvet that could not be more suitable and discreet. Her black velvet bonnet with green silk ribbons completed this picture of respectability. She looked at her reflection and sighed. She dearly loved pretty clothes. The prospect of several months of this drabness was infinitely depressing.

She was putting on her gloves when Aunt Adelaide bustled in to say that Ambrose was downstairs. "He means to see that you carry out this mad scheme," she said. "I think you've both lost your senses."

"Don't you approve of our fighting for our rights?"

"Not in an underhand way."

"But we must use our enemy's own weapons."

Aunt Adelaide sighed deeply. "Then here's one of them. The reference I've perjured myself to write for you."

Ambrose was waiting, full of excitement. He had been down to the docks and contacted the captain of a schooner to sail in two days' time for Trinidad. The captain promised him a journey that might be dull and uneventful, or full of the drama of hurricanes, or even attack by pirates.

"But Ambrose!" Sarah cried in alarm. "Is there danger? What use will Mallow Hall or a title be to you if you lie at the bottom of the ocean?"

Ambrose laughed, gratified by her dismay. "The fellow was only showing off. Of course there's no danger. Or what there is, if Blane could face it at sixteen"—his face hardened—"I can do the same at twenty-six."

"You're to sail so soon!"

Ambrose tilted her chin. "You yourself will soon be on your way to Mallow. Tell me, are *you* ready? You haven't lost courage?"

"Only for you, and the thought of those hurricanes."

"Would you like me to come part of the way with you in the cab?"

"No. I shall go alone."

"Remember, you must succeed," he said with a stony look in his eyes.

Sarah met his gaze levelly and straightened her shoulders. "I won't fail."

THE MORNING FOG had lifted, but only to show a low gray sky and the still shapes of trees to which the tattered leaves still clung. It was very cold for the end of October. The cab jogged across London, skirting Hyde Park and then proceeding down the Brompton Road. It was a long journey, and the driver was glad enough to wait outside the house in South Kensington to rest his horse. Sarah said she would not be more than fifteen minutes.

The cabbie was quite ready to trust the vivid face lifted to him. Despite her sober clothes, his passenger had the voice of a lady, and she smiled at him. She knew that he had a miserably chilly job in winter sitting up there, and that his bones got aches just as well as finer people's. Her warm smile told him all that. "I'll wait, miss. God bless yer."

This comforting voice kept Sarah's courage high as she walked up the steps. But when the front door swung open in response to her ring and the solemn-faced butler asked her her business, panic filled her.

She raised herself to her full height. "I should like to see Lady Mallow," she said firmly.

The butler stood aside for her to enter. "Take a seat, if you please. I will inquire if her ladyship is available. What is the name, please?"

"Miss Sarah Mildmay."

The butler bowed and withdrew. Sarah had scarcely time to look around the hall with its fine marble staircase, its tapestries and statuary, before there was a commotion. A little boy dressed in outdoor clothes was running down the stairs, pursued by a stout, untidy old woman with flying gray curls and lace cap askew.

"The great grizzly is catching you! *G-r-r-r! G-r-r-r!* Run for your life. Or he'll hug and hug you to death!"

The child flung himself into the arms of a nursemaid, who had come running down the stairs in their wake, and the old woman collapsed, panting, into the nearest chair.

"Well, Titus! Wasn't that a fine game? Don't you love to play with your grandmama? Now, off for your walk with Annie."

As they departed Lady Malvina fanned her face vigorously. She looked up and suddenly saw Sarah. "Who are you?"

Sarah bowed. "I'm waiting to see Lady Mallow."

The old lady's prominent pale blue eyes flicked knowledgeably over Sarah's sober and genteel appearance. "If you're wanting something, I warn you my daughter-in-law has a sharp tongue in the mornings. And she's been besieged by all sorts of people since the case. You know of the case, of course?"

"Yes, my lady."

Lady Malvina nodded contentedly. She was obviously ready to talk to anyone who would listen. "It's brought me great happiness. My son and grandson home again. But they're spoiling the child. Not my son, but my daughter-in-law, Amalie." She looked at Sarah in a friendly way. "Would you like a word of advice, my dear?"

"Thank you, my lady."

"Flatter her if you want something. That's the only way."

The butler had returned silently. "Her ladyship will see you upstairs in the morning room. Come this way, if you please."

Lady Malvina gave a flippant wave of a fat, beringed hand. Sarah resisted an impulse to wave back. She sensed in Lady Malvina an ally, if an irresponsible and unpredictable one, and followed the butler reluctantly.

"Flatter her," the old lady had said. Already prejudiced against the unknown Amalie, this thought filled Sarah with repugnance.

The butler opened a door and ushered Sarah into a room where a woman was sitting on a couch beside the fire. She was, Sarah saw at once, very elegant. Her gown was obviously new and too rich for morning wear; her hair was done in an elaborate arrangement of curls. No doubt it was her chief pride, for her face and figure were a little too thin, and her skin sallow. Her eyes were bright and restless.

The woman rose to her feet. "Yes, Miss Mildmay?" she said frigidly. "You wished to see me? What society is it you represent?"

"None at all, Lady Mallow. I'm sorry if I gave you that impression."

"Oh, it's only because I've been so bothered by representatives for various charities. As soon as one's name becomes prominent, one seems to represent easy game for all these people. What is your business, then?"

"I'm seeking a position," Sarah said, trying to sound meek.

"Here? In my house?"

Sarah opened her reticule and took out the newspaper clipping. "It says here that you might be requiring a governess for your son. I have excellent references—"

The woman cut her short with an angry gesture. "Really, Miss Mildmay, this is the greatest impertinence. In the first place, why didn't you come to the servants' entrance?"

Sarah flushed. "In England, Lady Mallow, a governess is considered one of the family."

Now she had said the wrong thing, she realized. Her quick indignation and lack of subservience were going to be her downfall.

"I don't require to be told what is the custom in England," Lady Mallow said icily. "Certainly not by a stranger."

"I didn't mean to do that, Lady Mallow." But the hasty meekness and downcast eyes were too late.

"Whatever your newspaper tells you, Miss Mildmay, I am not looking for a governess. Even if I were, I assure you that someone who had gained entry by false pretenses would have no hope of getting the position."

"Won't you look at my references, Lady Mallow?"

"Importuning me will get you nowhere." She pressed a bell. When the butler appeared she said, "Tomkins, show this—lady—out."

Quite apart from having to go home and tell Ambrose she had failed, Sarah had to tolerate being spoken to like that by an upstart from the West Indies who was only learning to be a lady. Sarah felt fury and a wild disappointment. She was almost in tears.

As she followed the butler into the downstairs hall there was a commotion. The front door burst open, and the nursemaid came in with the child. The little boy was not crying, but tears were not far off. Indeed, positive panic showed in his face as Lady Malvina pounced forward with loud cries of surprise and greeting. "What is it, Annie? Why are you back so soon? My little love, couldn't you bear to be away from Grandmama?"

"It's not that, my lady. It's too much champagne last night," Annie said bluntly, her voice full of bold disapproval.

"The little he had couldn't have hurt a fly!"

"He's feeling poorly, my lady. I'm taking him up to bed."

"Tch, tch, tch!" Lady Malvina exclaimed loudly. "Come to Grandmama, then!" But as she stretched out her arms to engulf the boy he panicked completely and, making an unexpected dart sideways, flung himself against Sarah, clinging to her skirts.

As his large dark eyes were lifted to hers she saw them full of entreaty. Sarah could not help herself. She lifted him into her arms, and he clung to her as to a refuge.

Lady Malvina came bustling up, waving her fan wildly. "Titus, you naughty little love, come to Grandmama."

Titus buried his face tightly against Sarah's neck and muttered desperately, "I won't!"

"I think," Sarah said, trying to be tactful, "you frighten him a little."

"Frighten him! Frighten my own grandson! What wicked nonsense! Tomkins, who is this young woman?"

Before Tomkins could reply, a door at the end of the hall opened and the tall dark man whom Sarah had last seen in the witness box in court came striding out. "What's going on here? What's the reason for all this noise?"

"Annie has the impertinence to say that too much champagne has made the boy ill," Lady Malvina said indignantly.

Sarah, feeling the little body clinging to her, calmly interjected, "If you have been giving a child of five champagne, I agree entirely with Annie. No wonder he's ill."

"And what the devil do you think you're doing?" the man asked.

"I'm comforting your son, who seems to need it."

"Well, I'll be damned! And who are you?"

Sarah did not flinch from his regard. Now at last she could see the face that hitherto had been at the other side of a badly lit courtroom. In selfishness and conceit it was all she had expected, and more. The haughty black brows, the moody eyes, the thin cheeks with lines showing signs of intolerance and an exceptionally strong will. But, holding his gaze, something stirred in Sarah, something jubilant and excited. For she recognized an adversary worthy of her. This man she could both admire and hate.

She said calmly, "My name is Sarah Mildmay. I've just been asking your wife, Lord Mallow, if I could be given the position of governess to your son. Unfortunately, she said you didn't intend engaging anyone at present. If I may express my opinion, your son is at an age where he requires more instruction than any nursemaid, no matter how capable"—she flashed a placating glance at Annie—"can give."

Blane Mallow (as she must consider him until she proved that that was not his name) stepped back a pace to regard her. "And why, may I ask, have you my son in your arms? Are you attempting to gain his affections?"

"No, he ran to me."

"Yes, he did that," Lady Malvina admitted fairly. "For some reason he flew to this young woman."

"I've told you to behave more quietly with him, Mama. He's not a strong child. What do you think?"

Sarah realized that the abrupt question had been directed to her. She felt the little boy's arms tighten around her neck. His heart was beating against her breast like a bird's. Unconsciously her voice softened. "Yes, he is too nervous. He needs gentleness. And time to become accustomed to such different surroundings, of course."

"Ha! You've been reading the case."

"Who hasn't?" said Sarah calmly. "Indeed, that's what brought me here. I've followed it with such interest. And when the newspaper reported that you might require a governess, I took the liberty of calling."

"But my wife would have none of you?"

Lord Mallow's mouth seemed to be twitching slightly. Sarah couldn't decide whether it was in amusement or anger.

"I was perhaps too impetuous."

"You have recommendations?"

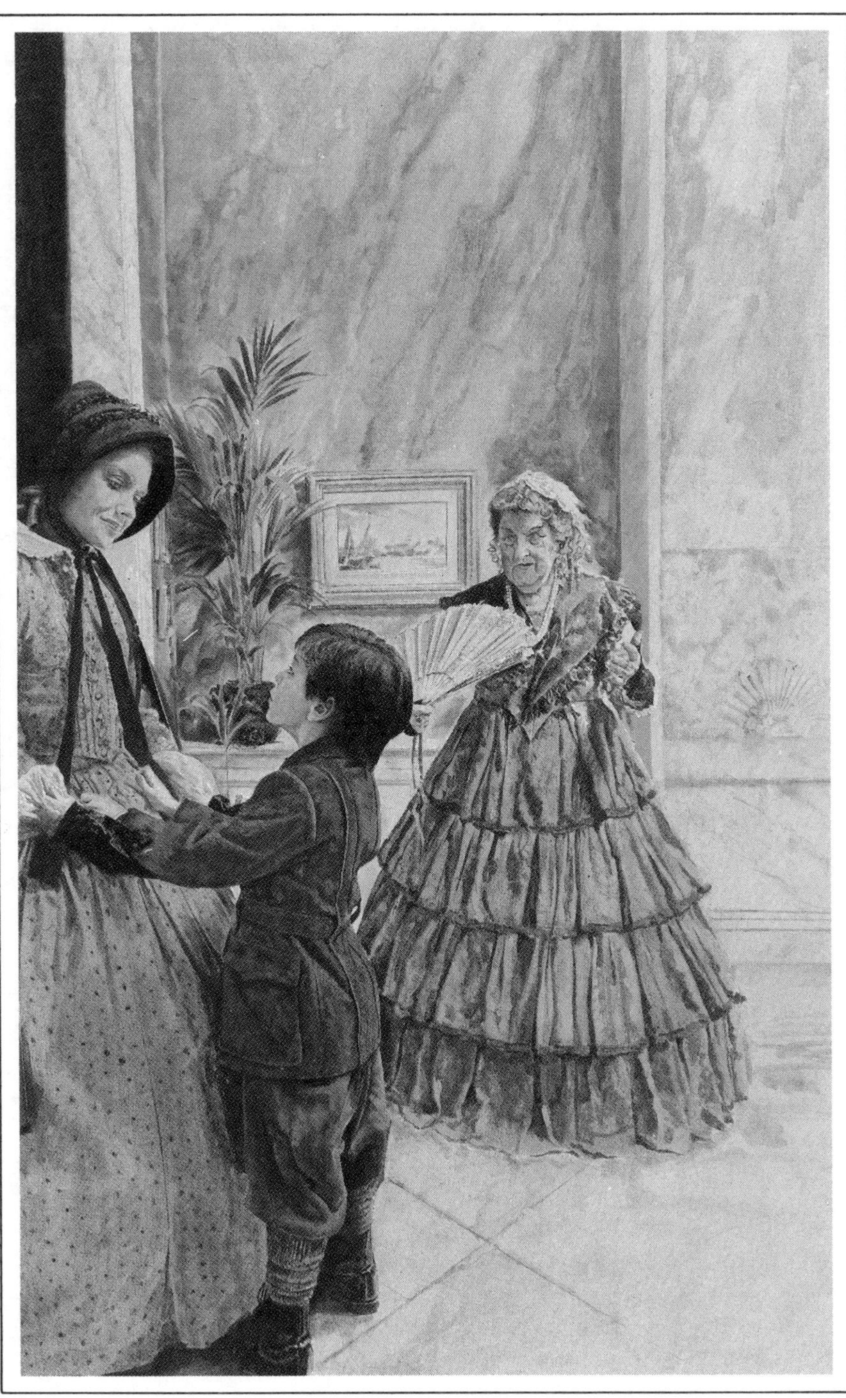

"Oh yes indeed. From Lady Adelaide Fitzsimmons, to begin with, and—"

Her guess that this forthright man would not bother with references, but would make his own decisions as to character, was right. Those brilliant black eyes examined her frankly. "Mama, Titus seems to like this young woman. Perhaps Miss Mildmay—"

Before the slightly ironic voice had finished, there was a cry from the stairs. "Blane, what are you doing down there? Is there something wrong with Titus?"

Blane looked up the curving staircase. He stepped back to give a slight bow. "Titus, my love, is suffering from too much *joie de vivre* last night. But he seems to have shown some acumen in choosing a governess."

Amalie came running down the stairs. "Blane, not that young woman who forced her way in! I've already dismissed her."

Blane went forward to meet his wife. He took her hand. "I think, my love, that perhaps you made a premature decision about Miss Mildmay. In any case, as you see, Titus has made his own decision."

"You can't tell me you are going to engage a servant"—again Amalie's use of the word made Sarah hot with fury—"on the passing fancy of a child."

"It's the child who will have to see the most of her," her husband retorted. "However, we'll perform the usual conventions. Perhaps, Miss Mildmay, you'd be good enough to step into the library and have a talk with me? Titus, go to your nurse." The little boy wept softly into Sarah's neck. "Titus!" The stern voice would tolerate no disobedience.

Sadly Titus detached himself from Sarah. Annie snatched him into her arms and hastened upstairs.

Blane bowed slightly. "This way, Miss Mildmay."

In the book-lined room, where a fire burned cosily, Blane waved her to a chair. "The boy's spoiled," he said abruptly.

"He seems a nervous child."

"Nervous? Perhaps. I know nothing about children."

Sarah bit her tongue, refraining from pointing out that he had had five years in which to learn. "A tropical climate is not good for a young child," she said primly. "Titus will grow much stronger in England."

"And grow to love the Atlantic winds rather than the Caribbean?" The man's eyes were ironic, as if the prospect of turning his son into a hardy English child amused him. "I want Titus to form an affection for Mallow Hall. I've wandered too much to care for any one place. But Titus is the heir. It would be a good thing if he came to love Mallow." He stopped.

"But we came in here to discuss you, not Titus. I intend you to join our household. For my wife's sake, however, tell me something of yourself."

This was the hardest moment of all—improvising, while the alert regard of those black eyes was bent on her. "My father is dead, Lord Mallow. He had misfortune in business and left my mother poorly provided for.

Consequently, my sisters and I have had to seek positions." She did not mention the amount of the fortune that her father had squandered. She thought fleetingly of her mother shutting up the house in Richmond, selling the elaborate furniture, shedding tears over the fashionable gowns that had to be discarded with her old way of life.

"I have been with Lady Adelaide Fitzsimmons for the last two years," Sarah went on, knowing that if he should take up her references Aunt Adelaide would be more than equal to the occasion.

"Do you mind my observing that no one looks less like a governess?"

Sarah had kept her face prim and lashes lowered. Now her eyelids flew up guiltily to meet again his frank and impudent scrutiny. "I can't help my appearance, Lord Mallow."

"Don't apologize for it. It's quite as satisfactory as your references. Can you begin tomorrow? We leave for Mallow the following day, and the journey may be tiresome. It would be better that Titus grow a little used to you in advance."

"Yes, I could be ready, sir," she answered. "If your wife wishes it also."

"The decision, Miss Mildmay, is mine."

Amalie had aroused no admiration in her, but did Titus' mother deserve this contemptuous disregard for her wishes? Sarah wondered.

"I shall be happy to pay you whatever you received in your last position," Blane went on. "If that isn't sufficient you have only to tell me."

"It is quite sufficient." Sarah stood up to leave. "Thank you, sir, for trusting me." The treacherous words escaped her without her realizing their import.

He gave a half smile. His eyes remained brooding. "On the contrary, thank you for trusting me. So far, very few people have."

As she left the house and returned to the waiting cab she was filled with triumph at her success. And the recounting of her experience to Aunt Adelaide and Ambrose was even more satisfying.

"I am to be ready in two days' time," she said, "to go down to Mallow Hall. We are all moving there for the winter."

"We!" Ambrose echoed in the greatest indignation.

"I am to be one of the household now, Ambrose. I'll soon get into Lady Malvina's confidence. Amalie, I'm afraid, is my enemy already."

"And the man?" Ambrose inquired stiffly.

Sarah gave a small retrospective smile. "I think I was a challenge to him just as much as he was to me. And there was the little boy clinging to me. Perhaps even he wasn't hard-hearted enough to resist that."

"Sarah, you almost make me believe you're as innocent as you sound," Ambrose cried exasperatedly. "Have you never looked in your mirror?"

Sarah opened her eyes in astonishment. "You mean he might have admired me? That he might have ideas of—of seduction?"

"He's a blackguard, isn't he?"

"But not in that way, Ambrose, not as far as we know. After all, he's respectably married. And if it should remotely come to that, I can take care of myself. Can't I, Aunt Adelaide?"

"If Sarah has the least trouble with her employer," said Aunt Adelaide, "she is to come home at once."

"And," said Ambrose, his eyes as hard as stone, "I shall kill him."

CHAPTER FIVE

AMBROSE WOULD NOT ALLOW Sarah to come to the docks to see him sail, for they could not risk being seen together, even in such an unlikely place. So they said their farewells in Aunt Adelaide's drawing room after Sarah returned from saying good-by to her two sisters. Ambrose was dressed for traveling, his face thin and pale and serious.

"How long shall you be away?" Sarah asked him.

"There's no telling. Three months, six, or even twelve."

"And I must stay at Mallow all this time?"

"Unless they discover what you are up to, or if, for any other reason, their behavior can't be tolerated."

"I will tolerate it."

"No, my love, you mustn't go beyond reasonable bounds. Even for me."

Sarah smiled. "I shall secretly pretend I'm mistress of Mallow."

"But with the right master."

"Ambrose, there's no need to remind me of that!" Nevertheless, a quick picture sprang into her mind of the dark-browed man she had last seen sprawling at ease with all the confidence of ownership in the firelit library in South Kensington.

"I shall send you news when possible by personal messenger," Ambrose said. "I couldn't risk posting a letter and having it fall into the wrong hands. If anything of importance happens to you, or you discover letters or documents that will help our case, communicate with me at once."

"You mean I'm to steal documents!"

"Let us say borrow." Ambrose gave his faint smile that was intended to be reassuring, but which Sarah privately wished had more warmth and tenderness. "Don't look so alarmed."

"I can't help thinking," Sarah said, "that it would be simpler if you were just to marry an heiress, after all."

The bitter intolerant look sprang into Ambrose's eyes. "And let this impostor win! As well as lose you? I love you, Sarah. I'll be back as soon as possible and all will be well. Now I must be off. The ship sails at full tide."

For a moment he clasped her in his arms. His cheek was cool against hers. If it hadn't been for the tightness of his embrace she would have thought him only half with her, even then his other half already in the hot sunshine of the West Indies, intent on revenge.

AMALIE WELCOMED SARAH with chilly courtesy. It was obvious that she had been compelled to make the best of an infuriating situation. "I'm afraid, Miss Mildmay, that until we get to Mallow Hall you will have to take charge of Titus completely. We've had to give Annie notice."

"I'm sorry about that, Lady Mallow."

"Servants, I am told, are becoming far too independent. Annie had some idea that her 'rights' were put upon, as she expressed it." The implication of Amalie's words was unmistakable.

"I shall be happy to do all I can, Lady Mallow."

"I warn you that Titus isn't easy. This sudden change in surroundings and climate has been too much for his delicate constitution. And then there's my mother-in-law—" But at that Amalie must have felt she was being indiscreet. She rang the bell for a maid to come and show Sarah to her room. "It is essential that Titus be in bed early," she said, "since we begin a long journey in the morning—and I'd suggest no noisy games."

Sarah was baffled, until she realized Lady Malvina was the difficulty.

"One more thing, Miss Mildmay. Since this is your first night here, perhaps you'd prefer supper on a tray in your room."

This gesture, Sarah knew, was no mark of thoughtfulness for her comfort. It was merely postponing the time when Sarah would share their table. But she welcomed it with inner excitement. While the family was at dinner, she could do a little quiet investigating.

She bowed her head. "Thank you, Lady Mallow."

The maid appeared and the cool, unfriendly interview was over. Blane had exercised his will, but Sarah knew she must not underestimate Amalie, who had her own weapons, and could make Sarah's position intolerable.

THE LITTLE BOY stood in the middle of the large nursery in his flannel nightshirt. He looked small and clean and troubled. His grandmother, exhausted from some recent activity, was sunk back in a chair fanning her flushed face. When Sarah came in she said wheezily, "Ah, here you are, Miss Mildmay. I have had the boy on my hands since that stupid Annie departed. But we've had a tremendous romp, haven't we, my love?"

Sarah took the child's hand. "You remember me, don't you, Titus?"

He nodded, but his sober face gave no sign of pleasure. The boy was so small and frail, and as tense as a wild kitten.

"We're going to be good friends," said Sarah. "I'm to teach you a great many things, like reading and drawing pictures and where all the countries in the world are. And we'll walk in the woods, and you'll have a pony."

"That's right," said Lady Malvina approvingly. "Teach the lad some spunk. He's scared of his own shadow."

"Some children are naturally shy and quiet," Sarah said. "But give Titus time. Wait until he's used to the country and rides his own horse."

"You seem a sensible young woman. But I must say, I thought you were most impertinent. So did my daughter-in-law. She was not at all pleased." The old lady paused to give a rich chuckle. "She suspected Blane had spied a new pretty face. He's a great one, my son, for pretty faces. There was the gamekeeper's daughter when he was only a schoolboy, but he's conveniently forgotten that. His amnesia serves him well. All the same I like a man to be vigorous, lusty. Better than that cold-blooded cousin of his."

Sarah lifted her eyes innocently. "Is that the person who would have inherited if your son hadn't returned, Lady Malvina?"

"Ambrose? Yes." Lady Malvina's lips were turned down in eloquent distaste. "Oh, he's well enough, perhaps. Industrious, righteous, doesn't gamble, has excellent taste. But he's a type I thoroughly dislike. Do you think he'd have paid my debts, taken me into his family, let me enjoy his children—if he ever begets any!" Lady Malvina chuckled again at her obviously bawdy thoughts and sailed out of the room.

Sarah burned with indignation, but at the same time she was conscious of an untidy warmheartedness about Lady Malvina. And there was no doubt that with her careless talk she was going to be of enormous help. Sarah resolved to keep a diary, to write down any snatches of conversation that her memory might not otherwise retain.

Titus meekly ate his bread and milk, and allowed himself to be put to bed in the firelit nursery.

"Have you traveled in a train before?" Sarah asked.

"No."

"Then that's very exciting, isn't it? Have you any toys you want to take?"

"No."

"But don't you have a favorite toy? Didn't you have any in Trinidad?"

"I had my friend José then."

This sparse information showed Sarah another side to Titus' quietness. He had lost a favorite playmate. He had not yet learned to play with an English child's toys. Well, there would be a rocking horse and toy soldiers and the pony. At least this part of her job, Sarah promised herself fiercely, she would do honestly.

"Good night, Titus. Sleep well. Shall I leave the candle for a little while?" The large dark eyes looked up at her beseechingly. She realized that this nervous little stranger to English nurseries had been left to go to sleep in the dark. "All right. I won't blow it out," she promised. "Are we going to be friends, Titus?"

"Why don't you call me Georgie?"

Sarah's heart missed a beat. "Why should I do that? Is that what"—she made a guess—"José used to call you?"

"Yes. And Mama too. When I was a baby."

"But when you came to England she started calling you Titus?"

"She said Georgie was a baby name."

"And Papa used to call you Georgie too?"

The little boy looked puzzled. "I think he called me Titus. When he came back from the sea."

"Was he away at sea a long time?"

"Ever so long. But Mama says he won't go to sea again. And I have to be called Titus because that was my grandpapa's name."

"It's a good name," Sarah said.

Already she had significant entries to make in her diary.

A very young maid named Lucy brought a supper tray to Sarah's room. After the maid left, Sarah set the tray to one side and tiptoed to the door. She opened it a crack and listened. Almost at once she heard the dinner gong, and a few minutes later the heavy tread of Lady Malvina on the stairs, followed by the lighter footsteps of Amalie. Blane must have been downstairs already, for there was no more sound.

It did not take long to discover which rooms on the second floor were Blane and Amalie's. The first door she opened was obviously Lady Malvina's, for she recognized the heavy scent of her cologne.

The next door she tried led to the master bedroom. The gas had been left burning low, and she could see the wide bed with its elaborate headboard and the shine of Amalie's discarded silk gown. A maid might come at any moment to turn down the bed, so Sarah moved swiftly. What was she looking for? She didn't know. Just anything significant.

Strangely, there was nothing masculine in this room. The dressing table held nothing but Amalie's possessions, the wardrobes only women's clothing. But of course—here was the communicating door leading to Blane's room. Sarah held her breath and turned the knob.

But the door didn't open. It was locked on the other side.

It took only a moment to tiptoe quickly down the passage and open the hallway door to Blane's room. The bed was quite narrow; Blane, at present, obviously occupied it alone.

Her cheeks hot, Sarah silently closed the door. This, at least, was none of her business, and she was ashamed of herself for discovering it.

But she must not let herself be deterred. Her real goal was the library. If there were any papers to be discovered, they would be in that room, in Blane's desk. There should be plenty of time to make a search while the family was at dinner. If she was disturbed, she could say that she had come to look for a book to read.

To reach the library she had to descend the stairs and actually pass the dining-room door. She could not resist stopping to listen a moment.

The only person talking was Lady Malvina. "Better than that sly Annie, anyway," she was saying. "And Titus seems to take to her."

"I thought she was remarkably forward and impudent for a person in her position," Amalie said coldly.

"Oh, that was just a pose. She obviously desperately needed this position, poor thing. Governesses are two a penny at present. And what else can an educated young woman do if she's forced to earn her own living? Anyway, the main thing is, Titus likes her. All that child needs is a little tenderness."

"I won't have him spoiled," said Blane. "If this girl is going to spoil him she'll have to go, tender heart or not, pretty face or not."

"I thought you said you hadn't noticed her face," Amalie said coolly.

Sarah, her cheeks flaming, moved on to the library, which again had a cosy, welcoming appearance. She had to overcome the impulse to stand by the warm fire and go instead to the desk, where writing materials were laid out and a letter begun. There was the name and address: Thomas Whitehouse, Esquire, and then a street name in Trinidad. "My dear Whitehouse, It is my wish to express my gratitude to you in some more tangible form than already . . ."

Whitehouse! That was the man whom Ambrose had sought, who had reputedly sailed for the West Indies. The man who swore he had known Blane since he first arrived in Trinidad. So he *had* been bribed!

Hesitating as to whether she should merely memorize the letter or take it with her as evidence, Sarah stiffened as she heard approaching footsteps. In a flash she crossed the room and concealed herself behind the heavy curtains drawn against the cold, foggy night.

The butler held the door open and bowed as Blane entered the room.

"I'll take my coffee in here tonight, Tomkins. I have some letters to finish."

"Very well, my lord."

Through the infinitesimal parting in the curtains Sarah saw Blane seat himself at the desk and pick up his pen. His dark head was bent as he began to write. Presently Tomkins returned with the coffee service on a silver tray. He put it down and withdrew.

The tantalizing smell of hot coffee reached Sarah's nostrils. She remembered that she had left her own supper tray untouched. But she must not make a noise. If she did and Blane discovered her, her bags would be packed within the hour. She must stand here until midnight, if need be, scarcely breathing. Sarah was almost in tears.

Perhaps half an hour went by, while the little French clock ticked on in its glass case on the mantelpiece and Blane's pen made a faint scratching.

Then abruptly the door burst open, and she heard Amalie's voice: "Blane! We've been waiting in the drawing room for you."

Blane scarcely looked up. "You heard me say I was coming here to work."

"But not until after your coffee. Oh, you've had it here."

"I have. And now, if you don't mind, I have urgent business to finish."

"But darling, I waited. You know I waited."

Now Amalie was referring to something that had nothing to do with the coffee, for her voice was uncertain, pleading, strangely humble.

Blane raised his head then, his brows drawn together in a look of barely controlled patience. "Yes, I know, and you know my answer to that."

"Blane! If you only thought a little—" She was in tears, groping for a handkerchief and looking intensely pathetic.

Sarah heard Blane give an impatient exclamation, then saw him spring to his feet and cross over to his wife. "Oh Lord! I can't stand this sort of tiresome behavior. Come, then. I'll have coffee with you in the drawing room and talk to Mama. And then you shall play and sing to me for half an hour, and we'll be a completely devoted couple."

Sarah slumped back wearily. She had been rescued by Amalie's display of temperament. Now she would always remember, when Amalie put on her haughty, confident air, that underneath it was this pathetic, pleading person, begging something of her husband that he was reluctant to give.

Baffled and more than a little disturbed, Sarah at last ventured forth and crept upstairs. She had been too distraught to read the remainder of Blane's letter to Mr. Whitehouse, but she had memorized the address. She must quickly write a letter to Ambrose so that when he received it he could call on Mr. Whitehouse in Trinidad.

CHAPTER SIX

THE DEPARTURE THE NEXT morning was complicated by the immense amount of luggage. In addition to her several trunks, Lady Malvina insisted on carrying a canary in a cage—a present for Titus, to amuse him on the journey. It was difficult to say which was the more dejected, Titus in his Norfolk jacket and cap or the canary silent on its perch.

Amalie was elegantly and discreetly dressed in dark blue, but for all her elegance she looked pinched and cold. She said she hoped there was some sort of heating in the train.

"You must learn to dress for our climate," Lady Malvina said. "I warrant you haven't a single flannel petticoat on."

Blane, who appeared in his traveling cape and top hat, got Titus and the ladies into the waiting cab with brisk efficiency. He himself followed with

Tomkins and the luggage in a second cab. Soames, the head groom at Mallow Hall, was to meet them with the carriage at Yarby, the railway station nearest to Mallow. Then there was a ten-mile journey across the marshes, but they expected to reach their destination before dusk.

They sat in reasonable comfort in the first-class railway carriage, its windows tightly closed against the smoke and soot. Titus was the most unfidgety small boy Sarah had met. In spite of the fact that it was his first train trip, he showed his excitement only by a tight grip of Sarah's hand and an increased pallor. It was his father who was restless. He spent the journey strolling up and down the corridor and occasionally opening the window to stick his head out and let in a blast of frozen, smoky air.

The canary remained silent, but Lady Malvina talked incessantly. After an hour had gone by she produced the hamper Mrs. Robbins, the London housekeeper, had packed, and distributed sandwiches and cold chicken. While Amalie was dozing, she also persuaded Titus to drink a little out of her glass of port. "It will put some color in his cheeks," she said.

Amalie woke up and exclaimed, "Mama, how can you be so foolish! Now he'll be ill. Miss Mildmay, couldn't you have had more sense?"

"I'm sorry," Sarah murmured meekly. How did one oppose this preposterous and determined old lady?

Sure enough, an hour later Titus was sick to his stomach. Afterward, shivering a little, he curled up on Sarah's lap and presently went to sleep. Sarah was aware of Blane's gaze on her. She had said nothing during the whole episode, merely cleaned up and comforted the child.

"I don't want you to spoil the boy," Blane said.

Sarah wondered indignantly if the poor baby, sick and tired, was expected to sit upright in his corner for the entire journey.

She raised her eyes innocently and said, "I won't spoil him, Lord Mallow. Indeed, I don't think he's at all spoiled. He's overexcited and bewildered by his new environment." Her voice was gentle and uncensorious. Was she being a little too rash? "But I did wonder last night why he asked me to call him Georgie. Is that a pet name?"

Amalie's eyes flickered slightly, but Blane's were composed. "His baby name, yes. But he's old enough to be called Titus now."

"You never told me that, Blane," Lady Malvina said. "Had you just that moment begun to call him Titus?"

"*Which* moment, Mama?"

"Why, when you appeared in my hall that day."

"Of course not. Good heavens, the child's full name is Titus Blane George Mallow. And I don't want him pampered."

For the first time Amalie spoke vaguely in Sarah's defense. "Being a bad traveler doesn't consist of being pampered. But this settles it. We don't travel any farther today. We spend the night at Yarby."

"Don't be absurd! Soames is meeting us with the carriage."

"Then he can be put up for the night. I, for one, don't intend to arrive at Mallow completely exhausted."

Blane shrugged. "Very well. I'll arrange for rooms at the George. If they can accommodate such a large party."

"Don't be silly, Blane," said Lady Malvina heartily. "You must remember Tom Mercer. He'd never turn anyone from Mallow away. And he'll be overjoyed to see you." But Sarah caught a flicker of uncertainty in Lady Malvina's eyes.

When they arrived, Soames, a dark little man with a narrow face, was waiting with the carriage, and in this they drove the short distance to the George Inn, where the ladies were ordered to wait while accommodations were being arranged.

Whether the owner, Tom Mercer, had recognized Blane at once, Sarah was not to know. But at least he acknowledged the importance of the arrivals by coming out to greet them with genuine pleasure.

"Well, Tom," said Lady Malvina, "do you recognize my scalawag son? Do you remember letting him drink too much ale when he was a schoolboy, and him coming home rolling drunk?"

"That I do, my lady," said Tom. "But if I may say so, Master Blane was not a lad you could say no to."

Lady Malvina chuckled reminiscently. "No, I grant you that."

"If you'd gossip a little less, Mama, and come inside," Blane said. "Rooms are being made ready, and there's tea in the parlor."

Early dusk was falling, and it was a relief not to have the long journey to Mallow that evening. Sarah found she was to share a room with Titus. Lady Malvina had the adjoining one, and Amalie and Blane had the large double chamber at the head of the stairs.

Sarah put Titus to bed immediately, and he fell asleep at once. Already, in twenty-four hours, she had settled herself into the part she was to play and was able quite meekly to offer her services to Lady Malvina or Amalie.

Lady Malvina was seated comfortably before a fire. "How kind, my dear," she said. "But I don't intend to dress this evening. I shall have a tray sent up here. How's the boy?"

"Asleep, Lady Malvina."

"Good. By the way, you didn't notice—" Her cheeks puffed in and out.

"Didn't notice what, Lady Malvina?"

"I was just curious. Many people have short memories for faces."

"You mean, did the landlord know him?" Sarah said boldly.

"But he must have, because we have all the attention, as usual. And tomorrow we'll be safely at Mallow. Ha-a!" She gave a great sigh. "I must buy some more jewels. My husband got a little eccentric for some time before his death. He became most parsimonious with money. I had to sell my pearls. But now Blane can get me some more. Yes, pearls. They're the kindest to aging throats."

"It has been quite a change of fortune for you, hasn't it, Lady Malvina?"

The old lady shot Sarah a quick, suspicious glance. But her love of a sympathetic listener got the better of discretion. "Yes, it has. Couldn't imagine my nephew Ambrose buying me jewels. He's a cold fish."

"Cold?"

"You know what I mean. Careful, minds about gossip, hates to be embarrassed. *Correct.* That's the word. I'd have embarrassed him greatly."

Sarah bit her lip. She didn't enjoy the old lady's ability to put people into words so effectively, whether the words were true or not. And of course they were not.

Sarah had scarcely gone back to her room before Amalie tapped at the door and came in. She had made a complete new toilette, and wore one of her taffeta dinner gowns, cut low over her shoulders. The color in her thin cheeks was high. "How is my son, Miss Mildmay?"

"He's asleep, Lady Mallow. I scarcely like to wake him for supper."

"I shouldn't. By the way, my mother-in-law isn't going down, so my husband and I will also dine in our room. Perhaps you'd make what arrangements you care to for yourself."

"Thank you, Lady Mallow."

She went out leaving a trail of scent behind her. She had not smiled, but she had been almost human—almost conspiratorial, as if something she had planned had worked out well.

Was it because tonight there could be no locked door between herself and her husband? It was Amalie who had insisted on breaking the journey, knowing that as a matter of course she and Blane would share a room.

Sarah made a note in her diary. *Lady M. extravagant and was embarrassed by debts when husband died. Looks to Blane to buy her new jewels. Determined to think Blane her son but is a little uncertain. Did Tom Mercer recognize Blane at once?*

Determined to find out something about Tom Mercer, Sarah went downstairs and asked for her supper to be served in the parlor. Luck was with her, for Tom himself carried in the tray. "We're short of help tonight, with so many unexpected guests. Hope this is to your liking, ma'am."

"Thank you," said Sarah. "I expect it was a great surprise for you to see Lord Mallow."

"It was that. I heard he was coming any day, but I didn't expect him unannounced like this."

"And would you have known him anywhere?" Sarah asked.

"Well, ma'am, speaking fairly, I can't say that I would have. It's twenty years, after all, and him only a lad when he left. But he's got that same proud look about him. That lad—only a schoolboy, and he could carry his liquor like an old-timer. He went away because he quarreled so deadly with his father. The two of them were too much alike, two hotheads. But now all's well, eh? And the little lad's the dead spit of him, only more delicate-like. It's a happy day for Mallow Hall. Well, ma'am, anything more you want, you just let me know."

She enjoyed her meal, thankful to have a little time alone. But when she returned upstairs Lady Malvina was standing at her door. She grabbed Sarah's arm and whispered, "Are those two downstairs or in their room?"

"In their room, I imagine."

Lady Malvina gave her deep chuckle. "That'll please her ladyship. At last, eh? Don't be shocked, Miss Mildmay."

The outrageous old woman pinched Sarah's cheek and retreated into her room. The door banged as Sarah stood there stiffly. In that moment the door of the double room at the head of the stairs opened and Blane came out. He was still dressed in his traveling clothes. Lifting his head, he saw Sarah and could not fail to notice her hot cheeks.

"What is it, Miss Mildmay? Has my mother been indiscreet, as usual?"

Sarah collected herself. "Nothing's the matter, thank you."

He stared at her, eyes overbright from some emotion, then gave a faint shrug. "Women!" he said under his breath, and went on down the stairs.

Titus awoke early in the morning. He said he was hungry, which was not to be wondered at since he had fallen asleep supperless. It was only six o'clock, but Sarah could hear stirring downstairs. She decided to find someone who would give her some milk and bread for Titus.

Putting a wrap on, she slipped quietly down the stairs. The parlor was empty and so was the dining room. She tentatively tried one or two doors, seeking a way to the kitchen. But one led to the bar parlor and the other to a kind of office. In this was a long leather couch, and stretched out on it, sound asleep, lay the new Lord Mallow.

Was he too drunk to climb the stairs? Or had Amalie this time been the one who locked the door in revenge?

Sarah closed the door softly and tiptoed away. She was stumbling on the wrong secrets. This was not amusing at all.

CHAPTER SEVEN

THE SERVANTS WERE LINED up in the hall. Blane, with Amalie clinging to his arm, acknowledged their bobs and curtsies with an offhand ease. He was the master come home. Standing a little behind them in the arched doorway of the old house, Sarah felt her blood rise, hot with resentment. She should have arrived at Mallow Hall for the first time as Ambrose's bride, and the deferential bobbing of the servants should have been to her, not to that haughty wife of Blane's who looked tired and sulky this morning, as if she hadn't slept well.

But when Sarah was inside the hall her heart sank. For at the foot of the stairs hung the controversial portrait that had had such significance at the hearings. The child in the picture was so remarkably similar to Titus that there was no explaining it away. Standing there, she attracted Blane's attention, and he came over. "Is there any hope for Titus, do you think?"

"I don't know what you mean, Lord Mallow."

"Starting from those beginnings," he said, waving toward the painting, "will he grow up to look like me?"

He was challenging her, she realized. Suddenly contempt filled her, and her confidence came back. "I am not good at predictions, Lord Mallow."

"One doesn't wonder without surmising. You, if I'm not mistaken, have been busily surmising ever since you arrived in my house."

Sarah had a flash of alarm. But if he noticed her involuntary look of guilt he had no time to comment on it, for Amalie had come up to say, "Let's go over the house room by room, my love. I long for you to show it to me."

"Certainly. Perhaps we could take Titus and Miss Mildmay to the nursery first. On the third floor. That's one direction I couldn't forget. I don't suppose a single thing has been changed in the nursery, has it, Mama?" he called out. "Although I remember being rather destructive."

Lady Malvina came bustling up, beaming with happiness at coming home. "You were very destructive indeed. We had to have new wallpaper after you went to school. Don't you remember?"

Blane laughed and took his mother's arm. "Let's go look at the nursery and decide what kind of wallpaper Titus shall have. It's most important, after all. One day he may have to tell a jury about it."

"Don't be absurd!" Amalie said sharply.

"Life is full of uncertainties and surprises," he returned.

Mallow Hall was not large, but it had been built with taste and discrimination. The proportions of the rooms and curving staircase were perfect although the furnishings were shabby. Amalie insisted on going over the entire house while Sarah was getting Titus settled in the nursery. Sarah heard their footsteps and occasionally Lady Malvina's loud voice.

A gauche, eager country girl called Eliza Matthews had been employed to help in the nursery. She had just come to work at Mallow, but her nervousness proved a good thing for Titus. It gave him confidence. For the first time Sarah heard him laugh.

"Miss Mildmay, Eliza doesn't know how to do anything. She's funny."

Eliza blushed and hung her head. She was a plump, healthy creature with bright cheeks and chilblains on her fingers.

"Have you any brothers and sisters, Eliza?"

"Yes'm. Seven."

"Then Titus is a child just like them, so don't be afraid."

"It's the old lady, ma'am," Eliza confessed in a rush. "I'm afraid of *her.*"

"That's Grandmama," Titus explained. "But she's only playing games, isn't she, Miss Mildmay? Eliza doesn't need to be afraid."

Already they were allies, the thin little boy and the awkward country girl. For Titus, at least, Mallow Hall would be good.

After getting the child settled, Sarah went to her own room next door. It looked out over the garden toward the lake. Early in November this view was melancholy and the wind pressed against the window. Halfway through her unpacking she felt intensely lonely. Her sisters, Amelia and Charlotte, envied her, thinking she would have some drama with this queer family. They didn't know she was grieving at being separated from Ambrose, and wondering how she could endure months of meekness and self-effacement in a house that should be her own.

Ambrose, with his elegant, pale good looks, would look so right in this house. She too, she thought, glimpsing her face in the mirror, would not look amiss. Better than Amalie, at least, with her overdressing and her sulks. Thinking of dinner, her first meal to be shared with her employers, Sarah halfheartedly shook out her modest dinner dress, a green taffeta from which she had reluctantly removed the expensive lace trimming.

Just then Lady Malvina came sweeping in and began poking about inquisitively, observing everything. "You haven't a lot of things, have you? But there's good material in that gown. I thought governesses were poor."

"It was given to me, Lady Malvina."

"No! By your last employer? Well, I'm afraid you won't get presents like that here. Not from the new Lady Mallow." Lady Malvina gave a short laugh and went on. "What do you think of Mallow?"

"It's a beautiful house."

"Falling to bits. Everything needs repair—the roof, the drains, the chimneys, the floor. After all, it's a hundred years old, even if they built well in those days. But my daughter-in-law intends to ignore the dull necessities and spend a fortune on furnishings. Carpets, curtains, pictures. All outward show."

"Does your son agree to this, Lady Malvina?"

"Of course he doesn't. He's thinking quite rightly of Titus' inheritance. There's money, but not that much. His silly wife will ruin him." Lady Malvina fiddled with the rings on her fingers. "And she forgets about me. I have requirements also. It's preposterous how little jewelry I have. Amalie forgets, or chooses to forget, how I had to sacrifice most of it. She wants to cut a dash. Her first opportunity, if you ask me. Where did she come from anyway? A shack that would collapse in a hurricane, I'll be bound." And she swept out as breezily as she had come in.

Sarah dressed for dinner with some nervousness. If Lady Malvina was feeling bored, or at odds with Amalie, she was likely to say anything. The results might be either entertaining or embarrassing. Nevertheless, it was impossible to dislike the old lady.

It was dark now, and lamps had been lit on the stairs, making yellow pools of light and leaving the high ceilings lost in darkness. The house was too far from a town to have had the new gas fittings installed. Now it smelled pleasantly of beeswax and candle smoke. The heavy curtains, frayed at the edges, had been drawn across the long windows and the sound of the dying wind shut out.

In the drawing room a fire crackled on the hearth. Amalie was there already. She stood facing the fire, the light shining on her ice-blue gown. She was a slim, graceful figure with her bent head and tiny waist. When she turned, her dark eyes glittered. "Well, Miss Mildmay, is Titus settled?"

"Very well, Lady Mallow. And he likes the new nursemaid."

"Splendid. Though what he likes or dislikes is not here or there according to my husband. He must not be spoiled. And he's such a little boy still. I'll go up to him presently. Ugh! What a drafty house this is. I've been shivering since we arrived."

"Then, as my mother recommends, you must wear more petticoats," came Blane's deep, pleasant voice from the doorway. "I'm glad to see you're joining us, Miss Mildmay. Do you agree with my wife that this is a cold house?"

"Perhaps it hasn't had time to be thoroughly heated yet, Lord Mallow."

"That's what I say. But my wife insists the furnishings are at fault. We're to import miles of Genoese velvet, acres of carpet, handpainted wallpapers and goodness knows what else. What, I ask you, does Titus care for all that?"

"Blane! This isn't only for Titus. We're living here."

"I came back solely for Titus, as you know. Let's simply preserve this place for him, as was our intention." Sarah was suddenly conscious of his black gaze on her. "Does that seem strange to you, Miss Mildmay? That I should want to preserve an inheritance for my son?"

"Blane, Miss Mildmay isn't interested in what you're planning to do," Amalie said sharply.

Blane grinned. A deep crevice showed in his cheek. "Isn't she? Not even in hearing I've promised to read the lesson in church tomorrow?"

Amalie clapped her hand to her mouth, stifling an exclamation. For the first time she seemed amused. "You!"

"Yes, I. The vicar called while you were resting. It's the custom to do this. My father always did."

Amalie was laughing openly. "Forgive me, my love. But how long is it since you opened a Bible?"

"If you think I'm more at home at sea, then I agree with you. All the same, you'll be at church tomorrow, and you'll take Titus. He might as well know what's in store for him."

Dinner at the candlelit dining table was amicable enough. Afterward Blane sprawled in a chair in front of the fire, while Lady Malvina dozed noisily and Amalie played the piano in a desultory way. Amalie was trying hard to be a fashionable lady.

"We must have dinner parties, Blane."

"We came down here to rest, don't you remember?"

"Oh nonsense. Nothing makes *you* tired. Besides, there'll be people here who expect to be invited to Mallow. Old friends. Isn't that so, Mama?"

Lady Malvina woke with a start. "Oh yes, there'll be plenty who expect it. But I warn you, everyone in these parts is as dull as ditchwater."

"Will you make up a list, Mama? After all, Blane can't be expected to know who lives here after twenty years away."

"No," Lady Malvina muttered. "But you'd remember the Fortescues, Blane?" Her voice was suddenly uncertain.

"The colonel? Of course. Is he still alive?"

Lady Malvina relaxed. "Do you think anything would kill him? And the Veseys and the Blounts. They're all still here."

"There you are," said Amalie triumphantly. "So we'll give a dinner party—soon. We must lead *some* kind of social life in the country."

When Sarah rose after coffee to take her leave, Blane sprang to his feet. "We'll expect to see you at church." His gaze lingered on her. Then he seemed to collect himself, saying lightly, "You might even rehearse me in my diction. You look skeptical, as if you really think I am an illiterate sailor."

Amalie said crisply, "Blane, Miss Mildmay is tired. Don't keep her standing. Good night, Miss Mildmay."

"Good night," Sarah murmured, and hastened up the stairs.

It was extraordinarily difficult to write in her diary that night. The man was such a hypocrite! Then Sarah remembered his determination to preserve the Mallow fortune for his son. No one would have doubted his sincerity when he said that.

There was no doubt also that Lady Malvina was uncertain of him and was scheming to get all that she could, money or jewels, while it was possible. Again, contrarily, she was deeply and genuinely attached to Titus, and certainly believed, or deceived herself, that he was her grandson.

Everything is a complex web, Sarah wrote by the light of the candle on her bedside table. *So far there is no tangible proof at all. But tomorrow I will observe closely the people at church and the way they greet the new family.* She closed and locked the little book, blew out the candle and settled down to sleep.

In the early hours Sarah heard Titus crying. She fumbled for matches to light her candle. She found the child half awake, but obviously frightened. He had heard strange noises, he said. "What sort of noises?" she asked. The wind had died and the big house seemed quite still.

"I don't know. From up there." He pointed to the ceiling, and Sarah's breath caught involuntarily. The floor above this one comprised the attic rooms. The servants slept up there, and it was in one of those rooms that the unhappy maid Bella, fifty years ago, had hanged herself.

"It was probably a mouse. You were asleep. You didn't hear properly. Now, go back to sleep. I'll leave the candle."

The little boy looked up at her with his docile gaze. The room was drafty, for the candle flame flickered constantly. Tomorrow, Sarah decided, she would arrange for a night-light, something in a globe that did not flicker, creating shadows. A child's imagination could so easily become distorted.

The house was very still. The uneasiness of the quiet was surely the product of her own distorted imagination.

It was a bright, cold morning, and they were all preparing for church. Sarah, going down early with Titus, had an opportunity to talk to Soames, who had brought the carriage to the door. This was the man who Ambrose believed had coached Blane in his knowledge of the past.

"The young master will be wanting a pony," Soames said. "I've just the one, a half brother to the one his father used to ride."

"Did you teach his father to ride, Soames?"

"Oh, aye. And a desperate rider he was, wanting to jump before he could canter. This wee lad, now, will be more cautious."

"You've noticed a great change in the master?"

"Not that much, miss. He's still the same devil-may-care person. This is a good day for the old place, miss. Never thought I'd live to see it."

"Then you wouldn't have cared for the—cousin—to be master here?"

"I've nothing against Mr. Ambrose—nothing personal-like. But if you ask me, he's not the type for Mallow."

Sarah's cheeks were hot with indignation. Ambrose not the type for Mallow indeed! He certainly wouldn't be the type for this nasty, sly creature who knew that dismissal would await him the moment Ambrose arrived. This surely confirmed Ambrose's opinion that Soames was in the conspiracy. That was two of them, Soames and the elusive Thomas Whitehouse.

But in church, Sarah was hypnotized by Blane's grave, beautiful voice as he stood tall and confident in the pulpit, reading the lesson. He did it as if he had been doing so every Sunday of his adult life. The entire congregation was utterly still and in his spell.

The man is a complete actor, Sarah thought angrily. How could he read the Bible so beautifully and be so false? As he finished and slowly closed the book, his moody gaze swept the church. It seemed to hold a sad irony, as if even he felt this was going a little too far.

But what a victory it was, for afterward, in the churchyard, he was besieged by eager people claiming recognition. Lady Malvina was always in the right place to say names clearly for the benefit of a lethargic memory. "Ah, Colonel Fortescue! Of course my son remembers you. And Mrs. Blount. Thank you, but you can't be as happy as I am. Let me present my daughter-in-law. And my grandson. Miss Mildmay, bring Titus."

The wind stirred in the long grass about the old gravestones. Even the stones, tilted with age, seemed to be bowing deferentially. Everyone, naturally, must be happy. The lord of the manor was home.

THE NEXT DAY, helped by one of the elderly servants, Sarah organized the schoolroom. The old woman was full of sentiment about the room. "Look, miss," she exclaimed triumphantly. "Here's where the master wrote on the windowpane. He borrowed his mother's diamond ring. There was such a row because he hid it afterward."

The childish scrawl on the lowest pane was perfectly visible:

I hate this room,
It's full of gloom.
I'd rather go away than stay.

"How old was he when he did that?" Sarah asked.

"Old enough to know better, miss. About ten or eleven. His father punished him severe."

Old enough to remember, Sarah thought.

"Look what naughty Papa did," Sarah said deliberately to Titus. "He wrote on the window and it will never come out."

Titus scrambled up to see. "What does it say?"

"Why don't you ask Papa to tell you?"

Titus' small fingers scratched at the indelible marks. "Does Papa know what it says?"

"If he wrote it he'll know, won't he?" Sarah smoothly changed the subject. "It's time for your walk. Go and tell Eliza to put on your things."

Titus, for all his timidity, was a sharp little boy. When he was taken down to the drawing room for an hour before his bedtime, he immediately approached his father and said, "Papa, what did you write on the window?"

Blane looked bewildered."On the window? What window?"

"In the schoolroom—you wrote with a diamond. How did you write with a diamond?"

Blane grimaced and said easily, "Looks as if my untidy childhood is catching up on me."

"But what does the writing say, Papa?" Titus persisted.

Blane looked at Sarah. "Is it illegible, Miss Mildmay? I know I was an almost illiterate child."

"No, it isn't illegible, Lord Mallow. It's quite a clever verse for a ten-year-old boy. I gather you were punished severely."

Blane merely shrugged and said, "Frankly, I haven't the slightest recollection of it. What does it say, Miss Mildmay?"

Sarah repeated the verse and Blane burst into a roar of laughter. "By Jove, it's deuced appropriate. It expressed my feelings. But I wonder where I picked up the diamond."

"Off your mother's dressing table," came Lady Malvina's voice from the door. She stood there, flushed and aggressive. "It was my most valuable ring. Afterward you hid it in a bird's nest in the gutter, and only confessed when your father whipped you. Disgusting child that you were."

Blane shrugged again, unperturbed. "This shows how fascinating the mind is. It deliberately shuts out unpleasant memories. Isn't that so, Miss Mildmay? You're the highly educated person here."

She answered carefully, "I believe the mind can do quite remarkable things, Lord Mallow. Personally, I would not have thought a child likely to forget an escapade like that. But there is, of course, your amnesia."

"It is true that I have the most extraordinary blanks. Isn't it, Mama?"

Lady Malvina agreed. "Especially as regards your misdeeds. That ring was an exceptionally good one, and I'd lost it for weeks. Most upsetting."

"Poor Mama. Then I must make belated amends. We shall find you another one."

Lady Malvina relaxed and glowed with pleasure.

CHAPTER EIGHT

AS THE DAYS WENT by, Sarah began to grow disheartened. She was making discoveries, but not the kind that were of any use to her. She knew, for instance, that Amalie was unhappy. Amalie had persuaded Blane to allow her to do some refurnishing, and the place had been littered with expensive materials. She had also had various people to call, and gone calling herself, driven by Soames in the carriage. But all this merely seemed to tighten her face and make her more moody. Something more than a passing quarrel was wrong between Amalie and Blane, but this did not constitute the kind of evidence for which Sarah was looking.

Titus' conversation was of no help. The past, when he had been called Georgie, rapidly slipped away from him as he became absorbed in his new surroundings. He was learning to ride his new pony and was overcoming his timidity. This pleased Sarah, for she was fond of the shy little boy.

As for Blane, he seemed restless and bored. What colossal nerve, thought Sarah, to oust Ambrose from his inheritance and then be bored with it himself. She felt as if she were up against a brick wall in proving him an impostor. He swept aside all awkward moments by pleading his unreliability as a child and his loss of memory. At other times his knowledge of Mallow Hall and the past seemed too uncannily accurate to be assumed. The only explanation for this was Soames, who was too familiar altogether, always hanging about. But even Soames could not have known some of the things Blane seemed to know.

The mystery was baffling, and Sarah had moments of wondering whether to give the whole thing up. But before very long she should hear from Ambrose, who must have arrived in Trinidad by now. She found she could scarcely remember Ambrose's face. Its pale elegance seemed to slip out of her mind each time she thought she had just secured it. This was the most disturbing thing of all.

After what had seemed an indefinite stalemate, a strange event happened. It was caused by a letter that arrived for Blane with the post at breakfast. Blane had been grumbling, but only halfheartedly, and he seemed to be in a good humor. "Fifty yards of silk damask, ten yards of French gray taffeta, one hundred yards of bottle-green embossed velvet. Are we setting up a drapery business? I hope you have something more cheerful than bills in your post, Mama."

"I have a letter from my jeweler," Lady Malvina answered. "He says he still has the pearl necklace I had to sacrifice when your father was being so eccentric about money. I can have it back for the same sum paid me."

"How much was that?" Amalie asked suspiciously.

"Only five hundred pounds. A trifle compared with all those fabulous materials you are getting, my dear. A hundred yards of embossed velvet. Tch, tch!"

"The materials are for the house. Which we all share," Amalie said pointedly.

"Be quiet!" Blane's voice was startling. He had a letter in his hand. He seemed very disturbed.

"What is it, Blane? Bad news?" asked his mother apprehensively.

Amalie half stood up. "Blane—"

Their tension, Sarah realized, was never very far below the surface. Was that a sign of guilt?

"Yes, I have some news," he said quietly, not adding whether the news was good or bad. "I'll have to go to London on the afternoon train."

"Blane, what *is* this unexpected news?" demanded Lady Malvina testily. "Aren't we to be permitted to know?"

Blane had recovered his poise. His eyes were sparkling now. He was a man to enjoy a fight. So there must still be something to fight over,

Sarah reflected. Whatever that letter had contained was not yet a defeat.

It was Amalie who could not hide her alarm. She had become very pale, and when Blane left the room she hurried after him to talk privately.

Sarah longed to follow. "Will you excuse me, Lady Malvina? I must go up to the schoolroom."

But Lady Malvina clutched her hand. "What was in that letter, do you think? Something's upset my son."

"I expect some business affair, Lady Malvina."

"It was more than business. Because it affected Amalie too. Did you see the way she looked? Oh dear, I hope nothing's gone wrong."

It was too late now. Amalie and Blane would be shut in the study, beyond overhearing. Sarah swallowed her disappointment.

"What do you think could go wrong, Lady Malvina?"

"Oh, things, things." Lady Malvina at last released Sarah's hand. "I tell you, Miss Mildmay, I'm never easy about my son. He's been so undisciplined and unpredictable. One always lives on tenterhooks with him. And now I'll be bound he'll go off to London without telling anyone why. That letter may even have been perfectly harmless, and he's trumping up an excuse to get away for a while. He's so restless."

"If that's the case, he acted very well," Sarah commented.

"Oh, acting. He would find that a very trifling difficulty."

Lady Malvina drummed on the table with her fingers; then, with her usual optimism, she suddenly brightened and exclaimed, "At least there's one good thing. If Blane's in London he can redeem my pearls."

Amalie had come back quietly into the room and heard the last words. A flash of vicious anger crossed her face. "There will be no time for that, I'm afraid. Blane has important business."

Lady Malvina pouted. "What sort of business?"

"I don't know. My husband doesn't worry me with details."

"Amalie!" Lady Malvina's voice held apprehension again. "It isn't anything to do with the case?"

"Of course not. You must realize that's finished and done with. Miss Mildmay, isn't it time for Titus' lesson?"

Sarah found it difficult to reply meekly. Why should she obey this shallow, petulant and, at present, very frightened woman? The mysterious thing that Blane, after a startled moment, intended to meet with his familiar confident arrogance had frightened his wife very much. She was not going to have an easy minute while her husband was in London.

If it came to that, neither was Sarah. Somehow she had to get her hands on that very interesting letter. She decided quite simply to go into the study at the time the maids cleaned it and say she had been sent by the master to get something out of his desk.

Indeed, the method was successful enough. The catch was that the letter did not appear to be there. Blane must be carrying it about in his pocket. It seemed she would remain in ignorance. This was intolerable! Ambrose would not have let an opportunity like this slip by. He would have found out who was meeting Blane, and why.

He would have followed Blane to London. . . .

IT WAS LATE the next day when Sarah rang the bell at the servants' entrance to the house in South Kensington. She had her face well muffled in a woolen scarf. The very young maid named Lucy opened the door and gave a little cry. "Lawks! Is it you, Miss Mildmay?"

"Yes, Lucy. I had to come to London to see the dentist."

"Oh, miss! Had you the toothache bad?" Lucy peered sympathetically.

"It's getting better now. I'll be all right after a night's rest."

"And me keeping you on the doorstep," Lucy exclaimed. "Come right in. There's only me and the housekeeper, Mrs. Robbins, here. And such a fuss when the master arrived yesterday!"

Following Lucy in, Sarah said, "Is the master here now?"

"Yes, he's waiting for someone, but no one's come. Right bad-tempered he's been. Saying why should he come to town on a wild-goose chase."

Sarah let the scarf drop from her face. Presently she would wash off the rouge that gave her the appearance of a high fever. Everyone, she was sure, had been quite taken in with her story of a night of agony and the necessity to see her own dentist in London immediately.

She had had a qualm about leaving Titus, however. Underneath the surface of his growing assurance he still had some deep insecurity.

"Are you going for ever, Miss Mildmay?" he had said.

"Titus, you silly little creature! Of course not! I'll be back tomorrow or the next day."

His gaze was full of uncertainty. He didn't attempt to embrace her but merely stood there, a little boy in a red velvet jacket, too old and too wise, looking at her with distrustful eyes. "Who will teach me my letters?"

"You may have a holiday until I come back. Eliza will take care of you, and Soames will take you riding."

"What if the mouse—"

"What mouse, Titus darling?"

"The one I hear in the night," he answered in a rush.

"But not every night, Titus. Only once, when you called me."

"It comes out of the fireplace. It's very large—it means to eat me."

"Titus! You're making that up to keep me here."

The little boy shook his head stubbornly. Sarah knelt and put her arms around him. How did she know what night fears he had? "I'll tell Eliza to sleep in the nursery with you, and always leave your light burning. Come, now. Surely you'll be all right for two nights while I get my tooth fixed."

He touched her face gently. “Promise to come back.”

Sarah had left in foolish tears, but this served to give proof of her assumed illness. Even Amalie, who looked to be in some kind of secret anguish herself, expressed wishes for Sarah’s quick recovery.

She had arrived at the London house in time, for apparently Blane had not yet accomplished the purpose for which he had come to town. He was expecting a caller—the writer of that letter, no doubt.

“I’ll go straight up to my room, Lucy. I would like a cup of tea, if you wouldn’t mind bringing it up. And Lucy, would you take care not to let the master know I’m here? It’s better not. He might think it impertinent, my coming here. Or he might think I expect to come down to dinner.”

At that moment there came the crash of the front door being banged shut.

“He’s gone out, thank goodness,” came Mrs. Robbins’ voice from the basement stairs. “Who do I hear you talking to, Lucy? Not that cheeky grocer’s boy again?”

“It’s Miss Mildmay, ma’am. She’s just come with the toothache.”

Sarah pressed her hand to her cheek. “I’m going up to my room, Mrs. Robbins. I’ve asked Lucy not to tell the master I’m here. He might worry about Titus. But I really had to see the dentist, I was suffering so.”

“You poor thing!” said Mrs. Robbins, coming upstairs. Plump and good-natured, she was full of sympathy. “You go right up to bed, my lamb. Lucy will bring you a tray.”

Sarah swayed. “I don’t want to worry anybody, particularly the master.”

“Neither you shall. Though why he shouldn’t be told we’re all human and get our aches and pains, I don’t know. Now he’s gone out leaving strict instructions if anyone calls I’m to keep them until he returns. He’s been expecting someone, but he’s got impatient waiting. Look, how’d it be if we all had a little drop of something? It’d do the tooth good. Keep the cold out for Lucy and me too.”

“No, thank you, Mrs. Robbins. I really must rest.” It was unbelievable luck that Blane had just gone out. Now she could slip into the library at once.

One would have thought he would have been much too careful to leave the letter lying about. But he must have expected Mrs. Robbins to be too uninterested and Lucy too illiterate to notice it. For there it was lying on the desk, in the envelope that had been readdressed painstakingly from this address to Mallow Hall:

Dear Blane,

Fancy, I thought you was dead. But I have just heard about you and all that business. You could have knocked me down with a feather. You never told me all that. So I am coming to London to see you. We have a lot to talk about. Expect me Thursday or Friday this week.

Yours faithfully,
Sammie

The postmark, Sarah noticed curiously, was Liverpool. Liverpool could mean someone who had just arrived on a ship. From the West Indies? Someone who had only just heard of the celebrated case and was eagerly expecting some share? Was he an old shipmate who thought he had stumbled onto a good thing—or a blackmailer?

Sammie. Soon Sarah would discover who he was. And the coming meeting between the two men promised to provide her with the vital evidence for which Ambrose was waiting. For if the writer of the letter thought the man who had received it was the true Blane Mallow and then found him to be an impostor, what would happen? Sarah sat with the door of her room ajar, listening.

An hour later the front doorbell pealed and she jumped convulsively, then ran softly to the head of the stairs. There was no difficulty in hearing Blane's loud and jovial voice. "Stoke up the fire in the library, Mrs. Robbins, and bring in the whiskey. It's a deuced cold night—my friend here is almost frozen stiff."

"Just about, gov'nor," came the reply in a cockney voice.

"Why are you standing there staring, Mrs. Robbins? Go and do as I say."

Sarah, in her extreme curiosity, ventured halfway down the curving stairs. She was just in time to see the two men disappear into the library; Blane's companion was a short man in a shabby, snow-covered cloak. How could a man like that have legitimate business with Lord Mallow?

They had shut the library door. Sarah waited until Mrs. Robbins had bustled in and out again, then she boldly went up to the door and put her ear to the keyhole. However, the door was inches thick and quite soundproof. She could hear only a confused murmur of voices. But fortunately for her she detected the sound of glasses put down and chairs moved—after a surprisingly short time, as if the business had been very brief indeed. She was just able to fly to the stairs before the door opened.

But her curiosity was her downfall. For, still looking around as she climbed the stairs, her foot caught in the hem of her skirt. She clutched wildly at the rail, failed to reach it and tumbled ignominiously to the bottom of the stairs.

For a moment she was conscious of nothing but pain. The gaslight danced above her in a luminous haze, then was blotted out by the shape of a head. She began to struggle up.

"Lor lumme! 'As she 'urt 'erself?" she heard the cockney voice saying.

Then she was aware of Blane leaning over her and the cold, furious anger in his face. Her heart turned over with its second shock, and faintness swept over her.

"Is she 'urt?" the other man repeated.

"I don't think so, Cabbie."

Cabbie! Was that all the stranger was? She had been brought to this predicament by trying to overhear a conversation between Blane and a London cabbie!

"Not seriously hurt, anyway," Blane said. "I'll see to her. You get on your way."

"Well, thanks, guv'nor, for the bit of good cheer. Wish all the gentry 'ad your kind 'eart. Sure you don't want me to stop at a doctor's with a message?"

"Good heavens, no! The young woman's only taken a tumble. Haven't you, Miss Mildmay? You're not hurt, are you?"

Sarah at last managed to sit upright. "N-not at all. I'm p-perfectly all right. Except for," she gasped, "the toothache."

After the shabby little man had gone out, Blane said, "I didn't know that the toothache came on from falling downstairs."

"I—had to come up to see the dentist. That's why I'm in London."

"And the dentist has applied a remedy that has made you dizzy? Allow me to assist you to your feet, Miss Mildmay."

He was too close to her. She wanted to shrink away. But he seemed to have controlled that moment of black anger and was wearing his look of ironic amusement again.

"I can at least look on your pain as a blessing," he went on. "Now I'll have someone to eat dinner with me. Why, I believe you *are* hurt."

For Sarah, on her feet, found herself quite unable to stand. She had broken several bones in her ankle at the very least! She had to cling desperately to Blane's supporting arm, and, just as Mrs. Robbins appeared, full of exclamations, felt herself swung into his arms.

"Lor, has the toothache taken her again, my lord?"

"Yes, in a curious place. Her ankle. Bring hot water and bandages, Mrs. Robbins."

Sarah was carried into the library and laid on the leather couch. The pain came back in a spasm as Blane took off her boot. He felt the ankle with a touch that was almost professional. "Not too serious, I think. Just a sprain, Miss Mildmay. But I'll warrant it's dispatched your toothache."

She believed he was laughing at her now. He was kneeling beside her, his face on a level with hers, the blackness of his eyes full of light.

"So you fell down the stairs," he said, and now the amusement was evident in his voice. "One could inquire what you were doing on the stairs just at that particular moment. Or even, indeed, why you should be seized with toothache the moment my back is turned."

Sarah summoned all her dignity. "If you must know what I was doing on the stairs, I was coming down to ask Mrs. Robbins for something soothing for my tooth. It is still very painful."

"But my dear young woman, you should have come to me for that remedy. I've just been dispensing it to the cabbie who drove me home from my club. He was almost frozen to his seat, poor devil. Now you shall have precisely the same mixture. Ah, Mrs. Robbins, bring the things here. You might bathe her ankle while I prescribe more effectively."

Blane poured a glass of rum and stood over Sarah. His face was full of impudence. Sarah knew he was thoroughly suspicious, but at the moment found herself quite unable to care. Her pain and her fury with herself, and with Blane for his extraordinarily intimate attitude, were too much.

"If that drink is to make me recover, Lord Mallow, I'd better have it at once." She took the glass out of his hand and drained the contents, choking a little over the unaccustomed fiery taste.

"May I ask you to be so good, my lord, as to leave the room while I remove Miss Mildmay's stocking?" Mrs. Robbins said primly.

"Of course. Of course." The impudent eyebrows were raised high. "And after that we'll take our dinner in here."

"Please excuse me, Lord Mallow. I would prefer to retire."

"The devil you would. But you can scarcely get upstairs without being carried. So you will have to wait my pleasure."

"Lor!" Mrs. Robbins murmured after he went out. "He is in a playful mood. It's being away from his wife, if you ask me."

As the rum had its effect the pain at last became tolerable. But her ankle seemed to be the size of two, and there was no doubt she was compelled to stay on the couch.

Presently Lucy, wide-eyed and scandalized, came in to prepare the table for dinner. "Lawks, Miss Mildmay, is he making you his prisoner?"

"Don't be foolish, Lucy!"

Lucy scampered out as Blane returned. "That's better, Miss Mildmay. You have some color again."

"I believe the drink has helped, Lord Mallow." Unaccustomed to strong liquor, she found her head was swimming. She felt strangely carefree.

"Now, let me take a look at Mrs. Robbins' bandage."

Before Sarah could prevent him, he had twitched off the lap robe that Mrs. Robbins had spread over her and his searching fingers were feeling the wrappings around her ankle. "Tch, tch! It'll have to be redone. Allow me. Now, why are you looking so outraged?"

"I believe you're merely enjoying yourself!" Sarah exclaimed. "The bandage is perfectly all right."

"On the contrary! It's giving you no support at all. See, this is how it should be."

There was no doubt that he was exceedingly skillful. "May I ask where you gained your experience, Lord Mallow? Are sprained ankles a natural hazard to a sailor's life?"

"Everything from sprained ankles to broken hearts. And an occasional case of bubonic plague, or perhaps a murder."

"In contrast, all this comfort must seem very pleasant."

"Pleasant but monotonous. A sailor's life is a man's life. If you're wondering what I'm doing here, it is, as I've already made clear, for my son. By the way, is Titus all right while you're away?"

"Perfectly all right, as I imagine he was before I came."

"He wasn't as well as all that, Miss Mildmay. You mentioned it yourself in no uncertain terms. But I believe he's growing fond of you now. There, does that feel better?"

Reluctantly Sarah had to admit that it did.

"Then we'll have some food."

Lucy had lit candles on the table. The yellow flames flickered bewilderingly. Sarah felt her face very hot. She must not be taken in for a moment. She *must* go on hating this man. "You accomplished your own business satisfactorily, I hope?" she said politely.

"No. As it happens, I haven't. The person I was to see has let me down. I shall wait only one more day, and then they can go to the devil."

His glance was completely without evasion. "We shall probably travel back to Mallow together. You'll have to tolerate my company since you'll need assistance with that foot."

A convenient way of keeping her under his eye? If so, she deserved it. But sitting up at the table, facing him over the candlelight, was an ordeal; and even more so was confining herself to thin broth for her supposed toothache while he ate the tantalizingly savory venison with great enjoyment.

She made herself wince now and then. This was almost overplaying her part, for Blane, with one of his acute glances, observed, "I believe your dentist hasn't done his job very well. You'd better see mine tomorrow."

"Oh no! I shall be quite recovered tomorrow."

He had opened a bottle of burgundy to drink with the meal. The meager half glass Sarah permitted herself increased her feeling of unreality. The face opposite her, she thought, fitted these surroundings well. With its strong lines and its boldness, it was eminently suitable. This was something she must not write in her notes for Ambrose. It was a discovery she had stumbled on and must forget.

"So unless I carry you upstairs, Miss Mildmay, it will be *you* for the couch tonight," he said, his eyes glinting with a wicked merriment.

Sarah started as the words penetrated her dulled mind. The couch! How was he aware that she had known about that night in Tom Mercer's inn?

"And your reason is as legitimate as mine was," he added smoothly.

"I—I was looking for the kitchen. For milk for Titus. I didn't mean—I thought you were asleep."

"And I thought you were snooping. You're much too attractive for that, Miss Mildmay. You're exceedingly attractive, do you realize? Wearing the Mallow diamonds, for instance. . . ."

Did he *know?* Sarah had a flash of alarm, realizing that just as she might succeed in unmasking him, so might he her.

"What an extraordinary thing to say, Lord Mallow!"

"Merely a fancy. My wife intends to wear them any day now. She's asked me to get them out of the bank. I'm not entirely sure she has quite the type of looks for them."

"Lord Mallow, I must demand to know why you said such an extraordinary thing to me."

He looked at her above the dancing candle flames. "Just a passing thought, Miss Mildmay. Nothing more, I assure you. Your eyes are as bright as diamonds tonight. Perhaps it's the wine."

He sat back, and his voice was suddenly curt. "You will go back to Mallow, Miss Mildmay. I accept your story that you had a severe toothache and that exhaustion after a long day caused you to be rather clumsy in descending the stairs. The outcome of that mishap is going to be much more inconvenient to you than anyone else. So we'll close the subject."

"Lord Mallow, are you suggesting that you might *doubt* my reason for being here?"

His eyes narrowed for a moment. Then he threw back his head and gave a disconcerting shout of laughter. "Never trust a pretty woman. I believe my wife was right when she wanted to send you packing. But you'll go back to Mallow because Titus has grown fond of you."

CHAPTER NINE

IT GREW DARK EARLY the next afternoon. The snow that had fallen over London had not touched the coast, but heavy clouds and an arctic wind persisted. No one knew why Miss Mildmay had not returned as she had promised. Soames had come back from the station reporting that no one at all had gotten off the train. Amalie was furious.

Yesterday she had had a tea party to occupy her and had been the grand hostess, dressed in expensive plum-colored taffeta with diamond eardrops glittering at her ears. It had been difficult to know what the Blounts and the Fortescues made of such elegance, Lady Malvina reflected. They had not been used to it at Mallow Hall. Her own parties had been haphazard affairs, and she didn't much relish Amalie, that little nobody from the tropics, queening it like this.

At least Lady Malvina could, for a few minutes, hold the floor when Amalie was called from the room to see some unexpected and uninvited visitor. Neither did she lose this advantage, for when Amalie returned she seemed distraught. "Just a sewing woman asking for work," she apologized vaguely. "The matter could have well waited. More tea, Colonel Fortescue? Oh, I see you have some. Mrs. Blount?"

"Did you employ her?" Lady Malvina asked.

"I've asked her to wait. I'll interview her later. Oh dear!" Amalie had knocked a cup of tea onto the carpet. "How clumsy of me!"

Lady Malvina glanced at her daughter-in-law in surprise. Amalie, even when upset, usually had the most calm and controlled movements.

"On your gown too. Never mind. If it stains, this new woman can take a tuck in the skirt. Now, when are you going to have Titus in?" Lady Malvina turned to the company. "You must all see the family likeness. It's remarkable. If anything convinced me I had my son home, that did."

Colonel Fortescue remarked irrelevantly, "I hear Ambrose sailed for the West Indies. Is there any particular reason? Unless," he added gallantly, "he's looking for a lady as charming as Lady Mallow."

Amalie's knuckles showed white where she gripped the tea table, but she said calmly, "I've scarcely had the opportunity to get acquainted with Ambrose. But my husband and I hope to remedy that."

"You can try," said Lady Malvina frankly. "Ambrose isn't a good loser. And what is he doing in the West Indies?"

"A sea voyage is a wonderful antidote for various ills," said Mrs. Blount. "So relaxing. Well, now, we must think of leaving. I shouldn't be surprised if it snows this evening."

All the company proceeded to take its departure, and when they were alone Amalie flung around on Lady Malvina. "Did you hear that? Ambrose has gone to the West Indies! Why? What does he expect to find?"

Lady Malvina's heart was fluttering again with that queer apprehension. "That would be for you to know, my dear."

The lids dropped over Amalie's uneasy eyes. "There's nothing beyond what has already been aired in court. But I wish Ambrose didn't distrust us so. Well, I suppose I must go and interview this wretched woman."

"Wretched?"

"Oh, she looks half starved, poor creature. I expect I must at least give her a trial, since she's come so far."

But Amalie was not a person to show pity, Lady Malvina had discovered. Was there something particularly pathetic about this woman? Something disturbing enough to make Amalie drop cups and lose her self-control?

Lady Malvina spent the next hour in the nursery with Titus, who seemed to be missing Miss Mildmay more than was reasonable. Then Amalie came in to give her brisk orders and say good night to her son.

"Is he all right, Eliza? Are you managing quite well?"

"Yes, ma'am. I'm to sleep in the nursery, Miss Mildmay said."

"Did she? I'm afraid I disagree. Titus isn't to be treated like a baby. You will sleep in your own room, Eliza."

"If the boy calls—" began Lady Malvina, distressed by his look of alarm.

"Why should he call?" said Amalie coldly. She bent to kiss her son's forehead. "Papa would be very angry, Titus, if you weren't a brave boy."

She was rustling out in her imperious way before Lady Malvina remembered to ask about the sewing woman.

"I engaged Mrs. Stone on a week's trial," Amalie answered. "I've put her in the room upstairs."

"Not Bella's room! Not the haunt—" Lady Malvina, belatedly thinking of the child, bit off her words.

"Don't be absurd, Mama. Of course the room isn't haunted. In any case it's the only empty one. But she must be kept busy, so give her any sewing you have. I won't be down to dinner, Mama. I have a headache."

The inquisitive Lady Malvina made a point of visiting the attic room. Mrs. Stone seemed harmless enough. The woman was below middle age, probably not much older than Amalie, but she was very poorly dressed and seemed pinched with cold. She spoke well enough, although with a furtiveness that Lady Malvina didn't care for.

"What brought you to Mallow, Mrs. Stone?"

"I'd heard there was a new mistress. I thought she might need help. Good situations are hard to come by nowadays."

"Where's your husband?"

"I'm a widow, my lady."

"Oh! That's a pity. Any family?"

Mrs. Stone shook her head.

"Well, I hope you'll be comfortable here. I'll give you plenty of work. I've been putting on some weight and my gowns need easing. None of this tight lacing for me. I'll send some up. Good night, Mrs. Stone."

"Good night, my lady."

The next day, when neither Blane nor Miss Mildmay turned up, seemed very long and full of tension. Titus had reverted to his pale-faced timidity, shrinking away from Lady Malvina's embraces. And Amalie couldn't sit still a minute, but walked up and down in her rustling gown, dressed as if for another tea party. Something was on her mind. She was worrying about Blane's mysterious business in London—and Miss Mildmay's overstaying.

"She was to get her tooth attended to and come back at once," Amalie stormed. "I almost believe she didn't have a toothache at all."

"But she was in tears of pain." Lady Malvina liked and trusted Sarah Mildmay, and intended to defend her.

"Then why is the business taking so long? Even if the tooth had to be extracted it would be done in a few minutes."

"There may have been aftereffects. Visits to the dentist are not usually pleasant. Or do you think"—Lady Malvina was suddenly malicious—"that my son finds her company agreeable? He's no saint, you know."

"I trust my husband, but I don't trust that sly creature," Amalie snapped. "Look at the way she inveigled herself into this household."

"Mrs. Stone came the same way and you had no objection to her. But then she's deplorably plain, isn't she?"

Amalie's face was icy. "I'm afraid my head is too bad for conversation. I shall spend the rest of the afternoon in my room."

So after that there was no one to talk to. Lady Malvina took a gown up to Mrs. Stone for alteration. Then sewing materials had to be found for her, since she had arrived without even a thimble. But the woman was disinclined to talk. When she was set to work, Lady Malvina left her and went to her own room, where, bored, she fell asleep in front of the fire.

She woke with a start much later to find the fire almost out and the room filled with pallid twilight. The wintry sky and forlorn tree branches gave her the creeps. She made her way to the window to pull the curtains closed, shutting out the loneliness of the country night. But, her hand on the heavy velvet, she paused and stared out into the gloom.

Was that a woman running? She could scarcely see. There was just that dark glimpse of bundled skirts and streaming hair. Then the form disappeared into the shrubbery and it was difficult to be sure whether she had seen it or not. The night was so still. Now nothing moved at all.

CHAPTER TEN

BLANE CAME INTO THE firelit room with his confident stride. Sarah, lying on the couch with her foot up, made to rise, but he tossed her a package and with a grin said, "Put that on."

"Put what on, Lord Mallow?"

"Open it and see. Lord, it's cold out tonight. And we have to be up at the crack of dawn to catch the first train."

"You have accomplished your business?" Sarah asked.

"No, but the post brought a note from my wife. We're to return at once. Now, do as I told you, Miss Mildmay. Open that and put it on. Or shall I do it for you?"

With a feeling of apprehension Sarah undid the wrappings, disclosing a long, slim jeweler's box. Her fingers were trembling as she opened it. The diamond necklace lay shimmering in the lamplight.

She stared at it for so long that Blane snatched up the necklace and unceremoniously fastened it around her neck himself. Then he stepped back to admire it. "It almost is worth perjuring oneself for, isn't it?"

Sarah's face was flaming. She fumbled for the clasp. "How dare you put them on me! How dare you!"

"My dear young lady, they won't contaminate you." But he was a little startled at her reaction, for he added placatingly, "I merely wanted to see them worn. By a beautiful woman. Diamonds should always be worn, and not hidden in a safety vault."

"Then find some other beautiful woman!" Sarah snapped, almost in tears. The Mallow diamonds, her rightful possession, put on her by this bragging impostor. And now their destination was Amalie's skinny neck.

"I'll undo it. Don't pull it to pieces."

"Please keep your hands off me, Lord Mallow."

Blane straightened himself to give his hearty roar of laughter. "What an unpredictable creature you are. I thought any woman would enjoy wearing a necklace like this, even if only for a few minutes."

"Your joke is in execrable taste."

"I believe *you* think so. Then I must ask you to forgive me. Now, if you'll allow me to unclasp that necklace, Miss Mildmay. I'm afraid the catch is complicated. Perhaps someday you'll tell me why you have this aversion to diamonds. To all diamonds, I wonder, or just these?"

The color deepened in Sarah's cheeks. She felt his probing eyes on her.

"If I were not Lord Mallow—" she heard him saying slowly.

But he did not finish the remark. Abruptly he swung the necklace away from her and tossed it into the velvet-lined box. "I expect these will please my wife. And I have my mother's pearls redeemed. And a present for Titus. So think of the welcome awaiting us tomorrow."

ON THEIR ARRIVAL, the first thing Sarah noticed was the way Amalie's face seemed to have grown even more thin and drawn. She was at the door as Blane helped Sarah from the carriage, and came running down the steps crying, "What's the matter with Miss Mildmay? Has she had an accident?"

Blane left Sarah to go and greet his wife. "Miss Mildmay had the bad luck to sprain her ankle rather severely, my love. She was quite unable to travel yesterday, although she wanted to."

It was impossible not to notice the quick suspicion in Amalie's face as she glanced at Sarah's feet. Sarah obligingly lifted her skirt a few inches to show the bandages and the clumsy slipper she was forced to wear.

Amalie flushed. "I don't disbelieve you, Miss Mildmay, though I don't see how a visit to the dentist involved you in this kind of accident. You'd better go up to Titus at once. He's in one of his difficult states."

Leaning on the stick Blane had acquired for her, Sarah slowly began to climb the steps to the front door. She was not acting now, for her ankle was still very painful and swollen. But she would have given a great deal to overhear Amalie and Blane's conversation.

Blane's voice did follow her. "I have the diamonds for you. You might even wear them at that ball you were talking of giving—"

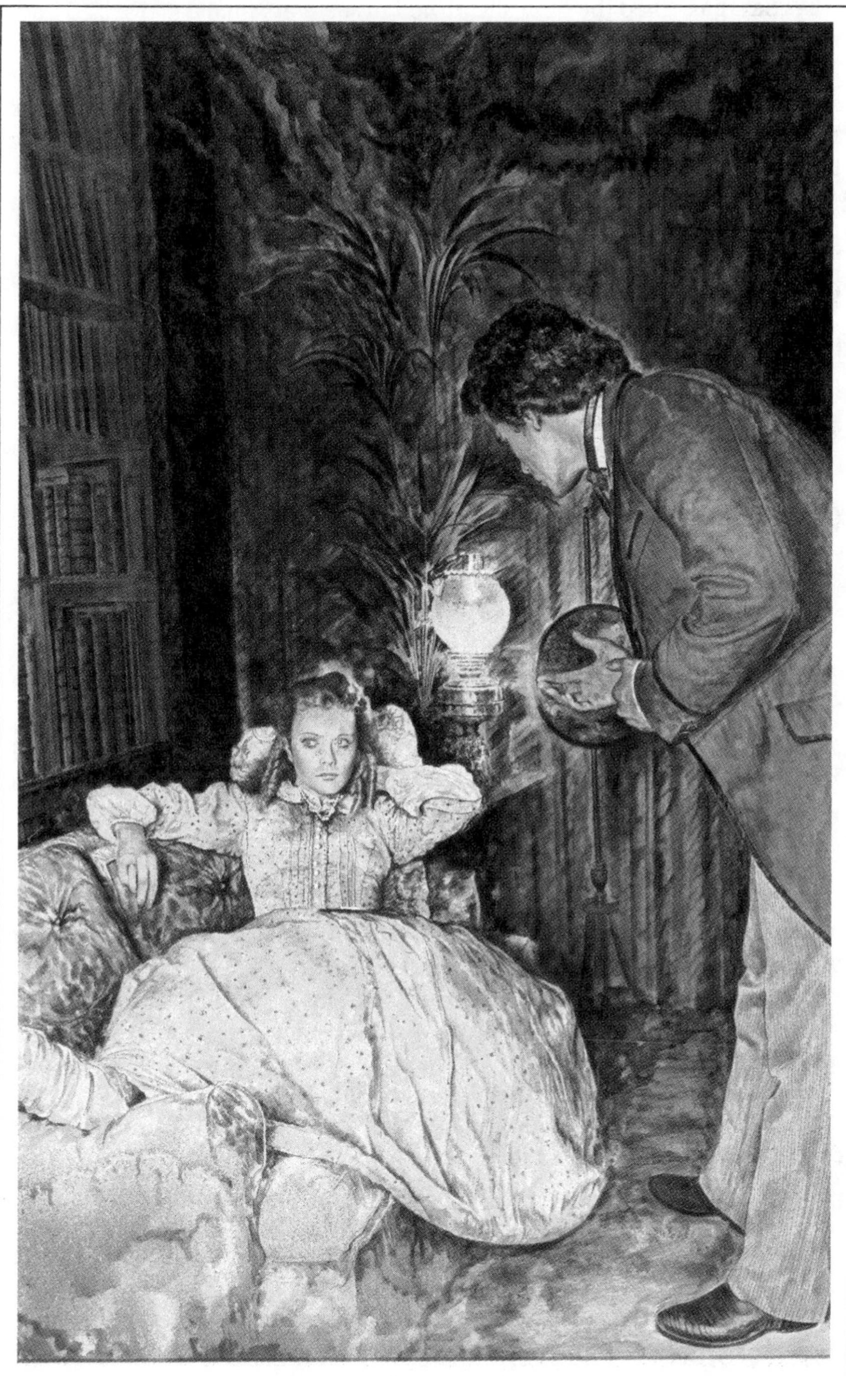

As Sarah reached the door she turned to see that Amalie had seized both of Blane's arms and was about to tell him something, or to embrace him. At that moment Blane chanced to look up and see Sarah pause. With what seemed undue deliberation, he bent his head and kissed his wife on the forehead, and then, more slowly, on the lips. Sarah hurried on, ignoring the pain in her ankle. Somehow she reached the third floor.

She forgot about Blane and Amalie when she was in the schoolroom. For Titus had completely lost the endearing gaiety and liveliness that she had encouraged in him. He sat silently at his desk, and when Sarah spoke to him he merely gazed at her with a look of hostility.

"Titus, come here and answer me when I speak to you."

Titus slipped off his chair and walked to the window, turning his back on her. What had happened to the child?

"Did you think I wouldn't come back?" Sarah asked gently.

"I don't care!" he muttered.

"But I did come back. And now you won't even speak to me. Eliza! Come and tell me what's wrong with Titus."

Eliza came from the nursery. "He had a nightmare."

"But you were sleeping with him?"

"No. You said I was to, but the mistress wouldn't allow it."

"I don't care," said Titus again loudly. "I wasn't frightened."

He resisted stiffly as Sarah lifted him into her arms. "You said you would come back and you didn't."

"But I've come now, Titus darling. I couldn't yesterday because I have a sore foot. Look, it has a bandage on it."

"Does it hurt?"

"It hurt a great deal at first. I fell down some stairs, which was very foolish. But now what's this about the bad dreams, Titus? Tell me."

"The light—went out," the child whispered. Suddenly his hostility melted and he flung his arms around Sarah's neck, holding her in a desperate embrace. "I heard someone crying."

"That was the second night," Eliza put in. "The first night he said someone had been walking in his room and leaning over him. I didn't take much notice. I said he'd been dreaming."

"Did you hear anything, Eliza? This crying, for instance?"

"I didn't until Titus called me, and then I thought I did. A sort of wild cry." Eliza shivered involuntarily.

"Was it a windy night?"

"Why, yes. The curtain was blowing, and the night-light had gone out. Don't tell the mistress, Miss Mildmay, but we were so scared that I took Titus into my bed."

"That seems most sensible, Eliza. I expect the wind was rattling a loose shutter."

Eliza nodded in nervous agreement. "I expect so, miss. It just seems scary in the middle of the night."

"I don't think Titus will have any more nightmares. Will you, my darling?" Sarah said to him. "Tonight you shall have hot milk when you go to bed, and you'll sleep so soundly you won't hear a thing."

"Will you be here?" the child whispered.

"Of course I'll be here. And Papa's home too. He has a present for you."

You will go back to Mallow because Titus has grown fond of you! It had been difficult to make herself meekly obey that autocratic voice. Now, watching the tremulous happiness in Titus' face, she knew that she had to stay until the end. Whatever the end might be. . . .

SARAH WOULD HAVE preferred to have made her injury an excuse for not going down to dinner that night. But she had a feverish desire to observe Blane and Amalie's manner. Would any comment be made on the failure of the mysterious Sammie to materialize?

As she was dressing, Lady Malvina came in in her unceremonious way. She was elaborately attired and wore the pearls Blane had brought home.

"Well, Miss Mildmay, between you and me, my daughter-in-law doesn't think a lot of your accident."

"I didn't try to fall, Lady Malvina."

"Well, I believe she thinks you did." Lady Malvina chuckled maliciously. "Have you never met a jealous woman, Miss Mildmay?"

"But she's not jealous of me!" Sarah gasped.

"She's jealous of everybody. In my opinion you're a great deal prettier than that foreign-looking creature. I suppose I shouldn't talk like this. But I confess I have little in common with my son's wife. Why she must take to her bed like a sick cat when her husband's away for a couple of nights, I don't know."

"Did she do that, Lady Malvina?"

"Apart from playing the grand lady at a tea party, yes. Someone told her that my nephew Ambrose had gone to the West Indies, and that seemed to alarm her."

Sarah spoke carefully. "Why should it do that?"

"I haven't the least idea." Lady Malvina's voice had grown loud and belligerent. "I might have known Ambrose wouldn't be a good loser. Blane says he'll fall in love with a Spanish beauty and stay in Trinidad. But for my part, I can't see Ambrose falling in love with anybody."

"Perhaps you don't know your nephew very well, Lady Malvina. Oh dear! Now I've torn my dress." In her anger at not being able to defend Ambrose more openly, Sarah had snatched at her dinner gown and caught it in the wardrobe door.

"Don't worry, my dear. We have a sewing woman now. A Mrs. Stone.

She'll mend that in a moment. You'll find her upstairs in Bella's room."

"The haunted room!"

Lady Malvina waved her fan. "My dear, I'm sure the room isn't haunted. And unless the other servants have told Mrs. Stone, she doesn't know the room's history. By the way, the boy missed you, Miss Mildmay. He was exceedingly naughty."

"He had nightmares again," said Sarah flatly. "He said someone walked about his room."

Lady Malvina's eyes seemed to protrude more than usual. "That's absurd," she said. "Who would go into his room at night? He must have heard that woman walking about overhead."

But it was impossible not to be aware of Lady Malvina's uneasiness over Titus' safety. Looking into the suddenly forlorn old face, Sarah didn't want to say more. "You are sure this woman will sew my dress?" she asked hurriedly. "I'll go up to her now."

"Yes, you'd better hurry. The dinner gong will be sounding shortly."

Sarah limped up the stairs and tapped at Mrs. Stone's door. A rather sulky voice bade her come in. The woman sitting at the table spread with sewing materials was thin and nondescript, though had she been a little plumper, her face would have had a certain rather common prettiness.

"Mrs. Stone? I'm Miss Mildmay, the governess. Lady Malvina said you would be kind enough to do this piece of sewing for me. I tore my gown."

"All right. Put it down. When do you want it?"

"For dinner this evening, if possible. In half an hour?"

The woman's pale eyes slid over Sarah with a rather unpleasant look. "So you're the young lady who got delayed in London," she said.

Sarah ignored the remark and said haughtily, "Will you bring the dress to my room when you've finished? I find the stairs very difficult."

"Very well. If you want it so quick, I'd better start it."

Sarah had no desire to linger. But something made her pause and say, "I hope you enjoy being here, Mrs. Stone."

"It's well enough. But I don't intend to stay long. Between you and me, I don't care for her ladyship."

"Then what brought you here?" Sarah was interested against her will.

"Have to keep myself since I lost my husband," the woman replied laconically. "I heard there were new folks at Mallow, so I came. But I shan't stay long. Just time enough to put a bit by."

SARAH WAITED THE half hour for Mrs. Stone to return her dress, and when it didn't come she made another painful climb to the attic. When she knocked at the door there was no answer, so she opened it and looked in. The lamp was burning and her dress was spread out, the needle and cotton still in it. But there was no sign of Mrs. Stone.

How exasperating! She would have to finish the sewing herself. It seemed to be nearly finished, but it was not done particularly neatly. Sarah looked in astonishment at the clumsy stitches. Either Mrs. Stone was a hoax and would be quickly found out, or she had considered the governess's work not worth bothering about.

Late as Sarah was going down, Amalie and Blane were later. Lady Malvina grumbled loudly at their unpunctuality. "This is very thoughtless. I get bad-tempered if I have to wait for my food. Oh, here's Blane at last. Where's Amalie?"

"Amalie isn't coming down. She isn't feeling well."

"Again! What's wrong with the woman?"

"She got caught in the rain out riding this afternoon. I think she has a chill. Well, what are we waiting for?"

His face was frowning and impatient. He hadn't given Sarah even a glance. It was clear that he was upset about something.

Lady Malvina pouted over her soup. "Well, I did think we'd have a little gaiety tonight. This house is like a tomb."

"Be thankful you're in it at all, Mama," Blane answered curtly.

His hair, Sarah noticed, was shining in the lamplight, as though he had just come in out of the rain.

"Well, Miss Mildmay, where's your appetite? I trust you haven't caught a chill too?"

Sarah winced at Lady Malvina's raucous voice. She bent her head over her soup, but not before Blane's moody glance had caught hers.

"Toothache again, Miss Mildmay?"

The sarcasm brought the color to her cheeks. But she answered composedly, "Only a little remaining tenderness, Lord Mallow."

"Then take your time. No one's hurrying you."

BLANE'S REMARK MIGHT have meant anything. One might have imagined him impatiently solicitous of her trifling ailments. But the letter from Aunt Adelaide the next day proved otherwise:

> My dear Sarah,
>
> Why did that fellow calling himself Lord Mallow come snooping here to ask about your testimonials? He got nothing from me, I assure you. I suggested it was a little late in the day to make inquiries, since you had already been with his family for several weeks. He made no explanations and admitted that you seemed to be an excellent governess, if a little unorthodox. Had you been unorthodox while in my employ? I enjoyed myself enormously inventing two daughters now at school in Paris who owed a great deal to your charming influence. I emphasized that his son could not be more fortunate in having you with him. He agreed with this. Then he took his departure, having discovered nothing he did not know already.

He cannot know about you and Ambrose, but I would not trust him one inch. What he determines to discover, he will. I tremble for you, my dearest Sarah, but I know you will be equal to this situation. However, come home the moment you feel there may be danger.

Your devoted aunt

So Blane *had* been growing suspicious of her. She hoped she would be able to go on perplexing him for longer than he perplexed her.

Sarah had read the letter in the privacy of her bedroom, but now Eliza had Titus ready for his morning lessons. Eliza was full of important information herself. "Miss Mildmay, that sewing woman has gone! The room's empty of all her things. She must have just left in the night."

For a moment Sarah had an involuntary picture of the room as she had seen it last night, with her green dress spread half-finished on the table and the lamp burning. But Mrs. Stone's belongings were still there then.

"In one way you can't blame her," Eliza went on. "Putting her in that room. She might have got feared and run off."

Later Amalie came to the schoolroom. Her face was pale and there were dark marks beneath her eyes. But when Sarah said, "I hope you're feeling better, Lady Mallow," she answered that she was perfectly recovered.

"The hot whiskey and milk my husband prescribed cured me. He's very good at remedies, as no doubt you discovered, Miss Mildmay, when you injured your ankle."

"Mrs. Robbins cared for me," Sarah answered coolly, then said, "Perhaps you'd like to see how well Titus is progressing with his letters?"

"Is he, the lamb? Come and show Mama, Titus."

It was the first time Amalie had come to the schoolroom. Her effect on Titus was to make him nervous and silent. She pouted when he edged away from her embrace, but in a moment said gaily, "Little boys don't like to be fussed over, do they? I'll just sit here quietly and watch."

She sat on the low chair by the smoky fire, silent for a while as she had promised, but with one foot tapping up and down and a far-off look in her eyes. Sitting there, she looked rather young and forlorn. The gray weather must depress her after the blue skies of the Caribbean, Sarah thought. She suddenly felt pity. "You no doubt miss the sunshine, Lady Mallow."

Amalie hugged her arms about herself. "I hate this weather! I hate it! And the sound of the wind in the night." She got up to stand looking out of the window. "My husband doesn't understand," she added, in a voice so low that Sarah scarcely heard.

Amalie flung around. "Why can't this place be gayer? We must have parties. Musical evenings. I enjoy playing and singing. I like to dance too. That's what we'll do." She lifted her skirts and twirled in a waltz. "Like that. Don't you think Mama should dance, Titus?"

Her face was bright with a kind of desperate gaiety. "We'll give a ball.

Why shouldn't we? We can afford it and we have plenty of servants. Oh, by the way," she said, dropping her skirts, "that wretched creature I engaged for sewing has gone already. Things are appalling, Miss Mildmay, when one only has to speak sharply to a servant and notice is given. I had to speak to Mrs. Stone about her very indifferent work."

"I noticed she sewed badly," Sarah said.

"Oh, you did? I'm glad you saw that too. She'd lied, of course, claiming to be an expert needlewoman. But I'd have given her another chance if she hadn't taken offense. She just packed her bag and went."

Amalie's eyes went to Titus. "But this isn't a subject for the schoolroom. And I'm interrupting lessons. What a pity, Miss Mildmay, that if we give a ball your ankle will scarcely be well enough for dancing." Whatever strange mood had possessed Amalie, now she was behaving true to her narrow and jealous nature again, making sly comments at Sarah's expense.

Sarah didn't give much thought to the strange woman who had so briefly occupied Bella's room. But later in the day some need for action—to ease her own sense of frustration—took her up to the now-empty room.

The lamp still stood on the table, but all the sewing materials had vanished. In the fading light the room was gloomy. Sarah admitted she wouldn't like to stay there long. Her eyes caught something that startled her. It looked like a black cat curled on the top of the wardrobe. What was it?

She stood on a chair to look. Then she gingerly put out her hand to retrieve the object. It was Mrs. Stone's black straw bonnet. But all her other belongings had gone. Why on earth should she hurry off and leave her bonnet? It wasn't even likely that she had had an alternative one to wear.

The chilly distaste the room gave her seemed to center in this limp, inanimate object dangling from her hand. She had an overwhelming impulse to drop it and run. But panic was foolish. This required investigating.

She went downstairs to the drawing room, where she knew she would find Amalie. The timing was fortuitous, for not only Amalie but Blane and Lady Malvina were there, finishing their tea.

Sarah pretended a naïve surprise. "Look what I found in Mrs. Stone's room. Why should she leave without her bonnet? I keep thinking of her in this cold wind with nothing on her head, poor creature."

"Poor creature!" Amalie was on her feet, her face blazing with anger. "No wonder she didn't take her disgusting old bonnet. Miss Mildmay, throw it on the fire. This minute."

"What on earth is all this?" demanded Lady Malvina. "Amalie, are you out of your head? Burning a servant's possessions! Surely the woman wasn't that bad."

"Bad!" Amalie exclaimed. "She only helped herself to some pieces of jewelry and other things out of my room, including that new bonnet you bought for me, Blane. My nicest one, the blue velvet with roses." Amalie snatched the shabby straw bonnet out of Sarah's hands and tossed it onto the flames. Then she rubbed her hands hard, as if rubbing off the contact. "Miss Mildmay, isn't it time you brought Titus down?"

"Before Miss Mildmay goes," drawled Blane from his chair by the fire, "perhaps she will tell us just what she was doing in Mrs. Stone's room."

"She was doing some sewing for you, wasn't she, Miss Mildmay?" Lady Malvina prompted helpfully.

"Yes, she was. But that was last evening." Sarah took a deep breath. "If Lord Mallow really wishes to know, I was testing a theory."

"What theory, Miss Mildmay? That Mrs. Stone was secreted in the wardrobe or behind the paneling?"

"Nothing so melodramatic, Lord Mallow. Merely that Mrs. Stone might have left because she was nervous about that room."

Blane regarded her with lazily narrowed eyes. "And what were your own reactions, Miss Mildmay? Did you sit up there in the dark and get pleasantly spooky?"

"I did find it rather uncanny," she said evenly. "But perhaps women are more susceptible to these influences."

"I can't believe Mrs. Stone was frightened away by a ghost," Lady Malvina said emphatically.

"This conversation is ridiculous!" Amalie screeched, as if her nerves were stretched beyond endurance. "The woman left because she couldn't sew. She was also a thief. And if Miss Mildmay is going to behave in this extraordinary way, she's not a suitable person to be in charge of Titus."

"Never mind Miss Mildmay," put in Lady Malvina impatiently. "If the woman's a thief the police should be informed."

Amalie sank into a chair, as if on the point of collapse. "She isn't worth the fuss. I only want to forget her."

CHAPTER ELEVEN

"BLANE, THERE'S NO NECESSITY to go. I settled the matter."

"Do you really think that will be the end of it?"

There was a momentary silence. Then Amalie said in a low voice, "I do." She began to laugh breathlessly. "Perhaps I make myself believe it because I can't bear you to go away again."

"Amalie! You know I don't like possessive women."

Sarah had begun to dread going down to dinner. She was no longer eager to eavesdrop. As strangers, impostors, usurpers, they deserved all the harm she could do them. But whatever else they might be, they were not strangers any longer. They were real people. Even Amalie. Foolishly, she hadn't visualized getting this involved. But so many things were spoiled. The thought of wearing the Mallow diamonds, or of Lady Malvina's being deprived of her home, or of Titus' being thrust back into insecurity, was difficult to contemplate.

Nevertheless, this accidentally overheard conversation revived her curiosity. Blane's reference to going somewhere must have meant that he still wanted to track down the mysterious Sammie. But Amalie disagreed.

Lady Malvina was coming down the stairs, her wide skirts making a great rustling. Sarah, caught lingering outside the drawing-room door, blessed the old lady for her obtuseness and waited for Lady Malvina to precede her into the room. The conversation within ceased. Amalie was holding her hands out to the fire, as if she were chilly in spite of the flush on her cheeks.

"Well, Amalie, I'm glad you've had some fresh air today," Lady Malvina said. "Didn't I see you down by the lake?"

"The lake? Oh yes. It must be a charming spot in summer, but in winter—*b-r-r-r!* However, one must walk somewhere."

"Are you bored with the ancestral home already?" Blane asked softly.

"No, but I think we should have more gaiety. We do nothing. We've been to church three times, and had people in to tea, and had a great deal of fuss and inconvenience with decorators, and that's the sum total of our exciting country life. I've been thinking about that ball, Blane."

"I must say that's a splendid idea," said Lady Malvina. "We can all wear our finery. Miss Mildmay, I hope you have brought a ball gown."

"I will be more than content to watch," Sarah said, surprised at Lady Malvina's imagining that a governess, naturally poor since she had to be a governess, should possess a ball gown. "I fear my foot—"

Amalie was tapping her own foot impatiently. "Mama, let's talk about more practical aspects. Whom we should invite, for instance. Of course, we will expect Miss Mildmay to bring Titus down for half an hour."

I CANNOT, CANNOT, cannot stand this kind of treatment any longer, Sarah wrote in her diary that night. *I didn't come here to be a doormat! And why should I look dowdy while Amalie dresses like a duchess? I am sorry, Ambrose, but this has been too much to ask of me. Though how can I forsake Titus now? What am I to do?*

It seemed that her mind was to be made up for her.

Out riding with Soames the next day, Titus had a fall. It wasn't a severe one, but Soames sensibly carried the child into his cottage, which was nearby, and then hurried up to the big house.

Blane had gone for a day's hunting, and Amalie was not to be found. "Her ladyship will be down at the lake, most likely," Soames said to Sarah in his knowing way. "She goes there most afternoons. Perhaps you'd come, miss, and see to the young master. He's not badly hurt, only shaken."

"Of course." As Sarah followed him across the park her gaze kept going toward the steely shine of water beyond the leafless trees. Why was that the only place Amalie cared to walk?

"There's a summerhouse there," Soames said, as if reading her thoughts. "It's shelter against the wind. It's a pity the mistress doesn't take more to riding."

"Better than sitting in a summerhouse in midwinter," Sarah burst out.

"That's what I thought, miss." Soames gave her a sideways glance, and she was sorry she had spoken. This man was not to be trusted.

Titus had recovered a good deal, though he still looked shaken and white. "Dandy threw me," he said importantly. "But I'll ride again tomorrow, won't I, Soames?"

"To be sure you will, Master Titus. You see, miss, he's just like his father was."

Sarah looked about the cosy, firelit room. A well-furnished room for a groom's cottage, she thought. Bribery might have bought the carpet and the carefully polished table and chairs.

"Come, Titus, we must go. Can you walk, or am I to carry you?"

"He can ride on my back," said Soames. "Won't be the first time I've carried the heir to Mallow."

Titus seemed to get over his fall quickly. He ate his supper as usual, and even romped a little with Lady Malvina. But by that time Amalie had heard the news, and came hurrying into the nursery. She snatched the child from Lady Malvina, exclaiming, "Are you sure he isn't hurt? Titus, my love, are you all right? Did you get a horrid fright?"

Titus immediately burst into tears.

Lady Malvina waddled to the door. "Well, of all the foolish behavior, Amalie! Miss Mildmay and I had the boy perfectly calm and happy, and now you're scaring the life out of him."

"Miss Mildmay and you! Of course you know best! You're both so wise. Especially Miss Mildmay! Then why did she allow this to happen to Titus?"

Amalie's startling outburst frightened Titus into crying harder. It convinced her that he was seriously hurt. "Don't cry, my lamb. You must go to bed at once. The idea of not putting you straight to bed when you're sick. Really, Miss Mildmay, I thought you'd have had more sense. You decide not to send for a doctor, not to have me told. Who's son is he, may I ask?"

Sarah bit back her swiftly rising anger. "I don't know what you mean, Lady Mallow. But I assure you Titus isn't hurt. He was merely a little dazed. He's had his supper. Eliza was just about to put him to bed."

Amalie sprang up with the sobbing child in her arms. "I'll put him there myself. Eliza! Get some bottles in the bed at once. And someone must go for the doctor. Mama, could you send Soames?"

"Really, I think you've gone crazy!" Lady Malvina exclaimed. "My son had falls enough, and simply got up and remounted. Do you want to turn the child into a mollycoddle?" She turned and swept out of the room.

Titus was still sobbing, but there was nothing Sarah could do, so she went to her room. Before long there was a sharp knock at her door, and Amalie swept in.

"Miss Mildmay, I want to know how Titus came to fall from his horse, and why you showed so little concern."

"So little concern!" Sarah repeated, astonished. "Are you accusing me of being careless of my duties?"

"More than careless. How did Titus come to fall?"

"I wasn't with him. Soames was there."

"You're sure? You're sure you weren't crossing the park and startled Dandy?"

"Just what are you suggesting?" Sarah whispered.

"I'm not suggesting anything. I'm trying to get to the bottom of the matter. For instance, Titus' nightmares. He never suffered from them before he came here—with you. He never complained of people walking in his room at night."

"But that happened while I was in London with a toothache!"

"And couldn't you have arranged to be away, to leave the child unprotected? And why were you so interested in Mrs. Stone? Even my husband noticed that. Is she a colleague of yours? You both got into this household in the same way, you remember, by simply arriving and asking for employment. I find it all exceedingly strange."

"You're not only suggesting that I might want to harm Titus," Sarah said icily, her chin high, "but that I may also be a thief. I fear, Lady Mallow, this is where we say good-by. I shall leave this evening. Your accusations are scarcely worth defending."

"Perhaps you can't defend them, Miss Mildmay. Perhaps I'm not so easily taken in as my husband by a pretty face."

Sarah started rapidly folding gowns and gathering up toilet things. Would she have to trudge the ten miles to Yarby, as apparently Mrs. Stone had had to do? Was she letting Ambrose down too badly? Or did her desire to escape from this intolerable family now include him too? She didn't know. She only knew she must go at once.

"Do I leave on foot?" she asked.

Amalie was watching from the doorway. She turned away and said, "I'll give orders for Soames to drive you to Yarby. I hope you will be ready within half an hour."

That, Sarah reflected, would allow her to get away before Blane returned. She wanted to avoid any fuss he might make. "I'll be ready, Lady Mallow. And I hope—"

"Yes?"

The words had escaped Sarah involuntarily. She had a poignant thought of Titus waking in the morning and looking for her, of the hurt and betrayal in his face. "I hope Titus will be well and happy."

"That need be no concern of yours, Miss Mildmay."

SOMEONE WAS HAMMERING on the door. Sarah had not been asleep. Her light put out, and sunk deep in the downy bed at the George Inn, she had been lost in a miasma of grief and exhaustion. Ambrose and Mallow Hall were lost forever. She had given them up. But the worst thing to contemplate was Titus' discovery of her desertion. Now someone was knocking on the door. She had to fumble for matches to light the candle, her hand shaking foolishly. Then, a wrap hastily flung on, she went to the door, holding the candle high. "Who is it?" she called. But she knew who it was.

The half-opened door showed her Blane standing in the lamplight, hair disheveled, clothes mud-spattered. "What the devil do you think you're up to, running off when my son is ill? Get dressed and come back at once."

"Titus isn't ill. It's only his mother who says so."

"He may not have been two hours ago, but he is now. He has a high fever, and is asking for you incessantly."

Sarah stepped back, making a move to shut the door, but his hand on it prevented her. "Titus was well when I left. What does the doctor say?"

"The symptoms hadn't developed so seriously when the doctor saw him," Blane said. "They came on after Titus had been told you had gone."

"Who told him at this time of night, when he was upset already? Couldn't that have waited until morning?"

"Or perhaps you could have delayed your departure until morning."

Sarah's eyes sparked angrily. "I may have no money, Lord Mallow, but I do have some pride as a human being."

For a moment she thought he was going to throw back his head and give his irreverent shout of laughter. Instead he said quietly, "My wife is waiting to apologize to you, so I hope you'll be equally tolerant. I'll wait downstairs while you dress. Be as quick about it as you can."

"I'm no longer in your employ, so I won't be ordered about like this."

"I'm not ordering you, Miss Mildmay. I'm merely stating the situation. If you can forsake a sick child, then you must." He turned to go, full of assurance. He knew that she would return to the house with him.

If she was to go back, she decided, this time she wouldn't weaken. She would see the thing through. And win.

Blane had driven in alone to get her. As she stepped outside, muffled in her cloak, he said briskly, "Get up in front. It will be company for me."

"It's a cold night. I'd prefer to ride inside."

"It won't be as cold as that. Come along. Up you go."

She didn't intend to pass the ten-mile drive by making small talk, but sat hunched in silence in the pale moonlight. The wind was very cold. It rustled the dead grass in the flat fields and caught the manes of the horses, tossing them wildly. Sarah was overcome with a feeling of desolation. This was the setting for an eerie play. The characters, already assembled, were about to make their entrance for the final dramatic act. How she knew this, she could not say. But something was about to happen. And she wished she were not to be there. She shuddered.

"Cold?" inquired Blane. "Sit closer so that I can keep the wind off you."

Sarah didn't reply. Neither did she move.

"Who are you, Miss Mildmay?"

That did elicit an indignant reply. "You know very well who I am, Lord Mallow. You've investigated my references yourself."

"You've puzzled me from the beginning. You're obviously too well bred to pursue a *cause célèbre* for mere sensation. Yet you came to my house, deliberately, to ask for a position."

"I needed work."

"But with your references that shouldn't have been difficult. Unless, of course, you're too attractive. That's a consideration, isn't it, where the husband may be susceptible and the wife—"

"You're being preposterous, Lord Mallow."

"And you, Miss Mildmay, are an impostor."

Sarah turned sharply to look at him, and he began laughing.

"You think me one, and I think you one," he said. "Isn't that so?"

"Do you think I would be a governess from choice? It's hardly a cheerful prospect. I have two sisters who are both unhappily doomed to the same life. Does that convince you?"

"What are their names?"

"Amelia and Charlotte. Why do you ask?"

"To make them seem more real. Are they as pretty as you?"

Sarah stiffened. She was now very angry and disturbed. But apart from leaping from the carriage, she couldn't escape. "Lord Mallow, I'm coming back to Mallow Hall because Titus is ill. Or so you tell me. But as soon as he's well I intend to prepare him for my departure."

"So you do mean to leave us. The novelty of the situation has worn off?"

"You may put it as you like." Her heart was beating wildly.

"What is *your* name, Miss Mildmay?"

She leaned forward. "Can't we go a little faster?"

Blane took the whip and lightly flicked it on the horses' rumps. They increased their pace, and the carriage rocked. Sarah clutched for something to support her. Blane's hand firmly on her arm steadied her.

"Sarah!" he said softly.

He was merely telling her that he knew her name. But did he need to speak it like a caress?

LADY MALVINA WAS IN THE NURSERY, rocking Titus gently in her capacious lap. Her raddled, pouched old face lit with pleasure at the sight of Sarah. "He's just fallen asleep," she whispered. "The fever seems a little less."

Sarah knelt beside Titus. "Had I known he was ill, I would never have left."

"Fevers come on children suddenly. And Amalie broke the news that you had gone rather callously. Thank heaven Blane caught you before you left for London."

Lady Malvina looked again at Sarah. "Are you all right yourself, Miss Mildmay? You haven't caught a chill, have you? You look flushed."

"I'm cold," said Sarah, and it was true that she was shivering.

"Ask Eliza to heat some milk. We'll all have some."

At that moment Titus stirred and opened his eyes. They widened as they fell on Sarah. "Mama said you went away," he said accusingly.

"Only for a few hours. That wasn't long, was it?"

"Yes, it was. I was sick. I cried for you." The little boy lifted his arms, and Sarah took him into hers. There was no sulking this time. He was too happy to see her. "You will stay now?"

"Yes. I'll stay," she said. He gave a satisfied murmur and dozed again.

"Amalie's a very difficult woman," Lady Malvina said to Sarah when Titus, tucked into his own bed, seemed to be sleeping more soundly. "There was an enormous row after you had gone. Blane was mad at her, really mad. He said you must be brought back at once, and if you weren't he would go back to sea and leave her to all this grandeur. Oh, it was a fine quarrel, and my son doesn't make idle boasts, as I learned long ago. I don't think he gives a fig for Mallow. He only wants it for his son."

"I believe he's quite ruthless," Sarah said. "He humiliates his wife. And because of me, a servant."

"I hardly think he regards you as a servant, Miss Mildmay," the old lady murmured slyly.

"I find his behavior intolerable."

"His behavior has always been intolerable. But the heart is there."

"Do you really believe that, Lady Malvina?"

"Now I do. Once, I admit, I worried a great deal. Blane wasn't a vicious boy, just uncontrollable. But now he's changed. He's basically good. It's a great relief to me."

The old lady gave Sarah a swift glance. Then she began to shake with laughter. "I'll warrant by the look on your face that my son's manners haven't changed. Was the drive from Yarby too long?" When Sarah didn't answer she went on. "My advice is to regard all this as a compliment."

"A compliment!"

"My dear, don't be a hypocrite. You must enjoy masculine admiration as well as the next woman. And you have the most exquisite color when he makes you angry. I like a young woman with spirit. So you just stay here and keep my grandson happy, and we'll say no more." She swept out of the room, giving Sarah no opportunity to reply.

Sarah left her door open that night so as to hear the slightest sound from Titus' room. She meant to sleep only lightly, but fatigue overcame her, and she had to struggle from a deep sleep when she heard the sound of her window curtains being pulled back. Pale, chilly early-morning light came in, and Amalie stood there in a flowing negligee, her dark hair hanging loose about her shoulders. "Good morning, Miss Mildmay," she said amicably. "It's getting light. Look, you can see the lake quite clearly now the trees are bare."

Sarah started up. "Titus—"

"Titus seems much better now. I'm glad you consented to come back. I behaved badly—I act on impulse. My husband says I can't go on engaging and then dismissing servants without real cause."

Amalie turned to go; then, as if drawn against her will, she went back to the window. "I didn't realize you had such a pleasant view from here. You can see almost the whole of the lake. In the summer we must have picnics down there. That is"—she came closer to the bed—"if you're still with us."

Her voice was perfectly friendly and amicable. It came as a distinct shock to see the hate glittering in her eyes.

CHAPTER TWELVE

IN THE DAYS THAT followed, Amalie seemed friendly enough. She spent a lot of time with Titus, who was recovering from his illness, which the doctor diagnosed as a sharp chill combined with the aftereffects of his fall. She also busied herself with arrangements for the ball. Acceptances came in as if all the countryside had been waiting for an invitation to Mallow Hall. Amalie was flattered and happy, but Sarah suspected that curiosity was bringing most of the people.

One significant thing happened, and that was a scrap of conversation Sarah overheard between Blane and Amalie.

"You'll have to get rid of Soames. He's getting insolent."

"Soames! Soames can't go. One has some loyalty. He's been here since I was a boy."

Amalie gave a derisive laugh. "I realize that's quite a long time, but that doesn't excuse his insolence. If you won't dismiss him, I will." She added in a low voice, "He watches me."

"I don't think so, my dear." Blane's voice was quite confident and quite cold. "Soames stays. You've had your fun at dismissing people."

IT WAS THE SUNDAY BEFORE THE BALL, and they were riding to church in the carriage, Titus crushed between Lady Malvina and Sarah, Amalie and Blane facing them.

Sarah suddenly exclaimed in surprise, "Why, you've found your blue velvet bonnet, Lady Mallow. Didn't Mrs. Stone take it after all?"

All eyes went to Amalie's attractive blue bonnet with the French silk roses. Lady Malvina said wheezily, as if she were suddenly asthmatic, "Then she must have gone without a bonnet at all. How extraordinary!"

"I didn't say it was this bonnet she took," snapped Amalie. "It was my other blue one."

"I didn't know you had two."

"Don't be foolish, Mama. I have dozens of bonnets."

"Then Mrs. Stone must have had quite a problem in making a choice," Blane murmured. His voice was gently ironic, but he was watching Amalie.

"She took my fur tippet too. And jewelry," Amalie said sulkily.

She had recovered. It had only been for a moment that that white look of fear had flashed into her face. Now the fear had left her, and settled instead in Sarah's heart. What she was afraid of she didn't know.

But nothing happened until the day before the ball. Eliza, who was allowed a night off once a week to spend with her family in Yarby, came back bursting with a secret.

"Oh, Miss Mildmay, I've got an important message for you."

"For me?" Sarah echoed.

"Yes. From a man arrived at the George. He said I was to hand it to you personally and not tell anyone else."

Without ceremony Sarah snatched the crumpled envelope from Eliza. This must be news from Ambrose at last. But the writer of the large, awkward script was a stranger:

> Dear Miss Mildmay,
>
> On instruktions from Mr. Ambrose Mallow, who I last seed in Trinidad, I have a packet to deliver to you. If you will communikate with me at the George and tell me where I can safely hand to you the said packet, it not to be trusted to the post, I will do my best to oblige.
>
> Your obed'nt servant,
> James Brodie

Where could she meet him? Sarah thought rapidly, momentarily forgetful of Eliza's burning curiosity.

"Tom Mercer said he was a sailor from the South Seas," the girl said breathlessly. "Is he really, Miss Mildmay?"

"Oh no, not the South Seas. But he's probably a sailor."

She would have to take the risk of trusting Eliza. "Eliza, this man has something for me from a—friend. How can I get a message to him?"

"Oh, Miss Mildmay! Have you got a secret lover?"

"Indeed I haven't. At least—" Sarah hesitated, realizing that this, of course, was what Eliza must be led to believe.

Eliza giggled conspiratorially. "I can see you have, Miss Mildmay. Is he on adventure in the South Seas? I do declare!"

"Now, Eliza, don't get ideas. And not a word of this to anyone. The thing is, how to get in touch with Mr. Brodie again?"

"If you'd write a message I could get it to him."

"Could you really? Without anyone knowing?"

"You can trust me. Ooh, Miss Mildmay! Isn't it romantic!"

Excitement kept Sarah from thinking clearly. She hastily wrote the first thing that came into her head:

> If you could come to Mallow Hall tomorrow afternoon I'll be in the summerhouse by the lake at five o'clock. Come by the path through the woods. No one is likely to see you.

When it was too late and the message had gone, Sarah reflected that the summerhouse was not such an ideal place, because of Amalie's habit of walking by the lake. But since tomorrow was the day of the ball, Amalie was not likely to be out of the house.

Eliza, now her willing ally, agreed to keep Titus happy and cover up for her absence. She hoped not to be gone more than half an hour.

SARAH PUT ON a cloak and slipped out by the garden door. It was very cold down by the lake. A few dead leaves rustled on the floor of the summerhouse, blown by gusts of wind. The lake was steely gray and empty even of wildlife. Now that the trees were bare the big house was visible, and in the deepening dusk lights sprang into the windows of the nursery, Lady Malvina's room and Amalie's. Only Blane's remained in darkness.

Fifteen minutes ticked past the appointed time and no one came. It passed through Sarah's mind that it was very odd Amalie should spend time down here, even if she was dreaming of the summer. But she had obviously been here very recently, for Sarah, seeing something shining among the dust and leaves on the floor, picked up a small jet brooch.

But that couldn't be Amalie's. It wasn't good enough. It was unobtrusive and inexpensive. It must belong to a servant. Perhaps more than one person made the summerhouse a rendezvous.

Sarah shivered and drew the cloak closely about her. She was getting anxious and impatient. She couldn't be out too long. Someone would be asking for her. And it was growing darker all the time.

Ah! Footsteps at last, crunching on the pebbles by the lakeside. She peered out of a window, trying to get a glimpse of James Brodie before he saw her. But the voice at the door of the summerhouse made her gasp.

"Amalie! What *are* you doing here? I can't understand this nonsense, mooning by a lakeside in midwinter. You surely can't be waiting for somebody. Or are you? Don't tell me it's a rendezvous."

It was Blane. Sarah stood petrified.

"Amalie, are you in a trance?"

Blane crossed over to Sarah, took her roughly by the arm and swung her around. "You!" he exclaimed. His fingers were pressing painfully into her flesh. His face was near hers. "What are *you* doing here, Miss Mildmay?"

Before she could speak, he went on. "You'll have to think hard to produce any explanation for being by the lakeside after dark. It can't be for the fresh air." He bent closer. Suddenly his voice was harsh and imperative. "Whom are you waiting for?"

Sarah managed to gasp, "No one, Lord Mallow."

"I don't believe you. Come now, a simple answer."

"I lost a brooch," Sarah said on an inspiration. "I thought it might have been down here."

"You mean you came down here after dark to look for something! Without a light? Oh come, Miss Mildmay, where's your ingenuity?"

"But I found the brooch. This is it."

She fumbled in her pocket and produced the modest ornament.

He struck a match and looked at the brooch, dismissing it scornfully. "I have yet to see you wearing something in that taste. Oh no, Miss Mildmay, think again."

"I'm afraid I haven't time to invent an explanation, Lord Mallow. I must go up to Titus."

She made to leave the summerhouse. Blane stood across the doorway, barring the way. "You're up to something. I should get rid of you. I should agree with my wife. But—"

His arms were about her before she could move. She was held in that same hard grip, and her head forced up so that he could find her mouth.

She couldn't have said how long the kiss lasted. She only knew that when he let her go she almost fell.

He was laughing softly. "What a fortunate thing you lost that horrible little brooch. Otherwise this couldn't have happened, could it?"

Even in her confusion she got his meaning. If she was in the summerhouse on some private affair, this episode must also remain private. As if she would want to talk of it!

"DID YOU GET it?" Eliza whispered eagerly, when at last Sarah arrived in the nursery.

Sarah shook her head. She had not meant to make Eliza her confidante, but she could not hide her distress. "Lord Mallow found me there."

"The master!" Eliza gasped.

"He wanted to know what I was doing. I said I was looking for a lost brooch. He came up to the house with me—I couldn't wait for Mr. Brodie."

"How clever you thought of the brooch," Eliza said admiringly.

Sarah fingered the piece of jet in her pocket. Strangely enough, she didn't want to tell Eliza that there *had* been a brooch. "Is Titus in bed?"

Eliza nodded. "And asleep," she said proudly. "I promised him if he went to sleep quick he'd be allowed up later for the ball. So he went off as good as gold. But Lady Malvina's been looking for you. I said you had a headache and wanted to snatch a breath of air before this evening."

Eliza learned quickly, Sarah reflected. Perhaps there was something devious in the simplest women.

Lady Malvina came in in her unceremonious way as Sarah was dressing. She looked splendid in her enormous crinoline of plum-colored silk, with the ropes of pearls on her massive bosom and her hair piled high in ringlets held with jeweled combs.

"Well, Miss Mildmay, how do I look?"

"Very impressive, Lady Malvina."

"Impressive! What an excellent choice of word. I like that. I was looking for you a while ago. Eliza said you had a headache. I hope it's better."

"It's nothing, Lady Malvina."

"Hmm. That's what I thought when I saw you coming up from the lake with my son. It was you, wasn't it, Miss Mildmay?"

Sarah could not escape the shrewd eyes.

"Why yes. Lord Mallow found me walking down there."

"Well, don't let my daughter-in-law catch you at it."

"Lady Malvina—"

"Don't explain, my dear. But be careful, for Titus' sake. Let him grow a little stronger before he loses you."

"I assure you you couldn't be more mistaken," Sarah said indignantly.

"But I often see someone down at the lake. Isn't it you?"

"Today was the first time. And my meeting with Lord Mallow was quite accidental."

"Then it must be Amalie. But she's not the type to moon by lakes, is she? Is she, Miss Mildmay? One night—" But Lady Malvina didn't go on with what she had been about to say.

Sarah, on an impulse, held out the jet brooch. "Other people do walk down there, because I found this. I should think it belongs to one of the servants, wouldn't you?"

Lady Malvina looked at the brooch with interest. "What a dreary piece of jewelry! Who have I seen wearing it?" All at once a strange, wary look came into her face. She closed her lips firmly.

"Should I ask the servants?" Sarah inquired.

"No, I don't think I'd do that, Miss Mildmay. I advise you to forget it."

It was after the ball had started, and she had led an excited Titus to a place of observation on the stairs, that a curious trick of memory made Sarah remember that she also had seen that jet brooch before.

It had been pinned at the modest, high neck of Mrs. Stone's drab gray dress.

CHAPTER THIRTEEN

TITUS WAS VERY EXCITED. He hung over the banisters looking at the gay scene and chattering incessantly. Standing beside him, Sarah too watched with interest as Amalie and Blane greeted their guests. The diamonds glittered around Amalie's neck. She was enjoying her moment of importance. Blane, Sarah could scarcely bear to watch at all. But she must, to observe every nuance of the greetings he was given by all these people whom he must pretend to know.

Tomkins was announcing the names so clearly that Blane was protected temporarily from mistakes. One would never have guessed from his demeanor that the evening was an ordeal. But was it? He was a gambler, a man who got tremendous zest from a challenge. And he had no conscience. If only for one moment, thought Sarah, she could have the satisfaction of seeing him at a loss, disturbed, defeated.

"The music's beginning," said Titus. "Are you going to dance?"

"I'm going to stay here with you."

"But you have your best dress on." He waited, then sighed, sliding his hand into hers contentedly. His eyes were shining. He had the entranced look of a child in fairyland. "How many candles are there burning? Doesn't Mama look pretty? Can we watch the dancing?"

"Yes. When it begins, we'll sit at the bottom of the stairs."

"Won't someone ask you to dance, Miss Mildmay?"

"I shall refuse."

But Blane would take no refusal. He had been dancing with his wife. Now Amalie was dancing with Colonel Fortescue and Blane had shamelessly left the ballroom to talk to the governess. "Get Eliza to stay with Titus," he said. "Come, Miss Mildmay, this is an order."

"Do you want a scandal?" Sarah muttered furiously.

"No. I merely want to go on asking you questions, and it will look much more natural if we're dancing than talking out here. For instance, that wasn't your brooch you picked up in the summerhouse, was it?"

Something wild and reckless seized her. "Very well. Since you insist. No, it wasn't my brooch. It was the person's you're afraid it was—Mrs. Stone's. I wonder what she was doing in the summerhouse."

"One might ask the same question of you, Miss Mildmay. So who was it you were waiting for?"

Titus was absorbed in watching the dancing. Sarah moved away a little from him and said in a low voice, "If you continue to persecute me in this way, Lord Mallow, I will be compelled to leave after all."

"I don't persecute you. I only find you so damnably secretive!"

"Blane!" Sarah started sharply at the sound of Amalie's angry voice behind them. "What are you doing out here? Why aren't you dancing?"

"My love, I'm endeavoring to. Miss Mildmay—"

Amalie no longer concealed her enmity. "Miss Mildmay! A servant! When you've scarcely spoken to your guests."

"*Your* guests, my dear," he said inexplicably.

"There's Soames!" Titus exclaimed, pressing his small face against the banisters and waving excitedly. "Have you come to dance?"

Sarah saw Soames approaching across the hall. The significance of his appearance in the house scarcely struck her, she was so fascinated by the change in Amalie's face. The rigid anger had given way to alarm.

"Good evening, Master Titus," Soames said, then turned to Blane. "I must speak to you, my lord."

Blane had more self-control than Amalie. He allowed nothing but impatience to show in his face. "It had better be something important."

A strange man had appeared in the hall, middle-aged with a weather-beaten face. Soames said in a low voice, "I'd send the boy away, my lord."

"Who's that?" Blane demanded, indicating the strange man.

"He says he lost his way, my lord. He found himself down by the lake, and saw the . . ." Soames lowered his voice to a whisper. Sarah could just make out the words. ". . . under the jetty. Caught against the piles. Must have drowned herself."

"Who?" whispered Amalie. *"Who?"*

The orchestra was playing a low, romantic waltz. It seemed macabre that the music continued to play with gaiety and heartlessness.

"The sewing woman, my lady," Soames said formally. "At least that must be who it is, because you said she stole jewelry. And she—the body—is wearing a diamond ring."

Involuntarily Amalie's hand went to the diamonds at her throat. "I told you she was a thief!" she shrieked.

"Be quiet, Amalie!" Blane took her arm. His face was somber, frowning, formidable. But he was quite calm.

"The police must be informed," he said, adding sharply, "Miss Mildmay, take Titus upstairs."

"Stop the music!" Amalie cried. "For God's sake, stop the music!"

Let there be silence for that dark bundle found floating in the steely water of the lake. The mysterious Mrs. Stone, whose taste had run to jet brooches and black straw bonnets, but who had finally left both behind, as well as the unfinished piece of work on her table.

Was it in that half hour, when Sarah had been waiting for her dress to be mended, that she had died? Sarah could remember every minute of that evening. Amalie had gone to bed early with a chill, and Blane had come in with his hair shining and glossy with rain. And afterward someone had slipped upstairs and packed Mrs. Stone's few shabby belongings, overlooking the black bonnet that was so hastily burned the next day.

Were these fantastic and horrible suspicions true? Or had the dreariness of life been too much for Mrs. Stone, and so she had voluntarily ended it?

The violins wailed to a stop. The gaiety had been short-lived.

FINALLY THE LAST carriage rolled away, and the ballroom with its half-burned candles was left to a few whispering servants. Soames had been sent posthaste to Yarby for the police.

Sarah scarcely remembered getting Titus upstairs. Fortunately the child hadn't realized what was happening. He was still captivated by his brief glimpse of what seemed a candlelit fairyland.

Sarah neither heard what he was chattering about nor noticed that Eliza had come in and was speaking to her. The girl had to seize her arm.

"Miss Mildmay! Didn't you see him downstairs? It's that Mr. Brodie. James Brodie!"

James Brodie had been asked to remain to answer the questions of the police, and was given food in the servants' hall. It was there that Sarah contrived to have a brief conversation with him, during which she hid under her shawl the letter he handed her.

"You were late," she whispered. "I couldn't wait."

"I mistook the way through the woods. I hung about hoping you might come down again. And then I saw this shape in the water. The moon caught it."

"Why shall you say you were there?"

"I'll say I was looking for a bit of poaching."

She noticed he had a creased, devil-may-care face. "You'll get jailed!"

"Pshaw! Not with all this excitement. And judging by the looks of the new lord, he won't be unfair."

Sarah thought that the letter felt cold through the silk of her gown, cold against her heart. She couldn't understand her dread of opening it.

"Do you know what's in this letter?"

"No, not a word, miss. But it's something important, judging by the gentleman's anxiety to get it to you."

As Sarah tried to slip back upstairs unnoticed, she encountered Blane coming from the library. His face was drawn into deep lines. She was afraid he would stop her, but he passed her as if she had been one of the servants.

She climbed the two flights of stairs to her room. At last she was alone and able to tear open the letter. The wind billowed the curtains and made the candle flame dip and gutter. Ambrose's fine, clerkly handwriting danced in a blur:

My dearest Sarah,

I am entrusting this letter to one James Brodie, who is perfectly honest and reliable, but naturally knows nothing of the circumstances. He is sailing immediately for England, and I am hopeful of following in a very short time.

Your letter regarding Thomas Whitehouse arrived safely and was valuable information, enabling me to finally unearth this gentleman. But unfortunately I could get nowhere with him. He has no doubt been well paid, for he remained loyal to my so-called cousin and merely repeated the story he had told in court about the length of time he had known Blane.

I have had some success following other clues and have discovered several curious facts—including a new tombstone, an entry in a church register and a woman called Samantha—that may prove to tie up with discoveries of yours.

I am assured we will have a very strong case for the court of appeal. So don't lose heart, my love. If your task has been disagreeable you are about to be amply rewarded. I hope the odious child has not been too intolerable, and that, in spite of your humiliating position there, you have grown to love Mallow. For I promise you it will be our home.

Keep up your spirits, remain observant of every smallest detail, and be on your guard if the woman Samantha should materialize.

Your devoted Ambrose

Samantha! The name was screaming in her head. Sammie!
Sammie was a *woman.*

CHAPTER FOURTEEN

EARLY THE NEXT MORNING, Mrs. Stone's shabby canvas traveling bag was also fished up from the lake, and in it, as well as her few clothes, were the fur tippet, ruby brooch and earrings, and garnet necklace of Amalie's that had been missing.

"Revenge followed by remorse!" the police sergeant said. "She must have taken the things to spite you, Lady Mallow, and then couldn't return or dispose of them without arousing suspicion. But you should have reported the theft."

"I didn't want trouble," Amalie said. "My husband and I had already been through so much." She raised her eyes appealingly, looking pale and fragile. For the first time since Sarah had known her she was dressed simply.

"And you employed her out of kindness, you say?"

"What could I do? What would you have done? She was in such despair and talked of taking her own life."

"I'd have sent the baggage packing," the sergeant said brusquely. But it was quite clear that Amalie had won his sympathy.

Everyone had to be questioned as to whether Mrs. Stone had been observed at the lake that last evening. No one had seen her there at that time, but Lady Malvina mentioned how, the night before that, she had seen a figure running up from the lake as if fleeing from some terrible destiny. Perhaps Mrs. Stone had been looking at it then with suicide in mind and her courage had failed.

The police sergeant obviously intended to waste little sympathy on a poor insignificant wretch of no importance. He was certainly not going to give any credence to the farfetched idea that if someone had helped Mrs. Stone to tumble into the lake, they were likely to pack her bag with valuables and throw it in after her. He even looked surprised when Sarah, at the end of her own short cross-examination, asked, "What was Mrs. Stone's first name?"

"I've never heard it, miss. But we'll find it out. Though what would you think that had to do with it?"

"Nothing, sir. It would just"—Sarah succeeded in looking confused—"make her seem more of a person."

After the police had left, Blane sent for Sarah to come to him in the library. His face was bleak and forbidding. Now, apparently, he no longer thought it necessary to keep up a façade. "Miss Mildmay, why were you meeting this man Brodie down by the lake?"

"Meeting him!"

"Come! None of that wide-eyed innocence."

"But I'd never seen James Brodie in my life. I haven't the slightest idea who he is. I thought he admitted he was looking for some poaching."

"With a strange degree of honesty that I don't trust." His hard, searching eyes were on Sarah. "Then what the devil *were* you doing down at the lake? My wife, it appears, has been haunting it morbidly, for fear this woman had carried out her threat. But that can't have been your reason. What *are* you up to?"

Sarah's voice was cool with dislike. "Why don't you dismiss me, Lord Mallow, if you find me so unsatisfactory?"

"You know I won't do that."

She couldn't escape his intent, disturbing gaze. She thought that if he took one step toward her she would have to run. Or stay to be kissed again in that violent way.

"Miss Mildmay, will you assure me that you weren't meeting a lover?"

"A lover! Good heavens, no!"

Her spontaneous astonishment seemed to satisfy him. He relaxed and all at once looked desperately tired. And haunted. As if Mrs. Stone's death was pressing on him.

He had gone to London to meet someone called Sammie, in response to a letter saying, "Fancy, I thought you was dead." But Sammie had meant to see him here, not in London, and instead had encountered Amalie.

Mrs. Stone had died by drowning certainly enough, but not of her own accord. Amalie knew. Blane knew. Probably even Soames knew. Someone in this house had helped the woman to die, and Sarah had to stay here, preserving her secret knowledge, until Ambrose returned.

Perhaps, without waiting for him, she should tell these things to the police. She should relate the burning of Mrs. Stone's bonnet, the way Blane's hair had shone with rain that night, Amalie's morbid haunting of the lake.

But she knew she would do none of this. Not because it was better for Ambrose to return with the strange jigsaw of suspicions pieced together, but because just now Blane had demanded to know whether she had been waiting for a lover. And she had indignantly denied it as if she had no lover. Not even Ambrose.

That night Titus had his nightmare again. Someone had been walking in his room and had blown out his light, he said. And sure enough, his light was out. "It was Sammie," Titus insisted in his sleep-blurred voice.

Sarah's heart stood still. "Who is Sammie?"

"I don't know. I heard someone say 'Sammie' one night. Is it the mouse again, Miss Mildmay?"

"There's no mouse and no Sammie," Sarah said firmly.

She held the trembling little boy in her arms, and thought she heard a door shut somewhere in the house. Whatever had woken Titus had infected her with its intangible fear. It might not be safe to keep silent, waiting for Ambrose, after all.

At the lunch table the next day she mentioned conversationally, "I'm sorry to say that Titus had that strange nightmare again last night. He thinks someone called Sammie came into the room and blew out his light."

There was no doubting that brief moment of suspended breathing. Then Lady Malvina said, "Sammie? I've not heard this before, Miss Mildmay. Who is Sammie?"

"I haven't the least idea, Lady Malvina. But I did wonder if by any chance Mrs. Stone's name was Sammie."

"What an extraordinary idea!" Amalie said sharply. "Whatever gives it to you, Miss Mildmay?"

"Only that the first time this happened was when Mrs. Stone was here."

"No one knows Mrs. Stone's first name," said Blane. "Not even the police as yet. So how, pray, could Titus?"

"Unless she told him," Sarah murmured.

Amalie gave an incredulous laugh. "You mean she'd creep in there late at night and tell my son her first name! What farfetched nonsense! Anyway, Sammie is a man's name."

"It could be short for Samantha," Sarah said.

Again there was that tiny bubble of silence. Again it was broken by Lady Malvina. "But Miss Mildmay, you aren't talking sense. For if this Mrs. Stone is by any chance called Sammie, or Samantha, it's certainly not her now going into Titus' room at night. How can it be when she's dead?"

"I merely meant that it might have been her the first time, and now if Titus is disturbed he imagines it's the same person disturbing him."

"I believe Miss Mildmay is suggesting that her ghost walks," Amalie said dryly.

Blane suddenly pushed back his chair. "Tomorrow Titus shall return to London." His statement was an order. Sarah was startled, but not as startled as the other women.

"Oh dear, I shall miss the boy," said Lady Malvina. "Do you mean this, Blane?"

"Of course he doesn't mean it!" Amalie exclaimed. "Titus can't go back to fogs and damp. Besides, my love, it was you who said his fancies mustn't be pampered." Her eyes widened. "Surely you're not suggesting he be sent away because of this unfortunate tragedy? Why, he knows nothing of it. And, if you ask me, Miss Mildmay has made such curious suggestions that one wonders how much of the nightmare was Titus'."

Blane looked directly at his mother. He behaved as if Amalie hadn't said a word. "Perhaps you'd like to go with him, Mama. He's grown fond of you, I believe."

Lady Malvina's face softened. "Why, of course. If you're insisting on his going. What about Miss Mildmay?"

"Miss Mildmay will stay here."

"Blane, what are you talking about?" Amalie exclaimed. "The woman is Titus' governess. Do we pay her to have a holiday in the country?"

Blane met his wife's anger with his hard, level gaze. "Miss Mildmay will be required at the inquest."

"Why will she be required more than Mama?"

Blane sighed and began a patient explanation. "Because, as I understand, you sent for Mrs. Stone at five o'clock that afternoon and dismissed her, telling her she could stay until morning but that she must be out of the house by daylight. Isn't that so?"

Amalie nodded.

"Miss Mildmay says she took some sewing up to Mrs. Stone at seven o'clock that evening. After that time no one else appears to have seen her. That makes Miss Mildmay the last person to have seen Mrs. Stone alive."

Amalie sprang up. "Then I shall take Titus to London myself."

"I think not."

"Am I a prisoner here?"

"If that's the way you want to look at it."

Amalie was not acting any longer. Her face wore an expression of extraordinary malevolence. "Oh no," she said. "I don't need to be a prisoner anywhere. You seem to forget that Titus is mine. And I shall do exactly as I please with him." She whirled around and left the room.

"Blane," said Lady Malvina. Her voice was that of someone very old and frightened. "Blane, what does she mean?"

"Mean?" Blane jerked himself to attentiveness. "Oh nothing, Mama. That's just Amalie in a tantrum. She enjoys theatricals."

"She wouldn't take Titus away?"

"You're taking him away, Mama. You can have him to yourself for a few weeks in London."

The old lady began to brighten. "Can I really? That would be tremendous fun. And the child needs a holiday. But not for too long, Blane," she added. "I want him to love Mallow."

"He's going to love Mallow. I don't know why you think he wouldn't."

SARAH WENT UPSTAIRS and found Amalie in the nursery, dressing Titus in his outdoor clothes while Eliza stood nervously watching.

"Where are you taking him?" Sarah burst out.

Amalie looked up. "I am his mother, Miss Mildmay. Had you forgotten? We're merely going down to look at the lake."

"No, you shan't take Titus near the lake!"

But Amalie took Titus' hand anyway. Suddenly he reverted to being the child Sarah had first met and began to scream and tug away from her. "No, I don't want to go! I won't go!"

"Darling! You're only coming for a walk with Mama. Don't you love Mama?"

"No, I'm not coming. I don't love you. I hate you!"

Red-faced and hysterical, Titus snatched his hand away and flew to Sarah. For the second time at a crucial moment he sought refuge in her arms. She picked him up, bundled in his tweed coat, and faced Amalie.

"So you've succeeded in spoiling him," Amalie said. "I always said you would. And you've done it deliberately. You're the most scheming woman I've ever met. You've stolen my husband and my son."

Sarah's mouth dropped open in sheer surprise.

"Don't bother to deny it, Miss Mildmay. And don't think you've gotten away with it. I shall ruin you, and my husband as well. I can, you know." She paused, then added significantly, "I only have to tell the police who Mrs. Stone really was."

"Then you did know her!"

Amalie laughed. "I didn't. But Blane did. She was his wife."

CHAPTER FIFTEEN

A BIGAMIST—AND A murderer too? Amalie's words had a deadly implication, for Blane could not afford to have a woman like that turning up to wreck all his plans. He would be as ruthless about her as he had been about everything else. And Amalie, suspecting what he had done, haunted by fear, had walked every afternoon at the lake to see if the body appeared. . . .

The police sergeant was back that afternoon. He spent a long time down by the lake, walking up and down, testing the ground and the rickety piles of the jetty. Afterward he came in and was shut in the library with Blane for a long time. Sarah kept trying to make up her mind whether she would tell the sergeant of the brooch she had found. Not in the mud by the lakeside, where it might presumably have fallen off, but in the summer-house. As if a struggle might have taken place there under the pretense of an embrace. If Mrs. Stone was really Blane's wife she might have welcomed his embrace, not suspecting its treachery.

But the sergeant left without asking to see anyone else, and Sarah felt sick with relief. She knew she had not meant to say anything about the brooch. She also could not believe that Blane had ever kissed Mrs. Stone's sour, secretive face.

And Amalie had certainly been bluffing when she had made those extraordinary statements, for she had made no attempt to see the police. She waited until they had gone, then came down to tea wearing a simple dark merino dress and a woolen shawl. She had a strange, extinguished look, as if her moment of madness in the nursery had burned out all her anger. She kept her eyes down as if she wanted to hide what was in them, but her voice was normal enough. "Where's Titus, Miss Mildmay?"

"Eliza's giving him his tea, Lady Mallow."

"Now it's so cold perhaps it's as well I didn't take him out." That was as near to an apology as she would ever get.

"We'll have to wrap up well for our journey tomorrow," Lady Malvina said.

"Titus has a fur-lined coat somewhere," said Amalie. "I'll look for it presently. And Mama, if you take him out walking in London do see he doesn't get wet feet. He catches cold so easily."

"I'll look after him like a cherished jewel."

"Thank you, Mama. I do trust you with him. I was overwrought earlier."

Then Blane came in, and without lifting her eyes Amalie said smoothly, "Tea, my love? I hope the police didn't detain you too long. What did they want this time?"

"Merely to verify suspicions."

"Suspicions?"

"Such as whether the woman's death was not suicide at all."

Amalie's eyelids flew up, then dropped again as she said calmly, "Have they discovered anything more about the woman's identity?"

"Only that she arrived by train at Yarby. She asked the porter the way to Mallow. She told him she'd come a long way and would have to walk the ten miles, since she had no money."

"And what did the sergeant make of that?" Amalie asked.

"He would have been very mystified if it hadn't been for Mrs. Stone's last remark. She said she'd had a lot of bad luck but hoped to catch some good from us." Blane took his teacup and turned to the fire. "The police have decided that the woman probably fell in the lake accidentally. The path around it is slippery. If it was very dark, she could easily have stumbled and fallen in. That would account for her bag in the lake too."

Lady Malvina leaned back in her chair. "That's the first sensible thing I've heard since this dreadful business began. The whole thing was an accident, of course. That will be the coroner's verdict, Blane?"

"I should think so, Mama. The woman seems to have been a vagrant and a sneak thief. I fear there'll be no sympathy wasted on her."

"And no one will identify her?" Sarah said in her clear voice.

Blane turned. He met her gaze levelly. "Unless someone turns up from her past."

"What about you, Lord Mallow?" Sarah asked.

"Me! But I'd never set eyes on her before." His gaze met hers unwaveringly and with astonishment. His answer had been quite spontaneous. But then, he was a devilishly clever actor.

Amalie was standing up, smiling. "Blane, let me congratulate you on finding Miss Mildmay. You recognized her talents when I was quite blind to them. She's so clever. So observant. And so good for Titus. I think you ought to give her a present. What about the diamond ring Mrs. Stone had?"

"Amalie!" Lady Malvina's voice was rough with shock. "What a peculiarly grisly thing to suggest! Anyway, you said the ring was yours."

"Not mine. Blane's. I believe it would fit Miss Mildmay. She has slim fingers too. Perhaps you've noticed the similarity, Blane? And governesses don't often have the chance to acquire valuable rings. Not if they're honest." For a moment, her face defiant and shrewish, she faced her husband. Then she said lightly, "I must look for Titus' fur coat for the morning. Will you excuse me?" and left the room.

"Blane!" Lady Malvina burst out pleadingly. "That ring wasn't Mrs. Stone's? Surely you didn't once give it to her!"

"I told you, Mama. I'd never seen the woman in my life."

"Then Amalie—" Lady Malvina began uncertainly.

"Go up to Titus, will you, Mama? Stay with him until Miss Mildmay comes."

Sarah also moved toward the door. "I'll go now."

"Stay here!" The harsh command stopped her.

"Lord Mallow, couldn't I go to London tomorrow with Titus?"

"What has my wife been saying to you?"

"Why, that—that—" She couldn't say the monstrous thing.

"Come, out with it!"

She should have flung the accusation in his face. He deserved it. But her heart failed. "She told me Mrs. Stone was your wife," she said flatly. "She said she intended to tell the police."

"And what did you think of this story?"

He didn't deny it, she noticed. She began to shiver. "I thought perhaps for some reason she wanted to hurt you."

"So she does," he muttered. "I believe she would swear that I pushed that wretched woman in the lake. My God!"

The unguarded horror in his face communicated itself to Sarah. "But Lord Mallow, surely you don't think—" This new suspicion was also unspeakable.

"You picked up that brooch in the summerhouse."

"Yes. It hadn't a very good fastening. It would have—fallen off. . . ."

"The diamond was on her finger. It was a bribe, of course. She hadn't stolen it. I give her credit for that. But when and where was she bribed?"

"And why?" Sarah asked.

The ghost of a smile touched his lips. "Amalie's right. You are observant, Miss Mildmay. Too observant. I think you're going to find out more than you will enjoy. That's what you want to do, isn't it? Outdo the judge and jury, and prove I don't belong here."

Somehow Sarah contrived to speak steadily. "If you think that, why didn't you dismiss me long ago?"

"Because your little plot amused me. That was the first thing. The second was that you proved enormously good for Titus. The third is that I've fallen in love with you."

She couldn't move. He didn't need to take her wrist in his hard grip to hold her there. "Why?" she whispered.

"Heaven knows. And a pretty mess you've made of all my plans."

"It's true you fall in love with every new face, as your mother says."

"But that was Blane Mallow. You don't believe I'm that person, do you? You've been trying to trick me into some admission ever since you've been here. You've taken pleasure in discovering any evidence you could."

"Then why—"

"Why do I love you? Because we're two of a kind. And we'll see this through together. Won't we?"

He had let her go, and she could have escaped had she wished. She stood rubbing her wrist. "Who *are* you?" she burst out in baffled anger.

He laughed, touching her cheek lightly with his fingers. "My dear Miss Mildmay, I fear you're going to find out very soon. So don't run away. I've too much trouble on my hands already. And anyway, I should find you."

Somewhere in the house a door banged. Sarah thought she heard Titus crying. With an enormous effort she pulled herself together. "I must go to Titus."

"Yes, go to him now. But he has to begin learning to do without you. That's why I'm sending him to London."

"So I've served my purpose!" Sarah flashed indignantly.

"Only that purpose—my dearest one!"

There were no complexities in his face now. Only longing. Tears sprang to Sarah's eyes. She must go before he saw them, and read something into them that was not there. For this was all crazy, crazy! He was married to Amalie, and she was waiting for Ambrose.

"Blane! Blane!" Lady Malvina's hoarse voice reached them long before she came bundling breathlessly down the stairs.

"What is it, Mama?"

"We can't find Titus. Eliza left him with his mother while he finished his tea. I came up soon afterward, but they were gone."

Blane was at the door. "Where's Amalie?"

"I don't know. I thought she meant to look for Titus' fur-lined coat for the morning."

"For now," said Blane, his face like stone.

"But why would she be taking him out now in the dark? She said herself it was too cold."

"The lake!" Sarah whispered.

Blane was ringing the bell for Tomkins, who came across the hall. Blane spoke curtly. "Have you seen Lady Mallow go out?"

"No, my lord."

"See if she's in the house, will you? Look in every room. Don't stop to knock at doors. And send someone for Soames."

Blane himself flung the front door open and started to run toward the lake. Sarah followed him, forgetful of the wind and the flakes of snow in the air. It was such a cold night. The water would be icy. . . .

But the lake was deserted. A curved moon hung upside down in the branches of the elm on the opposite side. The water shimmered faintly. The summerhouse was dark and empty. They were not too late, were they? The surface of the lake looked undisturbed, with no sinister bubbles or settling ripples. Blane stood a moment, a dark, brooding silhouette. Then he swung around and saw Sarah. "No, she wouldn't do it twice," he said. "She's not as stupid as that."

There was no time to ponder his deadly words. He was hurrying back to the house, and Sarah had to run to keep up.

Tomkins was waiting to report that Soames could not be found.

"Where is he?" Blane's voice was a lash.

"No one knows, sir. He's not in his house, and his horse is missing."

"I'll need my own horse," said Blane, and was off to the stables.

Soon he was back, riding his big chestnut hunter. He leaned down to say to Sarah and Lady Malvina, "All I can get out of Jim, that fool of a stable boy, is that he saddled a horse for Amalie and she rode off—with a bundle."

"A bundle," Lady Malvina echoed faintly.

"Soames followed," Blane said grimly. "God knows where they're heading. Soames knows this country like the back of his hand."

"Why should he be going?" Sarah asked.

"I thought I could trust him. I'd have sworn I could."

"Lord Mallow, I'm coming with you!"

Blane looked down at her. "Can you ride?"

"Of course I can."

"Then hurry. We'll get another horse."

It was dark, and she didn't mind if her petticoats flew up. She rode astride like a boy, as she had always done, except when her mother or governess had been there and forbade it in horror. This was action at last, and Sarah reveled in it.

Amalie and Soames could not have gotten far, and there was not a lot of cover in the marshes. As soon as they left the woods they would show up against the skyline. Unless Soames knew of some secret hiding place.

"Is she trying to kidnap Titus?" Sarah shouted, galloping up to Blane.

"More likely to kill him."

"*Kill* him! Is she mad?"

"When it comes to jealousy, yes."

The night was dark and the conventions far away. "You shouldn't have locked your door against her," Sarah said.

He turned to look at her. The wind streamed through his hair. "So you knew that too," he said, and that was all.

CHAPTER SIXTEEN

ELIZA COULD NOT BE made to stop crying. Finally Lady Malvina slapped her and exclaimed, "For goodness' sake, stop that noise! Nobody's blaming you. After all, you couldn't have been expected to defy your mistress."

"Miss Mildmay did, this afternoon," Eliza hiccuped. "She didn't let the mistress take Master Titus out walking."

"Miss Mildmay is another matter. She isn't a servant."

Lady Malvina heard herself speak the words with some surprise. She wondered why she had not realized earlier that Sarah Mildmay had never behaved with the slightest servility. She might have tried to, but her serene self-confidence had always shown through. Then who was she? If it came to that, who was anyone? Amalie, with her shrewishness and her vulgar ostentation; the poor drowned woman; the tall dark stranger who had just ridden off and who she had always known in her heart was not her son?

There was only Titus of whom she was sure, and Titus had been carried off, no one knew where. In the space of a few minutes her world had disintegrated. She was a forsaken old woman surrounded by weeping servants, with only her pearls to show that this had not all been a dream.

An hour went by, and it was quite dark when the sound of horses' hoofs came up the curving drive. Lady Malvina started up eagerly from her chair by the fire. Blane was back with Titus. She knew that all would now be well.

The doorbell rang. At the head of the stairs Lady Malvina waited tensely, listening for Tomkins' relieved welcome. All the servants had been hanging about, waiting and whispering.

Lady Malvina felt the wind sweep up the stairs from the opened door. She couldn't hear the voices. They were too low. Tomkins seemed to be hesitating. Then the door shut and there were footsteps across the tiled floor. Lady Malvina went down several steps to peer into the hall. She couldn't recognize the man who stood there in a riding cloak, with the lamplight glinting in his fair hair.

Was it someone with news? Lady Malvina began to run down in a flurry. "Who is it, Tomkins?"

"Mr. Ambrose, my lady."

"Mr. Ambrose!"

What did he want here at this hour? What was he poking his nose into now? Wasn't he supposed to be in the West Indies? Alarm shot through Lady Malvina's fuddled head. What had he discovered there?

She contrived to complete the descent of the stairs with dignity. Her face was highly flushed and her elaborate curls slightly adrift beneath her lace cap. But her greeting was cool and haughty. "Well, Ambrose, this is a surprise. You haven't visited me at Mallow for a very long time."

"No, Aunt Malvina. And I apologize for arriving so unceremoniously. But I just returned from Trinidad this morning. I came here immediately."

Lady Malvina's brows rose. "There was a reason for such urgency?"

"There are various questions I want to ask. Is Blane in?"

"No. He's out riding."

"Out riding! But it's late. It's dark."

"My son was always unpredictable. Don't you remember?" Lady Malvina gave her hoarse chuckle. She enjoyed baiting Ambrose. He had been a cold, dry stick of a boy. "If you insist on waiting until Blane returns, you'd better come into the library. We'll have some sustenance. It's a cold night."

"Very cold," said Ambrose, rubbing his hands. "Especially after the tropics."

"Ah yes. And how did you find the tropics?"

"Of great interest, Lady Malvina."

"Hmm. You'd better tell me. But first let us have some brandy. Will you pour it? We don't want the servants in. We have things to talk about."

"We certainly have things to talk about, Aunt. What's this I hear about a woman being drowned in the lake?"

"You didn't take long to hear that!"

"Everyone at Yarby is talking about it. There seemed to be a good deal of unpleasant speculation."

"She was a lying, thieving creature," Lady Malvina said bluntly.

"Was her name Samantha?"

Lady Malvina stared. "I haven't the least idea what her name was."

"Was she Blane's wife?"

"Good heavens, what nonsense are you talking?" Lady Malvina took a deep swallow of her drink. So Ambrose had come here to bluff, had he? Since he was asking questions, he obviously hadn't discovered the answers. But that sneaking, pasty-faced woman Blane's wife! She had to conceal the deep shock such a suggestion gave her. "I thought you had met Blane's wife. You surely did so at the time of the court proceedings."

"Amalie?" said Ambrose. "But I don't believe Amalie *is* his wife."

Lady Malvina stared. How priggish Ambrose looked. Priggish, superior, detestable. She threw back her head and laughed. "My dear boy, the hot sun in the tropics has affected your brain."

"I know she's the daughter of Thomas Whitehouse," Ambrose muttered. "I found that out. Now, if the court hears that Blane's chief witness is also his father-in-law, it might take a different view of the evidence."

"But you've just said Amalie isn't Blane's wife," Lady Malvina retorted.

A look of uncertainty crossed Ambrose's face.

"Don't you think the court might be aware of your ambitions too, Ambrose? And if you can't prove these extraordinary statements it isn't going to look very well for you."

"I've got to prove them! That's why I've come here. I intend to face this man you call your son, and Amalie, with some very suspicious facts. There's a newly erected gravestone in the British cemetery at Port of Spain. It has on it only 'Evan St. John. Aged 35 years. Died at sea.' "

"What of it?"

"You heard in court the story of how Blane was once the sole survivor when his ship sank in a hurricane. But a thing that didn't come out was that he came ashore, after floating on a spar for ten days, with a dead man."

"And you're telling me the dead man's name was Evan St. John?"

"That's what one assumes."

"Poor Blane," cried Lady Malvina, "to see his last companion die!"

"You don't understand what I'm getting at!" Ambrose exclaimed.

"Oh yes I do, you crafty devil!" Her voice rose richly with anger and contempt. "You're suggesting it was Blane who died, and this man came ashore to step into his shoes. He had seen the advertisements for the heir to Mallow and concocted a plot to come and take possession."

"Having, in those ten days at sea, in desperate straits, got all Blane's history from him," said Ambrose smugly.

"And this woman Samantha?"

"Or Sammie, as she was known. Blane's wife, of course. Who, I gather, turned up most inconveniently to denounce this impostor. Or to share in the spoils."

Lady Malvina sat very quietly for a moment. She wanted another drink, but she was afraid her hand would tremble too much to pour it.

"Admit, Aunt Malvina, that you always knew this man wasn't your son. Oh, I know you hadn't seen him since he was a boy of sixteen. But a mother must know her own son instinctively. And you didn't know this man. I swear it."

"Ambrose, you're impertinent!"

"You like being back at Mallow," Ambrose said softly. "You could have been just an impoverished old lady living unnoticed in some insignificant place. But with your son home all this has changed. It was very lucky for you, wasn't it, Aunt Malvina? Even if you had to perjure yourself in court and risk what would happen to you at the hands of these strangers."

"You have no real evidence," Lady Malvina said hoarsely.

"No, but I shall have when I've put my story together with Sarah's."

"Sarah's?"

"Sarah Mildmay, of course. She's clever, isn't she?"

"That girl! What has she to do with this?" Lady Malvina's face crumpled into bewilderment and despair. Was it true that her son was dead, and that she was to lose everything, even Titus?

Titus! Lady Malvina raised her sagging body and drew herself very erect. Her cap was askew, but her head was high, her eyes blazing with triumph. "Come with me, Ambrose. Take another look at this."

She led him into the hall, to the foot of the stairs. All the lamps were alight, and the portrait glowed in the radiance.

"Look!" she said commandingly. "You've seen Titus. Can you deny the likeness? Can any inscription on a tombstone or any marriage register explain that away? Can you say that boy can be anything but Blane's son?"

She pointed with her thick-ringed finger. Her voice rang out magnificently. "There's the heir to Mallow!"

Below stairs, Jim, the stable boy, came bursting unceremoniously into the kitchen. "I heered the church bell tolling!" he gasped.

All the servants looked at him askance. There was no sound but the wind blowing in the open doorway.

"You're hearing things," Tomkins said. "There's no church bell."

Then faintly from a long way over the marshes came the dull boom. They all heard it. "I told you!" Jim whispered. "Someone's dead!"

CHAPTER SEVENTEEN

They came out of the woods into the empty marshland. Blane drew rein to listen. Apart from the wind in the rustling winter grass, there was no sound. The horses fidgeted. The moon, coming from behind a dark streamer of cloud, showed a horizon empty of everything but wind-bent trees, a far-off farmhouse and, at the end of the curving, rutted road, the church tower.

"There's not a sound," said Sarah hopelessly.

But just as they set forth again a deep, reverberant sound boomed over the countryside. "What's that?" Sarah exclaimed.

"The church bell!" Blane spurred his horse. "Come on," he shouted. "The church, of course. Why didn't I think?"

Was Amalie frantically calling for help? Or Soames? Or was it some trick concocted by both of them?

The horses galloped down the muddy track. The gate that led to the churchyard stood open. Someone had come in a very short time ago, and in a hurry. Then Sarah saw the horses wandering saddled but untethered. Blane leaped off his own horse and ran up the slope to the church door. Sarah followed, her breath coming in gasps.

The door was open into the midnight darkness inside. Blane stood in the doorway. He put out an arm to bar Sarah, whispering to her to be quiet.

For someone was talking. It was Soames, his uncultured country voice strangely soft and persuasive. "It's no use hiding up there, my lady. Bring the lad down. I'll take him safe home. I'll say I found him in the woods."

There was a little silence. Then Amalie's voice, taut and full of furious anger, came from somewhere above them. "You're like all the rest, Soames. You only care about Titus. Titus, Titus, Titus! No one cares about me. What if I tell you he isn't Titus—that he's George?"

"He's Titus now, my lady. That can't be altered."

"You only want to think so. You and your precious Mallow. Why did you follow me? I was only taking the boy away. He's my son, and I can do what I like with him. I can even jump off the tower if I please. And if you try to come up here"—there was rising hysteria in her voice—"I will."

"Don't talk daft, my lady. Come down now. I promise I'll never tell a word of what I know."

"You're only bluffing, Soames! You don't know anything!"

Soames went on patiently and calmly, as if relating a story. "I'll say I never saw you in the summerhouse, my lady, with the woman, Mrs. Stone. No, nor I never heard a word of what you said to her, telling her she could have the ring—worth five hundred pounds, you said—if she went away and said nothing about being the master's wife. And I'll say I never heard Mrs. Stone laughing, crafty-like, and saying now she had the ring on her finger what was to stop her from having the master as well? So then you said you'd arrange for the master to meet her in the summerhouse the next night, when he got back from London. And that she might be sorry she hadn't met him there as she'd written saying she would, because here there was the lake, and sometimes people got drowned accidentally. Oh yes, I'll forget I saw her running back like a wild thing through the garden."

"What else have you—concocted, Soames?"

"My lady, I'm only saying the things I won't tell if you send Master Titus down safe. Such as the master being with me in the stables the next night at the time when you'd promised he'd be in the summerhouse to meet the woman. So someone else must have met her there. Someone who went back to the house alone, slipping in by the garden door. But if you bring Master Titus down now, my lady, my lips is shut forever."

"She slipped!" Amalie screamed. "She slipped in the mud. I couldn't go for help. It would have been too late."

Again there was the brief silence, as if the voices were lost and none of these terrible words had been said. Then, as footsteps began to grope on the stairs, Amalie's voice echoed through the dark church. "Don't come another step, Soames! I warn you! I'll jump with Titus. I'm right at the window." She must have moved sharply in the darkness, for suddenly the bell gave a muted boom and she screamed. "It's dark! I can't see!"

Sarah gripped Blane's arm. "Why doesn't Titus make a sound?"

"He's probably asleep. I suspect Amalie put some of her own sleeping draft in his tea. She couldn't risk him screaming."

Again it was silent, and they might have been alone in the dark building.

Blane whispered, "Stay here. I'm going to Soames."

Quiet as his approach down the aisle was, Amalie heard it, for she suddenly gasped, "Who's that? You've been lying, Soames. You've got someone there who's heard all you said."

Blane abandoned his caution and shouted in the deep, ringing voice with which, not long ago, he had read the lesson from the pulpit. "Amalie, don't move or the bell will strike you. Wait until I bring a light."

"You! Don't you dare come near me!"

"Don't move!" Sarah could hear Blane's swift footsteps. It was as if he could see in the dark, not tripping on the flagstones that covered older tragedies, older bones. "Soames and I are coming for Titus now, Amalie. Just keep quite still and you'll be safe."

"You won't get him! He belongs to me."

"He belongs to his grandmother and to Mallow Hall."

"I'll expose you! I'll tell everyone in England who you are. You'll be jailed. For years. I hope forever."

"Do what you like about me, Amalie! But let us get Titus safely down."

"Sammie would have killed him. She was going to kidnap him one night. I stopped her. I'm his mother, and I have a right to do exactly what I like with him. If hurting him is what hurts you most, my *dearest* love, I'll do it with pleasure. He's here on the floor asleep. He won't know a thing."

"Don't you *dare!*" Sarah couldn't help herself. She was stumbling down the aisle, bruising herself against the high pews that she couldn't see in the darkness. "You monstrous woman, don't you dare!"

"Ah! The clever Miss Mildmay too! I might have known. Then this is the end. I'm going to jump with Titus."

"Amalie!"

She gave a high, hysterical laugh. "You might have started pleading sooner, Blane. As I had to do with you. But I won't listen any more than you did. I'm going to—"

The sentence was never finished. For suddenly the great bell boomed deafeningly, and the fragments of a scream—or was that imagined?—were lost in the echoing sound.

"Blane!" whispered Sarah, groping for the rickety wooden stairs.

Someone struck a match. The frail light shone for the merest moment on Soames, hanging exhaustedly to the bell rope. Then it flickered out, and that deadly little picture too might have been imagined.

Blane sprang up the stairs, stumbling and blundering. After a long time, his footsteps began to descend slowly and heavily. "I've got Titus," he said tiredly. "He's quite unhurt—he was lying on the floor. Are you there, Sarah? Can you take him? He's still asleep."

Soames struck a match then, and for a moment his narrow face hung over the sleeping child. That was all. In that moment Sarah knew that the glimpse of Soames holding the bell rope, with the last terrible echoes dying away, was something that would be pushed into the back of all their memories. It would never be spoken of.

As Sarah took the sleeping child, there was a bustle at the front door and alarmed voices called out: "What's going on here? We heard the bell. Is there trouble?" It was the vicar and his wife. The vicar carried a lantern, and the scene was at last lit up: Soames with his face shining pallidly, Sarah disheveled and shocked, Titus wrapped in his warm coat asleep, with his head on her shoulder. Blane's face had its carved look, his eyes hollowed.

"There's been an accident," Blane said in a remote voice. "My wife was in the belfry. In the dark she must have stumbled against the bell. It swung back—as you heard."

"Good God! We must get help. Is she badly hurt?"

"I'm afraid it's too late."

"Oh, my dear boy!"

"I'm sorry, Vicar. She was always highly emotional and unpredictable. That poor drowned woman preyed on her mind."

The vicar bowed his head. "She came to my church for comfort."

The vicar's wife took Sarah's arm. "My husband will know what to do here. We'll take the boy to the house. What a good thing he's sleeping. He'll never know anything of this."

THOSE COMFORTING WORDS were still in Sarah's head as later they rode wearily home. Soames carried Titus on the saddle in front of him, tenderly and possessively. No one spoke much, until Soames turned to say, "This will blow over, sir." He no longer called Blane "my lord." "It'll cause talk, but there's always been talk about Mallow when the master's home."

"You have the master in your arms," Blane said briefly.

For a moment, in the moonlight, the two men's eyes met. Then Soames nodded. "You can trust me, sir."

"I know it, Soames. I apologize for ever thinking otherwise. You'd have died for that boy, wouldn't you?"

"As I would have for his father and his grandfather."

"Then make a man of him. Lady Malvina will help you. Now, ride on. I want to talk to Miss Mildmay."

When Soames rode ahead Blane said, "I'm going away as soon as Amalie's funeral is over. I'll never come back again. I've done what I set out to do."

"You mean, to get Mallow for your son?"

"Not my son. Blane Mallow's son."

"So you never were Blane!"

"No. I'm merely the younger son of another English family, who also set out to make his life at sea. Blane was my friend. We'd sailed together many times. He once saved my life. When I couldn't save his after our ship went down, I promised him to do all I could for his son. 'Get Mallow for him,' he said. I didn't know if I would ever reach land alive, but I promised."

"And did that mean you had to impersonate him?"

"It did, because I discovered that what should have been perfectly simple wasn't simple at all. You see, Titus is certainly Blane's son, but he's not legitimate."

Sarah stared. "Then Blane really was married to that awful woman, Mrs. Stone!"

"To Sammie. Samantha. Whatever her last name was. Yes, Blane was married to her. But she'd deserted him years ago, and he genuinely thought her dead when he married Amalie. However, she wasn't. They heard of her some time later, but hoped there'd be no trouble. Amalie had her marriage certificate and her baby. She didn't expect trouble because Blane was still the ne'er-do-well sailor Sammie had left. And Sammie knew nothing of the Mallow inheritance at that time."

"Why couldn't Amalie have brought Titus home and made the claim by herself?" Sarah demanded.

"She hadn't the courage. She knew her marriage was bigamous, and she needed support. It was she who noticed how much I resembled Blane, and during the ten days we'd spent floating in the Caribbean I'd heard every detail he could remember of his childhood, some related in delirium. I was pretty well equipped to make the attempt. In fact, I even had a scar beneath my ear that only needed a little improving on to fool the doctors."

"And you enjoyed doing all this! You didn't happen to think that you were depriving Blane's cousin Ambrose of his inheritance?"

"Ambrose could look after himself. Titus was only a child."

"So you had it all your own way. Lady Malvina was so delighted to have her son home that she shut her eyes to trouble, and Soames had this obsession about Titus, the true heir. They simply carried you through. What about the other man, Thomas Whitehouse?"

Blane grinned. "Amalie's father. He liked his daughter being a lady. He was quite prepared to swear he had always known me as Blane Mallow."

"You're incorrigible!" Sarah cried. "You did have it all your own way."

"No. You're wrong. It was far from that. You forget Amalie. And I completely underestimated her."

Sarah looked at the bleak outline of his face. "She fell in love with you."

"Passionately. Embarrassingly. She was shameless. She hadn't the modesty of an Englishwoman of your upbringing. I'd never expected to have to rely on locked doors. The plan had been that I was to stay here long enough to establish Titus and her and then go back to sea, and this time get completely lost. But Amalie began to make scenes. She refused to entertain the thought of my leaving."

Blane shrugged wearily. "Then you came and I, I confess, lost my head. I saw you standing in the hall looking furious with everybody because Titus was unhappy. I liked the way you so firmly took his side. I liked the way you looked. You were so full of spirit and indignation and tenderness. You were the kind of woman I had always looked for. So there it was. Your arrival was unconventional, your behavior was suspicious, but so was my situation, Amalie's, everyone's in that house. I overlooked what your coming would do to Amalie. I simply recognized that here in this queer business was something for me. So I determined you were to stay."

Sarah's voice was unsteady. "And it was worse than you had expected?"

"Oh, much worse. Well, it's all over now." He took a backward glance at the church tower. "But I never meant to bring her to this."

"She was the kind to destroy herself."

"Or others. Yes. You're right." After a little while he added, "I'll leave when the funeral's over. Everyone will think I have a broken heart. Titus will be all right. His grandmother will bring him up. You and Soames and Thomas Whitehouse, who would never betray his grandson, and I are the only living people to know the truth."

"How are you so sure I'm to be trusted?" Sarah asked.

"I have no doubt of it."

They were riding up the long, curving drive, the house standing pale and elegant across the meadow. "It's a beautiful place," Sarah said wistfully.

His voice was sharp with surprise. "Don't tell me that you had ambitions too!"

"Let's call them dreams." She slid wearily off her horse at the door.

Blane said, "What, Sarah? Had you some claim to this place?"

The door was flung open before Sarah could answer. Lady Malvina stood there, her arms outstretched. "Blane, have you brought back my grandson?"

"He's here, Mama. Soames has him. He's perfectly safe."

"Oh, thank God! Thank God! Ambrose and I heard the horses."

"Ambrose!" exclaimed Sarah.

Even before she saw Ambrose's lean, self-possessed figure in the background she was aware of Blane's eyes on her, his face hard with suspicion.

Ambrose came forward quickly to greet her. He obviously intended to make no secret now of their relationship. "My dear Sarah!" He took her hand and kissed it tenderly.

"You two appear to be old friends." Blane's voice came with detached interest. "Or should I say, more than friends?"

Ambrose answered him. "Sarah is my fiancée."

Sarah withdrew her hand. "We can talk later. Now Titus must be put to bed. Fortunately he's been asleep almost all the time. He knows nothing."

"Nothing of what?" The fear was naked in Lady Malvina's eyes. "Where's Amalie?"

"Lord Mallow will tell you, Lady Malvina." And Sarah went to take Titus from Soames.

"Blane, what is this?" Lady Malvina insisted.

"Amalie has had an accident, Mama."

The bleak words told her everything. "Not dead?"

"I fear so."

Lady Malvina clutched her throat. "Do you want to tell me how?"

"Not now, Mama."

"I believe she was quite mad, running off with Titus like that. Thank heaven he's safe. Blane, my poor boy! You look quite exhausted!"

"I'm all right, Mama. Shall we talk in the morning?"

"No," interposed Ambrose. "We must talk now. Sarah, give that child to the nursemaid. She's perfectly able to put him to bed."

Sarah obeyed, handing the child to Eliza. Titus stirred for the first time. "Grandmama?" Then he was asleep again.

"The little love," said Lady Malvina. "Now, come into the library and we'll have this out once and for all. But Ambrose, I ask you to have some delicacy, if you're capable of it. Blane has just lost his wife."

"If she was his wife."

"Oh, I know you have this fantastic story about Samantha and tombstones and suchlike, but we really can't believe them at this hour of night."

"Sarah must know the truth by now," Ambrose said pointedly. "You've been putting two and two together, haven't you, my dearest? Tell me what opinion you have formed. Is this man Blane Mallow? Was Amalie his wife? Is that boy his son? Come, you don't need to be afraid any longer to tell what you know. I'm here to protect you."

Blane had not spoken. He stood negligently leaning against the mantelpiece, his gleaming eyes fixed on Sarah. His expression told her nothing.

She looked from Blane to Ambrose. She had thought she loved Ambrose, she reflected in astonishment. He was so handsome, so elegant and cultured, so sure of himself. But she had not realized he was so cold. His eyes were the color of the lake water.

"Ambrose went to Trinidad to discover all these things," Lady Malvina said. "But he seems to have failed. He has no proof of anything. And with his trained legal mind too! Miss Mildmay, is it true that you're his fiancée? How could you be so deceitful?"

Sarah didn't enjoy meeting the hurt old eyes. Suddenly Blane answered for her. "The Mallow diamonds suited her very well. And she loves this house. Everyone has ambitions, Mama. Why shouldn't Miss Mildmay?"

He was an adventurer. He lied with amazing ease. He had tried to secure Mallow for a bastard. He had no sympathy for Ambrose's rights. But her decision as to how she would act in this situation had been made when she had seen Ambrose standing in the hall. Or had it been made weeks ago?

"I haven't found out anything of account, Ambrose. To the best of my knowledge this man is Blane Mallow and Titus is his son. As far as I know, Mrs. Stone was a dishonest vagrant and Amalie was Blane's wife. Both of these women are tragically dead, so now I fear we'll never know if anything is different from what we imagine."

Ambrose's gaze was narrowing in disbelief and a frightening, cold anger. Sarah had seen that expression only once before, just before he had sailed for the West Indies. She had fervently hoped never to see it again.

"So I must release you from your promise to me, Ambrose. You must marry an heiress, as I advised you at the beginning. You'll soon forget me, I assure you." She didn't add that she realized now she had never loved him. Poor Ambrose must be spared that final humiliation.

She turned to Lady Malvina to say sincerely, "I apologize for my deception to you, Lady Malvina. I thought at the time that I was justified, but I realize now that I was not. I also apologize to you, Lord Mallow."

The man at the fireplace didn't move.

"I shall leave tomorrow. Titus will be very happy with his grandmother, and a tutor might be hired for him. He's getting too big for a governess." She withdrew a step. "So may I say good night, and good-by?"

"Sarah!" Ambrose protested in a frozen voice.

"Leave her," said Blane.

"But Blane, must Miss Mildmay go like this?" Lady Malvina said peevishly. "I admit she's been very deceitful and secretive, but Titus loves her. And so do I." The old lady sank into her chair, her affectionate, blurred gaze on Sarah.

"I'm sorry, Mama. I'm afraid she must go." Blane turned to Sarah. "I shall take you to London myself. After all, everyone must agree, especially you, Ambrose, that this is no place for impostors."

"Sarah! Will you go with him? What would your family say?"

Her sisters, Amelia and Charlotte, with their dull existences, were going to be deeply envious, thought Sarah. And Aunt Adelaide was going to say dryly that as usual Sarah had done the unexpected, which was hardly the way to get a husband.

"Some day, Lord Mallow," she said, her eyes downcast to hide their leaping joy, "I hope you will meet my sisters, when they are free from their duties. As for myself, I don't intend to take another imprisoning situation. I haven't the disposition for this kind of life. I think I will travel. So I will be happy," she added, lifting her eyes to his shatteringly bright gaze, "to begin my journey with you."

River Rising

River Rising

A CONDENSATION OF THE NOVEL BY

JESSICA NORTH

ILLUSTRATED BY KARL SWANSON

A small painting, wrapped in newspaper—for Rochelle Dumont it was a vital clue to the mystery that was her dead father. Yet she dared trust no one with her shocking discovery. Rochelle had come to the small French-Canadian village to visit her mother's family. They lived on the cliffs above the St. Lawrence in an imposing mansion called River Rising. Years before, something terrible had happened at the Rising—something that had made her mother flee and never speak of the family again until she lay dying. Then came the frantic warning: "Don't believe them, Rochelle! Don't trust them!" Now Rochelle had to find out the truth for herself. Could she? Would they let her?

While writing *River Rising*, Jessica North lived by the St. Lawrence, absorbing the atmosphere of the region. Her book *The High Valley* appeared in Reader's Digest's *Six Gothic Tales*.

CHAPTER ONE

MY MIND, NOW THAT I can permit myself to remember all that has happened, returns always to the river, the great St. Lawrence pouring seaward from the cool heart of the continent, sweeping past the cities, farms and then wilderness of Quebec to merge with the Atlantic in that misty gulf whose reefs and shoals once made those waters a graveyard of ships and voyagers.

It was from the deck of a wooden sailing vessel journeying downriver that I saw the craggy headland and towering house known as River Rising, the place of my birth to which I now returned, a resentful stranger.

I was two years old when my mother took me into exile, and a little more than twenty years had passed since then. I could not possibly have remembered those granite cliffs, the slashed foam where waves battered the rocks of Wind-Whistle Cove. Yet when the schooner *Étoile Filante* rounded an island and the scene burst into view, my astonishment was mixed with a strange sense of the familiar, as though I had known that the house, starkly beautiful, would loom from the shore at this exact place.

"Look!" I exclaimed. "That must be the Rising!"

The ship's steward, leaning against the rail beside me, nodded. *"Oui. C'est magnifique."* Then, frowning, he muttered in accented English, "But it has a dark history." He studied the churning white water, the jagged rocks that could rend the strongest hull. "It is haunted, unlucky. There are many stories. . . ."

The ship did not believe him. Like the shooting star she was named for, she plunged ahead, canvas booming in the freshened breeze. Sunlight sparkled on the water, and the world that cool May morning was new-minted. But I had come filled with bitterness against the people who lived there, even though they were my only relatives. An unexplainable desire to do a favor for an old lady to whom I owed nothing had brought me. And perhaps there was a deeper reason. I felt rootless in the world. I had no country, no home. Why not visit my mother's people in Canada? At least I could see the cousins and the great-aunt who had done my mother such unkindness that she would not mention their names. When she finally did, in her last delirious hours, it was to warn me. "Don't trust them, Rochelle!"

Three solemn bell strokes rang across the water. The steward crossed himself, as though the notes echoing over the river were tolling for a death. Against my will I thought of Deirdre Cameron, and the morning suddenly seemed chill. Nonsense, I told myself. Nothing has happened to her.

"Quai Ste. Marie du Lac!" shouted the steward, leaving my side.

Atop the cliffs the mansard roofs and gables of an ancient town gleamed above tall sycamores and firs. Its beauty lulled me into believing that this might truly be a new beginning.

It was not, of course, a beginning. The enemy had already struck. Although I did not know it then, the first move had come in the crowded airport at Montreal, only minutes after my arrival in Canada.

"ROCHELLE! ROCHELLE Dumont!"

Startled, I looked in the direction of the voice. My flight from the West Indies had just landed and I had cleared customs. I now stood two steps inside Canada, and had paused to gather some first impression of my unfamiliar native country. But airports have no nationality.

"Rochelle!" called the voice again.

Who on earth? Even if my great-aunt, Regina Armitage, had sent someone to meet me, it could be no one who would recognize my face. Then I saw a girl waving at me. She, too, had just passed through customs, and was now fussing with the buckles of a canvas backpack that lay on the steel counter. Memories came back vaguely. College? Yes, Eastfield Hall.

She pushed past several people, the backpack dragging behind her, then threw her arms around me. "Rochelle, how wonderful!" she exclaimed.

"Deirdre Cameron?"

"Of course, Rochelle. I can't have changed in three years."

But it seemed to me a decade since I'd left Eastfield during my senior year to go home to Antigua. There had been my mother's illness and death, the losing struggle to continue the day school she had owned, finally selling it. Then several months in what seemed a vacuum, earning my living as a church organist and teaching piano to squirming children.

"You haven't changed," I said. "Only you're wearing your hair longer."

She smiled. "I used to yearn to have auburn hair like yours, and when girls talked about how unusual your green eyes were, my own must have almost turned green with envy."

"Deirdre, you can't be serious," I said.

"But I am."

In college we'd had little in common except that we were the only Canadians in our New England school. This formed no bond because I had no memories of Canada, so the warmth of her greeting surprised me until I recalled that sudden, effusive bursts of emotion were typical of Deirdre.

"Is anyone meeting you?" she asked.

"No."

"I'm alone, too. Let's have coffee at the snack bar."

Before I could refuse, she had captured a passing skycap, commanding him to take our luggage to *"le snack bar."*

I retrieved a bright yellow shawl that was lying on my suitcase.

"What's that?" she asked. "It's beautiful. Almost gold."

"A shawl. More a mantilla, I suppose. My great-aunt Regina made it. She wrote that it was to warm me in the Quebec spring."

"What gorgeous crocheting! Like lace on an old valentine." Taking possession, Deirdre draped it around her shoulders. I remembered then how she loved to borrow clothing. We were utterly unlike, I thought as we passed through swinging doors into the main hall of the terminal. My sensible suit paled beside the flare of Deirdre's rainbow-striped ankle-length skirt, her cheap sandals and sleeveless blouse defying the cool morning. The daughter of a rich Ontario family, she had called her attempts to wear a disguise of poverty "protest." It struck me as silly but harmless.

We had almost reached the snack bar when a hefty man, obviously late for a plane, charged through the crowd. *"Pardon! S'il vous—"*

I stumbled against the wall, dodging his attaché case. My ankle turned painfully and I felt the heel of my left pump give way, breaking off.

"What a boor!" Deirdre sputtered. "Are you all right?"

"I think it's just twisted, not a sprain." Leaning on her, I hobbled on one heel into the restaurant. I asked the skycap to put my suitcase beside me so I could find another pair of shoes, and opened my purse to tip him.

"No," said Deirdre. "He's mine. I caught him." She fumbled in her macramé bag. My eyes widened when she put two thick wads of money on the table of our booth, one crumpled stack Canadian, the other American—tens, twenties, fifties. Next she fished out a handful of coins.

The skycap's emphatic "Thank you, miss!" attested her generosity. As she stuffed the bills back into the bag I marveled that anyone could be so foolhardy. How much cash was she carrying? Several thousand dollars! Hadn't she heard of purse snatching? Or of traveler's checks?

Just then I heard my name called over the intercom. "Miss Rochelle Dumont. Please come to the information desk."

"I'll go for you," said Deirdre.

"Really, I'm all right. If I can just find another pair—"

"It's at the other end of the building. Give that ankle some rest." She left, calling back, "Order coffee for me."

I unzipped my suitcase and took out a pair of walking shoes. Who could be paging me? It had to be a member of the Armitage family. But Regina Armitage had been emphatic. "We won't meet you. You must have a chance to meet Canada first." As though I cared about their country! Or them. Family concern from the Armitages was twenty years too late!

I felt my ankle, finding it tender but not painful. I was determined to see as much of Montreal as possible this afternoon. After all, it was a vacation at Regina Armitage's expense, and while the family owed me nothing, they surely owed my mother a great deal. Guilt, I thought—Regina the matriarch salving her conscience for all the years my mother had spent alone. In her first letter several months ago, she had written of "this tragic estrangement," assuming I knew what she meant. I did not. What had they done to my mother while I was still a baby? Something so painful she had never been able to speak of them.

As a small child I had asked my mother about aunts, uncles and cousins. "They're far away and you wouldn't like them," she had said. And I knew the terrible finality of that tone. Charlotte Armitage Dumont could inspire awe, admiration and even fear, yet she had little power to evoke love. I felt myself an orphan who by an odd accident had a mother. A widow, she never spoke of the past but faced present and future with joyless courage. I could almost count the times I'd seen her smile with real warmth or burst into laughter. My loneliness would have been complete except for my music, which could hold me hour after hour, and for the love given me by my mother's only friend, Paul LaFarge.

A waitress came to the booth and I ordered two coffees. A moment later Deirdre arrived, flourishing an oversized envelope with a red maple-leaf design. "There was no one waiting, but this is for you."

My name was penciled in block letters. "Did they say who left it?"

"A skycap. Open it, Rochelle! Don't you love presents?"

Slitting the flap, I looked inside. "How strange. It's empty. Maybe my great-aunt's growing forgetful. But Regina Armitage sounds anything but senile in her letters."

Deirdre looked at me with new interest. "Armitage? You're not related to Morgan Armitage, are you?"

"I have a cousin named Morgan. Regina said he's a painter."

"A painter! Rochelle, your cousin may not be quite the most famous living Canadian artist, but most critics think he's the best. Didn't you know?"

"I don't know anything about my mother's family." Or my father's, either, I added silently.

"When I was thirteen, I had the most terrible crush on Morgan Armitage," Deirdre went on. "I saw him at the opening of an exhibition my mother dragged me to in Toronto. He was the handsomest older man I'd ever seen. I mooned about him for a month. Weren't you in love with someone, say an actor or musician, at thirteen?"

"No," I said, but a sudden flush gave me away.

Deirdre smiled. "Lying is a deadly sin."

"Well, there was an older man. A painter, too. Paul LaFarge from Martinique. But he wasn't famous. Just big and bearlike and rough and gentle at the same time."

Unwillingly I recalled Paul's red hair, the white duck trousers always paint-spotted, the kindness of his smile. There was no romance in what I felt for him—he was my mother's friend—but my happiest memories were of those summer days when his houseboat was moored in the cove near our cottage. When "Uncle Paul" was there, my mother's firm lips seemed fuller and her smiles less guarded. My love for him remained even during that terrible summer when I realized the truth: Paul LaFarge was my mother's lover. He came to the house when they thought I was asleep. I lay in adolescent torment. It was dishonest, I thought. Ugly. Why wouldn't my mother marry him? The world might call him a failure, a drifter who, I was told, painted with the fury of a madman but hardly sold enough to buy new canvas. If my mother really cared for him, none of this would matter. Only long after Paul's death could I force myself to admit that maybe he never wanted a wife, no matter how happy he seemed with us.

Now, as the waitress served our coffee, I forced my mind from the past and tried to listen to Deirdre. She had changed more than I had thought. Crescents darkened her lower eyelids and her gaiety seemed forced.

"Tell me about yourself," she said. "Are you still living in Antigua?"

"I don't live in the islands now. I'm visiting Canada."

"You're not on a concert tour, are you?" she asked.

I shook my head. "It turned out I don't have what they call an 'exploitable' talent. In other words, I'm not good enough."

She seemed honestly disappointed. "I remember that concert you gave at Eastfield. We all thought you'd be famous."

"I'm afraid not. I really don't know what I'll do."

"That makes two of us." Deirdre suddenly looked woebegone. "I'm having a bad time, Rochelle. I'm on the run. Hiding out."

"Hiding out? Deirdre, for heaven's sake!"

"Oh, not from the police! It's a personal thing." Her brown eyes became misty as she held back tears. "I hurt people I love. I don't mean to, but it happens. Afterward I run away. If only I could manage myself!"

I had no idea what she meant.

"I won't burden you with the troubles I've caused myself," she said. "I just want to get away where nobody can find me." She took several deep breaths, then her taut face relaxed. "What are your plans right now?"

I explained that I was going downriver to a village called Ste. Marie du Lac. "Regina Armitage arranged passage on the *Étoile Filante*."

"The old *Shooting Star*. What a wonderful way to see Quebec!"

"You know the ship?"

"I've made the trip twice. The *Star* is a real nineteenth-century sailing ship. Modernized for tourists, of course." She thought a moment, then said abruptly, "I'm going with you. Maybe to Quebec City, maybe all the way to Gaspé. I'll go right now to telephone for reservations."

I sat waiting, my feelings mixed about traveling with Deirdre. Then, remembering her woebegone look, I felt guilty. She returned shortly, face aglow. "I've got a cabin right next to yours."

"Lucky," I said, uncertain about what kind of luck this was.

Deirdre amazed me. Now that her next few days were settled, worry had evaporated. "How's your ankle?" she asked.

"Much better."

"Then I'll be your guide to Montreal. We don't sail until tonight."

As we rose to leave, my glance fell on the big envelope with its maple-leaf design. What had been left out when it was sealed? Someone at the Rising, I supposed, would clear up the mystery. But in this I was mistaken.

"WE'LL HAVE LUNCH at Le Coq d'Or," Deirdre said as our taxi sped into the city. "It's right at the wharf where the *Star* is moored. We can leave our luggage there until boarding time."

An overcast sky threatened rain, and patchy fog shrouded the river. "We're in Old Montreal now," said Deirdre as we passed docks and warehouses and narrow buildings with antique casement windows.

Le Coq d'Or was so haughty that it had no sign except a small brass plaque. Across the street I could see the masts of the *Étoile Filante*.

"Mademoiselle Cameron!" The doorman's greeting was enthusiastic.

"Hello, Charles. Good to see you. Please put these things in the coatroom. We'll return for them tonight."

The restaurant was dimly lit by candles and ships' lanterns. The maître d'hôtel, as cordial to Deirdre as the doorman had been, ushered us to a table beside a front window, snatching away a card proclaiming it reserved.

"Lunch, please, Armand. Whatever's best today."

"You're well known here," I said as he left.

"I should be. I ate here at least twice a week for months."

"You've lived in Montreal?"

She arched an eyebrow. "You might call it living. I was out of college and . . ." She hesitated. "I didn't graduate. The week before final exams I went to San Francisco. Fear of failing, I guess. I wandered around, then lived with my parents awhile, but I couldn't stand their stuffy friends. There was a terrific row and I came to Montreal."

"What did your father . . . ?"

She tossed her head defiantly. "He couldn't stop me. I'd come into my own money. Besides, they didn't know where I was. . . . I joined a group in an old house not far from here. We were into Zen and yoga and macrobiotic food." She shuddered. "Things that tasted like stewed bark. So I'd slip away and come here for a good meal."

"What finally made you leave?" I asked.

"I didn't really fit in. And I got tired of supporting a dozen people. One night when everyone was at a rock concert, I went home. It was terrible afterward. I got threatening letters. Actually blackmail! My father went to the police. I didn't want to get anybody in trouble, but what could I do?"

The waiter presented a steaming tureen of soup. Deirdre's gloom vanished. Exclaiming with delight, she fell upon it as eagerly as if she were still recovering from a soybean diet. I took my time, savoring the flavor, enjoying the candlelight on old silver and brass. I loved the diamond-shaped panes of the windows beside us, and my gaze wandered to the street.

No quaintness there, except the top rigging of the *Étoile Filante*. A solitary pedestrian strolled slowly by, a sailor or a longshoreman, to judge from the dark corduroy trousers, turtleneck sweater and navy-blue knit cap. He glanced toward the window and hesitated. Then, deliberately looking away, he slouched on. The sunglasses he wore had mirrored lenses that completely concealed the eyes, giving his swarthy face a robot look.

"Delicious." Deirdre sighed as she finished the soup. She clapped when the waiter returned bearing poached Gaspé salmon. "My absolute favorite!"

After the salmon course she said, "Excuse me. I have to congratulate the chef." And she bounded off to the kitchen.

I looked idly at the street, my thoughts returning to the man with the knit cap and reflector glasses. Strange, the way he had looked in the window, then turned his head so quickly. It had been furtive. Also, now that I considered it, how odd to wear sunglasses on a foggy day. Nonsense, I told myself. Deirdre's talk of threats had set my imagination running. It was ridiculous to be made uneasy by one glance from a passerby.

Deirdre, her smile radiant, returned to the table but did not sit down. "Coffee? Or should we start sightseeing?"

"Sightseeing." I reached for my purse. "Let's pay—"

"Nothing to pay. I took care of it in the kitchen. Don't say one word, Rochelle! This is my treat, and I loathe arguments about money." She was already heading toward the door.

Outside, the mist was like thin smoke. The wispy fog softened the outlines of buildings and quayside fences, yet the length of the street was visible. "The neighborhood's deserted," I said. "Should we call a taxi?"

"Oh, no. You have to see Old Montreal on foot," said Deirdre, moving ahead briskly.

The uneasiness I'd felt earlier returned strongly—almost a sense of being warned. I could find no valid reason for this until I seized upon the thought of Deirdre carrying so much money. I found myself glancing at the shadowed doorways. We passed several parked cars, forlorn in the mist as though abandoned forever. I kept wishing Deirdre would walk more slowly. My twisted ankle had started to ache.

"I'm afraid we'll have to take a taxi after all," I said at last. "My ankle will never make it."

"Oh, Rochelle! I'm sorry. There's a public phone across the street at the corner. You stay here. I'll go to call for one." She went on alone to the corner, and there turned to cross the street. The traffic signal was green her way as she stepped from the curb.

I will never know what made me look back at that exact second, as I think the motor was almost noiseless. Perhaps it was only the wariness that had been growing in me. But I did look. Then I screamed, "Deirdre!"

A gray panel truck hurtled toward her, flashing past me even as I screamed. I knew the driver could never halt in time and I ran forward, shouting. Warned by my scream, Deirdre had leaped back while the truck charged through the traffic signal. She had stumbled and now lay sprawled at the curb. When I reached her, she was gasping, feebly struggling to her feet. "Sit down," I commanded. "Sit on the curb and lower your head."

Weakly, she obeyed.

My heart hammered. The truck had missed her by inches, and if it had struck at such speed . . . I forced away the picture of her broken body.

"My fault, I suppose," she said. "But the light *was* green."

"*Not* your fault!" My fright was suddenly replaced by anger. "No one expects a truck to race through a crossing against the light. On a foggy day, too. The man must be crazy or blind!"

Perhaps it was the word "blind" that caused me to remember one fleeting impression. I had not really seen the driver; everything had happened too fast. But hadn't there been a flash of light from the face? Reflector sunglasses? Had I seen a blue knit cap? I thought so.

Deirdre rallied. "That man's a criminal! Did you get his license number?"

I struggled to remember. The truck had come from behind us, following the same street we had walked. I had watched it speed past Deirdre to the next corner, where it had swerved right, into the cross street. I could recall the sound of tires resisting the sudden turn. But what had I seen? A rear bumper and a taillight. What else?

"There wasn't any license plate," I said slowly.

Deirdre stared at me, bewildered. Then her features crumbled. Shuddering, she clutched Regina's yellow shawl around her shoulders. When at last she spoke, her voice sounded strangled. "He meant to kill me. He must have!"

CHAPTER TWO

WE FOUND OUR WAY back to the safety of Le Coq d'Or, a badly shaken pair. Deirdre went quickly to a rear table, far from the windows, and ordered two brandies. When the drinks arrived, she forced a wan smile. "I suppose all's well that ends well. I mean, no real harm was done."

"Just the same, we should report the driver to the police."

"The police? Don't think of such a thing! We haven't a license number or even a description. We'd be questioned for hours. You don't know what the Montreal police are like."

I didn't. But Deirdre, to judge from her reaction, was altogether too familiar with them. What had gone on while she lived with that group?

She finished her drink, and the smile, less artificial now, returned. "That stupid driver isn't going to spoil your first visit to Montreal. We'll take a long, slow taxi drive. You have to see Place d'Armes and . . ."

Either Deirdre had iron nerves or she could banish any unpleasantness by looking the other way. For me, the beauties of Montreal were lost. Whenever we left the taxi, I found myself glancing sharply right and left.

Deirdre's eagerness irritated me as we climbed the steps of a baronial art museum. Did she think I could concentrate on paintings today?

"This is special, Rochelle. Something you can't miss." She moved quickly past old masters and French Impressionists, then halted. "Look!"

We stood before a large canvas, and my breath quickened. Color blazed at me, writhing golds, twisting greens with wild flashes of orange. There were no identifiable shapes, for this was a painting of pure emotion, astonishing, beautiful. But its beauty conveyed a sense of frenzy, the outpouring of an artist whose hurt and rage had exploded in color. Moving nearer, I read the plaque. *Indian Summer*, by Morgan Armitage.

"Glorious," said Deirdre. "You should be proud of your cousin."

I nodded silently. But the Armitages were only a name to me, and my admiration for *Indian Summer* was mingled with uneasiness at the prospect of meeting the artist, a man who must be possessed by some private demon. It seemed impossible that this painter and my cool, emotionless mother could share the same background.

As we left the museum the painting haunted me. I knew little about art, but had no doubt that my cousin was a genius.

"If your ankle's not too tired, there's one last place I want to go before supper," said Deirdre. It was a curio shop. I sat while she explored.

"I'm buying this," Deirdre bubbled, displaying a music box. "Listen! When you lift it up, it plays 'Alouette.' " The famous French-Canadian song tinkled loudly. "How do you stop it?" she asked the clerk.

"Turn it over and set it down, miss. It's self-winding."

As we left the shop Deirdre was softly singing "Alouette" in English. *"Pretty skylark, pretty little skylark! Pretty skylark, I shall pluck you now!"* It had never struck me before that the words were rather sinister.

AT TEN THAT night the gay lanterns of the *Étoile Filante* twinkled a welcome. We mounted the gangplank with a throng of fellow passengers. Somewhere on board a concertina played a rollicking folk dance. As our tickets were checked Deirdre glanced eagerly around; then her smile faded. "Rochelle, I have to go ashore a moment. I'll be right back."

"What's wrong?"

She hesitated only an instant. "I forgot to tip Georges at the restaurant for taking care of our bags. Go to your cabin. I'll join you in a minute."

As she rushed down the gangplank I clearly remembered her handing a bill to the cloakroom attendant before I could reach for my own money. Why did she bother to lie? If she wanted to go ashore, she owed me no explanation. It was as though she had seen something that put her to flight. Something . . . or someone.

There were only two couples on deck, teenagers gazing across the river dim in misty moonlight. Then I realized another person was present, a tall man in an officer's cap and white uniform, inspecting the rigging. Could the sight of this man have sent Deirdre into sudden retreat? The lantern light revealed a face bronzed by sun and wind. But he seemed aloof and completely preoccupied, unaware of passengers.

A steward picked up my valise. I followed him, passing close to the silent officer, who glanced my way, then seemed about to speak. Automatically I said, "Good evening." Giving me the briefest possible nod, he turned away. Insolent, I thought, feeling foolish for having spoken first. Yet I was certain he had somehow recognized me, and I remembered Aunt Regina's letter saying she would mention me to her friend Captain McCabe.

"Is that Captain McCabe?" I asked the steward.

"Non, mademoiselle. Le Capitaine Lachance. Un marin très célèbre."

Captain Lachance might be a famous sailor, I thought, but he would win no prizes for friendliness.

After the steward left, I inspected the small, charming cabin. I tried to tell myself how comfortable it was, how exciting the voyage downriver would be. But it was useless. I felt only dread about going to River Rising, and my mother's dying words tormented me. Her fever-racked brain had slipped in and out of consciousness. She mumbled my father's name, then "River Rising . . . Morgan . . . Regina . . ." She seized my hand, and for a moment her voice was clear and strong. "Don't trust them! Don't believe them. Rochelle, I'm sorry. I should have told you . . . so many things. . . ." Then she slipped away. Months later when Regina Armitage's first letter arrived, the puzzling words came back to me, as they did again now: "Don't trust them! Don't believe them."

On the river a foghorn groaned. I rose quickly, as though in answer to a warning, and reached for my suitcase, ready to run from the ship before it was too late. Ready to go—where? I could think of nowhere. Then the decision was made for me. The *Étoile Filante* shuddered, and I heard the muffled clank of metal and the planks creaking as we weighed anchor.

A little while later Deirdre tapped on my door. "I'm in the next cabin, number eight." She frowned to see that I had changed to my dressing gown. "Rochelle, you can't go to bed so early! There's a band and dancing and lots of unattached males and . . ."

"Go and attach one. I just want a hot shower and a long sleep."

EITHER THE SHIP'S bell or a sudden ray of sunshine streaming through the porthole awakened me in the morning. I know my first thought was, This is a beautiful day. The gloom and uncertainty of last night had been banished by sleep, and as I brushed my hair I smiled in the mirror. Perhaps my moods were as mercurial as Deirdre's.

At the head of the companionway I halted, transfixed by the panorama of sky, river and shore. The wake of the *Étoile Filante* cut a white swath through the blue water, and faraway forests of pine and birch clothed rolling hills. I moved to the rail feeling that I had walked into a dream, and gazed on the same landscape my ancestors had first seen centuries before.

Only an appetite whetted by river air could have pulled me to the dining room. Even there the waiter led me to a table with a glorious view of the river. The room was almost deserted, but I was content to be alone. A card on the table announced we would make port in Quebec City early that afternoon. Passengers would have the rest of the day to explore the ancient town, and the ship would not sail until early the following morning.

I did not see Deirdre all morning, but she joined me at lunch, barricaded behind huge sunglasses. "You missed a wonderful party. I wore a black wig and a beret, very Montmartre and dangerous-looking."

"Did you find that unattached male?"

"Several. Especially one. A Hungarian poet. He lives in Quebec City because he says it's the only place in Canada that has a soul." She dipped her spoon into a steaming bowl of pea soup. "Are you getting acquainted?"

"Yes. With the river and with Canada." I hesitated, then said what strangely I had come to feel. "It's like coming home. I don't understand. I couldn't possibly remember this country from childhood. Longfellow's 'Evangeline' is all I know about Canada."

Deirdre laughed. " 'Evangeline' country is Nova Scotia, not here."

She looked past me toward the deck as Captain Lachance, a clipboard in hand, paused to make a note. He was accompanied by a dog, a powerful

German shepherd. "The *coureur de bois*," said Deirdre, scorn in her voice. "The legendary Canadian woodsman. The strong, silent folk hero."

"Do you know Captain Lachance?"

"No. I just don't like that arrogant type of Frenchman." She paused, then said, "Emil, the Hungarian poet, wants to show me Quebec City. Won't you come along? I'm sure he has a friend. We can double-date."

"No, thanks. I want to be on my own this afternoon."

EVERYTHING I HAD read about Quebec City was true. Hiring a horse-drawn carriage, I explored hillside streets lined with fanciful stone buildings. I stood breathless on the terrace of the Château Frontenac, gazing down hundreds of feet to the magnificent river. Only once did I see Deirdre. She was in a carriage with three young men and called, "See you tonight!"

Lured by a quaint restaurant on the wooden stairway to the Place Royale, I dined alone in luxury, lifting my wineglass in a toast to a wonderful day. No matter what lay ahead at River Rising, I had seen Quebec and would treasure it in my memory forever.

The night had turned chilly. Shivering in the taxi that took me back to the ship, I reminded myself to reclaim my yellow shawl from Deirdre. On board there was excitement and loud music. I found a note in my cabin. "Folk dance in dining room. Join us. Armand wants to meet you. D."

Armand? Probably one of the young men I'd seen in her carriage. I dropped the note in the wastebasket, and half an hour later fell asleep.

The nightmare seized me at some unknown hour. Someone, I felt, was in my cabin, standing over me, then stealthily moving back, while I fought against an inner voice that whispered, "You are only dreaming." I think a sharper sound, a thud, almost awakened me, yet I resisted, clinging to the false security of sleep even when I heard, *"Alouette, gentille alouette . . ."*

Slowly I forced my eyes open. The cabin was black except for a faint glow of moonlight against the porthole curtain. I sensed no presence, heard no breathing. Were there footfalls in the passage outside? I could not be sure. I found the light switch and the darkness vanished.

"Only a dream," I said aloud. But my uneasiness remained. I felt I had dreamed many more sounds than I could now recall. Had I been frightened by a muffled noise of something dragged across the floor? And the music. Had I actually heard Deirdre's music box through the thin wall?

Putting on slippers and a robe, I tiptoed to the door and opened it a few inches. To my surprise, no lanterns burned in the passageway. On deck a voice snapped, "Robichaud? Where the devil are you?"

"Here, Captain Lachance."

"What happened to the lanterns? You're on watch here."

"Just switched off, I suppose. *Oui*." A lantern blinked on. "Young people wanting a dark corner." The man chuckled.

Bolting my door, I returned to bed. Obviously in my sleep I must have heard Deirdre pick up the music box in her cabin. I drifted off again, and even the weighing of anchor hardly disturbed my rest.

I dressed quickly the next morning, not wanting to miss a moment of my last hours on board. When I reached deck, we had passed Île d'Orléans and the St. Lawrence was broadening, sweeping out to north and south.

After breakfast I went to Deirdre's cabin to get my shawl. No answer came when I tapped; then as I knocked harder the *Étoile Filante* tilted to meet a swell and the unlocked door swung open.

"Deirdre?" I said, stepping inside. No one had slept in the bed. There was no clothing, no rucksack. Deirdre had vanished—and so had my shawl, I thought angrily. No note had been left for me. Only one sign of Deirdre remained—her music box on the dresser.

Irritation mounting, I returned to my own cabin, taking the music box with me, fumbling with it, then remembering to turn it upside down to silence its tinkling. I tried to get a grip on my temper. Good riddance! I told myself. This, by Deirdre's own admission, was typical behavior. But the theft—and I could think of no kinder word—of the shawl was peculiar. It was out of the question that she could have forgotten who owned it, and out of character that she should walk off with it. Irresponsible, yes. Thieving? I didn't think so.

I tried to make sense of the situation. Deirdre must have debarked in the middle of the night, probably with her Hungarian poet. She would not have wanted to awaken me to explain. No doubt she had left the shawl with the steward. I asked him about it, and he directed me to the purser, an elderly man who was sitting on a high stool behind a counter when I entered his office. Captain Lachance was leaning against a desk, examining a list of figures. He glanced at me but did not speak.

When I inquired about the shawl, the purser shook his head.

"Did Miss Cameron leave any message for me?" I asked.

He glanced at the register, then spoke in a Scottish accent. "Cameron? I fear ye are mistaken, miss. No such passenger aboard."

"She *was* on this ship. We boarded together at Montreal."

"On the contrary, Miss Dumont." It was the abrupt tone of Captain Lachance. "You boarded alone. I saw you."

"Well, I meant we boarded at *almost* the same time. My friend went ashore for a moment."

The purser spoke firmly. "My register has cabin eight occupied by Miss Annabelle Lee of New York. Reservation by telephone, Montreal." His manner was courteous enough. The anger that surged up in me was directed at Captain Lachance, who seemed to enjoy my confusion.

"I don't care who the register says is in cabin eight," I snapped. "I've known Deirdre Cameron for years."

The purser scowled. "My register is kept with uncommon care."

No one was going to help me here. I whirled toward the door, but the captain halted me. "A moment. That's a name I remember." He had turned suspicious. "Mr. Andrews, give me file X, if you please."

The purser handed him a folder and he leafed through it. "Cameron. Here we are." He read silently a moment. When he looked at me again, I was startled by his taunting smile. "Our mystery is solved. Your friend boarded, but not under her true name. That would have been impossible. She has a prominent place in our dossier of unwelcome passengers."

"Unwelcome?" I blinked, astounded. "In what way?"

"You say you have known this person for years. Then you are familiar with her character. It is distasteful to speak of such matters."

"What nonsense! She's impetuous, but—"

"We will end this unpleasantness," he interrupted me. "A year ago Captain McCabe was ill, as he is now, and I was in command. Miss Cameron and her friends were noisy, obscene and using illegal drugs. One of them tried to sell drugs to another passenger. I put the whole group ashore but did not inform the police. Clearly, I should have."

He stood up, as though to terminate the conversation. "You say she left the ship last night. *Bien.* It saves me the trouble of throwing her overboard. Although that, perhaps, would be a pleasure." He glanced at his watch. "We raise Quai Ste. Marie du Lac in about two hours. I ask that you be ready to debark promptly. It is not a regular call. Captain McCabe arranged to have you put ashore there as a favor to your Aunt Regina."

"Why stop at all?" I asked hotly. "Just throw me overboard. That sort of thing seems to give you enjoyment."

His eyes met mine in a look that was at once a warning and a challenge. "I have lived all my life in Ste. Marie du Lac. I know your family well. Regina Armitage is a remarkable woman. A lady. Some women today fail to understand that word in any language."

"The word has a counterpart," I retorted. "A person known in English as a gentleman."

He left the office, touching his cap in either a salute or a gesture of contempt. I stood at the purser's counter, trembling with rage yet feeling an utter fool. I had no doubt that Captain Lachance had spoken the truth. Deirdre's peculiar behavior now made sense. She had not expected Lachance to be aboard, much less standing on deck. So she fled, to return when he was not watching. Also, I now understood the outlandish sunglasses and the black wig. She would have enjoyed this game of disguises.

Returning to my cabin, I finished packing. My anger at Captain Lachance did not cool. How dare he lump me with Deirdre? Then a voice whispered inside me: "Well, you were traveling together. You announced she'd been your friend for years."

All right, I had given the captain reasons for suspicion. Still, there was no excuse for his high-handed behavior. "Deirdre Cameron, I could kill you!" I cried. The words, not meant literally, of course, rang in my ears. Less than forty-eight hours ago someone had tried to do exactly that.

I sat still, forcing myself to be calm. Deirdre's Montreal acquaintances were far more sinister than I had suspected. Selling drugs on a public ship was a serious affair. No wonder Deirdre had fled her former companions. Then, almost a year later, the man in the mirror glasses had seen her and tried to take final revenge.

It fitted. But could I connect this with Deirdre's unannounced departure from the ship? I thought of my nightmare, the faint footsteps and tinkling tune. Suppose it had *not* been Deirdre in cabin eight? Suppose . . .

Nonsense. The simple explanation was that Deirdre had impulsively decided to remain in Quebec City, to study Hungarian poetry, I thought grimly. And I was a fool to worry about her. I rang for the steward, who took my suitcase to the deck. Captain Lachance, I resolved, would not be delayed one extra second on my account.

AN HOUR LATER I stood alone on the ancient stone pier of Quai Ste. Marie du Lac, wondering what to do next. Three empty fishing skiffs swung idly at their moorings. There were no buildings except two boathouses, their doors padlocked. I had known that Ste. Marie du Lac was in wilderness, but I had never imagined a place so utterly deserted. Surely someone would arrive soon.

A long time had passed when I heard a creak of wheels and then the voice of a man singing drunkenly, his French laden with the accent of the province. A home-built farm wagon rolled into view, a dapple-gray nag pulling it. I waved to the driver, a black-bearded giant, and he nodded his huge head. The parts of his face not concealed by whiskers and mustache were flaming red. Leaning from the wagon bench, he peered at me suspiciously.

"Bonjour," I ventured.

He inspected me and at last slurred the words: "*Mais oui.* This is what the daughter looks like." Swinging from the wagon, he hoisted my heavy suitcase as if it had been filled with feathers. Not eager to be lifted by him, I climbed aboard quickly, stepping on the axle hub. He mounted the wagon, flicked the reins. "Go, horse!"

"Did they send you to meet me?" I asked in French.

He shook his head. "*Anglais, non.* No speak."

"But I'm speaking French," I protested.

After deep concentration he decided this was so, and it seemed to trouble him. "Do they speak French in Australia?"

"In Australia?" It was my turn to be puzzled. "Some people do." I glanced at him uneasily. He was half drunk, perhaps he was also half-witted.

Daylight vanished as the road plunged into a forest that looked impenetrable, without paths or gaps. The tall trunks lining the road had towered here for generations, woodland giants, their branches intertwining to form a great vault of green and brown.

"I'm Gilles," the man beside me said. "They had to hire me to meet you. There was no one else. Everything is disarranged at the château. The police are searching for the criminal. The little girl was stolen last night. The little girl with the rag doll."

A kidnapping? I struggled to think of the French word for it and failed. "Tell me about it. What happened?"

"How should I know? It is not my affair." From under the bench he lifted an earthen jug and took a noisy gulp.

Aunt Regina's letters had given me no clue as to who this child might be. Morgan had a stepdaughter, but Regina had described her as "almost a teenager." A kidnapping. No wonder the household was "disarranged."

We entered a covered bridge, a long, barnlike structure in which the creaking wheels and the horse's hoofs blended with the churn of swirling water below. "Ste. Marie du Lac," Gilles said laconically as we emerged.

I had seen pictures and read descriptions of Quebec villages, but nothing had prepared me for Ste. Marie du Lac. A rolling green meadow flecked with new daisies and daffodils spread before us. Behind the hand-split rails of a fence a herd of khaki-colored cows quietly enjoyed the fresh grass. The village was in a valley with forest-clad hills rising on every side. To the north stretched a narrow lake. An ancient stone church stood a little apart, its ivy-wrapped spire guarding the village like a sentinel. There was one principal street, but the houses, twoscore or more, were scattered along lanes with no apparent plan, cottages of timbered stone boasting dormer windows with diamond panes, and a chimney at each end.

"Your town is lovely," I said.

Gilles shrugged. "I will stop for the mail. Then to the château."

Beyond the village and to the west a huge structure, walled and turreted, dominated a low rise of land. "What is that?"

"The abbey." He seemed surprised. "You should know that."

We drove down the deserted street. "Where is everyone?" I asked.

"Spring planting." Gilles tugged at the reins. The horse halted in front of a large, low building—apparently the commercial hub of Ste. Marie du Lac—housing a tavern, a general store and a butcher shop.

Gilles slouched into the store, and I was left to wait. An unreasonably long time seemed to pass. Then a raindrop splashed on my hand, and I realized the sky was becoming ominous. A little way ahead a narrow graveled road veered west to climb the slope and disappear into the woods. I supposed it led to the château. How far? I wondered. In a flurry of raindrops I climbed from the wagon, determined to make Gilles hurry.

The store was low-ceilinged and gloomy. The naked bulb dangling over the counter seemed only to create more shadows. I lingered just inside the door, accustoming my eyes to the dimness. The shelves displayed bolts of cloth, cheeses, canned goods, hardware and other oddly assorted items. Several men sat at two round tables, sipping coffee and playing cards. Gilles, his back to me, lounged against the counter, talking in low tones with a broad-faced woman in a white apron.

I had a feeling that the room had been lively with talk only a moment before and the utter silence was caused by my entrance. No one looked up, no one spoke a greeting. I seemed nonexistent.

I took a hesitant step forward. The woman must have whispered something to Gilles, for he looked over his shoulder. "I am still getting the mail," he said. I saw an envelope thrust in his hip pocket.

Behind me the door opened and one of the men muttered, "*Bonjour*, Madame Jeannette."

A rasping voice replied, "*Bonjour*, Bardot."

Turning toward the speaker, I saw a wizened crone shrouded in black, the fringe of her shawl giving an effect of tatters. Her gnarled hands were waxen, a startling contrast to the gypsy-brown face capped by a cascade of slate-gray hair that fell to her waist. The hunched shoulders straightened as she became aware of my presence, then she moved slowly toward me. Involuntarily I drew back. Pale, enormous eyes stared from hollow sockets into my face, a mad and malevolent scrutiny. The cardplayers leaned forward, and one made a sign of the cross.

I recoiled as the hag lifted her hand, clawlike fingers almost touching my face. "I know you," came the hoarse whisper. For a second we stood transfixed, until she whirled away, turning to the startled men, and her voice rose to a scream: "It is the murderer's daughter! The murderer's daughter has returned!"

CHAPTER THREE

THE HAG'S OUTBURST HAD come so unexpectedly that I stood stunned, not really grasping her meaning. Nor could I make sense of the babble of backwoods French that followed, catching only "Madame Jeannette" as the cardplayers tried to calm her. She was gesticulating wildly, screaming unintelligible abuse. In the midst of the confusion I heard a low chuckle and realized that Gilles, still at the counter, was leering at me.

Outrage brought me back to reality. Chin high, I marched from the store, slamming the door behind me. Mounting the wagon, I undid the reins, my hands trembling from sheer rage. When I exclaimed, "Go!" the horse plodded forward. If Gilles ran in pursuit, I would seek shelter at the nearest house; I was not riding another yard with him. But no one followed.

Anger had taken possession of me so completely that I gave no thought to the fact that I had not held the reins of a horse since childhood, nor did I stop to think I might be going in the wrong direction. I wanted only to leave Ste. Marie du Lac. The graveled road wound upward, and soon the wagon seemed engulfed by pine forest. "The murderer's daughter has returned." Madame Jeannette's scream rang in my head.

Could there be any meaning behind the words? Some timeworn gossip? I could not push away the memory of my mother's masklike face whenever I asked about my father. "He's dead, Rochelle. Why force me to remember?"

What did I know of this stranger who had fathered me? He was born in France and had no close relatives. He was an architect who met my mother when both were students at McGill University. He died young, by drowning, a tragic accident. My mother kept no photographs of him, no souvenirs, yet I was certain she had loved him deeply. Once I heard someone ask what her husband had been like. "A good man," she said. "A man of great tenderness." There was fierce pride in her voice, then she turned away. It was the only time I saw tears in her eyes.

Lightning streaked the sky. I urged the horse to move faster, but he held his dogged pace. The road turned sharply as we reached the crest and then, silhouetted against the thunderheads, River Rising loomed stark and solitary above the gray granite of the cliffs. The windswept height was scarred by upthrusts of rock. This was a place without pity.

We passed through open wrought-iron gates set in an arch. A marble plaque said RIVER RISING—1760—IN SAECULA SAECULORUM. For all the ages? Winds of more than two centuries had eroded the chiseled words, and the bold motto now seemed like an epitaph on an ancient tombstone. The words the steward had spoken came back to me: "It is haunted, unlucky."

Now, approaching the enormous house with its tall gables and shuttered windows, I understood why the Rising might inspire legends. Towering above wind-whipped trees, the château stood awesome and forbidding. Lights glimmered behind only a few of a hundred blind windows, and suddenly even these were extinguished as lightning split the clouds.

The horse quickened his pace, sensing the rage of the storm. We had just reached a lightless porte cochere fronting the main entrance when the deluge came. I hesitated on the wagon seat. The sprawling house, in blackness now, appeared deserted. Then, at a near window, I saw a moving light, and the massive door swung wide.

"Gilles?" a voice boomed. A bearlike woman stood in the entry, holding a lantern. She had the bosom of a giantess and her head, topped by a mop of grayish red hair, protruded above her shoulders as a turtle's pokes from its shell. "Mademoiselle Rochelle?"

"Oui."

"But where is Gilles?" She addressed me in English.

"In the village. Drunk," I told her.

"*Mon dieu!* Such a day! Ah, let me help you down. You're wet and shivering. *Zut*, that Gilles! I could tear his arms off."

Gilles, I thought, should beware. The woman had a strength that matched his as she lifted me from the wagon. "I'll get your valise," she said.

"It's very heavy. Let me help."

"What help would a twig like you be?" Her laughter bellowed as she hefted the valise with one arm.

"Did I steal the horse or does it belong here?" I asked.

"Would we have *this* bone-bag at the Rising? It belongs to Gilles, the monster. Gilles is my own cousin, but that is the crazy branch of the family. *Fou!*" She pointed a thick finger at her temple and rolled her eyes. "He had to be sent for you. There was no one else. The horse will go home by himself when the storm slackens."

Ushering me into a wide hall, she lighted an oil lamp. "Let me see you!" She stared, her look keen and probing. "*Mais oui.* The tiny one has blossomed into a beautiful lady. Those lovely green eyes . . . Why, it is as though Lady Judith had stepped from her frame in the gallery!"

"Lady Judith?"

My question unanswered, she threw her arms around me in a stifling embrace. "Welcome home, *poupée*. I am Tante Emma, as you have guessed."

Aunt Emma? A relative of my father's? The sharp eyes read my confusion. "*Poupée*, surely your mother told you about me. I have been here fifty years as cook, nurse and almost all else. When your mother stole jam as a child, who pretended to spank her? Tante Emma! Who rocked your own cradle?" She stopped abruptly, deeply offended.

"She must have talked about you," I said quickly. "But you know how children are. They pay no attention."

"It is of no importance." The disapproving set of her lips gave a clear opinion of the heedless young. Then her expression changed to surprise. "You spoke to me in French!"

"Yes. Not good French, I'm afraid."

"Splendid! When your mother took you away, I feared my little one would never hear our language again. Australia is so far from here."

Australia again. Gilles, now Tante Emma. Had my mother said we were going to Australia? I remembered Regina's first letter: "I would have written long ago, but I learned your address only this month."

Tante Emma took the lantern in one hand and my valise in the other. "My foolish mouth babbles while poor Rochelle shivers. Come, we will go up to the Captain's Country. I have prepared a fire in the hearth."

She talked on as we mounted the winding stairway. "The Captain's

Country is still as your mother must have described it to you. Her things are there—your things now. Your grandmother's bed, the rocking horse your grandfather rode as a child."

I did not disappoint her by saying I had no idea what the Captain's Country was. Besides, other questions crowded my mind.

"Gilles told me something terrible happened this morning. I think it was"—I used the English word—"a kidnapping."

"Kidnapping? I knew they could not teach you French in Australia. A painting was stolen, the portrait of a child."

"Thank heavens it was only that," I said. "I misunderstood."

We moved upward, the lantern casting a feeble circle of light. We reached a landing, and I felt an icy draft from an open hall to the left.

"The old gallery," said Tante Emma. A floorboard squeaked under her foot, and the lantern flickered. In the wavering light her enormous shadow swayed grotesquely. "Not a kidnapping, but a dreadful thing." She paused, turning to me, and lowered her voice as though someone might be listening. "Your aunt Regina surprised the thief at dawn. He was wearing a mask. No wonder my poor lady fainted and injured herself!"

"Is she seriously hurt?" Was it the eerie darkness that made me feel such concern for a great-aunt I had never met?

"I think not, but her wrist was very painful, and there was a bruise where her head struck the door. Monsieur Morgan insisted on driving her to the hospital. There was a great argument because of your arrival, but at last my lady consented." Tante Emma smiled rather grimly. "An astonishment. One does not win arguments with your aunt Regina."

"Then neither Aunt Regina nor Cousin Morgan is here," I said as we climbed to the second floor.

"No. And Monsieur Morgan's wife also wished to consult her doctor. Because of the shock, she said." A trace of contempt entered her voice. "Madame Dorothy suffers ill health with great *noblesse*."

At the head of the stairway Tante Emma hesitated. "Take the lantern, *poupée*, while I find the key. We will have lights again soon. The electric system is maintained by idiots." She fumbled with her keys, then moved down the hall to an arched doorway. Commanding me to wait, she unlocked the door and disappeared. I heard the scratching of matches, and despite the unnerving blackness of the corridor, I smiled to realize that Tante Emma was creating an entrance effect. The door opened wide. "Welcome to the Captain's Country, *poupée*."

Candles in pewter holders and two violet-shaded oil lamps suffused the large room with their glow, soft light blending with the brightness of flames in the fireplace. The paneling and heavy timbers of the ceiling might have made this room dismal, for the alcove windows seemed made to trap shadows. Yet the whole atmosphere embraced me, with warm friendliness radiating from the hand-hooked rugs and the gay print canopy of the bed. Even the grandfather clock chimed a greeting as I stepped into the room.

"It's like a museum!" I exclaimed.

"Not a museum. Your mother's room. *Your* room."

"I love it. Why is it called the Captain's Country?"

Tante Emma shrugged. "For some ancestor of yours who was a captain." She gestured toward a set of double doors. "There are two rooms. The other is the nursery." She sighed. "You were the last child there."

My mother's room, I thought, letting my gaze wander over the butternut cabinet, the sea chest, the finely stitched quilt on the bed.

"Was this also my father's room?" I asked.

"No." She bustled about, fluffing pillows. "Jean-Paul Dumont never lived at the Rising. When he married our Charlotte, they moved to the village. But she came back for you to be born here. All Armitages are born at River Rising."

"I'm not an Armitage," I said. "I'm Rochelle Dumont."

"*Zut!* You are a child of this house. Tante Emma could weep for joy." Opening the double doors, she gestured toward the dark adjoining room. "That is now your sitting room. Your cradle is still there."

I took a step into the room, then drew back, startled by a human figure in the dimness. Tante Emma chuckled. "A statue. We call her the Duchess of Glenway because she was the figurehead of a ship of that name, a ship lost on the rocks here." Tante Emma's face darkened. "The river claimed every soul but one. An Englishwoman, Lady Judith Crenshaw, reached shore. Her husband and baby were swept away."

"How terrible! Did you know her?"

"Child, this happened two hundred years ago. But many in this house have known her in nightmares. Lady Judith became Malachi Armitage's second wife, poor creature. He was a wicked man. In the village they say that even now his soul has no rest."

I gazed at the statue, feeling it was not the figurehead of the *Duchess of Glenway* but Lady Judith herself who might suddenly glide toward us. When the electric lights flickered, then flooded the Captain's Country with light, I sighed with relief.

"At last!" said Tante Emma. "Now enjoy a hot bath. Dinner in an hour and a half. You will hear the gong." Her glance darted around the room. "*Oui*, all is prepared—" She broke off sharply. I followed her astonished gaze to the bedside table, where a bud vase, filled with pale blossoms, stood beside a delft lamp. "*Sacrebleu!* Who could have done this?" She rounded the bed and seized the vase. "Monkshood. How can it be here?"

"Is it dangerous?" I was baffled. "Like poison oak?"

"Not like poison oak," she said grimly. "In the woods it is harmless. But monkshood in a house means . . . Never mind. I will take it away."

"No, wait. I want to know the meaning."

"Monkshood means that an enemy is near," she said as she started toward the door with the vase. "That strange child must have done this."

"What strange child?"

"Thalia. Monsieur Morgan's stepdaughter. Perhaps she thought to give you a gift. She may not know what monkshood means." She forced a smile. "Forget this, *poupée*. It is a blessing that you are home at last."

Alone, I stood listening to the rain pelting the windows and to the crackling hearth. The Captain's Country! I looked around this room that seemed mellow with the love of generations. How could my mother not have described it to me? I had always felt an emptiness because I knew nothing of my father, and now I realized that my mother had been almost equally a stranger. The causes of her silence were here at River Rising. Soon, I was determined, I would learn to know Charlotte Armitage Dumont.

I sat down, leaning back against the pillows on the bed and enjoying the security of the ancient walls against the storm outside. A line of poetry sang softly in my mind. *"Who loves the rain and loves his home and looks on life with quiet eyes . . ."* That, I knew, was what I longed for. All my life I had drifted. Not as a person who is aimless drifts, but as a fallen branch caught by the current moves without choice. I had to find a home, a life that was my own. Music had helped to fill an emptiness that I felt but could not understand. But always the music ended, and it was not enough.

I prepared for dinner, enjoying a bath in a big porcelain tub with claw feet. I inspected my limited wardrobe and chose the dress I had worn when I played my last recital in college—a deep maroon velveteen, long and flared, with tight bodice and sleeves, and fine lace at the cuffs and neckline. I had been playing Scarlatti and Vivaldi that night, and the gown seemed to go with baroque music. Now it felt right for River Rising.

Just as a gong sounded I heard a tap on my door. "Come in," I called.

I saw her first in the mirror, a pale girl of twelve or thirteen but tall for her age, with long flaxen hair and extraordinary large blue eyes. Turning toward her, I smiled. "You must be Thalia."

She nodded. Tante Emma had called her strange. Strangely beautiful, I would have said, with the translucent fairness of a dryad or sylph.

"Tante Emma thought you might have brought some flowers that were here when I came, Thalia," I said. "Thank you."

"No," she answered, her lips hardly moving. "I did not."

"Have you come to guide me to the dining room?" I asked. She nodded. "That's thoughtful of you. Shall we go?"

The passages and stairwell were faintly illuminated by gas jets adapted for electricity. Thalia paused on the landing between the first and second floors, and the boards creaked as they had when Tante Emma halted there earlier. "That arch leads to the gallery," she said.

"Where your stepfather's paintings are hung?" I asked.

"No. There are pictures, but it is not that kind of gallery. It was for minstrels. The ballroom is below. Would you like to see it?"

"Not just now, thanks."

"Are you afraid?" The question was expressionless.

"Yes," I told her. "I'm very much afraid of missing dinner."

We continued down the stairs, Thalia gliding beside me like a dancer, her forest-green skirt and blouse accenting her height and slenderness.

Crossing the entrance hall, we left the east wing of the house, and I found myself in another world. Ceilings had been lowered, huge rooms divided, so the study and sitting room were cheerful places, comfortable with rustic furniture and gaily patterned draperies. Then as we came into a short hall leading to the dining room I heard voices raised in sharp disagreement.

"Regina will never consent to it. Never!" The woman was angry.

A man replied with equal vehemence, "She'll have to face facts someday. She's not getting any younger. Or any richer!"

The argument was cut off abruptly by our entrance. A man and a woman, seated at opposite sides of a refectory table, turned their heads toward us, startled. Then both rose at once.

"Dear Cousin Rochelle!" The woman hurried to greet me, a plump cloud of rose chiffon. She was elderly, with a beehive of gray curls, yet rouged cheeks and fluttering gestures betrayed a determination to cling to the airs of youth. "Welcome to River Rising."

Cool lips brushed my face and I caught the scent of lavender. Taking both my hands in hers, she inspected me. "I'm Eunice Armitage, your cousin William's widow." Her round face beamed as she introduced me to her companion, who a moment before had been her bitter opponent. "Rochelle, this is our old friend Howard Palmer."

"Good evening, Mr. Palmer." I took his extended hand.

"Call me Howard, as your mother did. We were very dear friends."

"Did you also know my father?" I asked.

He chose his words carefully. "We were acquaintances. I had no opportunity to know him well. But Charlotte was like a sister."

I had no reason to doubt this, but I did. Howard Palmer, with his correct tweeds and military mustache, appeared the essence of respectability. Although the sandy hair was beginning to thin, he looked solid, even athletic. Yet there were cracks in the façade—a trace of cockney speech, untended fingernails, and a puffiness around his eyes that suggested too much whiskey. Still, he proved to be a good storyteller, a man whose wanderlust had led him to every corner of the world. During dinner he monopolized the conversation. Talk never turned to River Rising, the Armitage family or even this morning's burglary.

The meal was served by Angélique, an awkward girl who seemed freshly arrived from some remote farm. Eunice corrected her in an undertone. "*Non*, serve from the left. . . . *Non*, leave the service plate." Thalia sat removed, lost in her own world.

As we were finishing a dessert soufflé that Tante Emma had made light as foam, the note of a bell stroke penetrated the walls. Palmer ceased speaking in midsentence and Eunice looked up suddenly, as though prompted. "I forgot a message, Rochelle. From your Aunt Theresa. She hopes you'll call on her. She'll send you a note."

"Aunt Theresa?" I asked.

"Well, she's actually your mother's cousin, but Charlotte called her Auntie. Surely she spoke of Dame Theresa Armitage."

"I never heard of her. My mother never spoke of the family."

Palmer ran a thoughtful finger over his mustache, then said, "Charlotte certainly made a clean break."

"Perhaps she had good reason," I remarked, and turned to Eunice. "If you'd give me a list of relatives, I'd appear less rude when I meet them."

"A short list. The family has dwindled. There's Aunt Regina, of course, and I'm your cousin by marriage. Morgan is really a distant cousin, but Regina's brother Andrew adopted him as a small boy. That's all of us." She added an afterthought. "And Theresa."

"Tell me about her," I said. "Is 'Dame' a British title?"

Howard Palmer answered. "No. Theresa is a Benedictine nun, and they use the title 'Dame.' She went into the cloister at Clarendon Abbey more than twenty years ago."

"Is that the huge building I saw from the village?"

"Yes," said Eunice. "The nuns' property adjoins ours. The Lady Abbess is dying. The nuns are keeping vigils or whatever they do, so Theresa can't see you just now." She raised an eyebrow. "Theresa is the only Roman Catholic Armitage. Her entering the abbey was a dreadful shock to us."

"I'm glad she followed her convictions," I said, realizing that Dame Theresa and my mother must have had much in common.

"Well, Eunice, isn't it time for coffee and brandy in the living room?" Howard Palmer said, rising from the table.

THE LIVING ROOM was so skillfully furnished that I was hardly conscious of its baronial size. I admired the lovely japanned cabinet, the two teardrop chandeliers. Then I saw the harpsichord. It stood a little apart at the far end of the room, an ancient instrument so beautiful that I moved toward it with reverence and rested my fingers lightly on the mellow ivory keys.

"Do you play, Rochelle?" Eunice asked.

"Yes. May I?" Perhaps it was too fragile to be used.

"Please do, my dear." Eunice smiled benignly.

I sat at the stool, hesitated, then my fingers themselves made the selection. The living room rang with Mozart's "Turkish March"—not loudly, for the harpsichord's power lies not in volume but in brilliance and clarity. I played for myself and the instrument, hardly aware of listeners.

After the last chord ended, there was a long silence, broken at last by Thalia. "Lady Judith Crenshaw," she said.

Rising, I turned to the others. Eunice sat stiffly, her face blanched. Howard Palmer stared at me. "It's uncanny," he murmured. "Why didn't I see it before? Of course, it's the pose with the harpsichord."

"Not a pose," said Thalia. "Lady Judith. I knew when I first saw her."

Eunice suddenly applauded. "You play superbly, Rochelle! I had no idea you were a professional musician."

"Thank you, but I'm not. Thalia, what about Lady Judith?"

Howard Palmer answered for her. "Forgive this, my dear, but you're a throwback to one of your ancestors. Let me assure you, however, that Lady Judith was a remarkably beautiful woman."

"She was also a murderess." There was no condemnation in Thalia's remark; she was merely giving information.

Color rushed to Eunice's cheeks. "Really! Pay no attention, Rochelle. Thalia is trying to shock you."

"No, I'm fascinated. Tell me about Lady Judith."

Palmer was happy to oblige with yet another story. "It's just a legend, but part of it may be true. Captain Malachi Armitage founded the family fortune. As a fur trader he earned enough to buy the Rising from the Sulpician priests who built the first walls here. Soon his fortune multiplied because of some—well, lucky accidents."

"Shipwrecks," murmured Thalia. "He moved warning lights inland and lured ships to the rocks."

"He was in the salvage business," said Howard Palmer.

"Absolutely untrue," Eunice said angrily.

"True or not," Palmer continued, "one ship that foundered in Wind-Whistle Cove was the *Duchess of Glenway*. She'd sailed from Boston for western Quebec with a hundred souls aboard, most of them Tories fleeing the American Revolution. Fleeing with a great deal of money and jewels—"

Thalia interrupted. "Lord and Lady Crenshaw were aboard with their little son. Lady Judith was the only survivor."

"You might add that Captain Malachi rescued her," Eunice said. "At great cost to himself. He lost his right leg and lived out his life a cripple, as you can see in his portrait in the gallery here."

Palmer nodded. "Yes, and they were married a year later. Captain Malachi ordered that harpsichord from London for his bride."

The fire on the grate sputtered, and the wind whispered in the chimney, but otherwise the room was still. Howard Palmer seemed unwilling to go on. "Surely that's not all," I said. "The legend can't end there."

"It's said that eventually she learned about his murderous business, his part in causing the wreck. Then she took revenge."

"Nonsense," Eunice exclaimed. "He fell from the north cliff by accident. Why not? He was crippled, wasn't he?"

"It might have been an accident." Palmer spoke quietly.

Thalia leaned forward. "Then why does Captain Malachi walk at night and Lady Judith weep for her lost child? I've heard them. We all have."

"You mean River Rising is haunted?" I tried to smile.

"Idiocy!" Eunice said sharply. "A servant hears a shutter bang and the château is full of ghosts. I, for one, haven't heard anything."

"I think you will," Thalia replied with such calm certainty that I almost gasped. Thalia, the strange child, had suddenly changed a legend into present reality. I believed she sensed something unfathomable and menacing.

Howard Palmer suddenly checked his watch. "It's late and the rain's stopped. Bedtime for me."

Despite my curiosity I was relieved that this conversation was ending.

As we moved together toward the entrance hall Palmer linked his arm in mine in a gesture I did not appreciate. "I'm living at the guest cottage," he said. "You must drop in. The beautiful daughter of a dear friend is always welcome."

I withdrew my arm on the excuse of offering a handshake. "Thank you, Mr. Palmer. Good night."

Glancing back to the living room, he said in a rapid whisper, "My dear, this can be an unpleasant place. If you ever want to leave suddenly, I have a car at your disposal, no matter what the hour."

Before I could reply, Eunice joined us to say good night. "Don't worry about the corridor lights," she told me. "Madame Sud, the housekeeper, will turn them off." Then she assured me of Regina's early return in the morning.

I started up the stairway. It had been a peculiar evening, the conversation skillfully steered away from such subjects as my father and mother or even my own life. The only honest emotion had been Thalia's. She fully believed that the souls of the murderous captain and his vengeful wife prowled the passageways, believed it so strongly that I had been momentarily convinced.

Nonsense, I told myself. But as I reached the shadowy landing the floorboards creaked beneath my step and an icy draft from the gallery made me shiver. I could see nothing beyond the entrance, but I knew the portrait of Lady Judith hung there, as did that of Malachi Armitage. Were they side by side, the murderer and murderess unseparated even in death?

Then, from the gallery's depths, I heard a prolonged sigh that seemed neither human nor natural. "The wind," I whispered, not believing it. Reaching the upper corridor, my heart pounding, I paused to listen. The château lay shrouded in silence now. I stood chiding myself for letting my

fancy run wild, when I heard another sound. Hardly audible, the tones of a harpsichord rose from the stairwell.

I again blamed my imagination, the notes were so faint. But listening intently I discerned a melody, a minuet. Did it emanate from the harpsichord in the living room? Or did the hollow tones echo from the gallery? An eerie picture flashed through my mind, the portrait of Lady Judith coming alive, painted fingers touching painted keys, sending forth music from a phantom instrument. Now the notes seemed to resemble the tinkle of Deirdre's music box. The unknown musician broke off without finishing, and once again River Rising lapsed into the stillness of a tomb.

I made my way quickly to the Captain's Country and, safely inside, recovered my good sense. The sigh had been the wind, the music had been played by someone in the living room. "No more foolishness, Rochelle," I said aloud, using my mother's familiar command.

I prepared for the night, keeping my imagination in tight rein. I switched off all the lamps except the one on the nightstand, smiling to notice that Tante Emma had turned back the bed to welcome me after a long day.

Then my smile faded as I saw something else. Standing in its original place, as though never removed, was a vase of monkshood, the pale flowers silently repeating Tante Emma's words: "An enemy is near."

CHAPTER FOUR

I SLEPT BADLY THAT night, but did not wake until well after nine, when Angélique, the maid, delivered a huge Quebecois breakfast.

"Tante Emma said you are to be served in bed this morning, mademoiselle." She smiled shyly, but with a trace of mischief. "She also said you can fend for yourself in the dining room after today."

"*Merci*, Angélique. Has the family returned from the hospital yet?"

"More than an hour ago. Your aunt would like to meet you in her rooms when you are ready. She asked me to give you her most special greeting."

"Have you worked here long, Angélique?" I asked.

"*Non, mademoiselle.* No one stays long at the château. Will that be all?"

"Yes, thank you," I said.

Despite the restless night, I felt strong this morning and did full justice to Tante Emma's delicious cooking. Bathed and dressed, I opened the drapes.

The great river was agleam with sunlight, and I exclaimed at the sheer magnificence of it. A sleek liner moved majestically a mile or two offshore, dwarfing the fishing skiffs. Looking down, I felt a slight giddiness, for this wing of the house stood not far from the cliffs. But when I opened the window, the freshness of river air banished all imaginary specters so completely that I descended the stairs hardly glancing at the gallery entrance. Later I would explore it and lay to rest any fears of its darkness.

My aunt's rooms were flooded with morning light, dazzling as it reflected from walls and carpets of white and gold. Regina Armitage sat erect in a Sheraton chair, her right hand resting on a malacca cane. She rose slowly to greet me, the pain of moving almost concealed by a taut control that reminded me of my mother. "Rochelle," she said quietly.

For a moment we silently examined each other. She wore a long gown, Grecian in simplicity. Her left arm was supported by a sling made from a silk scarf as white as her curled hair. She was much smaller than I had supposed, but one felt her regal air, saw the elegance of fine bones and arched eyebrows. When she smiled, her face had a startling brilliance.

Moving toward me, she appeared taller and younger. Although over seventy, she had the carriage of a woman half her age. "Rochelle," she repeated. "I must kiss you because you are Charlotte's daughter." The touch of her lips on my cheek was warm and dry.

"Come, we'll sit near the window. It's too early for lilacs, but I thought I caught their perfume a minute ago. It is your being here. I have an illusion of summer." Again the captivating smile.

"On the contrary, I seem to have brought bad luck," I said. "A burglary and injury. I hope you're feeling better."

"The hospital visit was needless, but Morgan chose to smarm over me. However, Dorothy, his wife, did need medical attention. Her condition is always uncertain, and this stupid affair upset her. For me, the only serious consequence was that I could not be here to greet you." Her eyes radiated warmth and welcome. "Charlotte was a beautiful girl, but you surpass her, my dear." She spoke so simply that her remarks gave no impression of flattery. Everything about her confused and overwhelmed me. I was determined not to be taken in by her almost magical charm.

"I suppose the stolen painting was very valuable," I said to shift the conversation onto a less personal level.

"People seem to think that all Morgan's works are valuable. I am not a fan, but this one has great sentimental worth. It is a portrait of your mother as a child, done from memory, of course, and Morgan's memory is not very accurate. Still, it represented Charlotte, so I loved it. Most of his work is too abstract for my taste. This one was not."

We sat facing each other on matching settees, gilt with white upholstery.

"I am lost," she said lightly. "I have waited long for this moment, and now I can think of nothing to say. Tell me about your life, about Charlotte's."

I gave a brief, impersonal account, touching only on facts, but her changes of expression showed that she inferred much from the little I told.

"Not an easy life," she remarked. "Yet no real hardship. I suppose the most difficult part for you was that you didn't much like Charlotte."

I bridled at this. "I was devoted to my mother!"

Her pale eyes regarded me gravely. "No doubt. Still, there is a difference between liking and loving. You are Charlotte's daughter, so it will be natural for me to love you. But I may find I don't like you at all."

"This paradox is beyond me."

Her laughter tinkled like crystal. "Loving and liking need not be connected. I loved your mother with all my heart, yet she often exasperated me. Doubtless she felt the same toward me."

"I wouldn't know. She never mentioned you," I replied. "I told you that when I answered your first letter."

Against my will I regretted her wince of pain.

"Yes, you said you didn't know me. I took that to mean I was a shadowy character. Now I learn that Charlotte banished me utterly. That was cruel, cruel and undeserved."

"She must have had reasons for banishing all her family."

"You know only her side of the story."

"I've heard no side at all. Nothing! It's time I did."

The keen gaze studied me closely. "You mean you know nothing of your father and the . . . tragedy?" I shook my head. "My dear, I did not expect this." Her poise momentarily deserted her. Then she steeled herself. "Very well. I do not wish to upset you, but it is better that I tell the truth."

"The truth is what I want."

She regarded me doubtfully. "No, my dear. It is the last thing you want, but you must know it."

She rose, moving to the fireplace, then back to her chair. "Your mother's parents and Theresa Armitage's parents died when Charlotte was a baby and Theresa very young. The two couples were traveling together and were lost in a plane crash. The task of rearing the girls fell upon me, and I did not welcome it. I was occupied with my own career."

"Your career?"

"I was a gambler," she said with a glint. "Not at cards but with money. River Rising was heavily mortgaged, and I shared the estate with four brothers. Not one had a sense of business. Three of them died young, which is why I have the Rising today. I gambled first in small things, like marketing village crafts, handmade clothing and folk art. Then I moved on to cargoes and wheat futures. But that is another story.

"At any rate, I had the care of your mother and Theresa. My one surviving brother, Andrew, was a widower. He had to manage his difficult son, Philip François, and later Morgan. Morgan is not my nephew by blood, but I think of him as such."

"Eunice said he's another cousin," I told her.

"A distant one. He was born to relatives of ours who died in the bombing of London. As a child he was sent to Canada for safety, and

Andrew adopted him. We looked on him as Philip François' younger brother. Morgan has brought great fame to the family."

I caught a note of reserve. Was this, too, loving without liking?

"I was occupied with business, yet I considered myself a good foster mother to Theresa and Charlotte. I do not know how I failed!" The white cheeks became tinged with crimson. "First, I lost Theresa to the Benedictines, but I believe she is happy. It was losing Charlotte to Jean-Paul Dumont that was really too much to bear."

She uttered my father's name with a bitterness that shocked me.

"Do I surprise you? I will not disguise my opinion of Jean-Paul."

"Your hostility is too obvious to disguise," I retorted.

She glanced at me sharply. "Spoken like your mother's daughter. Jean-Paul was an architect, but his ambition was to be an artist. One summer he came to Ste. Marie du Lac with several students who worked with Henri Berthelot, a well-known painter who still lives here. Also, he came because he had met Charlotte at the university. The first time she brought him to dinner I saw that he was a dangerous, objectionable young man."

"You are speaking to that man's daughter," I said, hardly keeping my anger in check. "Do you think I'll listen to this?"

"You'll listen." Now her smile was not brilliant, but cynical. "You'll hear me out because it concerns you."

She moved about the room, seeming unable to stand still, her gestures giving emphasis to the words. "Jean-Paul had animal attractiveness—nothing wrong with that. I understood why Charlotte was fascinated. Still, a brief affair should have ended it. She knew he drank, knew he was violent. Three times he was locked in jail as a tavern brawler." Regina's small jeweled hand, protruding from the sling, clenched. "Of course I warned her. But she loved him beyond wisdom and, worse, beyond insight.

"Suspecting he was a fortune hunter, I disabused him of any illusions about Charlotte's money. But there I misjudged him. He answered with the rudeness I deserved, and at that moment I almost admired him."

"Bravo for my father!" I exclaimed. "At least one good quality. Or perhaps merely the absence of another bad one."

She turned to me, eyes flashing. "You think I was possessive and jealous of Charlotte's love? Quite right! I berated her, I pleaded, but she married Jean-Paul that summer. My young, lovely, impulsive niece! They lived awhile in Montreal, then returned to this village, renting a house that was little more than a shanty. They went hungry at times."

"You permitted this? And you claim you loved my mother!"

"Rochelle, now *you* are guilty of misjudgment." Her voice lost its anger. "Jean-Paul would accept nothing from me. I had insulted him, and he repaid me in full. Several times I gave friends money to buy his worthless paintings. When he discovered this, he came shouting drunken threats to me. Physical threats! Well, he chose the wrong woman. I had a pistol, and he knew I could use it."

"And I was born into this atmosphere of hate," I said. "How much better not to have known."

"No, Rochelle, no." She moved quickly to my side. "Never think that. Your birth changed things. I learned to respect what was good in Jean-Paul and to ignore the rest. I held my terrible tongue, and he held his terrible temper. You were a blessing to us."

She sat beside me, taking my hand. "My brother Andrew died, and his son, Philip François, turned idealistic. I detest idealists, they justify anything in the name of righteousness. It was a difficult time. Morgan had just reached manhood and became rebellious. Philip François dropped the Philip and demanded we call him François because he wished to be French—he announced his engagement to a penniless village girl and took on the task of educating a wild ragamuffin boy. It was you and Charlotte who held us together."

"And my father?"

"Your birth steadied him for a time," she said carefully. "He worked with an architectural firm in Quebec City and came here on weekends." She sighed. "And then one Saturday night in August we were destroyed. Several of the art students and their friends were drinking in the local tavern, and an idiotic political quarrel erupted between your father and François. Jean-Paul tried to attack François, he shouted threats against his life. The tavern owner ordered them out. Four of them, including your father, came to the Rising. They continued drinking on the porch of the studio built for Morgan, and the argument broke out again." She closed her eyes. "The night ended in murder."

"Murder?" My blood pounded. "My father was murdered? I thought—"

"No, Rochelle." She slipped an arm around me. "Jean-Paul killed François Armitage, my nephew, in a drunken rage."

"I don't believe it!" Madame Jeannette's words screamed in my brain: "The murderer's daughter has returned."

"Where is my father now?" I asked numbly. "In prison? Or . . . ?"

"By accident, or by his own intention, Jean-Paul plunged from the porch of the studio that same night. He was not the first those cliffs and the river have claimed."

"Was there proof of all this?" I asked desperately.

"There was proof. The weapon was an artist's framing hammer, with Jean-Paul's fingerprints. Two witnesses were almost close enough to prevent the tragedy. A third witness—Pierre Lachance—saw Jean-Paul fall."

"Were these other witnesses also from the village?"

"No. You have met one of them, Howard Palmer. The other was Morgan." Regina read my reaction instantly. "You are telling yourself that

Howard and Morgan might be guilty. Believe me, the police entertained this suspicion too, but it came to nothing. You are free to arouse dead suspicions—I hope you will not."

Regina seemed drained as she continued. "Charlotte blamed us all. She accused me of causing Jean-Paul to drink because we had exchanged angry words that day. She blamed Morgan for allowing the party to continue, although Morgan could hardly have controlled a man as violent as Jean-Paul. She left River Rising with you a week later, telling us she was going to Australia and we would not hear from her again."

"Did you ever try to find her?" I asked, my voice trembling.

"Not at first, because I believed she would return. Then I hired detectives, and wherever I traveled, I searched telephone directories. At last a friend vacationing in the West Indies sent me a newspaper clipping. A death notice." She looked away. "The first news and the final irony."

Her story left me dazed. "Why did you ask me to come here? Better to have left me in ignorance. This house can mean only unhappiness for me."

"That is what Morgan advised, what everyone advised." She squared her shoulders, lifted her chin. "Quite wrong! True, I did not know you were utterly ignorant of the past. But what's done is done. Why shouldn't Charlotte's daughter come home? Once Charlotte was happy at River Rising, why not Rochelle?"

"The villagers, for one thing. They—"

"No! If there was one quality both your parents had, it was pride. You are their daughter, you will hold up your head anywhere." Her fierceness vanished as she touched my hand. "You are my flesh and blood. I need you."

I hesitated, moved by the unexpected appeal. "I will stay awhile," I said. "I don't know how long. I am making no promises."

"I am asking none," she said. "One last thing. I meant my harsh words about your father. Yet I admit he and Charlotte were completely devoted. I cannot deny their love. It was total."

"Thank you. I needed to know that."

"And, Rochelle, my name is Aunt Regina."

I managed to smile. "Yes, Aunt Regina."

IF I HAD character, as Regina believed, the next hour was its heaviest test. Alone in my room I paced the floor, avoiding the window with its view of river and cliffs. "Don't trust them! Don't believe them." My mother's warning seemed futile. Against all my instincts, I was forced to accept Aunt Regina's story. Murder was a matter of fact, not opinion. Now I understood my mother's lifelong silence.

I could also understand Charlotte's choice of a lover in later years. Jean-Paul Dumont and Paul LaFarge had both been artists, but there all resemblance ceased. In Paul my mother had found gentleness, kindliness and peace. The two were also opposites in their work. My father had apparently been a dabbler. To Paul LaFarge, painting had been life itself. Tragic as my mother's life had been, I took comfort that two very different men had loved her deeply and she had returned their love.

I heard a light tap at the door and Angélique entered. "Monsieur Morgan asks if you will lunch with him on the sun porch, mademoiselle."

"I'll be happy to," I said falsely. I wanted only to be alone. Regina's story had altered all my perspectives.

On my way downstairs I felt the chill draft from the gallery and decided to look at Lady Judith's portrait. I walked calmly through the archway with no worries about spectral sighs or music. Yet I could not help admitting that this dark corridor was eerie. I passed family portraits of various eras, their gilt frames gathering dust. Then I saw Lady Judith, the portrait hanging in a section of the wall where a single ray of sunshine gave it dramatic emphasis. The painting, almost life-size, was executed with skill. Posed at the harpsichord, Judith Crenshaw appeared to have just looked up to smile at a welcome visitor. Now I understood the surprise I had caused last night, for this might indeed have been mistaken for a portrait of myself. The eyes, like mine, were green; the hair was similar but a deeper chestnut; and we had the same high cheekbones. I hoped my smile did not resemble Lady Judith's, for the upturned lips had a cruel tinge of mockery. Legend said she was a murderess. Had the painter predicted this?

Murderess. For an instant I felt she smiled for me, to taunt me. In a moment the full red lips would speak: "The murderer's daughter . . ."

Turning quickly, I hurried from the gallery. And I wondered if in time I would forget what my father had done, or if I would live with this terrible knowledge forever.

THE SUN PORCH, where I was to lunch with Morgan Armitage, lay at the rear of the house, a long veranda with French windows. Scattered the length of it were tables surrounded by cane chairs, giving the impression of a resort hotel. At the farthest table a tall, powerfully built man rose to greet me. He had to be over forty yet looked ten years younger. The light brown hair was close-cropped, and the sunlight gave it flecks of gold that seemed to reflect in his eyes. I could appreciate Deirdre Cameron's schoolgirl crush.

"Welcome to the Rising," Morgan said, and for a second the intensity of those eyes held me, a look too probing for comfort.

The table was laid for two, and he drew back a chair for me. "We'll sit in the sunshine. In Quebec every hour of sun is too precious to waste."

"You don't appear to have wasted any," I said. "Your suntan reminds me of Antigua. How do you manage it?"

"Hardy outdoor living." He chuckled. "Plus six weeks in Acapulco."

"You travel a great deal?"

"Dorothy, my wife, hasn't been well for three years. That and my stepdaughter's troubles have limited my wanderlust. You met Thalia last night. I hope she didn't annoy you."

"Annoy me? I only thought she was shy and much too silent."

"Silent, yes. But until yesterday never sinister."

"I don't understand."

"Tante Emma told me about the monkshood."

"That's hardly sinister. Just a superstition. Thalia probably didn't know the meaning. And she denies doing it."

"She knew," he said grimly. "Besides, monkshood is poisonous. I don't find the episode amusing. I'll speak to Thalia this afternoon." There was no mistaking Morgan's anger.

"Please be gentle with her," I said. "She meant no harm."

He said nothing, but he gave me a cool, hard stare. It vanished as quickly as it had come, yet it had given me a disconcerting glimpse of an implacable character. Morgan would not be an easy stepfather.

Looking past me, he smiled. "Madame Sud is here with our lunch. *Bonjour, madame.*"

A short, stout woman had entered carrying a tray. *"Bonjour, m'sieur. Bienvenue, ma'm'selle."* The housekeeper's swarthy face was expressionless, and thick-lidded eyes regarded me incuriously. After silently serving us, she glided from the sun porch, her thick-soled shoes soundless.

"Formidable, isn't she?" Morgan said. "But we're lucky to have Madame Sud and Tante Emma. Almost no one from the village will work here."

"Why not?"

"They believe the Rising is haunted. I can't deny we've had more than our share of trouble."

For a moment neither of us spoke; there was no need to discuss what "trouble" meant. Then he asked about my mother.

I told about our lives in Antigua, but despite his many questions I said less than I had to Regina. Pride and a sense of privacy made me describe Charlotte as happier than she had been, and I did not mention her lover. That would remain my secret.

He studied me doubtfully. "Strange that Charlotte never remarried."

"She never ceased to love the memory of my father. That's hard to believe, I suppose, if you agree with Aunt Regina that he was worthless and violent."

"Violent he certainly was. I never met a man as wild as Jean-Paul. The devil was in him."

"You're brutally blunt." I did not permit my voice to tremble. "Aunt Regina at least tempered her honesty with a little tact."

"I'm sorry to offend you with the truth. Remember, I *saw* what happened that night. And other nights."

Regina's words came back to me: "Two witnesses were almost close enough to prevent the tragedy." Morgan was one, Howard Palmer the other. Why should I believe the story they had told the police? Regina had warned me against arousing what she called dead suspicions, but I could not help it. What if my father had not been a murderer, but another victim? Victim of the man who now spoke with such compelling sincerity.

"I want your friendship and confidence," he was saying. "I loved your mother deeply. For her sake, I want to help you."

"Help me?" I asked. "How?"

"I've just talked with Regina. Her idea of keeping you here is madness. She hasn't considered the dangers to you."

"Dangers?" I was taken aback. "You exaggerate."

"I'm not given to exaggeration. I only returned a few hours ago, and already I know about your meeting with Madame Jeannette."

"A madwoman," I protested.

"Half the village will feel the same way. Regina doesn't realize that Charlotte left because she had to go. Did Regina want her to stay and be stoned in the streets?"

"You can't mean that!"

He leaned forward impatiently. "Jean-Paul did not commit an ordinary crime. François was a man many loved. The villagers wouldn't forgive Jean-Paul's wife, and they won't forgive his daughter."

"Monkshood. 'An enemy is near.' An appropriate greeting, wasn't it?"

"Leave, Rochelle. Quickly." It was almost a command. "Go to Quebec City or Montreal. It's senseless to suffer for what isn't your fault."

Morgan Armitage appeared honestly concerned about my welfare.

"Thank you," I said. "I need time to think. So much has happened—"

"Yes, and I'm afraid much more will." He rested his hand gently on mine. "You must not let Regina cloud your good sense."

His closeness confused me. A retreat into practicality seemed the best course. "I don't know how I'd make a living."

"From what I've heard about your talent for music, that's no problem. Also, you have plenty of money when you want to claim it."

"Manna from heaven?" I asked.

"No, the furnishings of the Captain's Country. Two rooms crammed with antique pieces. It's not a fortune, but it's yours."

With some surprise I considered all he had said. Yet I had made a promise to Regina and no quick departure seemed possible. I was about to explain this when I realized that Madame Sud, silent as a cat, stood at my side. I looked up quickly. Caught off guard, the inscrutable face could be read, and I saw a glare of malevolence. Her features composed themselves immediately. "Coffee, *ma'm'selle?*" she inquired stiffly.

"Yes, *merci.*"

As she began pouring my coffee she seemed to stumble. I jerked back so quickly that the scalding liquid only grazed my fingers.

"*Zut!* I am clumsy," she said. "Fortunately, you were not burned."

"Most fortunately!" I snapped, imagining the pain if the steaming coffee had struck my whole hand, as I was sure she had intended.

"What happened, madame?" Morgan asked, suspicion in his voice.

"An accident, m'sieur. I must remove the cloth before the stain sets and bring more coffee." If there was a trace of regret in her expression, I felt certain it came from her failure to scald me thoroughly enough.

"No coffee." I rose abruptly. "I find the service too dangerous."

Morgan also rose. Madame Sud's small act of malice had shown that all he warned about was true. No happiness would be permitted me at River Rising or in Ste. Marie du Lac. Looking at him I said, "Thank you for your advice. I will stay here only two or three days. I want to call on Dame Theresa at the abbey. Once I've done that, I'll be happily on my way."

Morgan hesitated, then nodded in agreement. "I'll try to make arrangements for you to see Theresa soon."

THAT AFTERNOON I strolled the broad grounds of the Rising, content with my decision. If there had been anything to keep me here, pride would have made me battle to stay. I hoped I had too much character to yield an easy victory to Madame Sud and the others who hated me because I was my father's daughter. But why struggle when I had nothing to win? I would go to Ste. Marie du Lac and walk the length of its main street with my head held high. In my few days remaining here I would show that the murderer's daughter was in no way ashamed of her parentage. If Madame Jeannette chose a second encounter, she would meet a prepared opponent!

Only once did my feelings waver. Lingering near the cliffside, gazing at the great river, I sensed that I belonged to these rocks and the white-churned cove. Had my father held me in his arms at this spot, and could that be indelibly imprinted on my memory?

I wandered beyond the west wing of the Rising, following a flagstone walk, and discovered a building at the brink of the precipice. A huge window on the north slope of the roof showed this was a painter's studio. I mounted three steps to a wooden porch that jutted out over the cliff, and there I saw a chain link fence almost shoulder height to guard against a fall to the rocks and eddies below. Certainly one would expect a guardrail, but hardly this tall, ugly barrier. Then Regina's words about my father's death came back with terrible clarity: "Jean-Paul plunged from the porch of the studio." The fence had been erected too late.

I knew I should turn away, should leave the porch and banish it from my mind, but I felt compelled to lean against the chain links and look down. Far below, the crosscurrents waged perpetual war against each other and against the jagged stones that confined them. Their turmoil was plainly audible even at the cliff top—a whirlpool to crush the timbers of a ship, to sweep away a man's body. Giddy and light-headed, I felt a terror that the fence would give way, that I would plunge downward.

I hardly heard the soft footfall behind me, and just as I realized someone was approaching, a heavy hand gripped my shoulder. Whirling in alarm, I found myself facing Tante Emma.

She spoke softly. "This is not a place for you, *poupée*."

What was she doing here? After all Morgan had said, I trusted no one.

But when she took my arm, her touch was gentle. "Come back to the house. Being here can only make you sad, and Monsieur Morgan angry."

"Angry? Why should he be?"

"This is his studio. He allows no one in. You must not come here again."

"I don't want to. Tante Emma, this is the place where . . ."

She nodded. "Where Jean-Paul killed François Armitage."

Late that afternoon there came a tap at the door of the Captain's Country. Before I could answer, Madame Sud slipped in carrying a large paper bag. "A message, ma'm'selle," she said tonelessly. "The Lady Abbess seems to be enjoying a miraculous recovery. You may visit Dame Theresa day after tomorrow. Also, this came for you." Madame Sud handed me the paper bag. No doubt she had already inspected the contents.

One glance inside revealed Aunt Regina's yellow shawl. I touched it and felt dampness, drew it from the bag and gasped. The beautiful shawl was ripped to tatters, spotted with black grease marks. How dared Deirdre send it back in such condition? I searched for a note, but the bag was empty. "Did Miss Cameron send no message with this?" I asked, furious.

"Miss Cameron?" Madame Sud conveyed an impression of total indifference. "I do not know of such a person. A village boy brought it."

"Surely there was some message!"

"It was delivered with the compliments of Captain Pierre Lachance."

She left me then. I stood looking at the remains of the shawl, slowly realizing that these were no ordinary rips. The cloth had been hacked, slashed, shredded with brutal force. Attacked, I thought. Attacked.

CHAPTER FIVE

I DELAYED SPEAKING TO Aunt Regina about the shawl and about my decision to leave. This was not hard, as I did not see her alone until the morning of my visit to Clarendon Abbey. Then practical matters had her full attention. I found her in the entrance hall, angrily shaking the telephone.

"Useless! The service is off again. I've tried for twenty minutes to reach either Louis Gagnon's garage or the one living taxi driver in Ste. Marie du Lac."

"Is it an emergency?"

"You want to get to the abbey. Of course, Morgan could drive you, but he's in his studio and it's worth our lives to disturb him."

"Why don't I drive myself? I'm sure I can find the way."

She shook her head. "My car is at the village garage, and Morgan's priceless automobile may be touched by no hand but Morgan's."

"Can't I walk?" I asked. "I'd enjoy it."

"It's easy enough to get there, downhill most of the way. But the climb back . . . I've solved it. Walk to the abbey, then go to the village and retrieve my car from Gagnon's garage. Just tell Louis I sent you."

She did not see me flinch. For all my planned defiance, I was not quite prepared to enter Ste. Marie du Lac and announce my name. Yet now was as good a time as any. "Louis Gagnon's garage?"

"Yes, a little repair shop with a gasoline pump in front." She was oblivious to any qualms I might have about the village. "Take the path through the garden, then follow the firebreak. But don't wander onto any of the side trails."

"Where do they lead?"

"Nowhere. Into wilderness." Moving forward impulsively, she took my hands in hers. "You'll like Theresa. Please tell her I love her deeply and she is often in my thoughts." The message, I felt, contained more than love; it was somehow a plea, an apology.

I crossed the garden separating River Rising from the forest and soon found the firebreak, a swath of cleared land running down the hillside. It was a long walk and there were indeed many side trails, yet I seldom lost sight of the abbey's forbidding stone turrets. I wondered how any young woman could bear to go behind those walls for life. Yet that was what Theresa Armitage had done—a quarter of a century ago, Regina said. As I approached the doors, nail-studded and set in a Gothic arch, I felt reluctant to pull the bell chain, unwilling to leave the sunlight even for an hour.

Unexpectedly, the bell had a merry peal, and when a small door cut into the great one opened, a beaming woman wished me good day. She wore a simple black habit almost concealed by a voluminous apron, faded blue. "You must be Rochelle Dumont. Dame Theresa is expecting you. Do come in!" Honest eyes studied me with friendly curiosity. "Follow me."

Inside I discovered that the somber walls were a mask. Clarendon Abbey was set in several acres of parks and gardens, where daffodils and tulips in full bloom lined the flagstone paths. Two young novices were playing a strenuous game of tennis on a clay court while a third girl applauded loudly. The corridor we entered had a vaulted stone ceiling, but the tinted windows warmed the walls with pale pink light.

I was ushered into a parlor, sparsely furnished with pleasant Victorian chairs, a plain room made extraordinary by the iron grille dividing it in half. This was the barrier beyond which I, an outsider, might not pass.

"Dame Theresa has been attending the Lady Abbess. She will be with you soon," said my guide, who then departed quietly.

I had the illusion briefly of being Alice in *Through the Looking Glass*, for the half of the room beyond the grille was almost the mirror image of the part I occupied. Then, when a door opened and Dame Theresa entered, the mirror illusion was irrevocably shattered. She moved in a rustle of sleeves and scapular. "Good morning, dear Rochelle. God bless you."

Dame Theresa was tall and slender, the flowing lines of the black habit emphasizing an imperial quality that reminded me of Regina. Our first few minutes were awkward as we spoke of the weather and my impressions of Quebec. Then she smiled. "You aren't sure how to address me, are you? Let's forget the title and I'll be Aunt Theresa. I was eleven years older than your mother, and I thought of her as my niece. Will that be all right?"

"Yes, Aunt Theresa."

"Also, you're bothered by the grille, aren't you?"

Reddening, I admitted this was true.

"Its bars are a reminder. In the world, Rochelle, each person has a private grille keeping him apart from all others. Here the bars are visible, but not so different from the invisible ones you've spoken through all your life." She spoke lightly, but the point had been made and the bars became less forbidding.

"Aunt Regina sends you her love," I said. "She thinks of you often."

"Oh? Charitable thoughts, I hope. I have always been certain of her love, less sure of the charity." I suspected Dame Theresa could be as tart as Regina and not a whit less frank.

When I talked of my mother's life and my own, she glanced at me several times with skepticism. "I'm thankful Charlotte had a happy life," she commented dryly. "I would not have expected it." She paused. "Rochelle, something is troubling you. Would it help to talk to me?"

"I'm not sure," I answered, yet I sensed I had found a woman wise and compassionate. "I've promised Aunt Regina that I would stay at River Rising. Now I intend to break my promise. I have to leave, but I feel incomplete. As though I had failed."

"Failed at what?"

"At finding my father, a man I can't remember. I ask questions, and all the answers seem wrong. Maybe I just can't face the truth. Did you know him, Aunt Theresa?"

"Not well. I came here a year before Charlotte married him."

"What did you think of him?"

"I knew him so slightly I had no opinion. Your parents brought you here

once as a baby. Jean-Paul seemed pleasant." She hesitated, then added, "I saw him a second time—only for a moment, and we did not speak."

She seemed to have nothing more to tell me on that subject. Our conversation turned to her life as a nun, but her manner had changed. I sensed she was evading me. "You've never wanted to leave?" I asked.

"Never," she replied firmly, then smiled. "I've told you a lie. At one time I not only wanted to leave, I did. I ran away like a midnight fugitive and was gone almost three hours." Her eyes did not meet mine and again I had the odd feeling that something was withheld.

When I left my newfound aunt, I felt pleased that I had discovered a member of my family I could love, yet regretful that her greater love lay elsewhere and our lives could only touch, never blend.

The road to Ste. Marie du Lac wound through pastureland. At the outskirts of the village I steeled myself, determined that no taunts would hurt me. Anger I could show, but nothing else.

The first passerby was a woman struggling with a stubborn porker tied by the leg with a length of clothesline. *"Allons!"* she snarled at it. The pig squealed and moved an unwilling step ahead.

"Bonjour, madame," I said.

"Bonjour." She hardly glanced at me. I felt relief, as though I had passed a first obstacle.

Gagnon's auto-repair shop proved to be a converted barn not far from the center of the village. Monsieur Gagnon received me with elaborate courtesy. He was "desolated." The car was not ready. Would I have the graciousness to return in perhaps an hour?

I walked to the main street, resolved that this would be my complete test of the villagers' feelings. I paid little attention to a young man in a light gray suit who was obviously not a villager. But I could not fail to notice the look he gave me. We passed, then he turned back quickly.

"Roxanne?" he asked. "It's Roxanne Dumont, isn't it?" He had sandy hair and a pleasant face dominated by horn-rimmed spectacles.

"I'm Rochelle Dumont," I said, puzzled.

"Rochelle, of course!" His smile broadened. "Sorry, my memory slipped. But I certainly didn't expect to see you here, of all places. I mean, just walking down the street."

"Yes, it's an out-of-the-way spot," I said, sparring for time. I had a vague memory of his face, but no name to connect to it.

"It's a wonder I recognized you at all," he continued. "You looked so different the last time I saw you."

"Forgive me, but when was that? I don't remember—"

"You couldn't possibly. You were playing a concert at Eastfield Hall. Afterward we were introduced, but there was a big crowd."

I could not help returning his infectious smile, but who was he?

"You've forgotten me," he said with an expression of mock tragedy. "The name that escapes you is Brad Copeland. My sister Gloria graduated from Eastfield two years ago."

A dim recollection stirred.

"When she was in college, I used to come down from Boston to prey on the young girls. I dated several. Elspeth Hurley, for instance, and Deirdre Cameron. You were on my list but escaped. Do you speak French?" he asked abruptly. When I nodded, he seemed about to applaud. "My life is saved! Would you explain to my landlady that I have to leave very early and need to borrow an alarm clock? You can't buy one here."

"I'll be happy to," I said.

Around the next corner was a tiny inn. Three tables with umbrellas stood on a patch of lawn, and a chalked sign advertised lunch.

The robust landlady turned deeply mistrustful when I asked her to lend a clock to her lodger. "I am already busy in the kitchen by five o'clock every morning," she said. "I will call the gentleman."

I translated, and Brad Copeland agreed that five was early enough. "Surely she doesn't think I'd steal her clock!"

"It has happened," said the woman in clear English. "No disrespect, but two alarm clocks have walked themselves away."

We chuckled and Brad directed me to the sidewalk café. "Lunch is on me. I have to pay for that needless translation work."

I hesitated only a second. My walk had whetted my appetite.

"Meeting you was a lucky coincidence," Brad said when we were seated. "What are you doing out in this wilderness?"

"Visiting my family. And you?"

"Vacation wandering in Quebec. I work in New York now."

The landlady did not bother to take an order. "You will have brook trout," she told us. "My husband caught them this morning. To start, I give you a tiny omelet with bits of smoked meat. *Formidable!*"

Brad Copeland was perhaps about thirty, but the boyish face gave him a naïve look. His genial manner and attractive smile must have appealed to many of my classmates, although I suspected Deirdre would have called him too square. "I miss those weekends at Eastfield," he said. "I wish I'd kept in touch with Elspeth. And especially with Deirdre. She's a fascinating girl. Weren't you and she friends?"

"Not really. We happened to be fellow Canadians."

"I'd forgotten that. Does she live near here?"

"No, she's from Ontario."

My answers seemed too curt, but conversation about Deirdre made me uncomfortable. I tried to forget the tattered shawl.

"You haven't seen her recently, have you?"

A girl brought glasses and a bottle of white wine, which gave me a chance to think before answering. Deirdre had been emphatic about keeping her whereabouts secret. "I don't know where she is," I answered truthfully.

Touching the wine bottle, he frowned. "Warm. If we're going to enjoy a *formidable* omelet and trout, we need chilled wine. Excuse me, Rochelle. I'll see what I can do inside."

He vanished into the inn and was gone a long time. The landlady brought puffy little omelets. "They will not keep," she warned me, glowering at the empty chair. "Your friend should learn to wait for his dinner."

Brad returned a moment later, bottle in hand. "I haven't improved things much. This place isn't rustic, it's downright primitive."

"Have you been here long?" I asked.

"No. I arrived this morning. I've been moving around—Montreal, Quebec City, Gaspé. Now here."

"That's a lot of driving."

"I'm flying. I borrowed the company plane."

The trout arrived, crisp and golden. He did not pursue the matter of Deirdre. Yet I felt a change in his manner. At moments he appeared distracted. The warning that things were not as they seemed came when a girl served our coffee. He glanced at the table absentmindedly, then said, *"Veuillez m'apporter du sucre, s'il vous plaît."*

"Remarkably good for a person who speaks no French," I said.

The boyish grin was turned on instantly. "You've just heard one of my five phrases. Should I show off the other four?"

"Not good enough," I said.

Who was this man, what was he attempting? I should have been suspicious when he was gone so long with the wine bottle.

"I'm cornered." He sighed. "I confess to four years in a Swiss prep school. But how else was I going to lure a pretty girl to lunch?"

I did not believe a word of this, and glanced uneasily about for the landlady. This supposedly chance meeting had been no accident. Then I caught sight of a jeep slowly approaching, an unwelcome figure at the wheel. It halted a few yards from us, and Brad Copeland exclaimed, "This is my lucky day for old acquaintances. Hello, Captain Lachance."

What game was being played? I felt uneasy, almost fearful.

The captain acknowledged Copeland's greeting with a salute and strode to our table, towering over me, the annoying ironic smile on his face.

"Rochelle, may I present Captain Pierre Lachance?" Copeland's voice was smooth with false innocence.

The captain bowed. "I have already had that pleasure."

"And I have not been spared it," I retorted.

"Join us for coffee, Captain." The invitation was superfluous. Lachance was already seating himself, and the girl had automatically appeared with a glass of nut-colored wine.

His uniform had been exchanged for a sailor's shirt and dungarees, yet casual dress did not lessen the air of authority. He might look like a gypsy, with the curling blue-black hair and jet eyes, but his least gesture made it clear that he was accustomed to taking charge. He said to Copeland, "Forgive my being delayed. I was not expecting your telephone call."

"Telephone call?" I asked, then realized why so much time had been spent with the wine. My impulse was simply to leave. Whatever game the two men were playing infuriated me. On the other hand, I was not going to be put to flight. "I already know who the captain is. But you, Mr. Copeland, or whatever your name is, are a complete stranger."

"My name *is* Copeland and everything I said was true. But I neglected to tell you that I am Deirdre Cameron's fiancé."

"Why didn't you say so?"

He leaned forward, intent. "You were with her when she disappeared. I've checked on you, and what I learned makes me uneasy."

"Checked on me!" I shot a look at Captain Lachance.

Copeland caught the look. "The captain gave me some facts but no opinion at all. I learned more in Ste. Marie du Lac."

"Village gossip!" My cheeks blazed. "What did you conclude?"

"That I ought to find out more. I remembered you were at Eastfield and telephoned a friend who works in the registrar's office."

"To discover what? That I barely passed algebra?"

"You had a scholarship in music. Even so, you couldn't afford to finish school. But you now take an expensive voyage on the St. Lawrence. Who paid for that, Miss Dumont? What was the plan?"

His questions were so preposterous that I felt anger changing to scorn. But before I could answer, Captain Lachance spoke quietly. "You will stop now, Mr. Copeland. When you called and asked me to join you here, I did not suspect an interrogation." He turned to me, the hard face almost gentle. "I assure you I did not share any plan of Mr. Copeland's. His pretense was unnecessary and, I think, rather contemptible."

"Now listen here, Captain!" Copeland was halfway to his feet. "After what I heard in the village I—"

"Sit down, Mr. Copeland." Lachance's tone would have sent a whole crew scurrying. Copeland sat. "For five days and nights you have been racing across this province. Your thinking no longer has logic. We will be reasonable now. When Miss Cameron left my ship—I will not say she disappeared—Miss Dumont concerned herself greatly. She took her friend's departure with more seriousness than I myself did. She will answer your questions if they are courteously asked."

"Don't take that for granted, Captain," I said. "Any questions might be better asked in a police station."

"Police!" Copeland's voice was bitter. "I've talked to the police in three cities. They write down Deirdre's name and then forget it. Another runaway girl! Even her father won't help. He says it's happened before." He sighed, his hurt and frustration painfully apparent. "I apologize, Miss Dumont. Really, I didn't plan to trick you. It was stupid and I'm sorry."

"We'd better forget it and start over again," I said, deciding that Deirdre was more important than my anger at her fiancé.

"So we will talk this through," said Lachance. "But not here. Madame Houard, the concierge, is almost falling out the window trying to hear us. Madame, the bill, *s'il vous plaît.*"

Captain Lachance drove us to a small park at the shore of the lake. Its benches were deserted. Brad Copeland began talking at once. "I met Deirdre when she was in college. We had several dates, but I thought she was too wild and I suppose she thought I was too dull. Six months ago we met at a party in New York. She had changed, grown quieter. We fell in love, or at least I did, and planned to be married last Friday. A legal ceremony at City Hall." He swallowed hard. "On Friday I went to the hotel where she lived, and they told me she'd checked out that morning. No message, no address. Nothing."

Tracing her had been simple. She was a girl who attracted attention. An airline clerk was certain he had sold her a ticket to Montreal. Deirdre had often talked of her favorite Montreal restaurant, Le Coq d'Or. Copeland had inquired there. The doorman had seen her board the *Étoile Filante*. "So I flew to Gaspé to meet the ship."

After talking with Captain Lachance, he tried Quebec City. There he first went to the police. "Then Montreal again and two more police stations. Absolute zero. I was desperate, so I came to see you, Rochelle."

"Doubtless it is not my affair," said Lachance gently, "but I wonder why you follow this young woman. Her intention seems clear enough."

Brad rubbed a hand across his eyes. "I don't know why. At first it was anger. Now it's something else. . . . I don't know. I'm just afraid." He avoided the captain's gaze. "I must seem a fool. . . ."

Pierre Lachance rested his hand on Copeland's shoulder, and his expression conveyed a depth of understanding and sympathy I would never have believed possible. Then he turned to me. "Now it is your turn. Tell us everything about your time with Miss Cameron."

I had not finished two sentences before he interrupted. "*Non, mademoiselle!* It is details we want. Go slowly. Omit nothing."

Pierre Lachance, a frown never leaving his rugged face, cross-examined everything I said. Incidents that really had nothing to do with Deirdre came back to me. I recalled the empty envelope delivered to me in the airport. When I mentioned the speeding truck, Brad uttered an exclamation, but Lachance merely nodded and asked more questions.

After the last wisp of information had been plucked from me, we were silent until Brad said, "I can't believe it. You sound as though some character from Deirdre's past tried to kill her."

"You find that incredible?" the captain asked.

"Yes, I do. Deirdre poured out the story of her life in Montreal to me. The people were weird, all right, but not violent."

"I'm sure she was frightened," I protested.

"Wouldn't you be if a truck nearly killed you?"

I had to agree. "I can't tell you more," I said, "but maybe Captain Lachance will explain about my shawl that Deirdre was wearing. It came back in damp shreds."

"A small mystery. A crewman noticed it while we were in Gaspé. It was fouled in the propeller of our emergency engine. But do not leap to a conclusion. Miss Cameron was seen on deck talking with a young man. She had draped the shawl over the rail. It might have fallen overboard."

"You could have sent a note explaining that."

He smiled faintly. "You forget the nature of our parting. I did not think our relationship encouraged the sending of notes."

As we rode back to the village I realized I had developed a respect for Pierre Lachance. His fairness had brought him immediately to my aid against Brad's outrageous suspicions, and I admired the firm way he took charge of a difficult situation. In any emergency I would want him on my side. But was he ever on anyone's side except his own?

"I'm going back to Quebec City," Brad said. "I'll look for a Hungarian named Emil who claims to be a poet." He got out at the inn, repeating his apologies and promising to telephone any news about Deirdre.

"I can walk from here to the repair shop," I told Lachance.

But he started the jeep before I could open the door. "This is your first trip to Canada, *non?*" he asked, and I nodded. "Before this trip you had no acquaintances here at all?"

"Not a soul."

Another abrupt question. "You are planning to leave soon?"

"You needn't sound so hopeful, Captain Lachance," I said, smiling. "I promise to avoid you carefully."

His hand slapped the steering wheel. "Do not play games! What kind of answer is that?"

My stubbornness arose. "I have made no plans."

"No plans? *Sacrebleu!* Can you not grasp that someone else may have made plans for you, Rochelle Dumont?"

He stopped the jeep at Gagnon's shop, then turned in his seat to study me, an unfamiliar expression in his dark eyes. Pity? I could not tell.

"I'm curious about something, Captain Lachance. You disliked me before we even exchanged a word. Will you tell me why?"

He hesitated. "You were a reminder of the past, and the past should stay buried. Regina made a mistake in resurrecting it, a dangerous mistake."

"I assure you I'm neither dangerous nor in danger. On the ship you showed a personal dislike. It doesn't matter, I was merely curious."

"You want my reasons?" He gave a Gallic shrug of indifference. "*Tant mieux!* We will clear the air. I asked myself what sort of young woman would accept a foolish invitation to a place where the past is bitter and memories long. Probably one seeking a fortune from an elderly relative, hoping to become Regina's heir."

"Of all the—"

"Do not protest. You asked for this. There was also the company you chose. I did not recognize Miss Cameron the first night out of Montreal. Her disguise fooled me. But I knew a girl you were traveling with behaved in a way to shock other passengers. That night she approached me on deck. I do not mind if an attractive girl tries to seduce me. But not in public when the girl is drunk and I am in command of a ship."

I stared at him, wondering what had happened. "Thank you for making things clear," I said, getting out of the jeep.

"A moment," he said. "This morning I talked with Regina. Now I realize you did not know the circumstances when you came here. You must forgive my first opinion." The faint half smile returned. "I still do not like your choice of traveling companions."

"How gracious of you to relent a little," I answered. "And, Captain, I suspect you are a prude."

His look shifted to one of extreme gravity. "You are at liberty to test that suspicion at a time of your choosing."

As I slammed the door of the jeep he saluted me.

LATE THAT NIGHT, alone in the darkness of the Captain's Country, I listened to the old clock chime midnight, then turned on the lamp. Sleep was impossible. I put on a warm robe, and pacing between bed and window, I forced my thoughts into some sort of order.

Morgan had urged me to leave River Rising. Pierre Lachance even indicated that I was in physical danger here—an exaggeration, I thought, but it was disconcerting. Yesterday I myself had felt that leaving was the wisest course, not out of fear but because in this house I would be forever uneasy. And lonely, as I was tonight. I envied Deirdre her Brad Copeland. She had hurt him deeply, yet he was searching the breadth of Quebec for her. How fortunate to have someone care so much.

I pushed this thought away and tried to think about tomorrow, when I should tell Aunt Regina I was leaving. But to go where? To become what? Quebec City had caught my imagination. I could go there. Morgan said I would have money enough from the sale of the antiques I had inherited. I hated the thought of parting with them, but they meant money to finish college.

I brushed my hand unthinkingly across the dresser, striking Deirdre's music box. It fell to the rug, where it tinkled thinly: *"Alouette, gentille alouette . . ."* The mindless tune played on and on. Thoughts of my own future were overwhelmed by the sensation that I was again on shipboard, lying in my cabin in the grip of the nightmare. Footsteps I could hardly hear, muffled sounds from Deirdre's cabin.

What if it had not been Deirdre, but someone else? Someone packing her clothes? The intruder could work unseen. Clothes do not cry out. The music box was different; lifted, it would play on and on unless one knew to turn it upside down. The music box had been left behind because someone did not know how to silence its voice. . . .

There was the sound of a heavy footfall in the corridor, and a muffled voice called, "Rochelle?"

"Yes, who is it?"

"Morgan."

I rushed to open the door, wondering what emergency could have brought him here at so late an hour. "Has something happened?" I asked.

He smiled. "No. I was just checking the house and I saw your light."

In his dark trousers and turtleneck sweater he seemed to blend with the shadows of the corridor. "Howard and I both felt uneasy after the burglary. We're going to do a bit of patrolling for a night or two. Enough for word to get back to the village that we're alert here. Howard has the harder job, he's outside. Look." Morgan crossed to the window and below, where he pointed, I made out the figure of a man leaning against a tree.

There was a metallic reflection in the moonlight. "Is he carrying a gun?" I asked. "A rifle?"

"He's armed to the teeth," said Morgan lightly. "Howard sets great store by his collection of guns. He's rather given to violence, I'm afraid."

Howard Palmer violent? I had dismissed him as drab and harmless. As the moon again touched the rifle barrel, I revised my opinion.

"But I don't want to talk about Howard," Morgan continued. "I want to talk about Rochelle. Have you decided where you'll go?"

"I was thinking about that tonight. Maybe Quebec City."

He nodded. "It is beautiful. I'd enjoy showing it to you."

"Thank you," I answered, suddenly uncertain of myself.

"It's right for you to leave here, best for you. But remember that the change won't make any difference with"—he hesitated—"with your family. You're one of us now. Wherever you go, we'll see each other often."

He took my hand, wishing me good night, a brief, casual gesture. Yet after he was gone I felt troubled by the feeling that his touch had not been that of a friend, but a lover.

CHAPTER SIX

"AN ENVELOPE WITH A maple-leaf design? I didn't send it," said Regina. I had joined her for breakfast on the sun porch, misnamed today. Rain and mist obscured the windows like a gauze veil. "A mistake, perhaps. Dumont is a common name and there must be other Rochelles."

"I'm sure that's the explanation," I said, not believing it.

Eunice entered in a pink robe and slippers with floppy rosebuds. "Pierre Lachance called. He's coming to dinner tonight."

"Is his wife coming with him?" I asked, a new thought crossing my mind.

"I hope not," said Regina tartly. "She died fifteen years ago."

"So long? He must have married young."

"Far too young. He was an inexperienced boy."

Eunice giggled. "You'd hardly call him inexperienced now. I'd say he's made up for lost time."

"You are repeating gossip, Eunice." Regina's look was a warning. "Pierre's passing amusements are none of our business."

Dismissing the matter, she glanced out the window. "What a sloppy day, but at least I have some good news this morning." Regina held up a letter. "A husband and wife who want domestic work. Since they don't speak French, they can't be corrupted by local nonsense about the Rising."

Eunice excused herself to dress. When she had gone, Regina said, "Madame Sud tells me Dorothy is feeling better. I took the liberty of sending word that you'd call on her this morning. I hope that's agreeable."

"Of course."

"But please don't feel you need see her frequently. She is an irritating woman, and was no less self-centered when she had her health."

"How unfortunate for Morgan."

"Don't waste sympathy. It was a marriage of convenience. Dorothy wanted to be the wife of a famous man, and Morgan is famous."

"And what did Morgan want?"

"Oh, she was attractive, had social connections, and I think Morgan was under the illusion that she was very rich."

"Surely Morgan didn't need to marry for money."

"His income has been high for many years. Almost as high as his outgo. He inherited quite a sum from my brother Andrew, but most of that was frittered away before Morgan got his hands on it."

"Doesn't River Rising belong partly to Morgan?"

"Morgan inherited a huge tract of useless land down the slope. River Rising belongs entirely to me."

The tiny Sevres clock on Dorothy Armitage's dressing table showed eleven fifteen. I had been in this stuffy room less than ten minutes, and it seemed an hour. Dorothy sat in bed, propped by a mountain of pillows. Her haggard face must once have had a feline prettiness. The large slanted eyes which Thalia had inherited could be called beautiful, I thought, but somehow they emphasized the small nose and sharp chin.

We had discussed the weather, the isolation of the village, the decor of the room, all meaningless small talk of interest to neither of us.

The presence of Madame Sud multiplied my discomfort. Seated in a window alcove, she carefully brushed the golden tresses of a wig. The wig block stood on a small table, its back toward me, giving the disconcerting impression that Madame Sud was ministering to a severed head. The thick yellow locks made a pathetic contrast to Dorothy's own lusterless hair.

"I suppose the remoteness of River Rising is good for my husband's work," Dorothy was saying, and I nodded mutely. Then she at last expressed a genuine feeling. "Also, it probably keeps him out of mischief. Morgan is terribly attractive to women, as you've no doubt noticed."

"Who could fail to notice? He's very handsome—for a middle-aged man." I hoped this would allay suspicion, but my remark was, of course, ridiculous. Morgan radiated youthful vitality.

"Middle-aged?" The tilt of her chin sharpened. "Age hasn't hindered girls from making fools of themselves over Morgan."

Then a puzzled look came over her face, as though she had forgotten the subject of conversation. "I'm much stronger than I was in the sanatorium," she went on. "If the weather clears, I'll walk in the garden today."

"I hope you can."

She studied me, then asked abruptly, "Do you believe in tarot cards?"

"You mean fortune-telling?"

"I'm learning how to read the tarot from an amazing old woman in the village. She comes twice a week. We've made remarkable forecasts." She became intent. "The cards foretold your coming here. I'll show you. Madame Sud, please bring the pack."

"Isn't this a strain for you?" I asked uncertainly. The color that flushed her pale cheeks seemed unnatural, and her breath came too rapidly.

Madame Sud placed a low table with a thin deck of cards on the bed. Dorothy made several gestures above the cards, then said, "Cut the pack four times. Lay the cards in the shape of a cross."

Reluctantly I did so, wishing Madame Sud were not so close.

Dorothy turned the cards, exposing their faces one by one, then stared vacantly at the pattern. "The drowned man is near you," she murmured. "The drowned man separates you from the hanged man. But are they one? The identity card is touching both."

The unsubtle reference to my father's death did not escape me.

"See how the deniers, the golden circles, have swarmed near you!" Her voice rose to a throbbing singsong punctuated by quick gasps. "But it is not gold coming to you. Yellow is danger for you, the color of death."

"This is enough," I said, rising. "You are under too much strain."

Dorothy Armitage did not hear me. "The old man is hidden from you, the philosopher, the wise King of Cups. He holds the answer, but you cannot find him. Go away. Safety is far from you. Go away. . . ."

The fortune-telling seemed over, yet she stared at the cards entranced.

"Who is teaching you this?" I asked. "Who is the woman from the village?"

"She is called Madame Jeannette." Dorothy's voice was toneless. "She knows the special reading, too. The one that can be done only on Friday at midnight. She sees a long life for me. She sees . . . everything."

Dorothy lay back on the pillows, her eyes closed. Madame Sud put her finger to her own lips, enjoining silence, and nodded toward the door.

I had never been happier to leave a room. The fortune Dorothy told was clearly prompted by Madame Jeannette and Madame Sud. Yellow meant the golden shawl, no doubt. But who was the philosopher who held the answer? "Go away" was the message—it was everyone's message to me.

The morning shower had moved southeast, crossing the river. I sat down at the harpsichord in the living room and began to play softly. Then I unconsciously shifted to an improvisation of chords and counterpoint, a confusion of themes reflecting my own emotions. I paused, sensing that someone was near, and found Thalia standing close to me, two great tears in her eyes. "You were playing a dream, weren't you?" she whispered.

"Something like that." I saw her glance at the keyboard, almost hungrily, then look away. "Do you play, Thalia?"

"I once did, just a little on the piano."

"You should play," I told her. "You're named for one of the Muses. Thalia is a lovely name."

"I like Ro-chelle better," she said, breaking the syllables. "I used to practice for hours. My father—" It was hard for her to say the word. "He liked to hear me. Maybe that's why I can't play anymore."

The bench was narrow, but I drew her to my side, my arm around her. "I lost my father, too. Maybe music gives him back to me, at least a little."

"No. Nothing could do that."

"Thalia, the rain is gone. Should we take a walk? Along the firebreak are bobolinks and larks. I saw a silver squirrel and a doe."

"No! I hate the forest. I'm afraid of it, I . . ." Sinking to the floor, she buried her face in my lap and wept, the suppressed pain pouring out. When no more tears would come, she began to tell the story of her father's death, bit by bit, and I understood a measure of what she felt.

After her parents' divorce and her mother's marriage to Morgan, Thalia lived with her father. A year ago last October he had taken her on a weekend vacation, first stopping at River Rising to visit Dorothy, then going to a rustic lodge twenty miles away. "To see the colors of the leaves," her father had said.

They were not far from the lodge when a blizzard struck, and foolishly they took shelter in the hollow of a tree, thinking the snowstorm would end quickly. But the swirling white became deeper, impenetrable, and the wind rose. "The wind screamed until we couldn't stand it. We had to escape."

Clinging together, they stumbled through a raging world where all landmarks were obliterated. The snow dazzled them with blinding white. Thalia's father, sightless, collapsed in a drift. They shouted against the wind, they tried to sing, hoping someone would hear. Her father's song became weaker and Thalia fell asleep. "When I awoke, Captain Pierre was holding me. He led the woodsmen who found us. I don't remember any more. But I still can't play any music, and I'm afraid to go in the woods."

Turning to the keyboard, I began to play tunes from childhood, pieces I had not thought of in years. "Now you play," I said firmly.

Thalia blanched. "I can't, Rochelle."

Putting her hands on the keyboard, I waited, hoping desperately. Then, hesitantly, she began. She did not understand the action of a harpsichord, but I recognized the familiar air of "Country Gardens," and at that moment no symphony could have been so beautiful.

A little later I found Tante Emma in the kitchen. "Exactly where does the monkshood grow, Tante Emma? Is it found near the garden?"

"What an idea! Monkshood is a devil of the woods."

It was as I suspected. Thalia never ventured into the forest. Whoever had put the monkshood in my room, it was not the child.

Next I called on Regina. "Aunt Regina, I'd like to go to the village. May I use your car?"

She smiled. "Kindly call it *our* car until you have your own. The keys are in the bowl in the hall. If you're going . . . I don't mean to burden you with errands, but Henri Berthelot telephoned. He has some endive for us."

"Berthelot?" The name seemed familiar.

"You remember. The artist—Morgan's teacher, and your father's. His house is on the main street. You'll see the name on the gate."

I looked forward to meeting anyone who had known my father, but my first task was the one I had left unfinished yesterday, the testing of the village of Ste. Marie du Lac.

THE TINY TOWN, from the first, had struck me as medieval. What I now saw on the church lawn surpassed any imagining. A score of men and women had gathered there, brilliant in fancy dress—hose and doublets, buckled shoes and plumed headgear. As I halted the car a small boy dressed as a page skipped past. "What's going on?" I asked.

"Rehearsal for the pageant. The Feast of Saint John the Baptist."

I lingered for a moment, but the participants gave me only cursory glances. I walked on, passing two girls who stared at me with open curiosity. I felt myself tense. They were looking at the murderer's daughter, of course, and without meaning to, I glanced away. Then I heard one say, "Her dress is *très chic*. From Paris, do you think?"

I almost laughed aloud in my off-the-peg jersey dress. The bit of flattery firmed my step for a harder test, entering the general store.

The dim room was deserted except for the proprietress. "I am looking for Monsieur Henri Berthelot," I said, gazing at her coolly.

"Across the street, second block on the corner."

The tone was polite, her expression bland, and I decided to go further. "Madame, as you know, I am newly arrived here. Were you acquainted with my parents?"

"Forgive me, mademoiselle, I did not know them. I, too, am a newcomer. Only seven years." Then she added, "I hope you were not too upset by Madame Jeannette. You must realize that she is a little mad."

"More than a little."

"I am told she was not always so. It was the tragedy of her daughter. . . ."

"What of her daughter?"

She lowered her eyes. "I do not know the details. Ask Monsieur Berthelot. He was here when the girl killed herself. I was not."

"Killed herself? Tell me, madame!"

"I was not here then," she repeated, shaking her head to dismiss me.

In front of his house Henri Berthelot had placed not a fence but a grape arbor. I could see that the vines had been trained so that in season clusters of fruit would hang on the public side of the stakes. A sign said TAKE WHAT YOU NEED. BUT LEAVE SOME FOR OTHERS. I suddenly liked Henri Berthelot.

The stone cottage resembled twenty others in Ste. Marie du Lac, but on the north side a clapboard studio with high windows had been added. An old man with a balding crown answered my knock, peering at me through thick lenses. His spectacles, combined with a bristling goatee, gave him the appearance of a mad scientist.

"Bonjour, monsieur, je—" I started to say.

He interrupted in English. "Rochelle Dumont! Such a pleasure. Regina phoned to say you were coming. My eyes are too old to see you clearly, but Regina tells me you are beautiful, as your mother and father were."

He spoke of my father without hesitation, and I was touched to hear Jean-Paul Dumont called beautiful. Inside, a single lofty room served for both cooking and dining. The walls were hung almost solidly with paintings, drawings and etchings.

"Take this chair, my dear," he said. "When you tire of my conversation, your eyes will rest on the south wall. My best paintings are there."

His work was delightful, the daily life of Ste. Marie du Lac glowing on the canvases—a girl milking a cow, a patriarch enjoying his mug of ale—homely subjects his strong brushstrokes had saved from sentimentality.

After pouring homemade wine into two water glasses, he sat down to savor his pipe. Conversation came easily. As we talked one painting kept catching my eye, a portrait, different from the others. "Who is that beautiful girl?" I asked. "The one in the white dress?"

"You like her? What a model she was! A beautiful wildcat. There was a glow about her—she was translucent. It was one of my last works."

"But who is she?"

"It is a portrait of Madame Lachance."

"The wife of Pierre Lachance?" I asked slowly.

"Yes, painted before she married him. She was sixteen then. And to think that only a few years later she hanged herself."

"Hanged herself?" I gasped. Then I remembered the remark of the woman in the store. "Did she come from the village?"

"Yes. Her mother scratched out a living by selling potions and herbs."

"Madame Jeannette?"

"Why, yes. Jeannette Massine. Her daughter was Giselle."

I stared at the portrait. The connection between Madame Jeannette and Pierre Lachance left me unbelieving. "Why did the daughter kill herself?"

"Thwarted ambition, I suppose. Giselle was engaged to marry François Armitage. It was a local sensation. How tongues wagged, Jeannette's among them. Giselle was going to be rich, to be known as the greatest beauty in Canada. But François died before the marriage took place."

"Yes," I said, "François died." And now I understood Madame Jeannette's malice toward me. My father's act of violence had destroyed her daughter's future. For years Madame Jeannette had nursed her hatred. Before, I had detested her; now I felt something closer to fear.

"A little later Giselle married Pierre Lachance, a boy, really, but handsome, the village athlete. It was not enough for Giselle. She left him at least once, something about trying to succeed in films or television. I have forgotten the details. In the end she died by her own hand."

Monsieur Berthelot glanced at my empty glass. "More wine? I am sorry I have upset you with this old tragedy."

"You haven't upset me. I'm grateful. It's important that I understand why people here behave as they do. But no wine—I must go now."

"Wait! I have two things for you." From the sideboard he brought a basket of crisp endive. "Grown in my tiny greenhouse." Then he handed me a rectangular parcel clumsily wrapped in newspaper.

"A drawing?" I could feel a frame. "Monsieur, you are too kind."

"A small painting done by one of my students and left here long ago. No, do not open it here. It is for you alone."

Leading me to the door, he said, "Return soon. We will talk of pleasant things, and the wine will have a brighter taste."

On the way back to River Rising I thought of Madame Jeannette's daughter, Giselle Massine. Pierre Lachance had been in love with the girl François Armitage intended to marry. Pierre had also been on the scene at the time of François' murder and my father's death. I saw the captain's dislike of me in a new light, and yet I could not be sure of what I felt.

But another matter was certain. Madame Jeannette was indeed my implacable enemy, and that enemy came and went freely within the walls of River Rising, the invited guest of Dorothy Armitage.

In the Captain's Country, I locked the door behind me before unwrapping the little painting. I knew what I hoped it would be. Monsieur Berthelot, I felt almost sure, had kept some work of my father's. Deliberately prolonging the suspense, I undid the paper so the back of the picture was toward me. My eyes fell on a label glued to the frame, and my heart leaped when I read it. "No. 183. Self-portrait by Jean-Paul Dumont."

I closed my eyes, afraid to turn it over. Would I have some vague memory of him? Would I, and this I hoped desperately, *like* him?

Then I looked and gasped.

Smiling at me across the years was the dearly familiar face of Paul LaFarge, my mother's lover.

HE HAD CHEATED death that night, had not been crushed on the rocks below River Rising! The words seemed to shout themselves, to shake the silent room where I stood holding the portrait with trembling hands.

"Paul," I whispered. "Paul."

My view of my whole life had just been swept away as by a hurricane. Nothing would be the same. I wanted to race through the corridors crying out the news. Charlotte had not left because she was ashamed or frightened, she had left to join her husband, to share the rest of his life.

Suddenly I loved my mother with a fullness I had never imagined. I had thought her cold and ungiving, yet she had given everything, chosen a life of exile where her love had to be concealed. My blaming her for not marrying Paul—I could not think of him as Jean-Paul Dumont, my father, yet—seemed cruel injustice. The danger of being recognized must have followed Paul every day of his life. My mother would never have allowed him to double that risk by living openly with him. They were right to keep their secret from me. As a child, I could have blurted out everything. At the end she had tried to tell me. But it was too late.

"The murderer's daughter," I said aloud, and the words had no sting. How could I be ashamed of being Paul's child?

Ever since coming to River Rising, I had harbored suspicions that someone else might be guilty of the death of François Armitage. I had secretly wondered about Morgan, and about Howard Palmer. Today I had found a motive pointing to the possible guilt of Pierre Lachance.

These suspicions vanished now. Paul's fleeing Canada showed his legal guilt. Yet I had known Paul, and if he had committed such a crime, he must have been driven to it. Regina was wrong, Morgan was wrong, everyone who had described my father to me was mistaken or deceived. Or lying.

The firm features and clear gaze of Jean-Paul Dumont's portrait gave me new resolution. The true story of that night had not yet been told, but it would be. And I would be the one to tell it.

CHAPTER SEVEN

"I HAVE AN ANNOUNCEMENT to make," said Regina.

We had gathered in the living room after dinner. The family was present except for Dorothy, and there were two visitors, if Howard Palmer could be described as one. The other was Captain Lachance, who joked easily with Regina, smiled at Thalia and ignored everyone else.

"We are going to celebrate Saint John's Eve as we used to, with a ball at River Rising."

Regina, who had expected delight, caused consternation instead. After dumbfounded silence came a chorus of objections.

"Where would you find servants?" Eunice looked lost.

"Would there be a lot of people here?" Thalia asked doubtfully.

Morgan scowled. "This will cost you a fortune."

"I *have* a fortune." Regina's eyes flashed. "And I intend to use it. Here is my beautiful niece, a stranger in her own country. Rochelle must meet people. And not merely villagers but our friends from Quebec City as well."

"A debut," said Captain Lachance with his irritating half smile. "Is not the debutante to be consulted? Perhaps Miss Dumont would not enjoy such a launching."

"Oh, stop calling her Miss Dumont, Pierre! This is Rochelle. You will end this annoying formality." Regina turned to me, her tone no longer imperious. "Of course I should have consulted you, my dear. But I regarded this as a delightful surprise. Have I been thoughtless?"

"On the contrary," I assured her. "But you see, Aunt Regina, it isn't . . ." I groped for words.

Pierre Lachance interrupted me. "Perhaps Miss Dumont—Rochelle—is trying to say that the Feast of Saint John the Baptist is a few weeks in the future and she may not be here."

Regina's expression showed hurt and astonishment.

"Please don't put words into my mouth," I said, and went quickly to her and kissed her cheek. "Of course I'll be here. But you must not go to extra expense or trouble for me."

She took my hand lightly but warmly. "Thank you. My motives are not as unselfish as you think. I myself intend to have a wonderful time. The Rising will be filled with music and celebration."

As I returned to my place on the couch, Thalia smiled at me, but hers was the only smile. Never had Pierre Lachance's face seemed more like granite. Morgan also gazed at me with disapproval. My decision annoyed both men, but what did it matter? I had every right to stay as long as Regina wished.

When I had resumed my seat, Lachance spoke. "I am happy you are eager to have guests, Regina." He managed a smile. "Now it is easier for me to ask a favor. Some vacationers wish to rent my house for a good deal of money. Alas, they do not care to rent me at the same time."

"You will come to the Rising at once, Pierre," Regina told him. "But I warn you, I may never permit you to leave."

"A pleasant captivity. We will arrive tomorrow. Both of us are grateful."

"Both?" Regina hesitated, then laughed. "Oh, Viking!"

"Your police dog?" Eunice sounded faintly panicky.

"A German shepherd," he explained. "They are sometimes used for police work, but are also gentle enough to be guide dogs for the blind."

Howard Palmer leaned forward. "Is he a good gun dog? I've been looking for one, or even two."

"Viking is a superb hunter. Unfortunately, he works only for me." Lachance paused and glanced at the empty spot above the mantel where the stolen painting had once hung. "He may be useful here."

"The burglar won't return," said Morgan flatly. "Art thieves never do."

"True, but I believe art thieves often send ransom notes. Oddly, that has not happened." He stood up and bade us good night. "Until tomorrow."

Later, in my room, I resisted a temptation to look at my father's portrait, which I had hidden in the sea chest. Tonight I must arouse no more emotions. Nor did I wish to think what the presence of Pierre Lachance in the house might mean to me. He was a disconcerting man. It was unexplainable that my anger rose so close to the surface when he was near. The stories of his youthful, tragic marriage and his frequent love affairs were nothing to me, I told myself.

PIERRE LACHANCE ARRIVED the next morning. I watched him approach from the Captain's Walk.

After breakfast I had climbed the steep stairs that led to the roof from the old nursery adjoining my room. At the top a small door opened to an outside walkway, the Captain's Walk, where a retired mariner might pace and gaze at the river and passing ships. The walk, fronted by a low parapet, was not visible from below, and behind it rose the great chimneys and gables of the uppermost attics. There was one attic window above me; otherwise, I had found the most commanding point at River Rising.

Looking down from the rather dizzying height, I saw the captain leave his jeep, a black-and-copper dog at his heels. A duffle bag was balanced on his left shoulder, and he carried a suitcase. A long visit, I thought.

I lingered a moment, held by the vista of the eternally moving water. Had my father painted this scene? The self-portrait evoked no memories of other pictures. The man I knew as Paul LaFarge worked on his ramshackle boat or in what he described as his "grass shack" studio on a nearby island. I had never seen it, and now realized its location had been deliberately kept from me. I did recall things he had drawn for me when I was a child. There was a purple pelican and a dancing flamingo.

Then the memory of pink-striped Sandy-Panda came back to me with a rush of sentiment. Somehow I had lost my favorite doll, left it on the beach and the tide had come in. Now I vividly recalled the strong, warm hands that comforted me. "*Tiens*, I will make you a new one, *ma petite.*"

I had not believed a big man like Paul could possibly make a doll, but that day I watched him create Sandy-Panda. I sat on the floor, wide-eyed, as he stitched with a sail-mending needle, then painted the gay stripes and the smiling bearlike face. "He is yours forever," he said, presenting him to me solemnly. "And he loves you almost as much as I do." Sandy-Panda slept at my side for years.

Shaking away my reverie, I started toward my room, careful to check the spring lock of the door to the roof behind me. I had just passed through the nursery when I heard an authoritative knock. "Come in," I said.

Pierre Lachance strode into the room, the dog moving, it seemed, in step with him. "*Bonjour*. I want you to meet your new friend, Viking. Viking, I present you to Rochelle, a lady we must never call Mademoiselle Dumont. We are under orders."

The dog's eyes, almond-shaped and deep amber, studied me. He sat at his master's side, pointed ears alert, an animal of power and pride.

"Does he shake hands?" I asked uncertainly.

Lachance looked pained. "Certainly not. Do you bark?"

"I have been known to," I said, making a tentative move forward.

"Non!" He shook his head impatiently. "Approach him confidently, but not too fast. Extend your right hand, with the palm down."

"Aye, aye, Captain." I obeyed with deep misgivings, then felt relief when Viking gently sniffed my knuckles.

Pierre took a brown envelope from his pocket. "These lozenges are Viking's favorites. Give him one now, and one each time he calls on you."

"Calls on me?" I asked, astonished. "Do you think that likely?"

"*Pourquoi pas?* Friends do call on each other."

Viking, a gentleman, took the lozenge I offered him carefully from my hand, pulverized it with one crunch of his jaws, then looked at me hopefully. I decided we might become friends after all.

"A good beginning," Lachance said. "Now you must change clothes. Your skirt will not do for a picnic in the woods."

"What?" I exclaimed.

"*Sacrebleu!* Control your panic. The child Thalia is frightened of the forest. She has confidence in you and, I think, in me. We are going to help her conquer her fear. So change into pants and meet us in the garden."

"So you have planned my day?" I said, my chin lifting. "Not everyone is a member of your crew, Captain Lachance."

"It is forbidden to call me anything but Pierre. Your aunt's command. And why this protest? You will enjoy yourself."

He turned to leave, and when Viking followed he made a quick gesture with his hand. The dog promptly sat and Lachance left, closing the door firmly behind him.

"Of all the arrogant . . ." But I couldn't help smiling. He was quite right, I wanted to go.

I put on a pair of jeans. Viking gave me a sympathetic look. But Viking, I thought, was more used to taking orders than I would ever be.

AT NOON WE turned onto the abandoned trail leading to the ghost town known as Castaways, Viking frisking a little ahead of us. It was a brisk day, the sky a shimmering, translucent blue. Spring wildflowers had opened in a profusion of pinks, reds and purples.

"Let's pick some," I said to Thalia, but she would not leave the trail.

Now, on the rutted corduroy road, Pierre said, "This settlement was called Castaways because its people were survivors of the shipwrecks on the river. They stayed though it was against the law."

"Against the law?"

"Englishmen were not supposed to settle among the French, but to go farther upriver. The castaways stayed here anyway. Their village lasted almost two centuries."

"But the Armitages were English," I said.

"Oh, they claim to be more English than the Queen. But most Armitage wives have been French. Thalia, you will soon see a very ugly but interesting place. We will call it the Sawdust Desert."

We emerged from forest into open space, barren ground, some of it a peculiar greenish blue, scarred by potholes and small craters. "You are looking at sawdust," said Pierre. "Miles of it, left by sawmills that once were here."

"My stepfather owns this, doesn't he?" asked Thalia. "I heard him talk about his fortune in sawdust."

"Ah, so small rabbits have long ears!" Pierre chuckled. "He owns this and most of Castaways. It was bought for Morgan with his own money, purchased by his guardian, François, before Morgan had control of things."

He glanced ahead. "And here is our city of specters." A collection of tumbledown shacks lay before us. Roofs had crashed down on rotted floors; marauders had carried away doors and window frames, leaving openings that gaped like wounds in the few remaining walls.

"No one lives here?" Thalia whispered.

"Only a watchman, a man named Gilles who has worked for Morgan for many years."

"I know Gilles," I said grimly.

We crossed a space that was once a village square and saw the single building that remained intact. Intact but unfinished, for the stone structure was solid below but had only steel girders for a second floor.

"That was to have been François' publishing center. Here he intended to print his magazine for an independent Quebec."

"In this wilderness? He must have been mad—insane," I remarked.

"You will not insult him." Lachance's voice was cool. "Eccentric, yes. He did foolish things, but also he bought me clothing when I was a child in rags, he gave me my first skates, my first skis. He paid for me to go to school. In life I repaid him badly. I can at least defend his memory."

"We see the man differently," I answered. "There's no reason for us to speak of him again."

"No reason at all." He whistled for Viking, who trotted to his side. "Now let us enjoy our picnic."

But the day had been spoiled. Pierre remained withdrawn, almost hostile. For Thalia's sake he attempted to conceal this, answering bird calls, pointing out game crossings and a salt lick. But my remark about François had struck some deep chord, aroused deep self-reproaches. Then as he absently patted Viking, eyes far away, I saw an expression that I understood because it sprang from an emotion we shared. Loneliness.

I was still thinking of this later that evening in my room as I tried to concentrate on a novel, distracted by my confused feelings. Firm footfalls sounded in the corridor, then a knock. "Who is it?"

"Le Capitaine Pierre Lachance et ami."

"Come in."

He and Viking were hardly inside the room before he was giving me another curt order. "Lock your door in the future. Anyone could have entered. No, do not argue with me again."

"This is a most unexpected visit," I said.

"*I* am not visiting you. Viking is. Sleep well, but behind a locked door, *s'il vous plaît.*" Then he left, releasing the catch of the lock and trying the door after he was outside.

I stared from the locked door to Viking, who gave me an amber-eyed look of sympathy. It was after ten o'clock. Could Pierre intend to leave the dog here all night? Viking, who appeared to read my mind, trotted to the foot of the bed and lay on the floor, tail wagging, perfectly at home.

"Well, I hope you're a quiet sleeper."

Yawning, he closed his eyes. The pointed ears lay back softly, an expression of peaceful lassitude. When I knelt to pet him, he rolled over on his back, suddenly clownish.

"So you want to be scratched! You're just a big baby. I don't think you'll be much use, though I admit you're lovable."

But thinking of my uneasiness when I learned Madame Jeannette made visits to the house, I decided that Viking might have his uses after all.

THE DOG STAYED with me the next night and the third, brought by Pierre rather late and leaving by himself early in the morning, signaling me with a polite scratch at the door. Pierre said nothing to the others about Viking's presence in the Captain's Country, nor did I.

The third night, as I prepared for bed, a shutter banged in the rising wind. Pushing back the draperies to hook the loose shutter, I gazed out at a troubled night. Dark clouds edged in silver moonlight scudded before the wind. The moon flickered, dimmed in cloud banks, then shone brilliantly again. My eyes traveled from the river, its waters swirling before the gale, to the cliff edge, then to the lawns of River Rising.

A figure moved along the drive, a hunched woman swathed in black. Madame Jeannette. Instinctively I drew back, and remembering Dorothy's words about a strange and special ritual at midnight, I glanced at my watch. It was not yet twelve, but soon would be, and this was Friday. So Madame Jeannette had come again to read the future. Read the future for a woman who hardly had a present, a grim thought.

The day, devoted to another long hike and a picnic, had exhausted me and I soon slept. The violent thunder and slashing rain outside did not disturb me, but I sat bolt upright, completely awake, when Viking uttered a loud, menacing growl.

Switching on the bedside lamp, I saw that the dog had moved near the corridor doorway and stood crouched, ears alert and nostrils quivering. Any thought of his being a playful puppy vanished as I stared at the bared fangs, the bristling coat. No intruder could have entered that door and survived. Getting out of bed, I called, "Who is it? Is someone there?"

No answer, but I felt a rush of cold air across my feet. From the adjoining nursery came the loud complaint of unoiled hinges. The door to the Captain's Walk must have blown open.

I shivered, chilled by the icy draft, then put on slippers and a negligee, too thin for the cold night but the first garment I could reach. "Come,

Viking," I whispered, and the dog, after a second suspicious snarl, moved with me toward the nursery.

"Is anyone there?" I called again, and still no answer came, only the roll of thunder and whine of the wind in the eaves. As I opened the nursery door I almost expected Viking to charge past me in furious attack, but he did not leave my side. I flicked the wall switch, but the nursery remained dark, the single lamp unresponsive. In the pale light from my bedroom the ancient ship's figurehead stared at me fixedly, expressionless. Nothing moved in the shadows except the door at the top of the stairs. I paused, knowing it had to be closed and locked, yet reluctant to enter the gloom of the narrow stairwell.

Go lock that door, I ordered myself, and stop these childish jitters. I moved ahead, but on the first step encountered a difficulty. Viking would neither lead nor follow, but insisted on remaining at my side, his shoulder pressing against my thigh, forcing me to the wall.

"Either go ahead or go back!" I said, but the dog ignored me and growled savagely as, crowded together, we went up step by step.

My hand had just touched the doorknob when I heard a faint, thin whisper in the darkness outside. "Ro-chelle, help me! Ro-chelle!" Holding the door tightly, ready to slam it at the first sign of danger, I listened, every nerve tingling.

Viking was wary, but his growling was stilled.

"Help, Ro-chelle. . . . Oh, please, Ro-chelle . . ."

Thalia, I thought, suddenly close to panic. Somehow she had climbed to the roof and was trapped among the steep, slippery gables. Injured, I thought wildly, as my name was whispered faintly again. "Ro-chelle . . . Ro-chelle . . . Help me. . . ."

I drew courage from Viking's sturdy assurance. The voice did not alarm him. "Thalia?" I said, and stepped outside, Viking still close to me.

The wind caught my loose hair, blowing it across my eyes. The force of the gale was far greater than I had thought. I took a few cautious steps forward, bracing myself against the parapet. "Thalia? Where are you?"

The whispered reply came at once. "Ro-chelle, help me. . . ."

Viking tensed, seemed uncertain. Then I whirled in alarm at a sharp bang behind me. The door I had left open was now shut. Rushing toward it, I seized the knob, twisted and pushed with all my weight, but it did not yield. The dog and I were trapped on the exposed Captain's Walk.

"Thalia!" I shouted. "Where are you?"

Fighting the heavy gusts of wind and flinging out an arm as if it could ward off the icy raindrops, I struggled along the walk toward its far end. The maddening whisper seemed to come from that direction, but as I heard it once more it sounded less like Thalia.

"Here, here . . . Oh, Ro-chelle . . ."

It had the bodiless, hollow tone of a specter. I forced myself not to think of Lady Judith. Yet as I fought the gale and tried to control my shivering, her image seemed to float in the shadows of the garret eaves, her voice enticing me toward . . . what? In terror I looked down at the Captain's Walk, fearing it might abruptly end, that I would step off into nothingness to plunge helplessly through the air to death below.

"Ro-chelle . . ."

But now I knew I must not answer, some primal instinct telling me that safety lay in silence. Viking's muzzle touched my hand gently, but I was not reassured. What was the matter with the dog? Why should the voice leave him unfrightened? Was this a voice that I alone could hear?

I stood still, straining to catch it again, but I heard only the rush of the storm and far away a frantic ringing of bell buoys that marked the river channel, clanging as the mounting waves tossed them.

For an instant the roof was illuminated in a flash of lightning, and in that split second I saw the ladder. It leaned against the face of a gable at the end of the Captain's Walk and reached to a high garret window, the very summit of River Rising. Now I moved more quickly. It was an ordinary household ladder, aluminum, light but strong. Wind tugged at my thin clothing, my teeth chattered with cold, and my shoulders trembled. It would be mad to climb the ladder in the darkness and storm, yet it tempted me. The window had neither bars nor shutters. I could break the glass with my slipper. An escape from a night of cold imprisonment on the roof. I rested my hand on a rung. Only ten steps, not so very high.

"Ro-chelle . . ."

Stifling a cry of fear, I drew back. Suddenly Viking broke into frenzy. Barking wildly, he leaped at the ladder, struggled to climb. Falling back, he threw himself against the wall, nails clawing the sheer sides as though he could scramble to the garret window and slash to pieces whatever was hidden above. Again he fell back, and this time his heavy body struck the ladder with tremendous force. It teetered, then plunged backward over the parapet. Thunder drowned the crash of its striking below.

Galvanized by Viking's action, I ran back to the stairway door and beat on the panel. "Help! Help!" I knew no one could hear, yet I cried out until my voice failed. Huddling behind the parapet, I sheltered myself as best I could. Viking's barks had changed to long howls of frustration, but I hardly heard him as a half-sleep of exhaustion settled over me. I could not tell how many hours passed, knowing only that it seemed an eternity.

Then a sound . . . an opening door? And a flood of light.

"Poupée? Alors, mon enfant!"

Vaguely I realized that Tante Emma, flashlight in hand, stood in the doorway. I tried to answer, but no sound came. She stepped toward me, but Viking leaped between us, daring her to move an inch closer.

KWS. 85

I tried to say "Captain Lachance," not sure that my rasping voice was audible. Then I drifted into a dream, puzzled that my bed was so hard and cold, wondering why the roof leaked. Had Tante Emma actually been there? I did not know. Next Pierre was speaking my name, lifting me in his arms. I felt the warmth and softness of my own bed. Voices confused me, but a man, I thought Pierre, spoke clearly: "A devil has done this."

As darkness enveloped me it seemed that Lady Judith stood beside the bed, mocking me with her painted smile.

FEVER DREAMS ASSAILED me. People came and went; I was given an injection by a doctor who asked me something, and perhaps I answered. Daylight faded and returned again, and I knew that Pierre, Thalia, Eunice and Regina often sat by my bed, but they were as unreal as the voice that forever called, "Ro-chelle . . . Ro-chelle . . ."

Once I thought Deirdre came. She was trying on my dresses, rejecting them, tossing them on the floor. "Stop it, Deirdre," I said, and she vanished, laughing.

Then I slept deeply, and awoke with complete clarity. I saw Regina sitting in the rocker crocheting.

"Good morning," I said, my voice hoarse. "Is it morning?"

"Sunday afternoon," she answered. "So you're awake at last." Coming to the bed, she sat on its edge. Her face looked worn and tired, but the fine features were smiling. "How are you, my dear?"

"I'm all right," I answered. "A bit weak."

"Food is what you need now." She turned the switch of a small electric kettle on the bedside table. "Hot consommé in a moment."

"How did Tante Emma happen to . . . ?" Speaking was a struggle, my throat still raw from an hour of shouting on the roof.

"Happen to find you? She kept dreaming of a howling dog, to her a sure sign of death, and awakened herself with fright. Then she realized the dog was real. Finally she discovered where the sound came from."

Regina poured the consommé into a cup. "She found you in the nick of time, too. You barely escaped pneumonia."

The broth tasted delicious. Regina refilled my cup, then said, "I'm surprised Pierre let Viking stay with you. He never lets that dog out of his sight. But then Pierre's not quite himself these days."

I gave her an inquiring look.

"He's tense. And I suspect he has told me a lie, which is unusual for him. I don't believe his house is rented. That was a pretext to stay at the Rising for a while." Regina frowned, perplexed. "If it were another man, I'd know it was an excuse to be near my beautiful niece. But you're not the type of girl Pierre usually pursues—or rather who pursues Pierre."

Regina rose. "I'll leave you now, Rochelle. We both need rest. Tante

Emma will bring you supper on a tray. Angélique has given notice. . . ."

She started to go, then turned back. "Theresa called from the abbey. She said you are not to worry about anything, she has you up her sleeve."

"Her sleeve?"

"In Benedictine jargon, she has been praying for you."

"How very kind."

"Theresa has no monopoly on communication with the Almighty. I spoke with Him myself soon after we found you."

She left quickly, a slight blush on her cheeks.

I AWOKE AGAIN a few hours later to a loud knock, and called, "Come in," expecting Tante Emma.

Pierre entered, Viking at his side. "I have brought your supper. Tante Emma is furious with me."

He carried a silver tray draped with a frilly cloth and adorned with sprigs of lilac. Pierre Lachance in his heavy boots, rough shirt and leather vest was incongruous as a waiter, and the decorated tray did not help matters. When I smiled, my chapped lips hurt and I was suddenly aware they were smeared with ointment. So were my cheeks and eyelids.

"Oui," he said pleasantly, "you look dreadful, but I have seen you worse than this—remember, I was on the Captain's Walk."

He set the tray beside me and sat down uncomfortably in the too-small rocking chair. Viking rested his muzzle on the bed, inspecting me.

"Eat first. Then tell me exactly why you were so foolish as to be on the Captain's Walk in a storm."

"Foolish? I'm not so stupid as to—" I hated the way my voice croaked, and did not appreciate his chuckle.

"Like a bullfrog," he said.

Tante Emma did not believe in starving an invalid, and at the end of the meal I felt amazingly stronger. I told the story, beginning with when I saw the figure I believed to be Madame Jeannette.

When I had finished, he shook his head. "You say Viking did not bark when you heard this voice. Such a thing is impossible."

"Then the impossible happened. The voice called my name, perhaps a dozen times. He paid no attention."

"The dog always barks. Could it have been a trick of the wind?"

"No, I heard every word. Plainly."

"It is not logical." Then he shrugged. "*Alors*, we must accept it."

"You don't believe me," I told him, suddenly weary.

"You are tired," he said softly. "We will talk no more for now."

"Thank you for bringing my supper."

"Ah, but I am a poor waiter. I am forgetting the tray." He suddenly smiled. "One last question, Rochelle. Who is this Scotsman you pine for?"

"Scotsman? What do you mean?"

"Perhaps not a Scotsman, but his name is Sandy. When you were feverish, his name was often on your lips. You called for him."

"So it is discovered," I said. "Sandy slept with me every night for years." I was pleased to see Pierre's surprise and then his frown.

"You are frank. Forgive me, I did not mean to pry."

"Sandy was a rag doll. His full name was Sandy-Panda."

Pierre smiled. "*Bien*. You are not so exhausted tonight, you are able to tease me." Then he became serious again. "I am going to tell everyone all you have said—the voice, the ladder, *tout*."

"They'll think I'm insane."

"That does not matter. Telling it will halt any further mischief for a time. *Bonne nuit,* Rochelle."

He left, seeming confident that all was well. But when Viking tried to follow, he commanded the dog to stay, and I noticed he tested the door from the outside to make sure it had locked.

CHAPTER EIGHT

I ENDURED THREE DAYS of bed rest, more than I thought necessary but the minimum Regina, Tante Emma and the village doctor would allow. One afternoon during this time Morgan visited me, and I did not enjoy telling my story again. "I suppose you think my imagination was running riot," I said.

"It is peculiar," Morgan said. "Viking is a superbly trained guard dog. Of course, there is one person he would ignore."

"Who?"

"Lachance himself, naturally."

My eyes widened. "Do you suggest—"

"I don't suggest. I merely wonder. You must know that Madame Jeannette was his mother-in-law, but do you know where she lives now?"

"No."

"On an abandoned farm near the firebreak. It's Lachance's house—it belonged to his family."

"Perhaps he'd find it awkward to evict her," I said.

Morgan got to his feet. "What's the use? You won't listen. Lachance has a way with women, they'll believe anything he tells them!"

"Perhaps you underestimate me," I said.

He paused. "I sound like a jealous rival, don't I? Well, perhaps that's the way I feel, Rochelle, and if it weren't for Dorothy . . ."

"But there is Dorothy," I said quickly. "She can hardly be forgotten."

His smile was rueful. "If you were a different type of woman, I'd say she could be forgotten easily. But you're not. Yet we both know that Dorothy will not recover, that it's only a matter of time. I can wait."

He left then, but what he had said haunted me.

On the morning following my enforced convalescence I went to Regina's rooms to say hello, but halted outside her open door when I heard her voice raised in anger.

". . . And I am telling you, Morgan, that I will brook no argument. Howard Palmer moves out of the guest cottage today. There are comfortable rooms in the house. He can use one."

"These servants you're importing from Montreal have a choice of twenty rooms here. It's unpardonable to push an old friend of the family around this way," said Morgan with considerable heat.

"Not a friend of the family, a friend of *yours*. I promised the Carltons a house of their own. They are coming to work here on that condition."

I left quickly, not from lack of curiosity but for fear that Morgan might storm out and find me eavesdropping. In the hall I met Palmer himself, whose beaming face revealed he had no hint of his coming eviction.

"You're looking marvelous, Rochelle," he said. "Completely recovered, eh? By the way, do you know if Captain Lachance is here?"

"I haven't seen him this morning."

"I'm buying a brace of hounds from this watchman who works for Morgan."

"Gilles?"

"Yes, that's the fellow, and I don't want trouble between these hounds and Lachance's dog. So I'll keep my dogs down at the cottage."

No, you won't, I thought, and escaped him to go outside.

LIFE AT THE Rising now began to flow as smoothly and evenly as the great river below us. But like the river, the house concealed deeper crosscurrents following their own hidden channels.

Regina and I were absorbed in preparations for Saint John's Eve. A seamstress from the city was installed on the second floor, creating costumes Regina had designed. "Everyone, including the servants, is to appear in seventeenth- or eighteenth-century dress," she decreed. "French, English or Canadian."

Mr. and Mrs. Carlton, now occupying the guest cottage, were marvels at handling domestic chores. Joseph Carlton was tall and bony, with an equine face. His wife, Marjory, seemed to match. "If only they stay!" Regina remarked, looking heavenward imploringly.

At times thoughts of Deirdre bothered me, but I kept assuring myself the police would soon find her. And during those days there was little opportunity for brooding. Regina seemed to be everywhere at once, directing and organizing, bargaining with caterers from the city. On the morning of June 23, a few hours before guests were expected, she inspected me critically while I was trying on my costume, an Evangeline outfit. "That costume is perfect," she declared.

"I hadn't realized Evangeline was the wealthiest girl in Canada," I said. The full, ruffled skirt was a dazzling rainbow of rich embroidery.

"Another thing," I remarked. "If Evangeline had been this décolleté, she would have been chased out of Nova Scotia." The neckline of the elegant blouse plunged dangerously close to the top of the laced bodice.

"Perfect," Regina repeated. "And the lace cap is like gossamer, but push it back a bit. We don't want to hide your hair."

"This is a party, Aunt Regina, not an exhibition."

"All parties are exhibitions. I want to show off my niece."

I changed into a modern beige-and-white suit in time to greet guests arriving for a garden-party luncheon. Regina performed introductions, and several people spoke warmly of my mother, with no implications or questions. I soon lost track of which name fitted which person in this curiously assorted group whose ages ranged from twenty to seventy-odd.

"Look over there," said Regina, lowering her voice. "The blonde with too much mascara is Sonia Kerr from Montreal. In wild pursuit of Pierre, as usual. I never cared for that girl."

"Then why did you invite her?"

"So Pierre could bask in some feminine admiration for a change." She gave me a look that I ignored.

That evening, gay in our costumes and harlequin masks, we all drove to the village for the torchlight pageant. Afterward we would return to the Rising for dancing and supper.

Julien Clouet, a young surgeon from Beauport who appointed himself my escort, seemed much too serious to be wearing the striped doublet and hose of a court dandy. "I am not the type for costumes," he said. "But later, with enough cariboo inside me, I promise to be festive."

"Cariboo?"

"A mixture of red wine and white alcohol. It is the world's most delicious dynamite."

A bystander handed Julien a tall white cane and gave him an inviting nod. "Observe," Julien said. "I pull off the top and it becomes a four-foot drinking flask. *À votre santé!*" He lifted the cane to his lips and took a long swallow, then offered me a drink.

I shook my head. "I'll wait for champagne at the Rising, thanks."

The cariboo seemed to have instantaneous effect. He put his arm around my waist and sighed contentedly. "A beautiful night, a beautiful girl, a beautiful place. I am glad my father's plans to buy River Rising for a hotel did not succeed. Otherwise, I would not be here at this party."

"For a hotel? Did Regina refuse?"

"She ordered him out. A formidable lady!"

We laughed together as the formidable lady herself, stunning in gold brocade, moved regally through the crowd.

"Several persons here lost fortunes because of that lady's refusal to sell," Julien said. "The land behind the Rising is of little value now. But combined with the main house and gardens as a winter resort, its worth would go up five times, maybe ten times."

"You mean Morgan's land?"

"Mostly Morgan's, but Eunice Armitage owns land, too, and the older servants have been given small pieces."

I realized there must have been bitter resentment of Regina's stand against selling, yet no one had shown a trace of it. At River Rising, I thought, matters were seldom what they seemed.

WHEN WE RETURNED to the château, the sprawling building twinkled with candles and lanterns, an enchanted world. I was now delighted that Regina had not allowed me to be too demure an Evangeline. In the ballroom, a buckskin-clad Pierre Lachance saluted me, Sonia Kerr clinging to his arm. I found myself whirled away first by Julien Clouet, then captured by a swarthy pirate afloat on cariboo. Morgan, transformed into a husky peasant in a Breton smock, rescued me.

"Enjoying yourself?" he asked.

"Yes. This is the way the Rising should always be."

Just as I spoke the ballroom doors banged shut, and a hundred candles flickered in a sudden gust of wind, some of their flames vanishing.

"I like this better," said Morgan. "Dim and romantic."

As the music quickened he spun me away. When I whirled back, Pierre Lachance had moved between us.

"Permit me, Morgan. I must have this dance."

We were off before Morgan could reply. "Did Miss Kerr sprain an ankle?" I asked.

"Who cares what Miss Kerr sprains? Come, we are leaving."

"Leaving? I certainly am not. I've just begun dancing."

"This is important. For once no argument, please."

The urgency of his tone silenced me. We danced through the ballroom doors, then we hurried up the stairs. "We have an experiment to perform," he said in a low voice. "Quickly! The wind is rising now, but if it dies we must wait for it. Days could pass."

When we reached my room, he said, "Go through the nursery and up the stairs to the Captain's Walk. Open the door, but do not go outside."

I felt gooseflesh rise on my arms as I mounted the stairway. When I opened the door at the top, the creaking hinges were a terrible reminder. I was happy to stand back and wait.

Outside, the wind was not so strong as on that other night, but powerful enough to bang shutters and rattle windows. Suddenly I felt a rush of air, and the door in front of me slammed violently.

I was still staring at it, unbelieving, when Pierre hurried up the stairs, his face aglow with triumph. "I do know something about winds and air currents, after all," he said.

"What did you do? The door was hardly moving, then—"

"Simple, and the effect, you will agree, seems supernatural. I had only to open the door from your room to the corridor, and *voilà!* An updraft strong enough to slam the door. Also, to lock it. The safety catch on the lock is old and worn. Or perhaps it has been loosened." His look of victory turned grim. "Someone knows this little trick and has put it to use."

"But I locked the door to the corridor earlier that evening."

Pierre shrugged. "So our mischief-maker has a key." He led me into my room. "Sit down, Rochelle. Do you now see what may have happened?"

I nodded slowly. "You think someone opened the door to the Captain's Walk, knowing the noise of the hinges would make me go to close it. Then he went to the corridor outside my room and . . ." I stopped, frowning. "No, there wasn't time."

"Then think of two mischief-makers. Call them Rooftop and Corridor. They must have a way of signaling each other. Once Rooftop lures you onto the Captain's Walk, a sign is given and Corridor unlocks your door to create the draft. Then you are trapped outside."

"But why?" I demanded, shuddering at the memory. "What could anyone gain by it? It was pointless and mad."

Pierre walked the length of the room and back, seeming to make a decision. Then he drew a chair close to mine and spoke quietly. "As you say, it was mad. Yet not pointless. The mischief-makers are real, and they failed. The great harm intended for you did not take place."

I swallowed. "Great harm? You mean someone intended my death?"

"You must at least suspect that. Then you will be on guard."

His voice compelled belief. It could have taken place as he said, yet there was no evidence that it had. My whole self rebelled at the notion that at least two people hated me enough to go to such lengths as murder.

"There is simply no reason for anyone to do me serious harm," I said. "Someone might want to drive me away, of course. But beyond that—"

"*Must* you be blind and stubborn? What if Regina decided to change her will? She is fond of you, she is rich. That would be a serious loss to Morgan and Eunice." His lips twisted in a saturnine smile. "And to me. She has said I am to have a small legacy. Maybe you endanger it."

"That's ridiculous. Regina has no intention of giving me anything at the expense of people she has known and loved for years."

"You are quite sure you don't stand between me and a fortune?"

Watching his face, I could not tell where mockery stopped and seriousness began. "I expect nothing from Regina," I said, "and she's a long way from dying." I rose, wanting to shake off the doubts he had caused in me. "Maybe someone worked my entrapment on the Captain's Walk, as you said. But it remains only a cruel trick."

"We are changing the locks on both of those doors. Not to do so would be madness." He stepped toward me, angry frustration in his face. "Will you not understand that nothing more serious happened because of Viking? No one knew he would be with you, and no one can stand against him except with a gun. But using a gun would spoil the effect of the accident that was planned for you. Rochelle, remember that ladder!"

"I never would have climbed it."

"The ladder was there for someone else to descend."

I imagined myself alone on the Captain's Walk, without Viking. I pictured a figure climbing silently down from the attic window, moving toward me, reaching out. "No," I said. "No." Faintly I heard the orchestra. My voice trembled. "Should we go back to the party?"

"I am not sure. There are too many masks, too many strangers."

"That's ridiculous." I fluffed out my skirt. "I intend to enjoy myself."

He stood barring the door. "I see I must protect you from your own rashness."

"And how will you do that?" I demanded.

Reaching out, he drew me close to him. "You will be with me every moment. Tonight *I* will be your only danger."

I looked up at his hard, weathered features, the fullness of the firm mouth. The embrace brought a flush to my cheeks, and feeling the response of my blood, I knew Pierre was right. I *was* in danger.

THE NEXT DAY I proved little help to Regina in returning the house to order. Pierre's demonstration of how my entrapment on the roof might have been accomplished preoccupied me. More than ever I felt sure it was Madame Jeannette I had seen from the window that night. Dorothy, I decided, could verify this. A little before noon I tapped on her door.

"Come in," she called. Dorothy sat propped against the pillows, a writing board in her lap. I was shocked at how wasted she looked, the hollowness of her face grotesquely emphasized by the blond wig she wore. "Excuse me, I'm just finishing an important letter," she said.

She added another line, signed her name, then folded the sheet and put it in an envelope. She addressed it in a shaky hand to Mr. Howard Palmer.

"I want Howard to see me today," she said. "I need his help. They are planning to send me away."

"Who is?"

"Morgan, Regina . . . all of them," she said vaguely.

"If you're sent away, it will be to a sanatorium for your own good," I said. "You need more care than you can be given here."

"You'd like to see me gone, it would give you a free hand with Morgan." When I ignored this, she went on, "I heard you met with an unfortunate experience on the roof."

"Yes." I decided to try a simple trap. "It happened the night Madame Jeannette told your special fortune."

"Yes. She said it would be an unlucky night for you. Her dead daughter's spirit spoke through the tarot cards. She asked for vengeance."

"Vengeance on me?"

"Of course." Dorothy leaned forward. "You don't believe in the ghosts of River Rising, do you, Rochelle? The only reason Regina invited you here was because of the ghosts. She was afraid, she needed help."

"Tell me about it, Dorothy," I said softly.

Dorothy's voice fell to a whispered chant. "Justine, Monique, Céleste. They were servants who left here because of the ghosts. Regina was faced with closing River Rising, and Morgan begged her to sell it, but she refused. I could hear them shouting." Dorothy's whisper was almost inaudible. "If she sold the Rising, Morgan would be rich. . . ."

The thin voice trailed into silence. I remembered my conversation at the dance with Julien Clouet.

"Last year Regina saw herself for what she is," Dorothy resumed. "A helpless, lonely old woman. And frightened. What if Morgan went away and persuaded Madame Sud to leave? He could, you know. There would be only Regina and Eunice and Tante Emma. Three old women alone in this house! Then she learned where you were. The long-lost niece."

"So she invited me to River Rising," I said slowly.

"She thought you would change things. She talked about having a young person here, a member of the family. Everyone knows Regina has promised you a fortune if you'll stay. She needs you. But it won't succeed. River Rising will destroy you just as it destroyed your father."

Her eyelids fluttered. "I'm tired. Will you take my letter to Howard?"

"Of course."

"Howard could make Morgan change his mind about sending me to a hospital. Howard has great influence on Morgan." She saw my expression of disbelief. "You think Howard isn't important. How little you know!"

When I left, my feeling of pity was almost unbearable. Not just for Dorothy, but for Morgan and, above all, for Thalia.

Howard Palmer now had rooms somewhere on the second floor of the west wing, an area of the house not familiar to me. The corridor was deserted. I wondered which of the dozen doors was Howard's. One stood half open, and I heard voices. I had no intention of eavesdropping, but Howard Palmer's tone and words were so surprising that I stood listening.

"You're a fool, Morgan. Every day she stays here adds to the danger."

"I know. But what more can I do?"

"Stop being weak! She has to be taken care of properly."

It seemed impossible that the speaker was Howard Palmer. His voice had a ring of command, almost contempt, while Morgan sounded defeated. Dorothy was right, I thought. They were planning to send her away.

I must have taken an unconscious step backward, for a floorboard creaked loudly, and there was instant silence inside the room.

"Hello," I called quickly. "It's Rochelle."

The door was flung wide. Howard Palmer, face white and tense, confronted me. Across the room stood Morgan.

"I have a letter from Dorothy," I said, awkward at having been caught listening. "I'm sorry. I couldn't help overhearing you."

"Yes?" Palmer's face was set, masklike.

"This letter is about what you were just saying," I told him. "Dorothy knows she is going to be sent away. I just came from her room."

"Really? Come in, my dear." The tone was suddenly genial, deferential. Palmer had undergone an instant change of personality.

He closed the door carefully. I handed him the envelope, which he took without speaking. The silence made me uneasy, and I said, "You're quite right about Dorothy's needing proper care. It's not my affair, but I was startled when I saw her."

For a moment neither man spoke, then Palmer nodded slowly. "I'm glad you agree. I was talking sternly to Morgan about it."

"I should go to Dorothy," said Morgan, and left quickly.

Palmer consulted his watch. "And you and I, my dear, are late for lunch. May I escort you?" He offered his arm with mock formality, and I had no choice but to take it. As I touched him I felt I was touching a chameleon.

CHAPTER NINE

I SAT IN THE parlor at Clarendon Abbey, looking through the grille into the tranquil face of Dame Theresa Armitage.

At River Rising the weeks of quiet had continued; Pierre's mischief-makers, if they really existed, remained inactive. But for me there had been little peace. Thoughts of two men created havoc with my feelings.

First, there was Pierre. I at last admitted to myself that I longed to be near him. No man had ever aroused such feelings in me, but my mind told me that this attraction would lead only to unhappiness.

Then there was my father, present in the portrait I kept hidden. The secret of his survival had become too much for me. I had to talk to someone.

"Aunt Theresa, this parlor is like a confessional, isn't it?" I asked haltingly. "I mean, things discussed here are private."

"Yes," she answered. "But, dear child, even if they were not, I trust you would rely on me. You can, you know."

This was true. I could trust her for wisdom as well as for silence.

"Jean-Paul Dumont did not die," I began, the words tumbling out. And the bars between us seemed to vanish. . . . "So you see, Aunt Theresa," I said, nearing the story's end, "I cannot accept my father in the role of murderer. He was too kind, too gentle. I'll never rest until I know the truth."

Dame Theresa studied me thoughtfully. "Are you searching for the truth," she asked, "or merely to confirm an illusion you cherish?"

"Why, the truth. There isn't any illusion. I *knew* my father."

Reaching through the grille, she took my hands in hers. "Rochelle, you must face facts. Jean-Paul, in his youth, was a violent man, especially when he had been drinking. He could be cruel even to Charlotte." I tried to protest, but she silenced me. "Your mother herself told me. She forgave him because she knew he could never forgive himself. Often he did not realize what he was doing, did not remember afterward. Then he was truly sorry.

"To take the life of another human being is a fearful act. Is it not possible that after François' death, remorse changed your father? Perhaps you have witnessed the miracle of conversion."

"People don't change that much," I said. "For instance, my father never touched liquor, not even a glass of wine."

"That is precisely what I mean, Rochelle. Suffering altered his life. I assure you he drank in Ste. Marie du Lac. I was an eyewitness."

I glanced at her in surprise.

"Yes." She smiled faintly. "At the time François was killed, I was too ill to know anything. But I must tell you of something that happened that summer. I avoided this matter when you came before, because it involves things that should be discussed only within the abbey. You see . . ."

She had lived at the Abbey four and a half years, she told me, and the time for her Solemn Profession, her vows to remain for life, was rapidly approaching. "I looked forward to that day with happiness that was far too mystical. Such fervor gives a dangerous, shaky foundation."

Her troubles began on August 13, her birthday. "As a child I always had presents and a party, and the foolish notion of being a 'birthday girl' had never quite left me. At the abbey the day passed unnoticed. I felt neglected. Nothing serious, but it was the start of what we call 'monsoons,' a violent wind that shakes your emotions and won't stop blowing."

That night she was unable to sleep, unable to pray. The abbey, which she had loved, became a prison. The next day brought no relief, and when evening came she was frantic. "It was late and I should have been sleeping. Instead, I slipped out to the garden." Memories of the outside world swept over her, tidal waves of loneliness that carried her almost unconsciously to a small gate at the rear of the garden. "Then I was outside and running. It was like a dream, the Rising just ahead, tall in the moonlight. I thought, If only I can reach it, I will be well again."

As she entered the garden of River Rising the spell suddenly broke. "I was horrified, I couldn't imagine why I had done this. Bewildered, I started to turn back. It was then I saw your father. He was lying on a long wooden bench. My position was mortifying. I would have fled, but he called out your mother's name. I thought he must be ill, so I went and spoke to him."

I saw the end of the story. "But he wasn't ill," I said.

"No." Dame Theresa hesitated. "In charity we should call him ill. He seemed to be half awake, yet not really conscious. It seemed wrong to leave him there. Clouds were gathering, rain was coming. I shook his shoulder, but couldn't rouse him. What a preposterous situation it was!"

She paused, and a note of ironic humor came into her voice. "You might say I was saved by the bell. It was the eve of Assumption Day, and at that moment the huge bell here rang for midnight to proclaim the feast. That bell was a command telling me where my duty lay. I started back to the abbey, and a few minutes later rain began to pour, a rain like ice. I came down with pneumonia, and I'm surprised Jean-Paul didn't."

"You never saw him again?" I asked.

"No. I was ill and in the hospital in Quebec City for several months. When I returned, François was dead, Charlotte had left. It was all over."

"Not quite all over. My father was very much alive." Unwillingly I added, "A changed man, as you said. I have to recognize that. Aunt Theresa, should I tell the truth? That he survived?"

The nun hesitated. "You raise a question of conscience, Rochelle. Duty does not require you to tell all you know. And you might injure three men who, I suspect, turned out to be loyal friends to your mother and father."

"What men? I don't understand."

She leaned toward me. "Morgan, of course, and Morgan's friend, whose name I do not remember. Then there is Captain Lachance."

"But how should my speaking injure them?"

"They were the witnesses to your father's plunge to the river. I remember those cliffs. Only a miracle could have saved him." Her lips were drawn in an ironic curve. "Miracles are part of my faith. But this particular miracle arouses my skepticism. Either Jean-Paul took wings or three men lied to cover his escape. Which is easier to believe?"

Just then there came a sharp knock at the door behind Dame Theresa. Turning in surprise, she called, *"Deo gratias."*

A frightened novice stepped in. *"Benedicite,"* she gasped. "Oh, Dame, forgive me, but the Lady Abbess is very ill and calling you."

Dame Theresa's cheeks paled. "I'll come at once."

THERE WAS A CARVED STONE BENCH outside the abbey, and pausing there, I considered my interrupted conversation. Little as I liked admitting it, Jean-Paul Dumont had been no saint. I remembered the nun's words: "Your mother forgave him because she knew he could never forgive himself."

Dame Theresa, in her wisdom, had discerned a truth that reconciled wild young Jean-Paul Dumont with gentle Paul LaFarge. Also, she had seen the most reasonable explanation for my father's miraculous escape. Morgan, Pierre and Howard Palmer had all lied, all helped him.

I heard the sound of a motor and, looking up, saw Pierre's jeep approaching, Viking sitting proudly in the rear seat behind his master.

"*Bonjour!*" Pierre called. "I thought you might like to ride back."

"Thank you," I said, distracted, yet delighted he had thought of me.

"You are too quiet," he said after we had driven a few minutes. "What troubles you? Some words of Dame Theresa?"

"Partly. Pierre, can a man's character change completely?"

"How many times?" he asked lightly.

"Please, I'm serious."

"So am I. As a boy I was the village roughneck. They pointed me out as gallows bait. Then I changed—"

"You passed the turn to the Rising," I said.

"I know. I want you to see my house, my bit of land."

We crossed the covered bridge, drove a mile or two toward the river, then turned sharply left onto a side road hidden by birches. When we came to another bridge, a small one of logs, he halted the jeep.

"Look upstream. My waterfall, not Niagara, but my own. We will pause here. The house is just beyond." He gave Viking a command. The dog leaped out and went across the bridge. "When Madame Gallet sees Viking, she will know I am coming soon, and coffee will be ready."

"Madame Gallet is your housekeeper?"

"What else?" he asked, his expression elaborately innocent. After a moment he said quietly, "You asked if a man changes. When I fell in love with Giselle Massine, I must have been different. . . ." He shook his head as though what had happened was beyond comprehension. "I knew she belonged to François Armitage, that she would marry him on her eighteenth birthday. I hated François, and I hated myself for feeling as I did. I owed him much—and repaid him by taking part of what was his."

"Did she love him?" I asked.

Pierre shrugged. "She loved the dream of the château . . . does it matter whether she loved the man or the dream? They came to the same thing." The knuckles of his hands showed white as he gripped the steering wheel. "For me it was a summer of agony. The joy of Giselle's kisses at night, then guilt when I saw François. When he was killed, I thought the guilt had ended, but it had only begun. I blamed myself for being pleased by my rival's death, happy that Giselle could belong to me. *Mon dieu,* what a childish illusion! François was dead, but Giselle's dream was not."

"Yet she married you," I said.

"Only when other ambitions had failed. Twice she left me for rich men's promises. In the end . . ." He did not need to finish. I knew the end.

Pierre turned his gaze full upon me, a vein throbbing in his temple but his features the unyielding flint I knew too well. "Does a man change?"

"You were a boy then, you were—"

"A boy in the beginning, very much a man at the end. I cannot now recognize the fool who wept openly at Giselle's funeral in the suicides' field."

I found no words for a moment, then I said, "The fool, the young man who wept . . . I like him. I wish we could meet one day."

He nodded. "I wish so, too." Then he started the jeep and drove ahead.

PIERRE'S HOUSE, BUILT of sand-colored stone and heavy timbers, stood on a shelf of land above the broad river. Madame Gallet greeted me with an air of surprise that made me think that if *le Capitaine*, as she called him, had as many affairs as gossip claimed, they must be conducted away from home.

The living room, where Madame Gallet served us coffee and slices of fresh-baked bread, held the fragrance of pine smoke, and I liked the leathery comfort of the chairs facing the hearth. One wall was lined with books and hand-carved models of clipper ships.

"I built part of the house myself," Pierre told me. "There is pleasure in living with what one has made."

"Your tenants keep it in beautiful condition," I said with a smile.

"Very good condition," he agreed, lifting an eyebrow.

After Madame Gallet had left us, Pierre said, "You must forgive me the scene at the bridge. I usually keep firmer control of myself."

"Perhaps you brood too much about the past."

"Good advice, Rochelle. I give it back to you."

"At River Rising the present and the past are always hand in hand." I put down my coffee cup. "Pierre, tell me about that night."

"The night François died? There is little to tell. I had been in the village. I walked back to the Rising very late. I lived there then, François had given me a room. There was some moonlight, but I carried my electric torch because I was near the cliff edge. I heard a terrible shout and a crash of wood. When I looked toward the studio porch, I saw Jean-Paul falling."

"How could you be sure?"

"I saw the flash of his yellow raincoat, a special coat that reflected light. There was no other like it in the village." He studied me, puzzled. "I do not understand. I speak of your father's death and it does not sadden you. Instead, you look relieved."

"I'm glad he didn't suffer."

Pierre accepted this, but his look was doubtful. I could not explain yet that he had lifted a burden by telling the truth. He had seen a falling raincoat, perhaps with something inside it, but nothing more. He had played no part in helping my father escape. The truth, if it became known, could not harm Pierre. Only two witnesses left, Morgan and Howard Palmer.

As we were leaving to return to the Rising, Pierre was called back inside to the telephone. I could hear explosions of provincial profanity. He came out scowling. "*Sacrebleu! L'Étoile Filante!* Will I never be free of that floating carnival? If Captain McCabe's pleurisy is to continue until the ice sets in, he should find someone else to take his place."

"Can't you refuse?" I asked.

"Not easily. McCabe's an old friend. He gave me my first command."

Viking, with a flying leap, took his accustomed place in the jeep. Getting in, I said, "It's a pity you feel that way about the ship. In spite of Deirdre, for me it was a beautiful voyage. One I'll always remember."

"It is not the ship but the people." He hesitated, his hand on the ignition key, then smiled. "If you enjoy it so much, why not come with me?"

I froze, unable to say, "Because I am afraid of my own emotions, because you could hurt me deeply."

"Why not?" he repeated.

This time it was a challenge. I hesitated only a moment. "How can I go with you?" I said quietly. "You haven't asked me."

"It is settled," he said, starting the motor. "We start for Montreal at five tomorrow morning."

As we crossed the bridge the great bell of the abbey sounded, telling the village that the Lady Abbess of Clarendon now rested in death.

OVER THE NEXT two weeks I learned what it must be like to be sixteen years old—and happy. I danced every night, and Pierre, to the astonishment of the crew, joined me. On deck I found myself chatting with complete strangers, boasting of the beauties of Quebec as if I had spent my life on this river. "I've turned into a magpie," I confessed to Pierre. "I can't help it. I have to make everyone realize how glorious all this is."

He smiled. "You make me see things for the first time again."

One day he took my hand and we stood at the rail as River Rising loomed into view. "Do you see the flag among the trees?" he said.

"Yes. A fleur-de-lis."

"That is my house. Look just below—you'll see a patch of water where the stream joins the river. To me this is the most beautiful place in the world. Much that I love is here."

That evening, anchored in the ancient port of Gaspé, Pierre said, "I've had news from home. I have talked with Regina. Dame Theresa Armitage has been elected Lady Abbess of Clarendon."

"The nuns chose wisely. What else did Regina say?"

"Dorothy Armitage has entered a private hospital."

New passengers boarded at Gaspé the next morning. As the ship turned back up the river Pierre dominated my thoughts. At supper that night in his cabin he said, "You are serious and far away from me this evening."

"I was dreaming." I flushed. "Wishing these days would go on forever, that River Rising and everything connected with it would vanish."

"All voyages end," he told me gravely. "Besides, you know you must return. There will be no peace or safety until you are sure about certain matters, until you know what happened to Deirdre Cameron."

"Deirdre!" I said sharply. "I've put her out of my mind. I want only to forget her."

He got up and stood beside my chair. "Do you think I invented tenants for my house and moved into the Rising without reasons? The day we talked with Brad Copeland, I decided you had both courage and honesty. Also, I was very attracted to you."

"Pierre, I—"

"Listen to me. I came to the Rising because I believed you were in danger. No one in Ste. Marie du Lac has ever seen you except as a tiny child, no one could recognize you. At the Montreal airport your name is spoken over a microphone—and who answers? A girl your age wearing a shawl Regina has sent to her niece. At the desk she claims a large, brightly colored envelope, an object anyone watching can see at a distance."

"I asked Regina about the envelope," I said. "She did not send it."

"No. Let me continue. Rochelle Dumont has now been identified. And what happens to this supposed Rochelle? Within hours she nearly meets with a fatal accident. The next night she disappears." His voice hardened. "Early the following morning there is a burglary at River Rising, a thing that has never happened before. Do you not see that wherever Rochelle Dumont goes, strange things take place?"

Pierre bent over me, holding my shoulders, gazing into my face. "You must return to the Rising. One cannot run away from an unknown enemy and live forever in doubt. The ways of making mischief at the Rising are limited. But if you leave, the possibilities for harm are endless."

For a moment fear held me, then I broke free of it. "I will not be afraid," I said. "And I will never run away."

Then his lips were pressed against mine.

THE FOLLOWING WEEK when I saw the old château mellowed by the end-of-summer sun, my apprehensions lessened. Aunt Regina welcomed me fondly, and Tante Emma served me a huge slab of cake she had baked for my arrival. Eunice greeted me with a vague kiss, then inquired coyly about the voyage. When I proved unresponsive, she turned to the subject of

Dorothy. "At least she's where the care is excellent. An invalid simply can't remain in a place as remote as the Rising."

"Are Thalia and Morgan with her?"

"Thalia left for a school near Montreal yesterday. She said she'll write you a letter every week. Imagine, having to answer all those letters! Morgan's here, preparing for an exhibition on the first of October in Ottawa. It's quite special. Even the Prime Minister will be attending!"

I was relieved to learn that Morgan was home. It had become imperative now that I talk with him.

"Oh, Rochelle," Eunice went on. "You missed the most hair-raising experience. Two nights after you left, all the service bells in the house began ringing all at once. And at the stroke of midnight! It was the exact anniversary, down to the moment, of François' death. Uncanny! Regina was shaken, and even Morgan seemed upset." She stopped abruptly. "Oh, I've brought up a subject painful to you."

"Not at all," I said honestly. "The past no longer disturbs me."

Later when I had tea with Regina, the bell-ringing incident was mentioned calmly. "It's what you expect from antique wiring," she said. "But I admit the timing was odd. Mr. Carlton found the electrical short and stopped the ringing." Regina appeared to concentrate on her teacup, then said, "About Pierre Lachance. I hope you're behaving wisely."

"I am not."

She smiled thinly. "Then I hope you're behaving well." She shifted the subject. "I took the liberty of accepting an invitation for you. If it's not agreeable, you can invent an excuse. Theresa wants you to spend next weekend at the abbey guest house. I have an impression she's very fond of you. I hope to heaven she isn't trying to recruit you."

"Small danger," I said, smiling. "I'll be delighted to go."

Morgan did not join us for supper, but after the meal I found him writing letters in the small library. He looked up at me inquiringly.

"I want to ask about a miracle," I said. "One that involves a man plunging over a cliff, then reappearing in Antigua quite undamaged. In fact, he enjoyed perfect health for ten years."

Morgan crossed to the door and closed it, then returned to his chair at the desk. "So you know," he said calmly. "Have you always known?"

"No. I learned it recently. I saw a picture of my father."

"Is that all?"

"All?" I stared at him, astonished. "Quite enough, isn't it?"

"I'm glad you've found out," he answered, thoughtful but unruffled. "I hope the truth will bring us closer together, Rochelle. As you've guessed, Howard and I lied to the police. We didn't want to, and Jean-Paul intended to stay and face his punishment."

"Then why did you lie?"

"For Charlotte. She heard the argument, arrived too late to prevent what happened and became hysterical. She said she wouldn't be parted from her husband, threatened suicide, and at last we gave in." Morgan sighed with deep weariness. "We were foolish, I think. But we were also very young, and in different ways, each of us loved Charlotte."

He rose and rested against the desk, looking older than I had ever seen him. "We hid Jean-Paul in an attic, then lied our heads off. He waited until the police were satisfied because there was a chance that Howard or I might be accused. In my case, it was a near thing."

"They suspected you?"

"They did indeed," he said bitterly. "Andrew Armitage was my father by adoption. He was fond of me, but he didn't think painters were to be trusted with money. In his will he gave François control of everything."

"So the police thought you had a motive and suspected you?"

"Yes. But people knew Jean-Paul's character, and there were his fingerprints on the hammer. So he didn't have to come forward and rescue me. When it was safe, we helped smuggle your father out of the country."

Morgan's telling of the story touched feelings deep within me.

"That isn't quite all," he said. "I worried about them, so I saw Jean-Paul about two years later."

"You came to Antigua?" I asked, astonished.

"Oh, no. That would have been much too risky. We met on St. Kitts, and I learned that Jean-Paul was having a hard struggle. He was too proud to accept money from me, so I persuaded my Toronto dealer to take a few of his paintings, but it didn't work out. I wish I'd been able to help."

Moving to him, I impulsively grasped his hand. "Thank you, Morgan. For giving my mother and father those added years, for giving me a chance to know my father. The secret is safe with me."

I went quickly to my room, ashamed of the suspicions I had harbored about Morgan and Howard Palmer. I could never like Howard, but both he and Morgan had taken great risks for my parents.

Only the three of us know the real truth, I told myself as I gazed down at the dark river before drawing the draperies. Then an annoying saying crossed my mind: "Three can keep a secret if two of them are dead."

I WAS PLAYING the harpsichord one afternoon the following week, and Viking lay on the carpet near me—a reminder that I had hardly seen Pierre since we had come back—when Howard Palmer entered the room. The dog growled a warning.

Howard was carrying a tape recorder. "How appropriate that I found you playing, Rochelle," he said. "Listen to this."

Beaming, he turned on the machine, and I heard a Mozart gigue. After a few measures I realized this was a recording of my own playing, made without my knowledge on a day when I was certainly not at my best.

"Brilliant!" Howard said. "I caught exactly the right selection."

"When did you . . ." The notion of a concealed recorder bothered me.

"I find electronics a fascinating hobby," he said. "I thought you would be more relaxed if you weren't aware a tape was being made. No doubt you have heard of Arturo Baroni?"

"No, I don't think so."

"He's an outstanding impresario who handles concert bookings all over the world. When I heard you play, I thought at once of Baroni, who is an old friend of mine. So I made this tape and sent him a copy."

"Really, you shouldn't have!" I felt painfully embarrassed at the thought of an expert listening to the music I had just heard.

"Baroni telephoned me an hour ago!" exclaimed Howard. "He's very impressed! He wants you to come to New York to audition."

"But that's impossible!"

"Not impossible, not even difficult, my dear. He guarantees expenses."

I stared at him, dumbfounded. Anyone who plays music seriously longs to believe in the gift of a major talent, but I knew the mediocrity of this performance. Mr. Baroni was either a swindler or a devoted friend repaying Howard Palmer for some past favor.

"It's impossible," I repeated.

"I understand how you feel," Howard went on. "You are afraid of failure. But there's no need for anyone to know *why* you are going to New York. If Baroni does not offer anything, only you and I—"

"Please! Howard, such miracles simply do not happen. It would take me months of practicing to prepare, even assuming I have an ability."

"Out of the question!" Palmer's smile faded. "Baroni leaves for Europe at the end of the week. You must go tomorrow or the next day. You disappoint me, Rochelle. I've gone to considerable trouble to arrange this."

"Not at my request!"

He changed tactics. "This came as a surprise to you. I'm sure you'll reconsider, but don't delay too long. Such a chance may not come again."

After he had left, I sat with my fingers resting on the silent keyboard. "I don't believe it," I said half aloud. There was probably some person named Baroni connected with music, but Howard's story seemed highly unlikely. I knew from Morgan that he had been kind to my parents. No doubt he was trying to be kind to me. My distrust of him was more instinctive than logical, but it persisted.

I HEARD A confusion of voices in the entrance hall the next morning, and then Regina calling my name. "Rochelle, come quickly!"

When I got there I saw two men from the village standing in the hall. "Your trunk has arrived from Antigua!" Regina exclaimed.

"There's no reason for excitement," I said, smiling. "It's only a few clothes, some books. Odds and ends. I wrote asking that it be sent here."

"Then the men can take it to my sitting room and I'll help you unpack it there. No need for them to climb all those stairs if most of the things in it are for the storeroom."

Unpacking took us only a few minutes. The trunk was hardly half full, and I wondered why I had bothered to keep most of its contents.

I thought Regina blinked back tears as she examined a photograph of my mother. I took a dozen treasured books from the trunk, then, like Regina, felt a tear in my eye as I touched two childhood gifts made for me by the man I now knew was my father.

Sandy-Panda, the garishly striped rag doll, had survived the years well, and when I placed him gently on the couch his painted grin seemed as friendly as ever. Then I paused to examine the last item in the trunk, a child's coloring book. The book had been a present for my fourth or fifth birthday. I had lacked the patience to fill the outlines with crayon, so Jean-Paul Dumont had done it for me, and in the margins had made whimsical sketches of me. As I put the book beside Sandy-Panda I realized that Regina was staring at the rag doll, a puzzled frown on her face.

"Did that belong to Charlotte?" she asked.

"No. It was made for me when I was about five years old," I told her.

She seized Sandy-Panda, scrutinizing the cloth animal with a strange intensity. "It's a copy of another toy. It has to be!"

"Sandy is a complete original. In fact, an improvisation. I remember the day he was stitched together and painted."

She seemed not to comprehend. "That's impossible. . . ." Picking up the coloring book, she leafed silently through the pages.

"Aunt Regina, dear, it was my father who drew the sketches for me, and he who made Sandy-Panda." Regardless of my promise to Morgan, Regina had to know the truth. "Jean-Paul did not die that night. He escaped, and lived in the islands near my mother for many years."

Regina's face turned chalky white. "How could he?" The words were whispered. "There were witnesses. Morgan and Howard swore that—" She suddenly raised her hands as though to ward off a blow. "Don't tell me any more. I don't want to know." She took an uncertain step toward me, catching the back of a chair for support. "Who else knows this?"

"Only Morgan and Howard."

"You must tell no one! I need time to think! I must have time!"

She was trembling, and her face had an alarming pallor. "Aunt Regina!" I started toward her, but she waved me away.

"Can an entire life be built on lies?" she said. "I must be, I have to be, mistaken." Her hands clutched at her throat and she crumpled to the floor.

Dr. Dorlan arrived quickly from the village, and by evening a specialist from Quebec City, Dr. Réal, had arrived by chartered plane. A nurse, Madame Corres, came with him.

"She has suffered a stroke," Dr. Dorlan told the assembled household, "but there is no cause for grave alarm. She cannot speak and there is paralysis of the right side, but we are convinced this is temporary."

"She should be taken to a hospital," said Morgan.

"She must not be moved! She requires complete rest and no visitors."

During the last hours I had been questioned first by Dr. Dorlan, then by the others about any emotional shock she might have had. "She found a photograph of my mother," I told them. "It brought painful memories."

Regina had pleaded with me to say nothing about my father's escape until she had time to think. I would give her that opportunity. But her strange question came back to me: "Can an entire life be built on lies?" Whose life had she meant?

CHAPTER TEN

ALONE ON THE SUN porch the next morning, I was finishing breakfast when Pierre came in. "Dr. Dorlan tells me that Regina is doing well," he said.

"Yes. Dr. Réal returned to Quebec City early this morning. He felt there was no danger."

We fell silent, both of us strangely awkward. Then he said, "The timing is unfortunate, but I must make a trip. In a few minutes I leave for Montreal."

"Really?" I took a quick sip of coffee, avoiding his eyes.

"I had a call yesterday. A Montreal firm needs a sailing master this winter for the Bahamas and Jamaica. They offer unusual pay and I know the vessel. She is beautiful."

"How exciting for you," I told him, studying the coffee cup.

"I spent hours thinking, pacing the floor."

"Is the decision so hard to make?"

"The decision may not be mine. This company may not want a married man. Also, a married man might not care to accept."

"No one is less married than you." I lifted my chin defiantly.

"With your help I expect to change that, Rochelle." He moved to my side. "I suppose you think I am saying this badly. But why should you expect me to talk drivel about love, although I am certain we love each other? I suppose we will have battles all the time. It is natural for me to give orders and natural for you to defy them. I am quite mad to ask you to marry me, and you are mad if you accept! *Alors*, what do you say?"

I was in his arms, we held each other. I do not remember saying yes, but he understood.

MY HAPPINESS FILLED THE OVERCAST morning with imaginary sunshine. Pierre had left Viking with me, and the dog caught my mood, capering like a puppy as I tossed a stick for him to retrieve. Pierre's image passed through my mind a dozen times in a dozen forms. The end of my drifting had come, and I wanted to shout the news, to make the old walls of the château ring with it, but we had agreed to say nothing until we talked to Regina.

Keeping a promise to Pierre who was worried about leaving me, I moved the few things I would need from my room to a small one on the ground floor just down the hall from Tante Emma's room. "Stay there tonight," he had told me. "Then you will be at the abbey until I return."

As I was hanging a few things in the old-fashioned armoire Mr. Carlton came to the door, carrying something that I took to be a radio. "Pardon me, miss. The gadgets I ordered to replace the old service bells have arrived, and you'll be needing one."

He placed a plastic box on the dresser and plugged a cord into a nearby electrical outlet. "To call the kitchen, press the red button. The blue one calls Madame Sud. I'll step to the kitchen now and we'll test it."

I looked at the device idly, expecting a ring or buzzing sound.

"Can you hear me, Miss Dumont?" The words came loudly and plainly, Mr. Carlton's voice only slightly distorted.

Then my hand flew to my mouth, stifling a cry. Another voice—human yet not human—came back to me, whispering, "Ro-chelle, Ro-chelle!"

"Miss Dumont, can you hear me, please?"

I paid no attention. My eyes moved to Viking, who lay quietly at my side, eyes half closed. The dog, always alert to human speech, ignored the sound. He did not respond because his keen sense of smell told him that no person was present. He would have been equally uninterested in a radio or a recording. Such sounds did not indicate danger.

But he was instantly alert when Mr. Carlton reappeared.

"No sound, miss? Must be something wrong with it." Patiently he explained again, and after he had gone I sat on the bed staring at the black box. It could have been concealed anywhere near the Captain's Walk.

My watch said noon. Pierre had promised to call me in the evening, but I couldn't wait. I could leave a message for him at the hotel in Montreal.

I hurried to the telephone at the front of the house. When I picked it up, the line was dead. As I turned away I heard a creaking on the stairway and caught a glimpse of a figure withdrawing quickly into the landing.

"Who is it? Who's there?"

"Ro-chelle." It was a papery whisper. "Ro-chelle."

"Thalia?" I asked, incredulous.

"Yes. I'm here."

I hesitated, but Viking pushed past me, bounding up the stairs, his tail wagging. Then the girl herself stepped into view to greet him.

"Thalia!" I exclaimed. "What are you doing here?"

She raised a finger to her lips and gestured for me to follow. A moment later we were in the Captain's Country, the door closed behind us.

"I've run away from the school. I'm never going back."

"Does your stepfather know you're here?"

"No. He doesn't care what happens to me. Neither does my mother."

"Your mother is ill, she's not responsible."

"If she cared for me, why did she ask the witch to come to the house when I begged her not to? The witch frightens me."

I took Thalia's hand; it was icy. "Madame Jeannette frightens me, too."

"After hearing Captain Pierre's story of the night you were locked on the roof, Aunt Regina told my mother that the witch must never come again. But she did! One night while you were away I heard her in my mother's room. I wanted her to be caught. Do you know what I did?"

"What, Thalia?"

"I went to the kitchen and pinched two wires together, so all the bells rang and woke everyone up. I'd heard Mr. Palmer tell my stepfather how the bells could be rung."

"Why would they have such a conversation, Thalia?"

"I think it was a joke on Aunt Regina. She and my stepfather quarreled every day because she wouldn't sell River Rising. And the servants were frightened of ghosts, so nobody would work here." Thalia moved to the window and stared down at the river. "Then you came and it was better."

Thalia confirmed what Dorothy had said earlier. The supposed haunting had been a very effective way of halting operation of the house, of forcing Regina's hand. My presence had been inconvenient. I could see why Morgan had urged me to leave. But that did not explain Regina's reaction to Sandy-Panda and the coloring book. Something still lay hidden.

The immediate problem, however, was Thalia. "The teachers at your school must be worried to death."

She shook her head. "I left a note saying I was going to visit my stepfather. They wouldn't worry much anyhow. It's a school for girls whose parents don't want them."

"Thalia, you mustn't feel this way," I said, going to her. "Your mother is ill and Morgan is preoccupied with his painting. He hasn't time to—"

"That's not true, Rochelle. He goes to his studio, but he doesn't paint. There's an attic window here from which you can see through the studio skylight. He plays solitaire or just paces the floor. I've watched."

"That happens to an artist. Times come when he can't work. Now, what am I to do with you? Morgan has to be told you're here."

"Please! Let me stay with you tonight! Then you can tell him."

"I can't do that, Thalia."

"Then I'll run away again," she said calmly.

Looking at her pleading eyes, I suddenly thought of Deirdre. Running away, frightened . . . to nowhere. "Very well, but just for tonight."

"Rochelle!" She threw her arms around me. "You're the only one who understands. You and Captain Pierre. I love you."

I was glad for her company. The house felt oppressive that night. Regina, the nurse said, was resting quietly. But for me there was little sleep.

In the morning I learned that Thalia had won a temporary reprieve. Morgan was not in the house and no one knew his whereabouts. I tried again to call Pierre, but telephone service had not resumed.

As the morning wore on, my uneasiness increased. I went to the small library, where Mr. Carlton had made a fire, and paced restlessly. Something about the ringing of the bells haunted me, some vital fact that lay just beyond consciousness. Trying to bring some order to my confused thoughts, I wrote down, "The bells. Midnight. August 14."

Tante Emma entered. "I have brought your lunch. The fireplace is cheering on this cold, gray day."

"Tante Emma," I said, "Eunice told me that the service bells rang here on the anniversary of François' death."

"That is so. To the very minute."

"But how is the minute known? Did Morgan or Howard look at a watch? It seems unlikely at such a moment."

"Why dwell on this?" she asked. "It was in statements they made to the police. The midnight bell of the abbey somehow enraged Jean-Paul. The sound triggered the attack. Now leave this matter alone."

I toyed with my lunch, troubled and unsatisfied. Suddenly Viking's ears lifted sharply, and I glanced over my shoulder to see Madame Sud.

"A telegram for you," she said, and gave it to me. I noticed the flap was open and looked at her. "It must have arrived like that. Monsieur Palmer accepted it." And Palmer, I thought, had read the contents.

As soon as she was gone, I drew out the message.

WORST FEARS ABOUT DEIRDRE CONFIRMED ON RADIO. I MUST CONTACT POLICE. GO TO ABBEY AT ONCE. REPEAT AT ONCE. I WILL RETURN QUICKLY. LOVE PIERRE.

This, I realized, was no time to hesitate or question. After a futile attempt to reach the abbey by telephone and an equally useless try to summon a taxi, I put the few things I would need in my shoulder bag. There was no way to get there but to walk.

Thalia sat reading a book in the downstairs bedroom. Her smile faded when she saw my face. "What's happened, Rochelle?"

Now every shadowed room of River Rising seemed filled with menace. I could not leave her here alone. "Thalia, do you know where Captain Lachance lives?" She nodded. "Take Viking and go there. Tell the housekeeper I sent you. You are to wait there until the captain returns."

Asking no questions, Thalia brushed her lips against my cheek, and a moment later she and Viking were on their way. I watched her, resolving that her future would be happier than her past. She would know that Pierre and I loved her, that she would never be alone.

Although the day was cool, even chilly, I did not take time to go upstairs for a coat. My wool dress with its matching cape and hood would give adequate warmth. From the bureau I took a small transistor radio.

When I reached the firebreak, I tuned it to a Montreal station. Eventually I heard the voice of a newscaster. There followed national and local announcements, but nothing about Deirdre.

I tried Quebec City, then stood completely still as I heard the first words: ". . . recovered from the river below Île d'Orléans, has been identified as Miss Deirdre Cameron, daughter of a prominent Toronto family. She had been missing . . ." The radio faded, then the sound returned: ". . . apparently a victim of foul play."

Foul play. I shuddered. More than ever I wanted to resist the belief that Deirdre had died in my place. *But she had.* Who should have been wearing the yellow shawl? Rochelle Dumont, of course. This terrible conviction chilled my shivering shoulders as much as the penetrating wind.

A storm was gathering, and I regretted not wearing a coat. I had been a fool to trust the Quebec weather even in September. Anyone venturing out too thinly clad was almost asking for pneumonia. After all, that had happened to Aunt Theresa all those years ago when—

I uttered a sharp exclamation. *When? Exactly when?*

Unexpectedly, a few flakes of snow swirled around, but I paid no attention, standing transfixed, struggling to recall Aunt Theresa's words.

On August 13, twenty years ago, a young nun had been seized by emotional storms that she called "monsoons." The following day she had lived in torment, and that night she had briefly run away. And what had called her back to the abbey? The great bell proclaiming Assumption Day, the bell she heard at midnight as she stood watching my father.

Midnight, August 14, the date and hour when François Armitage was killed on the porch of the studio. But at that moment Jean-Paul Dumont was in the garden, his presence there confirmed by a witness no one had known about—Theresa Armitage, now Lady Abbess of Clarendon. Why had she not spoken, cleared my father of the crime? Even as I asked, I realized the answer. When news of the murder electrified Ste. Marie du Lac, the nun was being taken to the hospital. She only learned of the tragedy months later, when she was told of the death but spared the details. Dame Theresa never knew the importance of what she had seen.

Lost in thought, I had ignored the thickening snow. Startled by it now, I knew I must hurry, for although the path along the firebreak was visible, the abbey's towers had disappeared in whiteness. I pressed on, astonished by this sudden storm. At the Rising there had been talk of snowstorms even in summer, but I had not imagined anything like this. It's almost blinding, I thought, pulling the hood of my cape forward to protect my face.

The sky was blotted out; nothing remained above me but white, spiraling and whirling. The silver trunk of a birch tree suddenly loomed in front of me, blocking my path. I halted, astonished, for no trees grew in the firebreak. Against my will I thought of Thalia and her father, how they had stumbled through a blind world. Don't remember them. Don't!

But I couldn't help it as, eyes to the ground, I struggled to retrace my steps and realized my footprints vanished instantly. Thalia and her father had stopped. I must keep going. A little farther, only a little farther.

Then a gust of wind momentarily cleared the view, and I caught sight of a stone building standing among tall timbers not far away. I hurried toward it, soon aware that it was not as near as I had hoped. But a few minutes later I crossed a rutted road I could not remember seeing before and reached the doorway.

I knocked twice and called loudly, but there was no answer, so I pulled a dangling latchstring and the door swung open. A deep-voiced "Moo!" greeted me. This was both a dwelling and a farm shed, one big room with an unpainted fence to divide human and animal occupants. Above it was a hayloft and, I supposed, a place used for sleeping, since I saw no beds.

"Is anyone here?" I asked loudly.

Only the cow replied from beyond the fence. Her calf looked up from nursing, while two black cats raced up the ladder to the loft.

I put my bag and radio on the table near the fireplace and hung my wet cape over the back of a wooden chair. The hearthstones were hot and the ashes gave a comforting warmth. I looked around the strange place.

Above the ladder to the loft was a large wooden box attached to ropes and pulleys, apparently a hay trolley to carry fodder from the loft to the animals' pen. The ropes to lower it were held by a hook in the wall and looked frayed. I stepped back, not caring to stand under it, and almost bumped into a set of open shelves lined with bottles and oddly shaped apothecary jars. In the dim light I saw herbs and sprigs, some whole, others ground to powder. In one of the large glass jars something green and slimy drifted, seeming neither quite living nor yet dead. A second jar of clear liquid displayed a small animal's skull. I turned away from this unsettling collection, wishing the snow would cease quickly so I could leave.

Two big cupboards stood against the opposite wall, and I went to one, hoping it might contain something I could wrap around myself. Success, I thought when I opened the door, for there was a patched blanket draped over some object leaning inside. I pulled the blanket away and gasped.

It was an oil painting, quite large and simply but perfectly framed. Even in the faint light I felt certain of what I had discovered. Taking it from its hiding place, I stood it against the wall. This had to be the painting stolen from River Rising just before I arrived.

It was a lovingly painted portrait of a little girl, face turned partly away, her loneliness poignantly shown in the droop of her thin shoulders, the emptiness of her hand as she reached toward a rag doll.

Tears came to my eyes, tears brought not so much by the beauty of the painting as by the way it spoke to me. The small girl wore a white cotton dress with a hibiscus print; the floor was covered with linoleum, a design of poppies. In the lower right corner I saw the signature "M. Armitage."

The squeak of wagon wheels outside snapped me from the spell. Running to the window, I wiped a small spot on the steamed glass and looked out. The snow no longer fell, and only a few yards away was a wagon carrying two passengers, Gilles and Madame Jeannette.

Madame Jeannette's house. Of course. The sinister-looking jars and bottles were the trappings of village witchcraft.

I thrust the painting into a corner and looked about desperately for a way of escape. There was none. Voices were approaching as I snatched up my things and scrambled up the ladder to the loft above.

The door opened, then closed again. There was a stamping of Gilles's boots, the scratch of a match, then pale candlelight.

"Cold," growled Gilles.

"I do not feel cold or heat," Madame Jeannette answered, her voice harsh. "My blood dried long ago. But put wood on the fire if you like."

After a long silence she said, "He is to meet you here, then?"

"So I was told."

In the deep dusk of the loft four luminous eyes stared balefully at me. The cats sat poised, ready to spring.

"Do you know what the plan is?" Madame Jeannette asked.

"I am not paid to know. My job is to watch the path and make sure she does not reach the abbey."

Not reach the abbey. I knew they were talking about me.

"The murderer's daughter seeks sanctuary in the abbey? A joke. What if she is already there?"

"She is not. The abbey gate is being watched."

Madame Jeannette's voice crackled with excitement. "So she might come down the path outside at any moment! What then, Gilles?"

"I take her to the place in Castaways. After that, I go home. I know nothing of what comes next."

"Then why the shotgun? Why the rope coiled in the wagon?"

"That is not my part."

Her tone softened, became a velvet purr. "Ah, I wish it were mine. My poor Giselle would like to watch the murderer's daughter die."

Horror at her words made me sit up, lean forward to listen. I moved my hand, touching something that began to move, to roll down the hay. I tried to snatch the object, but it eluded me, dropping to the floor with a thud.

"*Sacrebleu!* Is it raining pumpkins? Is someone in the loft?"

"They are stored up there. One dislodged itself, nothing more."

"Watch at the window. I will go up and see."

As I heard the first sound of his moving boots I drew back my arm, then threw it forward toward the cats, pretending to hurl something at them. They scampered down the ladder just as Gilles was starting to ascend. I held my breath, praying that somehow I might be made invisible.

"Cats." He chuckled, recrossing the room. "Only your devils of cats!"

I lay quietly, trying to still the pounding of my heart. In the ensuing moments a strange sensation took possession of me. I remained as alert as a cornered animal, yet part of my mind seemed to drift to a faraway place. I felt I was sitting on the floor of my mother's kitchen, with poppies scattered around me. No, not real poppies, but ugly, floral-patterned linoleum. "Do not wiggle, little one." It was Paul's voice. He bent over the table, deftly sketching with my crayons. Beside me on the floor lay Sandy-Panda.

The doll in the painting I had just seen! The doll the child reached for so sadly. But Morgan Armitage had never seen that doll, nor that linoleum. The painting was not a portrait of Charlotte, but of me. *I* was that child, and only one artist could have painted it—my father, Jean-Paul Dumont. What had Morgan said about trying to get a dealer to show my father's work? "It didn't work out." But it had! Very well indeed—for Morgan.

Regina's keen eye must have recognized Sandy-Panda at once. The coloring book, I suppose, had told her the rest. She had identified the style and knew Morgan's career was built on lies. No wonder she had collapsed.

"That is his car," said Madame Jeannette. "He is here."

Startled from my reverie, I tried to withdraw deeper into the loft, but my back was touching the wall. The unknown *he* was clearly the man who commanded. His first words were, "She did not come this way?"

"*Non, monsieur,*" the two answered together.

"She must have lost her way in the storm."

"*C'est bon!*" exclaimed Madame Jeannette. "Let her die in the forest, then. It saves trouble."

"No. We will find her. She's to be taken care of properly."

I knew the man's voice well, but only once before had I heard him use this steel tone of command. Howard Palmer had sounded like this when I overheard him talking with Morgan about Dorothy. *Dorothy?* No! *I* had been the subject of their conversation. Palmer had even used the same words: "She has to be taken care of properly." Taken care of on a trip to New York, perhaps?

"Monsieur Morgan watches near the abbey?" Madame Jeannette asked.

"Yes. Another reason we must find her. Morgan lacks nerve."

"You will not speak thus of Monsieur Morgan in my house! He is avenging François and Giselle. Do not insult him!"

"I was joking," Palmer answered with a trace of his false geniality.

So this was how they were using Madame Jeannette. Palmer and Morgan intended my death, and the deluded madwoman thought they were doing it out of some twisted sense of honor. She was mistaken. They had killed at least once for money, and I knew they would not hesitate to do so again.

"We should start looking," Palmer said. "You, madame, keep watch at the window here. Do you know how to fire this shotgun?"

"*Ave Maria!* Do you take me for a city idiot? Of course!"

"If you see her, fire into the air. Two shots. Do you understand?"

My mind raced ahead, planning my escape. Once the men were gone, I would somehow outwit Madame Jeannette. Lure her to the loft, perhaps? Could I do anything with the hay trolley or the ladder?

"What the devil!" Palmer exclaimed suddenly. "Why did you bring out that picture? You are paid to keep it hidden!"

"*Sacrebleu!* I did not touch it. Someone has been here."

"And what's this mess on the floor? A pumpkin?"

"It rolled from the loft. The cats pushed it," said Gilles.

Utter silence followed, and I knew that Palmer had made some gesture to command it. In a moment they would search the loft. You are not finished yet, I told myself. Fight back. Try anything. Forcing away my fear, I called out, trying to sound like a person just awakened. "Hello? Has someone come back?" I crawled to the top of the ladder and looked down. Gilles stood below, his foot on the lowest rung. "Gilles, please hold the ladder for me."

Mouth agape, he obeyed me, and I descended awkwardly.

When I reached the floor, I forced my lips into a smile. "Howard, how nice to see you! Have you taken shelter from the storm? I was freezing when I found this place. The loft seemed the warmest spot, and I fell asleep until just now!" I had no illusions that my performance would convince them, but I might win a little time.

"The painting! Did you take it from the cupboard?" Madame Jeannette demanded.

"Yes. I was looking for a blanket and I found it. Of course, the room was so dark I couldn't see it clearly." Pretending to stretch sleepily, I let my eyes dart over the room. Two guns leaned against the far wall, but no one was carrying a weapon. Gilles's menacing bulk barred any rush to the door, and Palmer had moved dangerously close. The hook to release the hay trolley was only inches from me, but I could think of no way to use it.

Palmer came a step nearer. "My dear Rochelle, I've been searching for you. So has Morgan. We thought you were lost."

"How kind of you to worry," I said quickly, as a desperate plan formed

in my mind. "Yes, I was lost awhile, until I met a man who guided me here."

"Indeed?" Howard was puzzled, almost convinced that I was lying, yet not quite sure. And he had to be sure. "Who was this guide?"

"I didn't catch his name." I glanced toward the loft in a furtive manner. "He was in a great hurry and had to leave at once."

I saw a shadow of suspicion in his face, and I pressed on. "How silly of me to be afraid when my friend Howard Palmer was on his way." I spoke his name in an unnaturally loud voice, as though to be sure that a concealed listener in the loft could not fail to hear it. "After all, you had read my telegram and knew I was going to the abbey."

Suddenly Palmer believed my deception. "Gilles," he shouted. "Search the loft. There's somebody else up there. She wasn't alone."

"No, no!" I protested, blocking the ladder. "I swear there's nobody."

Gilles thrust me roughly aside, and I pretended to stumble, to catch the ropes of the hay trolley for support. In those few seconds every eye was riveted on the loft while Gilles raced up the ladder. The instant he stepped on the floor above, I jerked the ropes of the hay trolley and let it crash.

As I plunged toward the door I saw the wooden box strike Palmer on the shoulder. He fell, seizing the loft ladder, bringing it down with him. I heard Gilles's shout and the screech-owl cry of Madame Jeannette, and then I was outside, running, expecting at any moment to hear the explosion of a shotgun.

CHAPTER ELEVEN

I DROPPED TO THE ground in a tiny clearing, blood pounding in my ears as I gasped for breath. The matting of pine needles felt damp, but except for patches the snow had quickly melted as the storm had spent itself. I gazed at the sky, wondering how much daylight was left. Sitting up, I strained to hear sounds of pursuit, but the woods were silent. No branch rustled, no birds called. I've lost them, I told myself, feeling a surge of relief.

Then, much as I longed to believe this, I stifled the hope. Howard Palmer was an experienced hunter, and Gilles must know every inch of this wilderness. Why expect to hear them? They would follow noiselessly.

Where was the abbey? I wondered. The village? Firs, maples and birches surrounded me, a world without directions.

"There is a way out, there has to be," I whispered, fighting against panic. If I could find the river, I could follow its shore to the Rising. I started out again, crouching low to disturb the foliage as little as possible, avoiding patches of snow that would hold telltale footprints. Yet leaving some tracks in wet ground was inevitable, and progress was painfully slow.

I had one advantage over my pursuers. They had to find me, while I had only to find any house, any party of hunters. Soon, perhaps even now, Pierre would be searching for me. Then I stiffened. In the distance I heard the baying of Howard Palmer's hounds. Spurred by terror, I ran ahead. I remembered the tricks of a hunted fox, doubling back, moving in loops to throw off a scent, but had not the strength to do such things.

The woods thinned. I saw a broad opening ahead. A farm, thank God. I ran into the open, and a chill swept over me as I realized I stood not on ground but on hard-packed sawdust, the man-made desert at Castaways.

Dusk was now changing to darkness. I could no longer run, but walked, drawing breath in gasps. Strangely, my fear had lessened. I believed that safety lay just ahead. At any moment Pierre would meet me, Viking at his side. I felt this so strongly that I almost saw him.

I could hear Palmer's dogs closer now, barking excitedly. Stumbling on, I recognized the ruined houses and old village square of Castaways. There stood the building François Armitage had erected. It had caused me to quarrel with Pierre on our first picnic. We would not quarrel so foolishly again, I decided. We would be too happy, we would—

A beam of light blazed in my face, blinding me. "Who is it?" I cried.

A hand seized my arm, and as I began to struggle I heard Gilles cursing me. I screamed, shouting for help, kicking at him, clawing his face with my nails. Suddenly a heavy cloth was thrown over me, stifling my cries. Still I fought, until something hard struck my head and I knew no more.

FAR AWAY A light flickered, moving unsteadily closer. My head throbbed, I did not want to enter the world again. I wondered who was trying to rouse me by slapping my cheek lightly. Go away, I thought. Let me alone.

Then someone said, "She's still out cold." And Morgan Armitage replied, "That's just as well."

Consciousness returned, but instinct told me not to move. I sat half sprawled in a corner, my back against a wall of stone. Covertly I opened my eyes just enough to learn where I had been taken.

We were in a large room lit by the glaring white of two gasoline lanterns. I had never seen this interior, yet I knew I was in François Armitage's building. I remembered the struggle with Gilles, but he seemed not to be here. Perhaps, as he had said earlier, what was to come now was not part of his job. Madame Jeannette sat on a stool near the closed metal door, the shotgun Palmer had given her leaning against the wall within her easy reach. Morgan and Palmer stood nearby, both tense with anger.

"Madame, I tell you to go home. You already know too much for your own good!" Morgan was not quite shouting.

"I stay until the end!" she flung back. "My Giselle is dead. You promised me vengeance if I would help you, and I will see it done."

"You'll see nothing," said Palmer.

She spat at him. Morgan moved to a table and took a swallow from a half-empty whiskey bottle. When he looked in my direction, I closed my eyes, but not before I had glimpsed a man in sheer torment. "There's got to be some other way out of this," he muttered.

"You're a coward, Morgan," Howard Palmer told him. "You don't mind paying to have a job done, like the one I arranged in Montreal—"

"Bungled!" Morgan retorted. "Five thousand dollars paid to a stupid thug who made matters worse. And now the Cameron girl's body is found!"

"Which is why you're a fool to delay any longer." Palmer's calm, untroubled tone was even more terrifying than his words.

"If we could have chosen our own time, when she was away from here, when there'd be no connection with the Rising, then—"

"Will you get it through your head that it's too late? We're no longer dealing with just the girl and Lachance. This morning it became a police matter."

Trembling inside, I forced myself to remain as still as one already dead.

"The thing to do now," Palmer was saying, "is to get this over fast."

His voice rose. "Morgan, put down that bottle and pay attention. We have to have a straight story. She must have been lost in the storm. There are hundreds of miles of wilderness out there. She'll never be found."

For a long time Morgan did not answer, and when he did he sounded numb and listless. "Is that the end? It seems a lifetime since we went to the islands and saw Jean-Paul."

"You've always had a squeamish conscience," said Palmer.

"Not conscience. When I brought those first paintings of his back to Canada, I knew they were good. It was hard to believe Jean-Paul had painted them, he'd changed so much."

"Well, he had plenty to make him change!"

"When I substituted my signature for his, I almost believed I *had* done the painting. It had everything I felt. I had no idea what it would lead to."

"A bloody fortune is what it led to! Will you shake off this heartbreaking self-pity so we can get on with business?"

Morgan seemed not to hear him. "A lifetime of lies. Always afraid that some stranger would tap me on the shoulder and say he recognized a painting. But it wasn't a stranger who came. It was Jean-Paul's daughter!"

"You make me cry, Morgan," Palmer answered. "You weren't too worried to pocket the money and hog the fame." He added with a sneer, "Jean-Paul's dear friend, his secret Canadian dealer who kept him going. A little hungry, maybe, and too poor to travel where he might see his own work with your name on it. Jean-Paul was a trusting fool."

"His daughter!" Morgan repeated, his voice growing shrill. "Isn't there something else we can do?"

I knew I must move now, before they did—make any attempt, however desperate, to confuse them. Delay was my only weapon. Someone would find us soon, Pierre would come—I had to believe that.

"Yes, there's another way out of this," I said loudly. Both men whirled as I struggled to my feet.

"I'm tired, Morgan," I told him with as much authority as I could. "Help me to a chair. We have to talk business."

Morgan stared at me blankly, then came forward and took my arm.

I sat in a chair at the table, keeping my hands in my lap so they would not be seen trembling. "If your blackmailing friend had had his way, I might be dead by now, Morgan, and that would have left you with no escape. By the way, he is a blackmailer, isn't he?"

Howard Palmer made a threatening move, but I ignored him. The look on Morgan's face had given me the answer. I continued, "We can come to an agreement, Morgan. I'm afraid it will be expensive for you, but really, you have no choice."

Morgan lifted the whiskey bottle, swallowed a heavy drink. "What the devil are you talking about?"

"First of all, Deirdre Cameron. You're an accomplice in her murder." I was improvising frantically. Morgan was a frightened, broken man, not thinking clearly. Howard Palmer remained the real threat, but I could see no way of dealing with him. It was Morgan I must confuse.

"Eventually the police will find your trail. I can probably invent some story about Deirdre to keep them away from you."

Palmer spoke, his mild tone carrying deadly threat. "I'm afraid you won't be around to tell the police anything."

"You are mistaken, Mr. Palmer, as you'll soon see." Looking at Morgan, I said, "When I saw your painting in the Montreal museum, I suspected it was my father's work. Then when the stolen portrait was described to me, I remembered the day it was painted. My father worked constantly, as you know. There must be a great many canvases that you've held back for the future. And I know what they are worth."

I glanced around the room at crated paintings, carefully wrapped in heavy brown paper. Several more, not wrapped, leaned against the wall. Then I swallowed hard. On the floor near the paintings was a coil of new rope, rope too strong and too heavy to be used to tie the crated paintings. It had to be the rope Madame Jeannette had spoken of.

"It's cold in here," I said, shuddering, then made myself continue the desperate game. "Shall we talk about my price?"

Morgan stared, seeming not to comprehend my words.

"Your price!" Palmer's face was twisted in a sneer. "You're not setting prices. You're a cool one, but it won't work."

I had to struggle to go on. Why didn't someone come? Surely Pierre—

Then, unaccountably, my mind went blank. I could not remember what I had said, what point I was trying to make.

My unexpected rescue came from Morgan, who prompted me without realizing it. "So what is your price?" he asked. He was rubbing his hands, clenching and unclenching the fingers.

"I will forget the past, forget today, make up some story about Deirdre. I'll even ignore the torment you've caused me while trying to drive me away."

"How generous," Palmer jeered. "For this you expect us to let you walk out of here?"

"I expect more than that," I retorted. "My price is one half the value of all the paintings you sell in the future."

Morgan raised his head, but I could read nothing in his face.

"What an interesting proposal," said Howard Palmer. He crossed the room to a tool rack that hung on the far wall, and I watched in horror as his fingers closed around the handle of a mat knife.

"Really, my dear," he said softly. "You sell too cheaply. Why take just half the value of the paintings? All of them belong to you. I assure you there's quite a fortune here." He paused, smiling. "But of course, you must be able to claim it."

"Yes, that's it!" I exclaimed. Hysteria was creeping into my voice. "How am I to prove who did these paintings? It would be my word against Morgan's. Years could go by before I had all the evidence. You understand that, don't you, Morgan? Morgan!"

His eyes were glassy, and when he spoke, it was not in reply to my question. "Why did all the bells at the Rising ring that way? At midnight. Was it Jean-Paul? Charlotte? But they're dead!"

"Come to your senses, Morgan!" Palmer said, and walked toward the coil of rope. Kneeling, but still watching me closely, he cut off a length of the heavy line, the razor-sharp mat knife slicing through it easily.

A rope to bind my hands, I thought. Or a rope to strangle?

"Are you accepting my bargain?" I demanded, my tone too shrill.

"I think we have a better solution," said Palmer, taking a slow step toward me. "But of course, what you said is worth considering."

His tone was velvet soft. He was trying to calm me, to delay any screams or struggle until it was too late. I rose from my chair in one last show of defiance. "Dame Theresa has a letter, to be opened only upon my death or disappearance. It explains all about the paintings."

I paused, then spoke directly to Morgan, playing my final card. "It also reminds Dame Theresa of the night she left the abbey, the night when she saw my father helpless in the garden at the moment you were killing François. For you killed him, Morgan. Worse than that, you convinced an innocent man that he was guilty. You pressed the hammer into his hand so his fingerprints would show. Howard helped you, and has blackmailed you ever since. You're guilty, Morgan, and Dame Theresa will soon know it."

Morgan's face crumpled. "It was an accident, I didn't mean it to happen!" he shouted. "François was squandering my inheritance, and he made fun of me, ridiculed my painting. The hammer was there on the table, and I . . . yes, I hit him. He drove me to it." He pressed his hands against his temples. "Jean-Paul had threatened to kill him. Why shouldn't Jean-Paul be guilty? He believed it himself!"

Morgan halted abruptly, astonished at the horror his own words evoked.

Howard Palmer cursed. "You're a babbling fool, Morgan. She's driven you into admitting it. Now we'll get this over."

His expression told me I had failed. He did not believe I had written a letter. He moved slowly toward me, holding the rope loosely in his extended hands. I stood paralyzed, riveted by terror.

Then an explosion ripped the air. Palmer turned back toward Morgan, who gave a strangled cry before his knees buckled. He reeled, half falling against the table. I saw blood on his shirt as he slipped to the floor.

Madame Jeannette stood near the door, the gun cradled in her arms, her face dazed. She had heard Morgan's confession, she had given final judgment. Now she spoke in a hoarse, mindless whisper, the dry lips hardly moving: *"Giselle . . . Giselle . . ."*

I moved toward the door, strangely unafraid. As I passed Madame Jeannette she did not see me. Her glazed eyes were fixed on Howard Palmer. I slid back the bolt, hardly hearing Palmer's whining, desperate voice: "I swear I didn't know, madame! It wasn't my fault. . . ."

I opened the door and stepped outside, no longer a prisoner. The night was cold, but I had no feeling of chill, no more than I had any real sense of hearing the blast of the second gunshot behind me.

Cloudy moonlight bathed the landscape, softening its edges. Ahead, not far away, I saw lights. Torches and lanterns carried by the men who were searching for me flickered in the darkness. Then a voice called my name, a beloved voice ringing through the night, even as I had imagined it.

"Rochelle, Rochelle!"

Not drifting, not uncertain or afraid, I moved across the Sawdust Desert toward him and toward the future.

ACKNOWLEDGMENTS

The condensations in this volume have been created by The Reader's Digest Association, Inc., and are used by permission of and special arrangement with the publishers and the holders of the respective copyrights.

Moonraker's Bride, by Madeleine Brent, copyright © 1973 by Souvenir Press, Ltd., is reprinted by permission of Doubleday & Co., Inc., and Souvenir Press, Ltd.

The Golden Unicorn, copyright © 1976 by Phyllis A. Whitney, is reprinted by permission of Doubleday & Co., Inc., and William Heinemann, Ltd.

Kirkland Revels, copyright © 1962 by Victoria Holt, is reprinted by permission of Doubleday & Co., Inc., and William Collins Sons & Co., Ltd.

Wings of the Falcon, copyright © 1977 by Barbara Michaels, is reprinted by permission of Dodd, Mead & Co., Inc., and Souvenir Press, Ltd.

Lady of Mallow, copyright © 1960 by Dorothy Eden, is reprinted by permission of The Putnam Publishing Group and the executors of the estate of Dorothy Eden.

River Rising, copyright © 1975 by Jessica North, is reprinted by permission of McIntosh & Otis, Inc.